CW00712721

HOLIDAY HOMES, COTTAGE
AND APARTMENTS
IN BRITAIN

AA

Editor: Penny Hicks
Designer: Gerry McElroy
Illustrations by Alan Roe

Gazetteer: Compiled by the Publications Research Unit in co-operation with the Accommodation Inspectorate both of the Automobile Association

Maps: Prepared by the Cartographic Services Unit of the Automobile Association

Cover picture: Long Byers, Brampton, Cumbria (Character Cottages)

Head of Advertisement Sales: Christopher Heard Tel 0256 20123 (ext 2020)
Advertisement production: Karen Weeks Tel 0256 20123 (ext 3525)
Advertisement Sales Representatives:
London, East Anglia, East Midlands, Central Southern and South East England: Edward May Tel 0256 20123 (ext 3524) or 0256 467568
South West, West, West Midlands: Bryan Thompson Tel 0272 393296
Wales, North of England, Scotland: Arthur Williams Tel 0222 620267

Filmset by: Vantage Photosetting Co Ltd, Eastleigh and London
Printed and bound in Great Britain by: William Clowes Ltd, Beccles and London

Published by the Automobile Association, Fanum House, Basingstoke, Hampshire RG21 2EA.

ISBN 0 86145 383 2
AA reference: 59569

Introduction

The growth of self-catering holidays has been quite remarkable in recent years and it is certainly one of the most comfortable ways of spending a holiday, offering a greater freedom than most hotels without the rigours of camping. Not only can you find a real home from home, you can often find something better than you have the rest of the year. It may be a pretty thatched cottage with roses round the door or the wing of a historic castle; a modern apartment looking out across the sea or a luxurious Scandinavian-style chalet amidst mountains and forests. We list around 15,000 places for you to choose from and every one has been thoroughly vetted by one of our team of inspectors to make sure it is of an acceptable standard.

Because of the first-hand knowledge gained by these visits, we were able to ask our inspectors which they considered to be the best of the establishments in their area and as a result of their co-operation, and subsequent judging, we have pleasure in announcing the results of our very first Holiday Home of the Year Awards. A special feature on the overall winner and the regional winners begins on page 7.

GRANADA MOTORWAY SERVICES

Caring for Travellers Nationwide

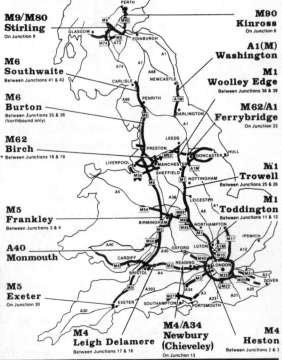

M9/M80 Stirling On Junction 9

M6 Southwaite Between Junctions 41 & 42

M6 Burton Between Junctions 35 & 36 (Northbound only)

M62 Birch Between Junctions 18 & 19

M5 Frankley Between Junctions 3 & 4

A40 Monmouth

M5 Exeter On Junction 30

M4 Leigh Delamere Between Junctions 17 & 18

M90 Kinross On Junction 6

A1(M) Washington

M1 Woolley Edge Between Junctions 38 & 39

M62/A1 Ferrybridge On Junction 33

M1 Trowell Between Junctions 25 & 26

M1 Toddington Between Junctions 11 & 12

M4/A34 Newbury (Chieveley) On Junction 13

M4 Heston Between Junctions 2 & 3

Wholesome food freshly prepared and served

Take away food and beverages

Variety and value

Petrol and diesel at competitive prices

GRANADA Lodge HOTELS

The Granada Lodge aim is to provide a high standard of bedroom accommodation at a budget price. Each bedroom has a private bathroom and colour television, radio wake up alarm, individual room heating and tea and coffee facilities are included

EXETER
- 58 Bedrooms with private bathroom
- Restaurant, bar and lounge
- Close to J30 of M5
- 3½ miles from city centre
- Weekend and Midweek Breaks
- Telephone (0392) 74044

STIRLING
- 36 Bedrooms with private bathroom
- Lounge
- Meals available in Country Kitchen restaurant adjoining
- At J9 of M9/M80
- 2½ miles from town centre
- Telephone (0786) 815033 or 813614

For further details please contact the hotel direct or
Sally Burton, Toddington (05255) 3881

Granada Lodge, Moor Lane,
Sandygate, Exeter, Devon EX2 4AR
Telephone (0392) 74044

Granada Lodge, Pirnhall Roundabout
Stirling, Scotland FK7 8EU
Telephone (0786) 815033

HOLIDAY HOME
of the year

Self-catering holidays have become more and more popular in recent years and we felt that the time was right to introduce an award for the top holiday home. Choosing the winner was a very difficult task – we list such a wide variety of properties, and different places suit different people. Nevertheless, we feel that we have come up with some very worthy first-time winners for this new award. In the pages that follow we tell you all about them – starting with the overall winner, Lynch Country House Holiday Apartments at Allerford, Somerset.

HOLIDAY HOME
of the Year
and West Region
WINNER

LYNCH COUNTRY HOUSE

HOLIDAY APARTMENTS

ALLERFORD, SOMERSET

The resident owners are Bernard and Janet Foster, a charming and friendly couple who have a keen awareness of self-caterers' requirements. They came to Lynch about three years ago, having previously worked in the hotel business, and, having their own apartment in the same house, are always on hand both to welcome visitors and to help out with any queries which may arise during their stay. Realising that self-caterers will probably want to take a rest from the cooking from time to time, Mrs Foster has set up a small dining room where she will provide simple, good value meals twice a week. A laundry room has also been installed in one of the outbuildings. The estate's gardener lives in a nearby cottage and, when he is not tending the lovely grounds, grows lots of vegetables which he will often sell to visiting holidaymakers. All in all this is a marvellous place for a holiday with its superb setting between Exmoor and the sea, its high standard of accommodation and the personal attention of its friendly and enthusiastic owners.

Our first-ever winner of the Best Holiday Home award is this delightfully converted Somerset mansion, set in several acres of hillside gardens above the Vale of Porlock. It was built of local grey stone around the turn of the century for a shipping magnate, but its old studded doors and huge mullioned windows give it a more ancient feel and each apartment retains much of the character of the house. Some have far-reaching views across the Vale to Dunkery Beacon and the sea, while others look out onto the National Trust's woods and meadows which surround the grounds. Each apartment is completely self-contained and beautifully fitted out with modern kitchens and bathrooms, pretty bedrooms and comfortable lounges, many having fine old pieces of furniture and grand fireplaces. Guests here have complete freedom to use the grounds, including the lovely old flagstone terraces around the house. There are sweeping lawns surrounded by shrubberies and borders, with the occasional wooden seat where visitors can relax and enjoy the peace and beauty of the views. There is a pretty little water garden too, and if you have an energetic nature, you can make use of the hard tennis court, the putting green or the squash court which is neatly hidden away in a rustic wooden barn on the hillside above the house. One interesting feature in the garden is the replica of Allerford's famous Packhorse Bridge. The first lady of the house had it constructed against the wishes of her husband while he was out of the country and it is still known today as 'Granny's Folly'.

9

KINGHAM LODGE

HOLIDAY HOMES

KINGHAM, OXFORDSHIRE

Three charming holiday homes have been created here within a Georgian country house and its grounds in the tiny Cotswold village of Kingham. Originally built in the 17th century, the house was later enlarged to become a gentleman's residence and it is this style and elegance which have been retained throughout its more recent conversion. Lots of restored woodwork, scrubbed pine and antique furniture enhances the spacious rooms and the two larger apartments will certainly provide a taste of gracious living. The largest of the apartments is the Coach House with four bedrooms, one of which has an en suite bathroom. The kitchen is fitted out with all the usual appliances, including a dishwasher, and is large enough to double as a dining room. The sitting room, too, is spacious with an open fireplace and french doors leading out onto a patio and small garden. There is also a separate study/playroom.

The Lodge is really the centrepiece with its Ionic colums supporting the central porch and a ballustraded balcony above. Within this grand exterior is a stylish apartment with spacious rooms, all beautifully furnished, including a kitchen/diner fitted with bespoke oak units. In contrast is the pretty little Yew Tree Cottage – the oldest of the properties – with oak beams, an old stained glass window on the landing and rooms of great character. Its garden of lawn and flower borders is enclosed in a dry-stone wall and its separate approach road and parking area gives it an extra degree of privacy.

Grounds extending to some 4½ acres are available to guests here and they include a croquet lawn and a hard tennis court. Owners Myles and Veronica Metcalfe are to be congratulated for this sympathetic conversion of an old house and for the standard of accommodation which they have created.

OAKFORD
COUNTRY COTTAGES
OAKFORD, DYFED

WINNER
Wales

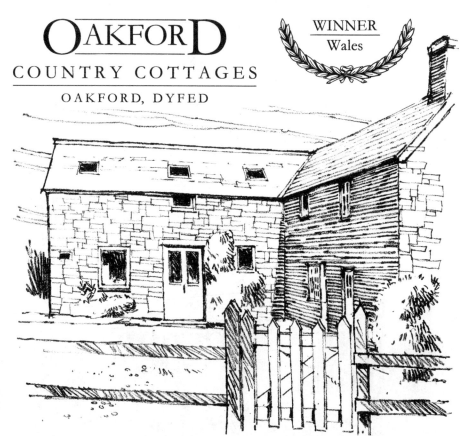

Originally the cottages and outbuildings of an estate, this group of five holiday homes is absolutely delightful. They have been thoughtfully converted, making the best use of the space available while keeping their cottagey character and the craftsmanship is superb, using traditional motifs and proper old-fashioned door latches. In all except the Coach House, which has a separate lounge with wood burning stove, the downstairs living accommodation is open-plan, with well-equipped modern kitchens and Scandinavian-style furniture. Bedrooms are comfortable and have plenty of cupboard and hanging space and the bathrooms are modern. Although furnished similarly, each cottage has its own distinctive character. Barn Owl, so named because owls have made their home in its roof for as long as anyone can remember, has a magnificent 18th-century inglenook fireplace; the Coach House, a listed building, has two enormous arched windows where the entrance doors originally were. There is a separate laundry room, properly equipped and at no extra charge, and in addition to each cottage's small garden, there is a large grassy paddock where children are safe to play. Owners Keith and Wendy Langley, who live about 200 yards away, are very friendly and put a lot of work into maintaining the cottages and offering exceptional service. Fresh flowers are put into each cottage before guests arrive and groceries can be ordered, to be ready on arrival. Information folders are provided, but should there be any queries during a stay here, someone will be on hand in the small site office. Plans are also afoot to have a selection of home-cooked frozen meals available to visitors and there is already a very adequate wine store on the site. We were most impressed with the thought that has gone into these holiday homes – the use of local pottery items, the welcoming gifts for return visitors, and the discount given when two people come to stay in a cottage designed for more.

11

THE OLD APPLE STORE

BROADWAY, HEREFORD & WORCESTER

This elegant and immaculate first-floor apartment is in a wing of a rambling 17th-century Cotswold manor house with extensive gardens. It is a very interesting house – former owners have included an ex-gaiety girl – and at some stage it was pulled down stone by stone and re-erected in the same form, but with all the principal rooms facing south. The apartment's living area is open plan with a modern, very well-equipped kitchen, cottage-style dining area and comfortable lounge area with chintz-covered furniture and a deep window seat looking out over the gardens. The bedroom has a beautifully tiled en suite bathroom and there is another suite of bedroom/bathroom available if required, although this is usually closed off. A coin-operated laundry room is also available. The apartment has its own small private garden, well screened by hedges, but the owner, Mrs Laura Nudd, is happy for guests to wander around the manor's own garden if they wish. Mrs Nudd is friendly and charming and goes to some lengths to cater for the needs of holidaymakers coming to Copgrove. She will order milk and papers, arrange for basic stores to be bought in before arrival and can even arrange for a complete dinner to be prepared locally and brought in and served on the first evening. If guests particularly wish to dine out at a place where advance booking is required, she will take care of this too and if they have a particular interest in some aspect of the area, she will find out all she can for them. General local information is always available. This is a stylish holiday home, set in a particularly lovely area and one where guests will be assured of a warm welcome.

BROCKWOOD PARK

WHICHAM, CUMBRIA

Only a short distance from the heart of the Lake District, Brockwood Park is a complex of 24 Norwegian wood lodges, surrounded by acres of attractive woodland. Unlike many holiday villages, this is a quiet site and one which has great concern for the environment and the surrounding wildlife. Brockwood means badger's wood and there are a number of badgers living in the area. Visitors here are encouraged to take an interest in these fascinating creatures – talks about badgers, and indeed about other aspects of the area's wildlife and environment, are given regularly – and anyone wishing to observe badgers can make use of the specially built hides. Bird watchers will be pleased to see that nest boxes have been fixed to many of the lodges.

The lodges, being Norwegian in design, are very well insulated and able to cope with anything that the vagaries of the British climate can offer. Triple glazing ensures that they remain warm on even the coldest day. The fittings and furnishings are luxurious and some lodges even have their own sauna in the bathroom. Those that don't can take advantage of the general sauna within the village and other facilities include an indoor heated swimming pool and a whirlpool. There is a bar and a small restaurant and take-away meals can be provided on request. The high quality of the accommodation and the care and consideration given to visitors' needs make this a very good centre for a self-catering holiday, particularly for those with an interest in nature and wildlife.

CRAOBH HAVEN

COTTAGES

BY LOCHGILPHEAD, ARGYLL

Our Scottish winner is part of an interesting new development on the west coast which centres on a specially constructed harbour and yacht marina. The eventual aim is to re-create the character and atmosphere of a traditional west highland village and the self-catering cottages form an integral part of this plan. Set apart from the main village street, this small row of cottages certainly has a picturesque appearance from the outside, but it is unlikely that the traditional west highland dweller would have enjoyed the same luxury as these interiors offer. They are built to a very high standard indeed, with spacious rooms and the use of natural timbers everywhere. High quality fitted carpets and comfortable furniture is provided and lots of pictures, ornaments and flower vases complete the homely feel. The kitchens are modern and superbly equipped with dishwashers, washing machines, tumble driers, food processors, coffee makers etc. Although there is full central heating, the cottages also have open fires in the lounge and logs are provided free. Each cottage has spectacular coastal views and visitors here can take advantage of the many recreational facilities which the village can offer – naturally with an emphasis on watersports and boating. Sailing, windsurfing, diving, fishing, water skiing etc are all on offer, with tuition available if required. There is also a riding stable and an exciting adventure playground for the children. This is a superb area for walking and birdwatching too. The village, built in the same style as the holiday homes, houses many of the people who work in the marina and a tightly knit community is fast developing. It also has a village shop, a craft shop/tea room and a pub where food is available.

14

About this book

The aim of this guide is to provide as much up-to-date information as possible for intending visitors to the houses, apartments, bungalows, chalets, cottages, etc which provide self-catering accommodation. However, we do not include places which offer bed-sitting accommodation or static caravans.

Gazetteer

Entries are arranged alphabetically by placename and cover the whole of Great Britain. If you are not sure which town you are looking for, it is probably a good idea to refer in the first instance to the location atlas or county list, details of which are given below.

County list

Our system of presenting the gazetteer in alphabetical order has proved to be most convenient for the majority of people. However, some have written to us stating a preference for places to be set out in county order. For this reason we have included a quick-reference list under county headings and this can be found on pages 264–269.

Location atlas

Another alternative is to plan your holiday around a certain area of the country and the easiest way to do this is to first consult the location atlas at the end of the book. Only those towns and villages which contain listed establishments are shown on the map, so you can easily see where to look in the gazetteer. Each town heading in the gazetteer includes a map reference too, so whichever way you decide to use the book, it is easy to see where you are and to consider all the alternatives.

NB For editorial reasons, the gazetteer is always completed after the atlas pages. Therefore, in some cases, deletions or new entries may not appear on the atlas. Always double-check the town/village names appearing on the map with the gazetteer entries.

AA Inspectors

All establishments in this guide have been inspected to ensure that premises come up to the required standards. The inspectors provide informed and unbiased reports upon which the Self Catering Establishments Committee can base its decisions.

Accommodation types

A wide range of accommodation types will be found in the guide and at the beginning of each description an abbreviation will indicate what type it is. We have accepted the inspectors' definitions of chalet, bungalow, cabin etc.

Booking

All entries contain an address for booking purposes. Where the booking address differs from the establishment address it follows the words "for bookings". When writing to book accommodation, please mention this guide. It is advisable to include a stamped, self-addressed envelope or an International reply paid coupon if enquiring from overseas. Some establishments include a number of units and in order to conserve space we have consolidated their entry. It is important to remember that in such cases it is possible that not all of the units at that location are approved by the AA. You should mention this guide when booking and ensure that the unit you book is among those that we list. It is advisable to book as early in the year as possible to avoid being disappointed.

The Tourism (Sleeping Accommodation, Price Display) Order 1977, compels self catering and other accommodation in Britain with four or more letting bedrooms to display in the reception area the maximum and minimum prices charged for each category of room. This order complements the voluntary Code of Booking Practice. Every effort is being made by the AA to encourage the use of the voluntary Code in appropriate establishments.

Cleaning and vacation of property

Tenants are usually expected to leave the premises clean and vacate the premises by 10am. Incoming tenants may normally arrive from

4pm. Please check these details carefully with the proprietor, since they can vary considerably.

Complaints

Any complaints about service or facilities should be made promptly, giving the proprietor or booking agency the opportunity to correct matters. If a personal approach fails, members should inform the AA regional office nearest to the establishment concerned.

Deposits

When you make the bookings for accommodation, in law you are entering into a contract. You are bound by the conditions which the proprietor stipulates before the contract is made, and the proprietor is equally obliged in law – if he accepts your booking – to give you what you stipulated in the negotiations leading to the confirmation of the booking. If a visitor does not turn up for accommodation, the proprietor must try to relet the accommodation if he can. Illness and accidents either preventing a person from taking up accommodation or obliging the visitor to leave prematurely do not allow the visitor to avoid his legal commitment to pay the proprietor or agency a proportion of monies due, although a reasonable proprietor or agency may, as a gesture, accept a nominal sum.

It is common practice to require a deposit, which may purport to be non-returnable in any event. In such a case, if the visitor breaches the contract, the deposit will be lost and the proprietor or agency may still be able to claim for extra losses suffered by him. But if a deposit is paid on such a basis and the proprietor or agency is shown to be in breach of contract, then the deposit may be recovered as part of the visitor's own claim for damages. (See under Insurance for more details).

Gazetteer entries

Description of accommodation type, layout, and sleeping arrangements are as observed at the time of inspection. Off-season variations in the published conditions and terms of hire, numbers accepted, charges etc may not be covered by the entry. Such matters can often be arranged by private negotiation. Self-catering units are recommended independently of any AA rating or classification which may have been applied to the complex or premises in which self-catering units may occasionally be found (ie hotels and caravan and camp sites).

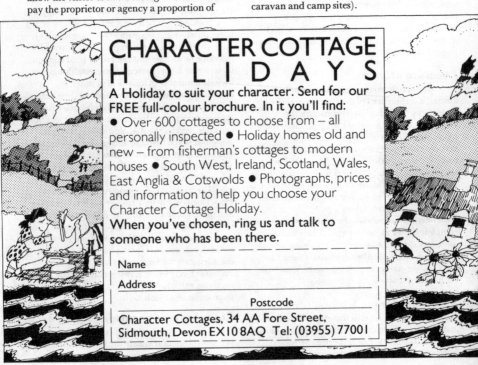

Heating

In each gazetteer entry, identification of source of heating in each gazetteer entry follows details of cooking facilities. The source of heating (other than central heating, indicated by a symbol) may be identified as gas, electric, open fires or coal fires. 'Electric' can mean anything from a fan heater to night storage heating.

High season

In general this is June, July and August, apart from at winter-sports centres.

Holiday complexes

Some of the holiday complexes included in this publication offer accommodation of various types, differing in sleeping arrangements, settings and prices. Full details are normally available from the operator and the maximum and minimum prices quoted are only a rough guide. It is wise to check details through current brochures.

Insurance

Enforced cancellation or curtailment of your holiday part-way through can involve you in considerable expense. It is unlikely that your deposit will be refunded and you will often have to pay the full cost of your holiday. In addition, if you were to lose your luggage or money, or were taken ill or met with an accident, this could completely ruin the enjoyment of your holiday. AA Travelsure is an exclusive policy for holidays and business trips which can help offset the effects of many of the mishaps that may beset the most careful holidaymaker. For full details call in at your local AA Centre or write to:

AA Insurance Services Ltd
FREEPOST
Newcastle upon Tyne NE99 2RP
– no need to use a stamp.

Licensed clubs

Club membership of licensed clubs cannot take effect – nor can a drink be bought – until forty-eight hours after joining

Linen

When booking check whether linen is charged for and the range which is supplied at the property. In some cases linen is available to overseas visitors only; this is indicated in the gazetteer entry.

Hoseasons – Britain's best choice in Holiday-Homes.

For the finest and widest selection of self-catering Holiday-Homes throughout England, Scotland and Wales, you'll find Hoseasons just can't be beaten.

Prices start from as little as £15 per person per week.

Countless activities. Plenty for both young and old alike. Heated swimming pools. Night clubs and a host of sports and relaxation activities. Or just the peace and quiet of beautiful scenery.

Clip the coupon or use our fast Dial-a-Brochure service, for your free brochure today.

Metered Electric/Gas

This can mean both coin operated meter or reading the meter at the end of the stay and a charge made for electricity or gas used.

Pets

Many places accept pets, although an additional charge is sometimes made. If you wish to take your pet, please check all relevant details with the proprietor/agency.

Prices

Rentals quoted are normally minimum/maximum per unit per week inclusive of VAT. Charges are those applicable as at June 1986.

Rent Act

Premises included in this guide are for holiday lets only and are exempt from security of tenure. No details are given of permanent or semi-permanent letting.

Restrictions

Some establishments are not let to single persons nor suitable for invalids. Please check carefully when making your booking to avoid disappointment. The AA publishes a guide specifically for disabled people, the AA Travellers' Guide for the Disabled 1986, available from AA offices (free to members, £2.25 to non-members), which gives details of accommodation suitable for disabled people as well as other useful information.

Standards of accommodation

When considering applications for listing in this guide the AA insists on standards which it considers are necessary for a comfortable stay. Minimum requirements are shown below under Accommodation, Furniture, fixtures and fittings, Services and Linen, also Inventory of Equipment on p.269, but it should be borne in mind that many units offer higher standards.

Accommodation

1 All units to be self-contained.

2 Bedrooms or sleeping areas to be of reasonable size in relation to the number of occupants; this number to be assessed according to the number of beds (single and double) provided. Convertible settees are acceptable in living rooms as extra bed-space but this should be included in the assessment.

3 Kitchen/Kitchenettes may not be sited in bedrooms.

4 Bath/shower Rooms and Lavatories: each unit to have a private bath or shower room (with wash-basin if any bedroom is without washbasin and mirror) and a flush toilet (with toilet paper and disposal bin).

5 Windows: each bedroom to have at least one window of reasonable size, which can be opened. Skylights are acceptable if in keeping with the style of building. All windows in sleeping areas to be fitted with adequate curtains or blinds. All living rooms and kitchens to have windows capable of being opened directly into the open air.

6 Ventilation: all passages, staircases, communal rooms, bathrooms and lavatories to have adequate ventilation.

7 Floors: all areas to have a suitable floor covering or finish.

8 At least 75% of units under one ownership within a complex to be up to AA standard and listed.

Furniture, fixtures and fittings

1 Beds: to be of comfortable proportions and in good condition, equipped with spring interior or foam mattresses. The following is a guide to minimum sizes: Single: 6'3" × 3' (190 × 90cms). Double 6'3" × 4'6" (190 × 135cm). Children's bunks and folding beds: 5'2" × 2'6" (157 × 76cms).

2 Furniture: adequate for the number of persons accommodated to include at least one dressing table or equivalent and a mirror and adequate wardrobe space equipped with hangers. All furniture to be kept in good condition.

3 Kitchen fixtures and equipment: each kitchen to be equipped with:

   a) Either a gas or electric cooker (or solid fuel cooker where appropriate) with not less than two rings or their equivalent, and a means of grilling or toasting.

   b) A ventilated food-storage cupboard or refrigerator.

   c) An impervious working surface for food preparation.

   d) A sink with draining board.

   e) A pedal bin or other covered refuse container.

4 Miscellaneous equipment: each unit to be provided with:

   a) Adequate dustbins outside the unit.

   b) Adequate ashtrays and waste-paper containers.

Services

Each unit supplied with:

a) Hot, cold and drinking water. Meters acceptable.

b) Lighting to be adequate in all areas including passages, corridors and staircases. Meters acceptable.

c) Heating levels to be adequate for the season when the unit is let. Meters acceptable.

d) Solid fuel (peat, coal etc as appropriate) where no other fuel is available.

Linen

Where linen is provided it must be changed between lets and spare linen should be available for lets of more than one week.

Inventory

An inventory of the equipment which must be supplied in each holiday home can be found on page 269

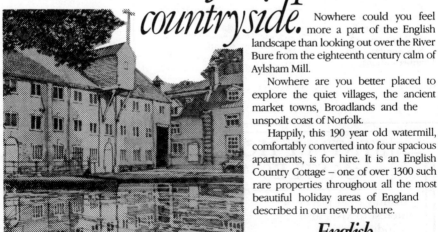

Explanation of a gazetteer entry

The example is **fictitious**

Map Reference
First figure is map page no. Then follows grid reference: read 1st figure across, (east) 2nd figure vertically (north).

Town Name
Appears in bold capitals in alphabetical order.

County Name
Administrative county names are used (both region and old county names are given for Scotland).

Classification
Cottage.

ALL STRETTON
Shropshire
Map **7** SO49

C   The Alders & Corner Cottage
for bookings Mrs E R Allen, Post Office Stores, Alstonefield, Ashbourne, Derbys DE6 2FX
☎Alstonefield(033527)201

Bookings
Address for bookings.

This small, white-washed 17th-century cottage comprises bathroom, kitchen, lounge/diner, double and single bedrooms and a good sized, secluded garden. A delightful situation with the Long Mynd as background.

Telephone Number for Bookings

Specific Details
Letting period, number of units, number of persons accommodated, facilities, terms. See 'Symbols and abbreviations'

All year   MWB out of season   2days min, 6wks max, 1unit, 1−4 persons ⊚ fridge open fires & storage heaters Elec metered ▯not provided ☎(1½m) TV ⊕3pin square   4P ⊇(1½m) ⊖ ♀(1½m)

Min£80 Max£150pw

Description
Description of establishment, sleeping arrangements, setting etc.

Gazetteer

The gazetteer gives locations and details of AA-listed self catering establishments in England, Wales and Scotland.
Locations on Islands are listed under the appropriate Island heading. The gazetteer text also gives suitable cross-references. A useful first point of reference is to consult the location maps which show where AA-listed establishments are situated. NB *There is no map for Isles of Scilly*

1986 prices quoted throughout the gazetteer.

Abbey Dore
—
Abercastle

ABBEY DORE
Hereford & Worcester
Map**3** SO32

H **Kerrys Gate Farmhouse**
for bookings Mrs M Jenkins, Blackbush Farm, Abbey Dore, Hereford
☎Golden Valley(0981)240281
A modernised, brick-built farmhouse situated in a quiet, picturesque village. Consists of lounge, dining room, kitchen/breakfast room, WC, two double bedrooms, one twin room, one bunk-bedded room and bathroom.
All year MWB out of season 1wk min, 6mths max, 1unit, 1–8persons ◆ ◆
⊚ fridge Electric Elec metered ⊔ can be hired ☎(20yds) Iron & Ironing board in unit TV ⊕3pin square P ⚓(4m)
⊖ ♨ (2½m)
Min£60 Max£85pw (Low)
Min£90 Max£110pw (High)

C **Poplar Cottage**
for bookings Mrs M Jenkins, Blackbush Farm, Abbey Dore, Hereford
☎Golden Valley(0981)240281
A detached brick cottage with its own garden overlooking the surrounding

---

countryside. Comprises lounge, bathroom, kitchen/dining area, two double bedrooms, and a twin-bedded room.
All year MWB out of season 1wk min, 6mths max, 1unit, 1–6persons ◆ ◆
⊚ fridge Electric Elec metered ⊔ can be hired ☎(30yds) Iron in unit
⊕3pin square P ⚓ ▥ ⚘(3m)
⊖ ♨ (2m)
Min£55 Max£80pw (Low)
Min£85 Max£100pw (High)

ABERCASTLE
Dyfed
Map**2** SM83

C **Ffesant & Cariad**
for bookings Coastal Cottage's of Pembrokeshire, Seaview, Abercastle, Mathry, Dyfed SA62 5HJ
☎Croesgoch(03483)7742
A beautifully restored stone barn, converted to form these two cottages. Both are well furnished and have good views across the valley and to the sea
Ffesant *comprises lounge/diner, well-fitted kitchen, bathroom one double bedroom, one twin and also one single bedroom.*
Cariad *comprises split-level sitting room and dining area, kitchen with built-in hob and oven, bathroom, one twin bedroom, one with two children's bunk beds and there is also a gallery bedroom, with double bed overlooking the sitting room.* →

All year MWB out of season 4days min,
2mths max, 2units, 2–6persons ◊ ◆
⊚ fridge ₩(calor gas) Gas & Elec
metered ⊞inclusive ☎(50yds) WM &
SD in units Iron & Ironing board in unit
☺ CTV ⊕3pin square 2P ⊞ ⚞(1m)
⊷ ⚱(1m)
Min£75 Max£320pw

ABERCRAF (Abercrave)
Powys
Map3 SN81

B   Dan-yr-Ogof Holiday Homes
for bookings Blakes Holidays, Wroxham,
Norwich NR12 8DH
☎Wroxham(06053)2917

Attractive bungalow style apartments for
2–8 people situated midway between
Brecon and Swansea on the A4067 in the
Brecon Beacons National Park. These well
appointed units are tastefully furnished
and decorated and set within a small
holiday complex offering good leisure
facilities including dry ski-slopes, squash
and sauna. All have mountain views from
lounges. There is a specially designed
chalet for disabled persons.

All year MWB out of season 1wk min,
17units, 1–8persons ◊ ◆ ⊚ fridge
Electric Elec inclusive ⊞inclusive ☎
Iron & Ironing board in unit   Launderette
on premises ☺ CTV ⊕3pin square
P ⚞(1m) ▭ ⚭Hard putting
⊷ ⚱ ♫

Details not confirmed for 1987

ABERDOVEY
Gwynedd
Map6 SN69

B & F   Landmaster Investment
Aberdovey Hillside Village Aberdovey,
Gwynedd LL35 0ND
☎Aberdovey(065472)522

This high class development of
bungalows, flats and split-level
apartments, most with ground level
entrances, has commanding views over
the Dovey estuary. Each apartment is well
furnished, with between one and four
bedrooms and all modern facilities
including dishwasher and freezer in four
of the units.

All year MWB out of season 3days min,
6wks max, 18units, 2–10persons ◊ ◆
◆ ⊚ fridge ₩(2units) storage/panel
heaters 16units Elec inclusive (2units)
Elec metered (except storage heaters,
16units) ⊞inclusive ☎ Iron & Ironing
board in unit [Launderette on premises]
☺ CTV ⊕3pin square P ⊞
⚞(300yds)
⊷ ⚐(1m) ⚱(300yds)
Min£75 Max£135pw (Low)
Min£230 Max£375pw (High)

F   1–4 Beach Cottages
for bookings Mr J D Menhinick, Beach
Cottage Holidays, 10 Glandovey,
Aberdovey, Gwynedd LL35 0EB
☎Aberdovey(065472)595

Abercastle
—
Aberfeldy

Former railway station converted into four
flats, situated near beach, sand dunes and
golf course. They have either a lounge or
lounge/diner, kitchen or kitchen/diner and
with the exception of Flat 2 which has a
bathroom/WC they have a shower/WC.
Flat 1 has four bedrooms and the others
have two bedrooms, all located on the first
floor.

Mar–Oct MWB out of season 1wk min,
1mth max, 4units, 2–8persons [◊] ◊
◆ ⊚ fridge Electric Elec metered
⊞not provided ☎(200yds) Iron in unit
☺ TV can be hired ⊕3pin square 8P
⊞ ⚞(200yds) ⊷ ⚐(50yds)
Min£56 Max£184pw

F   Mr & Mrs C A Bendall **Hafod**
Glandovey Terrace, Aberdovey, Gwynedd
LL35 0EB
☎Aberdovey(065472)418

These units consist of six maisonettes and
seven flats of varying size and design. All
are well furnished and newly-decorated
and are situated on the seafront in a
terrace of three houses.

All year MWB out of season 6wks max,
13units, 2–7persons ◊ ◊ ◆ ⊚
fridge ₩or Electric heaters
Elec metered ⊞can be hired
☎(100yds) Iron & Ironing board on
premises [Launderette on premises]
☺ TV can be hired ⊕3pin square
⚞(10yds)
⊷ ⚐(300yds) ⚱(100yds) ⚭(300yds)
Pitch & Putt(300yds)
Min£40 Max£90pw (Low)
Min£80 Max£200pw (High)

Ch   Plas Panteidal Holiday Village
for bookings Haven Holidays, PO Box 20,
Truro, Cornwall TR1 2UG
☎Truro(0872)40400

Lying 300ft above sea level, the detached
cedarwood chalets stand in 40 acres of
wooded hillside facing south over the
Dovey estuary. All chalets are detached,
with one, two, three or four bedrooms,
lounge/diner, kitchen, bathroom and WC.
Restaurant available.

Etr & Apr–Oct MWB 2days min, 92units,
2–8persons [◊] ⊚ fridge
Electric heaters Elec metered
⊞inclusive ☎(¼m) Iron & Ironing board
on premises [Launderette on premises]
☺ CTV ⊕3pin square P ⚞(¼m) ⚊
Childrens playground, table tennis games
room & Pool table
⊷ ⚐(3m) ⚱(200yds)
Min£61 Max£204pw (Low)
Min£140 Max£306pw (High)

F   Mr J D'Arcy **Rumbles** 17a Glandovey
Terrace, Aberdovey Gwynedd LL35 0EB
☎Aberdovey(065472)7792

A comfortable apartment on the first floor
of a seafront house. The accommodation

---

comprises a large open plan lounge, diner
and kitchen with two convertible single
bed-settees, separate bath/WC and one
twin-bedded room. A restaurant is
available on the premises if required.

All year MWB out of season 1day min,
6wks max, 1unit, 2–4persons ◊ ◆
⊚ fridge ₩storage & portable
Elec inclusive ⊞inclusive ☎(20yds)
[WM, SD & TD on premises] Iron &
Ironing board in unit ☺ ⊕ CTV
⊕3pin square ⊞ ⚞(40yds)
⊷ ⚐(½m) ⚱(40yds)
Min£95 Max£295pw

ABEREIDDY
Dyfed
Map2 SM73

C   Bank Farm
for bookings Coastal Cottages of
Pembrokeshire, Seaview, Abercastle,
Mathry, Dyfed SA62 5HJ
☎Croesgoch(03483)7742

A recently renovated cottage retaining
many of its original stone features,
situated close to the beach. It is
comfortably furnished and has a sheltered
sun terrace at the rear. Accommodation
comprises sitting room with open fire,
kitchen, dining room, bathroom, one
double bedroom with additional single
bed and one twin-bedded room.

All year MWB out of season 4days min,
2mths max, 1unit, 2–5persons ◊ ◆
no pets ⊚ fridge storage, open &
portable fires Elec metered ⊞inclusive
☎(1m) Iron & Ironing board in unit ☺
CTV ⊕3pin square 2P ⊞ ⚞(1½m)
⊷ ⚱(1½m)
Min£80 Max£340pw

C   The Villa
for bookings Coastal Cottages of
Pembrokeshire, Seaview, Abercastle,
Mathry, Dyfed SA62 5HJ
☎Croesgoch(03483)7742

A carefully restored and renovated
cottage, set quietly back off the beach with
a peaceful sheltered garden. The
accommodation is all on ground level and
comprises lounge, kitchen/diner,
bathroom/WC, two double bedrooms, one
bunk bedroom and one twin-bedded
room.

All year MWB out of season 4days min,
2mths max, 1 unit, 2–8persons ◊ ◆
no pets ⊚ fridge storage, open &
portable fires Elec metered ⊞inclusive
☎(1m) Iron & Ironing board in unit ☺
CTV ⊕3pin square 2P ⊞ ⚞(1½m)
⊷ ⚱(1½m)
Min£85 Max£370pw

ABERFELDY
Tayside *Perthshire*
Map14 NN84

Ch & G Mr & Mrs R S Middlemass
Aberfeldy Country Cottages Moness
Farm, Aberfeldy, Perthshire PH15 2DY
☎Aberfeldy(0887)20851

Well-equipped accommodation in pleasant surroundings. The cottages, standing on three sides of a sheltered courtyard garden, range in size from one bedroom to two bedroom units having spacious living area with convertible couch. Adjacent, set in former walled garden, are the spacious two bedroomed chalets. Their living rooms (with convertible couch) have large picture windows.

28Mar–Oct MWB out of season 2 nights min, 3wks max, 17 units, 1–6persons [◇ ◆] no pets ◎ fridge Electric Elec metered ⌂inclusive (except towels) ☎ [WM, SD & TD on premises] Iron & Ironing board in unit ☉ CTV ⊕3pin square 24P Ⅲ ⚏(½m)
↔ ♪(½m) ♀(½m) ✈(½m)
Sports centre(½m)
Min£97 Max£141pw (Low)
Min£181 Max£261pw (High)

ABERGAVENNY
Gwent
Map3 SO31

F Clytha Castle
for bookings Landmark Trust, Shottesbrooke, Maidenhead, Berkshire
☎Littlewick Green(062882)5925

Perched high above rolling Monmouthshire countryside and River Usk it offers very commendable and a quite unique style of accommodation. Stylish, spacious rooms adorned with period furniture promote their own distinct individuality offering comfort and character. It comprises lounge, kitchen, elegant dining room, spacious bathroom/WC, two twin-bedded rooms and a large circular double bedroom on the ground floor.

All year MWB out of season 7days min, 1unit, 1–6persons ◆ ◎ fridge storage heaters & open fires electric inclusive ⌂notprovided ☎(2m) Iron & Ironing board in unit ☉ ⊕3pin square ⊕3pin round 5P ⚏(3m)
↔ ♀(3m)
Min£275 Max£385pw

ABERGYNOLWYN
Gwynedd
Map6 SH60

F Dolgoch Falls Holiday Apartments
for bookings Shaws Holidays, Y Maes, Pwllheli, Gwynedd LL53 5HA
☎Pwllheli(0758)614422

Built of traditional slate and stone these modern apartments provide good comfortable accommodation. They comprise kitchen, lounge/dining room (one with double bed-settee), bath or shower/WC and between two and four bedrooms and sleeping 2–8 persons. Situated 200 yards from the falls.

All year wkd min, 6wks max, 6units, 2–8persons ◆ ◎ fridge Electric & storage heaters Elec metered ⌂inclusive (ex tea towels) ☎(100yds)

Iron & Ironing board in unit ☉ CTV ⊕3pin square Ⅲ ⚏(2¼m)
↔ ♀(2½m)
Min£93 Max£195pw

C Gamalit
for bookings Mrs M Jones, Tyn-y-Bryn Farm, Llanfihangel, Tywyn, Gwynedd LL36 9TN
☎Abergynolwyn(065477)277

On the Gwernol River in the centre of the village, this traditional farm cottage has beamed lounge, kitchen/diner and bathroom on the gound floor and three bedrooms on the first. With good views of Cader Idris range the cottage is approached by footbridge over river at rear of the chapel.

All year MWB out of season wkd min, 6wks max, 1unit, 2–5persons ◆ ◎ fridge Electric storage heaters & open fires (logs provided free) Elec metered ⌂can be hired ☎(300yds) Iron & Ironing board in unit ☉ CTV ⊕3pin square 2P Ⅲ ⚏(300yds)
↔ ♀(300yds)
Min£50 Max£180pw

ABERPORTH
Dyfed
Map2 SN25

F Mr R M L Morris Glan-y-Mor Apartments Aberporth, Cardigan, Dyfed SA43 2EN
☎Aberporth(0239)810861

Purpose-built apartments designed for up to four adults or ideal for families. One room can be divided into two at nights by a curtain type divider. Cooking facilities adjoin the dining/sitting area. Double bed-settee and twin beds provide the sleeping accommodation. The apartments are adjacent to the Morlan Motel.

All year MWB 1wk min, 23units, 2–4persons ◇ ◆ ◆ ◎ fridge ♨ Elec inclusive ⌂inclusive ☎ [Launderette on premises] ☉ ☯ CTV ⊕3pin square 25P ⚏
↔ ♀

Details not confirmed for 1987

ABERSOCH
Gwynedd
Map6 SH32

H 139 Cae Du
for bookings Shaws Holidays, Y Maes, Pwllheli, Gwynedd LL53 5HA
☎Pwllheli(0758)614422

Modern end of terrace house comprising kitchen/diner, lounge on ground floor and bathroom/WC, one double, one twin and one bunk-bedded room on the first floor. Located in a new private estate it is within walking distance of the beach and shops.

All year wkd min, 6wks max, 1 unit, 2–6persons no pets ◎ fridge Electric heaters Elec metered ⌂not provided ☎(200yds) WM in unit Iron & Ironing board in unit ☉ CTV ⊕3pin square ⚏(200yds)
↔ ♪(1m) ♀(½m) ♬(½m) ♪(½m)
Min£40 Max£165pw

C Tyn Don Holiday Cottages Tyn Don Farm
for bookings Mrs M J Bailey, The Dairy House, 21 Salisbury Rd, Burton, Christchurch, Dorset BH23 7JG
☎Christchurch(0202)486630

Five self-contained cottages with spacious rooms, beamed ceilings, open-plan pine staircase and modern furnishings including pine tables and chairs. Four of the cottages have showers, the other a bathroom. Llanengan 1½m SW unclass road.

Mar–Oct MWB out of season wkd min, 5units, 5–8persons ◆ ◆ ◎ fridge Electric Elec metered ⌂not provided ☎ Iron & Ironing board in unit Launderette within 300yds ☉ TV ⊕3pin square P Ⅲ ⚏(1m)
↔ ♀(1m)
Min£69 Max£80pw (Low)
Min£170 Max£215pw (High)

B Mrs J Jones **Tynewydd** Sarn Bach, Abersoch, Gwynedd LL53 7LE
☎Abersoch(075881)2446

Farm cottage recently modernised throughout. Accommodation consists of lounge/diner, large kitchen, one double bedroom and one sleeping three persons, bathroom/WC. From Abersoch take Sarn Bach road, on entering village turn right, cottage on left in private road.

All year 1wk min, 1mth max, 1unit, 1–5persons ◎ fridge ♨ Elec metered ⌂not provided ☎(½m) Iron & Ironing board in unit ☉ TV ⊕3pin square 2P Ⅲ ⚏(½m)
↔ ♪(1m) ♀(1m)
Min£60 Max£150pw

ABERYSTWYTH
Dyfed
Map6 SN58

F Ael-y-Don Holiday Flats Cliff Terrace
for bookings Mrs M Spear, Tidesreach, Borth, Dyfed SY24 5NN
☎Borth(097081)431

Ael-y-Don and Gwen-y-Don are two semi-detached houses situated about 50yds from the promenade, facing the sea. Both have been converted into self contained flats and sleep from 2–6 people. All flats comprise one bedroom and lounge with one or two bed-settees. Flat 1 has a bath all the others have showers.

Jul–Sep MWB in season 1wk min, 15units, 2–6persons no pets ◎ fridge ♨ Elec inclusive ⌂can be hired ☎(30yds) ☉ CTV ⊕3pin square Ⅲ ⚏(200yds) →

⊖ &(½m) ♨(150yds) 🎵(¾m)
Min£48 Max£135pw

ABOYNE
Grampian *Aberdeenshire*
Map15 NO59

Ch Aboyne Loch Caravan Park
for bookings Mr P Garioch, Tigh-na-Dee,
Drumoak, Kincardineshire AB3 3AU
☎Aboyne(0339)2244

Four modern semi-timber chalets set on wooded promontory of land with views over Aboyne Loch, which provides fishing and boating. They offer combined lounge/diner/kitchen, shower/WC and two bedrooms. Access from A93 ½m E of village.

Apr–Oct MWB out of season 3days min, 1mth max, 4units, 1–4persons ⓖ fridge Electric Elec metered Ⓛnot provided ☎ WM on premises Iron & Ironing board on premises ☺ TV ③3pin square 4P 🅃 ♨(½m)
⊖ &(300yds) ♨(½m) 🎵(½m) 🎵(½m)
Details not confirmed for 1987

C Kirkton Cottages
for bookings Holiday Dept 6, Estate Office, Old Station, Dinnet, Aboyne, Aberdeenshire AB35 5LL
☎Dinnet(033985)341

Twelve former poor houses (listed buildings) which have been modernised and converted into three holiday cottages. Each offers living room/diner, kitchen, two bedrooms and two shower rooms/WC. They are sited just west of Aboyne in open countryside with good views and limited traffic noise.

Mar–24Oct 1wk min, 1mth max, 3units, 1–4persons ◆ no pets ⓖ fridge Electric Elec inclusive Ⓛcan be hired ☎(2m) ☺ CTV ③3pin square P ♨(2m)
⊖ ♨(2m) 🎵(2m)
£89pw (Low)
£98pw (High)

ACRISE
Kent
Map5 TR14

F Mrs R M Patrick The Granary
Ladwood Farm, Acrise, Folkestone, Kent
☎Hawkinge(030389)3157 & Folkestone(0303)53077

A delightful converted granary dating back at least two centuries. This first-floor flat is built on the old flint walls of a cartlodge. The interior has planked walls and the original floor exists. The accommodation comprises two

Aberystwyth
—
Alcester

bedrooms; one with a double bed, the other with bunk beds. The lounge sofa converts into two beds if required. Modern bathroom and fitted kitchen.

All year MWB 1wk min, 3mths max, 1unit, 6persons ◆ ◆ no pets 🔥(Calor) fridge Coal & log burning fire, also electric Gas, coal & logs inclusive Elec metred Ⓛcan be hired Iron in unit ☺ CTV ③3pin square 2P 🅃 ♨(1½m)
⊖ ♨(2m) riding
Min£80 Max£130pw

AIRTH
Central *Stirlingshire*
Map11 NS98

H The Pineapple Dunmore
for bookings The Landmark Trust, Shottesbrooke Park, Maidenhead, Berkshire SL6 3SW
☎Littlewick Green(062882)5925

The Pineapple House was built by 18th-century stonemasons to celebrate the first pineapple grown in Scotland. A stone gazebo is topped by a pineapple-shaped roof. After restoration, the house has a high standard of décor and fittings, with fine furniture. Bedrooms and bathrooms are not internally linked with sitting room and modern kitchen. Situated just N of Airth and reached by ½m long track from the A905/B9124 junction.

All year MWB out of season 1day min, 3wks max, 1unit, 2–4persons ◆ ◆ ⓖ fridge Electric & open fires Elec inclusive Ⓛnot provided ☎(1m) Iron & Ironing board in unit ☺ ③3pin square P ♨(1m)
⊖ ♨(1m)
Min£133 Max£240pw (Low)
Min£170 Max£250pw (High)

ALCAIG
Highland *Ross & Cromarty*
Map14 NH55

B Cherrytree Cottage
for bookings Mrs M Macduff-Duncan, Alcaig, Conon Bridge, Ross-shire IV7 8HS
☎Dingwall(0349)61220

A detached, timber-clad bungalow with sun porch located on Alcaig farm, close to the main buildings, yet still retaining fine outlook. Pleasantly furnished accommodation comprises lounge/dining

room, kitchen, bathroom and three double bedrooms one with an additional single bed. Small neat garden with extensive views of Cromarty Firth and hills. 1m E of Conon Bridge.

2May–3Oct 1wk min, 1unit, 1–7persons ◆ no cats ⓖ fridge Electric & coal fires Elec metered Ⓛnot provided ☎(1m) WM in unit Iron & Ironing board in unit ☺ ③3pin square P 🅃
⊖ ♨(1m) 🎵(3m) 🐾(3m)
Min£57 Max£94pw

C Larchtree Cottage Alcaig Farm
for bookings Mrs M Macduff-Duncan, Alcaig, Conon Bridge, Ross-shire IV7 8HS
☎Dingwall(0349)61220

A detached cottage with sun porch on farm with pleasant outlook across surrounding countryside towards Wester Ross. Accommodation comprises a ground floor with kitchen, living room and two double bedrooms, one with additional single bed and an attic bedroom reached by way of a fixed extending ladder and ideal for a child.

2May–3Oct 1wk min, 1unit, 1–6persons ◆ no cats ⓖ fridge Electric & open fires Elec metered Ⓛnot provided ☎(1m) Iron & Ironing board in unit ☺ ③3pin square P 🅃(1m) ♨(1m)
⊖ &(3m) ♨(1m)
Min£50 Max£88pw

ALCESTER
Warwickshire
Map4 SP05

H Cold Comfort Farm Ragley Estate
for bookings Heart of England Cottages, The Barrel & Basket, The Market Place, Fairford, Gloucestershire GL7 4AB
☎Cirencester(0285)713295

Set in quiet picturesque rural setting this old farmhouse (part of which dates back to the 17th century) comprises sitting room with open fireplace, dining room, games room, large kitchen/diner, utility room, cloakroom with WC. The first floor has three twin and two double bedrooms, three bathrooms, one with WC and a separate WC.

All year MWB out of season 3days min, 6mths max, 1unit, 1–10persons ◆ ◆ ⓖ fridge 🍽 Elec inclusive Ⓛcan be hired (overseas visitors only) ☎ WM & TD in unit Iron & Ironing board in unit CTV ③3pin square 4P ♨(½m)
⊖ ♨(½m)
Min£185 Max£225pw (Low)
Min£240 Max£315pw (High)

H   Wood Bevington Manor 1 & 2 Wood Bevington
for bookings Heart of England Cottages, The Barrel & Basket, The Market Place, Fairford, Gloucestershire GL7 4AB
☎Cirencester(0285)713295

Ancient manor house steeped in history, situated at the top of a gentle rise above the hamlet of Wood Bevington. Number One is the largest and comprises flagged entrance hall, dining room, large drawing room both with open fireplaces, kitchen with dishwashing machine, twin-bedded room and bathroom/WC. Three bedrooms upstairs, two double-bedded, one twin-bedded and bathroom/WC. Number Two is the second half of this manor house and comprises sitting/dining room, kitchen all on ground floor and upstairs has one double-bedded room, two twin-bedded rooms (one with bathroom/WC). Can be rented as a whole (adjoining door) to sleep 14.

All year   MWB out of season   3 days min, 6mths max, 2 units, 1–8 persons   ◇ ◆
◎ fridge   ⌘ Elec inclusive   ⌷can be hired (overseas visitors only)   ☎ WM in unit   SD in unit(No 1)   Iron & Ironing board in unit   ⊕ CTV   ⊕3 pin square   10P   ⚒(½m)
⊕ ⚑ (¾m)

Min£95 Max£225pw (Low)
Min£110 Max£315pw (High)

ALDEBURGH
Suffolk
Map**5** TM45

C   Gallery Cottage Crabbe Street
for bookings Mrs J Cowan, 9 Crabbe Street, Aldeburgh, Suffolk IP15 2BW
☎Aldeburgh(072885)2909

Two-storey terraced cottage at rear of High Street just across from the beach: access is via a private garden. Accommodation comprises kitchen/diner, lounge with put-u-up settee, one double bedroom with extra single bed and bathroom/WC.

All year   MWB out of season   3 days min, 4wks max, 1 unit, 1–5 persons   no cats
◎ fridge   Electric   Elec metered
⌷not provided   ☎(100yds)   WM & SD in unit   Iron & Ironing board in unit   ⊕ ⊛
TV can be hired   ⊕3 pin square   ⊞   ⚒
⊕ ♪(1m)   ⚑ (200yds)

Min£50 Max£70pw (Low)
Min£75 Max£115pw (High)

F   4A King Street
for booking Mrs D M Neild, 44 Crag Path, Aldeburgh, Suffolk IP15 5BT
☎Aldeburg(072885)2218

Maisonette sleeping up to seven persons, and approached by three flights of outside stairs. Situated on the promenade overlooking pebble Beach and the sea.

All year   MWB out of season   7 days min, 8wks max, 1 unit, 2–7 persons   no pets
◎ fridge   Electric   Elec metered
⌷not provided   ☎(150yds)   Iron & Ironing board   ⊕ TV can be hired
⊕3 pin square   2P   ⊞   ⚒(100yds)

Alcester
—
Alford

⊕ ♪ ⚑ 𝄞 🎱
Min£60 Max£90pw (Low)
Min£100 Max£130pw (High)

H   The Martello Tower
for bookings The Landmark, Trust, Shottesbrooke, Maidenhead, Berkshire SL6 3SW
☎Littlewick Green(062882)5925

This is the largest and most northerly of the chain of towers put up by the board of ordnance to keep out Napoleon. Built in the shape of a quatrefoil for four heavy guns, nearly a million bricks were used in its construction. The accommodation has two twin-bedded rooms, with one stowaway bed and two solid hammocks, the latter put up in the lounge area. Children should be warned about being careful when crossing the moat bridge and of the cellar steps.

All year   MWB out of season   2 days min, 1 unit, 1–5 persons   ◆ ◎ fridge
Electric   Elec inclusive   ⌷not provided
☎(½m)   Iron & Ironing board on premises   ⊕ ⊕3 pin square   P   ⚒(1m)
⊕ ♪(2m)   🎱(1m)

Min£195 Max£305pw

ALDERNEY
See **Channel Islands**

ALDFIELD
North Yorkshire
Map**8** SE26

C   Mrs E I Graham, Druids Lodge, Druids Farm, Aldfield, Ripon, North Yorkshire HG4 3BE
☎Sawley(076586)216

Part of 160 year old farmhouse in attractive farm gardens with rural views. The cottage has a separate entrance and comprises ground-floor kitchen/diner/ sitting room with adjoining spacious bathroom and separate WC plus two bedrooms on the first-floor.

All year   MWB out of season   4 days min, 4mths max, 1 unit, 1–4 persons   ◇ ◆
no pets   🐕 fridge   Electric
Gas inclusive   Elec metered   ⌷can be hired   ☎(200yds)   Iron & Ironing board on premises   ⊕ TV   ⊕3 pin square   3P
⚒(3½m)   Riding stables
⊕ ⚑ (1½m)

Min£30 Max£40pw (Low)
Min£60 Max£85pw (High)

ALDSWORTH
Gloucestershire
Map**4** SP11

C   A & C Richards Swyre Farm,
Aldsworth, Cheltenham, Gloucestershire GL54 3RE
☎Shipton under Wychwood(0993)830252

Once the barns of Swyre Farm, these six cottages are grouped round a charming walled gaden, surrounded by four acres of fields and orchards. Apple and Pheasants Run 1 sleep two to four persons while Bramble and Pheasants Run 2 & 3 sleep up to six. Orchard is designed for the disabled visitor and has one twin bedroom and a further twin bedroom can be made available. All have fitted carpets, and are furnished with pine and cane. Table tennis and badminton.

All year   MWB out of season   2 night min, 3mths max, 6 units, 2–6 persons   ◇ ◆
no pets   ◎ fridge   ⌘ Elec metered
⌷inclusive   ☎(¾m)   WM in Apple   Iron in unit   Ironing board on premises   ⊕
CTV   ⊕3 pin square   12P   ⊞   ⚒(2m)
⊕ ⚑ (1m)

Min£115 Max£172pw (Low)
Min£149 Max£225pw (High)

ALFORD
Grampian *Aberdeenshire*
Map**15** NJ51

H   Balfluig Castle
for bookings Mr M I Tennant, 8 New Square, Lincoln's Inn, London WC2A 3QP
☎01-242 4986

A finely restored 16th-century castle which retains much of the original character and is furnished to a high standard throughout. The four-storeyed accommodation has kitchen, dining room and cloakroom/laundry on the ground floor. The great hall makes a spacious lounge on the first floor. There are two bedrooms (one with four-poster bed and one with twin-bedded room) and two fully-equipped bathrooms on the second floor; two bedrooms (one single and one double) and bathroom (no WC) on the third floor and one double bedroom with washbasin on the fourth-floor. A unique opportunity for an ideal holiday in the Scottish Highlands.

All year   MWB out of season   1wk min, 1mth max, 1 unit, 1–9 persons   [◇]
no pets   ◎ fridge   Electric & log fires
Elec metered   ⌷inclusive   WM & SD in unit   Iron & Ironing board in unit   ⊕ TV can be hired   ⊕3 pin square   P   ⊞
⚒(1m)
⊕ ♪ ⚑(1m)
£350pw

B & F   Site Warden Haughton House
Haughton Country Park, Alford, Aberdeenshire
☎Alford(0336)2107

The five flats are set in an 18th-century granite mansion and the bungalow is in the grounds of the extensive country park, which is wooded. The properties are decorated to a neat standard with modern furnishings. The bungalow sleeps six and the flats sleep between two and eight.

27Mar–5Oct   MWB out of season
2 days min, 1mth max, 6 units, 2–8 persons
◆ ◆   no pets   ◎ fridge   Electric
Elec metered   ⌷not provided   ☎ Iron & Ironing board on premises   Launderette →

25

on premises ⊕ TV ⊕3pin square 8P
⛟ ♨

⟷ 🛁(1m) 🚽(1m)

Min£75 Max£100pw (Low)
Min£80 Max£110pw (High)

ALLERFORD
Somerset
Map**3** SS94

F & C Mr & Mrs B T Foster **Lynch**,
Allerford, Porlock, Somerset
☎Porlock(0643)862800

*An attractive country house in an elevated,
woodland setting overlooking the sea and
moors. It offers six spacious, well-
appointed apartments and a three
bedroomed cottage within the seven-acre
landscaped gardens. The peaceful water
gardens are also an added delight. Tennis
and squash courts are available for
resident's use.*

**AA Holiday Home of the Year 1986–7 –
see page 7.**

Allyear MWM out of season 3nights min,
9units, 2–8persons ◈ ◆ no pets
(except in Gate Cottage & Stable Flat)
◎ fridge 🍴 Elec metered
🔲inclusive ☎ WM, SD & TD on
premises Iron & Ironing board on
premises ⊕ CTV ⊕3pin square P
⛟ ♨(½m) 🏌Hard pitch & putt
Squash

⟷ 🚽(1m)

Alford
—
Alstonefield

Min £90 Max £245pw (Low)
Min £115 Max £295pw (High)

ALSOP en le DALE
Derbyshire
Map**7** SK15

C Mrs M J Lapworth **New Inns Holiday
Cottages**, Alsop en le Dale, Ashbourne.
Derbyshire
☎Alstonefield(033527)203

*A row of four modern single storey
cottages converted from a former stone-
built stable block. One has two twin- and
one bunk-room, the other three have two
twin-bedded rooms. They each comprise
open plan lounge/diner/kitchen and
shower/WC. All have comfortable
furnishings and modern fixtures and
fittings. Situated in the grounds of
proprietor's Pub/Hotel on A515
(Ashbourne/Buxton road) in the Peak
National Park.*

Allyear MWB 4units, 4–6persons ◈
◎ fridge Electric Elec metered
🔲inclusive ☎ Iron in unit ⊕ TV
⊕3pin square 12P ⛟ ♨(1m)

⟷ 🚽

Details not confirmed for 1987

ALSTONEFIELD
Staffordshire
Map**7** SK15

C The Alders & Corner Cottage
for bookings Mrs E R Allen, Post Office
Stores, Alstonefield, Ashbourne, Derbys
DE6 2FX
☎Alstonefield(033527)201

*These two recently modernised cottages
are set in the centre of the picturesque
village of Alstonefield. In each cottage the
comfortable accommodation includes two
double bedrooms, one small bunk-bedded
room, large fitted kitchen/diner and large
lounge with wood-block floor. Both
cottages have open fires.*

Allyear MWB out of season 1wk min,
5mths(winter)max, 2units, 1–6persons
[◇] ◈ ◆ ◎ fridge 🍴 Electric &
open fires Elec metered 🔲provided
(overseas visitors only) ☎(50yds) WM in
unit SD in unit Iron & Ironing board in
unit ⊕ CTV ⊕3pin square P ⛟
♨(100yds)

⟷ 🚽 (150yds)

Min£75 Max£95pw (Low)
Min£100 Max£180pw (High)

C Rose Cottage Riverside
for bookings Mrs Y Bailey, 4 Woodland
Close, Thorpe, Ashbourne, Derbyshire
☎Thorpe Cloud(033529)447

*A tastefully modernised 200-year-old
detached cottage with pleasant paved*

Haughton House Country Park
Self Catering Accommodation

The upper and second floors of the Georgian Mansion house have been
converted into five flats, sleeping from three to eight persons, all
comfortably furnished and equipped with colour television. All windows
offer panoramic views of the surrounding countryside.

In the grounds there is a modern, fully equipped bungalow which sleeps
up to six persons. Also in the grounds are two fully equipped 20' caravans
for hire, each sleeping up to six persons and connected to mains electric
and water supply.

**Booking forms and prices are
available from**

**The Warden,
Haughton House Caravan
Site, Alford, Aberdeenshire
Telephone: Alford (0336) 2107**

*AA 1985 Best Caravan and
Camping Site in Scotland
Award*

front garden and situated in small, picturesque village, overlooking the River Dove. Accommodation comprises kitchen/ diner, bathroom/WC with shower, pleasant cosy lounge with exposed beams and two bedrooms.

All year 1wk min, 1unit, 6persons ◆ ◆ no pets ◎ fridge Electric Elec metered ▯not provided ☎(25yds) SD in unit ☉ ⊕3pin square 1P ▥ ▒(25yds) ◒ ☕(½m)

Min£70 Max£140pw

ALTARNUN
Cornwall
Map2 SX28

C CC Ref 3043
for bookings Character Cottages (Holidays) Ltd, 34 Fore Street, Sidmouth, Devon EX10 8AQ
☎Sidmouth(03955)77001

End of terrace cottage in the centre of Altarnun village. Accommodation comprises lounge/diner with flag-stone floors and woodburning stove, kitchen with cast iron range, bathroom and WC. Open plan stairs to one twin room, one double with one single off with either polished wood or carpeted floors. Furnished in keeping with the period of the cottage.

All year MWB out of season 2days min, 2mths max, 1unit, 5persons ◆ no pets ◎ fridge log & electric fires Elec metered ▯not provided ☎(100yds) SD in unit Iron & Ironing board in unit ☉ TV ⊕3pin square 1P ▥ ▒(100yds) ◒ ☕(1½m)

Min£86 Max£155

ALTON
Staffordshire
Map7 SK04

H Alton Station Alton Towers
for bookings The Landmark Trust, Shottesbrooke Park, Maidenhead, Berkshire SL6 3SW
☎Littlewick Green(062882)5925

The Station Master's house of the now disused Churnet Valley railway has been

Alstonefield
—
Alyth

carefully preserved and offers fine accommodation for up to seven people. Twin-bedded rooms are on each of the ground, first and second floors. Bathroom/ WC are on the ground floor and another WC is in the cloakroom off the hall. There is a lovely sitting room furnished with period Victorian and Edwardian pieces from the station's past. A combined kitchen/diner completes the accommodation. Two long flights of 18 steps down to the platform makes it difficult for the handicapped person.

All year MWB out of season 1day min, 3wks max, 1unit, 1–7persons ◆ ◎ fridge Electric Elec inclusive ▯not provided ☎(½m) Iron & Ironing board in unit ☉ ⊕3pin square P ▥ ▒(400yds) ◒ ☕(400yds)

Min£175 Max£305pw (Low)
Min£190 Max£305pw (High)

C Tythe Barn Holiday Homes Denstone Lane
for bookings Mrs J Ratcliffe, Orchard Bungalow, Saltersford Lane, Alton, Stoke-on-Trent, Staffordshire
☎Oakamoor(0538)702852

A 17th-century farmhouse with attractive garden on the edge of the village. Cleverly converted to provide two cottage style units, with simple, compact but comfortable accommodation, sleeping up to six persons in each in two–three bedrooms (including one family bedroom). One unit has combined lounge/kitchen/ diner the other a separate lounge and both have a modern bathroom/WC.

All year MWB out of season 1wk(in season)min, 3wks max, 2units, 6persons ◆ ◆ no pets ◎ fridge oil filled radiators & electric fires ▯inclusive ☎(½m) WM & TD on premises Iron & Ironing board in unit ☉ CTV ⊕3pin square 4P ▥ ▒(½m) ◒ ☕(30yds)

Min£85 Max£150pw

ALWINTON
Northumberland
Map12 NT90

B Barrow Mill
for bookings Mrs M Carruthers, Dunns Farm, Elsdon, Newcastle-upon-Tyne NE19 1AL
☎Rothbury(0669)40219

A modernised stone-built bungalow in attractive rural location close to the River Coquet and in the heart of the valley. Accommodation comprises of lounge/ diner, two bedrooms, kitchen and bathroom.

All year MWB out of season 2days min, 1mth max, 1unit, 2–6persons ◆ ◆ ◎ fridge ▯can be hired ☎ WM & SD in unit Iron & Ironing board in unit ☉ CTV ⊕3pin square 3P ▒(10m) ◒ ☕(½m)

Min£40 Max£140pw

C Elizabeth Johnson Low Alwinton & Reivers Cabin Alwinton, Harbottle, Morpeth, Northumberland NE65 7BE
☎Rothbury(0669)50224

A stone-built cottage and a contrasting Scandinavian style pine chalet situated in a tranquil setting in the Upper Coquet Valley, surrounded by the Cheviot Hills. **Low Alwinton** *has two double bedrooms plus a childrens loft room which accommodates up to three.* **Reivers Cabin** *has one twin and one double bedroom plus a single convertible bed in the living room.*

All year MWB out of season 2days min, 3wks max, 2units, 1–10persons [◇] ◆ ◆ ◁(Chalet) ◎(Cottage) fridge Electric & open/wood burning fires Elec metered ▯can be hired ☎(½m) Iron & Ironing board in unit ☉ CTV ⊕3pin square P ▥ ▒(2m) ◒ ☕(½m)

Min£50 Max£195pw

ALYTH
Tayside *Perthshire*
Map15 NO24

New Inns Holiday Cottages
Alsop-en-le-Dale, Ashbourne, Derbyshire
Telephone: (033527) 203

Situated in the heart of Derbyshire, 5 miles north of Ashbourne, ½ mile from Dovedale. Perfect for walking and cycling (cycles can be provided) holidays. Each cottage is fully equipped to a high standard for 4 and 6 people. Linen is provided, television, full sized cooker, refrigerator. All are ground floor level. Restaurant and bar facilities are available and pleasant gardens adjoin the Tissington Trail.

H Pictillum
for bookings Mr & Mrs M H Wilson,
Conifers, Blairmore Drive, Rosemount,
Blairgowrie, Perthshire
☎Blairgowrie(0250)2961

*A newly modernised farmhouse set in
open countryside close to Alyth. The
accommodation comprises kitchen,
dining/sitting room, lounge with
convertible settee and double bedroom on
ground floor and two bedrooms on the
first floor. Located at the end of a long
drive.*

All year 1wk min, 1unit, 1–8persons ◆
◆ ⊚ fridge ▥& open fires
Elec inclusive ⌶not provided ☎ WM &
SD in unit Iron & Ironing board in unit
⊙ TV ⊕3pin square 5P 4▥ ▥(2m)

⊖ δ(2m) ♀(2m)

Min£90 Max£110pw (Low)
Min£125 Max£150pw (High)

AMBLESIDE
Cumbria
Map7 NY30

During the currency of this guide the
dialling code for Ambleside will change to
(05394)

Ch & F   J D & D Irvin, **Eden Vale Holiday
Flats**, Lake Road, Ambleside, Cumbria
LA22 0DB
☎Ambleside(0966)32313

Alyth
—
Ambleside

*Eight flats and six single-storey chalets all
sleeping two people. In all the units the
lounge and sleeping area are combined in
a spacious room with a fold away bed;
there is also a small separate kitchen.*

All year MWB out of season 1day min,
3mths max, 14units, 2persons, nc15
no pets ₫ fridge ▥ Gas inclusive
⌶inclusive ☎(100yds) Iron & Ironing
board on premises [Launderette within
300yds] ⊙ CTV ⊕3pin square 15P
▥ ▥(100yds)

⊖ ♀(200yds) ▦(¼m) ♫(¼m)
▦(¼m) Sports centre(3m)

Min£85 Max£95pw (Low)
£105pw (High)

C   Horseshoe Cottage 3 Rydal View
for bookings Mr & Mrs Wiseman,
Wisemans Holiday Cottages, 37 Charles
Street, Blackpool FY1 3EY
☎Blackpool(0253)28936 (daytime) 43471
(evening)

*A traditional slate-built lakeland cottage in
a small terrace. Situated in quiet position
200yds from the centre of the village. There
are two double bedrooms and the second
floor has lovely views of the Fairfield
mountain range.*

All year MWB out of season 1night min,
4wks max, 1unit, 4persons ⊚ fridge
gas & electric Gas & Elec metered
⌶not provided ☎(200yds) Iron &
Ironing board in unit [Launderette within
300yds] ⊙ TV ⊕3pin square 1P ▦
▥(200yds)

⊖ δ(½m) ♀(200yds) ▦(200yds)
♫(½m) ▦(¼m)

Min£55 Max£85pw (Low)
Min£90 Max£145pw (High)

F & H   Mr & Mrs S Bateman, **Kirkstone
Foot Hotel**, Kirkstone Pass Road,
Ambleside, Cumbria LA22 9EH
☎Ambleside(0966)32232

*Twelve flats and a house situated in the
grounds of a country house hotel,
originally a 17th-century manor house.
Ashness is a family-sized house with two
bedrooms, lounge/diner (plus bed-settee),
well fitted kitchen and bathroom/WC.
Coachhouse flatlets are six units within
converted coaching house sleeping two
people in each, in either twin or double-
bedded rooms; small cosy lounge/dining
area, kitchen and bathroom/WC.
Penthouse Suite is on the top floor of a
converted coachhouse comprising open
plan lounge/diner, bathroom and sleeps
four to seven people. **Loughrigg** is also
situated in a converted coachhouse on
the ground-floor comprising one bedroom
sleeping up to three people. It has a
lounge/diner and modern bathroom.*

***Woodlands** are four, purpose-built flats with three offering a choice of a double-bedded room or twin-bedded room. The fourth has one double bedroom and a single. All are modern and well-equipped with open plan lounge/kitchen/diner. All the amenities of the hotel are available to guests.*

Allyear MWB 1night min, 1mth max, 13units, 2–7persons ◈ ◆ ◎ fridge ▥ Elec inclusive ◫ inclusive ☎ Iron & Ironing board in unit [Launderette within 300yds] ⊙ CTV ⊕3pin square 16P ▥ ⛟(¼m)

⊖ ⚲ (20yds) ♫(¼m) ♫(¼m) ⛫(¼m)

Min£84 Max£138pw (Low)
Min£182 Max£310pw (High)

AMMANFORD
Dyfed
Map**2** SN61

C **Brynderi Cottage** Pant-y-Llyn (3½m N off A483 beyond Llandybie)
for bookings Mrs D M Ridout, 19 St Edyths Road, Sea Mills, Bristol BS9 2EP
☎Bristol(0272)681967

Rurally situated small roadside cottage comprising pine furnished dining room, small sitting room with twin daybeds, kitchen and WC. The first-floor comprises a bathroom/WC and two bedrooms, one with a double and single bed, the other with a double bed.

6Jun–26Sep 4nights min, 1unit, 2–7persons ◈ no pets ◎ fridge Electric Elec metered ◫ inclusive ☎(25yds) SD in unit Iron & Ironing board in unit TV ⊕3pin square 3P ⛟(½m)

⊖ ⚲ (2m)

£100pw

AMROTH
Dyfed
Map**3** SN10

C **Sparrows Nest Cottage**
for bookings Coastal Cottages of Pembrokeshire, Seaview, Abercastle, Mathry, Dyfed SA62 5HJ
☎Croesgoch(03483)7742

A small detached stone cottage surrounded by woods and fields about 1½ miles from Amroth. It is comfortably furnished and comprises lounge/diner with french doors leading to the patio with barbecue, kitchen, shower room/WC, one single and two double bedrooms.

Allyear MWB out of season 2days min, 6wks max, 1unit, 2–5persons ◈ ◆ no pets ◎ fridge Storage heaters & portable heaters Elec inclusive ◫ not provided ☎(2m) Iron & Ironing board in unit ⊙ CTV ⊕3pin square 3P ▥ ⛟(2m) ≏(heated)

⊖ ⚲ (1½m)

Min£70 Max£275pw

APPIN
Strathclyde *Argyllshire*
Map**14** NM94

C **1 & 2 Creagan Cottage**
for bookings I & S Weir, Dungrianach, Appin, Argyll PA38 4BQ
☎Appin(063173)287

Two semi-detached cottages, each with its own garden and pleasantly situated overlooking Loch Creran. Each has a lounge/dining room, kitchenette, one double and one twin bedroom and bathroom/WC. Located on the A828 at the north end of the Loch.

Allyear MWB out of season 3days min, 3wks max, 2units, 1–4persons [◇] ◈ ◆ no pets ◎ fridge Electric Elec metered ◫ inclusive ☎ Iron & Ironing board in unit ⊙ CTV ⊕3pin square 6P ▥ ⛟(4m) Fishing, dinghies & cycles for hire, recreation room

⊖ ⚲ (¼m)

Min£75 Max£175pw

CH I & S Weir, **Appin Holiday Homes**, Dungrianach, Appin, Argylle PA38 4BQ
☎Appin(063173)287

Timber-built bungalows with small veranda and picture windows. Accommodation comprises two bedrooms, (one double, one twin) bathroom and kitchen/diner/lounge.

Allyear MWB out of season 3nights min, 3wks max, 10units, 1–5persons [◇] ◈ ◆ ◎ fridge Electric Elec metered ◫ inclusive ☎ on premises Iron & Ironing board in unit ⊙ CTV ⊕3pin square 1P ⛟(2m) Fishing, dinghies for hire, recreation room

⊖ ⚲ (¼m)

Min£75 Max£230pw

F **Kinlochlaich House**
for bookings Mr D E Hutchison, Kinlochlaich House, Appin, Argyll PA38 4BD
☎Appin(063173)342

A charming stone-built country house dating back 300yrs and showing both Gothic and Georgian influences; it stands in several acres of its own grounds which include a walled garden, in which a Garden Centre is situated. The three flats have been attractively converted, with tasteful furnishings and neat décor. Fresh garden produce available in season. In addition a maisonette close to the main house, accommodation includes double bedroom, lounge/diner/kitchen and bathroom first-floor accommodation is reached by a fairly steep pine staircase.

Mid Dec–Oct MWB out of season 1wk min, 5wks max, 4units, 1–6persons ◈ no pets ◐ ◎ fridge Electric [Gas/Elec] ◫ can be hired by overseas guests ☎ WM & TD on premises Iron & Ironing board on premises ⊙ TV ⊕3pin round P ⛟(2½m) Fishing, sailing & skiing

Min£52 Max£176pw

C **Laich Cottage**
for bookings Mr D E Hutchison, Kinlochlaich House, Appin, Argyll PA38 4BD
☎Appin(063173)342

A typical Highland building in its own grounds several yards from the main house. Simple but clean and well maintained accommodation with two bedrooms, one with bunk beds, tiled bathroom and kitchen, sitting/dining room with wood stove, and several extras such as flower arrangements. Tidy garden. Fresh garden produce available in season.

Mid Dec–Oct MWB out of season 1wk min, 5wks max, 1unit, 1–6persons ◈ no pets ◐ fridge Calor gas Gas/Elec metered ◫ can be hired by overseas guests ☎ WM & TD on premises Iron & Ironing board on premises ⊙ TV ⊕3pin round P ⛟(2½m) Fishing, sailing & skiing

⊖ ⚲ (2½m)

Min£76pw (Low)
Min£225pw (High)

APPLEBY
Cumbria
Map**12** NY62

H **Park House** Roman Road
for bookings Mrs M Wood, Gale House Farm, Roman Road, Appleby, Cumbria
☎Appleby(07683)51380

A three-bedroomed farmhouse which has been tastefully converted to a very comfortable holiday home. It comprises of three bedrooms (two doubles and one twin) and is in a peaceful situation on the north side of Appleby.

Apr–Nov 7days min, 21days max, 1unit, 6persons ◈ ◆ ◎ fridge storage heaters & electric fires Elec metered ◫ inclusive ☎(200yds) SD Iron & Ironing board in unit ⊙ CTV ⊕3pin square 4P ▥ ⛟(1m)

⊖ ⛳(3m) ⚲ (¼m)

Max£100pw (Low)
Max£125pw (High)

ARDBRECKNISH
Strathclyde *Argyllshire*
Map**10** NN02

B **Bungalow**
for bookings Mrs H F Hodge, Rockhill Farm, Ardbrecknish, Dalmally Argyll PA33 1BH
☎Kilchrenan(08663)218

A timber framed, shingle clad bungalow set in grounds of 200-acre livestock farm overlooking Loch Awe. Accommodation comprises lounge/diner, large kitchen, bathroom, two twin-bedded rooms and one with a double and single bed. Access via A819 Inveraray–Dalmally road.

Closed Xmas wk MWB out of season 2days min, 1mth max, 1unit, 1–8persons →

◆ ◉ fridge Electric Elec metered
🅻not provided ☎ SD in unit Iron &
Ironing board in unit CTV
⊕3pin round 4P 🎲 ♨(10m) Fishing
⊖ ⚲(2½m)
Min£65 Max£160pw

C Farm Cottage
for bookings Mrs H F Hodge, Rockhill
Farm, Ardbrecknish, Dalmally, Argyll
PA33 1BH
☎Kilchrenan(08663)218

*White-painted two-storey stone cottage on
200-acre livestock farm overlooking Loch
Awe. The cottage comprises lounge/diner/
kitchen, bathroom, separate WC and one
twin-bedded room on the ground floor, the
first floor comprises one twin-bedded and
two double-bedded rooms. Access is via
A819 Inveraray–Dalmally road.*

Closed Xmas wk MWB out of season
2days min, 1mth max, 1unit, 1–8persons
◆ ◉ fridge Electric Elec metered
🅻not provided ☎ SD in unit Iron &
Ironing board in unit ⊙ CTV
⊕3pin round 4P 🎲 ♨(10m) Fishing
⊖ ⚲(2½m)
Min£65 Max£160pw

ARDWELL
Dumfries & Galloway *Wigtownshire*
Map**10** NX14

Ch Ardwell Chalets
for bookings Mrs M McFadzean, Kilaser,
Ardwell, Stranraer, Wigtownshire
☎Ardwell(077686)294

*Six timbered chalets situated on the
foreshore at the edge of a tiny village with
fine views of the Galloway Hills and Luce
Bay. Accommodation which is functional
comprises open plan living room and
kitchenette, two small bedrooms (two
singles and two bunk beds) and
bathroom. In some chalets all storage/
cupboard space is in the living room.*

All year MWB out of season 1wk min,
2mths max, 6units, 1–6persons ◆ ◉
fridge Electric Elec metered
🅻not provided ☎(200yds) Iron &
Ironing board on premises ⊙ TV
⊕3pin square P ♨(200yds)
Min£40 (Low)
Min£120 (High)

ARISAIG
Highland *Inverness-shire*
Map**13** NM69

Ch Mr A Gillies **Kinloid Farm Holiday
Cottages** Arisaig, Inverness-shire
☎Arisaig(06875)666

*Two small, wood-built chalets both well-
equipped with modern fittings, with
outstanding views from the hillside over
the adjacent coastline.*

Etr–Nov MWB out of season 1wk min,
2units, 1–6persons no pets ◉ fridge
♨ Elec metred 🅻not provided
☎(1½m) SD on premises Iron & Ironing
board in unit ⊙ CTV ⊕3pin square
8P ♨(1½m) sea & trout fishing

Ardbrecknish
—
Ashburton

⊖ ♪(2m) ⚲(1½m)
Details not confirmed for 1987

ARNSIDE
Cumbria
Map**7** SD47

F Mr & Mrs A E & F W Anthony
Hampsfell House The Promenade,
Arnside, Carnforth, Lancs LA5 0AD
☎Arnside(0524)761285

*A spacious self-contained top floor flat
situated within a stone-built semi-
detached house standing on the
promenade with extensive views of the
Kent estuary and the Lakeland Hills. The
accommodation comprises one double
bedroom, one twin-bedded room (both
bedrooms with WHB), one single-bedded
room, lounge/diner, kitchen and
bathroom/WC.*

Mar–Nov MWB out of season
3days min, 1unit, 2–5persons, nc5
no pets ◉ fridge Electric
Elec metered 🅻can be hired ☎(½m)
SD in unit Iron & Ironing board in unit
⊙ CTV ⊕3pin square 2P 🎲
♨(100yds)
⊖ ♪(3m) ⚲(100yds)
Min£45 Max£60pw (Low)
Min£65 Max£105pw (High)
F Mrs A Mitchell, **The Moorings**,
Promenade, Arnside, Carnforth, Lancs
LA5 0AD
☎Arnside(0524)761340

*Large, well-furnished and comfortable flat.
On first floor of proprietor's stone-built
house on the promenade near Arnside
centre. Good views across the River Kent
estuary to the hills of South Cumbria. The
area has many nature trails and is popular
with ornithologists.*

Mar–Nov MWB out of season 1wk min,
1unit, 5persons ◉ fridge ♨ Elec
metered 🅻can be hired ☎(½m) Airing
cupboard on premises Iron & Ironing
board on premises TV ⊕3pin square
P ♨(300yds)
⊖ ⚲(300yds)
Max£110pw

ARRAN Isle of,
Strathclyde, Buteshire
Map**10**

BRODICK
Map**10** NS03

C Altbeg Cottage Corriegills
for bookings Altbeg Cottages, Room 355,
93 Hope Street, Glasgow
☎041-884 2706 & Brodick(0770)2386

*Three cottages, one a detached traditional
stone dwelling the other two recently built
semi-detached properties. The detached
cottage has its own little garden and
adjacent lawns and comprises lounge,*

---

*dining room, kitchen and three bedrooms,
one with bunks which is situated on the
ground floor. The other two cottages
comprise lounge/diner/kitchen, two
bedrooms and shower room. Corriegills
lies 250ft above sea level, 1m from Brodick
Pier.*

Etr–Sep 1wk min, 1mth max, 3units,
1–6persons, nc7 (in detached cottage
only) no pets ◉ fridge Electric fires
Elec metered 🅻not provided ☎(1m)
TD in unit (semi-detached cottages only)
Iron & Ironing board in unit ⊙ TV
⊕3pin square P 🎲 ♨(1m)
⊖ ♪(2m) ⚲(1m)
Min£80 Max£180pw

LAMLASH
Map**10** NS03

Ch Dyemill Chalets
for bookings Mrs & Mrs J T Cowie, The
Dyemill, Lamlash, Brodick, Isle of Arran
KA27 8NU
☎Lamlash(07706)419

*Six pinewood chalets of Finnish design set
in woodland, with beautiful views, close to
the Mona Mohr burn. Accommodation
comprises two bedrooms (one double, one
twin-bedded), lounge/diner, kitchenette
and bathroom/WC.*

mid Apr–Sep 1wk min, 1mth max, 6units,
1–4persons ◆ ◆ no pets ◉
fridge Electric Elec metered
🅻inclusive ☎(1m) Iron & Ironing board
on premises ◉ ⊕3pin square P 🎲
♨(1m)
⊖ ⚲(1m) 🎬(1m) ♫(1m)
Min£75 Max£160pw

H Dyemill House
for bookings Mr & Mrs J T Cowie, The
Dyemill, Lamlash, Brodick, Isle of Arran
KA27 8NU
☎Lamlash(07706)419

*A two-storey country house which is an
extension of the owner's house making a
self-contained unit, beside the Mona Muhr
burn in rural setting with good views. The
house is comfortable and spacious with
three bedrooms (one double, twin-bedded
and a single), sitting room, dining room/
kitchen and bathroom.*

All year MWB in season 1wk min, 1unit,
1–5persons ◆ ◉ no pets ◉
fridge Electric Elec metered 🅻inclusive
☎(1m) Iron & Ironing board on
premises CTV ⊕3pin square P 🎲
♨(1m)
⊖ ⚲(1m) 🎬(1m) ♫(1m)
Min£80 Max£170pw

ASHBURTON
Devon
Map**3** SX77

**B, F, & H Apartment 1, The Bungalow,
Lent Hill House & The Lodge**
for bookings The Manager, The River Dart
Country Park Ltd, Holne Park, Ashburton,
Newton Abbot, Devon
☎Ashburton(0364)52511

Three self-catering holiday properties set within grounds of the Country Park with the fifth, a large Georgian house, across the river. Follow Two Bridges road from Ashburton, Holne Park signposted on left hand side.
Apartment 1 – Three bedrooms, kitchen, lounge/diner and bathroom.
Lent Hill House – Detached house with shrubs and woodlands, five double bedrooms, one single, two bathrooms, two WCs, sitting room, TV room, kitchen, dining room, night-storage heaters. A garage is available.
The Lodge – Two twin, one double, twin bunks, two bathrooms, lounge, TV lounge, dining room, kitchen, own garden situated at entrance of park. A garage is available.
The Bungalow – A modern concrete built bungalow with its own garden, comprising three bedrooms, kitchen/diner, lounge and bathroom.
All year (Apr – Sep apartments 1) 1wk min, 6mths max, 4units, 1 – 14persons ◊ ✦
◎ fridge (Flat) ♨ Electric (3units) Elec metered ⌶can be hired ☎(& 1m) WM in Lent Hill House Iron & Ironing board in unit [Launderette on premises] ☉ CTV ⊕3pin square P ⚲(1m) ▭ ⤚Hard
⊖ ♪(1m) ♫(1m) 🎵(1m) ♬(1m) ⚙(1m)
Min£86 Max£141.50pw (Low)
Min£166 Max£340pw (High)

ASHREIGNEY
Devon
Map2 SS61

C JFH Ref CW46C Cottwood
for bookings John Fowler Holidays, Dept. 58, Marlborough Road, Ilfracombe, Devon EX34 8PF
☎Ilfracombe(0271)66666

Country cottage with large gardens and glorious views. Ground floor has large lounge/diner, stone open fire place with original bread oven and dark wood beams, kitchen and cloakroom. First floor has one double bedroom, one twin-bedded room, one single room and bathroom.
Mar – Oct MWB out of season 1wk min, 1mth max, 1unit, 3 – 7persons ◊ ✦

Ashburton
—
Ashurst

✦ ◎ fridge Electric Elec metered ⌶not provided ☎(½m) Iron & Ironing board in unit ☉ TV/CTV can be hired ⊕3pin square 2P ▥ ⚲(2m)
⊖ ♀(2m)
Min£67.85 Max£182.85pw

C JFH Ref LH57D
for bookings John Fowler Holidays, Dept. 58, Marlborough Road, Ilfracombe, Devon EX34 8PF
☎Ilfracombe(0271)66666

Large country cottage with own garden situated in wooded valley. Roomy kitchen, dining room with antique table and chairs, lounge, three bedrooms (one single, one double and one family room with bunk beds and cot), bathroom upstairs and extra WC on ground floor.
Mar – Oct MWB out of season 1wk min, 2wks max, 1unit, 5 – 7persons ◊ ✦
no pets ◎ fridge Electric Elec metered ⌶not provided ☎(1½m) Iron & Ironing board in unit CTV ⊕3pin square 4P ⚲(1½m)
⊖ ♀(1½m)
Min£56.35 Max£171.35pw

C JFH Ref N35D
for bookings John Fowler Holidays, Dept. 58 Marlborough Road, Ilfracombe, Devon EX34 8PF
☎Ilfracombe(0271)60666

A detached cottage comprising kitchen, sitting room and WC. On first floor there are two bedrooms and a bathroom.
Mar – Oct MWB out of season 3days min, 3wks max, 1unit, 3 – 5persons ◊ ◎
fridge Electric Elec metered ⌶not provided ☎(2m) Iron in unit CTV ⊕3pin square P ⚲(2m)
⊖ ♀(3m)

C JFH Ref N57C
for bookings John Fowler Holidays, Dept. 58, Marlborough Road, Ilfracombe, Devon EX34 8PF
☎Ilfracombe(0271)66666

Semi-detached 300-year-old cottage. Accommodation comprises lounge with chintz loose-covered seating and double bed-settee if required, WC, separate kitchen with adequate units and surfaces, first-floor bathroom and two bedrooms (a double and a twin).
Mar – Oct MWB out of season 3days min, 3wks max, 1unit, 5 – 7persons ◊ ◎
fridge Electric Elec metered ⌶not provided ☎(2m) Iron in unit CTV P ⚲ ♀(3m)

ASHTON
Cornwall
Map2 SW62

B & F Mr & Mrs B R C Winter **Chycarne Farm** Balwest Ashton, Helston, Cornwall TR13 9TE
☎Penzance(0736)762473

Converted single-storey farm buildings incorporating four bungalows and two flats. All have kitchen/living area with wall bed and one or two bedrooms, bungalows have bathroom/WC and flats shower/WC. 1m NW of Ashton on unclass road.
Mar – Oct MWB out of season 2days min, 4wks max, 6units, 1 – 8persons ◊ ✦
✦ ◎ fridge Electric Elec metered ⌶can be hired ☎(½m) Iron & Ironing board on premises ☉ CTV ⊕3pin square P ▥ ⚲
⊖ ♪(1½m) ♀(1½m)
Min£45 Max£95pw (Low)
Min£115 Max£180pw (High)

ASHURST
Hampshire
Map4 SU31

C Foxhills Cottages 211 Lyndhurst Road for bookings Mrs B M Davidson, 132 Woodlands Road, Ashurst, Southampton, Hants SO4 2AP
☎Ashurst(042129)2309

Two attractive red-brick cottages consisting of one double and two twin-bedded rooms, comfortable lounge/diner, kitchen and bathroom.
All year 1wk min, 4mths max, 2unit, 1 – 6persons ◊ ∂ fridge ♨ £9.00 charge for Gas/Elec ⌶can be hired ☎ →

WM Iron Ironing board ☺ CTV
⊕3pin square P ▥ ♨(500yds)
↫ ♪(3m) ♨(200yds)
Min£80 Max£140pw (Low)
Min£160 Max£210pw (High)

ASHWATER
Devon
Map2 SX39

H JFH P810B
for bookings John Fowler Holidays, Dept
58 Marlborough Road, Ilfracombe, Devon
EX34 8PF
☎Ilfracombe(0271)66666

Large modern detached country house.
The accommodation comprises kitchen/
diner with Rayburn and electric cooker,
spacious lounge with open fire and put-u-
up, three bedrooms, bathroom and WC.

Mar–Oct MWB out of season 1wk min,
1mth max, 1unit, 10persons ◆ ◆ ◎or
Rayburn on request fridge Electric
Elec metered ⊑not provided ☎(½m)
Iron & Ironing board in unit ☺ CTV
⊕3pin square 5P ▥ ♨(½m)
↫ ♨(½m)
Min£75.35 Max£205.85pw

AUCHENMALG
Dumfries & Galloway Wigtownshire
Map10 NX25

F Craig Lodge
for bookings The Hon. Mrs A Agnew,
Sweethaws Farm, Crowborough, E Sussex
☎Crowborough(08926)5045

A 19th-century mansion with extension
which has been converted into five flats.
Each flat has two/three bedrooms and
flats 1, 2 & 3 are particularly spacious. The
fifth flat has an open plan lounge/dining/
kitchen area. The building lies on its own
with only the road separating it from the
sea shore. Fine views out across Luce Bay.

All year MWB out of season 1wk min,
5units, 1–6persons [◆ ◆]· no pets
◎ fridge ▥(flat5) Electric
Elec metered ⊑can be hired (overseas
visitors only) ☎ SD in unit Iron &
Ironing board in unit ☺ CTV
⊕3pin square P ▥ ♨(7m)
↫ ♨(½m)
Min£50 Max£150pw

AUCHTERMUCHTY
Fife
Map11 NO21

C Orchard Cottage, High St
for bookings Mrs E J Dunlop, 6 Gladgate,
Auchtermuchty, Fife KY14 7AY
☎Auchtermuchty(0337)28496

Ashurst
—
Aviemore

19th-century stone cottage which has
been carefully renovated to provide
modern facilities whilst still retaining much
of its original character. Entrance is by
outside stairs to the first floor which
comprises living room, kitchen, bathroom
and three bedrooms upstairs.

All year MWB out of season 1wk min,
1unit, 5persons ◆ no pets ♪ fridge
▥ Gas/Elec inclusive ⊑inclusive WM
SD & TD in unit Iron & Ironing board in
unit ☺ CTV ⊕3pin square ▥
♨(50yds)
↫ ♪(3m) ♨(100yds)
Min£145 Max£235pw

H Weavers House 4 Gladgate
for booking Mrs E J Dunlop. 6 Gladgate,
Auchtermuchty, Fife KY14 7AY
☎Auchtermuchty(0337)28496

A traditional type house standing in own
gardens on elevated site in small village.
The house is well furnished and offers
lounge, dining room, modern kitchen and
shower with WC on the ground floor, one
bunk-bedded room, one double bedroom,
one twin-bedded room and modern
bathroom with WC on the first floor.
Access from A91 via Crosshills or
Gladgate.

All year MWB out of season 1wk min,
1unit, 1–6persons ◆ no pets ♪
fridge ▥ Gas/Elec inclusive
⊑inclusive WM, SD & TD in unit
Iron & Ironing board in unit ☺ CTV
⊕3pin square 1▥ ▥ ♨(200yds)
Fishing
↫ ♪(3m) ♨(200yds)
Min£175 Max£285pw

AULTBEA
Highland Ross-shire
Map14 NG88

CH Aultbea Lodges Drumchork
for bookings Mr R D Chapman, Torliath
House, Drumchork, Aultbea, Ross-shire
IV22 2HU
☎Aultbea(044582)233

Ten attractive 'A' frame chalets,
spaciously situated on a thirteen acre site
with stunning views over Loch Ewe and
beyond. Each unit is carpeted and
decorated to a high standard and
comprises kitchen, lounge/diner with
bed-settee, one twin and one double
bedroom, bathroom and balcony. Loch

---

fishing, sea fishing and boat hire can be
arranged.

All year MWB out of season 3days min,
5wks max, 10units, 4–6persons [◇ ◆
◆] ◎ fridge Electric Elec metered
⊑inclusive ☎(50yds) SD in unit Iron &
Ironing board in unit ☺ CTV
⊕3pin square 2P ▥ ♨(½m)
↫ ♨(50yds)
Min£78 Max£157pw (Low)
Min£154 Max£258pw (High)

AVENING
Gloucestershire
Map3 ST89

C Field Cottage 9 Mays Lane
for bookings Ms Susan Werner, 66
Stanthorpe Road, London SW16
☎01-769 4975

An attractive small detached stone
cottage with a pleasant garden, situated in
quiet lane surrounded by open
countryside on the edge of small Cotswold
town. Comprises living room, kitchen, one
double and one twin bedroom, and
bathroom.

All year MWB out of season 1wk min,
1mth max, 1unit, 1–4persons ◆ ◆
◎ fridge ▥& wood fire Elec metered
⊑not provided ☎(1m) Iron in unit
Ironing board on premises Launderette
within 300yds CTV ⊕3pin square 2P
▥ ♨(½m)
↫ ♪(2m) ♨(½m) ♫(2m)
Sports centre(3m)

AVIEMORE see also Carrbridge
Highland Inverness-shire
Map14 NH81

B 26 Callart Road
for bookings Mrs N Highmore, Tremayne,
Aviemore, Inverness-shire
☎Aviemore(0479)810694

On the north side of Aviemore, a modern
detached bungalow with dining/sitting
room (includes convertible couch), two
bedrooms, bathroom and kitchen.

All year MWB out of season 2days min,
1unit, 1–6persons ◎ fridge ▥
Elec metered ⊑inclusive ☎(½m) Iron
in unit Ironing board in unit ☺ TV
⊕3pin square 3P ▥ ♨(¾m)
↫ ♪(½) ♨(½m) ♫(1m)
♫(1m) ♨(1m)
Details not confirmed for 1987.

B Cedar Bungalow
for bookings Inverdruie & Glasnacardoch
Properties, Inverdruie House, Inverdruie,
Aviemore, Inverness-shire PH22 1QR
☎Aviemore(0479)810357

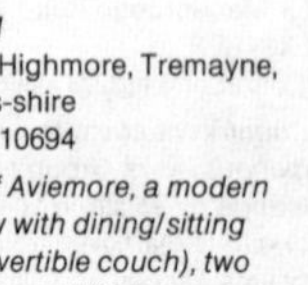

A cedarwood bungalow contained in the garden of an 18th-century country house. It has an open plan living/dining/kitchen, a double bedroom and a room with single bed & bunks. Access is from the B970 1m E of Aviemore.

All year MWB out of season 2 nights min, 1 unit, 1–5 persons [◇] ◆ ◆ ◎ fridge 🍴 Elec metered 🔲 can be hired 🍽 Dishwasher in unit Iron & Ironing board in unit [Launderette within 300 yds] ☉ CTV ⊕3 pin square 2P 🎞 Children's play area

↔ 🛈(1m) 🎵(1m) 🎵 (1m) 🐾(1m)
Min£80 Max£98pw (Low)
Min£180 Max£218pw (High)

Ch Dalfaber Estate Aviemore, Inverness-shire
☎ Aviemore(0479)810340

Scandinavian designed chalets situated in a 130 acre estate close to the River Spey and with views of the Cairngorm mountains. Each unit comprises a comfortable lounge/diner/kitchen with convertible bed-settee, and two bedrooms. Luxury lodges may also be available. Situated N of Aviemore on the B9152.

All year 5 days min, 6 wks max, 39 units, 1–8 persons [◇ ◈ ◆] ◎ fridge 🍴 Elec metered 🔲 inclusive ☎(200yds) Iron & Ironing board on premises [Launderette within 300yds]

Aviemore

☺ CTV ⊕3 pin square 2P 🎞 🛏(1m) ▭ 🛀 🎣 Fishing, squash, snooker, jacuzzi & bicycles for hire.

↔ 🛈 🎶 🎵
Min£195 Max£580pw

F Freedom Inn Aviemore Centre, Aviemore, Inverness-shire PH22 1PF
☎ Aviemore(0479)810781

A modern, low-rise building complex within the Aviemore holiday centre. The main room in each flat is multi-purpose, serving as bedroom, lounge, dining room and kitchenette – only the bathroom is separate. Rugged highland views over Spey Valley to Cairngorm Mountains. All the facilities of a hotel are available.

All year MWB 1 night min, 93 units, 1–4 persons ◇ ◈ ◆ ◎ (metered) fridge 🍴 Elec inclusive 🔲 inclusive ☎ ☉ ◐ CTV ⊕3 pin square P 🛏(1m) ▭(200yds)

↔ 🎣(½m) 🛈 🎶 🎵 🐾(200yds)
Min£101.20 Max£195.50pw

Ch High Range Self-Catering Chalets Grampian Road, Aviemore, Inverness-shire PH22 1PT
☎ Aviemore(0479)810636

Five comfortable and nicely furnished red cedar chalets set amidst silver birch trees and with views of the Cairngorms. Accommodation consists of kitchenette, lounge/diner, two bedrooms, each with shower/WC, and a convertible divan and Z-bed.

All year MWB out of season 1 wk min, 5 units 2–6 persons [◈ ◆] ◎ 'ridge Electric Elec metered 🔲 inclusive ☎ [Launderette within 300 yds] ☉ ◐ CTV ⊕3 pin square P 🎞 🛏(300yds)

↔ 🛈 🎶(500yds) 🎵(500yds) 🐾(500yds)
Min£120 Max£180pw (Low)
Min£200 Max£300pw (High)

F Inverdruie & Glasnacardoch Properties Inverdruie House, Inverdruie, Aviemore, Inverness-shire PH22 1QR
☎ Aviemore(0479)810357

18th-century stone-built country house standing in its own grounds and converted into two flats of varying sizes with spacious rooms and a mixture of traditional and modern style furnishings. Mountain and valley views. Access is from B970.

All year MWB out of season 3 nights min, 2 units, 4–6 persons [◇] ◆ ◆ ◎ fridge 🍴 Elec metered 🔲 can be hired ☎ Dishwasher Iron & Ironing board in unit [Launderette within →

33

300yds] ⊙ CTV ⊕3pin square 12P
Ⓜ ♨(1½m) Children's play area
⟗ ♨(1m) 🎜(1m) 🎝(1m) 🌳(1m)
Min£80 Max£98pw (Low)
Min£180 Max£218pw (High)

**Ch & F   Speyside-Craigellachie House
Flats & Chalets**
for bookings McWilliam – Speyside
Enterprises, Craigellachie House,
Aviemore, Inverness-shire PH22 1PX
☎Aviemore(0479)810236

Seven chalets varying in size and standard
from simplicity and compactness to luxury
and spaciousness; there are also two flats
in the main house. Situated in a sheltered
position at the S end of Aviemore village
with splendid views over the Spey Valley to
the Cairngorm Mountains, within short
distance of Aviemore Centre.

All year   MWB out of season   2nights min,
1mth max, 9units, 2 – 7persons   ◇ ♂
  🔘 fridge 🍴 Elec metered ☎(50yds)
Launderette ⊙ CTV ⊕3pin square
P ♨(500yds)
⟗ ♨(100yds) 🎜(1m) 🎝(1m)
🌳(1m) Fishing
Min£110 Max£200pw (Low)
Min£150 Max£300pw (High)

AXMINSTER
Devon
Map**3** SY29

H   CC Ref 7640L Dalwood
for bookings Character Cottages, 34 Fore
Street, Sidmouth, Devon EX10 8AQ
☎Sidmouth(03955)77001

Thatched Georgian listed country house
linked to an older farmhouse. Set in an
open plan garden the accommodation
comprises hall, dining room, large lounge
with log fire and french windows, modern
fitted kitchen, two twin bedded rooms
plus extra bed on landing and bathroom
with bidet.

All year   MWB out of season   2days min,
2mths max, 1unit, 6 – 7persons [◇] ◆
no pets 🔘 fridge electric fire & storage
heaters Elec metered Ⓛinclusive
☎(1m) WM SD & TD in unit Iron &
Ironing board in unit ⊙ CTV
⊕3pin square 1P ♨(1m)
⟗ ♨(1m)
Min£142 Max£297pw

B   The Lodge
for bookings Mrs S Clist, Annings Farm,
Wyke Green, Axminster, Devon.
☎Axminster(0297)33294

A modern detached stone-built bungalow,
which comprises a well furnished lounge/

Aviemore
—
Ballachulish

diner, modern fitted kitchen, one double
room with bunk beds, one twin-bedded
room, and a shower room. 1½m from
Axminster.

Mar – Nov MWB out of season   1wk min,
1mth max, 1unit, 1 – 6persons   ◇ ◆
  ♦ no pets 🔘 fridge Electric
Elec metered Ⓛnot provided ☎(1m)
Iron & Ironing board in unit ⊙ CTV
⊕3pin square 2P Ⓜ ♨(1m)
⟗ ♨(1½m)
Min£84 Max£144pw (Low)
Min£167 Max£190pw (High)

BACTON
Norfolk
Map**9** TG33

Ch   Kimberley & Glendale Chalets
New Zealand Way
for bookings Hoseasons Holidays,
Sunway House, Lowestoft, Suffolk
NR32 3LT
☎Lowestoft(0502)62271

These chalets occupy a level, grassed five-
acre site and many have sea views. They
are designed to sleep six in two double
bedrooms with double 'put-u-up' in
lounge/kitchen. Well-equipped and of
comfortable size. Small covered patio.
Manager on site.

Apr – Sep MWB out of season   1wk min,
54units, 2 – 6persons [◇ ◆] 🔘
fridge Electric Elec metered
Ⓛinclusive ☎(200yds) Iron on
premises ⊙ CTV ⊕3pin square P
🚲 🏌Putting Children's play area
⟗ ♨(½m) 🎜(2m)
Min£43 Max£115pw

Ch   New Zealand Bungalows
New Zealand Way
for bookings Hoseasons Holidays,
Sunway House, Lowestoft, Suffolk
NR32 3LT
☎Lowestoft(0502)62271

Nine detached chalets in quiet location,
each comprising kitchen, bathroom/WC,
two bedrooms sleeping up to five people,
plus double 'put-u-up' in the living room.

Apr – Sep MWB out of season   1wk min,
9units, 2 – 7persons [◇ ◆] 🔘
fridge Electric Elec metered
Ⓛinclusive ☎(100yds) [Iron on
premises] ⊙ CTV ⊕3pin square P
🚲(100yds) Children's play area

⟗ ♨(½m) 🎜(2m)
Min£45 Max£115pw

BALGEDIE
Tayside Kinross-shire
Map**11** NO10

Ch   Mr A Sneddon **Eagle Chalets** Stan-
Ma-Lane, Balgedie, Kinross, Kinross-shire
☎Scotlandwell(059284)257

A group of 18 chalets set together at the
foot of the Lomond Hills and looking out
over Loch Leven. Each has open plan
kitchen/dining area and either two or
three bedrooms, one of which may have
bunk beds. The chalets are compact but
modern. Balgedie lies 2m E of M90 and
some 3m NE of Kinross.

All year   MWB out of season   3days min,
18units, 1 – 6persons [◇ ◆] no pets
  🔘 fridge Elec metered Ⓛcan be
hired ☎ [WM & TD on premises] Iron &
Ironing board on premises ⊙ CTV
⊕3pin square P Ⓜ Children's play
area & games room
⟗ ♂(1m) ♨(100yds) 🎜(3m) 🎝(3m)
Min£65 Max£150pw (Low)
Min£100 Max£175pw (High)

BALLACHULISH
Highland Argyllshire
Map**14** NN05

C   Cormorant Cottage Glenachulish
for bookings Barrow & Butcher, The
House in the Wood, Glenachulish,
Ballachulish, Argyll PA39 4JZ
☎Ballachulish(08552)379

Large cottage designed to accommodate
up to 15 people and within easy reach of
Glencoe. Accommodation consists of
large kitchen/living room with french
windows overlooking the loch, five
bedrooms, shower, bath, three WC's and a
drying room.

All year   MWB out of season   1wk min,
1mth max, 1unit, 1 – 15persons   ◇ ◆
  🔘 fridge Electric & coal/log stove
Elec metered Ⓛnot provided ☎(½m)
SD & TD in unit ⊙ CTV
⊕3pin square 6P Ⓜ ♨(2m)
⟗ ♨(½m)
Min£190 Max£230pw (Low)
Min£250 Max£300pw (High)

Ch   Glenachulish Woodland Chalets
for bookings Barrow & Butcher, The
House in the Wood, Glenachulish,
Ballachulish, Argyll PA39 4JZ
☎Ballachulish(08552)379

Danish-design, timber chalets set in 5½
acres of rough woodland at the front of

Beinn a Beithir. Nearby are the shores of Loch Linnhe and Ballachulish Bay. The views are spectacular, and sailing and hill-walking facilities are available. Situated on the outskirts of Ballachulish near the southern approach to road bridge over Loch Leven on A828.

All year MWB out of season 1wk min, 28days max, 4units, 1–6persons ◆ ◆ ⊚ fridge Electric Elec metered ⊡not provided ☎(½m) SD in unit ☺ ⊕3pin square P ⊞ ♨(2m) ⊖ ☘(½m)

Min£75 Max£95pw (Low)
Min£120 Max£150pw (High)

C Seaview Cottage
for bookings Barrow & Butcher, The House in the Wood, Glenachulish, Ballachulish, Argyllshire PA39 4JZ
☎Ballachulish(08552)379

Large two-storey cottage overlooking Loch Linnhe. The ground floor has open plan kitchen/dining/sitting room, shower/WC; one room with two single beds. The first floor has four bedrooms and dormitory with two bunk bed units. The cottage is within easy reach of Glencoe and has been specially converted to suit groups of climbers, hill walkers and skiers.

All year MWB out of season 1wk min, 1mth max, 1unit, 1–15persons ◆ ◆ ⊚ fridge Electric Elec metered ⊡not provided ☎(½m) SD in unit ☺ CTV ⊕3pin square 3P ⊞ ♨(3½m) ⊖ ☘(½m)

Min£160 Max£200pw (Low)
Min£220 Max£270pw (High)

BALLANTRAE
Strathclyde Argyllshire
Map**10** NX08

B & H Balnowlart Lodge & Bungalow
for bookings Mrs A Young, Balnowlart Farm, Ballantrae, Girvan, Ayrshire
☎Ballantrae(046583)227

The properties are situated on the B7044 2 miles NE of the village and both have three bedrooms, combined lounge/diner and kitchen. The bungalow has a bathroom, the lodge has a shower. Furnishings and décor in tasteful modern style. Quiet, country location.

Ballachulish — Ballantrae

All year 1wk min, 2units, 1–6persons ◆ ⊚ fridge Open fires & ⅏(Bungalow) Electric fires (Lodge) Elec metered ⊡not provided ☎(2m) WM & SD in unit Iron & Ironing board in unit ☺ CTV ⊕3pin square P ♨(2m) ⊖

Min£40 Max£120pw

B Mrs C Scott **Balkissock Cottage**, Ballantrae, Girvan, Ayrshire
☎Ballantrae(046583)296

A modern three-bedroom bungalow with lounge/diner, kitchen (with oil fired stove), and bathroom. It is well maintained with neat décor and fitted carpeting throughout. Surrounded by rolling farmland, 3½m E of Ballantrae on unclassified road.

All year MWB out of season 2days min, 1unit, 1–6persons ◆ ◆ fridge ⅏ Elec inclusive ⊡not provided ☎(2m) Iron and Ironing board in unit TV ⊕3pin square 3P ♨(4m) Fishing ⊖ ☘(3m)

Min£50 Max£150pw

C Carrick, Horsehill & Kyle Cottages
for bookings J & R Stevenson Ltd, Balig, Ballantrae, Girvan, Ayrshire KA26 0JY
☎Ballantrae(046583)214

Three refurbished farm cottages of which **Kyle** and **Carrick** are semi-detached with communicating door and can be let singly or together. Each comprises two bedrooms. **Horsehill** is similar but detached. **Kyle** and **Carrick** have a shower room and **Horsehill** a bathroom. **Horsehill** also has a small private garden. Situated 300yds from private beach.

All year MWB All year 1wk min, 3wks max, 3units, 1 & 6persons [♢] ◆ ◆ ⊚ fridge Electric Elec metered ⊡not provided ☎(Kyle) ☎(1m) WM & SD in unit Iron & Ironing board in unit ☺ CTV ⊕3pin square 6P 4♨ ♨(1m)

⊖ ☘(1m) ♫(1m) Shooting & fishing available
Min£60 Max£175pw

H Drummaur & Kerr's Lodges
for bookings J & R Stevenson Ltd, Balig, Ballantrae, Girvan, Ayrshire KA26 0JY
☎Ballantrae(046583)214

Dating from around 1850 this large farmhouse has been renovated to provide two semi-detached units. **Drummaur Lodge** sleeps up to 10 people in three bedrooms plus sofa beds. Situated 300yds from the A77 on the A765, N of village. Private beach is 400yds.

All year MWB out of season 1wk in season, wknd out of season min, 3wks max, 2units, 1–10persons [♢] ◆ ◆ ⊚ fridge Electric & open fires Elec metered ⊡can be hired for overseas visitors only ☎(2m) WM & SD in unit Iron & Ironing board in unit ☺ CTV ⊕3pin square P ♨ ♨(1½m) Shooting & fishing ⊖ ☘(1½m) ♫(1½m)

Min£60 Max£180pw

C The Whim
for bookings J & R Stevenson Ltd, Balig, Ballantrae, Girvan, Ayrshire KA26 0JY
☎Ballantrae(046583)214

Attractive bungalow with small landscaped garden and burn. Accommodation comprises three bedrooms, sun lounge with sofa bed, large lounge/diner with open fire and kitchen with oil fired cooker. Situated 150yds from main road N of village.

All year MWB out of season 1wk in season, wknd out of season min, 3wks max, 1unit, 1–8persons [♢] ◆ ◆ Cooking by oil fired stove & open fires fridge ⅏ Elec metered ⊡can be hired for overseas visitors only ☎ WM & SD in unit Iron & Ironing board in unit ☺ CTV ⊕3pin square 4P ♨(1m) Fishing & shooting ⊖ ☘(1m) ♫(1m)

Min£65 Max£210pw

BALLATER
Grampian *Aberdeenshire*
Map**15** NO39

C   Ardgairn
for bookings Holidays Dept/6, Estate
Office, Dinnet, Aboyne, Aberdeenshire
AB3 5LL
☎Dinnet(033985)341
*A small south facing cottage with a wild
garden, set in heather clad hills beside the
River Gairn. It offers lounge with dining
area, kitchen, one double & one twin
bedroom and bathroom all on ground
level. 1m NW of Ballater. Trout fishing is
available by permit.*

Mar–25Oct   1wk min, 1mth max, 1unit,
1–4persons   ◆ ◎ fridge   Electric
Elec inclusive   ⌷can be hired   ☎(1m)
⊕3pin square   2P   ⚌(1m)

↭   ♂(2m)   ♞(2m)   ♫(2m)

£95pw (Low)
£110pw (High)

H   Candacraig
for bookings Holidays Dept/6, Estate
Office, Old Station, Dinnet, Aboyne,
Aberdeenshire AB3 5LL
☎Dinnet(033985)341

*Granite house, fully modernised and
furnished to a high standard. Large
comfortable rooms, pleasantly decorated.
Separate lounge, dining room and kitchen
with Rayburn and electric cooker. Four
bedrooms (double, twin, single and
bunks). 2m NW of Ballater.*

Mar–25Oct   1wk min, 1mth max, 1unit,
1–7persons   ◆ ◎ fridge   Electric &
open fires   Rayburn   Elec inclusive
⌷can be hired   ☎ WM   Iron & Ironing
board in unit   ☺ ⊕3pin square   P   ⚌
⚌(2m)   Fishing

↭   ♞(3m)

£125pw (Low)
£155pw (High)

C & B   Morvada Cottage & Bungalow
for bookings Mr & Mrs Nimmo, Morvada
Guesthouse, Braemar Road, Ballater,
Aberdeenshire
☎Ballater(0338)55501

*Detached two-storey cottage and modern
bungalow in the quiet gardens of Morvada
Guesthouse. The cottage comprises two
double bedrooms, two single bedrooms
ideal for children, lounge with dining area,
kitchen and sun porch. The bungalow has
two bedrooms, lounge and kitchen.*

All year   MWB out of season   1wk min,
2units, 4–6persons   ◆ ◎ fridge
Electric   Elec metered   ⌷not provided
☎(300yds)   WM in unit   Iron & Ironing
board in unit   CTV   ⊕3pin square   2P
▥   ⚌(300yds)

↭   ♂(½m)   ♞(300yds)

Min£70 Max£140pw

C   Morven West
for bookings Holidays Dept/6, Estate
Office, Old Station, Dinnet, Aboyne,
Aberdeenshire AB3 5LL
☎Dinnet(033985)341

Ballater
—
Bampton

*Small, semi-detached cottage in a
delightful glen surrounded by hills and
beside the River Gairn. Comfortable
accommodation with small, separate
kitchen, living room, two double
bedrooms, shower and WC. Ground-floor
accommodation and easy access making
the cottage suitable for elderly people. 2m
NW of Ballater.*

Mar–25Oct   1wk min, 1mth max, 1unit,
1–4persons   ◆ ◆ ◎ fridge
Electric   Elec inclusive   ⌷can be hired
☎(2m)   ⊕3pin square   P   ⚌(2m)   Trout
fishing

↭   ♞(3m)   ♫(3m)

£95pw (Low)
£110pw (High)

H   Seanchoille 12 Bridge Street
for bookings Mr & Mrs Chalmers, 8
Rubislaw Den South, Aberdeen AB2 6BB
☎Aberdeen(0224)314430 or 571433
*Homely little house forming part of a row
of buildings in centre of town off main
shopping street. The house is within a
garden courtyard and parking area.
Accommodation comprises lounge, small
kitchen, bathroom and twin bedroom on
ground floor. Two double bedrooms and a
box room on first floor.*

All year   1wk min, 1unit, 6persons   ◆ ◆
◎ fridge   open fire & electric heaters
Elec metered   ⌷inclusive   ☎(20yds)
WM in unit   Iron & Ironing board in unit
☺ CTV   ⊕3pin square   2P   ⚌(20yds)

↭   ♂(3m)   ♞(20yds)   ♫(100yds)

BALLINGHAM
Hereford & Worcester
Map**3** SO53

C   Carey Dene
for bookings Mrs R Price, Folly Farm,
Holme Lacy, Hereford, Herefordshire
HR2 6LS
☎Holme Lacy(043273)259
*Sandstone cottage situated on a mixed
farm, overlooking the River Wye, and
having comfortable lounge/diner, kitchen,
two bedrooms, bathroom and separate
WC.*

All year   MWB out of season   2days min,
6wks max, 1unit, 1–4persons   nc 5yrs
[◇]   no pets   ◎ fridge   Storage &
wood burner   Elec inclusive   ⌷inclusive
☎(250yds)   Iron & Ironing board in unit
☺ ☺ CTV   ⊕3pin square   2P   ▥
⚌(6m)

↭   ♞

Min£70 Max£90pw (Low)
£165pw (High)

BALNAIN (Glen Urquhart)
Highland *Inverness-shire*
Map**14** NH43

Ch   Tor Croft Chalets
for bookings Mrs E Mackintosh, Achmony,
Drumnadrochit, Inverness-shire IV3 6UX
☎Drumnadrochit(04562)357
*Five timber chalets set in an elevated
position with views over Loch Meikle
towards Glen Affric. Each offers open plan
lounge/kitchen/dining room, two
bedrooms and bathroom. Convertible
bed-settee in lounge.*

Etr–Oct   MWB out of season   1wk min,
1mth max, 5units, 2–6persons   ◆
no pets   ◎ fridge   Electric
Elec metered   ⌷can be hired   ☎(½m)
Iron & Ironing board in unit   ☺ CTV
⊕3pin square   8P   ⚌(3m)

↭   ♞(3m)

Min£70 Max£200pw

BAMPTON
Devon
Map**3** ST89

H   JFH Ref FM915A
for bookings John Fowler Holidays, Dept
58, Marlborough Road, Ilfracombe, Devon
EX34 8PF
☎Ilfracombe(0271)66666
*Victorian stone and slate farmhouse
situated in small country lane with 100
acres of farmland and own trout fishing.
Accommodation comprises two sitting
rooms, both with double bed settees, large
dining room with single bed settee, and
modern kitchen. On the first floor there are
three double bedrooms, a triple, a single
and a bathroom/WC. There is also an
outside WC.*

Mar–Oct   MWB out of season   3days min,
1mth max, 1unit, 1–15persons   [◇]   ◆
◎ fridge   Electric & log fires
Elec metered   ⌷not provided   ☎(½m)
Iron & Ironing board in unit   ☺ [TV]
⊕3pin square   3⚌   ⚌(½m)

↭   ♞(½m)

Min£90.85 Max£217.35pw

H   JFH Ref FC1114B
for bookings John Fowler Holidays, Dept
58, Marlborough Road, Ilfracombe, Devon
EX34 8PF
☎Ilfracombe(0271)66666
*Recently renovated former farmhouse set
in own grassed lawns bordered by a trout
stream. Accommodation comprises
spacious sitting room with huge inglenook
fireplace and double bed settee, modern
kitchen with Rayburn. Upstairs, three
double/family bedrooms, one bunk
bedded room, bathroom and WC.*

Mar–Oct   MWB out of season   3days min,
1mth max, 1unit, 1–14persons   [◇]   ◆
◎ & Rayburn   fridge   Electric & open
fires   Elec metered   ⌷not provided
☎(½m)   Iron & Ironing board in unit   ☺
TV   ⊕3pin square & 3pin round   5P
⚌(½m)   Fishing

↭   ♞(½m)

Min£90.85 Max£217.35pw

BANCHORY
Grampian *Kincardineshire*
Map**15** NO69

Ch Woodend of Glassel Banchory,
Kincardineshire AB3 4DB
☎Banchory(03302)2731

A group of compact, functional timbered chalets forming a small homely complex. Sheltered by woodland and situated 3 miles NW of Banchory. They comprise open plan kitchen/living/dining area, bathroom and either two bedrooms or one bedroom with single bedroom off, additional sleeping is available on a convertible settee.

mid Mar–mid Oct MWB out of season
1wk min, 7units, 1–5persons ◊ ◆
◆ ⊚ fridge Electric Elec metered
Ⓛcan be hired (overseas visitors only)
☎(1½m) SD on premises ☺ CTV
⊕3pin square P 🔟 ♨(1½m) Table tennis & snooker

⊖ ♂ ♀(3m) 🎜(3m)

Min£78 Max£99pw (Low)
Min£93 Max£120pw (High)

BANGOR
Gwynedd
Map**6** SH57

H Bryn Melyn
for bookings Menai Holidays, Old Port Office, Port Penrhyn, Bangor, Gwynedd LL57 3HN
☎Bangor(0248)362254

Detached modern house in secluded residential area. Comprises kitchen, dining room, lounge with coal fire, one double bedroom and bathroom/WC on ground floor. Two twin bedded rooms and WC on first floor. 1m SE A5122.

All year MWB in season 3days min,
6wks max, 1unit, 2–6persons ◊ ◆
no pets ⊚ fridge ♨(Gas) Gas & Elec metered Ⓛcan be hired ☎(½m) WM & SD in unit Iron & Ironing board in unit CTV ⊕3pin square 1P 1🔟 🔟 ♨(3m)

⊖ ♂(2m) ♀(3m) 🎜(3m) 🎵(3m) 🏌(3m) Sports centre(3m)

Min£120 Max£220pw

H Capel Ogwen, Penrhyn Park
for bookings Mrs H W Chamberlain, Menai

Banchory
—
Barnstaple

Holidays, Old Port Office, Port Penrhyn, Bangor, Gwynedd LL57 3HN
☎Bangor(0248)362254 or 351055

Large house near the Menai Straits in large park, once the gamekeeper's residence. The ground floor comprises kitchen (with dishwasher), lounge/diner (beamed), games room, WC and a twin-bedded room suitable for disabled. The first floor has three twin-bedded rooms and two double rooms with two bathrooms/WC. Salmon and sea trout fishing available.

All year MWB out of season 3days min,
6wks max, 1unit, 2–12persons ◊ ◆
⊚ fridge ♨& Electric Elec metered
Ⓛnot provided ☎ WM & TD in unit Dishwasher in unit Iron & Ironing board in unit ☺ CTV ⊕3pin square 6P 2🔟 ♨(½m)

⊖ ♂(3m) ♀(3m)

£220pw (Low)
Min£310 Max£350pw (High)

H 2 Flagstaff Gardens
for bookings Menai Holidays, Old Port Office, Port Penrhyn, Bangor, Gwynedd
☎Bangor(0248)362254 or 351055

A spacious semi-detached house with secluded lawns and gardens set almost on the quay at the fishing harbour. Accommodation comprises a large lounge/dining room, separate additional lounge, kitchen and WC. Upstairs there is one double, one twin and one single bedroom and bathroom/WC.

May–Oct MWB out of season
3days min, 6wks max, 1unit, 2–5persons
⊚ fridge ♨ Elec metered Ⓛcan be hired ☎(½m) WM & SD in unit Iron & Ironing board in unit CTV
⊕3pin square 2P 1🔟 🔟 ♨(1m)

⊖ ♂(½m) ♀(½m) 🎜(1m) 🏌(2m) Sports centre(2m)

Min£140 Max£240pw

BANKFOOT
Tayside *Perthshire*
Map**11** NO03

Ca Hunter's Cabins
for bookings Mr B Hunter, Hunter's Lodge, Bankfoot, Perthshire PH1 4DX
☎Bankfoot(073887)325

Group of six log cabins in the grounds of a popular restaurant. Each comprises lounge/dining area, small kitchenette, bathroom, a twin bedroom and one with a single bed and two bunks. An extra single bed can be set up in the lounge. The interiors, which are fully timbered, are simple and functional. Bankfoot is now by-passed by the A9, which although still conveniently close makes the environment pleasantly quiet.

All year MWB 1night min, 6units,
4–6persons [◊ ◊] ◆ ♠ fridge Gas Gas metered Ⓛinclusive ☎(50yds) Iron & Ironing board on premises [Launderette on premises] ☺ CTV ⊕3pin square 50P 🔟 ♨(200yds) 🏌Hard

⊖ ♀

Max£150pw (Low)
Max£195pw (High)

BARNSTAPLE
Devon
Map**2** SS53

C JFH Ref B6B
for bookings John Fowler Holidays, Dept. 58, Marlborough Road, Ilfracombe, Devon EX34 8PF
☎Ilfracombe(0271)66666

A country cottage overlooking the River Taw. It comprises kitchen, dining room with open fire, lounge with stone alcove, bathroom and WC. Upstairs is one double bedroom and two twin bedrooms, all light and well decorated.

Mar–Oct MWB out of season 1wk min,
1mth max, 1unit, 6persons ◆ no pets
⊚ fridge Electric fires & storage heaters Elec metered Ⓛnot provided ☎(½m) Iron & Ironing board in unit ♠ CTV ⊕3pin square 2P ♨(½m)

⊖ ♀(½m) 🎜(2m) 🏌(2m) 🏌(2m) Sports centre(2m)

Min£79.35 Max£205.85pw

BARR
Strathclyde Ayrshire
Map**10** NX29

H Mrs V Dunlop **Glengennet** Barr,
Girvan, Ayrshire
☎Barr(046586)220

Semi-detached wing of farmhouse
providing simply furnished, spacious
accommodation, comprising large
lounge/diner, separate kitchenette, double
bedroom on ground floor with twin and
double-bedded rooms on the first floor.
Set amidst hilly farmland on a sheep and
beef farm lying 1½m from the picturesque
village of Barr.

Mid-May–Oct 1wk min, 8wks max, 1unit,
1–6persons ◆ ◆ ◎ fridge
Electric fires Elec metered
⬜not provided ☎(1½m) Airing
cupboard in unit HCE in unit TV
⊕3pin square & ⊕3pin round P
🎣(1½m) Fishing & bird watching
↔ ☎ (1½m)

Details not confirmed for 1987

BARRA Isle of
Western Isles Inverness-shire
Map**13**

CASTLEBAY
Map**13** NL69

Ch **Monte Fracelma** Kentangaval
for bookings Mr G Campbell, 26
Kentangaval, Castlebay, Isle of Barra,
Inverness-shire
☎Castlebay(08714)328

This Norwegian-designed timber-clad
dwelling is well furnished, and contains
central heating and double glazing.
Spacious accommodation consists of
three bedrooms, large living room with
convertible settee, modern kitchen,
bathroom and WC. Views of Castle Bay.

All year MWB out of season 1wk min,
5wks max, 1unit, 1–10persons ◆ ◎
fridge Elec inclusive Elec metered in
winter ⬜inclusive ☎(½m) WM in unit
Iron & Ironing board in unit ⊕ CTV
⊕3pin square P 🎣(½m)
↔ ☎ (½m) 🎵(½m)
Min£50 Max£85pw (Low)
Min£100 Max£132pw (High)

C **1 Shore Cottage** Horve
for bookings Mr G Campbell, 26
Kentangaval, Castlebay, Isle of Barra,
Inverness-shire
☎Castlebay(08714)328

Close to water's edge at Kentangaval Bay,
this two-storey cottage consists of three
bedrooms, kitchen, dining room, sitting
room and shower room/WC.

Barr
—
Bath

All year MWB out of season 1wk min,
5wks max, 1unit, 1–8persons ◆ ◎ &
🍴 fridge Electric & open fires Elec
metered in winter ⬜inclusive ☎(1m)
CTV ⊕3pin square 🎣(½m)

↔ ☎ (½m) 🎵(½m)
Min£45 Max£80pw (Low)
Min£94 Max£115pw (High)

C **2 Shore Cottage** Horve
for bookings Mr G Campbell, 26
Kentangaval, Castlebay, Isle of Barra,
Inverness-shire
☎Castlebay(08714)328

A small renovated croft, standing by
Kentangaval Bay. Accommodation
comprises kitchen, dining/living room with
convertible settee, one large family
bedroom and shower room/WC.

All year MWB out of season 1wk min,
5wks max, 1unit, 1–5persons ◆ ◎
fridge Electric & open fires ⬜inclusive
☎ Iron CTV ⊕3pin square 🎣(½m)
↔ ☎ (½m) 🎵(½m)
Min£35 Max£70pw (Low)
Min£78 Max£95pw (High)

BASFORD
Staffordshire
Map**7** SJ95

H **Churnet Grange Farm**
for bookings Mrs C M Pickford, Lowe Hill
Farm, Ashbourne Road, Leek, Staffs
☎Leek(0538)383035

White-painted detached farmhouse in an
elevated position in rural surroundings.
Accommodation comprises lounge, dining
room, large kitchen and small bedroom,
with bunk beds. First floor comprises a
bathroom/WC, a large family bedroom, a
spacious triple-bedded room and a small
double.

All year MWB out of season 2days min,
1unit, 10persons ◆ ◎ fridge Electric
& open fires Elec metered ⬜can be
hired ☎ Iron & Ironing board in unit
⊕ TV ⊕3pin square 6P 1🎣 🎱
🎣(½m)
↔ ♪(1½m) ☎(½m) 🎵(3m) 🏠(3m)
Min£50 Max£120pw (Low)
Min£75 Max£180pw (High)

BASSENTHWAITE
Cumbria
Map**11** NY23

C Mrs P Trafford **Bassenthwaite Hall
Farm Cottages** Bassenthwaite, Keswick,
Cumbria CA12 4QP
☎Bassenthwaite Lake(059681)393

One cottage is converted from a barn
which adjoins the farmhouse; the other
two are also within the farm complex and
are in a tastefully converted 17th-century
building. All have spacious lounge with
feature fireplace, kitchen or kitchen/diner
and either two or three bedrooms. The
properties are ideal for children who can
catch minnows in the nearby stream or
feed the ducks and hens which roam
freely.

All year MWB out of season 2days min,
1mth max, 3units, 2–10persons [◇] ◆
◆ no pets ◎ fridge Storage heaters
& open fires Elec metered ⬜can be
hired ☎(200yds) SD in unit Iron &
Ironing board in unit ⊕ CTV ⊕3 pin
square P 🎱 🎣(½m) Fishing, pony
trekking
↔ ☎ (200yds)
Min£50 Max£200pw

BATH
Avon
Map**3** ST76

F **Bennet Street**
for bookings Mrs B Dunn, 12 Richmond
Road, Bath, Avon BA1 5TU
☎Bath(0225)311122

Situated opposite Bath's Assembly Rooms
in an elegant Georgian terrace the flat
comprises spacious lounge/diner, open
plan kitchen, one double and one twin
bedded room and bath/wc.

All year MWB 3days min, 4wks max,
1unit, 2–4persons nc5years no pets
◎ fridge night storage heaters
Elec inclusive ⬜can be hired ☎ Iron &
Ironing board in unit [Launderette within
300yds] ⊕ CTV ⊕3pin square
🎣(100yds)
↔ ♪(2m) ☎ (100yds) 🎵(½m)
🎵(½m) 🏠(½m) Sports centre(½m)
Min£100 Max£170pw

F Mrs I Lynall **Circus Mansions** 36 Brock
Street, Bath, Avon BA1 2LJ
☎Bath(0225)336462

One second-floor flat and one third-floor
flat in peaceful location in Georgian
residential area. Both comprise hall, fitted
kitchen, bathroom, one double bedroom
and living room. Comfortably furnished
and soundly appointed.

All year MWB 1day min, 1mth max,
2units, 1–4persons nc14yrs no pets
◎ fridge 🍴 Gas inclusive Gas & Elec
metered ⬜inclusive ☎(400yds) Iron &

Bath — Beauly

Ironing board on premises [Launderette on premises/within 300yds] ⊙ CTV
⊕3pin square 🔲 ♿(200yds)
↔ ♪(½m) ♀(200yds) ♫(¼m)
♫(1m) ♿(1m) Sports centre(1m)
Min£90 Max£135pw (Low)
Min£110 Max£150pw (High)

F Mr J Williams **Flats 2, 3 & 4**
1 Grosvenor Place
Bath, Avon BA1 6AX
Bath(0225)20537
*Ground, second and top floor flats in a spacious Bathstone townhouse having sitting room and kitchen. **Flats 3 & 4** have bathroom and **Flat 2** has a shower room. **Flats 2 & 3** have one bedroom. **Flat 4** has two. On E side of the city on A4.*

Allyear MWB out of season 2nights min, 3units, 2–4persons no pets ⓖ fridge ♨(Flats 3&4) Gas fires(Flat2) Elec & gas inclusive ⬜inclusive except towels ☎(20yds) WM, SD & TD on premises Iron & Ironing board on premises ⊙ CTV ⊕3pin square ♿(25yds) ↔ ♪(2m) ♀(30yds)
Min£85 Max£115pw (Low)
Min£110 Max£150pw (High)

F   Marshal Wade's House, 14 Abbey Church Yard
for bookings The Landmark Trust, Shottesbrooke, Maidenhead, Berkshire SL6 3SW
☎Littlewick Green(062882)5925
Unique, historical second- and third-floor flat situated in city centre overlooking the Abbey Church Square. Accommodation comprises large kitchen/diner, large lounge, two twin-bedded rooms, bathroom and separate WC.

Allyear MWB out of season 1night min, 3wks max, 1unit, 2–4persons ◆ no pets ⓖ fridge Storage & fan heaters Elec inclusive ⬜not provided ☎(200yds) Iron & Ironing board in unit ⊙ ⊕3pin square ♿(200yds) ↔ ♀(½m) ♫(¼m) ♫(¼m) ♿(¼m)
Min£170 Max£270pw (Low)
Min£190 Max£270pw (High)

BAYTON
Hereford & Worcester
Map**7** SO67

F Mrs M D Gregory **Broad Meadows Farmhouse**, Bayton, Clows Top, Worcestershire DY14 9LP
☎Clows Top(029922)304
This is a mainly 17th-century farmhouse with an older half timbered wing. It stands alone, south of the quiet village, commanding glorious views, and near to

---

the church. The two compact one bedroomed flats are well-equipped with lounge/kitchen/dining facilities, bathroom and WC.

Allyear MWB out of season 3nights min, 1mth max, 2units, 1–3persons, nc18yrs pets by prior arrangement ⓖ fridge ♨ Elec inclusive ⬜inclusive ☎(½m) WM & SD on premises Iron & Ironing board on premises ⊙ CTV ⊕3pin square 6P 🔲 ♿(1M) ↔ ♀ stables
Min£80 Max£95pw (Low)
Min£115 Max£130pw (High)

See advertisement under Cleobury Mortimer

BEACON
Devon
Map**3** ST20

C   CC Ref 7648L A & B
for bookings Character Cottages, 34 Fore Street, Sidmouth, Devon EX10 8AQ
☎Sidmouth(03955)77001
*Two converted thatched farm barns, situated in elevated position with sweeping views of East Devon countryside. **Cottage A** comprises lounge with woodburning stove, kitchen/diner, one double and two twin bedrooms plus bathroom. **Cottage B** comprises kitchen/diner, beamed lounge, french doors to garden, open plan staircase to one double, and one twin room with extra bed, plus bathroom. Both cottages are tastefully decorated with Laura Ashley fabrics and antique furniture.*

Allyear MWB out of season 2days min, 3wks max, 2units, 5–6persons [◇] ◆ no pets ⓖ fridge electric fires & wood burners Elec metered ⬜inclusive ☎(3m) WM & SD in unit Iron & Ironing board in unit ⊙ CTV ⊕3pin square 4P ♿(3m) ↔ ♀(3m)
Min£104 Max£258pw

BEARLEY
Warwickshire
Map**4** SP16

F   College Flat College Farm
for bookings Mr T E Tunnicliffe, 27 Meadow Sweet Road, Stratford-upon-Avon, Warwickshire CV37 7RH
☎Stratford-upon-Avon(0789)293518

Occupying the upper two storeys of a converted brick-built farmhouse, offering kitchen/diner, lounge, bathroom and three bedrooms, the comfortable accommodation is reached via an outside wooden staircase.

Allyear MWB out of season 7days min, 8mths max, 1unit, 1–6persons ◆ ⓖ fridge ♨ Elec metered ⬜inclusive ☎ Iron & Ironing board in unit ⊙ TV ⊕3pin square 🔲 ♿(1m) ♪ ↔ ♪(3m) ♀(½m)
Min£80 Max£160pw

See advertisement under Stratford upon Avon

H   Crescent Cottages
for bookings Mr T E Tunnicliffe, 27 Meadow Sweet Road, Stratford-upon-Avon, Warwickshire CV37 7RH
☎Stratford-upon-Avon(0789)293518
Two brick-built semi-detached houses situated in a quiet cul-de-sac, each comprising lounge, kitchen/diner, pantry and bathroom.

Allyear MWB out of season 7days min, 8mths max, 2units, 1–6persons ◆ ⓖ fridge ♨ Elec metered ⬜inclusive ☎ Iron & Ironing board in unit ⊙ TV ⊕3pin square 3P 🔲 ♿(1m) ↔ ♪(3m) ♀(100yds)
Min£80 Max£160pw

See advertisement under Stratford upon Avon

BEAULY
Highland *Inverness-shire*
Map**14** NH54

Ch Mr & Mrs D J Turner, **Dunsmore Lodges** Farley, Beauly, Inverness-shire IV4 7EY
☎Beauly(0463)782424
Nine Scandinavian-style wood chalets furnished and equipped to a high standard, set well apart on a wooded site. Eight of the chalets are two bedroomed, one has three bedrooms, and all have kitchen/diner/living room and bathroom. One chalet has been designed to suit disabled persons.

Allyear MWB out of season 9units, 1–7persons ◆ ⓖ fridge Electric Elec metered ⬜can be hired ☎ WM TD on premises Iron & Ironing board in unit ⊙ CTV ⊕3pin square P ♿(3½m)
Min£75 Max£85pw (Low)
Min£210 Max£240pw (High)

BEER
Devon
Map**3** SY28

H   CC Ref 7600
for bookings Character Cottages, 34 Fore
Street, Sidmouth, Devon EX10 8AQ
☎Sidmouth(03955)77001

*A well appointed neo-Georgian detached
house on three floors with views over the
village and Lyme Bay. Accommodation
comprises hall with utility room and WC off
stairs to two double bedrooms and one
twin room, bathroom with bidet. Further
wooden stairs lead to WC and cloakroom,
single bedroom, large kitchen and lounge/
diner with picture windows.*

Etr–Sep   MWB out of season   2days min,
3wks max, 1unit, 7persons   [◇]   ◆
no pets   ⏃ & ◎ fridge ▩(oil)   Gas Elec
& Oil inclusive   ⌂not provided
☎(200yds)   WM, SD & TD in unit   Iron &
Ironing board in unit   ⊙   CTV
⊕3pin square   1P   1🛏   ▥   ♨(200yds)
↩   ♨(100yds)   ♫(3m)
Min£271 Max£373pw

BELL BUSK
North Yorkshire
Map**7** SD95

C   Horseshoe & Rose Cottage
for bookings Mrs J Richardson, 563
Gisburn Road, Blacko, Nelson, Lancashire
☎Nelson(0282)66122

*Two stone-built cottages situated in the
centre of the village.* **Rose Cottage**
*comprises two double bedrooms, one
twin-bedded room, lounge, kitchen/dining
area and a bathroom.* **Horseshoe Cottage**
*has two double, one single and one twin-
bedded room plus a convertible settee in
the lounge, a kitchen/diner and bathroom.*

All year   MWB   3mths max, 2units,
2–8persons   ◆ ◆ ◎   fridge
Electric fires   ⌂can be hired   ☎(20yds)
Iron & Ironing board in unit   ⊙   CTV
⊕3pin square   P   ▥   ♨(20yds)
£54pw (Low)
Min£135 Max£150pw (High)

BEMBRIDGE
See **Wight, Isle of**

BERRIEW
Powys
Map**7** SJ10

C   Tanyfridd
for bookings Mrs M Williams, Llwyn-onn,
Brooks, Berriew, Welshpool, Powys
☎Berriew(068685)296

*18th-century detached cottage set in its
own lawns in lovely countryside. The
ground floor comprises lounge (with
inglenook) and dining room, with original
beams, divider, bathroom/WC, and
kitchen. On the first floor there are three
bedrooms.*

All year   MWB out of season   3days min,
6wks max, 1unit, 2–8persons   ◆ ◎
fridge   Electric storage heaters & open
fires (charge for logs)   Elec metered

Beer
—
Betws-yn-Rhos

⌂can be hired   ☎(½m)   SD in unit   Iron
& Ironing board in unit   ⊙   TV
⊕3pin square   2P   ▥   ♨(3m)
↩   ♨(3m)
Min£40 Max£110pw

BERRYNARBOR
Devon
Map**2** SS54

**Ch & F   Sandaway Holiday Park (chalets
& flats)**
for bookings Sandaway Holiday Park,
Berrynarbor, Ilfracombe, Devon EX34 9ST
☎Combe Martin(027188)3155

*These eight chalets and three flats of
modern design situated in a 20-acre
caravan and chalet park. There are fine
views of the sea and rolling countryside
with access to private beach. The village of
Combe Martin is ⅓m away. The
accommodation varies and sleeps from
2–8 persons.*

15Mar–Oct(chalets)
16Feb–14Jan(flats)   MWB out of season
2nights min, 1mth max, 11units,
2–8persons   ◆ ◆   ⏃(flats)
◎(chalets)   fridge   Electric   Elec
inclusive (except heating)   ⌂can be
hired   ☎(130yds)   [Iron on premises]
Ironing board on premises   [Launderette
within 30yds]   ⊙   CTV   ⊕3pin square
4P   ♨(30yds)   ☒   licensed bar
↩   ♫(½m)   ♫(½m)
Details not confirmed for 1987
See advertisement under Combe Martin

BETWS-Y-COED
Gwynedd
Map**6** SH75

C   Ty Capel & Ty Coch Rhiwddolion
for bookings The Landmark Trust,
Shottesbrooke, Maidenhead, Berkshire
SL6 3SW
☎Littlewick Green(062882)5925

*Set in the remote hills above Betws-y-Coed
these two cottages contain modern
facilities. They are modestly furnished
providing unusual and unique
accommodation adjacent to mountain
streams.* **Ty Capel** *is a converted stone
chapel comprising kitchen, lounge, diner
with log fire and a gallery with three single
beds plus bathroom/WC.* **Ty Coch**
*comprises lounge/diner with open fire,
kitchen, two bedrooms (one twin- and one
bunk-bedded) and bathroom/WC.*

All year   MWB out of season   2days min,
6wks max, 2units, 1–4persons   ◆ ◎
fridge   storage heaters   Elec inclusive
⌂not provided   ☎(1m)   Iron & Ironing
board in unit   ⊙   ⊕3pin square   2P
♨(2m)   ♪(2m)   ♨(2m)
Min£90 Max£190pw (Low)
Min£105 Max£200pw (High)

BETWS-YN-RHOS
Clwyd
Map**6** SH97

H   Coach House
for bookings Mr R A Lomax, 3 The Ffarm,
Betws-yn-Rhos, Abergele, Clwyd LL22 8AR
☎Dolwen(049260)287

*Converted and modernised Coach House
providing spacious and comfortable
accommodation. It comprises large
comfortable lounge, kitchen/dining room
on first floor and three bedrooms (one
double, two twin) and bathroom/WC on
the ground floor. It has a separate first-
floor entrance. Restaurant and bar
facilities are available on the complex.*

3days min, 6wks max, 1unit, 2–6persons
◆   no pets   ◎   fridge   storage heaters
Elec inclusive   ⌂can be hired
☎(100yds)   Iron & Ironing board in unit
⊙   CTV   ⊕3pin square   2P
♨(400yds)   ↩   ♨
Min£135 Max£248pw

F   Mews Flats
for bookings Mr R A Lomax, 3 The Ffarm,
Betws-yn-Rhos, Abergele, Clwyd LL22 8AR
☎Dolwen(049260)287

*Six flats in wooded position just off B5381.
Three flats are on the ground-floor of
converted stables and comprise lounge/
diner, kitchen, bathroom/WC and two
bedrooms sleeping up to five people. The
two second-floor flats comprise lounge/
diner/kitchenette, bathroom/WC and one
double bedroom. The maisonette has two
bedrooms, bathroom/WC, kitchen and
lounge/diner with a double put-u-up.
Restaurant and bar facilities are available
on the complex.*

All year   MWB out of season   3days min,
6wks max, 6units, 2–6persons   ◆
no pets   ◎   fridge   ▩   Elec metered
⌂can be hired   ☎(100yds)   Iron &
Ironing board in unit   ⊙   CTV
⊕3pin square   12P   ♨(400yds)
Min£55 Max£85pw (Low)
Min£115 Max£198pw (High)

Ch   Timber Chalets
for bookings Mr R A Lomax, 3 The Ffarm,
Betws-yn-Rhos, Abergele, Clwyd LL22 8AR
☎Dolwen(049260)287

*Compact timber chalets nestling in
woodlands and comprising lounge/diner/
kitchenette and shower/WC. Each chalet
has one double-bedded room, three have
a twin-bedded and three have bunk beds
in the second bedroom. Restaurant and
bar facilities are available within the
complex.*

Mar–Oct   MWB out of season   1wk min,
6wks max, 6units, 1–4persons   ◆
no pets   ◎   fridge   Gas & Electric
heaters   Gas/Elec metered   ⌂can be
hired   ☎(100yds)   Iron & Ironing board in
unit   ⊙   CTV   ⊕3pin square   12P
♨(400yds)
↩   ♨(100yds)
Min£65 Max£148pw

40

BEWCASTLE
Cumbria
Map**12** NY57

***C* Barn & Old Farm Cottages**
for bookings Mr & Mrs B Downer, Bank End Farm, Roadhead, Bewcastle, Carlisle, Cumbria CA6 6NU
☎Roadhead(06978)644

*Two cottages set in 20 acres of farmland with fishing rights on the Black Lyne river. **Barn Cottage** which adjoins the farmhouse, is a converted barn and comprises lounge (with two convertible bed chairs), kitchen, one double bedroom with original beam and bathroom/WC. **Old Farm Cottage** which adjoins Barn Cottage comprises three bedrooms, living room with convertible bed-settee, kitchen and bathroom/WC. Freezer facilities available.*

Allyear MWB out of season 2nights min, 1mth max, 2units, 2–8persons ◈ ◆ ◎ fridge 🔥& Electrical(Barn) Open fires(Old Farm) Elec inclusive Ⓛcan be hired ☎ WM, SD & TD on premises Iron & Ironing board in unit ⊙ CTV ⊕3pin square 6P Ⓜ ⛪(3½m)

⊖ ♀(3m)

Min£60 Max£180pw

BICKLEIGH (nr Tiverton)
Devon
Map**3** SS90

***C* CC Ref 679**
for bookings Character Cottages (Holidays) Ltd, 34 Fore Street, Sidmouth, Devon EX10 8AQ
☎Sidmouth(03955)77001

Situated in the east wing of a 16th-century farmhouse. Accommodation comprises a first floor with large comfortable lounge, one twin-bedded room, one double bedroom and bathroom/WC, and ground floor with kitchen/diner and a twin-bedded room.

end May–Sep 1wk min, 1mth max, 1unit, 2–6persons ◎ fridge Eletric Elec metered Ⓛcan be hired ☎ WM & SD in unit Iron & Ironing board in unit ⊙ TV ⊕3pin square ⊕2pin round P 🏠 Ⓜ ⛪(½m)

⊖ ♀

BICTON (nr Shrewsbury)
Shropshire
Map**7** SJ41

***B* Inglenook** Villa Lane
for bookings Mrs J M Mullineux, Fach-Hir, Brooks, Welshpool, Powys SY21 8QP
☎Tregynon(068687)361

A semi-detached bungalow with a small enclosed garden and lawn, located off the main A5, in a quiet cul-de-sac. The accommodation comprises lounge/dining room, kitchen, two double bedrooms and a bathroom/WC.

Allyear MWB out of season 1wk min, 3mths max, 1unit, 1–4persons, nc8 no pets ◎ fridge Electric Elec metered Ⓛinclusive ☎(60yds) WM & SD in unit Iron & ironing board in unit ⊙ Ⓦ CTV ⊕3pin square 2P 1🏠 Ⓜ ⛪(¾m)

⊖ ⛳(3m) ♀(¼m) ♫(3m) 🎥(3m)

Min£40 Max£100pw

BIDDLESTONE
Northumberland
Map**12** NT90

***H* Priests House**
for bookings Mrs M Carruthers, Dunns Farm, Elsdon, Newcastle-upon-Tyne NE19 1AL
☎Rothbury(0669)40219

Large, stone-built house in its own grounds, situated in the heart of the Cheviots. Accommodation comprises lounge, kitchen, four bedrooms, plus bed-settee if required, and bathroom.

Allyear MWB out of season 2nights min, 1mth max, 1unit, 6–10persons ◈ ◆ ◎ fridge Electric Elec metered Ⓛcan be hired ☎ SD in unit Iron & Ironing board in unit ⊙ CTV ⊕3pin square 5P ⛪(10m)

⊖ ♀(2½m)

Min£50 Max£60pw (Low)
Min£55 Max£160pw (High)

BIDEFORD
Devon
Map**2** SS42

***C* JFH BK6B**
for bookings John Fowler Holidays, Dept 58 Marlborough Road, Ilfracombe, Devon EX34 8PF
☎Ilfracombe(0271)66666

Country cottage with large garden and good views. Accommodation comprises on the ground floor: kitchen, dining room, lounge, single bedroom and bathroom; stairs lead to one single bedroom and two double bedded rooms all with oak beams.

Mar–Oct MWB out of season 1wk min, 3wks max, 1unit, 6persons ◈ ◆ no pets ◎ fridge Elec metered Ⓛnot provided ☎(¾m) Iron & Ironing board in unit CTV ⊕3pin square 4P Ⓜ ⛪(¾m)

⊖ ⛳(3m) ♀(1m) ♫(3m) ♫(3m)

Min£79.35 Max£205.85pw

***H* JFH BW4D**
for bookings John Fowler Holidays, Dept 58 Marlborough Road, Ilfracombe, Devon EX34 8PF
☎Ilfracombe(0271)66666

Part of a large country house on 100-acre estate. Comprises kitchen area, dining room, lounge, one double and one twin-bedded room and bathroom.

Mar–Oct MWB out of season 1wk min, 3wk max, 1unit, 4persons ◈ ◆ no pets ◎ fridge Elec metered Ⓛnot provided ☎(¾m) Iron & Ironing board in unit CTV ⊕3pin square 4P ⛪(¾m)

⊖ ⛳(3m) ♀(1m) ♫(3m) ♫(3m)

Min£56.35 Max£171.35pw

***C & B* CC Ref 574L 1–6**
for bookings Character Cottages (Holidays) Ltd, 34 Fore Street, Sidmouth, Devon EX10 8AQ
☎Sidmouth(03955)77001

Converted farm buildings consisting of five cottages and one bungalow in grounds of Kenwith Castle with marvellous views. Accommodation comprises open plan lounge, kitchen/diner, bathroom and WC. Three cottages sleep four in one double bedroom and one twin-bedded room. One cottage and the bungalow sleeps six in twin-bedded rooms and one double bedroom. Smallest cottage sleeps two in one double room. Decorated and furnished to a high standard.

end Mar–Oct 1wk min, 1mth max, 6units, 1–6persons ◈ ◆ no pets ◎ fridge Electric Elec metered Ⓛcan be hired ☎(1½m) Iron & Ironing board in unit ⊙ CTV ⊕3pin square 2P Ⓜ ⛪(1½m) ⛱ 🎾Hard

⊖ ♀(1m) 🎥(3m)

Min£103 Max£139pw (Low)
Min£169 Max£277pw (High)

C Mrs M Winsor **Heale Lodge** Yeo Vale, Bideford, Devon
☎Bideford(02372)77292

Semi-detached cottage attached to owners Victorian house, with views of river and countryside. Comprising lounge with log burning fire, two bedrooms, bathroom, well-equipped kitchen with backdoor onto patio, open plan, attractive garden.

Allyear MWB out of season 3nights min, 4wks max, 1unit, 1–5persons ◈ ◎ fridge Electric Elec metered Ⓛcan be hired ☎(50yds) WM & SD in unit Iron & Ironing board in unit TV ⊕3pin square 3P Ⓜ ⛪(2½m)

⊖ ♀(1m) 🎥(2½m)

Min£35 Max£45pw (Low)
Min£75 Max£95pw (High)

BINEGAR
Somerset
Map**3** ST64

***F* Forecourt & Lawnside**
for bookings Mrs A E Rich, Whitnell Farm, Binegar, Gurney Slade, Bath, Avon BA3 4UF
☎Oakhill(0749)840277

Two self-contained apartments in a manor house on a working farm with fine views of open countryside. The ground-floor apartment sleeps up to seven in three bedrooms, with comfortable lounge and inglenook fireplace, kitchen/dining area and bathroom. First-floor apartment comprises two bedrooms, lounge, kitchen and bathroom. Use of garden.

Allyear MWB out of season 3days min, 4wks max, 2units, 1–7persons [◇] ◈ →

no pets fridge Elec metered
can be hired (1½m) Iron in unit
Ironing board on premises CTV
3pin square 6P (2m)
δ(3m) (1½m)
Min£80 Max£190pw
See advertisement under Bath

BIRCHER
Hereford & Worcester
Map7 SX46

F   Stable House Bircher Hall
for bookings The Lady Cawley, Bircher
Hall, Leominster, Herefordshire
Yarpole(056885)218
*A recently modernised stable block
comprising a reception hall and WC on
the ground floor, and a twin-bedded room,
a single-bedded room, bathroom, kitchen
and lounge on the first floor.*
All year 1wk min, 6mths max, 1unit,
1–3persons no dogs   fridge   &
wood burning stove Elec metered   can
be hired   WM & SD in unit Iron in
unit   TV can be hired
3pin square 2P   (1½m)
(1½m)
Min£40 Max£110pw

F   West Wing Bircher Hall
for bookings The Lady Cawley, Bircher
Hall, Leominster, Herefordshire
Yarpole(056885)218
*A fully modernised apartment within
Bircher Hall, it has a private entrance and
comprises ground-floor bathroom,
kitchen/diner (with dishwasher), and
lounge; first floor with three twin bedrooms
and large bathroom.*
All year 1wk min, 6mths max, 1unit,
1–5persons, nc6   fridge
    SD & TD in unit, Iron & Ironing board in
unit   CTV 3pin square 2P
(1m)
(1½m)
Min£45 Max£70pw (Low)
Min£90 Max£120pw (High)

BIRCHOVER
Derbyshire
Map7 SK26

C   Keeling Cottage
for bookings Mr & Mrs E L Fisher,
'Ivydene', Birchover, Matlock, Derbyshire
DE4 2BL
Winster(062988)250
*Built of local stone in 1755 and situated off
the main street in the centre of a pleasant
Peak district village, this property has been*

Binegar
—
Blackboys

*modernised to a good comfortable
standard. Accommodation comprises
lounge/dining room, kitchen, one double
bedroom and one compact single
bedroom and bathroom/WC. Good décor
throughout.*
All year 1wk min, 1unit, 3persons, nc8
   no pets   fridge   & open fire
Elec inclusive   inclusive (200yds)
Iron & Ironing board in unit   CTV
3pin square 2P   (50yds)
(100yds)
Min£95 Max£115pw (Low)
Min£120 Max£130pw (High)

BIRMINGHAM
West Midlands
Map7 SP08

F   Maple Bank Church Road, Edgbaston
for bookings Mr E R Farrar, Residences
and Conferences, University of
Birmingham, PO Box 363, Birmingham
B15 2TT
021-472 1301 ext2167
*On the city centre side of the university
campus, groups of two-storey modern
blocks of six flats surrounding areas of
lawns. Flats consist of five bedrooms (four
singles and one twin) which are fairly small
but well equipped. A good size kitchen/
diner, bathroom and separate WC
completes the unit.*
Mid Jul–mid Sep 1wk min, 9wks max,
45units, 1–6persons   no pets
fridge   Elec inclusive
inclusive   Iron on premises
Ironing board in unit [Launderette on
premises] CTV can be hired
3pin square 100P   (½m)
Hard full sporting facilities
δ(⅜m)   (2m) (2m)
(2m)
Details not confirmed for 1987

BISHOP SUTTON
Avon
Map3 ST55

**C   Mrs J Quantrill Bonhill House
(Cottage)** Bishopsutton, Bristol BS18 4TU
Chew Magna(0272)332546
*Small detached cottage, converted from
the coach house and adjacent to the farm
house. Ground floor comprises: hall with
WC off, sitting room with bathroom off and
kitchen/diner. First floor has two*

---

*bedrooms, one double, one twin. Situated
on quiet country lane, near Chew Valley
Lake. Use of the garden at Bonhill House.
On site stabling and livery.*
All year 1wk min, 6wks max, 1unit,
4persons [ ]   fridge
Solid fuel Parkray Elec metered   can
be hired (overseas visitors only) (½m)
Iron & Ironing board in unit
CTV 3pin square 2P   (½m)
(½m)
Min£40 Max£90pw (Low)
Min£98 Max£145pw [High]

BLACKAWTON
Devon
Map3 SY84

**C   K & B Troup Hutcherleigh Farm
Cottages** Middle Hutcherleigh,
Blackawton, Totnes, South Devon
TQ9 7AD
East Allington(054852)377
*Situated in the midst of unspoilt
countryside of the South Hams the old
barns of this small farm have been
converted to provide comfortable well
furnished cottages. They are of traditional
design with thick stone walls and many
exposed beams. All cottages have
bedrooms and bathroom at ground level
with large open plan living area above.*
Granary and **Old Timbers** have three
bedrooms, one double, one twin and one
with bunk beds. Granary also has a sofa
bed. **Greystones** has two bedrooms, one
double and one twin plus a sofa bed. 6
miles S of Totnes along A381 take sign to
Blackawton, Middle Hutcherleigh
signposted ⅜m.
All year MWB out of season 1wk min
3units, 1–7persons   fridge
storage & electric heating Elec metered
can be hired   Iron & Ironing board
in unit [Launderette on premises]
CTV 3pin square 1P   (1½m)
childrens play area
(1½m)
Min£50 Max£90pw (Low)
Min£110 Max£220pw (High)

BLACKBOYS
East Sussex
Map5 TQ52

**C   C P & A S Wright Brownings Farm
Holiday Cottages**, Blackboys, Uckfield,
East Sussex TN22 5HG
Framfield(082582)338
*Five comfortable and well-equipped
cottages including two former oast houses
and a converted stable located on a 400-
acre farm. Each unit comprises two or*

---

three bedrooms, lounge, kitchen/diner and bathroom/WC. Situated between Heathfield and Uckfield.

All year 1wk min, 6mths max, 5units, 2–6persons ◇ ◈ ◆ no pets ◉
fridge 🍴 Elec inclusive ⊡inclusive
☎ WM in unit Iron & Ironing board in unit ☺ ⊗ CTV ⊕3pin square P
▣($\frac{1}{4}$m) 🚶 Farm trails Craft workshops
⊕ 🔋($\frac{1}{4}$m) 🐾(3m)

Min£95 Max£125pw (Low)
Min£165 Max£195pw (High)

BLACKPOOL
Lancashire
Map**7** SD33

F General Office **Almondbury Holiday Flats** 304 North Promenade, Blackpool, Lancashire FY1 2EY
☎Blackpool(0253)24757

Eight of sixteen modern holiday flats which all have lounge (with double foldaway beds), kitchen, shower/WC. Sleeping arrangements vary between single, twin and double-bedded rooms.

All year 3days min, 8units, 1–5persons ◈ ◉ fridge Electric fire
Elec metered ⊡inclusive ☎ Iron & Ironing board on premises [Launderette within 300yds] ☺ CTV ⊕3pin square
9P 🔲 ▣(300yds)
⊕ 🔋(1m) 🔋(50yds) 🎵(50yds)
🎵(50yds) 🐾($\frac{1}{4}$m)

Min£63 Max£125pw (Low)
Min£97 Max£184pw (High)

F Mr & Mrs D Middleton, **Berkeley Holiday Flats** 6 Queens Promenade, Blackpool, Lancashire
☎Blackpool(0253)51244

On a corner overlooking the sea and with various combinations of flats available, all of which have a modern standard of furnishings. There is a lift to all floors, a sun lounge and a launderette on the ground floor. The flats are fully self-contained and have either a bath or shower room.

Closed 2wks mid Nov MWB out of season 3wks max, 13units, 2–7persons ◈ ◉ fridge Electric Elec metered
⊡inclusive Iron & Ironing board on

Blackboys
—
Blair Atholl

premises [Launderette within 300yds]
☺ ⊗ CTV ⊕3pin square 13P 🔲
▣(200yds)
⊕ 🔋($\frac{1}{2}$m) 🔋(100yds) 🎵(100yds)
🎵(100yds) 🐾(1$\frac{1}{2}$m)

Min£44 Max£69pw (Low)
Min£128 Max£271pw (High)

F Mr G Shaw, **Florida Apartments**, 55–59 Dickson Road, Blackpool, Lancashire
☎Blackpool(0253)26950

A complex of newly furnished apartments above a row of shops close to the town centre. All comprise lounge, kitchen, bathroom or shower/WC with one to three bedrooms.

All year MWB out of season 1wk min, 8units, 2–6persons no pets ◉ fridge 🍴 Elec metered ⊡inclusive ☎ Iron & Ironing board on premises ☺ CTV
⊕3pin square 🔲 ▣
⊕ 🔋(2m) 🔋(20yds) 🐾($\frac{1}{4}$m)

Min£60 Max£95pw (Low)
Min£99 Max£180pw (High)

F Mr & Mrs J R H Battersby, **Havelock Court Flats**, 117 Coronation Street, Blackpool, Lancashire FY1 4QQ
☎Blackpool(0253)730140 & 23218

Converted Victorian building in a fine position in the centre of town close to the Central Beach and Tower but not on the seafront. There are 23 flats of which 18 are recommended, they comprise separate kitchens and ten have bathroom/WC and eight have shower/WC.

All year MWB out of season 2nights min, 18units, 2–5persons [◆ ◆] ◉
fridge 🍴 Elec metered ⊡inclusive
☎ Iron & Ironing board on premises
[Launderette within 300yds] ☺ CTV
⊕3pin square P ▣(20yds)
⊕ 🔋(100yds) 🎵(100yds)
🎵(100yds) 🐾(300yds)

Min£42 Max£90pw (Low)
Min£75 Max£170pw (High)

F Post House Holiday Flats
for bookings General Office, Almondbury Holiday Flats, 304 North Promenade, Blackpool, Lancashire FY1 2EY
☎Blackpool(0253)24757

Modern holiday flats each have twin-bedded rooms, shower/WC, the ground-floor flats have lounge/kitchen, first-floors having lounge and separate kitchen. All have double foldaway beds.

All year MWB 3days min, 4units, 1–4persons ◆ ◉ fridge 🍴
Elec metered ⊡inclusive ☎(20yds)
Iron & Ironing board on premises
[Launderette within 300yds] ☺ CTV
⊕3pin square 4P ▣(20yds)
⊕ 🔋(1m) 🔋(50yds) 🎵(50yds)
🎵(50yds) 🐾($\frac{1}{2}$m)

Min£80 Max£155pw

F Mr P Clarke, **Queens Mansions Holiday Apartments**, 224 Queens Promenade, Blackpool, Lancashire
☎Blackpool(0253)55689 & 061-485 4815

Superior self contained apartments with lounge, kitchen, bath/WC and one to three bedrooms. Situated on the seafront adjacent to shops.

All year MWB out of season 3days min, 15units, 1–8persons ◆ ◉ fridge
Electric Elec metered ⊡inclusive ☎
Iron & Ironing board on premises
[Launderette within 300yds] ☺ CTV
⊕3pin square 6P ▣(5yds)
⊕ 🔋($\frac{1}{4}$m)

Min£45 Max£85pw (Low)
Min£125 Max£235pw (High)

BLAIR ATHOLL
Tayside Perthshire
Map**14** NN86

C Mr S Richardson, **Vale of Atholl Country Cottages**, Blair Atholl, Perthshire PH18 5TE
☎Blair Atholl(079681)467

A charming complex of five 18th-century stone farm cottages in a courtyard layout with attractive garden and pond. The cottages are fully modernised and comprise lounge/diner/kitchen with beamed ceiling, bathroom and well-appointed bedrooms, **Rose Willow** *and→*

Pine sleeping four, **Heather** *sleeping six and* **Coach House** *eight. Arrangements can be made for private fishing and golf.*

All year MWB out of season 1wk min, 1mth max, 5 units, 4–8persons [◊ ◆] no pets no single sex groups under 25yrs ⊚ fridge 🍳 (Electric) Elec metered Ⓛinclusive ☎(100yds) [WM, SD & TD on premises] Iron & Ironing board in unit [Launderette within 300yds] ⊕ CTV ⊕3pin square 10P ▣(300yds) ▣(heated) Sports centre

⊖ ♪(300yds) ♨(¼m)

Min£125 Max£315pw

BLAIRGOWRIE
Tayside *Perthshire*
Map**11** NO14

Ca, Ch   Altamount Chalet Park
Blairgowrie, Pethshire
☎Blairgowrie(0250)3324

Detached and semi-detached luxury chalets and log cabins close to town centre. All have open-plan lounge/diner with patio windows and kitchen area. The chalets have either two or three bedrooms, two bedroom ones having showers, the three bedroom ones having a bathroom and shower. The cabins have one bedroom and bathroom. Interiors are of natural wood and matching furnishings. Within walking distance of town centre and shielded by pine trees.

All year MWB out of season 2nights min, 18units, 1–8persons [◊ ◊ ◆] ⊚ fridge 🍳 Elec metered Ⓛcan be hired ☎ Iron & Ironing board on premises ⊕ CTV ⊕3pin square P ▣ ▣(400yds) 🎾Hard ♪

⊖ ♪(400yds) ♬(400yds)

Details not confirmed for 1987

C & F   Mr & Mrs J Nicholson, **Craighall Sawmill Holiday Accommodation,**
Drimmie Road, Blairgowrie, Perthshire
☎Blairgowrie(0250)3956

A charming little complex comprising four cottage apartments in a converted stone sawmill and a separate cottage set in landscaped ground with lawns, gardens, trout pool and putting green. The cottage comprises three bedrooms, lounge, dining

---

Blair Atholl
—
Blockley

room, kitchen and bathroom. The cottage apartments have two bedrooms, lounge/diner/kitchen and bathroom.

All year MWB out of season 1wk min, 1mth max, 5units, 4–9persons ◊ ◆ ⊚ fridge Electric Elec metered Ⓛinclusive ☎ Iron in unit ⊕ CTV ⊕3pin square 12P ▣ ▣(1m)

⊖ ♪(2½m) ♨(1½m) ♫(2m) ♬(2m) Sports centre(2m)

Min£136 Max£250pw

BLAKENEY
Norfolk
Map**9** TG04

C   Driftwood Cottage 20 Westgate Street
for bookings Mrs K Nichol, Beaconfield Lodge, Langham Road, Blakeney, Holt, Norfolk
☎Cley(0263)740064 or 740819

Traditional flint-stone cottage situated 100yds from the historic Blakeney Quay. Accommodation consists of lounge, dining room, kitchen, bathroom and WC, rather steep stairs to four bedrooms – two twin-bedded and two single-bedded. There is a small enclosed courtyard at the rear of the cottage.

All year MWB out of season 3days min, 1mth max, 1unit, 6persons [◊] ◊ ◆ ⊚ fridge open fire Elec metered Ⓛcan be hired ☎(100yds) Iron & Ironing board in unit ⊕ ⊛ CTV ⊕3pin square ▣

⊖ ♨(50yds)

Min£65 Max£100pw (Low)
Min£150 Max£195pw (High)

C   46 High Street
for bookings Mrs M A Farrow, 45 Swafield Rise, North Walsham, Norfolk NR28 0DG
☎North Walsham(0692)405188 & 403369

Three-storey flint tiled detached cottage which offers modernised accommodation comprising of lounge, kitchen, bathroom and three bedrooms.

All year MWB out of season 3days min, 3wks max, 1unit, 1–6persons ◊ ◆ ⊚ fridge Electric Elec metered Ⓛnot provided ☎(500yds) Iron & Ironing board in unit ⊛ CTV ⊕3pin square ▣

⊖ ♨ (50yds)

Min£70 Max£100pw (Low)
Min£140 Max£200pw (High)

C   36 Morston Road
for bookings Mrs M A Farrow, 45 Swafield Rise, North Walsham, Norfolk NR28 0DG
☎North Walsham(0692)405188 & 403369

Flint and tiled terraced cottage with well maintained facilities, consisting of lounge, kitchen, bathroom and two bedrooms. There is a small garden to the rear.

All year MWB out of season 3days min, 3wks max, 1unit, 1–4persons ◊ ◆ ⊚ fridge Electric Elec metered Ⓛnot provided ☎(100yds) WM in unit Iron & Ironing board in unit ⊕ ⊛ CTV ⊕3pin square 1P ▣(500yds)

⊖ ♨ (50yds)

Min£50 Max£70pw (Low)
Min£100 Max£180pw (High)

BLEDINGTON
Gloucestershire
Map**4** SP22

C   Chestnut Cottage
for bookings Mrs M Forbes, Chestnuts, Bledington, Oxford, Oxon OX7 6XQ
☎Kingham(060871)308

Small semi-detached cottage with garden, overlooking village green, comprising kitchen, lounge, two twin-bedded rooms and bathroom.

Etr–Nov 1wk min, 3mths max, 1unit, 1–4persons, nc10 no pets ⊚ fridge 🍳 Elec metered Ⓛnot provided ☎(200yds) Iron & Ironing board in unit ⊕ CTV ⊕3pin square 1P ▣ ▣(10yds)

⊖ ♨ (10yds)

Min£75 Max£80pw (Low)
Min£85 Max£90pw (High)

BLOCKLEY
Gloucestershire
Map**4** SP13

C *The Cottage*, 4 Malvern House
for bookings Mr & Mrs H Da Silva, Glebe
House, The Square, Blockley, Moreton-in-
Marsh, Gloucestershire GL56 9ES
☎Blockley(0386)700354

*Small pretty cottage affording cosy living
room, kitchen/diner, two bedrooms and
bathroom/WC.*

Allyear MWB out of season 4nights min,
1unit, 3persons ◎ fridge 🍴
Elec metered Ⓛcan be hired
☎(200yds) Iron & Ironing board in unit
☺ CTV ⊕3pin square 2P 🔲
🛁(400yds)

↔ 𝄐(3m) 🚰(400yds)

Details not confirmed for 1987

C Lower Farm Cottages
for bookings The Manager, Lower Farm
House, Blockley, Moreton-in-Marsh,
Gloucestershire GL56 9DP
☎Blockley(0386)700237

*Situated down a brook on the edge of the
Cotswold village of Blockley. Set in 1¼
acres, all have been tastefully converted
from a group of period farm buildings.*
Badgers Den & Moles Cottages *have
been furnished in styles incorporating
original features and comprise three
bedrooms, kitchen, sitting/dining room,
bathroom/WC, plus separate WC.* ***Otters
Abode*** *is a spacious cottage featuring
exposed timbered roof and comprises
open plan kitchen, living/dining room with
a central spiral staircase leading to a
gallery with a double bedroom (the other
being on the ground floor), bathroom/
shower/WC, once the
granary, also sleeps four people.* ***Rattys
Retreat*** *is designed for two people and
comprises open plan living/dining room
and kitchen. The galleried bedroom with
bathroom en suite and Victorian half-
tester bed, is reached by a spiral staircase.
A mullioned window reaches from the
ground floor to the eaves.* ***Toads Hall*** *is a
spacious cottage with exposed beams
and comprises lounge/dining area, three
bedrooms, bathroom/WC plus a separate
WC. All the cottages are serviced twice
weekly or daily on request.*

Allyear MWB 2nights min, 1mth max,
6units, 2–6persons [◇ ◈ ◆]
no pets ◎ fridge 🍴 Elec & central

Blockley
—
Blue Anchor

heating inclusive Ⓛinclusive ☎
[Launderette on premises] Iron & Ironing
board in unit ☺ 🕭 CTV
⊕3pin square P 🔲 🛁(¼m)
↔ 𝄐(3m) 🚰(¼m)
Min£144.90 Max£394.45pw

F Flat 1 & 2 Malvern House
for bookings Mrs H Da Silva, Glebe House,
The Square, Blockley, Moreton-in-Marsh,
Gloucestershire GL56 9ES
☎Blockley(0386)700354

*Both flats offer two bedroomed
accommodation with bathroom, lounge,
kitchen and dining facilities; Flat 1 having
a patio overlooking a stream.*

Allyear MWB out of season 4nights min,
2units, 2–4persons ◎ fridge 🍴
Elec metered Ⓛcan be hired
☎(200yds) Iron & Ironing board in unit
☺ TV ⊕3pin square 4P 🔲
🛁(300yds)
↔ 𝄐(3m) 🚰(400yds)

Details not confirmed for 1987

C Val & Alan Savery, ***Mill Row Cottages***,
Blockley, Moreton-in-Marsh,
Gloucestershire GL56 9JS
☎Blockley(0386)700678

Authentic Cotswold cottages named
***Farthings, Jessica's, Honeysuckle &
Spinney****, set in 2½ acres of grounds of the
Mill House on the outskirts of the village.
The cosy accommodation comprises
beamed and panelled lounge/dining
room, kitchen and bathroom/WC on the
ground-floor. The upper floor has a
double and a twin-bedded room, and a
further single bed may be installed in each
cottage.*

Allyear MWB 2nights min, 4units,
2–8persons [◇] ◈ ◆ ◎ fridge
Electric (Gas in Spinney) Gas/Elec
metered Ⓛcan be hired ☎(½m) Iron &
Ironing board in unit ☺ CTV
⊕3pin square 8P 🛁(½m)
↔ 🚰(½m)

Details not confirmed for 1987

C 4 Northwick Terrace
for bookings Mrs H Da Silva, Glebe House,
The Square, Blockley, Moreton-in-Marsh,
Gloucestershire GL56 9ES
☎Blockley(0386)700354

*Attractively modernised, spacious,
terraced cottage affording lounge, well-
fitted kitchen, dining area, three
bedrooms, two bathrooms and a separate
WC.*

Allyear MWB out of season 4nights min,
1unit, 2–5persons ◎ fridge 🍴
Elec metered Ⓛcan be hired
☎(200yds) WC in unit SD in unit TD in
unit Iron & Ironing board in unit ☺ TV
⊕3pin square 2P 🔲 🛁(100yds)
↔ 𝄐(3m) 🚰(400yds)

Details not confirmed for 1987

H Old Mill Dene School Lane
for bookings Mrs W V Dare, 61 Kingston
Lane, Teddington, Middlesex
☎01-977 2502 or Blockley (0386) 700 457

*400-year-old house comfortably furnished
and decorated to a high standard, well-
fitted kitchen with breakfast area, dining
room, separate sitting room with open fire.
First-floor: two twin-bedded rooms, bath,
WC and shower: second floor: room with
canopied double bed, shower, and a
spacious room with bunk beds. The house
stands on the edge of the village, has a
beautiful garden, fine views and borders a
trout pool (dangerous for toddlers) and
stream. Additional folding beds available.*

Allyear wkd min, 1unit, 8–10persons
[◇] ◈ ◆ no pets ◎ fridge
🍴metered Ⓛcan be hired ☎
Dishwasher Iron & Ironing board in unit
☺ TV ⊕3pin square P 🛁(300yds)
Play area
↔ 🚰(300yds)

Details not confirmed for 1987

BLUE ANCHOR
Somerset
Map3 ST04

F Mr & Mrs Pope **Huntingball Lodge**
Flats Huntingball Lodge, Blue Anchor,
Minehead, Somerset TA24 6JP
☎Washford(0984)40076

*Flats 1, 2, 4 & 5 occupy part of Huntingball
Lodge which stands in 1½ acres of* →

MILL ROW COTTAGES
Val and Alan Savery welcome your enquiry for details
of Mill Row Cottages.
Lovingly renovated to a high standard whilst retaining
their authenticity and individual charm, the south
facing cottages are set in 2½ acres of landscaped
grounds, intersected by two streams which meet in
the mill pond. They have extensive views over the
surrounding rolling countryside on the outskirts of
Blockley, the village described by the tourist board as
"perhaps the finest and most unspoilt of Cotswold
Villages".
For free brochure and further particulars 'phone the
resident proprietors on **Blockley (0386) 700678.**

grounds, and most have splendid sea views. They comprise lounge, dining/kitchen areas, bathroom/WC, and varying size bedroom accommodation.

All year MWB out of season 2 days min, 4 units, 1–6 persons ◆ ◆ ◎ fridge Electric Elec metered ☐ inclusive ☎ WM & SD on premises Iron & Ironing board in unit ⊕ CTV ⊕ 3 pin square 8P ▥ ♨(2¼m)
↔ ♀ (100yds)
Min£42 Max£96pw (Low)
Min£100 Max£155pw (High)

BODMIN
Cornwall
Map2 SX06

B, C & F Barn Cottage, The Coach House, Orchard Cottage, The Tallet & Court Flat
for bookings Mr R E Crown, Washaway Court, Washaway, Bodmin, Cornwall PL30 3AD
☎ Bodmin (0208) 4951

Five tastefully converted properties. **The Coach House** has one double bedroom and one twin. **Orchard Cottage** has large kitchen/diner, lounge with bed-settee, three bedrooms, one double, one twin and one single, bathroom with shower fitting, and separate WC. **Barn Cottage** has a large open-plan lounge/kitchen/diner on the ground floor and two bedrooms and bathroom on the first. **The Tallet** is designed for two persons comprising open plan lounge/kitchen/diner on ground floor and one double bedroom with shower room on first floor. **Court Flat** a first-floor flat situated in the main house of Washaway Court, a former 18th century Inn, and comprising one double bedroom with ensuite bath/WC a further bedroom with access to bathroom through main bedroom, open plan lounge/kitchen/diner.

All year MWB out of season 3 days min, 1 mth max, 5 units, 1–6 persons ◆ ◆ ◎ fridge Electric ♨(Court Flat) Elec metered ☐ can be hired ☎(200yds) [WM SD & TD] on premises Iron & Ironing board in unit ⊕ CTV ⊕ 3 pin square P ▥ ♨(3m) ⊿
Min£65 Max£110pw (Low)
Min£115 Max£215pw (High)

Blue Anchor
—
Borgue

C Penbugle Cottage
for bookings Mrs Tidy, Penbugle Farm, Bodmin, Cornwall
☎ Bodmin (0208) 2844

Old farm cottage next to farmhouse and decorated to a high standard. Accommodation comprises lounge with inglenook, kitchen/diner, bathroom with WC, one double bedroom and another room with three single beds.

1 April – 30 Nov MWB out of season 1 wk min, 1 unit, 1–6 persons [◇] ◆ ◆ no pets ◎ fridge Woodburning stove Elec metered ☐ not provided ☎(1m)
Iron & Ironing board in unit ⊕ TV ⊕ 3 pin square 2P ♨(1m)
↔ ♀(1m) ♫(1m) ☂(1m) Shooting & fishing

Details not confirmed for 1987

BONCATH
Dyfed
Map2 SN23

C Madog, Myrddin & Taliesin Cottages
for bookings Mr & Mrs R Cori, Fron Fawr, Boncath, Dyfed SA37 0HS
☎ Boncath (023974) 285

Three luxuriously fitted cottages which were once a huge barn. Delightful décor combining colours, patterns and textiles. **Madog** and **Taliesin** both sleep up to six people with **Myrddin** sleeping up to five. All three cottages have vanity units and WHB in the main bedrooms, fully-tiled, heated bathrooms with drying facilities, well fitted kitchens and thick wool carpets and duvets in all bedrooms.

Closed Nov MWB out of season 1 wk min, 3 units, 2–6 persons [◇] ◆ ◆ no pets ◎ fridge Electric Elec metered ☐ inclusive ☎(½m) SD in unit Iron & Ironing board in unit ⊕ CTV ⊕ 3 pin square ▥ ♨(¾m)
↔ ♀(½m)
Min£172.50 Max£230pw (Low)
Min£285.20 Max£410.55pw (High)

BONTDDU
Gwynedd
Map6 SH61

F Nyth Bran Taicynhaeaf
for bookings Shaws Holidays, Y. Maes, Pwllheli, Gwynedd LL53 5HA
☎ Pwllheli (0758) 614422

This modern, comfortable ground-floor flat lies in a delightful wooded valley with mountain stream and waterfalls nearby. It comprises large lounge/diner/kitchen with double bed-settee, a small room with bunk beds and separate shower, WC

All year wknd min 6 wks max 1 unit 2–4 persons [◇] ◆ no pets ◎ fridge Electric Elec metered ☐ not provided ☎(200yds) Iron & Ironing board in unit ⊕ ⊕ TV ⊕ 3 pin square P ▥ ♨(1½m)
↔ ♀(1½m)
Min£70 Max£104pw

BORGUE
Dumfries & Galloway Kirkcudbrightshire
Map11 NX65

C Chapleton Cottage
for bookings G M Thomson & Co, 27 King Street, Castle Douglas, Kirkcudbrightshire
☎ Castle Douglas (0556) 2701

A comfortable semi-detached stone-built farm cottage comprising dining/living room, kitchen, bathroom, and two bedrooms both with twin beds. Convenient for Carrick and Sandgreen beaches.

Etr–Nov 1 wk min, 6 mths max, 1 unit, 1–4 persons no pets ◎ fridge Electric Elec inclusive ☐ not provided ☎(2m) Ironing board in unit ⊕ TV ⊕ 3 pin square P ♨(1m)
↔ ♀(2m)
Min£60 Max£95pw

C Drum Cottage
for bookings G M Thomson & Co, 27 King Street, Castle Douglas, Kirkcudbrightshire
☎ Castle Douglas (0556) 2701

Attractive semi-detached farm cottage situated ½m from village, comprising dining/living room, a bathroom, kitchen and three bedrooms, two with twin beds, and one with two three-quarter size beds.

Mar–Nov 1wk min, 6mths max, 1unit,
1–6persons ⊚ fridge Electric
Elec inclusive Ⓛnot provided ☎(½m)
Ironing board in unit TV ⊕3pin square
P Ⓜ ⚒(½m)
⊖ ⬮(½m)
Min£65 pw (Low)
Min£110 pw (High)

B Muncraig Shepherds Cottage
for bookings G M Thomson & Co, 27 King
Street, Castle Douglas, Kirkcudbrightshire
☎Castle Douglas(0556)2701

A modern bungalow surrounded by
farmland situated near the Solway Firth.
Consists of living room, dining room,
kitchen, bathroom and three bedrooms,
one with a double bed, two with a single
bed.

Mar–Nov 1wk min, 1unit, 1–4persons,
nc12 ⊚ fridge Electric Elec inclusive
Ⓛnot provided ☎(1m) TV
⊕3pin round P ⚒(2m)
⊖ ⬮(1m)
Min£70 Max£115pw

BORROWDALE
Cumbria
Map**11** NY21
See **Rosthwaite**

BOSCASTLE
Cornwall
Map**2** SX09

C Cargurra St Juliot
for bookings Mrs G M Elson, Hennett, St
Juliot, Boscastle, Cornwall
☎Otterham Station(08406)206

Remote semi-detached Victorian farm
cottage on private road, with glorious
views of Valency Valley. The well-
decorated accommodation consists of a
lounge/dining room with woodburning
stove, fully fitted kitchen, three bedrooms,

Borgue
—
Bournemouth & Boscombe

and a shower room with WC. 3m E off
B3263.

Closed 8 Jan–Feb 1wk min, 4wks max,
1unit, 1–6persons ◆ ◆ ⊚ fridge
storage heaters Elec metered
Ⓛnot provided ☎(200yds) WM in unit
Iron & Ironing board in unit ⊙ CTV
⊕3pin square P ⚒(2m)
⊖ ⬮(2m)
Min£60 Max£80pw (Low)
Min£100 Max£180pw (High)

C Cobblers Cottage High Street
for bookings Mr & Mrs Hall, Penrose
Burden, St Breward, Bodmin, Cornwall
PL30 4LZ
☎Bodmin(0208)850277 or 850617

Delightful end of terrace stone and slate
Cornish cottage in quiet area of Boscastle.
Modernised to a high standard it
comprises beamed lounge/diner, kitchen,
one double bedroom, one bedroom with
bunks plus a single bed and a bathroom/
WC.

All year MWB out of season 1wk min,
3wks max, 1unit, 1–5 persons [◇] ◆
◆ no cats ⊚ fridge Electric, log fire &
night storage Elec metered Ⓛinclusive
☎ Iron & Ironing board in unit ⊙
CTV ⊕3pin square 1P Ⓜ ⚒(½m)
⊖ ⬮(100yds)
Details not confirmed for 1987

C The Cottage
for bookings Mrs J Weekes, Lundy View,
Boscastle, Cornwall
☎Boscastle(08405)313

A stone-built converted coach house at
rear of Lundy View House. Comprising

---

kitchen with modern fittings, lounge/diner
and bathroom/WC. Two bedrooms with
double bed and single bed. Garden and
patio.

All year MWB out of season 3days min,
4wks max, 1unit, 1–6persons ◇ ◆
⊚ fridge Electric Elec metered Ⓛcan
be hired ☎(25yds) [WM on premises]
Iron & Ironing board in unit ⊙ CTV
⊕3pin square 4P Ⓜ ⚒(10yds)
⊖ ⬮(10yds) 🅹(1m)
Min£50 Max£75pw (Low)
Min£100 Max£175pw (High)

BOURNEMOUTH & BOSCOMBE
Dorset
Map**4** SZ09

F Aaron Holiday Flat
for bookings Mr M Lambert, 16 Florence
Road, Bournemouth, Dorset BH5 1HF
☎Bournemouth(0202)33503 or
Bransgore(0425)74020

Modern, purpose-built ground-floor flat in
a quiet road within easy walking distance
of shops and Boscombe seafront. It
comprises four bedrooms, large lounge,
dining room, kitchen and bathroom/WC.

All year MWB out of season 1wk min,
8mths max, 1unit, 2–10persons [◇ ◆
◆] ⊚ fridge 🍴 Elec metered Ⓛcan
be hired ☎ WM & TD in unit Iron &
Ironing board in unit [Launderette on
premises] ⊙ CTV ⊕3pin square 1P
Ⓜ ⚒(200yds)
⊖ ᵹ(1½m) ⬮(200yds) 🅹(300yds)
🐾(2m)
Min£229 Max£269pw (Low)
Min£349 Max£429pw (High)

F Mr & Mrs J K Seagrief **Annerley House
Holiday Flats** 2 Annerley Road,
Bournemouth, Dorset BH1 3PG
☎Bournemouth(0202)709271 ➔

Bournemouth & Boscombe

An attractive well-maintained detached house in quiet residential road. Accommodation in four ground- and first-floor flats (1, 2, 3 & 5) each with kitchen, lounge with double wall bed, shower room/WC (flat 5 bath/WC), and one bedroom (flat 3 has two bedrooms). Within easy reach of East Cliff and shops.

24May–20Sep 1wk min, 2mths max, 4units, 1–8persons [◈ ◆] no pets ◎ fridge Electric Elec metered 🄻can be hired ☎(300yds) Iron & Ironing board on premises [Launderette within 300yds] ⊙ CTV ⊕3pin square 7P 1🏠 Ⓜ 🏪(300yds)

⊖ ⛳(1½m) 🍷(50yds) ♫(¼m) 🎥(¼m)

Min£95 Max£278pw

F Mr & Mrs M J Batchelor **Azalea Park** 2 Milner Road, West Overcliff Drive, Bournemouth, Dorset BH4 8AD
☎Bournemouth(0202)761231

Located in two attractive houses with secluded gardens, in quiet residential area. The accommodation varies with each flat, each has kitchen, bathroom and either lounge and dining room or lounge/diner and varying number of bedrooms.

Allyear MWB out of season 2days min, 4wks max, 14units, 2–10persons ◇ ◈ ◆ ◎ fridge 🔥 Elec metered 🄻can be hired ☎ Iron & Ironing board in unit ⊙ CTV ⊕3pin square P Ⓜ 🏪(½m)

⊖ ⛳(2m) 🍷(½m) ♫(½m) ♫(¼m) 🎥(½m)

Min£90 Max£134pw (Low)
Min£213 Max£497pw (High)

F **Belle Reve** Studland Road, Alum Chine
for bookings Mr Callaghan, c/o Riviera Hotel, Burnaby Road, Alum Chine, Bournemouth, Dorset
☎Bournemouth(0202)765391

Detached building with dormer windows, set in a quiet residential area. Accommodation comprises lounge, kitchen, bathroom/WC, one bedroom and a lounge convertible. The flats are situated on three floors served by a lift.

Allyear MWB out of season 2days min, 4wks max, 12units, 2–7persons [◈] ◆ ◎ fridge 🔥 Elec metered 🄻inclusive ☎(200yds) Iron & Ironing board on premises ⊙ CTV ⊕3pin square 12P Ⓜ 🏪(1m) ⛱&⛵

⊖ ⛳(3m) 🍷 ♫ ♫ 🎥(2½m)

Min£120.75 Max£212.75pw (Low)
Min£287.50 Max£448.50pw (High)

F Mrs N Swift **Camellia Court Holiday Apartments** 23 Grand Avenue, Southbourne, Bournemouth, Dorset BH6 3SY
☎Bournemouth(0202)431038

Compact flats on 1st, 2nd and 3rd floors of this gabled villa property, very convenient to shopping centre and beach. Each comprises compact lounge with easy chairs plus dining table and chairs and an open area kitchenette sited within the lounge. Bath and shower room, bedroom accommodation varies, sleeping 2–5 people.

Allyear MWB out of season 3days min, 4wks max, 3units, 2–5persons ◈ ◆ ◎ fridge 🔥 & Electric heaters Elec metered 🄻can be hired ☎(700yds) Iron & Ironing board in unit ⊙ CTV ⊕3pin square 3P Ⓜ 🏪(700yds)

⊖ ⛳(2m) 🍷(½m) ♫(800yds)

Min£75 Max£125pw (Low)
Min£105 Max£195pw (High)

F Mr & Mrs J Brownlow ***Carnanton Holiday Apartments*** 5A Percy Road, Boscombe, Bournemouth, Dorset BH5 1JF
☎Bournemouth(0202)37838

House converted into apartments. All self-contained, with either double beds or twin beds and extra wall bed in lounge. All with kitchen, dining room and lounge. Six flats have bathroom/WC and five have shower/WC.

Allyear MWB out of season 3days min, 4wks max, 11units, 2–8persons [◇] ◈ ◆ ◎ fridge 🔥(4units) & electric Elec metered 🄻can be hired ☎ Iron on premises Ironing board on premises ⊙ CTV ⊕3pin square P 🏪(500yds)

⊖ 🍷(300yds) ♫(¼m) 🎥(1m)

Details not confirmed for 1987

F Mr R Cook **Chine View Holiday Flats** 5 McKinley Road, West Cliff, Bournemouth, Dorset BH4 8AG
☎Bournemouth(0202)769245

Self-contained flats in a large house, situated in a quiet residential area within walking distance of sea and shops. Flats can accommodate six persons in well-decorated spacious rooms.

Allyear MWB out of season 6units, 2–6persons ◈ no pets ◎ fridge 🔥 Elec metered 🄻can be hired ☎ Iron & Ironing board in units ⊙ CTV ⊕3pin square 8P 🏪(½m)

⊖ ⛳(1m) 🍷(½m) ♫(½m) ♫(½m) 🎥(1m)

Min£60 Max£90pw (Low)
Min£120 Max£255pw (High)

F Mrs M M Hubble **Delcot House** 55 Talbot Avenue, Talbot Woods, Bournemouth, Dorset
☎Bournemouth(0202)295248

Delcot House is a detached mellow red-brick building purpose built as four flats, two on the ground and two on the first floor. They vary in size, sleeping up to six people. The kitchens are fully appointed, and the lounge/dining rooms are traditionally furnished.

May–Sep MWB 1day min, 6wks max, 4units, 2–6persons ◈ ◆ ◎ fridge electric fires Elec metered 🄻inclusive ☎(600yds) WM & SD on premises Iron & Ironing board in unit CTV ⊕3pin square 6P 4🏠 🏪(600yds)

⊖ ⛳(½m) 🍷(½m) ♫(1m) ♫(1m) 🎥(1m)

Min fr£49 (Low)
Min fr£91 (High)

F Mr R Colman **Grand Lodge Holiday Flats** 14 Grand Avenue, Southbourne, Bournemouth, Dorset BH6 3SY
☎Bournemouth(0202)420481

Six flats within a double-fronted, detached, red-brick building located on a wide avenue in a residential area. All have a lounge/diner with kitchen area and bathroom/WC. They vary in size from one to two bedrooms.

Allyear MWB out of season 3days min, 1mth max, 6units, 2–4persons ◈ ◆ ◎ fridge 🔥 & electric fires Elec metered 🄻can be hired ☎ Iron & Ironing board on premises [Launderette within 300yds] ⊙ CTV ⊕3pin square P Ⓜ 🏪(250yds)

⊖ ⛳(½m) 🍷(½m) ♫(2m) 🎥(3m)

Min£55 Max£75pw (Low)
Min£95 Max£185pw (High)

F **Lyttleton Lodge Holiday Apartments** *for bookings* Mr M Lambert, 16 Florence Road, Boscombe, Bournemouth, Dorset BH5 1HF
☎Bournemouth(0202)33503 & Bransgore(0425)74020

Gabled villa linked to new purpose-built block, by carpeted reception hall. Five units in each section, all well equipped. In a quiet residential road near Boscombe shops and seafront pier.

Allyear MWB out of season 10units, 2–8persons [◇ ◈ ◆] ◎ fridge 🔥 Gas & Electric Gas & Elec metered 🄻can be hired ☎ Launderette on premises CTV ⊕3pin square P Ⓜ 🏪(200yds)

⊖ 🍷(200yds) ♫(300yds) 🎥(2m)

Min£63 Max£170pw (Low)
Min£99 Max£329pw (High)

F Mr & Mrs W E Wilkinson **Midchines** 14 McKinley Road, Bournemouth, Dorset BH4 8AQ
☎Bournemouth(0202)762974

Detached gabled villa located in a quiet area adjacent to Durley Chine. The flats have spacious rooms and are tastefully decorated. ***Flats 1 & 2*** *on ground floor have kitchen, bathroom and lounge/bedsitting room.* ***Flats 3, 4 & 5*** *first and second floor have kitchen, bathroom, lounge/diner and two bedrooms.* ***Flat 6*** *a first floor garden flat with kitchen, bathroom lounge/diner and one bedroom.*

Mar–Oct 1wk min, 1mth max, 6units, 2–6persons [◈ ◆] families only ◎ fridge 🔥 Elec metered 🄻can be hired ☎ Iron & Ironing board on premises [CTV] ⊕3pin square P 🏠 Ⓜ 🏪(1m)

⊖ ⛳(1m) 🍷(1m) ♫(1m) ♫(1½m) 🎥(1m) Sports centre(3m)

Min£40 Max£100pw (Low)
Min£90 Max£220pw (High)

F   Overcliffe Mansions East Cliff Holiday Flats, 1–3 Manor Road
for bookings Mrs D Daisley, 17 Clarendon Road, West Cliff, Bournemouth, Dorset BH4 8AL
☎Bournemouth(0202)764450

Detached red-brick block of eight purpose-built self-contained flats. Spacious, well equipped and comfortable. Comprising three double bedrooms (one double and two twin), lounge, kitchen/diner, bathroom and WC.

All year MWB out of season 3 days min, 3 mths max, 8 units, 1–6 persons, nc4
no pets 🐕 (1 unit) ◎ (7 units) fridge
♨(3 units) Electric(5 units) Gas/
Elec metered 🔲 can be hired
☎(25yds) Iron & Ironing board on premises ☉ CTV ⊕3 pin square P
🏛 ▥ ♨(500yds)
⊖ 𝄞(2m) ♬ (300yds) ♫(300yds)
♬(¼m) 🐾(1m)
Min£140 Max£200pw (Low)
Min£210 Max£295pw (High)

F   Saltaire Sea Road, Southbourne
for bookings Mr & Mrs D Counter, 'White Horses,' 47 St Catherine's Road, Southbourne, Bournemouth, Dorset BH6 4AQ
☎Bournemouth(0202)420296

Purpose-built holiday apartments, majority with balconies overlooking the sea and sandy beach. Shops and restaurants nearby.

All year MWB out of season 3 nights min, 3 mths max, 40 units, 2–7 persons [◇]
◆ ♦ ◎ fridge ♨ Elec metered
🔲 can be hired ☎ Iron & Ironing board on premises [Launderette on premises]
☉ [CTV] ⊕3 pin square P 🏛 ▥
♨(200yds) ▢ solarium
⊖ ♫ (230yds) ♬(1½m) ♫(1½m)
🐾(2m)

Bournemouth & Boscombe

Min£65 Max£120pw (Low)
Min£175 Max£340pw (High)

F   Salterton 17 Warren Edge Road
for bookings Mr & Mrs D Counter, 'White Horses', 47 St Catherine's Road, Southbourne, Bournemouth, Dorset BH6 4AQ
☎Bournemouth(0202)420296

Modern purpose-built block with high standard of furnishings and fittings. Most flats have fine views of Christchurch to Purbeck Hills. Use of facilities at adjoining Saltaire Flats.

Apr–Oct 1 wk min, 6 wks max, 5 units, 2–7 persons [◇ ◆ ♦] no pets ◎
fridge ♨ Elec metered 🔲 can be hired ☎ Iron & Ironing board on premises [Launderette on premises]
☉ [CTV] ⊕3 pin square 5🏛 ▥
♨(200yds) ▢(100yds)
⊖ 𝄞(2½m) ♫ (200yds) ♬(1½m)
♬(1½m) 🐾(2½m)
Min£100 Max£120pw (Low)
Min£250 Max£340pw (High)

F   Mr & Mrs K G Fraser Sheraton Park
7 Milner Road, West Cliff, Bournemouth, Dorset BH4 8AD
☎Bournemouth(0202)763305

An attractive well maintained red brick detached house in large garden. Situated in a quiet road at Westcliff. Close to cliff top and beaches. All flats are well appointed and quite spacious. Flats 1, 2 & 3 on the ground floor have lounge/diner, kitchen area, except Flat 1 where kitchen area is within lounge. Flats 4 & 5 on first floor have separate kitchen. Flat 6 on second floor has lounge/diner and separate kitchen. All flats have modern

---

well appointed bathrooms. The number of bedrooms and stackaway beds varies dependent on the unit.

All year MWB out of season 1 wk min, 4 wks max, 6 units, 2–8 persons ◇ ◆
◎ fridge ♨(except flat 6 which has storage heaters) Elec metered 🔲 can be hired ☎ Iron & Ironing board in unit
☉ CTV ⊕3 pin square P ▥ ♨(½m)
⊖ 𝄞(2m) ♫(½m) ♬(1m) ♫(1m)
🐾(1m)
Min£66 Max£78pw (Low)
Min£225 Max£319pw (High)

F   Skerryvore 64 Robert Louis Stevenson Avenue, Westbourne
for bookings Mrs M Cross, 165 Wilton Road, Salisbury, Wiltshire
☎Salisbury (0722)28193

A detached gabled house in residential road converted into three flats. Each comprising well-fitted kitchen, lounge/diner and bathroom/WC. Flat 1 has three bedrooms, Flat 2 one bedroom and Flat 3 two bedrooms and each has a double wall bed in the lounge. All are well furnished and decorated.

Jun–Sep 1 wk min, 3 mths max 3 units
2–8 persons ◆ ♦ no pets ◎
fridge ♨ & Electric Elec metered
🔲 can be hired ♨(500yds) Iron & Ironing board in unit [Launderette within 300yds] ☉ CTV ⊕3 pin square 4P
▥ ♨(500yds)
⊖ 𝄞(3m) ♫ (500yds) ♬(¾m)
♬(¾m) 🐾(¾m)
Min£75 Max£190pw

F   Col B A Lipscombe Stirling Court Holiday Flats 28 Manor Road, East Cliff, Bournemouth, Dorset BH1 3EZ
☎Bournemouth(0202)26646

Detached villa standing in its own grounds converted into self-contained flats. All have tasteful décor and modern furnishing and comprise either single, twin or double →

bedrooms, kitchen/diner, lounge with fold-up double bed and bathroom/WC. Located in the East Cliff area and near to seafront. Laundry room available.

All year MWB out of season 1 wk min, 4 wks max, 11 units, 2–7 persons [◆
◆] ◎ ◔ fridge 🍴 & Electric Elec metered ⬛ can be hired ☎ Iron & Ironing board in unit [Launderette on premises] ⊕ CTV ⊕3 pin square 25P 🚇 ♒(½m)
⟿ ♬(1½m) ♨(½m) 🎵(¼m) ⸱⸱🎵(¼m) 🏖(¼m)

Min£82.80 Max£164.45pw (Low)
Min£135.70 Max£316.25pw (High)

F Sycamores Town Centre Holiday Apartments 15 Surrey Road for bookings Mr G & Mrs J M Howard, 7 Seaway Avenue, Christchurch, Dorset, BH23 4EU
☎Highcliffe(04252)71066

Well furnished and maintained flats in a modernised detached corner residence overlooking Bournemouth's Central Gardens. One or two bedrooms depending on flat selected; each has a lounge, kitchen and bathroom/WC. Pets allowed in ground-floor flats only. Off Poole road via Queens road on edge of Westbourne.

All year MWB out of season 1 wk min, 5 mths max, 9 units, 2–6 persons [◇ ◆
◆] ◔ fridge Electric Elec metered ⬛ can be hired ☎ Iron & Ironing board on premises [Launderette within

---

Bournemouth & Boscombe

300yds] ⊙ CTV ⊕3 pin square 13P
🚇 ♒(300yds)
⟿ ♬(300yds) 🎵(½m)
🎵(½m) 🏖(½m)
Min£80 Max£110pw (Low)
Min£170 Max£240pw (High)

F John Norris **Villa Del Sol** 22 Surrey Road, Bournemouth, Dorset BH2 6BS
☎Bournemouth(0202)765246

Flat 1 on ground floor has a hall, bathroom, kitchen/living room and one bedroom with a double and two single beds. Flat 2 on ground floor has kitchen, bathroom, living room, two bedrooms one with a double bed plus two children's beds the other with two children's beds. Flats 3, 4 and 5 are on the first floor and each has kitchen, bathroom, living room and two bedrooms. Flat 3 has a family room and a single room. Flat 4 has a family room and a twin room. Flat 5 has a family room and a twin room for children.

All year MWB out of season 1 wk min, 1 mth max, 5 units, 4–6 persons ◆ ◆
◔ fridge🍴 Gas & Elec metered ⬛ can be hired ☎ Iron & Ironing board in unit ⊙ CTV 3 pin square 9P ♒(300yds)
⟿ ♬(1m) ♨(400yds) 🎵(1m)
🎵(400yds) 🏖(1m)

Min£50 Max£165pw (Low)
Min£110 Max£210pw (High)

F Mr & Mrs K J Garard **Westbrook Holiday Flats** 472/474 Christchurch Road, Boscombe, Bournemouth, Dorset BH1 4BD
☎Bournemouth(0202)36763 & 34820

Three-storey building comprising 23 flats adjacent to Boscombe shopping parade. Accommodation consists of kitchen/diner or kitchenette, lounge/bedroom, bathroom/WC and some have an extra bedroom.

All year MWB out of season 3 days min, 8 wks max, 23 units, 2–6 persons [◇ ◆
◆] ◔ fridge Gas or Electric fires Gas/Elec metered ⬛ can be hired ☎ Iron & Ironing board on premises [Launderette within 20yds] ⊙ CTV
⊕3 pin square P 🚇 ♒
⟿ ♨(150yds) 🎵(300yds)
🎵(300yds) 🏖(1m)
Min£34.50 Max£351.90pw

F Mr & Mrs A W Thompson **West Cliff Lodge** 4 McKinley Road, West Cliff, Bournemouth, Dorset BH4 8AQ
☎Bournemouth(0202)760925

Six flats located within a detached red brick villa standing in approximately ¼ acre of grounds in quiet residential area. The beach is within short walking distance and the local shopping area of Westbourne is only ½m away. All the flats have been modernised to a high standard.

22 Mar–Oct MWB out of season

1wk min, 6units, 2–8persons ◈ ◆
no pets ◎ fridge 🍴 Elec metered
Ⓛcan be hired ☎ [SD & TD on
premises] Iron & Ironing board in unit
⊙ CTV ⊕3pin square 9P 🎞 ♨(½m)
⊖ 🚲(½m) 🎵(½m) 🎵(½m) 🐾(½m)
Min£50 Max£295pw

F Mr & Mrs J H Holden **Wollaston Lodge**
Wollaston Road, Southbourne,
Bournemouth, Dorset BH6 4AR
☎Bournemouth (0202)422436

*Red brick detached house in quiet
residential road within 200 yards of cliff
top. All flats are self-contained, having
lounge (with bed-settee) small kitchen,
bath or shower room with WC & WHB, and
one double room with some having
additional single or bunk beds.*

AllYear MWB out of season 3days min,
3wks max, 6units 1–7persons [◈ ◆]
no pets ♦ & ◎ fridge Electric Gas &
Elec metered Ⓛcan be hired
☎(200yds) Iron & Ironing board on
premises [Launderette within 300yds]
⊙ CTV ⊕3pin square 10P 🎞
♨(200yds) Croquet Lawn
⊖ 🐾(1m) 🚲(350yds) 🎵(2m) 🎵(2m)
Min£74 Max£149pw (Low)
Min£180 Max£260pw (High)

F Mr Abrahams **Zena Court Flats** 9
Adeline Road, Boscombe, Bournemouth,
Dorset BH5 1EE
☎Bournemouth (0202)37101

*Detached red-brick gabled villa on corner
site in a dense suburban area.
Comfortable and well furnished. Near
main Boscombe shopping centre.*

AllYear MWB out of season 1wk min,
2mths max, 4units, 2–7persons ◈ ◆
◎ fridge Electric Elec metered
Ⓛinclusive Iron & Ironing board on
premises [Launderette within 300yds]
⊙ CTV ⊕3pin square P 🏠 🎞
♨(50yds)
⊖ 🚲(100yds) 🎵(100yds)
🎵(100yds) 🐾(1½m)
Min£40 Max£110pw (Low)
Min£80 Max£240pw (High)

BOURTON-ON-THE-HILL
Gloucestershire
Map**4** SP13

Bournemouth & Boscombe
—
Bourton-on-the-Water

C The Gable
for bookings Mr & Mrs Schuler, The Old
Sweet Shop, The Nettings, Hook Norton,
Oxon OX15 5NP
☎Hook Norton (0608)737496

*This 200-year-old property has been
extensively modernised whilst retaining the
character of a traditional Cotswold stone
cottage. The large open-plan living and
dining room, separated by a pine
staircase, leads to the spacious kitchen
and good sized garden. Upstairs are two
twin-bedded rooms with built-in
cupboards and a carpeted bathroom. The
cottage is located on the outskirts of the
village.*

AllYear MWB out of season 3nights min,
1mth max, 1unit, 1–4persons, nc13
no pets ♦ fridge 🍴 Gas inclusive
Ⓛinclusive ☎ WM TD Iron & Ironing
board in unit ⊙ CTV
⊕3pin square 1P 🎞 ♨(½m) Record
player, small library and cleaning service
⊖ 🚲(½m)
Min£133 Max£180pw

BOURTON-ON-THE-WATER
Gloucestershire
Map**4** SP12

F Mr & Mrs Wright **Farncombe** Bourton-
on-the-Water, Gloucestershire GL 54 2L G
☎Cotswold (0451)20120

*Newly converted flat built onto original
Cotswold stone house. Accommodation
comprises, on the ground floor: hall,
double bedroom with en suite bathroom,
on the first floor: spacious lounge with
double bed-settee, kitchen, dining room
and separate WC.*

AllYear MWB out of season 1 min,
1mth max, 1unit, 2–4persons no pets
◎ fridge storage heaters Elec metered
Ⓛcan be hired (overseas visitors only)
☎(100yds) Iron & Ironing board in unit
⊙ CTV ⊕3pin square 2P 🎞
♨(2½m)
⊖ 🚲(2½m)
Min£70 Max£140pw

C Greenmore Rectory Lane
for bookings The Heart of England
Cottages, Ridlands Cottage, Briston,
Melton Constable, Norfolk. NR24 2LU
☎Melton Constable (0263)861000

*Small Cotswold stone cottage in quiet
position with accommodation of utility
room, kitchen, comfortable lounge,
bathroom and three bedrooms.*

AllYear 1unit, 2–5persons [◇ ◈ ◆]
◎ fridge 🍴 & Gasfires Elec inclusive
Ⓛinclusive ☎ WM, SD & TD in unit
Iron & Ironing board in unit 🐾 CTV
⊕3pin square 1P ♨(50yds)
⊖ 🚲(100yds)
Min£110 Max£190pw

C Porch Cottage Clapton Row
for bookings Mr & Mrs R C Norman, South
Lawn, Victoria Street, Bourton-on-the-
Water, Gloucestershire GL54 2BT
☎Cotswold (0451)20813

*Facing the village green, this recently
renovated cottage offers leasing
accommodation of attractive lounge,
kitchen/diner, cloakroom, four bedrooms
and bathroom.*

AllYear 1wk min, 1unit, 1–8persons
[◇] ◈ ◆ no pets ◎ fridge 🍴
Elec inclusive Ⓛcan be hired
☎(100yds) WM & SD on premises, Iron &
Ironing board in unit 🐾 CTV
⊕3pin square 2P ♨(200yds)
⊖ 🚲(100yds)
Min£100 Max£200pw

C Mr & Mrs R C Norman **South Lawn
Cottage** South Lawn, Victoria Street,
Bourton-on-the-Water, Gloucestershire
GL54 2BT
☎Cotswold (0451)20813

*Situated within the grounds of the owners'
residence, this pretty cottage offers well-
kept accommodation comprising
cloakroom, attractive living room, kitchen,
two bedrooms and bathroom.*

AllYear 1wk min, 1unit, 1–4persons
[◇] ◈ ◆ no pets ◎ fridge 🍴
Elec inclusive Ⓛcan be hired
☎(100yds) WM & SD on premises Iron
& Ironing board in unit ⊙ 🐾 CTV
⊕3pin square 2P ♨(200yds)
⊖ 🚲(100yds)
Min£70 Max£170pw

BOVEY TRACEY
Devon
Map**3** SX87

C Stickwick Farmhouse Cottage,
Stickwick Farm
for bookings Mrs L. Harvey, Frost Farm,
Bovey Tracey, Devon TQ139PP
☎Bovey Tracey(0626)833266

A semi-detached cottage with own
garden, situated on the edge of the
Dartmoor National Park. It comprises
lounge, with open fire place, kitchen (with
microwave oven), one family and one twin
bedroom, separate bathroom and also
second WC

All year MWB out of season 3days min,
1mth max, 1unit 5persons ◊ ♦
by arrangement ◎ fridge Solid fuel
(inclusive) ⌸inclusive ☎(½m) WM &
TD in unit Iron & Ironing board in unit
⊕ CTV ⊕3pin square 2R 2🏠 🎞
🛁(½m)
↤ ♨(1½m) ♨(½)
Min£95 Max£175pw

H Stickwick House
for bookings Mrs L. Harvey, Frost Farm,
Bovey Tracey, Devon TQ139PP
☎Bovey Tracey(0626)833266

Part of an 18th century listed building, set
in own gardens with sweeping views of the
Devonshire countryside. Comprises
lounge with open fireplace, kitchen/diner
with exposed beams microwave oven and
Rayburn, bathroom and WC, six bedrooms
of various sizes one with en suite facilities.

Etr–Sep MWB out of season 3days min,
1mth max, 1unit, 9–11persons ◊ ♦
◎ fridge Solid fuel (inclusive)
⌸inclusive ☎ WM & TD in unit Iron &
Ironing board in unit ⊕ CTV
⊕3pin square 4P 🎞 🛁(½m)
↤ ♨(1½m) ♨(½m)
Min£185 Max£295pw

Bovey Tracey
—
Brampton

BOWMORE
See **Isle of Islay** Strathclyde Argyllshire

BOWNESS-ON-WINDERMERE
Cumbria
Map**7** SD49
See **Windermere**

BRADFIELD ST GEORGE
Suffolk
Map**5** TL96

H Old Farmhouse Littlecargate
for bookings Suffolk Holiday Cottages, 1
Lower Road, Glemsford, Suffolk
CO107QU
☎Glemsford(0787)281577

Located next to a working farm amidst
agricultural land, this L-shaped 16th-
century house comprises lounge, dining
room, kitchen, cloakroom/WC on the
ground floor and three bedrooms (one
twin, two double) all with exposed beams
and a bathroom on the first floor.

All year MWB out of season 1wk min,
1unit, 1–6persons ◊ ♦ ◎ fridge
🍴 Elec metered ⌸can be hired ☎
WM, SD & TD in unit Iron & Ironing board
in unit CTV ⊕3pin square 2P
↤ ♨(½m)
Min£70 Max£75pw (Low)
Min£155 Max£210pw (High)

BRAEMAR
Grampian Aberdeenshire
Map**15** NO19

B Somerset Cottage 25 Mar Road
for bookings Mr & Mrs Ramsay, 410 Great
Western Road, Aberdeen, Aberdeenshire.
☎Aberdeen(0224)316115

Modern bungalow tucked away on west
side of village, only five minutes walk from
centre. It comprises of lounge, kitchen,
bathroom, separate WC and three
bedrooms.

All year 1wk min, 1unit, 6persons
no pets ◎ fridge 🍴 Elec metered
⌸can be hired ☎(200yds) WM in unit
Iron & Ironing board in unit ⊕ CTV
⊕3pin square 2P 🛁(200yds)
↤ ♨(½m) ♨(200yds)
Min£140 Max£160pw (Low)
£180pw (High)

BRAITHWAITE
Cumbria
Map**11** NY22

C Hawthorn Cottage
for bookings Lakeland Holiday Cottages,
Yew Tree Cottage, Ullock, Keswick,
Cumbria CA125SP
☎Braithwaite(059682)493 or
Keswick(07687)72059

A comfortably modernised former
coachman's cottage in the heart of this
tiny village. It comprises beamed living
room with open fireplace, well appointed
kitchen, and bathroom/WC on the ground
floor and two bedrooms on the first floor.

All year 1mth max, 1unit, 2–6persons
◊ ♦ no pets ◎ fridge Storage
heaters & open fire Elec metered
⌸inclusive ☎(½m) Iron & Ironing board
in unit ⊕ CTV 🎞 🛁(½m)
↤ ♨(30yds) ♨(2m)
Min£93 Max£189pw

BRAMPTON
Cumbria
Map**12** NY56

C Long Byres Talkin Head
for bookings Mrs S Dean, Kirkhouse,
Brampton, Cumbria
☎Hallbankgate(06976)262

An attractive terrace of stone-built cottages tastefully converted from farm buildings, all with modern pine furnishings. The bedroom accommodation varies, sleeping from two to six people in one or two bedrooms plus some with a bed-settee in the lounge.

All year MWB out of season 2 nights min, 4wks max, 7units, 2–6persons ◆ ◆ ∂ fridge 🍴 Gas & Elec inclusive ⃞ inclusive 🎯 Iron & Ironing board on premises Launderette on premises ⊙ CTV ⊕3pin square 12P ▥ ≜ Horse riding & farm animals

↔ ♪(2m) ♨(½m)

Min£75 Max£100pw (Low)
Min£125 Max£170pw (High)

BRANCASTER STAITHE
Norfolk
Map**9** TF74

H Staithe Garden Cottage
for bookings Dr W T Mason, Church Barn, Great Shelford, Cambridge CB2 5EL
☎Cambridge(0223)844128

A comfortable family home built in traditional Norfolk flint and brick, in an idyllic secluded position overlooking the salt marshes and creeks of Brancaster and Brancaster Staithe, with approximately two acres of lawns and orchard. The house together with its guest flat offers six bedrooms a mixture of twin or double beds, one with en suite bath, one with a cot and one with bunk beds.

All year MWB 3 days min, 1 unit, 12persons [◇] ◆ ◆ no pets ◎ fridge 🍴(oil) Elec inclusive ⃞ inclusive WM & TD on premises Iron & Ironing board on premises ⊙ ⊗ CTV ⊕3pin square 8p ≜(½m) Barbecue Croquet

↔ ♪(1m)

Min£250 Max£500pw

BRANCSCOMBE
Devon
Map**3** SY18

C Margells Fountain Head
for bookings Landmark Trust, Shottesbrooke, Maidenhead, Berkshire SL6 3SW
☎Littlewick Green(062882)5925

Brampton
—
Brecon

A 16th-century thatched cottage, with great structural charm and beauty. The hallway has late medieval oak partitions leading the kitchen with feature stone open fireplace and dining area. The lounge also has a large open fireplace and both rooms have heavily moulded oak ceilings. Off the kitchen is the bathroom and WC. Upstairs there is one single bedroom and two twin-bedded rooms all with medieval wood panelling and high ceilings. One bedroom has a contemporary wall painting.

All year MWB out of season 1 day min, 1mth max, 1unit, 5persons ◆ Dogs accepted ◎ fridge Underfloor heating Elec inclusive ⃞ not provided ☎(50yds) Iron & Ironing board in unit ⊙ ⊕3pin square 2P(50yds) ▥ ≜(4m)

↔ ♨ (50yds)

Min£175 Max£355pw

BRAUNSTON
Leicestershire
Map**4** SK80

C Hideaway 21 Cedar Street
for bookings Rutland Holiday Cottages, 5 Cedar Street, Braunston, Oakham, Leicestershire LE15 8QS
☎Oakham(0572)2049

A mid-Victorian brick and stone cottage centrally located in a pleasant Rutland village. The accommodation is compact and freshly decorated, comprising kitchen/dining room, and comfortable lounge with open fire. The first floor has a traditionally-furnished bedroom sleeping three, and another with bunk beds suitable for children. There is a combined bathroom and WC.

All year MWB 1wk min, 1unit, 4persons [◇] ◆ no pets ◎ fridge open fires, night storage & electric heaters Elec metered ⃞ inclusive ☎(500yds) Iron & Ironing board in unit TV ⊕3pin square ▥ ≜(500yds) Fishing & sailing

---

↔ ♨(100yds) 🚲(2m)

Min£60 Max£70pw (Low)
Min£80 Max£90pw (High)

F 2 & 2A Wood Lane
for bookings Rutland Holiday Cottages, 5 Cedar Street, Braunston, Oakham, Leicestershire LE15 8QS
☎Oakham(0572)2049

Ground-floor and first-floor flats in a two-storey Edwardian house standing opposite the churchyard near the centre of the village. Each has a kitchen/diner, lounge, bathroom/WC and a traditionally furnished double room.

All year 1wk min, 2units, 2persons [◇] ◆ no pets ◎ fridge Electric storage heaters Elec metered ⃞ inclusive ☎(500yds) Iron & Ironing board in unit ⊙ TV ⊕3pin square ▥ ≜(500yds)

↔ ♨ (200yds) 🚲(2m)

Min£60 Max£70pw (Low)
Min£80 Max£90pw (High)

BRECON
Powys
Map**3** SO02

C Coach House & Stable Cottage
for bookings Mrs F R Harries, The Court, Cradoc Road, Brecon, Powys
☎Brecon(0874)2028

The Coach House is an attractive conversion featuring oak beams and stone arches comprising kitchen/dining room plus bedroom on ground-floor with lounge, two bedrooms and bathroom/WC on the first floor. **Stable Cottage** has been converted into an attractive unit retaining original beams and comprises.sitting room with dining area and kitchen. There are two bedrooms plus bathroom/WC on the first floor.

All year MWB out of season 2units, 5–6persons [◇] ◆ ◆ ∂ fridge 🍴 Gas & Elec charged Nov–Mar ⃞ inclusive ☎(300yds) Iron & Ironing board in unit [Launderette within 300yds] ⊙ CTV ⊕3pin square 2P 1▥ ≜(300yds)

↔ ♪(200yds) ♨ (200yds) 🚲(300yds)

Min£84 Max£108pw (Low)
Min£115 Max£235pw (High)

F   Court Flat
for bookings Mrs F R Harries, The Court,
Cradoc Road, Brecon, Powys
☎Brecon(0874)2028

*Converted from a hay loft, the flat with its
panoramic views, stands above the
original cowshed which is now a
veterinary surgeon's premises. It is
comfortable and spacious with sitting/
dining room, kitchen, two bedrooms and
bathroom/WC. The flat is reached by
outside stairs.*

All year   MWB out of season   1 unit,
2–4 persons   [◇] ◆ ◆ ◎ fridge
🍴 Gas/Elec charged Nov–Mar
Ⓛ inclusive ☎(300yds) Iron & Ironing
board in unit   [Launderette within
300yds] ⊙ CTV ⊕3pin square 2P
🛁(¼m)

⊖ ♪ (¼m) 🍴(¼m) 🐾(¼m)
Min£84 Max£108pw (Low)
Min£100 Max£210pw (High)

BREDON
Hereford & Worcester
Map**3** SO93

B   St Michael's
for bookings Mrs B Trigg, St Mary's, Dock
Lane, Bredon, Tewkesbury,
Gloucestershire GL20 7LG
☎Bredon(0684)73110

*A modern bungalow standing in gardens
adjacent to River Avon. Accommodation
comprises two bedrooms, kitchen,
bathroom/WC and lounge/dining room
with bed-settee.*

All year   1 wk min, 4 mths max, 1 unit,
1–6 persons ◆ ◆ ◎ fridge 🍴
Elec metered Ⓛcan be hired ☎(¼m)
Iron & Ironing board in unit   CTV
⊕3pin square 2P 🔲 🛁(¼m)

⊖ ♪(¼m) 🎵(3m) ♫(3m) 🐾(3m)
Min£55 Max£65pw(Low)
Min£80 Max£90pw(High)

BRIDGERULE
Devon
Map**2** SS20

F   The Chancellry
for bookings Mr D A Dudley & Mrs G M
Wakefield, Glebe House, Bridgerule,
Holsworthy, Devon EX22 7EW
☎Bridgerule(028881)272

*A ground-floor, spacious apartment of
Glebe House, a stone built Georgian
rectory in five acres of gardens with
superb views. Accommodation comprises
large lounge, kitchen/diner with freezer,
four bedrooms, one with en-suite facilities,
and a master bathroom. Designed to
accommodate disabled people.*

Mid Feb–mid Nov & mid Dec–mid Jan
MWB out of season   2 nights min,
6 wks max, 1 unit, 1–12 persons   [◇] ◆
◆ no pets ◎ fridge 🍴 Ⓛ inclusive
☎ Iron & Ironing board on premises
Launderette on premises ⊙ CTV
⊕3pin square P 🔲 🛁(400yds)
Games room   Croquet lawn

⊖ ♪(3m) ♀(¼m)

Brecon
—
Bridport

Min£145 Max£495pw

See advertisement under Bude

**C   Coach House, Mews, Granary,
Forge, Little Barn & Old Stables Cottages**
for bookings Mr D A Dudley & Mrs G M
Wakefield, Glebe House, Bridgerule,
Holsworthy, Devon EX22 7EW
☎Bridgerule(028881)272

*Well-equipped and furnished converted
cottages originally a coach house and
stables, set in a five acre estate. Consisting
of large lounge, kitchen/diner with split-
level cooker, bathroom/WC and either two
or three bedrooms, sleeping 2–8 people.*

Mid Feb–mid Nov & mid Dec–mid Jan
MWB out of season   2 nights min, 6 units,
2–8 persons   [◇] ◆ ◆ no pets ◎
fridge 🍴 Ⓛ inclusive ☎ Iron &
Ironing board on premises   Launderette
on premises ⊙ CTV ⊕3pin square
P 🔲 🛁(400yds) Games room
Croquet lawn

⊖ ♪(3m) ♀(¼m)
Min£60 Max£358pw

See advertisement under Bude.

BRIDGNORTH
Shropshire
Map**7** SO79

**C   Mrs M A Crawford-Clarke Eudon
Burnell Country Cottages** Eudon Burnell,
Bridgnorth, Shropshire
☎Middleton Scriven(074635)235

*Semi-detached, red brick, Victorian
cottages in quiet lane, 3m SW of
Bridgnorth off B4363, with lovely views
over open farmland. They comprise three
bedrooms, kitchen with dining area, sitting
room and ground-floor bathroom/WC.*

All year   MWB out of season   2 nights min,
2 mths max, 3 units, 1–6 persons, ◆ ◆
◎ fridge 🍴(in No. 1 only) Storage
heaters & open fires   Elec metered
Ⓛcan be hired   WM in unit   Iron &
Ironing board in unit ⊙ ◎ CTV
⊕3pin square 6P 🛁(3m)

⊖ ♪(3m) ♀(¼m) 🎵(3m) ♫(3m)
🐾(3m)
Min£60 Max£110pw (Low)
Min£100 Max£120pw (High)

H   The Gatehouse
for bookings Mrs W Cash, Upton Cressett
Hall, Bridgnorth, Shropshire
☎Morville(074631)307

*An attractive, spacious 16th-century red-
brick gatehouse with two octangular
turrets on either side of a central archway
and twenty-six transomed and mullioned
windows. On the first floor there is a
shower/WC and two double bedrooms,
which are tastefully furnished and have
exceptional plasterwork ceilings. The
second floor has a large open lounge with
exposed roof rafters and beams providing*

---

*an ideal relaxing atmosphere. The kitchen
is the other side of the archway and
contains the dining table. 3m W of
Bridgnorth.*

Mar–Dec   MWB   3 nights min, 6 wks max,
1 unit, 1–5 persons, nc8yrs ◎ fridge
Electric   Elec metered Ⓛcan be hired
Iron & Ironing board in unit ⊙ ◎
CTV ⊕3pin square 2P croquet

⊖ ♪ (2½m) 🐾
Min£75 Max£175pw

BRIDLINGTON
Humberside
Map**8** TA16

F   22 Belgrave Road
for bookings Mrs D Morgan, 4 Hymers
Avenue, Hull, Humberside HU3 1LN
☎Hull(0482)41380

*Two self-contained flats on ground and
first-floors of a semi-detached house
situated close to the beach. Sleeping
accommodation for up to six people with
one double-bedded room, one twin room
and a double bed-settee in the lounge is
included in each unit. Both flats contain
kitchen and bathroom (separate WC in the
first-floor flat).*

1 May–30 Sep   MWB out of season
1 wk min, 1 mth max, 2 units, 1–6 persons
◆ no pets ◇ & ◎ fridge Gas &
Electric fires   Gas/Elec metered
Ⓛnot provided ☎(100yds) TV
⊕3pin square 🔲 🛁(200yds)

⊖ ♀(¼m) 🎵(¼m) ♫(¼m) ⊠ 🐾(¼m)
Max£65pw (Low)
Max£70pw (High)

F   7 & 9 Swanland Avenue
for bookings Mrs M Smith, 9 Swanland
Avenue, Bridlington, Humberside
YO15 2HH
☎Bridlington(0262)674351

*Two first-floor and one ground-floor flat in
an Edwardian terrace near the North Bay
shopping and beach areas. All the flats
have two bedrooms, lounge/diners and
kitchens. One of the first floor flats has one
bedroom with en suite shower/WC.*

All year   1 wk min, 3 units, 1–6 persons ◆
◆ no pets ◇ fridge Gas fires   Gas &
Elec metered Ⓛcan be hired
☎(300yds) Iron & Ironing board on
premises [Launderette within 300yds]
CTV ⊕3pin square P 2🔲 🔲
🛁(200yds)

⊖ ♀(200yds) 🎵(400yds)
♫(500yds) 🐾(300yds)
Min£50 Max£130pw

BRIDPORT
Dorset
Map**3** SY49

**F   Mrs N Vaughan Coniston Holiday
Apartments** Coniston House, 69 Victoria
Grove, Bridport, Dorset DT6 3AE
☎Bridport(0308)24049

*Three flats located within detached, red
brick gabled villa in residential road off
A35 through Bridport. The ground floor*

flat sleeps 7, first-floor flat sleeps 6 and second-floor flat sleeps 9. There is a children's play area in the grounds.

All year MWB 1wk min, 1mth max, 3units, 2–9persons [◇] ◆ ◆ ◎ fridge Electric Elec metered ☐ not provided ☎(150yds) WM & SD in unit Iron & Ironing board in unit [Launderette within 300yds] ⊙ Ⓦ CTV ⊕3pin square P ⊞ ⛟(120yds) ⛵

⊖ δ(2½m) ♀(120yds) ♬(273yds) ♬(273yds) 🎥(328yds)

Min£35 Max£65pw (Low)
Min£55 Max£160pw (High)

BRIDSTOW
Hereford and Worcester
Map**3** SO52

C **The Lodge**
for bookings Wye Valley Leisure Ltd, Wye Lea, Bridstow, Ross-on-Wye, Herefordshire
☎Ross-on-Wye(0989)62880

Modernised to a very high standard, this gatehouse of a Georgian country house has its own garden and comprises kitchen, lounge/dining room, two bedrooms, bathroom/WC and a utility room. Suitable for disabled persons.

All year MWB out of season 3days min, 56days max, 1unit, 1–4persons ◆ ◆ no pets ◎ fridge ⛽ [Elec] ☐ inclusive ☎(½m) WM&TD in unit Iron & Ironing board in unit ⊙ Ⓦ CTV ⊕3pin square 2P ⊞ ⛟(¾m) grass putting green Fishing

⊖ δ(3m) ♀(¾m) ♬(2m) ♬(2m) 🎥(2m)

Min£126.50 Max£146.05pw (Low)
Min£158.70 Max£204.70pw (High)

See advertisement under Ross-on-Wye.

F **Pear Tree & Wysteria**
for bookings Wye Valley Leisure Ltd, Wye Lea, Bridstow, Ross-on-Wye, Herefordshire
☎Ross-on-Wye(0989)62880

Two first floor suites that form part of a Georgian house. The ***Pear Tree suite*** *has one bedroom/lounge, kitchen/diner and bathroom and the* ***Wysteria*** *suite has kitchen, lounge/dining room and two bedrooms with en suite facilities. Both are furnished to a high standard.*

All year MWB out of season 3days min, 56days max, 2units, 1–4persons ◆ ◆ no pets ◎ fridge ⛽ [Elec] ☐ inclusive ☎(½m) WM(in Wysteria) SD in unit TD(in Wysteria) Iron & Ironing board in unit ⊙ Ⓦ CTV ⊕3pin square 4P 2⌂ ⊞ ⛟(¾m) (grass) putting green Fishing

⊖ δ(3m) ♀(¾m) ♬(2m) ♬(2m) 🎥(2m)

Min£96.60 Max£128.80pw (Low)
Min£120.75 Max£180.55pw (High)

See advertisement under Ross-on-Wye.

BRIGHTON
East Sussex
Map**4** TQ30

Bridport — Brixham

F **12B Brunswick Road** Hove
for bookings Mrs S J Chapple, 44 Hill Brow, Hove, East Sussex BN3 6QH
☎Brighton(0273)507381

Basement flat situated in Victorian house ¼m from sea-front and near shops. It has two bedrooms, open plan lounge with divan, kitchen/diner, bathroom/WC and separate shower/WC.

Jun–Sep 1wk min, 3mths max, 1unit, 1–4persons ◆ ◆ no pets ◎ fridge ⛽ Gas & Elec metered ☐ inclusive except tea towels ☎(¼m) Iron & Ironing board in unit [Launderette within 300yds] ⊙ TV ⊕3pin square ⊞ ⛟(100yds)

⊖ δ(2½m) ♀(¼m) ♬(¼m) ♬(¼m) 🎥(¼m)

Min£95 Max£135pw

H **54 Cornwall Gardens**
for bookings Mrs A H P Beater, Teme House, Lancing College, West Sussex BN15 0PW
☎Shoreham(07917)2219

Three storey house in pleasant residential area to the north of the town. Accommodation comprises kitchen, lounge/diner and WC on the ground floor. One double and one single bedroom, bath/WC on first floor. One twin and one single bedroom, shower and WC on the top floor.

End Jun–Sept 1wk min, 3mths max, 1unit, 1–6persons ◎ fridge ⛽ Elec inclusive ☐ inclusive ☎(500yds) WM & SD in unit Iron & Ironing board in unit CTV ⊕3pin square ⌂ ⊞ ⛟(500yds)

⊖ δ(2m) ♀(500yds) ♬(1m) ♬(1m) 🎥(½m) Sports Centre (1m)

Max£230pw (High)

BRISTOL
Avon
Map**3** ST57

F Mrs D M Ridout, **19 St Edyths Road**, Sea Mills, Bristol, Avon BS9 2EP
☎Bristol(0272)681967

Small, soundly furnished, self-contained flat on the first floor of a double fronted semi-detached house in a quiet residential position, 3–4m from city centre. It comprises one double-bedded room, one single and a single put-u-up, bathroom/WC, kitchen with dining area overlooking garden and a separate lounge.

All year MWB out of season 2wks min, 2mths max, 1unit, 2–4persons, nc5 no pets ◎ fridge Electric Elec metered ☐ inclusive ☎(50yds) SD in unit Iron & Ironing board in unit ⊙ CTV ⊕3pin square ⛟(50yds)

⊖ δ(1m) ♀(½m) 🎥(3m)

Min£65pw (Low) Min£100pw (High)

BRISTON
Norfolk
Map**9** TG03

C **Holly & Ivy Cottages** Edgefield Road
for bookings Mrs R Webb, 33 Blackmores Grove, Teddington, Middx TW11 9AE
☎01-977 4197

Early 19th-century flint and brick cottages situated on the edge of the village. They are tastefully modernised and well-equipped and both have three bedrooms, living room with storage heaters for winter use, kitchen/diner and bathroom/WC. A large garden is available for the use of both cottages. The steep staircase in ***Holly Cottage*** *makes it unsuitable for the elderly and infirm.*

All year MWB out of season 3days min, max by arrangement, 2units, 1–6persons [◇] ◆ ◎ fridge Electric & open fires & storage heaters Elec metered ☐ not provided ☎(½m) Iron & Ironing board in unit TV ⊕3pin square P ⛟(100yds)

⊖ ♀(½m)

Min£45 Max£65pw (Low)
Min£55 Max£110pw (High)

C **2 & 4 Mill Road**
for bookings Mrs R Webb, 33 Blackmores Grove, Teddington, Middx TW11 9AE
☎01-977 4197

Modernised and comfortably-appointed flint and brick cottages situated on the Briston village green, which is about 4m W of Holt. No2 has three twin-bedded rooms, one of which is on the ground-floor and No4 has four bedrooms, all on the first-floor. Both have sitting rooms with storage heaters for winter use, dining room, kitchen and bathroom/WC. A small private garden is available for each cottage in addition to a larger shared garden. The steep staircase in the cottages make them unsuitable for elderly or infirm persons.

All year MWB out of season 3days min, max by arrangement, 2units, 1–8persons [◇] ◆ ◎ fridge open fires & storage heaters Elec metered ☐ not provided ☎(¼m) Iron & Ironing board in unit TV ⊕3pin square P

⊖ ♀(¼m)

Min£45 Max£65pw (Low)
Min£55 Max£130pw (High)

BRIXHAM
Devon
Map**3** SX95

B Mrs B Baker **Fishcombe Cove Holiday Homes** Fishcombe Cove, Brixham, Devon TQ5 8RD
☎Brixham(08045)51800

Fifteen detached and five terraced purpose-built bungalows in pleasant grounds with fine views of Torbay. Each bungalow comprises one double and one twin-bedded room, lounge with double put-u-up, kitchen/diner and bathroom.

All year MWB out of season 2days min, 20units, 2–6persons ◆ ◆ no pets ◎ fridge Electric Elec metered ☐ can→

be hired ☎(100yds) Iron & Ironing
board on premises [Launderette within
300yds] ⊙ TV ⊕3pin square 20P
🛁(100yds) Childrens play area
↩ ♨(100yds) ♬(100yds)

Min£52 Max£90pw (Low)
Min£115 Max£230pw (High)

C Georgian Cottages Mount Pleasant
Road
for bookings Mr J W Griffith, 51 Wall Park
Road, Brixham, Devon TG5 9UF
☎Brixham(08045)2625

*Two attractive fishermen's cottages on a
hill overlooking the harbour. Each unit
comprises lounge with stone fireplaces
and beamed ceilings, kitchen/dining
room, bathroom/WC and four double
bedrooms two of which have wash hand
basin.*

All year MWB out of season 1wk min,
2units, 8–10persons ◈ ◆ ◎ fridge
Storage heaters Elec metered 🅻can be
hired ☎(200yds) Iron & Ironing board in
unit [Launderette within 300yds] ⊙
CTV ⊕3pin square P ▥ 🛁(200yds)
↩ ♨(3m) ♨(200yds) ♬(200yds)

Min£87 Max£160pw (Low)
Min£200 Max£373pw (High)

F Halfway House Holiday Flats Heath
Road
for bookings Mr C Manser, 'Upover',
Victoria Road, Brixham, Devon
☎Brixham(08045)3845

*Colonial style, architect designed block of
holiday flats in superior residential area
with four ground-floor and four first-floor
flats. Each comprise lounge/diner/kitchen,
bathroom/WC, one double and one twin-
bedded room plus a double bed-settee in
lounge.*

All year MWB out of season 3days min,
1mth max, 8units, 2–6persons ◈ ◆
no pets no single sex groups ◎
Electric fires Elec metered 🅻inclusive
☎(100yds) Iron & Ironing board on
premises [Launderette on premises]
⊙ CTV ⊕3pin square 12P ▥
🛁(150yds)
↩ ♨(2m) ♨(½m) ♬(1m) ♬(1m)
Min£50 Max£220pw

**·F Mr & Mrs Howard, Headland Court
Holiday Flats,** Lower Rea Road, Brixham,
Devon TQ5 9UD
☎Brixham(08045)7361

*Modern, purpose-built holiday flats, each
with its own balcony giving magnificent
sea-views towards Torbay. There are three
ground floor and three first floor flats each
comprising lounge/diner, kitchen,
bathroom/WC, one double and
one twin-bedded room and also a double
studio couch in the lounge.*

All year MWB out of season 2days min,
1mth max, 6units, 6persons ◈ ◆ pets
by arrangement ◎ fridge night
storage & Elec fires Elec metered 🅻can
be hired ☎(400yds) Iron & Ironing
board in unit ⊙ CTV ⊕3pin square
6P ▥ 🛁(400yds)

**Brixham
—
Broad Haven**

↩ ♨(3m) ♨(½m) ♬(¾m) ♬(¾m)
Min£50 Max£156pw (Low)
Min£106 Max£214pw (High)

Ch Landscove Holiday Village Berry
Head
for bookings Hoseasons Holidays Ltd,
Sunway House, Lowestoft, Suffolk
NR32 3LT
☎Lowestoft(0502)62281

*117 modern chalets surrounded by several
acres of well laid-out gardens and
grassland. Adjoins Berry Head Country
Park.*

Apr–Oct MWB out of season 3days min,
1mth max, 117units, 2–6persons
[◇ ◈ ◆] no pets ◎ fridge
Electric Elec metered 🅻inclusive ☎
[Iron & Ironing board on premises]
[Launderette on premises] ⊙ ⑭ CTV
⊕3pin square 250P 🛁 🖾
Licensed clubhouse Pitch & Putt
↩ ♨(3m) ♨ ♬ ♬
Min£50 Max£225pw

C Winkle Cottage Roseacre Terrace
for bookings Mr J W Griffith, 51 Wall Park
Road, Brixham, Devon TQ5 9UF
☎Brixham(08045)2625

*Georgian cottage only ½m from town
centre and ½m from St Mary's Bay.
Accommodation comprises lounge with
put-u-up, separate kitchen and dining
area. One double bedroom and one room
with bunk beds. Bathroom with washbasin
and WC. Street parking. Out of town
centre into Bolton Street, left into Rea Barn
Road, terrace on the left.*

All year MWB out of season 1wk min,
1unit, 4–6persons, nc6 ◎ fridge
Electric Elec metered 🅻can be hired
☎(200yds) Iron & Ironing board in unit
[Launderette within 300yds] ⊙ CTV
⊕3pin square ▥ 🛁(300yds)
↩ ♨(3m) ♨(½m) ♬(¼m)
Min£44 Max£100pw (Low)
Min£120 Max£215pw (High)

BROAD CAMPDEN
Gloucestershire
Map**4** SP13

C Mr & Mrs J V Rawcliffe, **Lion Cottage**,
North End, Broad Campden, Chipping
Campden, Gloucestershire GL55 6UR
☎Evesham(0386)840077

*North end of attractive Cotswold stone
cottage with pretty garden; the other end
is occupied by the owners. The well
appointed accommodation comprises an
open plan lower floor with lounge, dining
facilities and kitchen while upstairs are
three bedrooms, bathroom/WC plus
separate shower room/WC.*

31Jan–19Dec MWB out of season
3nights min, 1unit, 1–6persons ♉
fridge 🍴 Elec metered 🅻can be

---

hired ☎(10yds) Iron & Ironing board in
unit ⊙ CTV ⊕3pin square 2P ▥
🛁(¾m)
↩ ♨(3m) ♨(200yds)
Min£55 Max£125pw (Low)

BROAD HAVEN
Dyfed
Map**2** SM81
See also **Ratford Bridge**

C Bank House
for bookings Coastal Cottages of
Pembrokeshire, Seaview, Abercastle,
Mathry, Dyfed SA62 5HJ
☎Croesgoch(03483)7742

*A period cottage situated within a short
walk of Broad Haven sands. Recently
modernised, it comprises lounge with
open fire and beamed ceiling, kitchen/
diner, one double, one single and one
bunk-bedded room. There is also a small
back garden.*

All year MWB out of season 2days min,
6wks max, 1unit, 2–5persons ◈ ◆
◎ fridge 🍴& open fire Elec metered
🅻inclusive ☎(50yds) WM & SD in unit
Iron & Ironing board in unit ⊙ CTV
⊕3pin square P ▥ 🛁(100yds)
↩ ♨(50yds) ♬(100yds)
Min£70 Max£250pw

B Mr & Mrs P Bauer, **Timber Hill**, Broad
Haven, Haverfordwest, Dyfed SA62 3LZ
☎Broad Haven(043783)239

*Sixteen out of 44 detached cedarwood
bungalows set in 130 acres on the
southern slopes of a valley within the
Pembrokeshire Coast National Park.
These well furnished properties each have
a verandah, three bedrooms, well-
equipped small kitchen, lounge/diner and
a bathroom/WC. 2m N of Broad Haven.*

Mar–Oct MWB out of season 1wk min,
16units, 1–6persons [◇] ◈ ◆ ◎
fridge Electric Elec inclusive
🅻inclusive ☎ Iron & Ironing board in
unit [Launderette on premises] ⊙
CTV ⊕3pin square P ▥ 🛁(2m)
↩ ♨(2m)
Min£90 Max£230pw

Ch 30 Timber Hill
for bookings Mr & Mrs J Thatcher, 30
Albemarle Gate, Pittville, Cheltenham,
Gloucestershire GL50 4PJ
☎Cheltenham(0242)529268

*Situated on a small wooded development
of detached cedar bungalows. It
comprises of open lounge/diner, separate
kitchen and bathroom, three bedrooms
(one double, one twin and one with
bunks). There is a verandah at the front.
Located on the southern slopes of a quiet
valley.*

Etr–Oct 1wk min, 1unit, 1–6persons ◈
◆ ◎ Electric Elec inclusive 🅻can be
hired ☎ Iron & Ironing board in unit
[Launderette on premises] ⊙ CTV
⊕3pin square 2P ▥ 🛁(1½m)
↩ ♨(1½m) ♬(1½m) ♬(1½m)
Min£67 Max£200pw

BROADWAY
Hereford & Worcester
Map**4** SP03
See also **Stanton & Snowshill**

C   Bibsworth Lodge
for bookings Heart of England Cottages,
The Barrel & Basket, Market Place,
Fairford, Gloucestershire GL7 4AB
☎Cirencester(0285)713295

An attractive two-storey lodge standing by
the entrance to Bibsworth House. It has its
own small garden. The accommodation
comprises lounge, dining room, kitchen
and bathroom/WC on the ground-floor
and one twin-bedded room and one
double bedroom on the first-floor.

All year   MWB out of season   3days min,
6mths max, 1unit, 1–4persons ◆ ◆
no pets ◉ fridge Electric Elec metered
(night storage inclusive) ⌷can be hired
☎ WM & SD in unit   CTV
⊕3pin square 2P ▥ ♨(½m) Putting
↩ ⬤(¾m)

Min£75 Max£85pw (Low)
Min£95 Max£125pw (High)

**F   The Old Music Room & The Old Apple
Store**
for bookings Heart of England Cottages,
The Barrel & Basket, The Market Place,
Fairford, Gloucestershire GL7 4AB
☎Cirencester (0285)713295

A beautiful 17th-century Cotswold House
with lovely enclosed garden. The **Old
Apple Store – Midlands Holiday Home of
the Year** – see page 12 – is a first floor flat,
comprising sitting room with views over
the garden, kitchen, one twin-bedded
room with en-suite bathroom. A second
suite of bedroom and bathroom can be
made available. The **Music Room** is a later
addition to the house and has been
converted into a ground-floor apartment
with spacious dining room, sitting room
with inglenook fireplace, twin bedroom
with fitted wardrobes and a large
bathroom.

All year   MWB out of season   wkd min,
2unit, 2–4persons nc no pets ◔ or
◉ fridge ♨& electric fires Gas & Elec
inclusive ⌷inclusive ☎(1m) [WH & TD
on premises] Iron & Ironing board in
unit CTV ⊕3pin square 2–4P ▥
♨(1m)

Broadway
—
Broughton-in-Furness

↩ ♂(3m) ⬤(½m)
Min£110 Max£210pw

BROADWINDSOR
Dorset
Map**3** ST40

C   Hursey Farm Cottages
for bookings Mrs Poulton, Hursey Farm,
Hursey, Broadwindsor, Beaminster, Dorset
DT8 3LN
☎Broadwindsor(0308)68323

Three stone-built cottages set in quiet
rural countryside. First cottage comprises
ground-floor lounge/diner, separate
kitchen. Two bedrooms (one double and
one with two single beds, extra bed
available), combined bathroom/WC on
first-floor. Middle cottage consists of
ground-floor lounge/diner, separate
kitchen, combined bathroom/WC. Two
bedrooms on first-floor comprising one
double-bedded room and one with twin
beds or bunks plus single bed. Third
cottage consists of ground-floor
accommodation only, lounge, kitchen/
diner, combined bathroom/WC, two
bedrooms.

All year   MWB out of season   3days min,
4wks max, 3units, 2–5persons [◇] ◆
be hired ☎(½m) Iron & Ironing board in
unit ⊖ CTV ⊕3pin square 2P ▥
♨(½m)
↩ ⬤(½m)
Min £50pw Max£138pw

BROADWOOD KELLY
Devon
Map**3** ST60

C   J F H MD46D
for bookings John Fowler Holidays, Dept
58 Marlborough Road, Ilfracombe, Devon
EX34 8PF.
☎Ilfracombe(0271)66666

Thatched country cottage with own small
garden. It comprises entrance hall, dining
room, lounge with exposed beams and

---

inglenook fireplace with original bread
oven, small modern kitchen, bathroom/wc.
There is one double and one twin-bedded
room and also a bed settee in the lounge
which sleeps 2.

Mar–Oct   MWB out of season   1wk min,
1mth max, 1unit, 6persons ◆ ◉
fridge Elec metered ⌷not provided
☎(½m) Iron & Ironing board in unit ⊖
CTV ⊕3pin square 5P ▥ ♨(½m)
↩ ⬤(2½m)
Min£79.35 Max£205.85pw

BRODICK
See **Arran, Isle of,** Strathclyde Buteshire

BROUGH
Cumbria
Map**12** NY71

F   Mrs J Atkinson **Augill House Farm**,
Brough, Kirkby Stephen, Cumbria
☎Brough(09304)305

A small ground-floor flat situated adjacent
to the farmouse in a pleasant and
peaceful location. It accommodates four
people in one double-bedded room and a
convertible double sofa in the living room.

All year   MWB out of season   3days min,
3mths max, 1unit, 4persons ◆ ◆ ◔
fridge ♨ Gas inclusive Elec metered
⌷can be hired ☎(1m) Iron & Ironing
board in unit CTV ⊕3pin square 2P
▥ ♨(1m)
↩ ⬤(1m)
Min£50 Max£70pw

BROUGHTON-IN-FURNESS
Cumbria
Map**7** SD28

F   Mr & Mrs K M Shaw **The Dower House**
High Duddon, Duddon Bridge,
Broughton-in-Furness, Cumbria LA20 6ET
☎Broughton-in-Furness(06576)279

A charming house set in seven acres of
woodland and gardens. It has recently
been converted to provide four flats.
Rawlinson has a family room sleeping
four and a double convertible settee.
Woodside has two double bedrooms plus
double convertible. **Orchard Corner** has
one double room. **Chimneys** has one
double and one triple room. Also the →

LOWER PORTWAY FARM

Forge Cottage (illus.), Manor House and Georgian
farmhouse converted into self-contained apartments,
set in lawned gardens amid beautiful countryside in
quiet village. Equipped to very high standard of
comfort. Colour TV. Ample parking. Sleep 2 to 6.
Personally supervised by owner. Sorry no pets. Ideal
touring centre for Cotswolds and Vale of Evesham,
with Stratford, Cheltenham and Worcester nearby.
**For bookings contact: Mrs. D Stow,
Lower Portway Farm, Sedgeberrow,
Evesham, Worcestershire.
Tel: (0386) 881298**
See gazetteer under Sedgeberrow

converted Coach House has **Stable Loft** with a double, a twin room plus double convertible and **Coach House** has one double and two twin rooms. All are furnished and decorated to a high standard.

All year MWB out of season 2 days min, 6 units, 2–6 persons ◇ ◆ no pets in Dower House ◎ fridge & freezer ❄ & storage heaters Elec inclusive ⌸ inclusive ⚡ [WM & TD on premises] Iron & Ironing board in unit ⊕ CTV ⊕ 3 pin square 20P ▥ ♨ (1¼m) Lounge bar games room
↔ ♬ (1m)
Min£74 Max£230pw

C Mr & Mrs M Tyson **Wreaks End Cottage** Wreaks End House, Broughton-in-Furness, Cumbria LA20 6BS
☎ Broughton-in-Furness(06576)216
An attractive stone-built cottage adjoining main house comprising spacious kitchen, utility room, living room and four bedrooms. Gardens to front and rear. Located 1m SE of village in rural setting.

All year MWB out of season 1 night min, 1 mth max, 1 unit, 6–8 persons ◇ no pets ◎ fridge Electric inclusive ⌸ not provided ⚡ (1m) WM, Iron & Ironing board in unit ⊕ ⊕ CTV ⊕ 3 pin square 1P ▥ ♨ (1m)
↔ ♬ (1m)
Min£100 Max£150pw

BRYNSIENCYN
Gwynedd
Map**6** SH46

H **Ty Coch**
for bookings Menai Holidays, Old Port Office, Penrhyn Bay, Bangor, Gwynedd.
☎ Bangor(0248)362254 or 351055
A large detached house set in 1½ acres of lawns and gardens, situated about one mile from Menai Straits. It comprises utility room, kitchen, lounge/diner and separate WC. Upstairs there is one double and one twin bedded room, both with en suite facilities, and a further two twin bedrooms with separate bath/shower room and WC.

May–Sep MWB out of season 3 days min, 6 wks max, 1 unit, 8 persons ◎ fridge ❄ Elec metered ⌸ can be hired ⚡ (½m) WM & SD in unit Iron & Ironing board in unit ⊕ CTV ⊕ 3 pin square 6P ♨ (1m)
↔ ♬ (1m)
Min£190 Max£230pw (Low)
Min£295 Max£350pw (High)

BUCKDEN
North Yorkshire
Map**7** SD97

C Mr & Mrs D Lusted **11 Dalegarth**
Buckden, Skipton, North Yorkshire
☎ Kettlewell(075676)877
A cluster of cottages set in a small cul-de-sac in the centre of the village. They comprise of kitchen, large lounges, two bedrooms (one double, one twin) plus convertible settees in the lounge, and

---

Broughton-in-Furness
—
Buckingham

bathroom/WC. They include such designs as first-floor lounges and deck terraces and some have their own saunas. Disabled visitors are catered for.

All year MWB out of season 10 units, 1–6 persons ◇ ◆ small dogs only ◎ fridge ❄ Elec metered ⌸ inclusive ⚡ Iron & Ironing board in unit [Launderette on premises] ⊕ CTV ⊕ 3 pin square ♨ ▥ ♨ (200yds) ▨ games room
↔ ♬ (100yds)
Min£128.80 Max£280.60pw

C **Low Greenfield Farm Cottage**
for bookings Mr & Mrs D Lusted, 11 Dalegarth, Buckden, Skipton, North Yorkshire
☎ Kettlewell(075676)877
Set along a gated road in the middle of the Dales, it is ideal for those seeking peace, privacy and tranquillity. Well-furnished, it comprises a large kitchen, lounge with inglenook fireplace and oak beams, two bedrooms (one twin, one double). Situated on a working sheep farm.

May–Oct 1 wk min, 1 unit, 1–4 persons ◇ ◆ no pets ◎ fridge ❄ & log fire Elec metered ⌸ inclusive ⚡ (3m) Iron & Ironing board in unit ⊕ 3 pin square 2P ♨ (6m) trout fishing
Min£103.50 Max£178.25pw

BUCKIE
Grampian Banffshire
Map**15** NJ46

C **Oystercatcher & Sandpiper** Bowie's Lane, Buckpool
for bookings Blantyre Holiday Homes Ltd, West Bauds, Findochty, Buckie, Banffs AB5 2EB
☎ Buckie(0542)31773
Two completely renovated early 19th-century fishermen's cottages on the seafront in the old town area of Buckie. The accommodation is all on the ground-floor and comprises lounge/diner with bed-settee, one double bedroom, one twin-bedded room, modern kitchen and bathroom.

Etr–Oct MWB out of season 1 wk min, 3 wks max, 2 units, 1–6 persons [◇ ◆] ◎ fridge Electric Elec metered ⌸ can be hired ⚡ (1m) Iron & Ironing board in unit ⊕ CTV ⊕ 3 pin square P
↔ ♬ (2m) ♬ (100yds) ♫ (2m) ♫ (1½m)
Min£64pw (Low)
Min£145pw (High)

BUCKINGHAM
Buckinghamshire
Map**4** SP63

B **The Bungalow** Church End
for bookings Mrs S Goodall, Hillesden Holiday Homes, Home Farm, Hillesden, Buckingham, Bucks MK18 4DB
☎ Steeple Claydon(029673)256
Modern bungalow with two bedrooms. Surrounded by garden and facing the village church.

All year 1 wk min, 1 unit, 2–6 persons [◇] ◇ ◆ ◎ fridge Electric Elec metered ⌸ inclusive ⚡ (100yds) SD on premises Iron & Ironing board in unit ⊕ TV ⊕ 3 pin square 2P 1♨ ▥ ♨ (1m) Trout lake, river fishing
↔ ♬ (3m) ♬ (1m) ♫ (3m)
Min£75 Max£198pw

C **4 Church End**
for bookings Mrs S Goodall, Hillesden Holiday Homes, Home Farm, Hillesden, Buckingham, Bucks MK18 4DB
☎ Steeple Claydon(029673)256
Modernised semi-detached cottage with three bedrooms and lounge/diner. Close to village church.

All year 1 wk min, 1 unit, 2–6 persons [◇] ◇ ◆ ◎ fridge Electric Elec metered ⌸ inclusive ⚡ (100yds) SD on premises Iron & Ironing board in unit ⊕ TV ⊕ 3 pin square 2P 1♨ ▥ ♨ (1m) Trout lake, river fishing
↔ ♬ (3m) ♬ (1m) ♫ (3m)
Min£75 Max£198pw

H **College Farmhouse**
for bookings Mrs S Goodall, Hillesden Holiday Homes, Home Farm, Hillesden, Buckingham, Bucks MK18 4DB
☎ Steeple Claydon(029673)256
A charming 17th-century house divided into two units situated in quiet village with open rural views. Each comprises three double bedrooms, lounge, dining room and kitchen with access to own well kept garden.

All year 1 wk min, 2 units, 2–6 persons [◇] ◇ ◆ ◎ fridge Elec metered ⌸ inclusive ⚡ (½m) SD on premises Iron & Ironing board in unit ⊕ TV ⊕ 3 pin square P ▥ ♨ (½m) Trout lake Fishing
↔ ♬ (2m) ♬ (1m) ♫ (2m)
Min£80 Max£211pw

H **Lower Farm House**
for bookings Mrs S Goodall, Hillesden Holiday Homes, Home Farm, Hillesden, Buckingham, Bucks MK18 4DB
☎ Steeple Claydon(029673)256
Luxurious and spacious period farmhouse with five large bedrooms and three bathrooms. Set in peaceful surroundings with lovely views overlooking countryside.

All year 1 wk min, 1 unit, 2–14 persons [◇] ◇ ◆ ◎ fridge ❄ Elec inclusive ⌸ inclusive ⚡ (½m) SD in unit Iron & Ironing board in unit ⊕ CTV ⊕ 3 pin square 6P 2♨ ▥ ♨ (1m) Trout lake, river fishing
↔ ♬ (3m) ♬ (1m) ♫ (3m)
Min£120 Max£388pw

BUCKLAND
Gloucestershire
Map**4** SP03

C   Pear Tree Cottage
for bookings Heart of England Cottages,
The Barrel & Basket, Market Place,
Fairford, Gloucestershire GL7 4AB
☎Cirencester(0285)713295

A 100-year-old two-storey Cotswold stone
cottage comprising kitchen/diner/lounge
with open fireplace and a divan bed. The
first-floor comprises one double and one
single bedroom and bathroom/WC.

Allyear MWB out of season 3days min,
6mths max, 1unit, 1–5persons ◇ ◆
◆ no cats ♨ fridge ♨♨ Gas/
Elec metered Ⓛcan be hired
☎(100yds) Iron & Ironing board
Launderette ☉ TV ⊕3pin square
1P 🛏 ♨(1m)

↩ ♨

Min£80 Max£90pw (Low)
Min£110 Max£140pw (High)

BUCK'S CROSS
Devon
Map**2** SS32

Ch F & H   Bideford Bay Holiday Park
for bookings Haven Holidays, PO Box 20,
Truro, Cornwall TR1 2UG
☎Truro(0872)40400

Bradgate House is a stone built period
house. The ground floor has the lounge/
diner, well equipped kitchen and
bathroom/WC while upstairs are one
double, one twin, two bunk bedrooms, one
having two additional single beds, and an
extra bathroom/WC. The *Chalets* are semi
detached and built of stone and timber.
They comprise lounge/diner with put-u-up,
kitchen area, bathroom, one double and
one twin bedroom. The *flats* are either in
the main Manor House or the converted
stables. All have an open plan lounge/
kitchen/diner and bathroom/WC
bedrooms vary sleeping 1–8 persons.

Etr & May–Sep MWB 2days min,
203units, 1–10persons [◇ ◇ ◆]
◉ fridge Electric Elec metered
Ⓛinclusive ☎ [Launderette on
premises] ☉ CTV ⊕3pin square P
🛏 ♨ ⊡ ⇗ Pitch & Putt ♨

Games room, children's play area Sauna,
restaurant

↩ ♨ 🎲 ♫

Min£77 Max£262pw (Low)
Min£171 Max£421pw (High)

BUDE
Cornwall
Map**2** SS20

F   Mr & Mrs I Phillips, *Downland Holiday
Flats* Maer Lane, Bude, Cornwall
☎Bude(0288)4994

Fourteen purpose-built flats, seven are
ground-floor units and seven are first-floor
flats set in 2 acres of grounds. The
properties are situated adjacent to a
holiday park, and enjoy views over open
fields. The ground-floor flats contain a
small hall with shower/WC, kitchen/diner,
lounge with foldaway bed, and two
bedrooms. The accommodation is similar
in the first-floor flats except they have one
bedroom.

28May–28Sep MWB out of season
1wk min, 4wks max, 14units, 1–6persons
◇ ◆ ♨ fridge Electric fires
Elec metered Ⓛcan be hired
☎(50yds) [Launderette within 300yds]
☉ TV ⊕3pin square 28P ♨(50yds)
↩ ♨(1½m) ♨(50yds) 🎲(50yds)
♫(50yds) ♨(1½m)

Details not confirmed for 1987

BUDLEIGH SALTERTON
Devon
Map**3** SY08

F   Mr & Mrs Skelding, **Cliff House Flats**
Cliff House, Cliff Terrace, Budleigh
Salterton, Devon EX9 6JY
☎Budleigh Salterton(03954)2432

Situated in quiet residential road, 200 yds
from the beach. The first floor flat
comprises kitchen/diner, lounge with
double bed-settee, one double bedroom,
one single bedroom and wash hand basin,
bathroom and WC. The lower ground-floor

flat has open-plan kitchen/lounge/dining
area, one twin and one double bedroom
and shower/WC. Both flats have their own
entrance.

Allyear MWB out of season 1wk min,
6wks max, 2units, 1–5persons [◇] ◉
fridge ♨♨ Elec inclusive Ⓛcan be
hired ☎(220yds) Iron & Ironing board in
unit ☉ CTV ⊕3pin square 1P 🛏
♨(100yds)
↩ ♨(½m) ♨ 🎲 ♫ ♨

Min£80 Max£95pw (Low)
Min£115 Max£140pw (High)

CC   CC Ref 681E
for bookings Character Cottages
(Holidays) Ltd, 34 Fore Street, Sidmouth,
Devon EX10 8AQ
☎Sidmouth(03955)77001

Large cottage in grounds of country
house estate. Good tarmac approach.
Porch, attractive lounge, styled fireplace,
dining room, fitted kitchen, three twin
bedrooms. Expensive and fine furnishings.

Allyear MWB out of season 1wk min,
1mth max, 1unit, 2–6persons ◇
no pets ◉ fridge Electric
Elec metered Ⓛnot provided ☎ WM,
SD & TD in unit Iron & Ironing board in
unit ☉ CTV ⊕3pin square
⊕2pin round P 🛏 ♨(½m)
↩ ♨(1m)

Min£105 Max£160pw (Low)
Min£235 Max£340pw (High)

H   CC Ref 6034
for bookings Character Cottages
(Holidays) Ltd, 34 Fore Street, Sidmouth,
Devon EX10 8AQ
☎Sidmouth(03955)77001

A modern, brick-built detached residence
with a large garden. On the ground floor is
a large lounge, dining room, kitchen, WC
and one double bedroom. On the first floor
are two double bedrooms and a
bathroom/WC.

Allyear 1wk min, 6mths max, 1unit,
2–6persons ◇ ♨ fridge Electric &
gas Gas/Elec inclusive Ⓛcan be hired
Iron & Ironing board in unit [Launderette
within 300yds] ☉· TV ⊕3pin square
⊕2pin round P 🛏 🛏
↩ ♨(1½m) ♨(½m) 🎲(½m) →

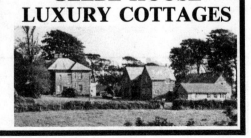

Min£129 Max£160pw (Low)
Min£215 Max£291pw (High)

H   CC Ref 7023P
for bookings Character Cottages
(Holidays) Ltd, 34 Fore Street, Sidmouth,
Devon EX10 8AQ
☎Sidmouth(03955)77001
*A spacious stone-built house, on the
seafront. It comprises lounge with balcony,
dining room, kitchen/breakfast room,
bathroom and WC. One of the bedrooms
has a bathroom/shower en suite and two
have wash hand basins.*

All year   MWB out of season   1wk min,
1mth max, 1unit, 1–8persons ◆ ◎
fridge 🍴 Elec inclusive
🔲not provided ☎(100yds)   SD in unit
Iron & Ironing board in unit ⊕ CTV
⊕3pin square   3P   2🛏 🎛 🛁(100yds)
↔ ♪(½m)   ♨ (100yds)
Min£119 Max£199pw (Low)
Min£255 Max£325pw (High)

C   CC Ref 7690
for bookings Character Cottages, 34 Fore
Street, Sidmouth, Devon EX10 8AQ
☎Sidmouth(03955)77001
*A cottage in the centre of East Budleigh
village, set within a small walled garden.
The accommodation comprises lobby,
lounge/diner with exposed beams and
open stone fireplace with log burner, a
step leads to small kitchen and bathroom/
WC. Stairs from lounge to one double and
one single bedroom.*

All year   MWB out of season   3days min,
2mths max, 1unit, 3persons, nc5yrs
no pets ◎   fridge   🔲not provided
☎(100yds)   Iron & Ironing board in unit
CTV   ⊕3pin square   🛁(20yds)
↔ ♪(3m)   ♨(100yds)
Min£71 Max£149pw

Ch   CC Ref 7691
for bookings Character Cottages Ltd, 34
Fore Street, Sidmouth, Devon EX10 8AQ
☎Sidmouth(03955)77001
*Wooden chalet situated in the elegant
gardens of Sunways House on the edge of
Budleigh Salterton. Accommodation
comprises kitchen/lounge/diner, one small
double bedroom, one single bedroom,
shower room and WC.*

Mar–Oct   MWB out of season   3days min,
2mths max, 1unit, 3persons ◆ ◎
fridge   electric heaters   Elec inclusive
🔲charged   ☎(½m)   Iron & Ironing board
in unit ⊕ CTV   ⊕3pin square   2P 🎛
🛁(½m)
↔ ♪(½m)   ♨(½m)
Min£84 Max£149pw

Budleigh Salterton
—
Burgh by Sands

BUILTH WELLS
Powys
Map3 SO05

C   The Forge Cottage & The Folley
Nant-yr-Arian
for bookings Mr & Mrs A H P Beater, Teme
House, Lancing College, Lancing, West
Sussex BN15 0RN
☎Shoreham-By-Sea(0273)452219

*The Forge is a restored stone cottage
offering comfortable accommodation. It
comprises lounge with original black slate,
small dining room, kitchen, bathroom/wc,
one single and two twin-bedded rooms.
The Folley is an extension of Forge
Cottage, and still contains the forge. It has
a combined lounge/diner, small
kitchenette, one bedroom with twin beds
and a separate shower room/WC.*

All year   MWB out of season   2days min,
6wks max, 2units, 2–5persons ◆ ◆
◎   fridge   Storage & Radiators
Elec metered   🔲inclusive   ☎(½m)   SD in
unit (Forge Cottage only)   Iron & Ironing
board in unit ⊕ CTV   ⊕3pin square
3P 🎛   ♪(½m)
↔ ♪(½m)   ♨(½m)   🎵(1m)   🐾(1m)
Sports centre(1m)
Min£40 Max£50pw (Low)
Min£110 Max£145pw (High)

BURFORD
Oxfordshire
Map4 SP21

**C & F   Mrs R M Jennings The Mill at
Burford** Burford, Oxford OX8 4DN
☎Burford(099382)2379

*Three modernised properties grouped
around the restored Mill House and the
mill stream. Tail Race is a 17th-century
cottage with kitchen, lounge/diner, shower
and WC, and three bedrooms, one with
four poster bed. Windrush is a ground-
floor flat with two bedrooms and
Millstream a first-floor flat with one
bedroom. Both flats have kitchen and
lounge/diner.*

All year   MWB out of season   2nights min,
3units, 1–5persons [◇] ◆ ◆ ◎
fridge 🍴 Elec inclusive 🔲inclusive
☎ [WM, SD & TD on premises]   Iron &
Ironing board on premises ⊕ ⊗ CTV
⊕3pin square   5P 🎛 🛁(500yds)
↔ ♪(1m)   ♨ (200yds)   Boats, bicycles,
fishing and barbecue.

Min£85 Max£115pw (Low)
Min£125 Max£210pw (High)

C & F   Widford Farm Cottages
for bookings Mrs E Buxton, Widford
Manor, Burford, Oxford OX8 4DU
☎Burford(099382)2152
*Six cottages and one flat built of old
Cotswold stone and all have lounge/
dining room, well-equipped kitchens,
bathroom and WC. Widford Manor Flat is
self-contained and has one double
bedroom plus bed-settee. Whitehill
Cottage is semi-detached with three
bedrooms, two twin-bedded rooms and
one with bunk beds, plus an additional
sofa-bed. Woodmans Cottage is semi-
detached with three bedrooms, one twin-
bedded room, one triple-bedded room and
one bunk-bedded room, a sofa in the
lounge can sleep one additional person.
Clock House is converted from farm
buildings and has full central heating with
two twin-bedded rooms and one room
with bunk beds plus a double bed-settee
in lounge. Shepherd's Cottage has two
twin-bedded rooms and one room with
three single beds plus a folding bed.
Gardeners Cottage has one double
bedroom and another room with three
single beds plus a folding bed. Widford
End, self-contained ground-floor
accommodation with two bedrooms, one
double room and the other having bunk
beds plus a convertible bed-settee in
lounge. Each unit has its own garden. 2m
E of Burford on unclassified road.*

All year   1wk min, 7units, 2–8persons
[◇] ◆ ◆   no pets except dogs   ◎
fridge   Electric wood stove & open fires
Elec metered   🔲can be hired   ☎   WM,
SD & TD on premises   Iron & Ironing
board in unit   Freezer ⊕ ⊗   TV (CTV
can be hired)   ⊕3pin square
⊕3pin round   30P 🛏 🎛 🛁(2m)
🐟Hard   Trout fishing, table tennis &
bicycles for hire
↔ ♪(2m)   ♨ (1m)
Min£75 Max£125pw (Low)
Min£110 Max£210pw (High)

BURGH BY SANDS
Cumbria
Map11 NY35

C   Hollygarth Cottage Monkhill
for bookings Rev L Higdon, The Vicarage,
4 St Georges Crescent, Stanwix, Carlisle,
Cumbria CA3 9NL
☎Carlisle(0228)24978
*Modernised Georgian farmworker's
cottage in tranquil hamlet amidst beautiful
countryside, ideal for touring the lakes,
Roman wall and Scottish Borders.*

The Mill at Burford
18th Century Cotswolds watermill setting, secluded and peaceful, yet only 5
minutes walk from centre of Burford. Cottage (sleeps 6) and four delightful
holiday flats (sleep 4, 3, 2 and 2) gathered around millstream and garden.
Enjoy our boats, bicycles and fishing (we also have a local club membership).
Every comfort — colour television, fitted carpets, central heating, antiques.
Open all year.   **Ring Ruth Jennings: Burford 2379**

Accommodation comprises cosy lounge, kitchen, bathroom/WC and two bedrooms.

All year MWB out of season 1wk min, 1mth max, 1unit, 2–5persons ◆ ◆ ⏚ fridge Electric & gas fires Gas & Elec inclusive ⌷inclusive ☎(100yds) WM & SD in unit Iron & Ironing board in unit ⌾ TV ⊕3pin square 2P ▥ ▦(1½m) ↔ ☕ (100yds)

Details not confirmed for 1987

BURGH CASTLE
Norfolk
Map**5** TG40

Ch Waveney Valley Holiday Village
Butt Lane
for bookings Hoseasons Holidays, Sunway House, Lowestoft, Suffolk NR32 3LT
☎Lowestoft(0502)62271

One hundred units with small patios, designed to sleep four in two bedrooms plus a double put-u-up in lounge/diner. Set in a quiet rural location.

Apr–Sep MWB out of season 1wk min, 100units, 2–6persons [◆] ⓦ fridge Electric Elec metered ⌷inclusive ☎(¾m) ⌾ CTV ⊕3pin square P ▦ ☕ ↔ ♫(2m)
Min£45 Max£115pw

BURNOPFIELD
Co Durham
Map**12** NZ15

H The Banqueting House Gibside
for bookings The Landmark Trust, Shottesbrooke, Maidenhead, Berkshire SL6 3SW
☎Littlewick Green(062882)5925

An exceptional 18th-century Gothic building, once the banqueting house of the now derelict Gibside Hall. Restored by local craftsmen, it is peacefully situated in a delightful woodland setting overlooking the Derwent Valley. Accommodation, all on ground-floor, comprises kitchen, bedroom and elegant, stately lounge with open fire and two single convertible beds.

All year MWB out of season 3nights min, 7nights max, 1unit, 4persons no cats ⓦ fridge Electric & open fires Elec inclusive ⌷inclusive ☎(2m) Iron & Ironing board in unit ⌾ ⊕3pin square ⊕3pin round 4P ▦(2m) ↔ ♪(1m) ☕(1m) ♫(2m) ♫(2m)
Min£133 Max£220pw (Low)
Min£155 Max£240pw (High)

BURTON IN LONSDALE
North Yorkshire
Map**7** SD67

C Badger Gate Barn & Poachers Cottage Leeming Lane
for bookings Mrs G S Wood, The Goodies Farmhouse, Firbank, Sedbergh, Cumbria
☎Sedbergh(0587)21087

Burgh by Sands
—
Bute

Two delightfully furnished old cottages full of character and interest. **Badgers Gate Barn** includes a spacious lounge on the first-floor, two ground-floor bedrooms (one twin, one double) plus bed-settee in the lounge. **Poachers Cottage** includes bedrooms (one double, one with three single beds), well furnished lounge and shower room. Both have oak beams and stone walls.

All year MWB out of season 1wk min, 2units, 2–6persons ⓦ fridge ᴹ Elec metered ⌷not provided ☎(200yds) Iron & Ironing board in unit ⌾ CTV ⊕3pin square 1P ▥ ▦(500yds) ↔ ♪(3m) ☕ (200yds)
Min£75 Max£85pw (Low)
Min£115 Max£180pw (High)

C Greta Holiday Cottages Bridge End
for bookings Mrs C Brown, Bridge Cottage, Burton in Lonsdale, Carnforth, Lancs LA6 3LJ
☎Bentham(0468)61874

Two, modernised, but very old and beamed cottages situated by the River Greta on the outskirts of the village. Accommodation comprises two bedrooms, lounge, kitchen/diner and a bathroom on first-floor.

All year MWB out of season 1wk min, 1mth max, 2units, 2–5persons ◆ ◆ ⓦ fridge Electric Elec inclusive ⌷inclusive ☎(¼m) SD in unit Iron & Ironing board in unit ⌾ CTV ⊕3pin square 4P ▥ ▦(¼m) ↔ ♪(3m) ☕ (¼m)
Min£65 Max£85pw (Low)
Min£90 Max£105pw (High)

BURWASH
East Sussex
Map**5** TQ62

F Mr & Mrs M A Ramsden **Southover Place** Spring Lane, Burwash, East Sussex TN19 7JA
☎Burwash(0435)882445

New luxurious apartments, created from a restored monastery, set in seven acres of beautiful countryside, they comprise either 1, 2, 3, or 6 bedrooms, lounge/diner with mahogany dining suite, regency style log effect fire, remote controlled television and wall folding double bed. Open plan luxury kitchen with ceramic top cooker, deep freeze, microwave oven and dishwasher. The en suite bathroom/WC with shower attachment is fully tiled.

All year MWB out of season 1wk min, 6mth max, 15units, 1–8persons, nc12 no pets ⓦ fridge Electric Elec metered ⌷inclusive except tea clothes & towels ☎ [WM, SD & TD on

premises] Iron & Ironing board in unit ⌾ CTV ⊕3pin square 20P ▥ ▦(1m) sauna, solarium, snooker table, Horse riding ▨ ✚hard ↔ ♪(3m) ☕(1m) ♫(1m)
Min£99 Max£204pw (Low)
Min£189 Max£441pw (High)

BURWELL
Cambridgeshire
Map**5** TL56

F Adventurers
for bookings Mr D Whitehouse, 123 North Street, Burwell, Cambridgeshire CB5 0BB
☎Newmarket(0638)741948

The Flat is part of a 17th century house with its own separate entrance located in a very peaceful part of the village. It comprises lounge/dining room, kitchen, two bedrooms (one double and one bunk-bedded) and bathroom/WC. It is tastefully decorated and has an open fireplace and exposed beams.

All year MWB out of season 3days min 2wks max 1unit 1–4persons [◇] ◆ ◆ no pets & single sex groups ⓦ fridge storage heaters Elec metered ⌷inclusive ☎(½m) [WM, SD & TD on premises] Iron & Ironing board on premises ☎ ⊕3pin square 2P ▥ ▦(½m) fishing ↔ ☕(½m) ♫(½m) ♫(½m)
Min£70 Max£130pw

BUTE, Isle of Strathclyde Buteshire
Map**10**

ROTHESAY
Strathclyde Buteshire
Map**10** NS06

C & F Prospect Cottage A Prospect House Flats 1 & 2 Marine Road
for bookins Mr & Mrs Shaw, Morningside, Mount Pleasant Road, Rothersay, Isle of Bute
☎Rothesay(0700)3526

Five self-contained flats located within large white-painted house, situated in own grounds, 20yds from the sea. All comprise lounge/kitchen/dining room, one or two bedrooms and bathroom except for one flat which has two bedrooms with shower/ WC's en suite. Some flats have sofa bed in lounge and all are well decorated and furnished. Small cottage in grounds adjoining the flats, comprising large bedroom sleeping up to three, bathroom, kitchen/diner and lounge with double bed-settee.

All year MWB 2days min, 4wks max, 6units, 1–6persons ◆ ⓦ fridge ᴹ Elec metered except hot water & heating ⌷inclusive ☎ WM & SD in one unit only Iron & Ironing board in unit ⌾ CTV ⊕3pin square P ▦(100yds) ↔ ♪(½m) ☕(½m) ♫(½m) ♫(1m)
Min£89 Max£145pw (Low)
Min£125 Max£185pw (High)

BUTTERSTONE
Tayside *Perthshire*
Map**15** NO04

Ca   Butterstone Log Cabins Ltd
Butterstone, Dunkeld, Perthshire
☎Butterstone(03504)234/205

A group of ten sturdy Scandinavian spruce log cabins lying in sheltered wooded clearing by small burn. Each has three bedrooms – a double, one with two single beds and a bunk bed above each and one room with bunk beds. There is a living/dining room with small open-plan kitchen area, a bathroom with bath and shower (hand). Butterstone village is 5m E of Dunkeld on A923 amidst loch and mountain scenery.

All year   MWB out of season   1wk min, 1mth max, 10units, 1–8persons ◆ ◎ fridge   Electric   Elec inclusive Ⓛinclusive ☎(200yds) ☺ CTV ⊕3pin square   2P Ⓜ ♨(4m) Fishing
£156pw (Low)
£270pw (High)

BUXTON
Derbyshire
Map**7** SK07

F   Mr & Mrs D A Swain **Hillside** 1 Spencer Road, Buxton, Derbyshire SK17 9DX
☎Buxton(0298)5451

A well furnished, spacious stone-built flat situated in quiet road close to town centre. Accommodation comprises lounge, well-equipped kitchen, spacious bathroom/WC and two bedrooms (one double & one twin)

All year   MWB out of season 1wk min 1unit 2–4persons nc12 no pets ◎ fridge ♨ Elec inclusive Ⓛinclusive ☎(½m) WM, SD & TD in unit   Iron & Ironing board in unit   ☺ ❀ CTV ⊕3pin square ⚽ Ⓜ ♨(½m) ⊖ ♪(1m) ♀ (50yds) 🎵(½m) ♫(½m)
🏓(½m)

Min£100 Max£140pw

BYRNESS
Northumberland
Map**12** NT70

C   **Rose Cottage**
for bookings Mr R H Armstrong, Border Park Service Station, Byrness, Otterburn, Newcastle upon Tyne NE19 1TR
☎Otterburn(0830)20271

Single-storey cottage converted from a village school room. Accommodation comprises living room, two twin-bedded rooms with two additional bunk beds in one, modern kitchen and bathroom/WC.

All year   MWB out of season 1wk min, 3mths max, 1unit, 1–6persons ◆ ◎ fridge ♨ Elec metered Ⓛnot provided ☎(½m) WM & SD in unit Iron & Ironing board in unit   ☺ CTV ⊕3pin square P ♨(60yds)
⊖ ♀ (100yds)

Min£40 Max£60pw (Low)
Min£70 Max£140pw (High)

Butterstone
—
Caernarfon

CADBURY
Devon
Map**3** SS90

F   **East & North Wing Flats & Gable Flat**
for bookings Mr D Fursdon, Fursdon House, Cadbury, Thorverton, Exeter, Devon EX5 5JS
☎Exeter(0392)860860

*Flats situated in two wings of a delightful country mansion, secluded within a large estate. Accommodation varies, with **North Wing** having one bedroom with four-poster and one with bunk-beds and **East Wing** having two twin-bedrooms and one single. **Gable Flat** comprises double bedroom, lounge/diner, kitchen and bathroom/WC. All offer fine views over the estate.*

All year   3days min, 4wks max, 3units, 1–5persons [◇] ◆ ◆ no pets 𝄢 ◎(Gable Flat) fridge ♨ & open fires Gas & Elec inclusive(lighting) Elec metered(heating) Ⓛcan be hired WM & SD on premises   Iron & Ironing board in unit   P Ⓜ ♨(2m) 🎵grass Croquet
⊖ ♀ (2m)

Min£60 Max£100pw (Low)
Min£145 Max£175pw (High)

H   **Lime House**
for bookings Mr D Fursdon, Fursdon House, Cadbury, Thorverton, Exeter, Devon EX5 5JS
☎Exeter(0392)860860

Detached stone-built house set in a garden within the grounds of Fursdon House. Accommodation includes kitchen, dining room, lounge, four bedrooms, bathrooms/WC and separate WC.

All year   MWB out of season   3days min, 4wks max, 1 unit, 1–8persons ◎ fridge Electric & open fires Elec metered Ⓛcan be hired   Iron, & Ironing board in unit ☺ CTV ⊕3pin square P Ⓜ ♨(2m) 🎵grass Croquet

Min£65 Max£140pw (Low)
Min£185 Max£220pw (High)

H   **East Wing,** Fursdon Barton
for bookings Mr D Fursdon, Fursdon House, Cadbury, Thorverton, Exeter, Devon EX5 5JS
☎Exeter(0392)860860

Wing of old stone farmhouse located within the grounds of a large estate. Accommodation comprises kitchen/diner with Rayburn, lounge, three bedrooms, bathroom and WC. Delightful position and good standard of furnishings and fittings.

All year   3days min, 4wks max, 1unit, 1–6persons ◎ fridge Elec & wood burning stove Elec metered Ⓛcan be hired   Iron & Ironing board in unit   ☺ CTV ⊕3pin square P Ⓜ ♨(2m) 🎵grass Croquet
⊖ ♀ (2m)

Min£40 Max£65pw (Low)
Min£100 Max£200pw (High)

CADGWITH
Cornwall
Map**2** SW71

C   **CC Ref 307 EL**
for bookings Character Cottages (Holidays) Ltd, 34 Fore Street, Sidmouth, Devon EX10 8AQ
☎Sidmouth(03955)77001

Stone-built cottage with patio and five steps to beach. The accommodation consists of large lounge and modern kitchen and an open-tread staircase to two double and two single bedrooms and a bathroom/WC.

All year   MWB out of season   1wk min, 1mth max, 1unit, 2–6persons ◆ ◆ ◎ fridge Electric Elec metered Ⓛcan be hired ☎(50yds) Iron & Ironing board in unit ☺ TV ⊕3pin square ⊕2 pin round P Ⓜ ♨(50yds)
⊖ ♀

Min£101 Max£158pw (Low)
Min£179 Max£245pw (High)

F   **CC Ref 316 EL (1,2 & 3)**
for bookings Character Cottages (Holidays) Ltd, 34 Fore Street, Sidmouth, Devon EX10 8AQ
☎Sidmouth(03955)77001

*Three maisonettes located in a block and timber building near to the sea. Flats 1 & 3 have a ground floor with one twin and one single bedroom and a first floor with living room, well appointed kitchen, double bedroom and bathroom/WC. **Flat 2** also has two floors comprising two twin-bedded rooms, one double-bedded room, 'L' shaped living room with an open ceiling, kitchen/diner, bathroom and separate WC.*

All year   MWB out of season   1wk min, 1mth max, 3units, 2–6persons ◇ ◆ no pets ◎ fridge ♨ Elec inclusive Ⓛcan be hired ☎(50yds) Iron & Ironing board in unit ☺ TV ⊕3pin square ⊕2pin round P Ⓜ ♨
⊖ ♀

Min£76 Max£107pw (Low)
Min£142 Max£194pw (High)

CAERNARFON
Gwynedd
Map**6** SH46

F   **The Bath Tower**
for booking Landmark Trust, Shottesbrooke, Maidenhead, Berkshire SL6 3SW
☎Littlewick Green(062882)5925

Facing the Menai Strait this converted tower forms part of the 13th-century town wall. It comprises a modern kitchen, combined lounge/diner and bathroom on the entrance floor. A spiral staircase descends to an immense bedroom with three single beds and separate WC. There is also a twin-bedded room with terrace on the first floor.

62

All year MWB out of season 2 nights min,
6 wks max, 1 unit, 2–5 persons ◆ ◎
fridge Storage heaters & electric fire
Elec inclusive ▢not provided
☎(200yds) Iron & Ironing board in unit
☉ ⊕3 pin square 🔲 ▥(300yds)
↤ ♪(3m) ♀(100yds) ♫(¼m)
Min£154 Max£275pw (Low)
Min£185 Max£285pw (High)

Ch Glan Gwna Private Riverside Chalets
for bookings Mr P G Hill Turner, Ivy
Cottage, 20 Mount Scar, Swanage, Dorset
BH19 2EZ
☎Swanage(0929)426360

Wood and slate chalets comprising an
open-plan kitchen/diner, lounge, two or
three bedrooms and combined bathroom/
WC. There is a bed settee in the lounge.

15Mar–31Oct MWB out of season 1mth
max, 6 units, 1–8 persons [◇ ◆ ◆]
pets charged for ◎ fridge Electric
Elec metered ▢inclusive ☎(200yds)
[Launderette within 300yds] ☉ CTV
⊕3 pin square P ▥(200yds) ⌂
↤ ♪(3m) ♀(200yds)
Min£50 Max£205pw

CALCETHORPE
Lincolnshire
Map**8** TF28

C Lincolnshire Wolds Cottages (Swift & Swallow)
for bookings C V Stubbs & Sons, Warren
Farm, Welton-le-Wold, Louth, Lincolnshire
LN11 0QX
☎Louth(0507)604207

A pair of semi-detached, two-storey, brick-
built farmworkers' cottages dating from
the 1920s standing in a quiet country lane
in the midst of the Lincolnshire Wolds.
Situated off the A157, about 5m W of
Louth. The accommodation comprises
one double bedroom, lounge/diner and
kitchen on the ground floor and one
single-bedded room and one twin-bedded
room on the first-floor.

All year MWB out of season 1wk min,
2 units, 5 persons ◆ ◎ fridge
Electric Elec metered except heating
▢can be hired ☎(1½m) Iron & Ironing

Caernarfon
—
Calvine

board in unit TV ⊕3 pin square P
▥(3m)
↤ ♀(3m)
Min£66 Max£80pw (Low)
Min£92 Max£120pw (High)

CALLANDER
Central Perthshire
Map**11** NN60

Ca Strathyre Forest Cabins
for bookings Forestry Commission, (Dept
A.A.) 231 Corstorphine Road, Edinburgh
EH12 7AT
☎031-334 0303 or 334 2576

A complex of 17 log cabins set on a
secluded, elevated site with views over
Loch Lubnaig and surrounding hills. The
cabins offer combined lounge/diner/
kitchen, one twin-bedded and one single-
bedded room (plus double bunks) and
shower room/WC.

Closed Nov MWB out of season
3 days min, 6 wks max, 17 units,
1–5 persons ◆ ◆ ◎ fridge
Electric Elec metered ▢inclusive ☎
Iron & Ironing board on premises
[Launderette on premises] ☉
⊕3 pin square 17P ▥(3m) fishing
canoeing
↤ ♪(3m) ♀(2m) ♫(3m) ♬(3m)
Min£67 Max£225pw

CALSTOCK
Cornwall
Map**2** SX46

H The Danescombe Mine
for bookings Landmark Trust,
Shottesbrooke, Maidenhead, Berkshire
SL6 3SW
☎Littlewick Green(062882)5925

Converted from the ruined tower of a
disused pump house, beautifully situated
in wooded valley. There are stone steps to
the split level lounge, kitchen and dining
area, a metal staircase leads to the second
level with a twin bedroom and WC. Further

---

metal stairs to the third level with another
twin bedroom and bathroom.

All year MWB out of season 1 unit,
4 persons ◆ ◎ fridge
Underfloor heating Elec inclusive
▢not provided ☎(1m) Iron & Ironing
board in unit ☉ ⊕3 pin square 2P
▥(2m)
↤ ♀(1m)
Min£126 Max£255pw (Low)
Min£170 Max£255pw (High)

CALVER
Derbyshire
Map**7** SK27

C Mrs S V Brooks Whitegates Riddings
Lane, Curbar, Calver, Derbyshire S30 1YN
☎Hope Valley(0433)30300

In a rural position, this semi-detached
cottage with attractive gardens comprises
lounge with bed settee, dining room,
kitchen, shower/WC, one double bedded
room and one twin bedded room.

All year MWB out of season 1wk min
1 unit 1–5 persons ◆ ◎ fridge 🍴&
electric fires Elec metered ▢inclusive
☎(¼m) Iron & Ironing board in unit
CTV ⊕3 pin square 3P 1🏠 🔲
▥(¾m)
↤ ♀(¼m) ♫(2m)
Min£45 Max£150pw

CALVINE
Tayside Perthshire
Map**14** NN86

C Cuildaaloskin Cottage
for bookings Mrs Wendy Stewart, Clachan
of Struan, Calvine, Pitlochry, Perthshire
PH18 5UB
☎Calvine(079683)207

Quaint little detached former shepherd's
cottage surrounded by grazing land.
Accommodation comprises living room
(with double bed-settee), dining room,
kitchen and upstairs a twin bedroom, a
bedroom with one double and one single
bed, and bathroom. Décor furnishings
and fitments are simple but the cottage is
not without charm or character. Lies just
off B847 close to the River Errochty 1½m W
of Calvine, which itself is on the A9 12m N
of Pitlochry. →

Etr–Oct MWB out of season 1wk min,
1unit, 1–5persons ◆ ◆ ◎ fridge
Electric Elecmetered ⎣can be hired
☎(1½m) Iron & Ironing board in unit
☉ TV ⊕3pin square 4P ♨(1½m)
⊖ ♀(1½m)
Max£110pw

CAMBRIDGE
Cambridgeshire
Map5 TL45

H **20 Water Street** Old Chesterton
for bookings Mrs S J Mackay, 'Roebuck
House', 28 Ferry Lane, Chesterton,
Cambridge
☎Cambridge(0223)60000
*A semi-detached house built in 1936 and
located in a quiet part of Cambridge.
Accommodation comprises lounge, dining
room, kitchen and cloakroom/WC on the
ground floor and two doubles and one
single bedroom, bathroom and separate
WC upstairs. The rear garden gently
slopes down to the banks of the River
Cam.*

Allyear MWB out of season 2nights min
1mth max, 1unit, 1–5persons [◇] ◆
◆ ◔ fridge ♨ Gasinclusive ⎣can
be hired ☎ [WM & SD in unit] Iron &
Ironing board in unit ☉ ⑭ CTV
⊕3pin square ⫙ ♨(200yds) fishing
bicycle hire
⊖ ♀(10yds) ☷(1½m) ♫(1½m)
⚘(1½m)
Min£125 Max£150pw (Low)
Min£205pw (High)

F Mr & Mrs S J Wilson **Whitehouse
Holiday Apartments** Conduit Head Road,
Cambridge CB3 0EY
☎Cambridge(0223)67110 & Madingley
(0954)211361

Calvine
—
Cannich

*A block of eight flats on two floors each
comprising one double- and one single-
bedded room, lounge with double bed-
settee, kitchen and bathroom. Maid
service is available at extra cost. Located
1¼m from the centre of Cambridge just off
the A1303.*

Allyear MWB 2days min, 42days max,
8units, 1–5persons [◇] ◆
◔(3units) ◎(5units) fridge ♨ Gas/
Elecmetered ⎣inclusive ☎ Iron &
Ironing board in unit [Launderette on
premises] ☉ CTV ⊕3pin square
25P ⫙ ♨(1m)
⊖ ᶑ(2m) ♀(½m) ☷(1m) ♫(1m)
⚘(1m)
Min£89.70 Max£100.63pw (Low)
Min£158.70 Max£172.50pw (High)

CAMELFORD
Cornwall
Map2 SX18
See **Helstone**

CAMPBELTOWN
Strathclyde *Argyllshire*
Map10 NR72

C Col & Mrs W T C Angus **Kilchrist
Castle Holiday Cottages** Campbeltown,
Argyll PA28 6PH
☎Campbeltown(0586)53210
*The 17th-century Old Byre of Kilchrist has
been rebuilt to provide one three-
bedroomed, three two-bedroomed and
one one-bedroomed cottages, the
smallest of which is detached. The one-
bedroomed, circular-shaped former*

---

*gatehouse has also been rebuilt and is
detached. All have lounge/diner/kitchen
and small shower room. The
accommodation is surrounded by
farmland in the grounds of Kilchrist Castle.*

Etr–Oct MWB 1wk min, 6units,
1–6persons ◆ ◆ ◎ fridge
Electric Elecmetered ⎣inclusive
☎(600yds) Iron & Ironing board in unit
☉ CTV ⊕3pin square P ♨(1m)
Children's playground
⊖ ♀(3m) ☷(3m) ♫(3m) ⚘(3m)
Min£68 Max£91pw (Low)
Min£120 Max£160pw (High)

C **Oatfield Cottage**
for bookings Mrs G E Staples, Oatfield
House, Southend Road, Campbeltown,
Argyll PA28 6PH
☎Campbeltown(0586)52601
*Formerly the coachman's cottage, this
small cottage stands beside Oatfield
House within seven acres of grounds and
woods. The simple accommodation
comprises downstairs kitchen, with dining
table, separate lounge with steep staircase
leading to two upstairs bedrooms. Off
A842 Campbeltown/Southend road, 3m
from Campbeltown.*

Etr–Oct 1wk min, 1unit 1–4 persons
◇ ◆ ◆ ◎ fridge Electric
Elecmetered ⎣inclusive ☎(½m) Iron &
Ironing board in unit CTV
⊕3pin square P ♨(1½m)
⊖ ♀(3m) ☷(3m) ♫(3m) ⚘(3m)
Min£85 Max£135pw

CANNICH
Highland *Inverness-shire*
Map14 NH33

C **The Croft** Tomich
for bookings Col J A Fraser, Tomuaine,
Tomich, Beauly, Inverness-shire
☎Cannich(04565)220

Stone cottage rebuilt in 1979 situated at the foot of a tree-studded hillside in a secluded south facing position. The accommodation comprises living room with two single beds, one twin-bedded room, kitchen/diner and bathroom/WC.

18Apr–26Sep 1wk min, 1mth max, 1unit, 1–4persons [◈] ◎ fridge Electric Elec metered ⌷not provided ☎(½m) Iron & Ironing board in unit ⊙ CTV ⊕3pin square 2P ▦(4m) Fishing

Min£70 Max£90pw

Ch & C D J Fraser **Guisachan Farm Chalets** Tomich, Cannich, Beauly, Inverness-shire IV4 7LY
☎Cannich(04565)332

The six chalets are situated in a clearance in the woods. Each has a verandah and balcony, open plan kitchen/diner/lounge with convertible settee, bathroom, cloakroom, one double and two twin-bedded rooms. The cottage is a listed property that has been tastefully modernised. Situated beside the farm complex, it comprises large kitchen/diner, small sitting room with bed settee, cloakroom, one twin bedroom and bathroom.

Etr–Oct 1wk min, 5wks max, 7units, 4–8persons [◈ ◆] ◎ fridge electric Elec metered ⌷can be hired ☎(150yds) Iron & Ironing board in unit ⊙ CTV ⊕3pin square P ▦(4m) ⊠(heated at nearby Farm complex) games room

Min£64 Max£180pw

H   University of Kent
for bookings The Conference Officer, The Registry, University of Kent, Canterbury, Kent CT2 7NZ
☎Canterbury(0227)69186

Clustered around informal quadrangles, these units comprised of two-storey apartments each containing either four bedrooms (one twin-bedded) and a lounge; or five single bedrooms. All have kitchen/diner and shower/WC.

4Jul–19Sep MWB in season 1wk min, 40units, 2–5persons [◈] no pets noise restriction after 11pm ◔ fridge 🍴 Gas inclusive ⌷inclusive except towels ☎(200yds) Iron & Ironing board in unit [Launderette within 300yds] ⊙ TV can be hired ⊕3pin square 1P ▦ ⚲Hard Squash, badminton & library
⊖ ♫(3m) ⊠(3m) ⚐(200yds) ♫(3m) ♫(3m) 🎮(3m)

£130pw (Low)
£175pw (High)

Cannich
—
Cardinham

H   White Owl Farmhouse
for bookings Mrs P J H Packwood, Rookery Farm, Brockhurst, Canwell, Sutton Coldfield, West Midlands B75 5SR
☎021-308 1039

Brick-built farmhouse standing in its own garden overlooking the surrounding countryside. Accommodation comprises kitchen, dining room and lounge both with open fires, bathroom/WC and three bedrooms.

All year MWB 1night min, 3wks max, 1unit, 1–7persons [◇] ◈ ◆ no pets ◎ fridge Electric & open fires Elec metered ⌷can be hired ☎(1m) WM & SD in unit Iron & Ironing board in unit ⊙ ⊛ CTV ⊕3pin square 4P ▦(2m) Farm produce available
⊖ ♫(3m) ♪(1½m) 🎵(1½m)

Min£57.50 Max£77.50pw (Low)
Min£67.50 Max£87.50pw (High)

F   Coach House (Flats)
for bookings Mr & Mrs Hobbs, Cilbronnau Mansion, Llangoedmor, Cardigan, Dyfed SA43 2LP
☎Llechryd(023987)254

Two flats located within a converted coach house, the Ground-floor flat comprises two bedrooms, lounge with bed-settee, kitchen/diner, shower and WC. The First-floor flat has lounge with convertible settee, one double-bedded room, kitchen/diner and bathroom/WC. 1m E of Cardigan on B4570.

All year MWB out of season 3nights min, 2units, 4–6persons ◈ ◆ ◎ fridge Electric Elec metered ⌷can be hired ☎(400yds) WM & SD on premises Iron & Ironing board in unit ⊙ CTV ⊕3pin square 4P ▦(2m)
⊖ ♫(4m) ♪(1½m) 🎵(2m)

Min£60 Max£185pw

C   Tycanol (Middle House)
for bookings Mrs Y Davies, Trenewydd Farm, St Dogmaels, Cardigan, Dyfed
☎Cardigan(0239)612370

One of three cottages on this 12-acre smallholding. Converted from farm buildings, they have an attractive modern design and are close to the National Park. Ideal for a family of five, Tycanol has two bedrooms, one with a double bed and one single and the other with two singles. Also there is a combined bathroom and WC, sitting room and kitchen. 3m W of Cardigan off B4546.

All year MWB out of season 3nights min, 1unit, 5persons ◈ ◆ ◎ fridge 🍴 Electric Electric metered after 150 units ⌷inclusive ☎(1½m) WM & SD in unit

---

Iron & Ironing board in unit ⊙ CTV ⊕3pin square P ▦ ▦(1½m)
⊖ ♪(1½m) 🎵(3m)
Min£90 Max£255pw

C   Tymawr (Big House)
for bookings Mrs Y Davies, Trenewydd Farm, St Dogmaels, Cardigan, Dyfed
☎Cardigan(0239)612370

Set out on two levels, there is a double-bedded room, a twin-bedded room and a further room with bunks on the ground floor, and a pleasant sitting room and kitchen/diner, combined bathroom and WC on the first floor. 3m W of Cardigan off B4546.

All year MBW out of season 3nights min, 1unit, 6persons ◈ ◆ ◎ fridge 🍴 Electric Electric metered after 150 units ⌷inclusive ☎(1½m) WM & SD in unit Iron & Ironing board in unit ⊙ CTV ⊕3pin square P ▦ ▦(1½m)
⊖ ♪(1½m) 🎵(3m)
Min£95 Max£285pw

C   Tytwt (Small House)
for bookings Mrs Y Davies, Trenewydd Farm, St Dogmaels, Cardigan, Dyfed
☎Cardigan(0239)612370

Compact and nicely appointed two-bedroomed cottage with lounge/diner, separate kitchen and combined bathroom and WC. 3m W of Cardigan off B4546. 2½m from Poppit Sands.

All year MWB out of season 3nights min, 1unit, 4persons ◈ ◆ ◎ fridge 🍴 Electric Electric metered after 150 units ⌷inclusive ☎(1½m) WM & SD in unit Iron & Ironing board in unit ⊙ CTV ⊕3pin square P ▦ ▦(1½m)
⊖ ♪(1½m) 🎵(3m)
Min£85 Max£240pw

F   Courtyard, Coachhouse, Hayloft & Stable Flats
For bookings Mrs A M Kerslake, Cardinham House, Cardinham, Bodmin, Cornwall PL30 4BL
☎Cardinham(020882)297

Four converted flats within wing of Cardinham House set in four acres. All comprise lounge/kitchen/diner, bathroom/shower/WC (except Hayloft which has shower/WC), one or two bedrooms and a bed-settee in lounge.

All year MWB out of season 4units, 1–6persons [◇ ◈ ◆] no pets except dogs ◎ fridge Electric Elec metered ⌷not provided (except for overseas visitors) ☎(200yds) SD in unit except Hayloft Iron & Ironing board in unit ⊙ CTV ⊕3pin square P ▦ ▦(2m) ⚲ Children's play area
⊖ ♪(3m)
Min£75 Max£140pw

CARLISLE
Cumbria
See **Welton**

CARRBRIDGE
Highland *Inverness-shire*
Map**14** NH82

Ch Mrs E Reed **Fairwinds** Carrbridge,
Inverness-shire PH23 3AA
☎Carrbridge(047984)240

Two and three bedroom chalet
bungalows, sleeping up to six people. Set
in the 7-acre grounds of Fairwinds Hotel.
Full use of hotel facilities.

All year MWB out of season 2 days min,
6 units, 1–6 persons ◆ ◆ ⊚ fridge
卿 Elec metered 🔲 inclusive
☎(200yds) WM Iron & Ironing board in
unit ⊙ CTV ⊕3 pin square 15P
🛁(300yds)
⊖ ♪(500yds) 🍴 🎵(400yds)
Min£130 Max£160pw (Low)
Min£235 Max£285pw (High)

Ch Manager **Lochanhully Lodges**
Carrbridge, Inverness-shire (or any AA
Travel Agency)
☎Carrbridge(047984)234

Fifty timber-constructed Finnish chalets
with south-facing views. They are set
amidst birch trees ½m E of Carrbridge and
the A9 on the A938 Grantown road. Each
chalet consists of a double-bedded room,
bunk-bedded room, bathroom, large living

Carlisle
—
Castlebay

room (with double bed-settee, pine table
seating, french windows and balcony) and
kitchen area. Lochanhully Lake is well
stocked with rainbow trout. There is also
an artificial ski slope and a games room
on site.

Closed Nov–13 Dec MWB 5 wks max,
50 units, 1–6 persons ◆ ◆ ⊚ fridge
Electric Elec inclusive 🔲 inclusive ☎
Airing cupboard in unit Iron & Ironing
board on premises Launderette on
premises ⊙ CTV ⊕3 pin square P
🛁(½m) ▭
⊖ ♪(½m) 🍴 🎵(½m)
Min£135 Max£285pw

C Mrs M Sinclair **Slochd Cottages**
Carrbridge, Inverness-shire
☎Carrbridge (047984)666

Situated 4m N of Carrbridge just off the A9,
three stone-built cottages in a clearing
surrounded by hills with distant views over
the Cairngorms. Accommodation consists
of two bedrooms, lounge, kitchen and
shower/WC.

All year MWB out of season 1 wk min,
2 wks max, 3 units, 2–6 persons ◆ ⊚
fridge electric & open fires

Elec metered 🔲not provided ☎(4m)
Iron & Ironing board on premises P
🛁(4m)
Min£85 Max£99pw (Low)
Min£120pw (High)

CARSAIG
Strathclyde *Argyll*
See **Mull, Isle of**

CARTMEL
Cumbria
Map**7** SD37

F Mr & Mrs E Smith **Aynsome Manor
Park** Cartmel, Cumbria LA11 6HH
☎Cartmel(044854)433

Five attractive flats situated on Aynsome
Manor Estate with its eight acres of
farmland, woodland and informal
gardens. Sleeping two to four people.

All year MWB out of season 2 days min
3 mths max 5 units 2–4 persons nc 8 yrs
no cats ⊚ fridge storage heaters
Elec metered 🔲can be hired ☎(½m)
[WM on premises] CTV ⊕3 pin square
15P 🎬 🛁(½m)
⊖ ♪(1m) 🍴(1m)
Min£25 Max£35pw (Low)
Min£75 Max£125pw (High)

CASTLEBAY
Western Isles *Inverness-shire*
See **Barra, Isle of**

CASTLE DOUGLAS
Dumfries & Galloway *Kirkcudbrightshire*
Map11 NX76

B   Ardencaple
for bookings G M Thomson & Co, 27 King Street, Castle Douglas, Kirkcudbrightshire DG7 1AB
☎Castle Douglas(0556)2701 & 2973

One unit of a divided bungalow in a quiet residential part of the town centrally situated just off town centre, near hospital. Consists of double-bedded and twin-bedded rooms, small sitting room with bed-settee, compact basic kitchen (calor gas cooking), bathroom and WC.

Mar–Nov 1wk min, 1unit, 1–5persons
◆ no pets no ball games ◎ fridge
Electric Elec inclusive ⌷not provided
☎(200yds) CTV ⊕3pin square P ▥
▨(200yds)
↔ ♪(200yds) ♨(200yds) ♫(200yds)
♬(200yds) ♨(200yds)

£80pw (Low)
£140pw (High)

C   Ellislade
for bookings G M Thomson & Co, 27 King Street, Castle Douglas, Kirkcudbrightshire DG7 1AB
☎Castle Douglas(0556)2701 & 2973

A neat roadside cottage with its own garden, situated in pleasant farmland on B975 2m from Castle Douglas. It comprises

---

**Castle Douglas
—
Caswell Bay**

two double-bedded rooms, sitting room with bed-settee, dining room and small kitchen.

Etr–Oct & Xmas–New Year 1wk min,
1unit, 1–5persons ◎ fridge
electric fires Elec inclusive
⌷not provided ☎(2m) Iron & Ironing board in unit ⊕ ◐ CTV
⊕3pin square P ▥ ▨(2m)
↔ ♪(2m) ♨(2m)

£85pw (Low)
£155pw (High)

C   Livingstone Cottage Balmaghie
for bookings G M Thomson & Co, 27 King Street, Castle Douglas, Kirkcudbrightshire DG7 1AB
☎Castle Douglas(0556)2701 & 2973

A simple, single-storey stone-cottage in peaceful woodland setting, reached by way of a short track. It comprises two bedrooms, living room and small kitchen, and is situated just past Livingstone House (see below).

Mar–Nov 1wk min, 1unit, 1–4persons
◎ fridge Electric & open fires
Elec inclusive ⌷not provided ☎(2¼m)
Iron & Ironing board in unit TV
⊕3pin square P ▨(5m)

£80pw (Low)
£140pw (High)

H   Livingstone House
for bookings G M Thomson & Co, 27 King Street, Castle Douglas, Kirkcudbrightshire DG7 1AB
☎Castle Douglas(0556)2701 & 2973

A fine 18th-century country house on three floors with spacious accommodation; dining room, sitting room, large kitchen, games room, WC, two bathrooms and five bedrooms sleeping a total of eight people. Large 24-acre garden beside River Dee. Access via B795 towards Laurieston. Turn right after crossing Glenlochar Bridge. After 2m house on right.

Mar–Nov 1wk min, 1unit, 1–8persons
◆ ◎ fridge Electric & open fires
Elec inclusive ⌷not provided ☎ WM & SD in unit Iron & Ironing board in unit
⊕ TV ⊕3pin square P ▨(5m)
Fishing

£150pw (Low)
£315pw (High)

CASWELL BAY
West Glamorgan
Map2 SS58

F   309–310 Redcliffe Apartments
for bookings Mr & Mrs B & M Davies, Bar Marc Holiday Properties, 7A Redcliffe, Caswell Bay, Swansea, W Glamorgan SA3 3BT
☎Swansea(0792)69169 →

Self-Catering in luxury
Scandinavian Lodges from only
£3.90 per person per night

Lochanhully Lodges set in spectacular Highland scenery seven miles from Aviemore. Fully equipped Scandinavian self-catering lodges that sleep 6 comfortably from £140 per week per lodge.

Local activities include golf, fishing, pony-trekking, hill walking and skiing. Or, take a dip in our very own heated indoor swimming pool.

For more details contact your local AA Travel Agent. Or book direct to: Lochanhully Lodges, (AAS/C), Carrbridge, Inverness-shire PH23 3NA. Tel: 047 984234.

LOCHANHULLY LODGES

Situated in an apartment block at the water's edge. Purpose-built accommodation of open plan design with large lounge (and double bed-settee), balcony, double bedroom and shower room/WC.

All year MWB out of season 1wk min, 3mths max, 2units, 2–4persons ◆
no pets ◎ fridge Electric
Elec metered 🗔not provided
☎(300yds) ☺ CTV ⊕3pin square
P 🛁(¾m)
↔ ♀(½m)
Max£72pw (Low)
Max£149pw (High)

CATLOWDY
Cumbria
Map**12** NY47

C Mr & Mrs J Sisson **Bessiestown Farm**
Penton, Carlisle, Cumbria CA6 5QP
☎Nicholforest(022877)219

Three stone cottages converted from an old barn and stable in farmhouse courtyard, comprising open plan lounge/diner/kitchen on the first floor which affords panoramic views of the Borders and Solway countryside. All have two double bedrooms (additional bunk beds on request) and a bathroom/WC on ground floor.

All year MWB out of season 3nights min, 3units 4–6persons ◆ ◆ fridge

---

🍴(part) Elec metered 🗔not provided
☎(100yds) ⊕3pin square 20P
🛁(100yds) ▣ Games room, horse riding
↔ ♀
Min£60 Max£100pw (Low)
Min£160 Max£190pw (High)

CAULDON
Staffordshire
Map**7** SK04

C Mrs N Burndred **Park View Cottage**
Park View Farm, Cauldon, Waterhouses, Staffordshire ST10 3EP
☎Waterhouses(05386)233

Red brick semi-detached cottage situated on the edge of Peak National Park in Staffordshire moorlands, offering comfortable accommodation. Ground floor comprises of lounge, kitchen/diner, bathroom and separate WC, whilst upstairs there are three bedrooms.

All year MWB out of season 1unit, 6persons ◇ ◆ ◆ fridge 🍴 &
Electric Elec inclusive 🗔inclusive
☎(300yds) WM in unit Iron & Ironing board in unit ☺ ⑮ CTV
⊕3pin square 2P ▥ 🛁(300yds)

↔ δ(2m) ♀(½m)
Min£65 Max£80pw (Low)
Min£85 Max£110pw (High)

CAULKERBUSH
Dumfries & Galloway *Kirkcudbrightshire*
Map**11** NX95

H **Oakbank**
for bookings G M Thomson & Co, 27 King Street, Castle Douglas, Kirkcudbrightshire DG7 1AB
☎Castle Douglas(0556)2701 & 2973

A chalet-style house comprising three bedrooms, kitchen, living room and bathroom. It lies by the roadside 1m outside the village, set high with views of the Solway Firth.

Mar–Nov 1wk min, 6mths max, 1unit, 1–6persons ◆ ◎ fridge 🍴
Elec inclusive 🗔not provided ☎(2m)
SD in unit Ironing board in unit CTV
⊕3pin square P 🛁(2m)
↔ δ(3m) ♀(3m)
Min£90 Max£170pw

CAWOOD
North Yorkshire
Map**8** SE63

B **Cawood Park Bungalows** Ryther Road
for bookings Mr W G Archer, Wharfe Cottage, Ryther Road, Cawood, Selby, North Yorkshire YO8 0TT
☎Cawood(075786)578 or 450

Bessiestown Farm

Catlowdy, Penton, Carlisle, Cumbria.

Five modern bungalows facing an attractive two-acre lake. Accommodation comprises lounge with double bed-settee, kitchen, bathroom/WC, one double and one twin-bedded room.

All year   MWB in season   2 days min, 3mths max, 5units, 6persons ◊ ◆ ◎
fridge ♨ Elec metered ⌴ inclusive
☎(200yds) Iron & Ironing board in unit
[Launderette within 300yds] ⊕ CTV
⊕3pin square 5P ⩜(200yds) Fishing
↫ ☀(200yds) ♫(200yds)
Min£92 Max£195pw

CAYTON
North Yorkshire
Map**8** TA08

B   24 Green Park Road
for bookings Mrs Nicholson, Edelweiss, North Drive, Bramhope, Leeds LS16 9DF
☎Leeds(0532)673487
Modern bungalow with small garden and garage. Situated one mile from the sea at Cayton Bay. Accommodation comprises: Hall with phone, breakfast kitchen with dishwasher, fridge/freezer, microwave etc, dining room with french windows to patio, lounge, two double bedrooms (one on the first floor) also a single divan in the dining room, bathroom with shower.

All year   MWB out of season   2 nights min, 1mth max, 1unit, 1–5 persons ◊ ◆
◎ fridge ♨ Elec inclusive
⌴ not provided ☎ WM in unit Iron & Ironing board in unit ⊕ ⊗ TV & CTV
⊕3pin square 3P 1⚓ ⩜(150yds)
↫ ☀(3m) ☀(100yds) ♫(3m)
☀(3m) ☙(3m)
Min£58 Max£195pw

B   Scaran Bungalow
for bookings Mr Griffiths, Country & Coastal Self Catering Holidays, 9 Birdgate, Pickering, North Yorkshire
☎Pickering(0751)75058
Detached spacious bungalow with four bedrooms, large dining room, kitchen, bathroom and separate WC on the ground floor and a lounge on the first.

All year   MWB out of season   1 day min, 3mths max, 1unit, 1–8persons [◊] ◊
◆ ♫ fridge ♨ Gas/Elec metered
⌴can be hired ☎(100yds)
[Launderette within 300yds] TV & CTV
⊕3pin square 2P ⫟ ⩜(100yds)
↫ ☙(1m) ☀(2m) ☀(3m) ♫(3m)
☀(3m)
Min£50 Max£250pw

CENARTH
Dyfed
Map**2** SN24

C   Mr & Mrs B J Swatton Penwernfach
Ponthirwaun, Cardigan, Dyfed SA43 2RL
☎Newcastle Emlyn(0239)710694
Modernised stone cottages offering comfortable accommodation and lying some three miles north of Cenarth. Six acres of grounds available with goats, donkeys, ponies and ducks. Telfi and Cych are terraced cottages comprising

---

Cawood
—
Challaborough Bay

---

open-plan dining room/lounge, kitchen, bathroom and two family bedrooms on the first floor. Towy, a ground-floor cottage, has open-plan dining room/lounge, kitchen, shower room and two bedrooms sleeping up to five persons. Taf is a first-floor cottage the same as Towy except with bath/WC. Gwaun is a detached cottage with combined lounge/dining room, one double bedroom and shower room. All have patios with tables and chairs. 1½ miles North off B4570.

Apr–Oct   MWB out of season   1wk min, 5units, 1–8persons [◊] ◊ ◆ ♦
fridge Electric Gas inclusive
Elec metered ⌴ inclusive ☎ Iron & Ironing board in unit [Launderette on premises] ⊕ CTV ⊕3pin square P
⫟ ⩜(3m)
↫ ☙(1m)
Min£65 Max£100pw (Low)
Min£140 Max£245pw (High)

CERNE ABBAS
Dorset
Map**3** ST60

F   1 & 2 The Annexe & The Cottage
for bookings Mr Paul, Giants Head, Old Sherborne Road, Cerne Abbas, Dorset
☎Cerne Abbas(03003)242
Two chalet-type, single-storey flats comprising hallway, kitchen/diner with older style fitments, lounge with single put-u-up, one flat has double-bedded room the other a twin-bedded, one flat has shower and separate WC the other a bathroom and separate WC. The cottage flat adjoining the main farmhouse comprises lounge with extra bed space for one, kitchen/diner with older style cupboards, one double and one twin-bedded room, bathroom and WC.

Etr–Oct   MWB out of season   3days min, 1mth max, 3units, 2–5persons   no pets
◎ fridge electric fires Elec metered
⌴ inclusive ☎(2m) Iron & Ironing board in unit ⊕ TV ⊕3pin square 2P ⫟
⩜(on site)
↫ ☙(2m)
Min£35 Max£125pw

CHAGFORD
Devon
Map**3** SX78

C   Coach House, Granary, Mews & Tackery
for bookings Mr Bennie, Beechlands Farm, Chagford, Newton Abbot, Devon
☎Chagford(06473)3313
Converted from stables these attractive cottages have been well decorated and carpeted throughout. Granary has four bedrooms, Coach House and Mews comprise three bedrooms, Tackery has one double bedroom. All comprise

---

bathroom/WC, kitchen and open plan lounge/diner with additional sofa bed.

Mar–Dec   MWB out of season   3days min, 6wks max, 4units, 1–7persons
◊ [◊] ◎ fridge Electric
Elec metered ⌴ not provided ☎(½m)
Iron & Ironing board in unit ⊕ CTV
⊕3pin square 6P ⫟ ⩜(½m) Fishing
↫ ☙(½m) ♫(½m) ♫(½m)
Min£50 Max£80pw (Low)
Min£100 Max£190pw (High)

C   Coombe Farm Barn
for bookings Mrs S M Bowater, Coombe Farmhouse, Chagford, Devon TQ13 8DF
☎Chagford(06473)3593
Surrounded by woodland this converted 17th-century barn offers split-level open plan kitchen/dining/living room with wood burner; three double bedrooms, and modern bathroom. At Sandy Park Inn follow Castle Drogo signs, turn sharp right 1m.

Apr–Oct   MWB out of season   1wk min, 2mths max, 1unit, 1–6persons [◊] ◊
◆ no pets ◎ fridge Electric & open fire Elec metered ⌴ inclusive ☎(1m)
SD in unit Iron & Ironing board in unit
⊕ TV ⊕3pin square 1P 1⚓
⩜(1½m)
↫ ☙(1½m) ♫(1½m)
Details not confirmed for 1987

B   CC Ref 542 ELP
for bookings Character Cottages (Holidays) Ltd, 34 Fore Street, Sidmouth, Devon EX10 8AQ
☎Sidmouth(03955)77001
A newly constructed block building with Tyrolean finish. Accommodation comprises lounge/diner, one bedroom, one single bedroom, lounge with french windows to patio cloakroom and washbasin and bathroom/WC.

All year   MWB out of season   1wk min, 1mth max, 1unit, 2–6persons ◊ ♦
fridge ♨ Electric Gas/Elec inclusive
⌴can be hired ☎(½m) Iron & Ironing board in unit ⊕ CTV ⊕3pin square
⊕2pin round P ⫟ ⩜(½m)
↫ ☙(½m)
Min£95 Max£132pw (Low)
Min£157 Max£206 (High)

CHALLABOROUGH BAY
Devon
Map**2** SX64

B   Mr & Mrs B Carter Beachdown
Challaborough Bay, Bigbury-on-Sea, Kingsbridge, Devon TQ7 4JB
☎Kingsbridge(0548)2282
Situated in a valley with direct access to beach in an area of some 2¼ acres adjacent to a holiday caravan site. Each unit has one double and one twin-bedded room plus double put-u-up in lounge/diner, kitchen and bathroom/WC.

All year   MWB out of season   3days min, 13units, 2–6persons [◊ ◊ ◆] ◎
fridge ♨ Electric Elec metered
⌴ not provided ☎ Iron & Ironing board→

69

on premises [Launderette within 300yds] ⊕ CTV ⊕3pin square 25P ♨(250yds) Children's play area

⊖ ♪(½m) ♀(300yds) ♬(300yds)

Min£46 Max£145pw (Low)
Min£175 Max£270pw (High)

CHANNEL ISLANDS
Map16

ALDERNEY
Map16

C & Ch Pine Springs
for bookings C/O Grand Island Hotel, Alderney, Channel Islands
☎Alderney(048 182)2848

Hope, Faith and Charity are Swedish-style log cabins and Woodmans, which is a two-storey Swedish-style log and brick cottage, are situated in a wooded valley. The timbered interiors of the chalets comprise lounge/bedroom with twin beds, separate bedroom, kitchen/diner and bathroom/WC. Woodmans has a lounge/bedroom on the ground floor and kitchen/diner, one bedroom and bathroom/WC on the first floor. Situated on the edge of the island's town.

Apr–Oct MWB in season 1wk min, 6mths max, 4units, 4–7persons [◆ ◆]
∅ fridge Gas fires Gas/Elec inclusive
🔲can be hired ☎each unit Iron & Ironing board in unit ⊕ ⊕ CTV
⊕3pin square P ♨ [♪hard]

⊖ ♪ ♀ ♬ ♬ ♨

Min£108 Max£291pw

GUERNSEY
ST PETER PORT
Map 16

B La Collinette Hotel, Self Catering Cottages St Jacques, St Peter Port, Guernsey, Channel Islands
☎Guernsey(0481)710331

A group of seven bungalow cottages of modern construction in a quiet location. Each has a lounge/diner, well-equipped kitchen, bathroom, one double, one twin and one bunk-bedded room (for children). Use of the hotel's solarium, sauna, jacuzzi and restaurant are available.

All year MWB 3mths max, 7units, 4–6persons [◇] ◆ ◆ no pets ⊕
fridge Electric convectors Elec metered
🔲inclusive ☎ [WM & TD on premises]
Iron & Ironing board in unit ⊕ CTV
⊕3pin square 7P ♨(½m) ♨(heated)

⊖ ♪(2m) ♀ ♬(½m) ♬(½m)
Sports centre(½m)

Min£65pw (Low)
Min£150 Max£365pw (High)

Challaborough Bay
—
Charmouth

ST SAVIOUR'S
Map16

C L'Atlantique Cottages L'Atlantique Hotel, Perelle Bay, St Saviour's, Guernsey, Channel Islands
☎Guernsey(0481)64056

Attractive linked bungalow units in grounds of hotel opposite the rocky Perelle Bay beach. The units have modern and comfortable furnishings. Facilities of the hotel including a swimming pool, bistro type bar and restaurant are available. Also hotel laundry service.

All year MWB 1wk min, 10units, 4persons [◇ ◆ ◆] no pets Electric rings & Sunbeam multi cooker fridge
♨& electric fires Elec metered
🔲inclusive ☎ [WM on premises] Iron & Ironing board in unit ⊕ CTV
⊕3pin square 10P 🔳 ♨(½m) ♨

⊖ ♀ ♬

Min£90 Max£125pw (Low)
Min£170 Max£300pw (High)

CHARLTON
West Sussex
Map4 SU81

H Foxhall
for bookings The Landmark Trust, Shottesbrooke, Maidenhead, Berkshire SL6 3SW
☎Littlewick Green(062882)5925

A delightfully renovated 'folly' dating back to the 1700s. Accommodation comprises an elegantly decorated lounge/dining room, fully equipped kitchen, one twin-bedded room, one double bedroom in recess adjacent to lounge and bathroom/WC. Foxhall is immaculately kept and located in a very picturesque Sussex village.

All year MWB out of season 1day min, 2wks max, 1unit, 1–4persons nc 12
no pets ⊕ fridge ♨ Elec inclusive
🔲not provided ☎(100yds) Iron & Ironing board in unit ⊕ ⊕3pin square
⊕3pin round 2P 🔳(4days) ♨(1m)

⊖ ♀

Min£180 Max£260pw (Low)
Min£195 Max£275pw (High)

CHARMOUTH
Dorset
Map3 SY39

H Char View Catherston Lane
for bookings A Loosmore, Manor Farm, Charmouth, Bridport, Dorset DT6 6QL
☎Charmouth(0297)60226

Semi-detached modern house situated on outskirts of village. Accommodation comprises two double and one twin-bedded room, kitchen/diner, lounge, bathroom and separate WC. Located off A35 on east side of Charmouth. Backing onto Camping Park with use of the facilities.

All year MWB out of season 1wk min, 3wks max, 1unit, 2–6persons [◆ ◆]
⊕ fridge ♨ Elec metered
🔲not provided ☎(200yds) Iron & Ironing board in unit [Launderette within 300yds] ⊕ CTV ⊕3pin square 3P
♨(200yds)

⊖ ♪(2½m) ♀ (250yds) ♬(3m)
♨(3m)

Min£110 Max£250pw

B Holcombe Pine Catherston Lane
for bookings A Loosmore, Manor Farm, Charmouth, Bridport, Dorset DT6 6QL
☎Charmouth(0297)60226

Detached modern bungalow situated in own grounds. Accommodation comprises kitchen/diner, lounge, two double bedded rooms, one twin bedroom, bathroom and separate WC. Off A35 east side of Charmouth. Use of Manor Farm camping site facilities.

All year MWB out of season 1wk min, 3wks max, 1unit, 2–6persons [◆ ◆]
⊕ fridge ♨ Elec metered
🔲not provided ☎(200yds) Iron, Ironing board in unit [Launderette within 300yds] ⊕ CTV ⊕3pin square 3P
♨(200yds)

⊖ ♪(2½m) ♀ (250yds) ♬(3m)
♨(3m)

Min£115 Max£295pw

C Mr & Mrs P R S Allen The Lilacs The Street, Charmouth, Bridport, Dorset DT6 6QH
☎Charmouth(0297)60747

An attractive thatched cottage situated in Charmouth's main street comprising of kitchen, lounge/diner with inglenook fireplace, separate shower room and WC and one twin-bedded room.

29Mar–1Nov 1wk min, 1mth max, 1unit, 1–2persons no children no pets ∅
fridge Electric & gas fires Gas & Elec inclusive 🔲not provided ☎(100yds)
WM & SD in unit Iron & Ironing board in unit ⊕ CTV ⊕3pin square 1P 🔳
♨(50yds)

70

⊖ ƙ(2m) ⚑(50yds) 🎵(50yds)
🍴(2½m)

Min£70 Max£155pw

H 1, 2, 3, 4 & 5 Manor Court
for bookings Mr R A Loosmore, Manor
Farm, Charmouth, Bridport, Dorset
DT6 6QL
☎Charmouth(0297)60226
Numbers 1, 2 & 3 are purpose-built stone
terraced houses, comprising lounge with
convertible bed-settee, kitchen, two
bedrooms and a bathroom. Number 4 is
similar but detached. Number 5 is semi-
detached with two double-bedded rooms
and one twin-bedded. On entering the
village of Charmouth from Bridport, the
houses are situated in the main street.

All year MWB out of season 1wk min,
3wks max, 5units, 4 – 6persons [◆ ◆]
no pets ∅ ◎ fridge Gas/
Elec metered ⓛincluded ☎(100yds)
Iron & Ironing board in unit [Launderette
within 300yds] ⊙ CTV ⊕3pin square
P ⚎(100yds) Use of Manor Farm
Campsite facilities
⊖ ƙ(3m) ⚑(100yds) 🎵(3m) 🍴(3m)

Min£100 Max£250pw

CHEDDAR
Somerset
Map**3** ST45

C Mrs S Blakeney Edwards **Stable &
Orchard Cottages** Fairlands House,
Cheddar, Somerset
☎Cheddar(0934)742629

Semi-detached stone cottages converted
from old stables, set in large orchard in
private grounds of country house, with
views of Mendip Hills and Cheddar Gorge.
Accommodation comprises open-plan
lounge/kitchen/diner; first floor has two
bedrooms, one with a double bed and the
other with twin bunks and bathroom/WC.

Etr – Sep 1wk min, 3wks max, 2units,
4 – 6persons ◇ ◆ ◆ no pets ◎
fridge Electric Elec metered
ⓛinclusive ☎(200yds) Iron in unit
Ironing board in unit [Launderette within
300yds] ⊙ TV ⊕3pin square 2P 📺
⚎(150yds)
⊖ ⚑(200yds) 🎵(½m)

Details not confirmed for 1987

CHELTENHAM
Gloucestershire
Map**3** SO92

C R & J Champness, **1, 2 & 3 Church
Court Cottages** Mill Street, Prestbury,
Cheltenham, Gloucestershire
☎Cheltenham(0242)525385 or 529280

Attractive and well-appointed cottages,
converted from stone farm buildings, in a
small courtyard. They are full of character
and furnished to a high standard. **No 1**
has a hall, kitchen and dining room with
two twin bedrooms and a bathroom/WC;
the first floor has a double bedroom with
en suite bathroom and lounge. **No's 2 & 3**
have a hall, one double and one twin
bedroom and separate bathroom/WC; on

---

the first floor an attractive lounge and
fitted kitchen/diner.

All year MWB out of season 3days min,
3mths max, 3units, 2 – 6persons ◆
no pets ∅ ◎ fridge Gas & Elec
inclusive ☎ WM & TD in
unit Iron & Ironing board in unit ⊙
CTV ⊕3pin square 3P 📺 ⚎(100yds)
⊖ ƙ(2½m) ⚑(20yds) 🎵(2m)
🎵(2m) 🍴(2m) Sports centre(2m)

Min£158 Max£194pw (Low)
Min£303 Max£400pw (High)

CHERITON BISHOP
Devon
Map**3** SX79

H CC Ref 478
for bookings Character Cottages
(Holidays) Ltd, 34 Fore Street, Sidmouth,
Devon EX10 8AQ
☎Sidmouth(03955)77001

A converted farm cottage in secluded
position, with access along farm road. Set
on hillside with garden area and parking,
overlooking woods. There is a kitchen with
modern fittings, rear entrance and
cloakroom/WC and large lounge. On the
first-floor there is a bathroom, two double
bedrooms, one room with three singles.

All year MWB out of season 1wk min,
6wks max, 1unit, 1 – 7persons ◆ ◎
fridge Electric Elec inclusive ⓛcan be
hired ☎(1m) WM, SD in unit Iron &
Ironing board in unit ⊙ CTV
⊕3pin square P ⚎(1m)
⊖ ⚑(1m)

Min£78 Max£118pw (Low)
Min£148 Max£209pw (High)

CHESWICK
Northumberland
Map**12** NU04

C Garden Cottage
for bookings Lt Col H Crossman,
Cheswick House, Berwick-upon-Tweed,
Northd TD15 2RL
☎Berwick-upon-Tweed(0289)87234

A semi-detached cottage in the grounds of
Cheswick house, ½m from the A1. The
ground-floor accommodation comprises
lounge, kitchen, bathroom/WC and one
twin-bedded room and first floor has two
twin-bedded rooms.

Apr – Oct MWB out of season 1wk min,
1mth max, 1unit, 2 – 6persons [◇] ◆
◆ ∅ fridge Electric & coal fire central
heating Gas/Elec metered ⓛinclusive
☎(½m) ⊙ CTV ⊕3pin square 1P
📺 ⚎(5m)
⊖ ƙ(1m) ⚑(½m)

Min£30 Max£40pw (Low)
Min£65 Max£85pw (High)

H West Lodge
for bookings Lt Col H Crossman,
Cheswick House, Berwick-upon-Tweed,
Northd TD15 2RL
☎Berwick-upon-Tweed(0289)87234

Single-storey stone-built lodge in the
grounds of the Victorian mansion,
Cheswick House. Accommodation
consists of two twin-bedded rooms, living
room, bathroom/WC and kitchenette. 4m
from Berwick and 1m from the sea.

Apr – Oct MWB out of season 1wk min,
1mth max, 1unit, 1 – 5persons ◆ ◎
fridge 🍴and open fires Elec metered
ⓛinclusive ☎(400yds) ⊙ TV
⊕3pin square P ⚎(5m)
⊖ ƙ(1m) ⚑(1m)

Min£25 Max£35pw (Low)
Min£55 Max£75pw (High)

CHEW MAGNA
Avon
Map**3** ST56

B Baliffs House
for bookings Mrs S E Lyons, Chew Hill
Farm, Chew Magna, Bristol BS18 8QP
☎Bristol(0272)332496

A detached, pebble dashed, dormer
bungalow in grounds of a farmhouse.
Situated in a rural setting with open views
from an elevated position.
Accommodation comprises a ground floor
with dining room, kitchen, lounge and WC
and first floor with twin-bedded room, two
single-bedded rooms and bath/WC.
Access from the A38, Bristol to Bridgwater
road, or A37, Bristol to Shepton Mallet
road, then by B3130 to Dundry Hill.

All year MWB out of season 1wk min,
4wks max, 1unit, 2 – 4persons ◎ fridge
Electric Elec metered ⓛinclusive
☎(2½m) Iron & Ironing board in unit
⊙ TV ⊕3pin square P ⚎(2½m)

Min£100 Max£200pw (Low)
Min£140 Max£200pw (High)

B East Lodge Chew Hill
for bookings Mrs S E Lyons, Chew Hill
Farm, Chew Magna, Bristol BS18 8QP
☎Bristol(0272)332496

A detached dormer bungalow in a quiet,
rural setting with open views across the
valley and lake. Accommodation
comprises lounge, dining room, kitchen
and WC on the ground floor and one twin-
bedded room, two single bedrooms and
bathroom/WC on the first floor. Access
from the A38 Bristol to Bridgwater road, or
A37, Bristol to Shepton Mallet road, then
by B3130 to Dundry Hill.

All year MWB out of season 1wk min,
4wks max, 1unit, 2 – 4persons ◎ fridge
Electric Elec metered ⓛinclusive
☎(1m) Iron & Ironing board in unit ⊙
⊕3pin square P ⚎(1m)

Min£100 Max£200pw (Low)
Min£140 Max£200pw (High)

H West Lodge Limeburn Hill
for bookings Mrs S E Lyons, Chew Hill
Farm, Chew Magna, Bristol BS18 8QP
☎Bristol(0272)332496 →

71

A colour washed, Victorian lodge, offering simply-furnished accommodation, standing at entrance to farm house in a quiet, rural setting with good views. The ground floor comprises dining room, lounge, kitchen and bathroom/WC. The first floor comprises one twin and two single bedrooms.

All year   MWB out of season   1wk min, 4wks max, 1unit, 2–4persons   ◉   fridge   Electric   Elec metered   ☐ inclusive   ☎(2½m)   Iron & Ironing board in unit   ☉   TV   ⊕3pin square   P   🏠   ♨(2½m)

Min£80 Max£140pw (Low)
Min£110 Max£140pw (High)

CHILLENDEN
Kent
Map**5** TR25

C   Whitehorn
for bookings The Cottage Secretary, Knowlton Estate Office, Knowlton Court, Wingham, Canterbury, Kent CT3 1PT
☎Sandwich(0304)617344

Small comfortable cottage in the village of Chillenden. Accommodation comprises one twin-bedded and one bunk-bedded room, dining room, kitchen, sitting room and bathroom/WC. Private garden.

All year   MWB out of season   1wk min, 1unit, 1–4persons   [◇]   ◆   ◉   fridge   Electric   Elec metered   ☐ can be hired   ☎(½m)   Iron & Ironing board   ☉   TV   ⊕3pin square   🔟   ♨(1m)

↤   ♿(½m)

Min£65 Max£80pw (Low)
Min£95 Max£125pw (High)

CHIPPING CAMPDEN
Gloucestershire
Map**4** SP13

C & B   Mr & Mrs F Morrall **Orchard Retreat, Poplar Cottage and Paddock End** Charingworth Grange, Chipping Campden, Gloucestershire.
☎Paxford(038678)342

Orchard Retreat is a comfortable, detached bungalow, in its own garden with hall, sitting room, kitchen/dining area and a separate dining room, bathroom, separate WC, one double and two twin bedrooms. *Poplar* and *Paddock End* are two semi-detached cottages of great character and charm. *Poplar* offers hall, living room, kitchen, two double bedrooms and one single, bathroom, and WC. *Paddock End* offers hall, sitting room, kitchen/dining room, bathroom and separate WC; upstairs is one double, one twin and one single bedroom and a second bathroom/WC. All kitchens have dishwashers, there is an indoor games area, stables and facilities provided for guests' horses.*

All year   MWB out of season   2days min, 3mths max, 3units   1–6persons   ◆   ◆   no pets   ◉   fridge   🔥oil, coal fires   Elec inclusive   ☐ inclusive   ☎   Iron & Ironing board in unit   Launderette within

---

300yds   ☉   CTV   ⊕3pin square   6P   3🏠(winter)   🔟   ♨(2½m)   ⛵(Hard)

↤   ♿(1½m)
Min£130 Max£320pw

C   Primrose Cottage 3 The Bank
for bookings Heart of England Cottages, The Market Place, Fairford, Glos GL7 4AB
☎Cirencester(0285)713295

An attractive and well-appointed terrace cottage with secluded garden, in quiet village close to the church. It comprises living room, kitchen, shower room and WC; on the first floor one double, one twin and one single bedroom and bathroom/ WC.

All year   MWB out of season   4days min, 1unit, 1–5persons, nc10   [◇]   no pets   ♨   fridge   Gas charged   ☐ inclusive   ☎   SD in unit   Iron & Ironing board in unit   ☉   ◐   CTV   ⊕3pin square   1P   🔟   ♨(1m)

↤   ♿(200yds)

Min£125 Max£150pw (Low)
Min£165 Max£190pw (High)

CHRISTCHURCH
Dorset
Map**4** SZ19

C   Pebbles West 2 Fishermans Bank
for bookings Mrs J Long, 23 East Weare Road, Portland, Dorset DT5 1ES
☎Portland(0305)826683 & Christchurch (0202)479704

Semi-detached waterside cottage built some 100 years ago. Accommodation on the ground floor comprises a large carpeted kitchen/diner, a small lounge, one twin-bedded room, and a shower room with WC. The cottage affords direct access to the harbour and slipway.

Etr–Sep   1wk Min, 1mth max, 1unit, 2persons   ♨   fridge   Electric   Elec inclusive   ☐ inclusive   ☎(160yds)   Iron & Ironing board in unit   ☉   TV   ⊕3pin square   2P   🔟   ♨(60yds)

↤   ♿(3m)   ♿(100yds)

Min£65 Max£75pw (Low)
Min£80 Max£95pw (High)

CHRISTOW
Devon
Map**3** SX88

C   CC Ref 446 ELP
for bookings Character Cottages (Holidays) Ltd, 34 Fore Street, Sidmouth, Devon EX10 8AQ
☎Sidmouth(03955)77001

One of five cottages in a beautiful area, comprising lounge with put-u-up, one double bedroom, twin-bedded room, WC, bathroom and kitchen/diner.

All year   MWB out of season   1wk min, 1mth max, 1unit, 2–6persons   ◆   ◉

---

fridge   Electric & Calor gas   Elec metered   ☐ can be hired   ☎   Iron & Ironing board on premises   ☉   TV   ⊕3pin square   ⊕2pin round   P   🔟   ♨(200yds)

↤   ♿(½m)   🔟   ♫

Min£45 Max£82pw (Low)
Min£84 Max£138pw (High)

CHUDLEIGH
Devon
Map**3** SX87

C   Cider, Stable & Swallow Cottages
for bookings Mr & Mrs R Smith, Coombeshead Farm Holiday Cottages, Coombeshead Cross, Chudleigh, Newton Abbott, Devon TW13 0NQ
☎Chudleigh(0626)853334

Three cottages in a converted L-shaped stone barn situated on a non-working Farm. They all have two bedrooms, one of which is family sized, and bathroom. Cider has a lounge/diner and kitchen. Stable has a lounge with bed-settee and kitchen. Swallow has lounge with bed-settee and exposed beams and kitchen/diner. All have been converted to a high standard with modern amenities but retaining old charm.

Mar–15Jan   MWB out of season   1wk min, 3mths max, 3units, 1–8persons   [◇]   ◆   ◆   no pets   ◉   fridge   Electric   Elec metered   ☐ can be hired   ☎(1m)   WM & SD in unit   Iron & Ironing board in unit   ☉   CTV   ⊕3pin square   6P   ♨(1m)

↤   ♿(3m)   ♿(1m)   🔟(1m)   ♫(1m)

Details not confirmed for 1987

CHURCH STRETTON
Shropshire
See **Wall under Heywood**

CHURSTON FERRERS
Devon
Map**3** SX95

B   CC Ref 403E
for bookings Character Cottages (Holidays) Ltd, 34 Fore Street, Sidmouth, Devon EX10 8AQ
☎Sidmouth(03955)77001

Modern split-level, semi-detached bungalow, 1½m from seafront with views over Torbay. There are three double bedrooms, lounge/diner, kitchen, bathroom and WC.

All year   MWB out of season   1wk min, 6mths max, 1unit, 2–6persons   ◆   no pets   ◉   fridge   Gas/   Elec metered   ☐ not provided   ☎(150yds)   SD   Iron & Ironing board in unit   ☉   TV   ⊕3pin square   ⊕2pin round   P   🏠   ♨(150yds)   Sailing

↤   ♿(1m)   🔟(1m)   ♫(2m)   🍴(2m)

Min£91 Max£129pw (Low)
Min£188 Max£252pw (High)

CHWILOG
Gwynedd
Map**6** SH43

72

H Mrs C Jones **Chwilog Fawr** Chwilog Pwllheli, Gwynedd LL53 6SW
☎Chwilog(076688)506

This south-facing wing, part of an 18th-century stone farmhouse in elevated position, comprises lounge, dining room, kitchen, two double-bedded rooms, one twin-bedded, and bathroom/WC. 1½m from village.

May–Sep 1wk min, 4wks max, 1unit, 1–6persons ◇ ◈ ◆ no pets ◎ fridge ⑭ Elec metered Ⓛsupplied ☎(400yds) [WM on premises] TD Iron & Ironing board in unit ☉ CTV ⊕3pin square 3P ⑪ ♨(1m)

↭ ♪(3m) ♀(1m) 🎵(3m)

Min£100 Max£225pw

Ch **Wernol Farms Caravan Park**
for bookings Mrs C Jones, Chwilog Fawr, Chwilog, Pwllheli, Gwynedd LL53 6SW
☎Chwilog(076688)506

Five purpose-built timber chalets on quiet caravan site close to beaches and mountains. Four units have lounge/diner, kitchen, one twin-bedded room, one double and one with bunk beds, bathroom/WC. The other has lounge/kitchen/diner, bathroom/WC and two bedrooms, one with twin beds, the other with double.

Mar–Oct MWB out of season 1wk min, 4wks max, 5units, 1–6persons ◈ ◆ ♨ fridge Electric Elec metered Ⓛcan be hired ☎(200yds) WM on premises SD on premises CTV ⊕3pin square 2P ⑪ ♨(1m)

↭ ♪(3m) ♀(1m) 🎵(3m)

Min£70 Max£150pw

CIRENCESTER
Gloucestershire
Map**4** SP00

F & C **Trewsbury Holiday Cottages**
for bookings Mr & Mrs P J Willmett, Trewsbury House, Coates, Cirencester, Gloucestershire GL7 6NY
☎Kemble(028577)306

The holiday cottages and flat, are set within the 40 acres surrounding Trewsbury House. They have been modernised, yet retain their character and charm. Stable flat comprises kitchen/diner, double-bedded room, lounge with double convertible settee and bath/WC. Stable Cottage comprises lounge, dining room, kitchen, shower/WC, one double and two twin bedrooms, bath/WC. Garden Cottages 1 & 2 comprise lounge, kitchen/diner, one double and one twin bedroom, bath/WC. Rose Cottage has a lounge, kitchen/diner, cloakroom with WC, one double and two twin bedrooms, bath/WC.

Etr–Oct MWB in season 2days min, 6wks max, 5units, 4–6persons ◈ ◆ pets in Stable & Rose Cottage only ◎ fridge night storage or solid fuel (Stable Cottage) Elec metered Ⓛinclusive ☎ WM, SD & TD on premises Iron & Ironing board in unit ☉ CTV ⊕3pin square P ⌂(Stable Flat & Rose Cottage only)

Chwilog
—
Cleobury Mortimer

⑪ ♨(2m) ⌇(heated with cover) Games room and stables nearby

↭ ♪(3m) ♀(1m) 🎵(2m) 🎵(2m) ⑩(2m) Sports centre(2m)

Min£90 Max£245pw

CLACHAN-SEIL
Strathclyde *Argyllshire*
Map**10** NM71

B **Dorus Mor**
for bookings Highland Hideaways, 5/7 Stafford Street, Oban, Argyll PA34 5NJ
☎Oban(0631)62056/63901

Luxuriously appointed bungalow, superbly situated overlooking the Sound of Seil. Many attractive features include lounge with open fireplace and timber ceiling, kitchen, utility room, and dining room with patio doors. Also three bedrooms, bathroom, cloakroom, and a fourth bedroom with bathroom en-suite.

Etr–Oct MWB out of season 1wk min, 1unit, 1–7persons no pets ◎ fridge ♨ & open fires Elec inclusive Ⓛnot provided ☎ WM & TD in unit Airing cupboard, Iron & Ironing board in unit HCE in unit ☉ ⑯ CTV ⊕3pin square 3P 2⌂ ♨(1m)

↭ ♀(1m)

Min£117 Max£255pw

C **Seil Island Cottages**
for bookings N & E Kenyon, Seil Island Cottages, Clachan Seil, Oban, Argyll PA34 4QZ
☎Balvicar(08523)440

Two modern detached cottages set on a hillside on Seil Island. Each cottage contains living/dining room with two divans, double bedroom, room with bunks and kitchen. The properties are 5m from the A816 on the B844 and are reached by crossing the famous, 'Bridge over the Atlantic'.

All year MWB out of season 3days min, 2units, 1–6persons ◇ ◆ no pets ◎ fridge Electric Elec metered Ⓛprovided ☎(100yds) Iron & Ironing board in unit ☉ ⊕3pin square CTV P ♨(1½m)

↭ ♀(150yds)

Details not confirmed for 1987

CLACTON-ON-SEA
Essex
Map**5** TM11

Ch **Highfield Holiday Park** London Road
for bookings Hoseasons Holidays Ltd, Sunway House, Lowestoft, Suffolk NR32 3LT
☎Lowestoft(0502)62292

A holiday park approx 2m from the seafront with good recreation facilities

---

and children's amusements. Caribbean chalets comprise two double bedrooms, living room, kitchen & bathroom.

Apr–Sep MWB out of season 1wk min (high season), 1night min (low season), 68units, 1–6persons [◈ ◆] no pets ◎ fridge ⑭ Elec metered Ⓛinclusive ☎ [Launderette within 300yds] ☉ CTV ⊕3pin square 500P ♨(200yds) ⌇ Children's play area

↭ ♪(3m) ♀ 🎵 🎵 ⑩(2½m)

Min£45 Max£175pw

CLAPHAM
North Yorkshire
Map**7** SD76

C **Clapham Woods Cottages**
for bookings Mrs R Crossiand, Clapham Woods Farmhouse, Clapham, Lancaster LA2 7AS
☎Clapham(04685)609

Two newly converted cottages, developed from a large barn each with large lounge with stone fireplace, kitchen/diner, three twin-bedded rooms and bathroom/WC. Set in peaceful countryside.

All year MWB 1day min, 1mth max, 2units, 2–6persons ◇ ◈ ◆ ◎ fridge ⑭ & open fire Elec metered Ⓛinclusive ♨(1m) ☉ CTV ⊕3pin square 4P ♨(1m)

↭ ♀(1m)

Min£75 Max£105pw (Low)
Min£105 Max£145pw (High)

CLEE HILL
Shropshire
Map**7** SO57

C **Titterstone Hill Cottage**
for bookings Heart of England Cottages, The Barrel & Basket, Market Place, Fairford, Gloucestershire GL7 4AB
☎Cirencester(0285)713295

A remote 200 year old stone cottage set on the slopes of Clee Hill comprising lounge/dining room, kitchen, bathroom and three first floor bedrooms. Comfortably furnished.

All year MWB out of season 3days min, 2mths max, 1unit, 1–5persons ◈ ◆ ◎ fridge & log burning stove Elec inclusive Ⓛinclusive ☎(¾m) WH&SD in unit Iron & Ironing board in unit ☉ ⑯ CTV ⊕3pin square 4P ⑪ ♨(2m)

↭ ♀(2m)

Details not confirmed for 1987

CLEOBURY MORTIMER
Shropshire
Map**7** SO67

F **Station House**
for bookings Heart of England Cottages, The Barrel and Basket, Market Place, Fairford, Gloucestershire GL7 4AB
☎Cirencester(0285)713295

Five self-contained apartments retaining many original features and set on the edge of the Wyre Forest. Four units comprise lounge/kitchen/diner with →

convertible double bed-settee, one double bedroom and bathroom/WC. One unit had lounge with convertible double bed/settee, kitchen/diner, one bedroom with one double and one single bed and bathroom/WC.

MWB 3nights min, 3mths max, 5units, 1–5persons ◆ ◎ fridge ▓ Elec inclusive (Sep–May) Elec metered (Jun–Aug) ⌴inclusive ☎(60yds) WM Iron & Ironing board on premises CTV ⊕3pin square 6P ⸗Hard

↔ ⬤ (60yds)

Min£110 Max£235pw

CLEVEDON
Avon
Map**3** ST47

C Newhouse Farm Moor Lane
for bookings Summer Cottages, Northernhay House, The Grove, Dorchester, Dorset PT1 1UL
☎Dorchester(0305)67545

This cottage is an annexe to the owner's farmhouse which dates from 1630 and is within an attractive craft centre. Accommodation comprises sitting room, with large inglenook, dining room, kitchen, bathroom/WC and three bedrooms, one with WHB. A garden with garden furniture is available.

Apr–Sep 1wk min, 1unit, 6persons ◆ ◎ fridge Wood burning stove & electric fire Elec metered ⌴can be hired by overseas visitors only ☎(1m) WM & SD in unit Iron & Ironing board in unit ⊕ CTV ⊕3pin square 2P ▥ ▣(¾m) Restaurant

↔ ᦔ(1½m) ⬤(¾m)

Details not confirmed for 1987

CLIPPESBY
Norfolk
Map**9** TG41

Cleobury Mortimer
—
Clynnog Fawr

B, C & F Clippesby Holidays Clippesby, Great Yarmouth, Norfolk NR29 3BJ
☎Fleggburgh(049378)367

A complex of properties converted from the old country hall, cottages and outbuildings all set within this 30-acre estate between Norwich and Great Yarmouth. **Arbroath & Tiree** are semi-detached bungalows each having two bedrooms **Banff & Nairn** are two bedroomed flats both on first floor. **Glenrose & Galbraith** are bungalows each having three bedrooms, large lounge/diner, kitchen and bathroom. **Grampian** is a large two-storey property well-equipped and designed to sleep eight. **Montrose & Angus** are flats, both on the first floor, comprising one bedroom and a fold-down bed in the lounge/diner. **Lomond** is a two-storey chalet with spacious lounge/diner with fold-down bed and two bedrooms. Overlooks spacious lawns. **Mendip & Cheviot** are flats attached to the former old Hall each having three bedrooms. **Moray** is a flat with two bedrooms and a fold-down bed in the spacious lounge/diner.

16May–26Sep MWB out of season 3days min, 6wks max, 13units, 1–8persons [◇ ◆ ◆] ◎ fridge Electric Elec metered ⌴inclusive ☎ [Iron & Ironing board on premises] [Launderette on premises] ⊕ TV ⊕3pin square P ▥ ▣ ⌂ ⸗grass Games room, Licenced Bar Putting green

Min£51.75 Max£166.75pw (Low)
Min£92 Max£218.50pw (High)

CLYNNOG FAWR
Gwynedd
Map**6** SH44

B, C, H & F Bach Wen
for bookings Mr & Mrs P Smith, The Knoll, Hightown, Liverpool L38 3RT
☎051-929 2209

Five properties grouped together within 20 acres only 100yds from private beach, all having sea views. The **Bakery** has been converted to a comfortable compact flat with stone walled lounge/diner, and sleeps two. **Brochwel** is a modernised farmhouse and sleeps up to six; **Cadfan** is the modernised west wing of a farmhouse with extensive views of Caernarvon Bay and sleeps up to nine. **Cadwallon** is a converted granary with arched doors and stone loft steps and the sitting room faces the sea; it sleeps up to eight. **Gwyddaint** is a converted stone-built shippon with small bell tower at the gable end; it sleeps up to eight.

All year MWB out of season 1wk min, 4wks max, 5units, 2–9persons (nc or pets in Bakery) ◆ ◆ ◎ fridge Electric (Elec inclusive in the Bakery) Elec metered ⌴not provided ☎(Cadfan, Brochwel & Cadwallon) ☎(½m) WM (Cadwallon) TD in unit Iron & Ironing board in unit ⊕ CTV ⊕3pin square P ▣(½m)

↔ ⬤(½m) fishing

Min£80 Max£170pw (Low)
Min£100 Max£295pw (High)

F Flat 3, St Beuno's Court
for bookings Mr R Brown, 3 Bell Orchard, Alveley, Bridgnorth, Salop
☎Quatt(0746)780434

School house converted into flats. The unit consists of a lounge/diner, separate kitchen, bathroom/WC, one room with bunks and single bed and one double room. On A499 Pwllheli-Caernarfon road.

All year MWB out of season 1wk min, 1unit, 4–5persons ◆ no pets ◎ fridge Electric Electric inclusive ⬜not provided ☎(50yds) ☉ TV ⊕3pin square 1P 1🏠 ⬛(50yds) Sea trout & salmon fishing

Min£65 Max£90pw (Low)
Min£100 Max£105pw (High)

COGGESHALL
Essex
Map5 TL82

B 2 Albert Gardens Albert Place
for bookings Mrs M Ratcliffe, Ashes Farm, Cressing, Braintree, Essex CM7 8DW
☎Silver End(0376)83236

Modern bungalow in quiet cul-de-sac close to town centre. The bungalow has its own small garden and comprises spacious lounge/diner, bathroom, kitchen with split level cooker, two twin-bedded rooms one with en-suite shower.
All year MWB 3days min, 3mths max, 1unit, 4persons, nc7yrs no pets ◎ fridge under floor heating
Elec inclusive ⬜can be hired ☎(200yds) SD in unit Iron & Ironing board in unit ☉ CTV(charge) ⊕3pin square 1P 📺 ⬛(50yds)
⊖ 🏃(300yds)
Min£80 Max£110pw

COLATON RALEIGH
Devon
Map3 SY09

C Mrs Jean Daniels, Drupe Farm Cottages (No's 1–7&9–15) Drupe Farm, Colaton Raleigh, Sidmouth, Devon
☎Colaton Raleigh(0395)68838
Fourteen delightful cottages converted from old farmhouses and outbuildings, set around a courtyard. Each has a lounge/diner with kitchen area, and sleeping accommodation which varies with either two or three bedrooms. Excellent standard of furnishings and fittings.
All year MWB out of season 1wk min, 3mths max, 14units, 1–7persons [◇] ◆ ◎ fridge ♨ Elec inclusive ⬜inclusive ☎ Iron & Ironing board in unit [Launderette on premises] ☉ CTV ⊕3pin square P 6🏠 📺 ⬛(½m) Games room & children's play area
⊖ ♪(3m) 🏃(¼m)
Min£45 Max£85pw (Low)
Min£142 Max£250pw (High)

COLCHESTER
Essex
Map5 TL92

Clynnog Fawr
—
Coll, Isle of

F University House Avon Way
for bookings University of Essex, Catering & Accommodation Office, PO Box 23, Wivenhoe Park, Colchester, Essex CO4 3SQ
☎Colchester(0206)868510
Modern flats in three-storey buildings. Each flat consists of four or six bedrooms, bathroom and kitchen. One bedroom can be converted into a small lounge if required. All campus facilities are available to guests. Flats situated 1½m from town centre and University campus.
11Jul–12Sep 1wk min, 9wks max, 63units, 2–6persons ◆ ◎ fridge ♨ Elec inclusive ☎ WM & SD on premises Iron & Ironing board on premises TV can be hired
⊕3pin square P 📺 ⬛(150yds)
⊖ ♪ 🏃 🎵 🛍
Min£156.40 Max£175.95pw

COLERNE
Wiltshire
Map3 ST87

C Cottage in the Garden
for bookings Mrs S Gifford, Thickwood House, Colerne, Chippenham, Wiltshire SN14 8BN
☎Box(0225)742329
Fine conversion of an original 17th-century cowshed into two units, each has sitting/dining room, with quality furnishings, bedroom, modern bathroom and small kitchen.
All year MWB out of season 2days min, 2mths max, 2units, 1–2persons, nc no pets ◎ fridge ♨ Elec metered ⬜inclusive ☎(100yds) Iron & Ironing board in unit ☉ CTV ⊕3pin square 4P 📺 ⬛(1½m)
⊖ 🏃(1½m)
Min£95 Max£110pw

COLL, ISLE OF
Strathclyde Argyllshire
Map13 NM25

H Breachacha Farm
for bookings Mrs C K M Stewart, Estate Office, Isle of Coll, Argyll PA78 6TB
☎Coll(08793)339
A stone-built house within the farm steadings, facing lovely sandy bay in a splendid location on the SW end of the island. Accommodation comprises sitting/

dining room with bed-settee and open fire; kitchen with bathroom and WC leading off, and a double bedded room. Two spacious bedrooms on the 1st floor are reached by a steep staircase.
Apr–Oct MWB out of season 1wk min, 1mth max, 1unit, 2–8persons [◆ ◆] ◎ fridge Electric & open fires Elec metered ⬜can be hired ☎ Iron & Ironing board in unit ⊕3pin square 2P ⬛(5m)
Details not confirmed for 1987

F Malin & Hebrides Arinagour
for bookings Mrs C K M Stewart, Estate Office, Isle of Coll, Argyll PA78 6TB
☎Coll(08793)339
Situated approximately ¼m from Coll pier in the small coastal settlement of Arinagour, these two modernised first-floor flats are situated above the local shop. Both offer neatly-furnished lounge/dining room, modern kitchen and bathroom/WC. Malin has one twin and two single bedrooms and Hebrides contains one double, one single and one family room. Superb views over loch and islands. Accommodation unsuitable for invalids.
All year MWB out of season 1wk min, 1mth max, 2units, 2–8persons [◆ ◆] ◑ fridge Electric & open fires Gas/ Elec metered ⬜can be hired ☎(100yds) ☉ ⊕3pin square 1P ⬛(20yds)
⊖ ♪ 🏃 🛍
Details not confirmed for 1987

B Minches Arinagour
for bookings Mrs C K M Stewart, Estate Office, Isle of Coll, Argyll PA78 6TB
☎Coll(08793)339
Cedar clad bungalow situated to rear of local shop overlooking lawn, ¼m from Coll pier. It comprises lounge dining room with double bed-settee, kitchen and two bedrooms, all with modern furnishings.
All year MWB out of season 1wk min, 1mth max, 1unit, 2–6persons [◆ ◆] ◑ fridge Elec & open fires Gas/ Elec metered ⬜can be hired ☎(100yds) ☉ ⊕3pin square 1P ⬛(20yds)
⊖ ♪ 🏃 🛍
Details not confirmed for 1987

B Stronvar Breachacha Bay
for bookings Mrs C K M Stewart, Estate Office, Isle of Coll, Argyll PA78 6TB
☎Coll(08793)339
Large, timber-built bungalow with splendid views of sandy beach, Breachacha Bay, and two castles (one →

14th and one 18th century). Spacious accommodation comprises kitchen, sitting/dining room, four bedrooms (one double, one twin, one single and one with bunk beds) all with WHB and bathroom/ WC. Accommodation unsuitable for invalids.

Apr–Oct MWB out of season 1wk min, 1mth max, 1unit, 2–8persons [◊ ◆]
◎ fridge Electric Elec metered ⬜can be hired ☎ ⊙ ⊕3pin square 2P
🏠(5m) Loch fishing
↩ δ ♀ 🎜

Details not confirmed for 1987

COLONSAY, ISLE OF
Strathclyde *Argyllshire*
Map**10** NR38/40

C Alister Annies Kilchattan
for bookings Mrs E McNeill, Machrins Farm, Isle of Colonsay, Argyll
☎Colonsay(09512)312

Painted pebbledash cottage on small hilltop overlooking Loch Fada. Accommodation comprises kitchen/diner, lounge with sofa bed and bathroom on ground floor and two attic bedrooms, one double, one twin which are reached by steep ladder type staircase. The cottage is set back from single track road that encircles the island.

All year MWB out of season 1wk min, 1unit, 1–6persons ◊ ◎ fridge
open fires Elec metered ⬜not provided
☎(3m) ⊙ ⊕3pin square P 🏠(3m)
↩ δ(1m) ♀(3m) 🎜(3m)
Max£97.75pw (Low)
Max£162.50pw (High)

C Avenue Cottage Kiloran
for bookings Mrs E McNeill, Machrins Farm, Isle of Colonsay, Argyll
☎Colonsay(09512)312

Single-storey cottage in gardens of Colonsay House, comprising lounge/ diner, kitchen, two twin and one double bedroom and bathroom/WC.

All year MWB out of season 1wk min, 1unit, 1–6persons ◊ ◎ fridge
open fires Elec metered ⬜not provided
☎(½m) ⊕3pin square 2P 🏠(3m)
Tennis court at Colonsay House
↩ δ(3m) ♀(3m) 🎜(3m)
Max£103.50pw (Low)
Max£175.50pw (High)

C Baleromindubh Cottage
Baleromindubh
for bookings Mrs E McNeill, Machrins Farm, Isle of Colonsay, Argyll
☎Colonsay(09512)312

Remote cottage situated on the SE side of the island with views towards Jura. It is heated by open fires. The accommodation is simple and comprises one double bedded room, one bunk-bedded, sitting room with bed-settee and kitchen/diner.

All year MWB out of season 1wk min, 1unit, 1–6persons ◊ ◎ fridge
open fires Elec metered ⬜not provided
☎(2m) ⊕3pin square P 🏠(2m)

Coll, Isle of
—
Colonsay, Isle of

↩ ♀(2m) 🎜(2m)
Max£97.75pw (Low)
Max£162.50pw (High)

H Baleruminmhor Farmhouse Cable Bay, Scalasaig
for bookings Mrs E McNeill, Machrins Farm, Isle of Colonsay, Argyll
☎Colonsay(09512)312

Stone farmhouse in superb position overlooking islands of Jura and Islay. It has three bedrooms and a bathroom on the first floor. On the ground floor there is a lounge and a large kitchen/diner, additional bathroom, cloakroom and double bedroom. Facilities are modest. Very rough approach road of 1m.

All year MWB out of season 1wk min, 1unit, 1–10persons ◊ ◎ fridge
open fires Elec metered ⬜not provided
☎(3m) ⊕3pin square P 🏠(3m) Loch & sea fishing, boat for hire
↩ δ(3m) ♀(3m) 🎜(3m)
Max£175.50pw (Low)
Max£276pw (High)

C Cnoc Na Ban Kilchattan
for bookings Mrs E McNeill, Machrin's Farm, Isle of Colonsay, Argyll
☎Colonsay(095 12)312

Croft-style cottage with attic bedrooms, access at each end of the cottage by narrow staircase. Also one double bedroom on ground floor. Sitting room has attractive stone fireplace, and compact kitchen and bathroom leading off. Reached by a short rough track, the cottage is on W side of island.

All year MWB out of season 1wk min, 1unit, 1–6persons ◊ ◎ fridge
open fires Elec metered ⬜not provided
☎(3m) ⊕3pin square 2P 🏠(3m)
↩ δ(1m) ♀(3m) 🎜(3m)
Max£103.50pw (Low)
Max£162.50pw (High)

C Cnoc-na-Fad Kilchattan
for bookings Mrs E McNeill, Machrins Farm, Isle of Colonsay, Argyll
☎Colonsay(095 12)312

White painted stone cottage half way between Loch Fada and Port Mhor on island road. Accommodation is all on the ground floor and comprises sitting room, kitchen/diner, bathroom, three bedrooms – one double, one twin and one bunk-bedded.

All year MWB out of season, 1wk min, 1unit, 1–6persons ◊ ◎ fridge
open fires Elec metered ⬜not provided
☎(3m) ⊙ ⊕3pin square 1p 🏠(3m)
↩(1m) ♀(3m) 🎜(3m)
Max£103.50pw (Low)
Max£178.25pw (High)

F Colonsay House Flats Kiloran
for bookings Mrs E McNeill, Machrins Farm, Isle of Colonsay, Argyll
☎Colonsay(09512)312

Nine self-contained flats forming a wing of Colonsay House and set on either ground, first or second floor level. They vary in size but each has sitting/dining room, kitchen, bathroom and one to three bedrooms.

All year MWB out of season 1wk min, 9units, 2–6persons ◊ ♂ fridge
Calor gas or solid fuel fires Elec metered
⬜not provided ☎ [Launderette] on premises ⊙ ⊕3pin square 20P
🏠(3m) ↩Hard.
↩ δ(3m) ♀(3m) 🎜(3m)
Max£92pw (Low)
Max£175.50pw (High)

H Farm House Kiloran
for bookings Mrs E McNeill, Machrins Farm, Isle of Colonsay, Argyll
☎Colonsay(095 12)312

Largest house on the estate situated adjacent to entrance of Colonsay House garden. Comprises lounge with open fire, kitchen/diner, one double bedroom and two bathrooms downstairs and four twin-bedded rooms upstairs.

All year MWB out of season 1wk min, 1unit, 10–12persons ◊ ◎ fridge oil fired Rayburn & open fires Elec metered
⬜not provided ☎(¼m) ⊕3pin square 6P 🏠(3m) Tennis at Colonsay House
↩ δ(3m) ♀(3m) 🎜(3m)
Max£175.50pw (Low)
Max£276pw (High)

C Garta Ghoban Kilchattan
for bookings Mrs E McNeill, Machrins Farm, Isle of Colonsay, Argyll
☎Colonsay(095 12)312

Two-storey stone cottage situated on west side of island. Comprising sitting/dining room/kitchen with open fire. There is a double bedroom and bathroom on the ground floor with two twin-bedded rooms on the first floor.

All year MWB out of season 1wk min, 1unit, 1–6persons ◊ ◎ fridge
open fires Elec metered ⬜not provided
☎(3m) ⊕3pin square 2P 🏠(3m)
↩ δ(1m) ♀(3m) 🎜(3m)
Max£103.50pw (Low)
Max£178.25pw (High)

C Glen Cottage Scalasaig
for bookings Mrs E McNeill, Machrins Farm, Isle of Colonsay, Argyll
☎Colonsay(095 12)312

Small white painted stone cottage located close to Scalasaig Pier comprising kitchen, sitting room, bathroom and one double bedded room on the ground floor. A steep staircase leads to two twin-bedded attic bedrooms.

All year MWB out of season 1wk min, 1unit, 1–6persons ◊ ◎ fridge
open fires Elec metered ⬜not provided
☎(200yds) ⊙ ⊕3pin square P
🏠(200yds)

⊕ ♨(¼m) 🎵(¼m)
Max£103.50pw (Low)
Max£178.25pw (High)

C Port Mhor Kilchattan
for bookings Mrs E McNeill, Machrins
Farm, Isle of Colonsay, Argyll
☎Colonsay(095 12)312

*Stone cottage comprising living room,
kitchen with adjoining bathroom and a
double-bedded room all on the ground
floor. There are two twin-bedded rooms in
the attic.*

All year MWB out of season 1wk min,
1unit, 1–6persons ◆ ◎ fridge
Open fires Elec metered ⌷ not provided
☎(3m) ☉ ⊕3pin square 2P ♨(3m)
⊕ ♭(1m) ♨(3m) 🎵(3m)
Max£103.50pw(Low)
Max£178.25pw (High)

C School & Sgreadan Cottages
Kilchattan
for bookings Mrs E McNeill, Machrins
Farm, Isle of Colonsay, Argyll
☎Colonsay(095 12)312

*Both cottages overlook Loch Fada and
are set back from the single road that
circuits the island. They comprise of
sitting/dining room with open fire, kitchen,
bathroom and double bedroom. The first
floor has two twin attic bedrooms reached
by a steep staircase.*

All year MWB out of season 1wk min,
2units, 1–6persons ◆ ◎ fridge
Open fires Elec metered ⌷ not provided
☎(3m) ☉ ⊕3pin square 4P ♨(3m)
⊕ ♭(1m) ♨(3m) 🎵(3m)
Max£103.50pw (Low)
Max£178.25pw (High)

C Uragaig & Kiloran Bay Cottages
Kiloran Bay
for bookings Mrs E McNeill, Machrins
Farm, Isle of Colonsay, Argyll
☎Colonsay(095 12)312

*Two cottages overlooking Kiloran Bay,
close to sandy beaches. Each comprises
lounge/diner with open fire, kitchen and
double bedroom on ground floor plus two
twin attic bedrooms reached by steep
staircase.*

All year MWB out of season 1wk min,
2units, 1–6persons ◆ ◎ fridge

Colonsay, Isle of
—
Combe Martin

Open fires Elec metered ⌷ not provided
☎(3m) ⊕3pin square 6P ♨(3m)
Tennis at Colonsay House
⊕ ♭(1m) ♨(3m) 🎵(3m)
Max£103.50pw (Low)
Max£178.25pw (High)

COLWELL BAY
See **Wight, Isle of**

COLWYN BAY
Clwyd
Map**6** SH87

F Sprindrift Holiday Flat Mr R W Gibson,
16 Mostyn Road, Colwyn Bay, Clwyd
LL29 8PB
☎Llandudno(0492)79228

*Comfortable 1–3 bedroomed flats within
Edwardian house in pleasant residential
area close to sea, park and shops. They all
contain kitchen/diner, lounge, bathroom/
WC. Owners supervision.*

Apr–Oct 1wk min, 6wks max, 3units,
2–7persons ◆ ◎ fridge Electric
Elec metered ⌷ can be hired
☎(100yds) Iron & Ironing board in unit
☉ CTV ⊕3pin square 3P 🎛
♨(100yds)
⊕ ♭(2m) ♨(100yds) 🎵(¼m)
🎵(¼m) 🥾(150yds)
Min£50 Max£95pw (Low)
Min£75 Max£165pw (High)

COLYTON
Devon
Map**3** SY29

**C & F Byre, Cider House, Dairy,
Granary & Farm Wing**
for bookings Mrs R E Davies, Barritshayes
Farm, Colyton, Devon EX13 6DU
☎Colyton(0297)52485

*Set in a converted barn on a 5-acre
smallholding, overlooking the countryside,
all the units offer tastefully furnished
accommodation and good facilities. The
Byre is a one bedroomed flat, with living/*

---

*dining room, kitchen area, bathroom and
WC. The Dairy and Granary cottages both
have two storeyed accommodation
comprising living/dining room, kitchen
area, two bedrooms, bathroom and WC. A
third cottage, Farm Wing consists of
kitchen/dining room on the ground floor
leading to lounge, two bedrooms,
bathroom and WC on the first floor, with
third bedroom in the attic. The Cider
House consists of: on the ground floor a
combined lounge with double put-u-up,
open plan kitchen and dining area, and
double bedroom; On the first floor one
treble bedroom and bathroom/WC.*

Etr–Oct MWB out of season 1wk min,
1mth max, 5units, 1–7persons ◇ ◆
♦ no pets ◎ fridge Electric fires
Elec metered ⌷inclusive ☎(2m) WM
on premises Iron & Ironing board in unit
☉ CTV ⊕3pin square 10P 🎛
♨(2m) ≏ Games room
⊕ ♨(2m) 🎵(2m)
Min£60 Max£165pw (Low)
Min£120 Max£215pw (High)

C CC Ref 7540 LP
for bookings Character Cottages
(Holidays) Ltd, 34 Fore Street, Sidmouth
Devon EX10 8AQ
☎Sidmouth(03955)77001

*A detached stone-built cottage, situated in
a quiet lane. It comprises pine fitted
kitchen/breakfast room, dining room and
WC on the ground floor, with lounge, two
bedrooms and bathroom, WC on the first
floor.*

All year 1wk min, 1mth max, 1unit,
1–5persons ◆ ◎ fridge Electric
Elec metered ⌷inclusive ☎ Iron &
Ironing board in unit ☉ CTV
⊕3pin square 1P 1🏠 🎛 ♨(150yds)
⊕ ♨(200yds)
Min£77 Max£126pw (Low)
Min£146 Max£189pw (High)

COMBE MARTIN
Devon
Map**2** SS54

B Beachside
for bookings Mrs P J Norman, Waters
Edge, Newberry Road, Combe Martin,
Ilfracombe, Devon EX34 0AP
☎Combe Martin(027 188)3321 →

Modern semi-detached bungalow situated on the seaward side of the main road to the W of the village. Within 100yds of the beach and close to the sea. The accommodation is spacious and well-furnished and consists of two double-bedded rooms, one with an extra single bed, lounge/diner, kitchen and bathroom, and WC. There is a fenced rear yard.

Mar–Nov MWB out of season 3days min, 6wks max, 1unit, 2–5persons [◇ ◆ ◆] ♂ fridge Electric Elec inclusive Gas metered ⬜inclusive ☎(300yds) Iron & Ironing board in unit [Launderette within 300yds] ⊕ CTV ⊕3pin square 2P

⊖ ♀(300yds) 🎏(300yds) ♫(1m)

Min£75 Max£100pw (Low)
Min£125 Max£160pw (High)

F Drake Flat Boronga road
for bookings R J Norman, Waters Edge, Newberry Road, Combe Martin, Ilfracombe, Devon EX34 0AP
☎Combe Martin(027 188)3321

Attractive cottage-style flat located above a gift shop, 100yds from the sea. Beamed entrance hall, living room with kitchen off, two bedrooms and bathroom/WC. Car parking on payment in garage opposite or public car park, 100yds.

Mar–Nov MWB out of season 3days min, 1mth max, 1unit, 1–4persons [◇ ◆ ◆] ☺ fridge Electric Elec metered ⬜inclusive ☎(50yds) Iron & Ironing board in unit [Launderette within 300yds] ⊕ TV ⊕3pin square 🍴 ♨

⊖ δ(2½m) ♀(50yds) 🎏(50yds) ♫(½m)

Min£75 Max£100pw (Low)
Min£125 Max£160pw (High)

F The Flat
for bookings R J Jordan & M Raffle, Lion Inn, Victoria Street, Combe Martin, Devon EX34 0LZ
☎Combe Martin(027 188)2485

First-floor flat located within a public house comprising three bedrooms, lounge/diner with a single put-u-up, kitchen area and shower room with WC.

Combe Martin

All year MWB out of season 4days min, 1mth max, 1unit, 1–9persons [◇] ◆ ◆ no pets ☺ fridge Electric Elec metered ⬜not provided ☎(5yds) Iron & Ironing board on premises TV ⊕3pin square 2P 🍴 ♨(¼m)

⊖ ♀ 🎏(½m) ♫(½m)

Ch & F Glenavon Park
for bookings Mr & Mrs R Griffin, Glenavon Park, Combe Martin, Devon EX34 0AS
☎Combe Martin(027 188)2563

Ten flats and 17 chalets situated in wooded and secluded grounds near sea and beach. The **Chalets** *comprise of kitchenette/living room, with double studio couch, bathroom/WC and two bedrooms.* **Flat No. 1** *and* **No. 4** *in the* **Coach House** *both have three bedrooms, while* **Nos. 2 & 3** *have two bedrooms each. All flats have varying sized lounge/dining/kitchen areas, and a bathroom. The six* **Flats** *are located in a Victorian-style house. Two have one bedroom with studio couch in lounge; two have two bedrooms, while the sleeping accommodation of the other two is a divan and a studio couch in the lounge. All have bathroom and kitchen or kitchenette.*

Flat all year **Chalets** 15Mar–Oct MWB in season 3days min, 3wks max, 27units, 1–8persons [◆ ◆] (no dogs ☺ fridge Electric (🍴in Manor House Flats) Elec inclusive ⬜inclusive ☎(100yds) [Launderette on premises] ⊕ CTV ⊕3pin square P 🍴 ♨ ⌂

⊖ δ(3m) ♀ 🎏(1m) ♫(1m)

Min£60 Max£90pw (Low)
Min£130 Max£235pw (High)

F R J Jordan & M Raffle Jacaranda Lodge The Lion Inn, Victoria Street, Combe Martin, Devon EX34 0LZ
☎Combe Martin(027188)2485

A first-floor flat with southerly views across rural valley. Entrance to the flat is through the Inn courtyard. Accommodation comprises lounge/diner, kitchen area, put-u-up in lounge, two double bedrooms and

---

a third room with bunks and two single beds; shower and separate WC.

All year MWB out of season 4days min, 1mth max, 1unit, 1–10persons [◇ ◆ ◆] ☺ fridge Electric Elec metered ⬜not provided ☎ Iron & Ironing board on premises ⊕ CTV ⊕3pin square 2P 🍴 ♨(¼m) δ

⊖ 🎏(½m) ♫(½m)

F Loverings Maisonette
for bookings Mrs M D Lovering, Woodlands Court, Combe Martin, Devon EX34 0AN
☎Combe Martin(027188)3613

A self contained maisonette comprising dining room, well fitted kitchen, two double bedrooms, bathroom and, on top floor, a shower and WC, a plus lounge with doors to paved patio. Well equipped and furnished, situated centrally in Ilfracombe, 100yds from beach.

Etr–Nov MWB out of season 4days min, 1mth max, 1unit, 1–5persons [◇] ◆ ◆] ♂ fridge 🔥gas wall fires Gas & Elec inclusive ⬜inclusive ☎(5yds) Iron & Ironing board in unit [Launderette within 300yds] ⊕ 🐟 CTV ⊕3pin square 2P 🍴 ♨(50yds)

⊖ δ(3m) ♀(50yds) 🎏(½m) ♫(½m)

Min£90 Max£120pw (Low)
Min£150 Max175pw (High)

C Lyncliff Cross Street
for bookings Mrs P J Norman, Waters Edge, Newberry Road, Combe Martin, Ilracombe, Devon EX34 0AP
☎Combe Martin(027 188)3321

Small, semi-detached cottage style property comprising lounge/diner, kitchen, one double-bedoom, one twin-bedded room and bathroom/WC.

Mar–Nov MWB out of season 3days min, 1mth max, 1unit, 1–4persons [◇] ◆ ◆ ☺ fridge Electric Elec metered ⬜inclusive ☎(50yd) Iron & Ironing board in unit [Launderette within 300yds] ⊕ CTV ⊕3pin square 2P 🏠 🍴 ♨(20yds)

⊖ δ(3m) ♀(50yds) 🎏(50yds) ♫(½m)

Min£80 Max£120pw (Low)
Min£140 Max£175pw (High)

C   1 Mimosa & 2 Roseus Cottages
for bookings R J Jordan & M Raffle, Lion Inn, Victoria Street, Combe Martin, Devon EX34 0LZ
☎Combe Martin(027 188)2485

*A pair of semi-detached, pebble-dashed cottages converted from stables. **Mimosa** comprises open plan lounge/diner and kitchen area divided off, with open plan stairway leading to two bedrooms and shower room/WC. **Roseus** has kitchen/ diner on ground floor with open plan stairway leading to first-floor lounge with bed-settee, two bedrooms and shower room/WC.*

All year   MWB out of season   4 days min, 1 mth max, 2 units, 1–5 persons [◇ ◆]
◆ ◎ fridge Electric Elec metered
🅛 not provided ☎ Iron & Ironing board on premises ⊖ TV ⊕3pin square 4P
📺 ♨(½m)

Details not confirmed for 1987

Ch   Moory Mead Sea Close
for bookings Mrs P J Norman, Waters Edge, Newberry Road, Combe Martin, Ilfracombe, Devon EX34 0AP
☎Combe Martin(027 188)3321

This neat little detached chalet of older design, clad in wood, is tucked away behind shops, on the seaward side of the main road through village about 150yds from the beach. The furnishings are traditional and the accommodation comprises two double-bedded rooms, compact kitchen with dining area off, lounge and shower with WC.

Mar–Nov   MWB out of season
3 days min, 6 wks max, 1 unit, 2–4 persons
[◇ ◆ ◆] ◎ fridge Electric
Elec metered 🅛inclusive ☎(20yds)
Iron & Iron board in unit [Launderette]
⊖ TV ⊕3pin square P 📺 ♨(20yds)
⊖ ♀(300yds) 🎵(300yds) ♬(300yds)
Min£60 Max£80pw (Low)
Min£100 Max£125pw (High)

H   Sea Close
for bookings Mrs P J Norman, Waters Edge, Newberry Road, Combe Martin, Ilfracombe, Devon EX34 0AP
☎Combe Martin(027 188)3321

Combe Martin
—
Compton

A detached Victorian house with fine views of coast, close to shops and beach. The accommodation consists of lounge, dining room, kitchen, four bedrooms, two with wash hand basin and bathroom and WC.

Mar–Nov   MWB out of season
3 days min, 6 wks max, 1 unit, 2–8 persons
[◇ ◆ ◆] ♨ fridge Electric
Elec inclusive Gas metered 🅛inclusive
☎(300yds) Iron & Ironing board in unit
[Launderette within 300yds] ⊖ CTV
⊕3pin square P 📺 ♨(200yds)
⊖ ♀(300yds) 🎵(300yds) ♬(1m)
Min£120 Max£280pw

F   Sundora Flats, 1 2 & 3 Cross Street
for bookings Mrs P J Norman, Waters Edge, Newberry Road, Combe Martin, Ilfracombe, Devon EX34 0AP
☎Combe Martin(027 188)3321

One ground- and two first-floor flats, all comprise kitchen, lounge/dining room, bathroom and WC. Ground floor has three bedrooms and sleeps up to seven, the others have two bedrooms.

Mar–Nov   MWB out of season
3 days min, 1 mth max, 3 units, 1–7 persons
[◇ ◆ ◆] no pets in first-floor flats
◎ fridge Electric Elec metered
🅛inclusive ☎(50yds) Iron & Ironing
board in unit [Launderette within 300yds] ⊖ CTV ⊕3pin square 4P
📺 ♨(30yds)
⊖ ♭(3m) ♀(50yds) 🎵(50yds)
♬(½m)
Min£80 Max£120pw (Low)
Min£120 Max£175pw (High)

B, C & H Mr T Massey **Wheel Farm Country Cottages** Wheel Farm, Berry Down, Combe Martin, Ilfracombe, Devon EX34 0NT
☎Combe Martin(027 188)2100

*Seven well-kept cottages and a farmhouse of a high standard situated on the fringe of the Exmoor National Park. **Stable, Byre, Shippon** and **Granary** have three*

bedrooms each, whilst **Old Dairy** and **Linhay** have two and **Hayloft** has one with a four poster. Hayloft can be interconnected with the Byre, all cottages are well furnished and have open plan lounge/diner, kitchen and bathroom. **Wheel Farmhouse** has two double-bedded rooms, one twin and one room with bunks. Ground-floor comprises spacious lounge, a dining room, kitchen and shower/WC. Maid service is available.

Mar–4 Jan (Farmhouse May–Sep)
1 wk min 4 wks max, 8 units, 1–8 persons
[◇ ◆ ◆] ◎ fridge
storage heaters 🍳 Elec metered
🅛inclusive ☎(1m) [Launderette on premises] Iron & Ironing board on premises ⊖ CTV ⊕3pin square 13P
📺 ♨
⊖ ♀(200yds) 🎵(2½) ♬(2½m)
Min£74 Max£105pw (Low)
Min£169 Max£363pw (High)

COMPTON
Devon
Map **3** SX86

C Mr & Mrs J N Songer **Compton Pool Farm** Compton, Paignton, South Devon TQ3 1TA
☎Kingkerswell(08047)2241

*Old stone barns, grouped around a central fountained courtyard, have been converted into six cottages each with individual character and retaining many period features. Each cottage has a lounge/diner, pine fitted kitchen and bathroom/WC. **The Coach House** is a two-storey cottage with natural stone walls, one double bedroom and one family bedroom. **Old Barn** is the largest cottage with one twin, one bunk bedroom and a family bedroom. It also has an additional shower room/WC. **Old Farm Cottage** was part of the original farmhouse, it has a twin bedroom and a family room with a four poster bed. **Cider House** is the other half of the farmhouse with a family room, and a twin bedroom with intercommunicating bunk bedroom. **Garden Cottage**, formerly the old milking parlour, has its own small patio area and comprises a family bedroom with WHB and four poster bed and a twin bedroom. **The Hayloft** offers first floor →*

accommodation with a double bedroom with four poster and two single bedrooms.

Etr–Oct 1wk min, 6units, 2–8persons [◇] ◈ ◆ pets by arrangement ◎ fridge storage heaters & electric fires Elec metered ⊡inclusive (except towels & tea towels) ☎ [WM & SD on premises] Iron & Ironing board in unit [Launderette on premises] ⊖ ⊗ CTV ⊕3pin square P ⊞ ⊠(heated) ⊅Hard

⊖ ♪(3m) ⚲(⅔m) ♫(3m) ♬(3m) ⛺(3m) Sports centre(3m)

Min£85 Max£175pw (Low)
Min£115 Max£310pw (High)

CONISTON
Cumbria
Map**7** SD39

F Thurston House
for bookings Mr & Mrs M Smith, Woodhow, Staveley in Cartmel, Ulverston, Cumbria
☎Newby Bridge(0448)31223

Traditional large lakeland slate house, in quiet position with views of the lake, Grizedale Forest and the Coniston mountain range. First and second-floor flats with accommodation in various combinations.

Allyear MWB out of season 3days min, 3wks max, 4units, 4–6persons ◈ ◆ ◎ fridge Electric Elec metered ⊡can be hired ☎(100yds) Iron & Ironing board in unit ⊖ [TV] ⊕3pin square 7P ⊞ ⛼(50yds)

⊖ ⚲(100yds) ♬(100yds)

Min£40 Max£60pw (Low)
Min£70 Max£120pw (High)

CONNEL
Strathclyde Argyllshire
Map**10** NM93

B Ashfield & Cullreigh
for bookings Mrs I Campbell, Druimbhan, North Connel, Oban, Argyll
☎Connel(063171)424

Two bungalows situated on the north side of Loch Etive, one mile from the junction of the A828. Accommodation comprises three compact bedrooms, spacious kitchen and lounge.

Compton
—
Connel

Allyear MWB out of season 2nights min, 1mth max, 2units, 1–6persons ◈ ◆ ◎ fridge Electric Elec metered ⊡inclusive ☎(1m) WM, SD in unit Iron & Ironing board in unit ⊖ CTV ⊕3pin square 2P a unit ⛼(2m)

⊖ ⚲(½m)

Min£60 Max£175pw

C Cruachan & Linnhe View Cottages
South Ledaig
for bookings Mr A McIntyre, Eilean Beag, South Ledaig, Connel, Argyll
☎Connel(063171)597

Renovated farm building converted to two semi-detached cottages each with kitchen, sitting room, one double bedroom with wash hand basin, one twin bedroom and bathroom. Shared large garden. Cruachan has a terrace. Two miles from Connel on main A828 to Fort William.

Apr–31Oct 1wk min, 4wks max, 2units, 1–4persons ◈ no pets ◎ fridge Electric Elec metered ⊡not provided ☎(1m) Iron & Ironing board in unit ⊖ CTV ⊕3pin square 4P ⛼(2m) Rough Shooting, pony trekking, gliding & fishing

⊖ ⚲(1m)

Min£80 Max£160pw

C Diarmid Cottage Tigh-na-Mara
for bookings Highland Hideaways, 5/7 Stafford Street, Oban, Argyll PA34 1NJ
☎Oban(0631)62056/63901

Single-storey cottage with its own lawn sloping down to the sea. Accommodation consists of a fitted kitchen, front facing dining room with access to lawn, back lounge with fireplace, and three bedrooms sleeping up to six people. Heating is included in the rental.

Etr–mid Oct 1wk min, 3mths max, 1unit, 1–6persons no pets ◎ fridge Electric Elec metered ⊡not provided ☎(½m) Iron in unit CTV ⊕3pin square P ⛼(½m)

⊖ ♪(2½m) ⚲(2½m) ♫(2½m) ♬2½m) ⛺(2½m)

Min£70 Max£245pw

H Fingal House Tigh-na-Mara
for bookings Highland Hideaways, 5/7 Stafford Street, Oban, Argyll PA34 1NJ
☎Oban(0631)62056/63901

Elegant house forming the main part of Tigh-na-Mara House. It has a lounge, kitchen, dining room, double-bedded room with dressing room, double room, single room, and two bathrooms with WC. Heating included in rental.

Etr–mid Oct 1wk min, 3mths max, 1unit, 1–7persons, nc15 no pets ◎ fridge Elec metered ⊡not provided ☎ Iron & Ironing board in unit ⊖ CTV ⊕3pin square P ⛼(½m)

⊖ ♪(2½m) ♫(2½m) ♬(2½m) ⛺(2½m)

Min£100 Max£279pw

B & C Rhonelin & Tigh Grianach
for bookings Mrs I Campbell Achnacree Bay, North Connel, Argyll
☎Connel(063171)288

A semi-detached bungalow and a detached cottage situated on the north side of Loch Etive, one mile from the junction of the A828. The accommodation comprises three compact bedrooms, spacious kitchen and lounge.

Allyear MWB out of season 2nights min, 1mth max, 4units, 1–6persons ◈ ◆ ◎ fridge Electric Elec metered ⊡inclusive ☎(1m) WM & SD in unit Iron & Ironing board in unit ⊖ CTV ⊕3pin square 2P per unit ⛼(2m)

⊖ ⚲(½m)

Min£60 Max£175pw

C Somerled Cottage Tigh-na-Mara
for bookings Highland Hideaways, 5/7 Stafford Street, Oban, Argyll PA34 1NJ
☎Oban(0631)62056/63901

A cottage on two floors being the central section of Tigh-na-Mara House. The ground floor comprises an entrance hall, central dining room, lounge, modern kitchen, bathroom/WC, separate WC and a large double bedroom with a dressing room. Upstairs has a further two bedrooms. Heating included in rental.

Etr—mid Oct MWB out of season
1wk min, 3mths max, 1unit, 1–6persons
no pets ⓦ fridge Elec metered
Ⓛnot provided ☎(½m) Iron & Ironing
board in unit ☺ CTV ⊕3pin square
P 🏠 ⚊(½m)
⊖ δ(2½m) ⚌(2½m) 🎵(2½m)
♫(2½m) ⚏(2½m)
Min£74 Max£250pw

CONTIN
Highland *Ross & Cromarty*
Map14 NH45

Ch Craigdarroch Chalets
for bookings R E Hendry, Craigdarroch
Drive, Contin, Strathpeffer, Ross-shire
☎Strathpeffer(0997)21584
*Five attractive detached chalets
containing two bedrooms, bathroom and
lounge/kitchen with convertible settee.
The chalets are grouped together at the
end of a driveway that runs from A382, 1m
NW of Contin.*

11Apr–4Oct 4days min, 5units,
1–6persons ⓦ fridge ⚒ Elec metered
Ⓛinclusive ☎(100yds) Iron & Ironing
board in unit ☺ CTV ⊕3pin square
P ⚊(1m) Horse riding & fishing
⊖ δ(3m) ⚌(100yds) 🎵(3m)
Min£120 Max£165pw (High)

COPMANTHORPE
North Yorkshire
Map8 SE54

C Mr J Hughes **Holiday Cottages**
Copmanthorpe Grange, Copmanthorpe,
York YO2 3TN
☎Appleton Roebuck(090484)318
*Restored and converted farm building
previously a specialist stud-farm set in
attractive rural surrounds of open farmland, 4m S of York. These 8 units sleep
from 1–6persons with either bathroom/
WC or shower room/WC and combined
lounge/dining room and kitchen.*

All year MWB 3days min, 6mths max,
8units, 1–6persons [◇] ◈ ◆ ⓦ
fridge Electric Elec inclusive
Ⓛinclusive ☎(1m) Iron on premises
Ironing board in unit ☺ CTV
⊕3pin square 20P ⚏ ⚊(1m)
⊖ δ
Min£78 Max£108
Min£118 Max£168

See advertisement under York

CORNHILL
Grampian *Banffshire*
Map15 NJ55

C **Bogroy Cottage**
for bookings J & J Palphramand, West
Reidside, Cornhill, Banffshire
☎Cornhill(04666)381
*Conversion of roadside cottage into a
comfortable holiday home of character. It
comprises modern kitchen with dining
facilities, cosy lounge, bathroom and two
bedrooms. Situated 3m S of Portsoy and
Moray Firth coast.*

Connel
—
Crackington Haven

All year 1wk min, 1unit, 1–4persons ⓦ
fridge Electric & open fires
Elec metered Ⓛcan be hired ☎(1½m)
☺ TV ⊕3pin square 4P ⚏ ⚊(1½m)
⊖ ⚌(1½m)
Min£80 Max£175pw

CORWEN
Clwyd
Map6 SJ04

H **Plau Uchaf** Llangar
for bookings Landmark Trust,
Shottesbrooke, Maidenhead, Berkshire
SL6 3SW
☎Littlewick Green(062882)5925
*A restored 15th-century Hall with a
magnificent beamed hall featuring a large
open stone fireplace. Accommodation
comprises lounge, kitchen, bathroom/WC
and two twin-bedded rooms (one with Z-
bed).*

All year MWB out of season 1day min,
3wks max, 1unit, 2–5persons ◆ ⓦ
fridge storage & portable heaters/open
fire Ⓛnot provided ☎(1m) Iron &
Ironing board in unit ☺ ⊕3pin square
4P ⚊(1½)
⊖ ⚌(1½m)
Min£154 Max£275pw (Low)
Min£180 Max£275pw (High)

COSHESTON
Dyfed
Map2 SM90

H **West Farm**
for bookings Powells Cottage Holidays, 55
High Street, Saundersfoot, Dyfed
☎Saundersfoot(0834)812791
*Large modern detached house with large
garden set in quiet lane with good views
over estuary. Comprises lounge, dining
room, large kitchen, one double, one twin
and one family bedroom, bathroom/WC
and shower/WC.*

May–Sep MWB out of season 1wk min,
1unit, 1–6persons ◆ ⓦ fridge ⚒
Elec inclusive Ⓛnot provided ☎(2m)
WM in unit Iron & Ironing board in unit
☺ CTV ⊕3pin square 2P ⚏ ⚊(1m)
⊖ ⚌(1m)
Min£165 Max£351pw

COVENTRY
West Midlands
Map4 SP37

F **Hurst & Redfern Flats**
for bookings The Vacation Flats
Administrator, University of Warwick,
Rootes Hall, Gibbet Hill Road, Coventry,
West Midlands CV4 7AL
☎Coventry(0203)523507

*Modern blocks of flats set in extensive
landscaped grounds on the University
campus. Ideal for sports enthusiast. Each
comprises kitchen/dining area, bathroom,
WC and five or six single bedrooms all with
wash hand basins. Bedrooms can be
converted into twin rooms upon request.*

11Jul–19Sep MWB Aug & Sep
4days min, 8wks max, 50units,
1–12persons [◇] no pets ◑ fridge
⚒ Gas & Elec inclusive Ⓛinclusive
☎ Iron [Launderette within 300yds]
⊕3pin square 70P ⚏ ⚊(300yds)
⟿ ◐Hard & grass δ Sports centre,
sauna & croquet
⊖ δ(3m) ⚌ 🎵 ⚏
Min£161 Max£189pw

See advertisement on page 82

CRACKINGTON HAVEN
Cornwall
Map2 SX19

B **CC Ref 331 P**
for bookings Character Cottages
(Holidays) Ltd, 34 Fore Street, Sidmouth,
Devon EX10 8AQ
☎Sidmouth(03955)77001
*Semi-detached bungalow with integral
garage situated in corner of cul-de-sac.
Accommodation comprises small hall,
cloakroom/WC, living room, modern
kitchen/diner, two bedrooms (one with
double bed, one with twin beds), modern
bathroom and WC. Good position, just
over 1m from beach.*

All year MWB out of season 1wk min,
1mth max, 1unit, 2–4persons ◆ ⓦ
fridge Electric Elec metered
Ⓛnot provided ☎(½m) Iron & Ironing
board in unit ☺ TV ⊕3pin square
⊕2pin round P 🏠 ⚊(1½m)
⊖ ⚌(1½m)
Min£52 Max£104pw (Low)
Min£168 Max£194pw (High)

F Mr & Mrs A Grauers **Gunnedah**
Crackington Haven, Bude, Cornwall
EX23 0JZ
☎St Gennys(08403)265
*Pebble-dashed bungalow type flats
situated 200yds from the beach, and
enjoying glorious views. The units vary in
size from one to four bedrooms and each
have a lounge/diner, kitchen, and
bathroom/shower/WC.*

All year MWB out of season 2days min,
3wks max, 5units, 1–11persons [◇ ◆
◆] ⓦ fridge Electric Elec metered
Ⓛinclusive ☎(100yds) [WM & TD on
premises] Iron & Ironing board on
premises ☺ CTV ⊕3pin square 5P
5🏠 ⚏ ⚊(200yds)
⊖ ⚌(100yds)
Min£80 Max£290pw

C **East & West Emetts**
for bookings Mr & Mrs A Cummins,
Mineshop, St Gennys, Bude, Cornwall
EX23 0NR
☎St Gennys(08403)338 →

A pair of cottages (one of them thatched, the other slated), about a mile from the beach at Crackington Haven. One comprises open plan living room with wood/coal burner and kitchenette; one double bedroom and twin-bedded room, bathroom and WC. The other cottage has room with bunk beds, one double bedroom and studio couch in lounge.

All year MWB out of season 1wk min, 6wks max, 2units, 2–6persons ◆ ◎ fridge Night storage Elec metered ⌂can be hired ☎(300yds) Airing cupboard Iron & Ironing board in unit HCE in unit CTV ⊕3pin square P 🛁(20yds)
⊖ 🛉(1m)
Min£55 Max£75pw (Low)
Min£102 Max£165pw (High)

CRANTOCK
Cornwall
Map**2** SW76

C Halwyn Farm Cottage, Scantlebury & Trevalsa Cottages West Pentire
for bookings J A & P A Eastlake, Treago Farm, Crantock, Newquay, Cornwall
☎Crantock (0637)830277

These properties are located at West Pentire, ½m from Treago Farm. **Halwyn Farm Cottage** comprises dining room, lounge, kitchen, bathroom, separate WC and two large bedrooms. **Scantlebury & Trevalsa** have been converted and modernised for holiday letting, both sleep

Crackington Haven
—
Craobh Haven

up to six people with Trevalsa having kitchen with dining area, lounge, bathroom and WC; two double bedrooms and one with two single beds. Scantlebury has two double bedrooms and one with two bunks, kitchen, large lounge with dining area, bathroom and WC. All the above properties have some main rooms that overlook the beach and sea.

Mar–Oct MWB 1wk min, 3mths max, 4units, 1–6persons ◆ ◎ fridge Electric Elec metered ⌂not provided ☎(½m) Iron & Ironing board in unit ◎ CTV ⊕3pin square P 🅼 🛁(½m)
⊖ ♪(2m) 🛉(2m) 🎵(2m) ♫(2m)
🛅(2m)
Min£70 Max£92pw (Low)
Min£200 Max£230pw (High)

C Treago Malthouse & Treago Cottage
for bookings J A & P A Eastlake, Treago Farm, Crantock, Newquay, Cornwall
☎Crantock (0637)830277

The **Malthouse** is a modern purpose-built holiday cottage on the site of the old malthouse and backs onto the farm courtyard. It comprises three bedrooms, bathroom, separate WC on the first floor and large lounge, open plan kitchen with breakfast bar, on the ground floor. **Treago**

Farm Cottage is a typical old Cornish cottage with thick stone walls and beamed ceiling. The accommodation comprises two bedrooms plus a landing bedroom with single bed; kitchen, lounge/dining room and bathroom/WC.

All year MWB out of season 1wk min, 3mths max, 2units, 1–6persons ◆ [◆Malthouse] no dogs[Malthouse] ◎ fridge Electric Elec metered ⌂not provided ☎(100yds) Iron & Ironing board in unit ◎ CTV ⊕3pin square P 🅼 🛁(30yds)
⊖ ♪(2m) 🛉(2m) 🎵(2m) ♫(2m)
🛅(2m)
Min£70 Max£92pw (Low)
Max£230pw (High)

CRAOBH HAVEN
Highland Argyll
Map**10** NM70

C Mrs A Hampton **Craobh Haven Cottages** Craobh Haven, Lochgilphead, Argyll PA31 8QR
☎Barbreck (08525)266 & 666

Part of the new Leisure Village and Marina Complex. The cottages combine traditional character with high standards of modern comfort. Accommodation consists of semi-open plan lounge/ kitchen/diner. Upstairs **Scarba, Luing** and **Islay** have a double bedroom with wash hand basin, a twin room and bathroom. **Lunga, Seil, Shuna, Torsa** and **Jura** have one double and one twin bedroom each

with wash hand basin, an additional bunk room and bathroom. Located off the A816, 14 miles north of Lochgilphead. **Scottish Holiday Home of the Year – see pages 7–14.**

All year MWB out of season 8units, 1–6persons [◇] ◆ ◉ fridge 🍴, electric & open fires Elec inclusive Ⓛinclusive ☎(50yds) WM in unit TD in unit Iron & Ironing board in unit ⊕ CTV ⊕3pin square 4P ♨(25yds) Riding centre, playground

⊖ 🏠(100yds)
Min£143 Max£157pw (Low)
Min£175 Max£275pw (High)

F Mrs A Hampton **Honeymoon Flat**
Craobh Haven Cottages, Craobh Haven, Lochgilphead, Argyll PA31 8QR
☎Barbreck(08525)266

The flat is situated on the first floor above the Arts and Crafts shop overlooking the harbour and village green.
Accommodation comprises open plan living area, bedroom featuring Italian kingsize brass bed and bathroom. It has been furnished and fitted to a high standard and designed for a romantic holiday.

All year MWB out of season 1unit, 2persons ◉ fridge electric Elec inclusive Ⓛinclusive ☎(25yds) Launderette(100yds) Iron & Ironing board in unit ⊕ CTV ⊕3pin square 2P ♨(25yds) riding centre Water sports centre
Min£153 Max£175pw (Low)
Min£168 Max£250pw (High)

CREDITON
Devon
Map**3** SS80

F **CC Ref 5009 L Shobrooke**
for bookings Character Cottages (Holidays) Ltd, 34 Fore Street, Sidmouth, Devon EX10 8AQ
☎Sidmouth(03955)77001

A 1st floor flat attached to an old farmhouse, situated in extensive grounds. The accommodation comprises well-equipped pine fitted kitchen/diner, lounge with double put-u-up, one double and one twin bedroom, a bathroom and WC.

Jun–Sep 1wk min, 1mth max, 1unit, 1–6persons ◆ ◉ no pets ◉ fridge Electric Elec metered Ⓛinclusive ☎(160yds) SD in unit Iron & Ironing board in unit ⊕ CTV ⊕3pin square 3P 1🏠 🎲 ♨(4m)

⊖ 𝄐(3m) ♨(2m)
Min£148 Max£175pw

C **JFH Ref WC68D** Bow
for bookings John Fowler Holidays Dept 58, Marlborough Road, Ilfracombe, Devon EX34 8PF
☎Ilfracombe(0271)66666

Spacious end of terrace cottage, consisting of lounge with open fire place (logs provided), dining room with arch to kitchen area, two twin bedrooms and one double, bathroom/WC and extra WC, also

---

Craobh Haven
—
Criccieth

a utility room. Arrangements can be made for guided farm tours.

Mar–Oct MWB 1wk min, 1mth max, 1unit, 6persons ◆ ◉ no pets ◉ fridge Electric heaters & log fire Elec metered Ⓛnot provided ☎(1½m) Iron & Ironing board in unit ⊕ CTV ⊕3pin square 2P ♨(1½m)

⊖ 🏠(1½m)

CRESSING
Essex
Map**5** TL72

C **1 & 2 Red Lion Cottages** Lanham Green Road
for bookings Mrs M Ratcliffe, Ashes Farm, Cressing, Braintree, Essex CM7 8DW
☎Silver End(0376)83236

Two small country cottages with exposed beams, each with lounge/dining room, two bedrooms, bathroom and kitchen. There are good views of surrounding open countryside and the cottages, which have been converted from an old country pub, are only 2m from the market town of Braintree.

All year MWB out of season 2units, 2–5persons nc7 no pets ◉ fridge Electric Elec inclusive Ⓛcan be hired ☎ SD Iron & Ironing board in unit ⊕ TV can be hired ⊕3pin square P 🎲 ♨(3m)

⊖ 🏠(¼m) 🎵(3m) 𝄐(3m) 🐾(3m)
Min£70 Max£90pw

CRIANLARICH
Central Perthshire
Map**10** NN32

Ch Elaine & Trevor Taylor **Portnellan Lodges** Loch Dochart, Crianlarich, Perthshire FK20 8QS
☎Crianlarich(08383)284

Situated 2½m E of Crianlarich at the foot of Ben More these. Finnish pine lodges are comfortable and well equipped. All have splendid views and comprise large lounge with open-plan kitchen and dining area. Most lodges have one double and one twin-bedded room, but three bedroom lodges are also available.

Apr–Dec MWB 3days min, 8units, 1–8persons ◆ ◉ fridge Elec metered Ⓛinclusive ☎ Iron & Ironing boad in unit [Launderette on premises] ⊕ ◉ CTV(charge) ⊕3pin square 16P 🎲 ♨(1½m) Game fishing, canoes, rowing boats, clay pigeon shooting

⊖ 🏠(1m)
Min£99 Max£185pw (Low)
Min£136 Max£225pw (High)

CRICCIETH
Gwynedd
Map**6** SH43

B **Bro Elfion**
for bookings Mr & Mrs G Lloyd Jones, Bro Dewi, Ynys, Criccieth, Gwynedd, LL52 0NT
☎Garn Dolbenmaen(076675)334

18th-century store recently converted to a single storey cottage type dwelling of high standard throughout. Accommodation comprises of lounge, kitchen/diner, two double and one twin-bedded room. Take B4411 from Criccieth.

Mar–Oct MWB out of season 1wk min, 6wks max, 1unit, 1–6persons ◇ ◆ no pets ◉ fridge Electric Elec metered Ⓛnot provided ☎(2m) Iron & Ironing board on premises ⊕ CTV ⊕3pin square 3P 🎲 ♨(3m)

⊖ 🏠(2m)
Min£60 Max£110pw (Low)
Min£125 Max£160pw (High)

F **Clifton House** Mr E A Roberts, 27 Marine Terrace, Criccieth, Gwynedd
☎Criccieth(076671)2220

Two flats located within building situated on the seafront 400yds from village centre. Each comprise of kitchen; lounge/diner a single folding bed, bathroom/WC, one bedroom with three single beds and one bedroom with double and single or bunk beds.

10Jan–30Nov MWB out of season 3days min, 1mth max, 2units, 2–6persons ◇ ◆ no pets ◉ fridge Electric Elec metered Ⓛinclusive ☎(100yds) [Launderette within 500yds] CTV ⊕ ⊕3 pin square 🎲 ♨(100yds)

⊖ 🏠(¼m) 🎵(¼m)
Min£65 Max£90pw (Low)
Min£100 Max£150pw (High)

C **Refail Bach Cottage** Rhoslan
for bookings Mrs E W Roberts, Cae Canol Farm, Criccieth, Gwynedd
☎Criccieth(076671)2351

A traditional Welsh cottage, tastefully modernised with delightful views of Snowdonia and Cardigan Bay. Comprises a lounge, kitchen/diner, one twin-bedded room and two double rooms, and bathroom/WC. Good accommodation in pleasant rural setting.

All year MWB out of season 2days min 6wks max 1unit 2–6persons [◆] ◉ fridge storage heaters & electric fires Elec metered Ⓛnot provided ☎(½m) Iron & Ironing board in unit ⊕ TV can be hired ⊕3pin square 3P ♨(2½m) Fishing, shooting

⊖ 𝄐(2½m) 🏠(2½m) 🎵(2½m)

F Mrs Broadley **Vista Marina** 30 Marine Terrace, Criccieth, Gwynedd
☎Criccieth(076671)2139

Very well run and clean flats in an end of terrace house which faces S over the beach and Cardigan Bay. To the W is a green and another sea view. Within walking distance of town centre. Two flats have a shower instead of a bath.

Mar–Oct MWB out of season 1wk min, 4wks max, 5units, 3–6persons ◇ ◆ ◉ fridge Electric Elec metered Ⓛcan →

be hired ☎(200yds) SD on premises
Iron & Ironing board in unit ⊕ CTV
⊕3pin square P 🔟 ♨(½m)
⊖ ♪(½m) ☎(300yds) 🎵(½m)
Min£60 Max£94pw (Low)
Min£88 Max£152pw (High)

CRIEFF
Tayside *Perthshire*
Map**11** NN82

H   Craigeuan
For bookings Mrs J S Scott, Easter
Dowald, Crieff, Perthshire PH7 3QX
☎Crieff(0764)3285

*A large secluded farmhouse with
panoramic views situated 100yds off A85,
2m E of Crieff. It comprises large living
room, one double bedroom, WC and
shower/WC on ground floor, with four
bedrooms and bathroom on first floor.*

Mar–Nov 1wk min, 1unit, 1–12persons
◆ no pets ◎ fridge Electric
Elec metered 📥can be hired ☎(½m)
Iron & Ironing board in unit ⊕ CTV
⊕3pin round 6P 1🏠 ♨(2m)
⊖ ♪(2m) ☎(100yds)

Ch   Mr A A Colquhoun **Loch
Monzievaird Chalets** Ochtertyre, Crieff,
Perthshire PH7 4JR
☎Crieff(0764)2586

*Scandinavian chalets spaciously grouped
in secluded mature parkland below
hillside and overlooking Loch
Monzievaird. Accommodation varies, one
chalet having two bedrooms and twelve
having three. All have open plan lounge/
diner, kitchenette and bathroom plus one
chalet with sauna. They are completely
pine panelled with matching furnishings
and are finished to a high standard. 2m W
of Crieff off A85. Three ponies are
available free of charge to Chalet
occupants with previous riding
experience.*

All year MWB out of season 1night min,
13units, 1–8persons [◇] ◆ ◆ ◎
fridge 🍴 Elec inclusive 📥inclusive
☎ Iron & Ironing board in unit
[Launderette on premises] ⊕ CTV
⊕3pin square P 🔟 ♨(2m) Trout
fishing and sailing instruction available
⊖ ♪(3m) ☎(2m) 🎵(2m) 🎵(2m)
Min£101.20 Max£321.20pw

Criccieth
—
Croesgoch

CRINAN
Strathclyde *Argyllshire*
Map**10** NR89

F   Kilmahumaig Barns
for bookings Mr M Murray, Kilmahumaig,
Crinan, Lochgilphead, Argyll
☎Crinan(054683)238

*A converted barn containing three flats
situated ½m E of Crinan on B841. Two of
the flats have open-plan kitchen/living
area with two divans on the ground floor
and a double-bedded gallery bedroom
upstairs. The larger unit has separate
living room, kitchen/dining area
downstairs and two bedrooms. All have a
steep spiral staircase.*

All year MWB out of season 3days min,
3mths max, 3units, 1–6persons ◆ ◆
no pets ◎ fridge 🍴 Elec metered
📥not provided ☎(½m) ⊕
⊕3pin square P ♨(1½m)
⊖ ☎(½m)
Min£55 Max£96pw (Low)
Min£108 Max£165pw (High)

CROCKETFORD
Dumfries & Galloway *Dumfries-shire*
Map**11** NX87

C   Stable & Byre Cottages
for bookings A W & M M S McDonald,
Brandedleys, Crocketford, Dumfries
DG2 8RG
☎Crocketford(055669)250

*Two adjoining cottages converted from
old farm buildings and lying next to
owners house with caravan park.* **Stable
cottage** *has an open plan lounge/dining
room/kitchen area, large double bedroom
and shower room with WC.* **Byre cottage**
*has an open plan lounge/dining room,
separate kitchen, twin and double
bedrooms and shower room with WC.
Brandedleys lies in elevated position and
both cottages have splendid views from
their lounge and patio overlooking open
countryside to Auchenreoch Loch. Guests
are free to use the caravan park facilities.*

Jan–Nov MWB out of season
3days min, 3mths max, 2units,
1–7persons 🍴 ◎ fridge 🍴
Elec metered 📥available to hire
☎(50yds) [Launderette on premises]
⊕ CTV ⊕3pin square 2P ♨ ☐
⚓Hard putting Games & TV rooms
⊖ ☎ 🎵(½m)
Min£72 Max£105pw (Low)
Min£160 Max£220pw (High)

CROESGOCH
Dyfed
Map**2** SM83

C & H   Valley Fach Holidays
for bookings L J Richards, West Lodge
Farm, Butterhill, St Ishmaels,
Haverfordwest, Dyfed SA62 3TN
☎Dale(06465)514

*Valley Fach is a carefully restored
farmhouse, known to be over 200 years
old and formerly a mill. A stream runs
through the lower part of the secluded
gardens. Accommodation comprises one
double and one twin bedded room, both
with WHBs and facing south. The lounge
has a beamed ceiling and stone fireplace
and is linked to the dining room, there are
comfortable chairs which convert into
single beds. The modern kitchen and
quality bathroom/WC are on the ground
floor.* **Melin Fach** *was built in 1974 and
extended in 1981, it is particularly
comfortable with the notable feature of
pine ceilings throughout. There is one
double bedroom with additional single
bed and one twin-bedded room, if
required one of the single beds can be
replaced with bunk beds. The modern
fully-equipped kitchen is linked to the
lounge and dining room and there is a
modern bathroom with separate WC.*
Hafan Fach *is the smallest of the cottages
and was originally the milking parlour. The
upstairs living room and kitchen/dining
area have splendid views to the south and
west. On the ground floor is the bedroom
with a double bed and bunk beds and
adjacent is the shower room/WC.*

All year MWB out of season 5days min,
3units, 5–6persons ◆ ◆ no pets
◎ fridge Storage & Convector heaters
Elec metered 📥inclusive ☎ Iron &
Ironing board in unit ⊕ CTV
⊕3pin square 6P ♨(1m)

⊕ 🛏(1m)
Min£55 Max£70pw (Low)
Min£165 Max£240pw (High)

CROPTON
North Yorkshire
Map**8** SE78

Ca   Keldy Castle
for bookings Forest Holidays, Forestry
Commission (Dept A.A.) 231 Corstorphine
Road, Edinburgh EH12 7AT
☎031-334 0303 or 2576

*A vast, rambling complex set in pinewoods
on the fringe of the National Park. The
cabins are compact with an open plan
living area and all sleep six, each having
one double bedroom and four bunk beds
split between the living area and a
separate room, and a shower room/WC.*

Closed endJan – midFeb   MWB out of
season   3nights min, 1mth max, 60units,
1–6persons ◈ ◉ fridge
Electric heaters   Elec metered
⊡inclusive   ☎ [Launderette on
premises]   ☺ TV can be hired
⊕3pin square   60P   ♨ Table tennis,
squash, badminton, riding
⊕ 🛏(2m)
Min£85 Max£240pw

CROSCOMBE
Somerset
Map**3** ST54

H   The Old Hall Church Street
for bookings The Landmark Trust,
Shottesbrooke, Maidenhead, Berkshire
SL6 3SW
☎Littlewick Green(062882)5925

*Once the great hall of a medieval manor, it
is set off a quiet lane in the village centre.
Accommodation comprises kitchen, large
flagstoned hall, lounge with log burning
stove, two bedrooms (one with two singles,
the other with three single beds) and
bathroom.*

All year   MWB out of season   1wk min,
6wks max, 1unit, 1–5persons ◈ ◉
fridge   🍲(ground floor only)   Electric
Elec inclusive   ⊡not provided
☎(200yds)   Iron & Ironing board in unit
☺ ⊕3pin square   2P   🖾 ♨(100yds)
⊕ 🍷(3m) 🛏(100yds) 🛏(3m)
Min£140 Max£255pw (Low)
Min£160 Max£255pw (High)

CROSSGATES
Powys
Map**3** SO06

Ch   Park Motel Chalets Park Motel,
Crossgates, Llandrindod Wells, Powys
LD1 6RF
☎Penybont(059787)201

Croesgoch
—
Crymych

*Modern brick-built chalets with views of
gardens and swimming pool. All have
kitchen/diner (with bed-settee if required),
twin-bedded room and combined shower/
WC. Daily maid service available*

Closed Xmas & Jan   MWB   1night min,
7units, 4persons ◈ ◆ ♪ fridge
🍲 Gas inclusive   ⊡inclusive
☎(20yds)   ☺ CTV   ⊕3pin square   P
🖾 ♨(400yds)   ⊅   Licensed restaurant
and bar.
⊕ 🍷(3m)
Min£110.90 Max£138.60pw

CROSSMICHAEL
Dumfries & Galloway*Kirkcudbrightshire*
Map**11** NX76

H   Culgruff Lodge
for bookings G M Thomson & Co, 27 King
Street, Castle Douglas, Kirkcudbrightshire
DG7 1AB
☎Castle Douglas(0556)2701 & 2973

*A pleasant detached stone-built house
situated off the drive to Culgruff House
Hotel and containing sitting room,
kitchen/diner and sleeping up to four
people.*

Mar – Nov   1wk min, 1unit, 1–4persons
◉ fridge   Electric & open fires
Elec inclusive   ⊡not provided
☎(400yds)   Iron & Ironing board in unit
TV   ⊕3pin square   P   ♨(300yds)
Coarse fishing on Woodhall Loch
⊕ 🛏(300yds)
Min£85 Max£155pw

H   Dane Vale Stable Court Dane Vale
Park
for bookings G M Thomson & Co, 27 King
Street, Castle Douglas, Kirkcudbrightshire
DG7 1AB
☎Castle Douglas(0556)2701 & 2973

*Full conversion of stables property into a
comfortable house within grounds of
Dane Vale House. Spacious
accommodation comprises dining room,
lounge, kitchen, bathroom and three
bedrooms and bathroom upstairs. Dane
Vale lies on A713 between Crossmichael
and Castle Douglas 1m south of former.*

Mar – Nov   MWB out of season   1wk min,
6mths max, 1unit, 1–6persons ◈
no pets   Aga ◉ fridge   Electric & open
fires   Elec inclusive   ⊡not provided
☎(1m)   ☺ CTV   ⊕3pin square   P
♨(1m)

⊕ 🍷(3m) 🛏(3m) Fishing
Min£90 Max£170pw

CROWS NEST
Cornwall
Map**2** SX26

C   3 West Darite Terrace
for bookings Mr & Mrs Brend, 4 West
Darite Terrace, Crows Nest, Liskeard,
Cornwall PL14 5JL
☎Liskeard(0579)43462

*A mid-terraced, former miner's cottage
situated approximately 4 miles from
Liskeard in the village of Crow's Nest. It
comprises a lounge with exposed beams,
kitchen/diner, one double bedroom and
one bunk bedroom through which the
bathroom/WC is reached.*

Mar – Oct   1wk min, 1mth max, 1unit,
4persons   [◇] ◈ ◆
◉ & microwave   fridge   Electric fires
Elec metered   ⊡inclusive   ☎(300yds)
WM & SD in unit   Iron & Ironing board in
unit   ☺ CTV   ⊕3pin square   P   🖾
♨(½m)
⊕ 🛏(300yds)
Min£80 Max£120pw

CROYDON
Gt London
See **Purley**

CRYMYCH
Dyfed
Map**2** SN13

B   Brengast, Hafan & Hafod
for bookings Mr & Mrs E Rees, Esgairordd
Farm, Crymych, Dyfed SA41 3SQ
☎Crymych(023973)275

Three bungalows facing the Preseli Hills.
Brengast *has spacious lounge with patio
doors onto a terrace, modern kitchen/
diner, bathroom and separate WC. Two
double bedrooms and one with twin beds
(a convertible settee in lounge if required)
completes the accommodation.* **Hafan &
Hafod** *are semi-detached and have good
sized lounges, kitchen, dining area, one
double bedroom, one twin bedroom,
bathroom and separate WC.*

All year   MWB out of season   3nights min,
3units, 4–8persons ◈ ◆ ◉ fridge
🍲inclusive   Elec metered
⊡not provided   ☎(1½m)   Iron & Ironing
board in unit   ☺ TV   ⊕3pin square
2P   1🛁 🖾 ♨(1½m)   Trout fishing
⊕ 🛏(1½m)
Min£80 Max£1650pw

CULKEIN
Highland *Sutherland*
Map**14** NC03

Ch **Bayview & Brisbane**
for bookings Mrs V MacLeod, 7 Mount
Stuart Road, Largs, Ayrshire KA30 9ES
☎Largs(0475)672931

*Two modern timber chalets in a beautiful
and isolated position, on foreshore of
Culkein bay overlooking sandy bay.*
Bayview *comprises lounge/diner/kitchen,
shower/WC, one twin-bedded room, one
double and one with bunk beds.* ***Brisbane***
*has lounge/diner/kitchen, shower/WC and
two bedrooms, one twin- and one double-
bedded.*

21Mar–17Oct 1wk min, 4wks max, 2units,
2–8persons ◆ ◆ ◎ fridge
Electric Elec inclusive 🔲 not provided
☎(1m) SD in unit Iron in unit ⊙ CTV
⊕3pin square 4P ♨(3m)

Min£98 Max£175pw

Ch **Burnside Chalet**
for bookings Mrs V MacLeod, 7 Mount
Stuart Road, Largs, Ayrshire KA30 9ES
☎Largs(0475)672931

*Chalet on stilts facing sandy bay where
Atlantic rollers break. There are two
bedrooms, open plan lounge and kitchen,
bathroom and verandah.*

21Mar–17Oct 1wk min, 1unit,
1–6persons ◆ ◆ ◎ fridge
Electric Elec inclusive 🔲 not provided
SD, Iron in unit ⊙ CTV ⊕3pin square
P ♨(3m)

Min£98 Max£175pw

CULLERCOATS
Tyne & Wear
Map**12** NZ37

F Mrs G E Aitken **Everitt House Holiday
Flats** 46 Beverley Terrace, Cullercoats,
North Shields, Tyne & Wear
☎091-252 1568

*An imposing Victorian terraced house,
overlooking Cullercoats Bay, tastefully
converted to offer five comfortable flats.
Three have one bedroom and two have
two bedrooms, but extra beds are
available in four of the flats. All have
modern fitted kitchens, bathrooms and
comfortable living areas. There is double-
glazing throughout and facilities include a
video system with films for each flat.*

All year MWB out of season 3days min,
6mths max, 5units, 2–6persons ◆ ◆
𝄐 fridge 🍲 Gas metered
🔲 inclusive ☎ [WM, SD & TD on
premises] Iron & Ironing board in unit
[Launderette on premises] ⊙ ⑱ CTV
⊕3pin square 📺 ♨(100yds)

Culkein
—
Dale

↩ ♪(1m) 🔊(100yds) 🎵(100yds)
♫(½m) 🐕(1m)

Min£50 Max£95pw (Low)
Min£60 Max£150pw (High)

CULLIPOOL
Strathclyde *Argyllshire*
See **Luing, Isle of,**

CULLODEN MOOR
Highland *Inverness-shire*
Map**14** NH74

C & F **Cherry Tree Flat, Rosevally &
Stabledene Cottages**
for bookings Miss M Skinner, Clava Lodge
Holiday Homes, Culloden Moor, Inverness
☎Inverness(0463)790405 & 790228

*Occupying part of the top floor of Clava
Lodge,* ***Cherry Tree Flat*** *is well appointed
and offers accommodation of lounge,
kitchen/diner, bathroom and one
bedroom. Nearby,* ***Rosevally Cottage*** *is
situated by the riverside and has lounge,
dining room, kitchen, bathroom and two
bedrooms. Also in the surrounding
grounds is* ***Stabledene****, a stone-built and
tastefully converted cottage with
comfortable accommodation consisting of
an open plan lounge/diner/kitchen, three
bedrooms (one double, one twin and one
single) and bathroom.*

mid May–end Sep 1wk min, 6mth max
(Cherry Tree Flat), 3units, 1–6persons
◆ ◆ ◎ fridge 🍲 (Stabledene)
Electric fires & open fires in Rosevally
Elec metered 🔲 can be hired
☎(Rosevally) ☎ WM in unit Iron &
Ironing board in unit ⊙ CTV
⊕3pin square 12P 📺 ♨(2m)
putting green fishing

↩ ♪(1m) 🎵(1m)

Min£40pw (Low)
Min£80 Max£100pw (High)

CURY
Cornwall
Map**2** SW62

B Mr & Mrs Mills **Franchis Holiday
Bungalows** Cury Cross Lanes, Helston,
Cornwall TR12 7AZ
☎Mullion(0326)240301

*Modern bungalows located in a secluded
position at the end of 10 acres of private
woodland, adjacent to a select rural
camping site. They are well appointed and
furnished and comprise of two twin-
bedded rooms, lounge/diner, kitchenette
and shower/WC. Additional folding bed*

---

*available. Pleasant location off A3083 6m
S of Helston.*

Mar–Oct MWB out of season 3days min
(out of season), 5units, 1–5 persons ◆
◆ 𝄐 fridge Gas fires Gas/
Elec inclusive 🔲 inclusive ☎(1m) Iron
& Ironing board in unit ⊙ CTV
⊕3pin square P ♨

↩ ♪(3m) 🔊(3m) 🎵(1m) ♫(1m)

Min£63 Max£85pw (Low)
Min£138 Max£165pw (High)

DALAVICH
Strathclyde *Argyll*
Map**10** NM91

Ca **Lochaweside Forest Cabins**
for bookings Forestry Commission, (Dept
A.A.) 231 Corstorphine Road, Edinburgh
EH12 7AT
☎031-334 2576 or 0303

*Quietly situated on the western shore of
Lochawe, the cabins are of varying
designs and located in clusters around the
edge of woodland, in forest sites or by the
lochside. Accommodation comprises open
plan kitchen/dining/lounge area with
either sofa or bunk beds, two bedrooms
(one double, one bunk-bedded), shower
and toilet. Each cabin has its own terrace
and although compact, they are well
furnished and fitted. Although designed
for six, a maximum of four adults is more
desirable. Four cabins are suitable for
disabled persons.*

mid Feb–mid Jan MWB out of season
3days min, 1mth max, 44units,
1–6persons ◆ ◆ 𝄐 fridge
Electric Elec metered 🔲 inclusive ☎
Iron & Ironing board on premises
[Launderette on premises] ⊙
⊕3pin square P ♨(100yds) Social
club facilities, fishing

↩ ♪(50yds)

Min£78 Max£240pw

DALE
Dyfed
Map**2** SM70

F **Ashlee**
for bookings Powells Cottage Holidays, 55
High Street, Saundersfoot, Dyfed
☎Saundersfoot(0834)812791

*Ground-floor flat located in modern
detached house comprising small lounge/
dining room, breakfast bar/kitchen, one
double bedroom one bunk bedroom.*

May–Sep MWB out of season 1wk min,
1mth max, 1unit, 4–6persons [◇] ◆
◆ no pets ◎ fridge 🍲
Elec metered ☎(50yds) Iron in unit
Ironing board in unit ⊙ CTV
⊕3pin square 2P Dinghy available

⊖ 🍴(200yds) 🎵(200yds) in summer
Min£99 Max£222pw

DALRY (St John's Town of)
Dumfries & Galloway *Kirkcudbrightshire*
Map**11** NX68

C   Grennan Mill Cottage
for bookings Miss S Harrison, Grennan
Mill, Dalry, Castle Douglas,
Kirkcudbrightshire DG7 3XQ
☎Dalry(06443)297

*Single-storey post-war cottage peacefully
situated behind the main house within 20
acres of wooded grounds. The cottage is
simply decorated and furnished but has
many objéts d'art which give it a charming,
homely atmosphere. There are two
bedrooms, living room and compact
kitchen. The rocky Garpel Burn and
working Water Mill are just a few yards
from the cottage. The cottage's own
donkey and poultry augment the area's
bird and wildlife.*

Apr–Nov MWB out of season 1wk min,
1unit, 1–6persons ◆ ◎ fridge
Electric & open fires Elec metered
⊡not provided ☎(½m) WM, Iron &
Ironing board in unit ☉ ⊕3pin square
P ♨(½m) Trout fishing
⊖ ♪(2m)   🍴(2m)
Min£65 Max£95pw (Low)
Max£135pw (High)

DARLINGSCOTT
Warwickshire
Map**4** SP24

C   Camperdown & Ivycliff Cottages
for bookings Heart of England Cottages,
The Market Place, Fairford,
Gloucestershire GL7 4AB
☎Fairford(0285)713295

*Two old stone cottages comfortably
furnished in a very quiet hamlet.
Accommodation in both comprises
lounge/diner, kitchen, cloakroom with WC
on ground floor.* **Camperdown** *has two
twin-bedded rooms (one with private
bathroom) and one single room,
bathroom and bathroom/WC.* **Ivycliff** *has
three bedrooms (one double, one twin,
one single) and a bathroom. Both
cottages have use of rear garden.*

Dale
—
Dartmouth

All year 1wk min, 2mths max, 2units,
1–5persons ◆ ◆ ◎ fridge Storage
heaters & open fires Elec metered
⊡can be hired ☎ WM & SD in unit
Iron & Ironing board in unit ☉ CTV
⊕3pin square 2P 2♨ ♨(1½m)
⊖ 🍴(2m)
Min£90 Max£110pw (Low)
Min£95 Max£155pw (High)

DARTMOUTH
Devon
Map**3** SX85
C   Bake Hill Cottage 4 Broadstone
for bookings Mrs S R Ridalls, The Old
Bakehouse, 7 Broadstone, Dartmouth,
Devon TQ6 9NR
☎Dartmouth (08043)4585

*A terraced cottage of great character with
odd shaped rooms and low ceilings, close
to town centre, shops and harbour.
Accommodation comprises: shower and
WC on ground floor, lounge and kitchen
on 1st floor, double bedroom and landing
area with bunk beds on 2nd floor.*

All year MWB out of season 3days min,
1mth max, 1unit, 2–4persons [◇] ◆
◆ ◎ fridge Storage heaters
Elec metered ⊡inclusive ☎(600yds)
WM & SD in unit Iron & Ironing board in
unit [Launderette within 300yds] ☉
CTV can be hired ⊕3pin square 🚽
♨(200yds)
⊖ 🍴(100yds) 🎵(250yds)
🎵(250yds) 🍴(200yds)
Details not confirmed for 1987

F   No 1 Clare Court 2 Newport Street
for bookings Mr & Mrs G Powell, 20 South
Town, Dartmouth, Devon
☎Dartmouth(08043)2638

*Ground-floor flat in modern block situated
opposite the market in town centre. Large
lounge, one double- and one twin-bedded
room, neat galley-style kitchen and
separate bathroom. Own carport.*

All year MWB out of season 2days min,
3mths max, 1unit, 2–4persons [◆]

[◆] ◎ fridge Electric Elec metered
⊡not provided ☎(50yds) Iron & Ironing
board in unit [Launderette within
300yds] ☉ CTV ⊕3pin square 1P
♨(10yds)
⊖ ♪(3m) 🍴(50yds) 🍴(200yds)
Min£30 Max£50pw (Low)
Min£72 Max£130pw (High)

C   The Cottage
for bookings Mrs S R Ridalls, The Old
Bakehouse, 7 Broadstone, Dartmouth,
Devon TQ6 9NR
☎Dartmouth(08043)4585

*Compact 'olde world' style terraced
cottage, with beamed ceilings and stone
fireplace, adjacent to town centre. On the
ground floor is lounge, kitchenette and
double bedroom, first floor has another
bedroom and bathroom/WC. Meals
available.*

All year MWB out of season 3days min,
6wks max, 1unit, 2–6persons [◇] ◆
◆ ◎ fridge Electric Elec metered
⊡can be hired ☎(800yds). Iron &
Ironing board in unit ☉ CTV can be
hired ⊕3pin square 🚽 ♨(200yds)
Boat for hire
⊖ 🍴(200yds) 🍴(200yds)
Details not confirmed for 1987

F   Harbour Views 26B South Town
for bookings Mr & Mrs G D Powell, 20
South Town, Dartmouth, Devon TQ6 9BN
☎Dartmouth(08043)2638

*Terraced property with living
accommodation on first floor, (above its
own lock-up double garage) reached by
external steps. Comprises lounge, diner/
kitchen with double put-up in lounge.
Downstairs a double-bedded room and
separate bedroom with twin bunk beds,
also bath/WC. Fine views across estuary.*

All year MWB out of season 2days min,
1mth max, 1unit, 2–6persons [◆ ◆]
◎ fridge Elec (night storage)
Elec metered ⊡can be hired
☎(600yds) Iron & Ironing board in unit
☉ CTV ⊕3pin square 🚽 🚽
♨(600yds)
⊖ 🍴(600yds) 🎵(600yds)
🎵(600yds) 🍴(½m)
Min£35 Max£60pw (Low)
Min£110 Max£198pw (High)

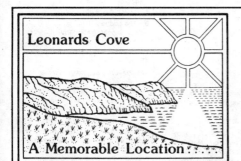

F Mrs A Day **Redwalls (Flats 1–3 & 5, 6 & 8)** Townstal Road, Dartmouth, Devon TQ6 9HT
☎Dartmouth(08043)4222

Substantial building converted into self-contained apartments and standing in its own large grounds, offering views of both river and estuary. Nicely furnished and equipped.

Mar–Oct MWB out of season 3days min, 2mths max, 6units, 2–4persons ◎ fridge Electric Elec metered 🄻can be hired ☎ Iron & Ironing board in unit ⊙ TV ⊕3pin square 8P 🄼 ♒(¼m) Boats for hire

⊖ ♀(¼m) 🎥(¼m)

Min£50 Max£100pw (Low)
Min£85 Max£182pw (High)

F Second Flat
for bookings Mrs S R Ridalls, The Old Bakehouse, 7 Broadstone, Dartmouth, Devon TQ6 9NR
☎Dartmouth(08043)4585

Ground-floor flat forming part of the Old Bakehouse, comprising lounge/dining room with beamed ceiling, kitchenette, one double and one twin bedroom. Shower room/WC. Meals available.

All year MWB out of season 3days min, 6wks max, 1unit, 2–4persons [◇] ◈ ◆ ◎ fridge Electric Elec metered 🄻can be hired ☎(800yds) Iron & Ironing board in unit ⊙ CTV can be hired ⊕3pin square 🄼 ♒(200yds) Boat for hire

⊖ ♀(200yds) 🎥(200yds)

Details not confirmed for 1987

Dartmouth — Dawlish

DAWLISH
Devon
Map**3** SX97

H Coach House
for bookings Mr & Mrs J Patrick-Mitchinson, Edencliffe, Holcombe Drive, Holcombe, Dawlish, Devon EX7 0JW
☎Dawlish(0626)863171

Converted Coach House with private path to the beach 300yds away. Accommodation comprises two double bedrooms and one with twin beds and bunk beds, lounge, kitchen, enclosed patio/diner with skylight, shower room and WC.

Apr–Oct 1wk min, 1mth max, 1unit, 2–8persons [◇] ◈ no pets ◎ fridge 🍳 Elec metered 🄻can be hired ☎(300yds) [WM, SD & TD on premises] Iron & Ironing board on premises ⊙ CTV ⊕3pin square P ♒(½m)

⊖ ♀(½m) ♬(1½m) ♫(1½m) 🎥(1½m)

Min£65 Max£215pw

F Edencliffe
for bookings Mr & Mrs J Patrick-Mitchenson, Edencliffe, Holcombe Drive, Holcombe, Dawlish, Devon EX7 0JW
☎Dawlish(0626)863171

A flat located within a house which was rebuilt in 1928 from John Nash's original 19th-century plans. Impressive views overlooking Lyme Bay towards Babbacombe. Beach within 300yds. Accommodation comprises two bedrooms (one large double, one small child's room), lounge/diner, kitchen and bathroom.

Apr–Oct MWB 1wk min, 1unit, 4persons [◇] [◈] no pets ◎ fridge 🍳 Elec inclusive 🄻can be hired ☎(300yds) WM, SD & TD on premises Iron & Ironing board on premises ⊙ CTV ⊕3pin square P ♒(½m)

⊖ ♀(½m) ♬(1½m) ♫(1½m) 🎥(1½m)

Min£57 Max£181pw

F 28 Park Road (Flats 1 & 2)
for bookings I & J Bulpin, Little Down, Breakneck Hill, Teignmouth, Devon TQ14 9NZ
☎Teignmouth(06267)6040

First- and second-floor flats over shop in Dawlish shopping area, ½m from seafront. Both flats have lounge with put-u-up or divan, two bedrooms with either double, twin and single/bunk beds, separate kitchen and shower room/WC.

All year 1wk min, 8mths max, 2units, 2–8persons ◈ ◆ ◎ Electric Elec metered 🄻can be hired ☎(100yds) SD in unit Iron & Ironing board in unit [Launderette within 300yds] CTV ⊕3pin square ♒(20yds)

⊖ ⛳(2m) ♀(20yds) ♬(½m) ♫(½m)

Min£65 Max£110pw (Low)
Min£125 Max£165pw (High)

F Mr & Mrs R A Potter **Gaycourt Holiday Flats** 8 Marine Parade, Dawlish, Devon EX7 9DJ
☎Dawlish(0626)862846 & 863385

Six flats of varied accommodation located on the seafront with spectacular sea views. Ample forecourt parking.

All year MWB out of season 1wk min, 6mths max, 6units, 2–6persons [◇] ◈ ◆ ◎ fridge 🍳 Gas & Electric Gas/Elec metered 🄻can be hired ☎ Iron & Ironing board in unit [Launderette within 300yds] ⊙ CTV ⊕3pin square P ⌂ 🄼 ♒(200yds)

⊖ ⛳(2¼m) ♀(100yds) ♬(100yds) ♫(100yds)

Min£95 Max£117pw (Low)
Min£144 Max£181pw (High)

F High Trees
for bookings Mr & Mrs D J Richmond, Oak Park Holiday Flats and Houses, Oak Park Cottage, Old Gatehouse Road, Dawlish, Devon EX7 0DG
☎Dawlish(0626)863113

*Eleven self-contained flats in pleasantly converted hotel. All have lounge/diner with double convertible bed-settee, kitchen and bathroom with shower attachment (except Flat 18, see below). The sleeping accommodation is as follows: **Flat 12:** two bedrooms, one with double, one twin-bedded room and bunk bed. **Flats 14, 15, 16** and **19:** one bedroom with double and bunk bed. **Flat 17:** two bedrooms, one with double and single plus shower and basin, one with two single beds. **Flat 18:** flatlet for two people, kitchen, bathroom and lounge with double wall bed. **Flat 20:** one bedroom with four single beds. Double wall bed in lounge and breakfast bar in kitchen. **Flat 21:** spacious two bedroom flat, one with double and bunk beds, one with two singles and bunk beds. **Flat 22:** one bedroom with double bed and bunk beds which convert to one single. **Flat 23:** one bedroom with two singles and bunk bed.*

All year MWB out of season 7days min in season, shorter breaks in low season, 8mths max, 11units, 1–8persons ◈ ◆ no pets ◎ fridge 🍳 Elec metered (Except lighting) 🄻inclusive ☎ Iron & Ironing board in unit [Launderette within 100yds] ⊙ CTV ⊕3pin square P 🄼 ♒

⊖ ⛳(3m) ♀(400yds) ♬(½m) ♫(1m)

Min£39 Max£82pw (Low)
Min£109 Max£233pw (High)

F Mr & Mrs R A Potter **Lisburne Holiday Flats** Westcliffe, Dawlish, Devon EX7 9DN
☎Dawlish(0626)863385 & 862846

Three-storey building in an elevated position overlooking Marine Parade and sea. The flats are on the first, second and third floors, some with sea views. Five of the flats each have kitchen, lounge, double beds and studio couch in lounge. Four with shower, one with bath. Another three flats on the second floor have lounge with studio couch, bedroom with bunk beds, double bedroom, kitchen and bathroom with WC.

All year MWB out of season 1wk min, 6mths max, 8units, 2–6persons [◇] ◈ ◆ no pets ◎ fridge Electric Elec metered 🄻can be hired ☎(100yds) Iron on premises Ironing board on premises [Launderette within 300yds] ⊙ TV ⊕3pin square P ⌂ 🄼 ♒(200yds)

⊖ ⛳(1¾m)

Min£85 Max£125pw (Low)
Min£128 Max£185pw (High)

B The Lodge
for bookings Mr & Mrs J Patrick-Mitchinson, Edencliffe, Holcombe Drive, Holcombe, Dawlish, Devon EX7 0JW
☎Dawlish(0626)863171

Self-contained bungalow with own garden and private path to the beach. There are two double bedrooms, lounge/diner with double studio couch, kitchen and bathroom.

All year MWB out of season 1wk min, 1unit, 6persons [◇] [◈] no pets ◎ fridge 🍳 Elec metered 🄻can be hired ☎(300yds) WM, SD & TD on premises Iron & Ironing board on

premises ☺ CTV ⊕3pin square P
♨(½m)
⟷ ⚲(½m) 🎵(1½m) ♫(1½m) 🏌(1½m)
Min£65 Max£224pw

F Oak Park House
for bookings Mr & Mrs D J Richmond, Oak
Park Holiday Flats, Oak Park Cottage, Old
Gatehouse Road, Dawlish, Devon
EX7 0DG
☎Dawlish(0626)863113

*Nine self-contained flats in converted
hotel on ground and first-floor levels.
Accommodation as follows:* **Flat 1** *two
bedrooms, one with double and single
beds with shower/WC en suite, one with
two singles and bunk bed, kitchen,
bathroom and lounge/diner with bed-
settee.* **Flat 2** *two bedrooms, one with
double bed and one with two single beds,
kitchen, bathroom and lounge/diner with
bed-settee.* **Flat 5** *one bedroom with
double and bunk bed, kitchen, bathroom
and lounge/diner with convertible.* **Flat 6**
*one bedroom with double bed and two
single beds, bathroom and large lounge/
kitchen/diner.* **Flat 7** *three bedrooms, one
with double bed and shower/WC en suite,
one with four singles and one with a 4ft
double, kitchen, bathroom and lounge/
diner with convertible.* **Flat 8** *two
bedrooms, one with two singles, one with
one double, kitchen, bathroom and
lounge/diner.* **Flat 9** *two bedrooms, one
with double and single, one with bunk
beds, kitchen, bathroom and lounge/*

Dawlish

diner. **Flat 10** *three double bedrooms, one
with double and en suite shower room,
one with two singles and vanity unit and
one with bunk beds, kitchen, bathroom
and lounge/diner with double bed-settee.*
Flat 11 *one bedroom with one double and
one single, kitchen, bathroom and lounge/
diner. All flats have baths and showers.*
All year MWB out of season 7days min in
season, 8mths max, 9units, 1–9persons
◇ ◆ no pets ◎ fridge 🍴
Elec metered (except lighting)
🔲inclusive ☎ Iron & Ironing board in
unit [Launderette on premises] ☺
CTV ⊕3pin square P 🎲 ♨
Children's play area
⟷ 🐾(3m) ⚲(400yds) 🎵(½m) ♫(1m)
Min£50 Max£84pw (Low)
Min£148 Max£239pw (High)

H Shell Cove House Flats
for bookings Mrs A A Jameson, Shell Cove
House, Old Teignmouth Road, Dawlish,
Devon EX7 0LA
☎Dawlish(0626)862523

*Large Georgian house with new wing.
Situated within six acres of grounds with a
secluded beach. All units are spacious
and comfortably furnished, with beautiful
sea views and patios overlooking lawns*

*and sea. Each unit contains living room,
1–3 bedrooms, kitchen and bathroom/
WC. Communal TV lounge, games room
and laundry room.*
All year MWB 2days min, 5mths max,
10units, 2–7persons [◇] ◆ ◆ ◎
fridge 🍴 Gas/Elec inclusive (Elec
metered in low season) 🔲inclusive ☎
[WM on premises] TD & SD on premises
Iron & Ironing board on premises ☺
CTV ⊕3pin square P 🎲 ♨
🔥(Heated) 🏊Hard, Badminton, croquet,
playground
⟷ ⚲(½m) 🎵(1m) ♫(1m) 🏌(2½m)
Min£66 Max£110pw (Low)
Min£150 Max£360pw (High)

H Shell Cove Lobster Cottage
for bookings Mrs A A Jameson, Shell Cove
House, Old Teignmouth Road, Dawlish,
Devon EX7 0LA
☎Dawlish(0626)862523

*Shell Cove Lobster Cottage has been
tastefully modernised. Situated within
grounds of Shell Cove House sharing all
amenities and direct access to beach.
Accommodation comprises: Porch with
cloakroom, modern kitchen, large lounge
diner with doors to patio. Downstairs twin
bedroom with shower. Upstairs three
bedrooms and coloured bathroom suite.*
All year MWB out of season 1wk min,
5mths max, 1unit, 8persons [◇] ◆
◆ ◎ fridge 🍴 Elec metered
🔲inclusive ☎ [WM on premises] SD & →

TD on premises Iron & Ironing board on premises ☺ CTV ⊕3pin square P
🎦 ♨ ⌇(Heated) ✍Hard, Badminton, croquet, games room
↩ ♀(¼m) 🎵(1m) 🎵(1m) ☕(2½m)
Min£120 Max£380pw

H Shell Cove Shrimp Lodge
for bookings Mrs A A Jameson, Shell Cove House, Old Teignmouth Road, Dawlish, Devon
☎Dawlish(0626)862523
Detached property in grounds of Shell Cove House sharing all amenities and direct access to secluded beach. Accommodation comprises lounge, separate kitchen, and one single bedroom on the ground floor; one double bedroom and one twin-bedded room on the first floor; also separate bathroom/WC. Off the A379 Dawlish to Teignmouth road.
All year MWB out of season 1wk min, 5mths max, 1unit, 1–5persons [◇]
[♦ & ◆] ◎ fridge Gas & Electric fires Gas/Elec inclusive (metered in low season) Ⓛinclusive ☎ Iron & Ironing board on premises [Launderette on premises] ☺ CTV ⊕3pin square 2P 1🎦 🎦 ♨ ⌇(heated) ✍Hard, Badminton, croquet, games room
↩ ♪(2½m) ♀(¼m) 🎵(¼m) 🎵(¼m) ☕(3m)
Min£100 Max£280pw

DEGANWY
Gwynedd
Map**6** SH78

F Berklay Court
for bookings Mr & Mrs J Williams, 20 Marine Crescent, Deganwy, Conwy, Gwynedd
☎Deganwy(0492)83464
Three-storey house containing two flats, each comprising two bedrooms, kitchen, lounge/dining area, bathroom, WC and separate shower room. On seafront 400yds from village centre.
All year 1wk min, 1mth max, 2units, 4persons ◎ fridge Electric Elec inclusive Ⓛinclusive ☎ Iron & Ironing board on premises Launderette on premises ☺ ⊛ CTV
⊕3pin square P 🎦 ♨(750yds)
↩ ♪(750yds) ♀(750yds) 🎵(750yds)
Min£140 Max£160pw (Low)
£190pw (High)

F Clova
for bookings Mr & Mrs J Williams, 20 Marine Crescent, Deganwy, Conwy, Gwynedd
☎Deganwy(0492)83464
Ground-floor flat on seafront containing kitchen, lounge with dining area, bathroom separate shower room and two bedrooms. Good décor and furnishings.
All Year 1wk min, 1mth max, 1unit, 2–4persons ◎ fridge Electric Elec inclusive Ⓛinclusive ☎ Iron & Ironing board on premises Launderette on premises ☺ ⊛ TV

Dawlish
—
Docklow

⊕3pin square 2P 🎦 ♨(750yds)
↩ ♪(750yds) ♀(750yds) 🎵(750yds)
Min£140 Max£160pw (Low)
£190pw (High)

DENHOLM
Borders *Roxburghshire*
Map**12** NT51

C & Ch Mrs Pat Leslie **Hazeldean Holiday Centre** Hassendeanburn, Denholm, Roxburghshire TD9 8RU
☎Denholm(045087)373
Teviot Lodges are four fully modernised traditional whinstone and slate-roofed cottages in an attractive courtyard. Three ground floor and one first floor, comprising lounge/kitchen/dining room, double and twin-bedded room and a third with bunk beds and bathroom. Denholm Lodges, also in the courtyard, have the same accommodation as Teviot Lodges, without the bunk bedroom. Hazeldean Lodges are six 'A' frame timber lodges with open plan lounge/dining room/kitchen containing twin sofa beds. There is one double bedroom, bathroom and at gallery level a twin bedroom reached by ladder stairs. Double-glazed windows open onto a balcony. Facilities include fishing, archery, games room, bar and riding school.
All year MWB out of season 1wk min, 12units, 1–6persons [◆ ◆] ◎ fridge Elec inclusive (in season) Elect metered (out of season) Ⓛinclusive [WM, SD & TD on premises] Iron & Ironing board on premises ☺ CTV ⊕3pin square 20P 🎦 ♨(3m)
↩ ♪(3m) ♀ 🎵(3m) ☕(3m)
Min£147 Max£188pw (Low)
Min£206 Max£263pw (High)

DENT
Cumbria
Map**7** SD78

F Mr H Sutcliffe **Seedsgill Barn Flat**
Dent, Sedbergh, Cumbria
☎Dent(05875)362
This 17th-century converted haybarn and shippon is in a peaceful and typically unspoilt Dales village, with extensive views of the surrounding countryside. The accommodation consists of a spacious open plan kitchen/lounge, bathroom and three bedrooms.
All year MWB out of season 1wk min, 1unit, 2–6persons ◇ ◆ ◆ ◎ fridge Electric & open fires Elec metered Ⓛcan be hired
☎(30yds) Iron in unit ☺ ⊛ TV
⊕3pin square 3P 🎦 ♨(200yds)
↩ ♀(50yds)
Min£50 Max£80pw (Low)
Min£100 Max£140pw (High)

DERVAIG
Strathclyde *Argyllshire*
See **Mull, Isle of**

DINNET
Grampian *Aberdeenshire*
Map**15** NO49

H Monandavan
for bookings Holidays Dept/6, Estate Office, Dinnet, Aboyne, Aberdeenshire AB3 5LL
☎Dinnet(033985)341/2
A stone house standing in National Nature Reserve with pine woods and fine views. The house offers lounge/diner and a twin-bedded room on the ground floor, with one twin and one double bedroom and bathroom on the first floor. Access by narrow country road from A93 at Dinnet.
Mar–25Oct 1wk min, 1mth max, 1unit, 1–6persons ◇ ◆ ◎ fridge Electric & coal fires Elec inclusive Ⓛcan be hired ☎ CTV ⊕3pin square P ♨(1m)
↩ ♀(1m) 🎵(1m)
£135pw (Low)
£152pw (High)

H Wisdomhowe
for bookings Holidays Dept/6, Estate Office, Dinnet, Aboyne, Aberdeenshire AB3 5LL
☎Dinnet(033985)341/2
A traditional stone house set in the heart of a nature reserve and surrounded by moorland. The accommodation offers living/dining room, kitchen and one double bedroom on the ground floor and two twin-bedded rooms and bathroom on the first floor. Good access road from the A93.
Mar–25Oct 1wk min, 1mth max, 1unit, 1–6persons ◇ no pets ◎ fridge Electric & coal fires Elec inclusive Ⓛcan be hired ☎(2½m) ☺ CTV
⊕3pin square 3P ♨(2½m)
↩ ♀(1m) 🎵(2½m)
£130pw (Low)
£145pw (High)

DOCKLOW
Hereford & Worcester
Map**3** SO55

C Mr & Mrs M Ormerod **Docklow Manor**
Docklow, Leominster, Herefordshire
☎Steens Bridge(056882)643
These cottages were originally ancillary buildings to the manor house. They are constructed of local stone and grouped around a walled pond. Set in 10 acres of garden and grounds. Each cottage is differently furnished, all to a high standard, several with wood burning stoves. Cottages cater for two, four or six people. Some are single storey without steps.
All year MWB in season 2days min, 6wks max, 10units, 1–6persons [◇] ◆ ◆ no dogs ◎ fridge Electric Elec inclusive Ⓛinclusive ☎ Iron & Ironing board on premises [Launderette

90

on premises] ☺ CTV ⊕3pin square
P ▥ ♨(5m) ⌂ ⚲ Croquet lawn
↔ ♨(½m)
Min£94.50 Max£110.40pw (Low)
Min£159.85 Max£247.25pw (High)
See advertisement under Leominster

F   Budlea Cottage
for bookings Mrs M R M Brooke, Nicholson
Farm, Docklow, Leominster, Herefordshire
HR6 0SL
☎Steens Bridge(056882)269

Recent conversion of a small wing of this
344-year-old farmhouse. The ground floor
has a large kitchen/dining area and the
sitting room, with exposed beams and
studio couch, is on the first floor together
with a double bedroom and shower/WC.
Use of garden.

All year   MWB in season   2days min,
1mth max, 1unit, 1–3persons, nc3yrs
[◇] ◆ ◉ fridge Storage heating
and electric fires   Elec metered ⊔can be
hired ☎(1½m) WM & TD on premises
Iron in unit ☺ CTV ⊕3pin square
6P ▥ ♨(1¾m) Trout and carp fishing
↔ ♨(1m)

Details not confirmed for 1987

B   The Cedars, Firs & Honeysuckle
for bookings Mrs M R M Brooke, Nicholson
Farm, Docklow, Leominster, Herefordshire
HR6 0SL
☎Steens Bridge(056882)269

A large modern, cedar-clad building
converted into three comfortable units
each with dining/sitting rooms, well fitted
kitchen, bathroom/shower and WC.
Honeysuckle sleeps up to four, Firs up to
six, and Cedars as many as eight and also
has solid fuel fire in the lounge. Units on
one level and suitable for wheelchairs.

All year   MWB out of season   2nights min,
1mth max, 3units, 1–8persons [◇] ◆
◉ fridge Storage heaters (free) ⊔can
be hired ☎(1½m) WM & TD on
premises   Iron in unit ☺ CTV
⊕3pin square 6P ▥ ♨(1¾m) Trout
fishing

↔ ♨(1m)

Details not confirmed for 1987

DOLGELLAU
Gwynedd
Map6 SH71

H   Plas Hen Brithdir
for bookings Mrs H Richards, 2 Bishops
Walk, Barnack, Stamford, Lincolnshire
PE9 3EE
☎Stamford(0780)740480

16th-Century Welsh manor house with
large garden, and beautiful mountain
views. Comprising of two lounges, kitchen/
diner, utility room and WC on ground floor
and first floor with one double, two twin-
bedded, one single room and fifth
bedroom with double & single bed. Also
separate WC and bathroom

18Apr–1Jan   MWB out of season
4nights min, 6mths max, 1unit,
2–8persons ◆ ◉ fridge Storage

Docklow
—
Downderry

heaters & open fires   Elec metered
⊔not provided ☎ WM Iron & Ironing
board in unit   CTV ⊕3pin square 4P
♨(2½m) Fishing
↔ ♬(3m) ♨(3m) ♫(3m)
Min£125 Max£180pw (Low)
Min£190 Max£230pw (High)

DOLLERIE
Tayside Perthshire
Map11 NN92

C & H   Mr A G Murray Dollerie Estate
Dollerie House, Crieff, Perthshire PH7 3NX
☎Crieff(0764)3234

Scattered around the 500-acre Dollerie
Estate are three houses and three
cottages built of stone with slate roofs.
East Tuckethill is a small farm cottage
comprising lounge/diner and two
bedrooms. Muir of Dollerie Farm Cottage
also has lounge/diner and two bedrooms.
Muir of Dollerie Farmhouse is large and
comprises kitchen with dining area, sitting
room and five bedrooms. Dollerie Annexe
is attached to the Lairds Mansion and
comprises sitting room, dining room, three
bedrooms and a study/bedroom. Dollerie
Cottage is a converted coach house
comprising lounge/dining room, two
double bedrooms and a small single.
Dollerie Lodge has sitting/dining room
and two bedrooms. The properties are well
furnished and decorated and equipped to
a high standard including dishwashers,
with the larger houses having TV and
washing machine.

15Mar–31Oct   MWB out of season
1wk min, 6units, 1–10persons [◆ ◆]
no cats ◉ fridge Electric
Elec metered ⊔not provided ☎(2½m)
SD in unit   Iron & ironing board in unit
☺ ⊕3pin square ⊕3pin round 12P
▥ ▥ ♨(2½m)
↔ ♬(2½m) ♨(2½m) ♫(2½m) ♫(2½m)
Min£70 Max£185pw (Low)
Min£150 Max£275pw (High)

DORNOCH
Highland Sutherland
Map14 NH78

**Ca   Mrs E M Grant Pitgrudy Farm
Holidays, The Cabins** Pitgrudy Farm,
Dornoch, Sutherland IV25 3HY
☎Dornoch(0862)810291

Two timber-framed cabins comprising
wood-panelled lounge/dining room,
modern kitchen, two bedrooms and
shower/WC. Modern well-maintained
equipment.

All year   MWB out of season   1wk min,
2units, 4–5persons ◆ ◉ fridge
Electric Elec metered ⊔not provided
☎(1½m) [Launderette within 300yds]
CTV ⊕3pin square P ▥ ♨(1m)
↔ ♨(1m) ♫(1m) ♫(1m)

Min£80pw (Low)
Min£145pw (High)

**C   Mrs E M Grant Pitgrudy Farm
Holidays, The Cottages** Pitgrudy Farm,
Dornoch, Sutherland IV25 3HY
☎Dornoch(0862)810291

Pitgrudy Farm is situated approx 1m from
the historic burgh of Dornoch and enjoys
panoramic views of the Kyle of Sutherland
and Ross-shire hills beyond. There are
four modern cottages, each comprising
lounge/kitchen with breakfast bar, two
bedrooms with modern furniture (a
convertible settee is also available) and
modern bathroom/WC.

All year   MWB   out of season   1wk min,
4units, 4–5persons ◆ ◉ fridge
Electric Elec metered ⊔not provided
☎(1½m) [Launderette with 300yds]
CTV ⊕3pin square P ▥ ♨(1m)
↔ ♨(1m) ♫(1m) ♫(1m)
Min£80pw (Low)
Min£145pw (High)

**Ca   Mrs E M Grant Pitgrudy Farm
Holidays, The Log Cabin** Pitgrudy Farm,
Dornoch, Sutherland IV25 3HY
☎Dornoch(0862)810291

Log cabin situated near to the farm house,
with panoramic views of the Kyle of
Sutherland and Ross-shire hills.
Accommodation of open plan layout,
comprises bathroom, lounge/kitchen with
bed-settee and heavy curtains to bedroom
area with bunk beds.

All year   MWB out of season   1wk min,
1unit, 2–4persons ◆ ⚃ fridge Calor
gas heating   Gas/Elec inclusive
⊔not provided ☎(1½m) [Launderette
within 300yds] CTV P ▥ ♨(1m)
↔ ♬(½m) ♨(1m) ♫(1m) ♫(1m)
Min£70pw (Low)
Min£125pw (High)

DOUGLAS
See **Man, Isle of**

DOWNDERRY
Cornwall
Map2 SX35

C   CC Ref 306 ELP
for bookings Character Cottages
(Holidays) Ltd, 34 Fore Street, Sidmouth,
Devon EX10 8AQ
☎Sidmouth(03955)77001

Converted coastguard house with a
garden, adjacent to beach.
Accommodation comprises three small
bedrooms, lounge, kitchen/diner,
bathroom and WC.

All year   MWB out of season   1wk min,
1mth max, 1unit 2–7persons ◆ ◉
fridge Electric Elec metered ⊔can be
hired ☎ Iron & Ironing board in unit
☺ CTV ⊕3pin square ⊕2pin round
P ▥ ♨(200yds)
↔ ♨(200yds) ♫200yds)
Min£76 Max£122pw (Low)
Min£150 Max£243pw (High)

C   CC Ref 3060
for bookings Character Cottages
(Holidays) Ltd, 34 Fore Street, Sidmouth,
Devon EX10 8AQ
☎Sidmouth(03955)77001

*End of terrace cottage overlooking the
beach at Downderry. Accommodation
comprises lounge with child's single room
off, dining area, kitchen, stairs to double
room with beach views, twin-bedded room
and bathroom/WC.*

All year   1wk min, 8wks max, 1unit,
5persons [◇] ◆ no pets ◎ fridge
🎄radiators electric & log fires
Elec metered   ⌷not provided ☎(½m)
SD in unit   Iron & Ironing board in unit
☺ CTV ⊕3pin square 2P 🎲 ⌂(½m)
⊖ 🍴(½m)
Min£73 Max£231pw

F   JFH Ref S57B
for bookings John Fowler Holidays, Dept
58, Marlborough Road, Ilfracombe, Devon
EX34 8PF
☎Ilfracombe(0271)66666

*First floor flat situated above the
Smugglers Inn with views of Seaton. The
'olde worlde' accommodation comprises
stairs to landing, lounge off with a double
bed-settee, double bedroom, shower/WC,
more stairs to kitchen/diner and further
bedroom with three single beds. Use of all
adjacent holiday site facilities.*

Mar–Oct   MWB out of season   2days min,
6wks max, 1unit, 7persons [◇] ◆ ◎
fridge convector heaters   Elec metered
⌷not provided ☎ Iron & Ironing board
in unit   [Launderette on premises]
CTV(metered) ⊕3pin square   2P
🎲(adjacent) ⤳Hard Club
entertainment, snooker, table tennis,
arcades, putting
⊖ 🍴 🎵(on site) ♫(on site)
Min£79.35 Max£205.85pw

DREWSTEIGNTON
Devon
Map**3** SX79

C   CC Ref 506 LP A & B
for bookings Character Cottages
(Holidays) Ltd, 34 Fore Street, Sidmouth,
Devon EX10 8AQ
☎Sidmouth(03955)77001

*Two semi-detached thatched cottages in
rural surroundings, recently restored and
modernised. Accommodation comprises
two double bedrooms, oak-beamed
lounge, large fitted kitchen/diner and
combined bathroom and WC.*

All year   MWB out of season   1wk min,
6mths max, 2units, 2–4persons ◆ ◎
fridge Electric Elec metered ⌷can be
hired ☎(200yds) Iron & Ironing board in
unit ☺ TV ⊕3pin square
⊕2pin round P 🎲
⊖ 🍴(2m)
Min£58 Max£87pw (Low)
Min£102 Max£125pw (High)

Downderry
—
Drumnadrochit

DRIMNIN
Highland *Inverness-shire*
Map**13** NM55

**B & C   The Bungalow, Tom Mor &
Keepers Cottage** Killundine Estate
for bookings Mr W Lauder, Higher
Longcombe, Totnes, Devon TQ9 6PN
☎Totnes(0803)863059

*The simple traditional bungalow and the
two semi-detached cottages command
excellent views over the Sound of Mull and
are situated close to the remote Killundine
farmhouse. The Bungalow and Tom Mor
Cottage can accommodate four people
and Keepers Cottage six people. All have
sitting rooms with open log fires, kitchen
and bathrooms with bath, wash hand
basin and WC.*

29Mar–31Oct   MWB out of season
1wk min, 3units, 1–6persons ◆ ◆
◎ fridge Electric & open fires
Elec metered ⌷not provided ☎(4m)
Iron in unit (bungalow) ☺
⊕3pin square P 🎲 ⌂(8m)
Min£37 Max£50pw (Low)
Min£75 Max£105pw (High)

DRUMBEG
Highland *Sutherland*
Map**14** NC13

C   Achd Cottage
for bookings Elizabeth Johnson, Low
Alwinton, Morpeth, Northumberland
NE65 7BE
☎Drumbeg(05713)236

*This modernised stone croft house is set in
the wild, rugged country of the Sutherland
west coast, approximately ½m from
Drumbeg Village. Accommodation
comprises open plan lounge/diner with
linked kitchen area, one double bedroom
and bathroom on ground floor, and one
double and one twin-bedded room on the
first floor. Access from B869 Lochinver/
Ullapool Road.*

All year   MWB out of season   1wk min,
3wks max, 1unit, 1–8persons ◆ ◆
◎ fridge electric heating
Elec metered ⌷not provided ☎(½m)
SD in unit Iron & Ironing board in unit
☺ CTV ⊕3pin square 2P ⌂(½m)
⊖ 🍴(½m)
Min£80 Max£175pw

DRUMNADROCHIT
Highland *Inverness-shire*
Map**14** NH53

Ch   Mrs E Mackintosh Achmony Chalets
Drumnadrochit, Inverness-shire IV3 6UX
☎Drumnadrochit(04562)357

*Eight wooden chalets set in pairs at
different levels on a steep hillside
overlooking Drumnadrochit with views to
Loch Ness. Accommodation comprises*

---

*wood panelled dining/sitting room,
kitchen, two good sized bedrooms and
bathroom.*

Etr–Oct   MWB out of season   1wk min,
1mth max, 8units, 2–4persons ◆
fridge Electric Elec metered ⌷can be
hired ☎(½m) Iron in unit ☺ CTV
⊕3pin square P 🎲(½m) Pony trekking
& bowling
⊖ 🍴(½m)
Min£70 Max£180pw (Low)
Min£90 Max£180pw (High)

Ch   The Chalet
for bookings Mrs W D Ross, Strone,
Dumnadrochit, Inverness-shire
☎Drumnadrochit(04562)351

*Attractive timber chalet in delightful
situation overlooking Urquhart Bay with
extensive views of Loch Ness. It provides
three bedrooms, lounge/kitchen, shower/
WC and has wood panelling throughout.*

Mar–Oct   MWB out of season   2days
(out of season) min, 4wks max, 1unit,
1–6persons ◆ no pets ◎ fridge
Electric Elec metered ⌷can be hired
☎(1m) Iron & Ironing board in unit ☺
CTV ⊕3pin square 4P ⌂(1m)
⊖ 🍴(1m) 🎵(1m) ♫(1m)
Min£75 Max£170pw

B   Strone Cottage
for bookings Mrs W D Ross, Strone,
Drummadrochit, Inverness-shire
☎Drumnadrochit(04562)351

*Modern detached bungalow located just
off the A82, ⅓m N of Urquhart Castle
offering excellent views of Loch Ness.
Accommodation comprises lounge,
kitchen/diner, three bedrooms and
bathroom/WC.*

Mar–Oct   MWB out of season   2days
(out of season) min, 4wks max, 1unit,
1–6persons ◆ no pets ◎ fridge
Electric Elec metered ⌷can be hired
☎(1m) SD in unit Iron & Ironing board
in unit ☺ CTV ⊕3pin square 3P
🎲(1m)
⊖ 🍴(1m) 🎵(1m) ♫(1m)
Min£75 Max£170pw

B   Tor-Na-Brach
for bookings Mrs W D Ross, Strone,
Drummadrochit, Inverness-shire
☎Drumnadrochit(04562)351

*Modern detached bungalow in elevated
position overlooking Lewiston and
Drumnadrochit towards Loch Ness. It
comprises of lounge, kitchen/diner, three
bedrooms and bathroom/WC.*

Mar–Oct   MWB out of season   2days
(out of season) min, 4wks max, 1unit,
1–6persons ◆ no pets ◎ fridge
Electric Elec metered ⌷can be hired
☎(½m) SD in unit Iron & Ironing board
in unit ☺ CTV ⊕3pin square 5P
🎲(1m)
⊖ 🍴(1m) 🎵(1m) ♫(1m)
Min£75 Max£170pw

DRYBROOK
Gloucestershire
Map**3** SO61

B **The Bungalow** Starve Beech
for bookings Mrs H I Smith, Old Kilns,
Howle Hill, Ross-on-Wye, Herefordshire
☎Ross-on-Wye(0989)62051

*A 1950s style Bungalow in a very secluded
setting with woods to the rear and
extensive forward views. It comprises two
double bedrooms, one convertible double
divan settee and two folding beds. There is
also a lounge, dining room, kitchen and
bathroom. A large garden is also available
for guests use with garden furniture and
barbecue.*

Allyear MWB 1daymin, 1unit,
1–8persons [◇ ◈ ◆] ◎ fridge
Night storage, electric & open fires
Elec metered Ⓛcan be hired ☎(½m)
Iron & Ironing board in unit ⊙ CTV
⊕3pin square 2🏠 Ⅲ ⚊(1m)
↩ 🎤(1m) 🎞(3m) 🎵(3m) 🐾(3m)
From £25pw

DUFFTOWN
Grampian *Banffshire*
Map**15** NJ34

C **Gordon & Richmond Cottages**
Tullochallum
for bookings Mrs E Innes, Ardlair, Insch,
Aberdeenshire AB5 6YR
☎Dufftown 20216 or 20172

*Semi-detached cottages lying on their own
on road to farm. They are simply
decorated and furnished and comprise
small kitchen, lounge/dining room, one
double and two twin bedrooms, and
bathroom. There is a fine outlook across
farmland with Dufftown in the distance.*

Apr–Oct MWB out of season 1wk min,
2units, 2–6persons ◆ ◆ ◎ fridge
Electric Elec inclusive Ⓛcan be hired
☎(1½m) SD in unit Iron & Ironing board
in unit ⊙ CTV ⊕3pin square 4P Ⅲ
⚊(1½m)
↩ 𝛿(3m) 🎤(1½m)
Min£75 Max£110pw

DUIRINISH
Highland *Ross & Cromarty*
Map**13** NG73

Drybrook
—
Dulverton

Ch **Allt Duirinish Chalets**
for bookings Duirinish Lodge Holidays,
Dept AA, Duirinish, Kyle, Ross-shire
IV40 8BE
☎Plockton(059984)268

*A group of seven chalets situated on the
edge of mature woodlands. Six have open
plan kitchen/lounge/dining room, two
twin-bedded rooms and a bunk-bedded
room. One has two twin-bedded rooms.
Located on an unclass road some ½m E of
Duirinish.*

mid Mar–Oct MWB out of season
1wk min, 5wks max, 7units, 1–6persons
[◆] ◆ ◎ fridge Electric
Elec metered Ⓛcan be hired ☎(½m)
SD, Iron & Ironing board in unit ⊙ CTV
⊕3pin square P ⚊(2m)
↩ 🎤(2m)
Min£60 Max£215pw

DULNAIN BRIDGE
Highland *Morayshire*
Map**14** NH92

C **Mrs G M Whittle Easter Laggan
Cottage** Dulnain Bridge, Grantown-on-
Spey, Moray PH26 3NT
☎Dulnain Bridge(047985)283

*The white stone cottage, which dates from
1786, is situated in a secluded spot about
¾m from the A95, Aviemore to Grantown-
on-Spey road, at the end of a private farm
road 1m from the village. It stands in 5
acres of hilly land with fine views over the
river Spey and across the Forest of
Abernethy to the Cairngorm mountains.
The accommodation consists of three
bedrooms, sitting room which contains a
piano and a wood burning stove, kitchen,
cloakroom/WC and bathroom/WC. The
fittings and furniture are of a good
standard and the décor is clean but
simple.*

Mar–Nov 1wk min, 1unit, 2–6persons
◆ ◆ no pets ◎ fridge 🐾
Elec metered Ⓛnot provided ☎ WM &
SD in unit Iron in unit ⊙ [TV]
⊕3pin square P ⚊(1m)

↩ 🎤(2m)
Min£110pw (Low)
Min£110 Max£135pw (High)

H **Glencarr**
for bookings Mrs E Hamilton,
Tullochgribban Mains, Dulnain Bridge,
Grantown-on-Spey, Morayshire PH26 3NE
☎Dulnain Bridge(047985)333

*A large traditional country house with four
bedrooms and two bathrooms, large
lounge, dining room and kitchen with
dining area. It is decorated and furnished
to a very high standard and there are
open views across the Spey valley to the
Cairngorms.*

Allyear MWB out of season 4days min,
1unit, 1–8persons ◆ ◆ no pets ◎
fridge Electric Elec metered Ⓛcan be
hired ☎ WM & SD in unit Iron &
Ironing board in unit ⊙ CTV
⊕3pin square 4P 2🏠 Ⅲ ⚊(1m)
↩ 𝛿(3m) 🎤(1m) 🎞(3m)

Details not confirmed for 1987

DULVERTON
Somerset
Map**3** SS92

H **JFH HF711B**
for bookings John Fowler Holidays,
Dept 58, Marlborough Road, Ilfracombe,
Devon EX34 8PF
☎Ilfracombe(0271)66666

*Part of a period farmhouse on a 122-acre
holding in the heart of Exmoor, which is
remote but not isolated. There are two
sitting rooms, both with bed settees if
required, and a superb inglenook
fireplace, kitchen with breakfast bar and
dishwasher, bathroom and WC. Upstairs
there are two double bedrooms, one with
one extra single bed and the other with
two. The farmhouse is beamed
throughout.*

Mar–Oct MWB out of season 3days min,
1mth max, 1unit, 1–11persons [◇] ◆
◎ fridge Electric & log fire
Elec metered Ⓛnot provided ☎(2m)
Iron & Ironing board in unit ⊙ TV
⊕3pin square 2P 2🏠 ⚊(2m)
↩ 🎤(2m) Min£79.35 Max£205.85pw

DUNBAR
Lothian *East Lothian*
Map**12** NT67

F **East Wing**
for bookings Mrs Moira Marrian,
Bowerhouse, Dunbar, E Lothian EH42 1RE
☎Dunbar(0368)62293

*The East wing of a 19th-century mansion
house which stands in 25 acres of ground,
is surrounded by farmland and lies 2½m S
of Dunbar. First-floor level comprises
double bedroom, a twin bedroom, open
plan lounge/dining room (with double
bed-settee), large kitchen and a
bathroom. The ground floor has a
generous hall area, single bedroom and a
WC.*

All year 1unit, 6–8persons ◎ fridge
Electric Elec metered ⬜can be hired
☎(2m) Iron & Ironing board on
premises TV ⊕3pin square 2P ▥
▣(2½m)

⊖ δ(3m) ⬚(2m)

Min£90 Max£115pw (Low)
Min£150 Max£180pw (High)

C **Laundry Cottage**
for bookings Mrs Moira Marrian,
Bowerhose, Dunbar, E Lothian EH42 1RE
☎Dunbar(0368)62293

*Converted from the former laundry,
adjacent to the mansion house, this small
building has been attractively redesigned
to give lots of character. Living/dining
room (with double bed-settee) and kitchen
on split level, one twin bedroom, one with
two single bunks and a bathroom. Private
walled garden to rear.*

All year 1unit, 4–6persons ◎ fridge
Electric Elec metered ⬜can be hired
☎(2m) Iron & Ironing board on
premises TV ⊕3pin square 2P ▥
▣(2½m)

⊖ δ(3m) ⬚(2m)

Min£70 Max£85pw (Low)
Min£115 Max£150pw (High)

DUNMORE
Strathclyde *Argyllshire*
Map**10** NR76

C **Campbell, Fraser, MacMillan & Ross
Cottages**
for bookings Mr & Mrs M Kerr, Dunmore
Court, Dunmore, Tarbert, Argyll
☎Tarbert(08802)642

*Formed from converted farm buildings
these well-furnished cottages offer two
and three bedroomed accommodation, as
well as having lounge, kitchen/diner,
bathroom and WC. Some have vanity units
in bedrooms and feature fireplaces.*

All year MWB out of season 2days min,
1unit, 1–7persons [◆ ◆] ◎ fridge
Electric & log fires Elec metered ⬜can
be hired ☎(15yds) WM & SD in unit
(Campbell & MacMillan only) Iron in unit
Ironing board on premises ⊕ ⊕ CTV
can be hired ⊕3pin square P ▣(7m) Boats for hire

Details not confirmed for 1987

Dunbar
—
Dunster

H **Bar-Na-Criche**
for bookings Mr & Mrs M Kerr, Dunmore
Court, Dunmore, Tarbert, Argyll
☎Tarbert(08802)642

*Spacious bungalow with loch views,
affording kitchen/diner/lounge and four
bedrooms. One bedroom has en-suite
bathroom and one has a vanity unit. 9m
from Tarbert.*

All year MWB out of season 2days min,
1unit, 1–8persons [◆ ◆] ◎ fridge
⊯ Elec metered ⬜can be hired
☎(2m) WM, SD & TD in unit Iron in unit
Ironing board on premises ⊕ ⊕ CTV
can be hired ⊕3pin square P ▣(9m)
Dishwasher & Freezer Boats for hire

Details not confirmed for 1987

H **Dunmore Villa**
for bookings Mr & Mrs M Kerr, Dunmore
Court, Dunmore, Tarbert, Argyll
☎Tarbert(08802)642

*Attractive villa on north shore of Loch
Tarbert, having lounge with superb views,
bathroom, dining room, kitchen and five
bedrooms, one of which has luxury en-
suite bathroom.*

All year MWB out of season 2days min,
1unit, 1–10persons [◆ ◆] ◎
fridge ⊯ Elec metered ⬜can be
hired ☎ WM, SD & TD in unit Iron in
unit Ironing board on premises ⊕ ⊕
CTV can be hired ⊕3pin square P
▣(6m) Freezer Boats for hire

Details not confirmed for 1987

H **Taylor Cottage**
for bookings Mr & Mrs M Kerr, Dunmore
Court, Dunmore, Tarbert, Argyll
☎Tarbert(08802)642

*Three bedroomed semi-detached house
with lounge, kitchen/diner, and bathroom.
Comfortable family accommodation.*

All year MWB out of season 2days min,
1unit, 1–8persons [◆ ◆]
◎&Rayburn fridge Electric & log fires
Elec metered ⬜can be hired
☎(15yds) WM in unit Iron in unit
Ironing board on premises ⊕ CTV can
be hired ⊕3pin square P ▣(7m)
Boats for hire

Details not confirmed for 1987

DUNNING
Tayside *Perthshire*
Map**11** NO01

H **Coachman & Gean Tree Cottages**
for bookings Mrs J R Marshall, Dalreoch,
Dunning, Perth PH2 0QJ
☎Dunning(076 484)368

*Two semi-detached and recently
modernised stone houses forming part of
the old stable block which belong to
Duncrub House. The larger house sleeps
eight in three twin and one double
bedrooms; the smaller house has one*

---

*bedroom with double and single beds plus
bed-settee in the lounge. Indoor games
centre (June – Aug) and table tennis
always.*

All year MWB out of season 1wk min,
2units, 1–8persons ◆ ◆ ◎ & solid
fuel fridge Electric & open fires
Elec inclusive ⬜inclusive ☎ WM, SD &
TD on premises Iron & Ironing board in
unit ⊕ CTV ⊕3pin square 6P
▣(½m)

⊖ δ(½m) ⬚(½m)

Min£95 Max£295pw

DUNNINGTON
North Yorkshire
Map**8** SE65

C **Crest Cottage** York Road
for bookings Mrs Hanby, The Paddocks,
Low Catton, York, N Yorkshire YO4 1EA
☎Stamford Bridge(0759)71375

*A large cottage extended and modernised
in rural surroundings on the edge of the
village. Accommodation for up to five
people in two double-bedded rooms and
one single room. There is a spacious and
comfortable lounge, dining room, well-
fitted modern kitchen, bathroom/WC and
a separate WC.*

All year MWB out of season 1wk min,
1mth max, 1unit, 1–5persons ◆ ◆
◎ fridge ⊯ Elec inclusive
⬜not provided ☎ Iron & Ironing board
in unit ⊕ CTV ⊕3pin square 2P
1🏠 ▥ ▣(500yds)

⊖ ⬚(½m)

Min£90 Max£170pw

DUNS
Borders *Berwickshire*
Map**12** NT75

H **No's 1 & 2 Printonan**
for bookings Mrs Mather, Printonan, Duns,
Berwickshire TD11 3HX
☎Leitholm(089084)378

*These two simply appointed farmhouses
stand in a quiet location and share views
of both Lammermuir and Cheviot Hills.
Accommodation comprises lounge/diner,
kitchen and three bedrooms. Number 2
sleeps six while number 1 sleeps four. No
children in number 1.*

May – Sep MWB out of season 1wk min,
2units, 1–6persons ◆ ◆ no pets ◎
fridge Electric fires Elec metered
⬜not provided ☎(3m) WM in No. 2
Iron & Ironing board on premises ⊕
TV ⊕3pin round 4P ▣(3m)
⊖ ⬚(3m)

Details not confirmed for 1987

DUNSTER
Somerset
Map**3** SS94

C **Clover Cottage** 3 St George Street
for bookings Miss M & M Clarke, The Old
Rectory, Selworthy, Minehead, Somerset
TA24 8TW
☎Minehead(0643)862233

94

An attractive terraced cottage in a village setting comprising downstairs, a small sitting room, kitchen, compact dining room, and bathroom/WC; first floor comprises two bedrooms.

All year MWB out of season 2nights min, 1unit, 2–4persons [◇] ◈ ◎ fridge Electric Elec metered Ⓛcan be hired ☎(150yds) Iron & Ironing board in unit ⊙ CTV ⊕3pin square 1P ▥ ⩘(25yds)
↤ ♦(2m) ♨(100yds) ♫(2m)
♬(2m) ☖(2m)

Min£40 Max£80pw (Low)
Min£100 Max£130pw (High)

DUNS TEW
Oxfordshire
Map4 SP42

C Mr R F Moffatt **Daisy Hill Farm** Duns Tew, Oxford, Oxfordshire
☎Steeple Aston(0869)40293

Ten converted cottage-type units set in a picturesque Cotswold village. The accommodation varies to include one, two and three bedroomed units. All have open plan kitchen with dining area, sitting room and bathroom/WC. Modern furniture and equipment.

All year MWB out of season 3nights min, 10units, 2–8persons ◈ ◆ ◎ fridge ⦿ Electric Elec inclusive Ⓛinclusive ☎ Iron & Ironing board on premises Launderette on premises ⊙ CTV ⊕3pin square 25P ▥ ⩘ Games room
↤ ♨

Min£105 Max£210pw (Low)
Min£170 Max£330pw (High)

DUNSYRE
Strathclyde *Lanarkshire*
Map11 NT04

C **Mountview Cottage**
for bookings Lee & Carnwath Estates, Estate Office, Carnwath, Lanark ML11 8JY
☎Carnwath(0555)840273

Small, single-storey, stone cottage built in 1820 and modernised in 1974, it has its own pleasant garden offering superb views of Black Mount and Medwin Valley. Accommodation comprises lounge with open log-fire (logs provided), modern kitchen/dinette, two twin-bedded rooms and a bathroom/WC.

All year MWB out of season 1wk min, 1mth max, 1unit, 2–4persons [◇ ◆] ◎ fridge Storage heaters (off peak), electric & log fires Elec metered Ⓛcan be hired ☎(incoming) Iron & Ironing board in unit ⊙ CTV ⊕3pin square P ⩘(3m) Fishing

Min£105 Max£157pw (Low)
Min£130 Max£185pw (High)

H **Shawfield House**
for bookings Mr McDonald-Lockhart, Lee & Carnwath Estates, Estate Office, Carnwath, Lanarkshire ML11 8JY
☎Carnwath(0555)840273

Dunster
—
Eastbourne

An extended and fully modernised late Victorian, stone built house, with good garden area and superb views. On the ground floor is the lounge/diner, two twin bedrooms with WHB, kitchen and bathroom and on the first floor another twin-bedded room. Out-door pursuits include fishing.

All year MWB out of season 1wk min, 1mth max, 1unit, 2–6persons [◇ ◆] ◎ fridge ⦿ Elec metered Ⓛcan be hired ☎(2m) Iron & Ironing board in unit ⊙ CTV ⊕3pin square 3P ▥ ⩘(2m)

Min£120 Max£179pw (Low)
Min£147 Max£210pw (High)

DUNVEGAN
Highland *Inverness-shire*
See **Skye, Isle of**

EASTBOURNE
East Sussex
Map5 TV69

F **Beach House** 34 Beach Road
for bookings Mrs K E Jones, Manor Cottage, 31 Elven Lane, East Dean, Eastbourne, Sussex BN20 0LJ
☎East Dean(03215)3032

A semi-detached late 19th-century fisherman's house skilfully converted into two flats, each comprising two bedrooms, lounge, kitchen and bathroom/WC. Set in quiet suburban area of Eastbourne. 500yds from eastern end of seafront.

All year MWB out of season 8mths max, 2units, 1–5persons ◈ ◆ no pets ◎ fridge Electric Elec metered Ⓛinclusive ☎(300yds) Iron & Ironing board on premises ⊙ ⦾ TV ⊕3pin square P [🏠] ▥ ⩘(50yds) ⫻Hard putting
↤ ♨(¼m) ♫(¼m) ♬(1m) ☖(1m)

Min£55 Max£75 (Low)
Min£70 Max£135pw (High)

F Mr S W Dawkins, **Caithness Holiday Apartments** Willmington Square, Eastbourne, East Sussex BN21 4DX
☎Eastbourne(0323)30610

Self-contained one and two bedroom flats comprising lounge/diner, bathroom/WC en suite, and kitchen. Set in a three-storey Victorian terraced house in King Edwards Parade, off the seafront. Lift to all floors.

Mar–Nov 1wk min, 4wks max, 14units, 1–8persons ◈ ◆ no cats ◎ fridge Electric Elec metered Ⓛcan be hired ☎(100yds) Iron & Ironing board on premise ⊙ ⦾ CTV ⊕3pin square ▥ ⩘(100yds)
↤ ♨(1¾m) ♫(¾m) ♬(¾m) ☖(¾m)

Min£60 Max£120pw (Low)
Min£155 Max£225pw (High)

F **Carlisle Court** 49 Carlisle Road
for bookings Mr & Mrs R H Greenwood, 11 The Brow, Friston, Eastbourne, East Sussex BN20 0ER
☎East Dean(03215)2130

Modern well furnished and equipped accommodation on four floors, comprising two flats with two bedrooms, sleeping six–seven persons, and one flat with one bedroom sleeping three persons, all with bathroom and WC.

All year MWB out of season 1wk min, 6mths max, 3units, 1–7persons, nc18mths [◈ ◆] no pets ◎ fridge freezer ⦿ Elec metered Ⓛcan be hired ☎ Iron & Ironing board in unit [Launderette on premises] ⊙ CTV ⊕3pin square ▥ ⩘(½m)
↤ ♦(1m) ♨(½m) ♫(½m) ♬(½m) ☖(½m)

Min£53 Max£79pw (Low)
Min£117 Max£190pw (High)

F Mrs Anne Billings **Chesleigh Holiday Flats** 4 Marine Parade, Eastbourne, East Sussex BN21 3DX
☎Eastbourne(0323)20722

Three self-contained flats with twin-bedded rooms kitchen/diner and bath or shower/WC. Well appointed and overlooking the sea.

12Apr–6Dec 1wk min, 1mth max, 3units, 1–2persons, nc, no pets ◎ fridge Electric Elec metered Ⓛcan be hired ☎(100yds) Iron & Ironing board on premises [Launderette within 300yds] ⊙ ⦾ CTV ⊕3pin square ▥ ⩘(50yds)
↤ ♦(1¾m) ♨(50yds) ♫(50yds) ♬(50yds) ☖(50yds)

Min£66 Max£130pw

F Mr R H Brooker **Holiday Flats** 3 Jevington Gardens, Eastbourne, East Sussex BN21 4HR
☎Eastbourne(0323)29998

Part of a terraced house, situated in quiet residential part of town 50yds from Winter Gardens. Two of the three flats have one bedroom (four single beds) plus a large lounge with two folding beds. The other flat is small with just two folding beds in the lounge. All have modern furnishings, fittings and fitted carpets. Large bathroom/WC.

All year MWB out of season 2days min, 6mths max, 3units, 1–6persons ◈ ◆ no pets ◎ fridge ⦿ Elec metered Ⓛinclusive ☎(10yds) Iron & Ironing board on premises ⊙ ⦾ CTV ⊕3pin square ▥ ⩘(200yds)
↤ ♨(250yds) ♫(300yds) ♬(300yds) ☖(1m)

Min£90 Max£170pw

F Mr & Mrs C A Manchester **Marine Court Holiday Apartments** 33 Marine Parade, Eastbourne, East Sussex BN22 7AY
☎Eastbourne(0323)644568

Modern, well-maintained studio apartments facing the sea, the →

accommodation comprises an open plan bedroom/lounge/dining area with double beds, and either bath or shower/WC. Some flats have their own roof patio or balcony.

All year MWB out of season 2nights min, 28days max, 6units, 1–4persons, nc5 no pets ◎ fridge Electric fires Elec metered ⌷inclusive 🕿(20yds) Iron & Ironing board on premises [Launderette within 300yds] ☺ CTV ⊕3pin square ♨(500yds)
⊖ ⌇(3m) ⬥(½m) ♫(½m) ♫(½m) ▓(¼m)
Min£55 Max£120pw (Low)
Min£110 Max£185pw (High)

F Meads Holiday Flats
for bookings Mr & Mrs J N Weaver, Meads Lodge Holiday Flats, 1 Jevington Gardens, Eastbourne, East Sussex BN21 4HR
🕿Eastbourne(0323)27895 & 24362

Five-storey Edwardian building which has been renovated and converted into 14 modern flats. Situated in quiet residential part of Eastbourne, 400yds from sea and Devonshire Park. Units comprise kitchenette, bathroom/WC or shower/WC, one bedroom and lounge with one or two fold-away beds. Outdoor solar heated swimming pool available at Lodge Holiday Flats, 1 Jevington Gardens.

Closed Feb MWB out of season 1wk min, 1mth max, 14units, 1–6persons [◇ ●] ◎ fridge Electric Elec metered ⌷ can be hired 🕿 Iron & Ironing board on premises ☺ ⑭ TV ⊕3pin square ▥ ♨(100yds)
⊖ ⌇(1m) ⬥(200yds) ♫(½m) ♫(¾m) ▓(1m)
Min£69 Max£207pw

F Mr & Mrs J N Weaver, Meads Lodge Holiday Flats, 1 Jevington Gardens, Easbourne, East Sussex BN21 4HR
🕿Eastbourne(0323)27895 & 24362

Detached house skilfully converted into four self-contained flats. Decorated and furnished to a high standard. Ideally situated in one of the best parts of Eastbourne. The rear garden contains an outdoor solar heated swimming pool, and patio area, and is available to all resident holiday clients (during opening hours).

Mar–Oct MWB out of season 1wk min, 4wks max, 4units, 2–4persons [◇ ●] ◎ fridge ▓(inclusive) Elec metered ⌷ can be hired 🕿 Iron & Ironing board on premises ☺ ⑭ TV ⊕3pin square ▥ ♨(200yds)
⊖ ⌇(2m) ⬥(200yds) ♫(200yds) ♫(½m) ▓(600yds)
Min£69 Max£172.50pw

Eastbourne
—
East Prawle

C Mill Cottage 13 Watts Lane
for bookings Mrs K E Jones, Manor Cottage, 31 Elven Lane, East Dean, Eastbourne, East Sussex BN20 0LJ
🕿East Dean(03215)3230

One of four cottages about 200-years-old, constructed of pale pink stone with white shutters. It comprises of sitting room/ dining area, kitchen with pine panelled walls and ceiling, small lobby with bathroom/WC, all on the ground floor, and two bedrooms on the first floor.

All year MWB out of season 2days min, 6mths max, 1unit, 2–4persons ◇ ● no pets ◎ fridge ♨ Elec inclusive ⌷inclusive ♨ iron & ironing board in unit [Launderette within 300yds] ☺ ⑭ CTV ⊕3pin square ▥ ♨
⊖ ⌇(2m) ♫ ♫ ▓
Min£60 Max£135pw

F Mowbray Court Lascelles Terrace, Eastbourne, East Sussex BN21 4BJ
🕿Eastbourne(0323)501490

Seven self-contained flats; four flats sleep two to three in a separate twin bedroom with third bed in lounge. Two studio flats sleep two in the lounge and a third flat sleeps three. All flats have separate kitchenette and bathroom.

Mar–Oct 1wk min, 4wks max, 8units, 1–3persons, nc7 no pets ◎ fridge Electric Elec metered ⌷ can be hired 🕿 Iron & Ironing board on premises ☺ ⑭ CTV ⊕3pin square ▥ ♨(100yds)
⊖ ⬥ ♫ ♫ ▓
Min£51 Max£61pw (Low)
Min£128 Max£145pw (High)

F Netherby Holiday Flats 17 Cambridge Road, Royal Parade
for bookings Mrs P Knowles, Reymar, 2 Cambridge Road, Eastbourne, East Sussex BN22 7BS
🕿Eastbourne(0323)26003

An end-terraced house, 100yds from sea, converted into six flats. All have one bedroom (double or twin beds) plus fold-away beds in the lounge. Top two flats sleep three, remainder four. Two flats have separate kitchen, remainder have combined lounge/diner/kitchenette. Modern equipped kitchen. Five flats have showers, the other has a bath.

All year MWB out of season 6mths max, 6units, 1–4persons ◇ ◎ fridge

---

Electric Elec metered ⌷ can be hired 🕿(10yds) [Launderette within 300yds] ☺ TV ⊕3pin square P 🏠 ♨(300yds) ⌇
⊖ ⬥(30yds) ♫(1m) ♫(½m) ▓(¾m)
Details not confirmed for 1987

EAST DEAN
East Sussex
Map**5** TV59

Ch, B Birlingdean 81 Michel Dene Road
for bookings Miss P G Elkins, 26 Lymington Court, All Saints Road, Sutton, Surrey SM1 3DE
🕿01-644 7271 or East Dean(03215)2303

This three-bedroomed detached chalet-bungalow stands in a quiet residential area on elevated ground with extensive views of the Downs and sea (1½m). The accommodation consists of three double bedrooms (one on ground floor), cloak room, lounge/dining room, kitchen, bathroom, hall and garage. Visitors met on arrival.

All year MWB out of season 1wk min, 5mths max, 1unit, 1–6persons ◇ ◎ fridge ⌷ can be hired SD in unit Iron & Ironing board in unit ☺ CTV ⊕3pin square 🏠 ♨(¾m)
⊖ ⬥(1m) ♫(3m) ♫(3m) ▓(3m)
Min£50 Max£150pw (Low)
Min£170 Max£250pw (High)

EAST PORTLEMOUTH
Devon
Map**3** SX73

F Mr L Richards **Gara Rock Hotel** East Portlemouth, Salcombe, Devon
🕿Salcombe(054884)2342

This hotel complex was once a coastguard station and consequently affords fine views. Thirteen flats are purpose-built and stand in the hotel grounds while six form part of the main hotel building. Use of private beach.

Etr–Oct MWB out of season 1wk min, 3mths max, 19units, 2–6persons ◇ ◇ ● ◎ fridge Electric Elec metered ⌷inclusive 🕿(20yds) WM & TD on premises Iron & Ironing board on premises ☺ ⑭ CTV ⊕3pin square 100P ▥ ♨(2m) ⌇ ✂ Games room
⊖ ⬥(20yds) ♫(20yds)
Min£130 Max£175pw (Low)
Min£260 Max£395pw (High)
See advertisement under Salcombe

EAST PRAWLE
Devon
Map**3** SX73

B   CC Ref 4051L
for bookings Character Cottages
(Holidays) Ltd, 34 Fore Street, Sidmouth,
Devon EX10 8AQ
☎Sidmouth(03955)77001

*A new bungalow in the centre of a small
village. Accommodation comprises
lounge, kitchen/dining room, three
bedrooms, bathroom/WC and shower
room/WC.*

All year   MWB out of season   1wk min,
1mth max, 1unit, 1–6persons   ◈
no pets   ◎   fridge   Electric
Elec inclusive   ⌷inclusive   ☎(50yds)
Iron & Ironing board in unit   ⊙   CTV
⊕3pin square   2P   1🏠   ⅲ   ♨(3m)
⟊   🍴(50yds)
Min£97 Max£166pw (Low)
Min£181 Max£226pw (High)

EAST PRESTON
West Sussex
Map**4** TQ00

C   Kingston Corner Cottage Kingston
Corner, Kingston Gorse, East Preston,
W Sussex BN16 1SE
☎Rustington(0903)782723

*Modern detached cottage on quiet, private
residential estate within easy reach of the
beach. Accommodation comprises one
double and one twin-bedded room, one
en-suite, one situated on ground-floor, the
other on first-floor, a comfortably
furnished lounge/diner and kitchen. 2m E
of East Preston on unclassified road.*

Feb–Nov   MWB out of season
4days min, 1unit, 1–4persons, nc3   ♦
fridge   🍴Gas inclusive   Elec metered
⌷inclusive   ☎(½m)   Iron & Ironing board
in unit   ⊙   ⊕   TV   ⊕3pin square   2P
1🏠   ⅲ   ♨(1m)
⟊   ♪(1½m)   🍴(1m)   𝄞(3m)   𝄞(3m)
Min£110 Max£140pw

EASTRY
Kent
Map**5** TR35

C   2 & 3 Tickenhurst Cottages
for bookings The Cottage Secretary,
Knowlton Estate Office, Knowlton Court,
Wingham, Canterbury, Kent CT3 1PT
☎Sandwich(0304)617344

*A pair of cottages set in rural
surroundings. One has three bedrooms,
large sitting room/dining room, kitchen
and two bathrooms. The other has two
bedrooms, sitting room, dining room,
kitchen and bathroom.*

All year   MWB out of season   1wk min,
2units, 1–10persons   [◇]   ◈   ♦   ◎
fridge   🍴   Electric   Elec metered
⌷inclusive   ☎(1m)   Iron & Ironing board
in unit   ⊙   TV   ⊕3pin square   P   ⅲ
♨(1m)
⟊   🍴(1m)
Min£65 Max£85pw (Low)
Min£95 Max£140pw (High)

East Prawle
—
Edinburgh

EAST TAPHOUSE
Cornwall
Map**2** SX16

F   Five Acres
for bookings Mr & Mrs R A Edwards, East
Taphouse Farm, Liskeard PL14 4NH
☎Liskeard(0579)20355

*The solid stone walls of a traditional
Cornish barn have been cleverly utilized to
provide four apartments of character and
charm. **Lapwing** and **Wagtail** are both two
bedroomed flats with lounge/dining room,
kitchen and bathroom, furnished to a high
standard. **Wren** and **Robin** offer one
bedroomed accommodation with lounge/
diner, kitchen and bathroom, well-
equipped and tastefully decorated.*

Mar–Dec   MWB out of season
2nights min, 1mth max, 4units,
1–5persons   ◇   ◈   ♦   ◎   fridge
Electric   Elec metered   ⌷inclusive
☎(200yds)   Iron & Ironing board in unit
⊙   CTV   ⊕3pin square   6P   ⅲ
♨(250yds)
Min£70 Max£195pw

ECKINGTON
Hereford & Worcester
Map**3** SO94

C   Japonica & Juniper Cottages
for bookings Mrs L Leyland, The Manor
House, Manor Road, Eckington, Pershore,
Worcs
☎Evesham(0386)750315

*A Victorian stable block converted into two
cottages each providing accommodation
of a very high standard. Each comprises
two bedrooms, Japonica's are the first-
floor and Junipers on the ground-floor.
There is a large lounge with open fire (logs
supplied), kitchen/diner and bathroom/
WC.*

All year   MWB out of season   2days min,
6mths max, 2units, 1–5persons   [◇   ◈]
◎   fridge   🍴 & open fires
Elec inclusive   ⌷inclusive   ☎   SD & TD
on premises   Iron in unit   [Launderette on
premises]   ⊙   CTV   ⊕3pin square   4P
ⅲ   ♨(½m)   🏌Hard   putting   Croquet
lawn, fishing & sailing
⟊   ♨(½m)
Min£115 Max£135pw (Low)
Min£145 Max£230pw (High)

EDALE
Derbyshire
Map**7** SK18

F   Flat 3 Edale Mill
for bookings The Landmark Trust,
Shottesbrooke, Maidenhead, Berkshire
SL6 3SW
☎Littlewick Green(062 882)5925

*A self-contained flat on the second floor of
a renovated 18th-century cotton mill,
featuring original beams and comprising*

---

*two bedrooms with twin beds and two
folding beds. Situated in the very pleasant
village of Edale.*

All year   MWB out of season   1day min,
3wks max, 1unit, 2–4persons   ◎   fridge
🍴   Elec inclusive   ⌷not provided
☎(100yds)   ⊙   ⊕3pin square   P   ⅲ
♨(100yds)
⟊   ♨(1m)
Min£112 Max£235pw

EDINBURGH
Lothian *Midlothian*
Map**11** NT27

F   Controller of Catering & Residences
Heriot-Watt University Riccarton, Currie,
Edinburgh EH14 4AS
☎031-449 5111 ext2178

*Ideal self-contained flatlets in three
modern blocks on the University Campus.
Each flat has a lounge/kitchenette, with
twin-and-single-bedded rooms, shower
and WC. Full campus amenities available.*

28Jun–27Sep   MWB   1wk min,
3mths max, 36units, 3–6persons   ◎
fridge   Elec inclusive   ⌷inclusive   ☎
Iron & Ironing board in unit   [Launderette
on premises]   ⊙   ⊕3pin square   P   ♨
🏌Hard   Sports complex
⟊
Details not confirmed for 1987
See advertisement on page 98

F   Keyplan Apartments Linton Court,
Murieston Road, Edinburgh EH11 2JJ
☎031-3374040

*Forty-two units within newly developed
block of flats with lift and laundry room. All
flats with fully equipped kitchens and
bathrooms, reception and chambermaid
service. Situated on the main bus route
one mile from city centre.*

All year   MWB   1day min, 42units,
1–7persons   [◇   ◈]   ♦   ◎   fridge
🍴   Elec metered   ⌷inclusive   ☎   Iron &
Ironing board in unit   [Launderette on
premises]   ⊙   CTV   ⊕3pin square
♨(100yds)
⟊   ♨(½m)   🍴(1m)   𝄞(1m)   🎳(1m)
Min£121 Max£297pw
See advertisement on page 98

F   Vacation Accommodation (BOX AA)
Pollock Halls of Residence 18 Holyrood
Park Road, Edinburgh EH16 5AY
☎031-667 1971

*Student flats within halls of residence and
conference centre amidst extensive
grounds on south side of city. The four
person flats comprise two bedrooms with
wash hand basin, lounge/diner which can
be used as an additional bedroom,
bathroom, WC and kitchen. The two
person flats, comprise small bedroom,
lounge/diner; bathroom/WC and kitchen.
The two bedroomed flats plus one of the
four bedroomed flats have two ringed
Baby Belling cookers. The
accommodation is basic but functional.*

4Jul–26Sep   1wk min, 10units,
1–5persons   ◎   fridge   Electric

Elec inclusive ⬜inclusive ☎(100yds)
[WM & TD on premises] Iron & Ironing
board on premises ⊕3pin square P
🏠 ♨(½m) squash courts
⊝ 𝄢(½m) 🍴(¼m) 🎵(1m) 🎵(1m)
🍽(1m)

Min£63 Max£171pw

EGHAM
Surrey
Map**4** TQ07

H   Penrose Court Highfield Road,
Englefield Green
for bookings Miss S Simpson, Conference
Office, Royal Holloway and Bedford New
College, Egham Hill, Egham, Surrey
TW20 0EX
☎Egham(0784)34455 ext 3047

Sixteen identical terraced houses set
around the courtyard in the grounds of
this splendid Victorian College. The
accommodation comprises four or six
single study bedrooms, both with shower
and WC, kitchen and diner combined.

Jul–Sep MWB in season 1wk min,
11wks max, 16units, 1–6persons no pets
🍴 fridge 🍲 ⬜inclusive ☎(200yds)
Iron & Ironing board in unit [Launderette
on premises] ⊕ ⊕3pin square P
♨(500yds) ✄Hard Sports centre
subject to availability
⊝ 𝄢(2m) 🍴(½m) Sports centre(1m)
from£120pw

ELLARY
Strathclyde Argyllshire
Map**10** NR77

C & F   Holiday Homes at Ellary
for bookings Castle Sween Bay (Holidays)
Ltd, The Estate Office, Ellary,
Lochgilphead, Argyll PA31 8PA
☎Ormsary(08803)232 & 209 or
Achnamara(054 685)223

Two spacious flats located within Ellary
House and five cottages of varying sizes
and in different location, at the mouth of
Loch Sween and on Loch Caolsport. The
flats have three bedrooms, the cottages
have two or three. The flats are in an
elevated position with magnificent views.

All year MWB out of season 2nights min,
7units, 1–8persons ⊚ fridge Electric &
coal fires Elec metered ⬜not provided
☎(3m) ⊙ TV ⊕3pin square P 📺
♨(11m) Windsurfing Cycles for hire
fishing

Min£103 Max£111pw (Low)
Min£204 Max£222pw (High)

ELRIG
Dumfries & Galloway Wigtownshire
Map**10** NX34

H   The Anchorage
for bookings Mr J H G Korner, House of
Elrig, Port William, Wigtownshire DG8 9RF
☎Port William(098 87)242

Detached two-storey traditional stone
house in small rural hamlet. On the
ground floor there is a small sitting room,
dining room, double bedroom, bathroom
and kitchen. Upstairs are three twin-
bedded rooms and additional bathroom.
A spacious house with plenty of storage
space. Elrig is located in the heart of
pleasant farming countryside but still only
10 minutes' drive from the sea. Tennis
available at Elrig House (1½m). 2½m N of
Port William and reached by unclassified,
signed road off A747.

Apr–Oct (Nov–Mar 2wks min) MWB out
of season 2wks min, 1unit, 1–8persons
◊ ⊚ fridge 🍲 & open fire
Elec metered ⬜not provided ☎ WM in
unit Iron & Ironing board in unit ⊝
CTV ⊕3pin square P 📺 ♨(3m)
✄Hard Fly-fishing
⊝ 🍴(3m)

Min£105 Max£175pw

C   Lochside of Elrig
for bookings Mr J H G Korner, House of
Elrig, Port William, Wigtownshire DG8 9RF
☎Port William(098 87)242

Only a country road separates this
restored and extended gamekeepers
cottage from the shores of Loch Elrig. The

house, which is neatly appointed, provides three bedrooms, two bathrooms (one with shower), lounge, dining room, large kitchen, all on ground floor. Tennis available at Elrig House (1½m). 2½m N of Port William and reached by unclassified, signed road off A747.

Apr–Oct (Nov–Mar 2wks min) MWB out of season 2wk min(Jul&Aug), 1unit, 1–5persons [◇] ◆ ◉ fridge ⋔ & open fire Elec metered ⬛ not provided ☎ WM in unit Iron & Ironing board on premises ⊙ CTV ⊕3pin square 6P 1🛏 🎞 ♨(4m) Fly fishing
Min£90 Max£160pw

ELSDON
Northumberland
Map**12** NY99

C Bilsmoor Foot Farm
for bookings Mrs M Carruthers, Dunns Farm, Elsdon, Newcastle upon Tyne, NE19 1EL
☎Rothbury(0669)40219

A two-storey stone-built farm cottage with three bedrooms and bathroom/WC on first floor with lounge, kitchen/diner on ground floor. Situated in the Coquet Valley on the B6341 Rothbury–Otterburn road.

All year MWB out of season 3nights min, 3mths max, 1unit, 1–6persons ◇ ◆ ◉ fridge Elec metered ⬛ can be hired ☎(1m) Iron in unit ⊙ TV ⊕3pin square P ♨(4m) Fishing
⊖ ♨(3m)

Min£40 Max£50pw (Low)
Min£55 Max£150pw (High)

EPPERSTONE
Nottinghamshire
Map**8** SK64

C The Cottage
for bookings Mrs S Santos, Eastwood Farm, Hagg Lane, Epperstone, Notts NG14 6AX
☎Nottingham(0602)663018

Two-storey 150-year-old cottage adjoining proprietors' own farmhouse. Accommodation comprises one double and one single-bedded room on first floor, a lounge/dining room on ground floor, small, but adequately-equipped kitchen with larder, and a combined bathroom/ WC. Simple décor and furnishings. Situated 10m NE of Nottingham. Leave A6097 (Doncaster/Leicester) opposite a garage and head for Epperstone village. Turn left at T junc and right into Hagg

Elrig
—
Evesham

Lane. Eastwood Farm is ⅜m on the left hand side.

All year 1wk min, 1unit, 3–4persons ◇ ◆ ◉ fridge ⋔ & electric Elec metered ⬛ can be hired ☎(⅜m) WM in unit Iron & Ironing board in unit ⊙ TV· ⊕3pin square P ♨(1m)
⊖ ♨(1m)
Min£54 Max£80pw

F The Mews
for bookings Mrs S Santos, Eastwood Farm, Hagg Lane, Epperstone, Notts NG14 6AX
☎Nottingham(0602)663018

First-floor accommodation over garage and outbuildings comprising one double and one twin-bedded room, small lounge/ dining room, small kitchen providing basic essentials, combined bathroom/WC.

All year 1wk min, 1unit, 5persons ◇ ◆ ◉ fridge ⋔ & open fires Elec metered ⬛ can be hired ☎(⅜m) WM in unit Iron & Ironing board in unit ⊙ TV ⊕3pin square P 🏠 ♨(1m)
⊖ ♨(1m)
Min£54 Max£80pw

ERMINGTON
Devon
Map**2** SX65

C CC Ref 412 LP
for bookings Character Cottages (Holidays) Ltd, 34 Fore Street, Sidmouth, Devon EX10 8AQ
☎Sidmouth(03955)77001

16th-century detached cottage with large garden in rural setting. Accommodation consists of large kitchen, small dining room, lounge, ground-floor bathroom, separate WC, three bedrooms, one with bunk beds, one double room and one room with three beds. WC on first floor. Very well decorated and furnished.

All year MWB out of season 1wk min, 6wks max, 1unit, 1–7persons [◇] ◆ ◆ ◑ fridge ⋔ Gas inclusive Elec metered ⬛ can be hired ☎ Iron & Ironing board in unit ⊙ TV ⊕3pin square 4P 🎞 ♨(1½m)
Min£74 Max£133pw (Low)
Min£176 Max£224pw (High)

ESKDALE
Cumbria
Map**7** NY10

C Mrs J A Hall, **Fisherground Farm**, Eskdale, Holmrook, Cumbria CA19 ITF
☎Eskdale(09403)319

Two cottages of charm and character, recently converted from farm buildings, on a traditional lakeland fell farm. Both have open plan kitchen, dining room and lounge, one cottage has one double, one twin and one bunk-bedded room, the other has one double and one family bedroom. Facilities include a miniature railway and a pond with raft for children to play on.

All year MWB out of season 2days min, 1mth max, 2units, 1–6persons ◇ ◆ ◉ fridge ⋔ & Coal fires Elec metered ⬛ not provided ☎(200yds) [WM, SD & TD on premises] Iron & Ironing board in unit ⊙ CTV ⊕3pin square 10P 🎞 ♨(1m)
⊖ ♨(400yds)
Min£50 Max£70pw (Low)
Min£105 Max£190pw (High)

EVESHAM
Hereford & Worcester
Map**4** SP04

C Mrs P Jeffrey, **Abbey Manor Farm** Worcester Road, Evesham, Worcs.
☎Evesham(0386)3802

Limetree is a fully modernised and sympathetically restored detached cottage with excellent views of the surrounding countryside. It comprises one double and one twin bedroom, bathroom, kitchen and lounge which has a feature brick fireplace. **Pippins, Plums & Pears** are three semi-detached cottages which have been converted from an old barn. **Pippins** is the largest with one double, one twin and one bunk-bedded room, **Plum** has one double and one twin bedroom and **Pears** has one double bedroom and one with bunks. All have kitchen/dining areas, living rooms and bathrooms. They are comfortably furnished and have retained original beams and attractive brickwork.

All year MWB out of season 2days min, 1mth max, 4units, 4–6persons [◇] ◆ ◆ ◉ fridge ⋔ (Pippins, Plum & Pears) Logburner (Limetree) Elec inclusive ⬛ inclusive ☎(500yds) [WM & TD on premises] Iron & Ironing board in unit [Launderette on premises] ⊙ CTV ⊕3pin square 8P 🎞 ♨(⅛m) →

⇿ ♪(2½m) ♨ (500yds) ♫(1m)
♫(1m) 🦯(1m)
Min£80 Max£100pw (Low)
Min£85 Max£175pw (High)

EXETER
Devon
Map**3** SX99

H   72 Barrack Road
for bookings Exeter Holiday Homes,
Barnfield End, 4 Spicer Road, Exeter
EX1 1SX
☎Exeter(0392)71668

Modern link house in residential area of
Exeter 1m from city centre. On the ground
floor there is a lounge, separate dining
room and modern fitted kitchen. On the
first floor there is one double, one twin and
one bunk-bedded room, and separate
bathroom/WC/wash hand basin.

All year   MWB out of season   1wk min,
6mths max, 1unit, 2–8persons   [◇] ◆
◎ fridge 🍳 Elec metered ⌶can be
hired   Iron & Ironing board in unit ☉
CTV ⊕3pin square   🔟 🚿(½m)
⇿ ♪(2m) ♨(½m) ♫(1m) ♫(1m)
🦯(1m)
Min£98 Max£180pw (Low)
Min£132 Max£240pw (High)

C   CC Ref 7098 L
for bookings Character Cottages
(Holidays) Ltd, 34 Fore Street, Sidmouth,
Devon WX10 8AQ
☎Sidmouth(03955)77001

An attractive ground-floor cottage,
adjoining owner's Georgian house. The
accommodation comprises well-equipped
kitchen/diner, bathroom, separate WC,
lounge with beamed ceiling and one
double bedroom. A most attractively
decorated and thoughtfully furnished
property.

All year   MWB out of season   1wk min,
1mth max, 1unit, 1–2persons   no pets
◎ fridge 🍳 Elec inclusive
⌶inclusive ☎(1½m) WM, SD in unit
Iron & Ironing board in unit ☉ CTV
⊕3pin square   2P 🔟 🚿(1½m)
⇿ ♪(2m) ♨(3m) ♫(3m) ♫(3m)
🦯(3m)
Min£90 Max£100pw (Low)
Min£117 Max£155pw (High)

F   1 Denmark Road
for bookings Exeter Holiday Homes,
Barnfield End, 4 Spicer Road, Exeter,
Devon EX1 1SX
☎Exeter(0392)71668

Two flats, one on each floor of an end-of-
terrace house in a relatively peaceful street
very near the centre of Exeter. In excellent
condition and ably managed by owner
who lives 100yds away and is constantly
on call.

All year   MWB out of season   7days min,
6mths max, 2units, 1–10persons   ◆ ◆
◎ fridge 🍳 Gas/Elec metered ⌶can
be hired   ☎ Iron & Ironing board in unit
[Launderette within 300yds]   ☉ ⊛
CTV ⊕3pin square ♨ 🔟 🚿(150yds)
⇿ ♨ ♫ ♫ 🦯

Evesham
—
Exmouth

Min£92 Max£192pw (Low)
Min£124 Max£280pw (High)

F   Lafrowda
for bookings Miss B Newton, Cornwall
House, St German's Road, University of
Exeter, Devon EX4 6TG
☎Exeter(0392)3508

Modern purpose-built university campus
hall of residence in a parkland setting,
only a short distance from the city centre.
Each unit comprises studio type single
rooms with kitchen/diner and bathroom/
WC.

Jul–Sep   1wk min, 1mth max, 40units,
3–12persons ◆ no pets ☞ fridge
🍳 Gas inclusive ⌶inclusive ☎ [WM,
SD & TD on premises]   Iron & Ironing
board in unit [Launderette on premises]
☉ TV can be hired ⊕3pin square
100P 🚿(250yds) ♨(heated) 🏓Hard
Sports centre
⇿ ♪(3m) ♨ ♫(½m) ♫(½m) 🦯(½m)
Min£143.75 Max£212.75pw

F   18 Watermore Court Pinhoe Road
for bookings Exeter Holiday Homes,
Barnfield End, 4 Spicer Road, Exeter,
Devon EX1 1SX
☎Exeter(0392)71668

A modern flat on the second floor of a
purpose-built block ⅜m from city centre,
ideal touring base for Devon. In
immaculate condition, owner on call ⅜m
away.

All year   MWB out of season   7days min,
6mths max, 1unit, 1–5persons ◆ ◆
◎ fridge Electric Elec metered ⌶can
be hired   ☎ Iron & Ironing board in unit
☉ ⊛ CTV ⊕3pin square P 🔟
🚿(50yds)
⇿ ♨ (50yds) ♫(½m) ♫(1m) 🦯(½m)
Min£92 Max£148pw (Low)
Min£124 Max£198pw (High)

EXFORD
Somerset
Map**3** SS83

B & C   Westermill Farm Cottages
for bookings Mrs A Edwards, Westermill
Farm, Exford, Minehead, Somerset
TA24 7NJ
☎Exford(064383)238

Six Scandinavian log cottages in small
paddocks and a further cottage attached
to the farmhouse, all situated on a working
farm. **Bracken, Molinia** and **Gorse**
comprise lounge/dining room with pine-
fitted kitchens off, shower/WC and two
twin- (Gorse three twin-) and one bunk-
bedded room. **Whortlebury, Ling** and
Holly comprise open plan kitchen/lounge/
diner, shower/WC, one twin- and one
bunk-bedded room. **The Cottage** attached
to the farmhouse has a small compact
kitchen, lounge/diner, bathroom/WC and
two twin- and one bunk-bedded room.

15Mar–30Nov (cottage attached to
farmhouse Feb–Nov) & Xmas   MWB out
of season   1wk min, 4wks max, 7units,
1–8 persons, nc3 (Bracken & Molinia)
[◇ ◆ ◆] ◎ fridge Convectors/Oil
filled radiators Elec metered
⌶not provided ☎(100yds) Iron &
Ironing board in unit ☉ CTV
⊕3pin square 8P 🔟 🚿 (Spring
BH–Oct)
⇿ ♨(3m)
Details not confirmed for 1987

EXMOUTH
Devon
Map**3** SY08

B   CC Ref 7571
for bookings Character Cottages Ltd, 34
Fore Street, Sidmouth, Devon EX10 8AQ
☎Sidmouth(03955)77001

A modern bungalow in a residential area
approximately 1½ miles from the seafront.
Accommodation comprises hall, lounge,
kitchen/diner with modern units and pine
table with benches, one double bedroom,
one twin bedroom with cot, bathroom/WC
and a small enclosed garden.

All year   MWB out of season   3days min,
2mths max, 1unit, 4persons ◆ no pets
◎ fridge 🍳&fires Gas metered
⌶not provided ☎(1m) WM in unit Iron
& Ironing board in unit ☉ CTV
⊕3pin square 2P 1🛏 🔟 🚿(1m)
⇿ ♪(3m) ♨(1m) ♫(2m) ♫(2m)
🦯(2m) Sports centre(2m)
Min£68 Max£194pw

F   (Flat 4 & 5) Ardenny Court Douglas
Avenue
for bookings Mr C R Lenn, St Andrews
Holiday Homes, Channel View, The
Esplanade, Exmouth, Devon EX8 2AZ
☎Exmouth(0395)264189

Flat 4 is a modern, well-equipped, second-
floor apartment comprising one double,
one twin bedroom, modern kitchen,
lounge/diner (with double bed-settee),
bathroom/WC and balcony with access
from lounge. Flat 5, a cosy garden flat, has
lounge, door to patio and garden, modern
kitchen, bathroom, one twin-bedded room
with extra sleeping accommodation for
two on bed-settee. Close to the beach.

All year   MWB out of season   1wk min,
2unit, 2–6persons ◆ ◆ no pets ◎
fridge 🍳 Elec metered ⌶can be
hired ☎(½m) Iron & Ironing board in
unit ☉ CTV ⊕3pin square 1P 🔟
🚿(½m)
⇿ ♨(½m) ♫(½m) ♫(½m)
Max£106pw (Low)
Min£87 Max£177pw (High)

**F   Mr C R Lenn St Andrews Holiday
Homes, Channel View (Flats 1, 3 & 4)** The
Esplanade, Exmouth, Devon EX8 2AZ
☎Exmouth(0395)264189

Spacious first- and second-floor flats
overlooking the seafront, each comprising
lounge, kitchen/diner, bathroom and
sleeps six to nine people.

4Jul–3Oct 1wk min, 6mths max, 3units, 6–9persons ⬖ ◆ ⌀ & ◎ fridge Electric Gas/Elec metered 🅻can be hired ☎(100yds) WM in unit SD in unit Iron & Ironing board in unit ⊙ CTV ⊕3pin square 3P 🅼 ⛼(¼m)

⊖ 🍷(¼m) 🅹(¼m) ♫(¼m)

Min£119 Max£209pw

***B* 27 Linden Close**
for bookings Mr C R Lenn, St Andrews Holiday Homes, Channel View, The Esplanade, Exmouth, Devon EX8 2AZ
☎Exmouth(0395)264189

A modern brick-built bungalow in a quiet residential estate, accommodation comprises, well-equipped modern kitchen, lounge/diner with double bed-settee, one double and one twin bedroom, bathroom and WC. There is also an enclosed patio/ sun room.

Allyear MWB out of season 1wk min, 1unit, 2–6persons ⬖ ◆ no pets ⌀ fridge 🔥 Gas/Elec inclusive 🅻can be hired ☎(300yds) Iron & Ironing board in unit ⊙ Ⓦ CTV ⊕3pin square 2P 1🏠 🅼 ⛼(200yds)

⊖ 🍷(½m) 🅹(½m) ♫(½m)

Max£106pw (Low)
Min£106 Max£177pw (High)

***H* Lovering Farm Cottage** Marley Road
for bookings Eagle Holiday Flats, Eagle House, The Strand, Exmouth, Devon EX8 1AL
☎Exmouth(0395)271661

Detached farm cottage situated 1¾m from town centre. Accommodation offers lounge with two folding beds, dining room, kitchen, two twin and one single bedroom, and bathroom/WC.

Allyear MWB out of season 1wk min, 1mth max, 1unit, 1–7persons ◎ fridge Electric Elec metered 🅻not provided ☎(½m) Iron & Ironing board in unit ⊙ TV ⊕3pin square 2P 1🏠 🅼 ⛼(½m)

⊖ ⛳(3m) 🍷(1m) 🅹(1½m) ♫(1½m)

Min£74 Max£121pw

***F* Flat 2 Mamhead View**
for bookings Eagle Holiday Flats, Eagle House, The Strand, Exmouth, Devon EX8 1AL
☎Exmouth(0395)271661

A first-floor flat situated on the seafront enjoying good coastal views. The flat is within a Victorian brick building, and the accommodation incorporates a lounge with upholstered suite converting to a single and double bed, kitchen/diner, one bedroom with twin beds, and bathroom/ WC.

Exmouth — Fairwarp

Allyear MWB out of season 1wk min, 3wks max, 1unit, 1–5persons ⬖ ◆ ◎ fridge Electric Elec metered 🅻not provided ☎(200yds) Iron & Ironing board in unit CTV ⊕3pin square 1P 🅼 ⛼(200yds)

⊖ 🍷(200yds) 🅹(½m) ♫(½m)

Min£58 Max£105pw

***F* 23 Morton Road**
for bookings C R Lenn, St Andrew's Holiday Homes, Channel View, The Esplanade, Exmouth, Devon EX8 2AZ
☎Exmouth(0395)264189

A recently converted ground-floor flat with an open-plan lounge/kitchen/diner, one family bedroom and shower/WC.

4Jul–3Oct 1wk min, 6mths max, 1unit, 2–6persons ⬖ ◆ ◎ fridge Electric Elec metered 🅻can be hired ☎(100yds) SD in unit Iron & Ironing board in unit ⊙ CTV ⊕3pin square 🅼 ⛼(50yds)

⊖ 🍷(¼m) 🅹(¼m) ♫(¼m) 🎥(¼m)

Min£77 Max£128pw

***F* Flat 1** 15 Raleigh Road
for bookings Mr C R Lenn, St Andrews Holidays Homes, Channel View, The Esplanade, Exmouth, Devon EX8 2AZ
☎Exmouth(0395)264189

A well-furnished and decorated ground-floor flat within a terraced house, comprising lounge with bed-settee, kitchen, bathroom/WC and two bedrooms.

4Jul–3Oct 1wk min, 6mths max, 1unit, 6–8persons ⬖ ◆ ◎ fridge Electric Elec metered 🅻can be hired ☎(50yds) SD in unit Iron & Ironing board in unit ⊙ CTV ⊕3pin square P 🅼 ⛼(¼m)

⊖ 🍷(200yds) 🅹(½m) ♫(½m) 🎥(½m)

Min£80 Max£134pw

***F* 88 St Andrews Road (Flats 1, 2 & 3)**
for bookings Mr C R Lenn, St Andrews Holiday Homes, Channel View, The Esplanade, Exmouth, Devon EX8 2AZ
☎Exmouth(0395)264189

Three well-furnished and decorated two-bedroomed flats situated within a terraced house close to the beach, offering well-furnished accommodation of lounge, kitchen, bathroom/WC; Flat 2 has a shower/WC.

4Jul–3Oct 1wk min, 6mths max, 1unit, 5–8persons ⬖ ◆ no pets ⌀ (Flat 1) ◎ (Flats 2&3) fridge Electric Gas/ Elec metered 🅻can be hired ☎(100yds) SD in unit Iron & Ironing board in unit ⊙ CTV ⊕3pin square P 🅼 ⛼(200yds)

⊖ 🍷(¼m) 🅹(¼m) ♫(¼m)

Min£87 Max£155pw

***F* Flats 1, 2, 3 & 4** 90 St Andrews Road
for bookings Mr C R Lenn, St Andrews Holiday Homes, Channel View, The Esplanade, Exmouth, Devon EX8 2AZ
☎Exmouth(0395) 264189

Four self-contained modern and well-equipped flats within a terraced house close to the town centre. They comprise open plan lounge/kitchen/diner plus double bed-settee, except Flat 3 with bed/ sitting room and separate kitchen/ breakfast bar. All have shower and WC, Flats 1 and 2 have one bedroom and Flat 4 has two bedrooms.

4Jul–3Oct 1wk min, 4units, 1–7persons ⬖ ◆ ◎ fridge Electric fires Elec metered 🅻can be hired ☎(200yds) Iron & Ironing board in unit ⊙ CTV ⊕3pin square P 🅼 ⛼(100yds)

⊖ 🍷(½m) 🅹(½m) ♫(½m)

Min£45 Max£148pw (High)

***F* 44 The Strand (Flats 1 & 2)**
for bookings Eagle Holiday Flats, Eagle House, The Strand, Exmouth, Devon EX8 1AL
☎Exmouth(0395)271661

Two recently converted flats each comprising lounge with convertible bed, one double bedroom, kitchen/diner and modern bathroom.

Allyear MWB out of season 1wk min, 1mth max, 2units, 1–4persons ⬖ ◆ ◎ fridge Electric Elec metered 🅻not provided ☎(100yds) Iron & Ironing board in unit CTV ⊕3pin square 🅼 ⛼(20yds)

⊖ 🍷(100yds) 🅹(100yds) ♫(100yds)

Min£45 Max£84pw

FAIRWARP
East Sussex
Map**5** TQ42

C Mrs J Clark **Bracken Cottage** Browns Brook, Fairwarp, Ashdown Forest, East Sussex
☎Nutley(082571)2304

Bracken is a delightful period cottage peacefully situated on the edge of the forest. Accommodation comprises two double bedrooms, bathroom with shower and WC, cosy lounge/dining room with open fire and fitted kitchen. There is a lovely well-stocked garden to the rear. →

All year MWB 3days min, 2wks max, 1unit, 4persons, nc12 no cats ◎
fridge ⚙ Elec inclusive Ⓛcan be hired (overseas visitors only) ☎(½m)
Iron & Ironing board in unit ⊙
⊕3pin square 2P 📺 ♨(6m)
⊖ ☏(½m)
Min£115pw(Low)
Min£125pw(High)

FALMOUTH
Cornwall
Map2 SW83

F Mr & Mrs J Morgan **Anchorage Apartments** Gyllyngvase Road, Gyllyngvase Beach, Falmouth, Cornwall TR11 4DJ
☎Falmouth(0326)312164

Nine one- or two-bedroomed apartments adjacent to Gyllyngvase Beach and within a few minutes' walk of town centre and famous tropical gardens. Each offers a high standard of facilities comprising separate lounges and adjoining well-equipped fitted kitchens, luxury bathroom/ WC.

All year MWB out of season 1wk min, 2wks max, 9units, 1–7persons [◇ ◆]
◎ fridge Electric Elec metered Ⓛinclusive ☎ Iron & Ironing board in unit ⊙ CTV ⊕3pin square 1P 📺 ♨(½m)
⊖ ☏(2m) ☏(½m) 📻(½m) ♫(½m) 🐾(½m)
Min£50 Max£80pw(Low)
Min£170 Max£220pw(High)

F Mr John Bedford **Cheriton House Holiday Flats** 11 Stracey Road, Falmouth, Cornwall TR11 4DW
☎Falmouth(0326)312784

The property, once a hotel, is set in its own grounds facing south overlooking the beach; now converted into flats of varying accommodation.

All year MWB out of season 1wk min, 4wks max, 6units, 2–8persons ◇ ◆
no pets ◎ fridge Electric Elec metered Ⓛinclusive ☎ Iron & Ironing board in unit ⊙ CTV ⊕3pin square 2P 📺 ♨(½m)
⊖ ☏(1m) ☏(50yds) 📻(½m) ♫(½m) 🐾(¾m)

Fairwarp
—
Falmouth

Min£55 Max£150pw(Low)
Min£126 Max£210pw(High)

F D Hesketh **Courtenay Holiday Flats** Swanpool Beach, Falmouth, Cornwall
☎Falmouth(0326)311416 or 314774

Purpose-built blocks of flats in a secluded position. Good standard of furnishings. Picture windows with good views from most units of sea and Swanpool.

All year MWB out of season 1wk min, 4wks max, 20units, 2–6persons [◇]
◇ ◆ ◂ fridge Electric Gas inclusive Elec metered Ⓛcan be hired ☎ [Launderette within 300yds] [WM, SD & TD on premises] Iron & Ironing board on premises ⊙ CTV ⊕3pin square P 📺 ♨(1m)
⊖ ☏(½m) ☏(1m) 📻(1m) ♫(1m) 🐾(1m)
Min£60 Max£80pw(Low)
Min£75 Max£160pw(High)

F **Crossways Holiday Flats** Pennance Road
for bookings S A Higgs, Crossways, Seaview Road, Falmouth, Cornwall TR11 4EA
☎Falmouth(0326)313985

Complex of five flats situated within a former hotel in convenient position at corner of Pennance Road and Sea View Road, north-west of Gyllyngvase Beach. Flat 1 on ground floor comprises one bedroom with twin beds, lounge with double folding bed, bathroom/WC and kitchen area. Flat 2, also on the ground floor, comprises two bedrooms, one with double bed, one with a single bed, lounge with bed-settee, separate kitchen and shower/WC. Flat 4 is located on the first floor with two bedrooms, one double with additional single bed, the other with a single bed, lounge with bed-settee, separate kitchen and shower/WC. Flat 5 is also on the first floor with lounge/kitchen, separate double bedroom and bathroom. Flat 6 is on the second floor with twin-bedded room, kitchen, bathroom and

---

large partitioned lounge with twin beds and bed-settee.

mid Mar–mid Nov MWB out of season 1wk min, 5units, 1–6persons, nc2
no pets ◎ fridge Electric Elec metered Ⓛinclusive ☎(300yds) Iron & Ironing board on premises ⊙ CTV ⊕3pin square P 📺 ♨(400yds)
⊖ ☏(1m) ☏(300yds) 📻(½m) ♫(1m) 🐾(1m)
Min£55 Max£75pw(Low)
Min£88 Max£221pw(High)

F Mr & Mrs J Griffin **Gayhurst Holiday Apartments** 10 Pennance Road, Falmouth, Cornwall TR11 4EA
☎Falmouth(0326)315161

Five self-contained flats within a detached house, well-equipped and comfortably furnished. All have kitchen areas, bathroom/WC, lounge (four with double bed-settee and one with a single bed-settee), and various sized bedrooms. The flats are situated within easy reach of all Falmouth's amenities.

Mar–Oct MWB out of season 3days min, 3wks max, 5units, 1–6persons ◇ ◆
◎ fridge Electric fires Elec metered Ⓛinclusive ☎(100yds) Iron & Ironing board in unit ⊙ CTV ⊕3pin square 5P 📺 ♨(½m)
⊖ ☏(1m) ☏(100yds) 📻(100yds) ♫(100yds) 🐾(1m)
Min£55 Max£160pw

C & F **22 Greenbank**
for bookings Mrs B Morris, 2 Stratton Place, Falmouth, Cornwall TR11 2ST
☎Falmouth(0326)314853

Two flats situated on the first- and second- floors with separate entrances from rear stairs, comprising open plan kitchen/lounge/diner, two bedrooms, bathroom and WC. There are magnificent views from the front bedrooms and lounges. The carefully converted Fisherman's Cottage is tucked away behind the main house. It has a split-level kitchen/diner, two bedrooms (ground-floor bedroom has own shower room/WC), bathroom/WC and lounge with access to small paved area and garden. All the properties have been converted to a high

standard, creating an atmosphere of character and charm.

All year 1wk min, 8wks max, 3units, 2–4persons, nc5 no pets ◎ fridge Electric Elec metered ⨅ can be hired ☎(60yds) Iron & Ironing board in unit ⊙ CTV ⊕3pin square ⊞ ⌂(½m) ⊖ ♪(3m) ♀(60yds) 🎞(½m) ♫(½m) 🛁(½m)

Min£60 Max£80pw (Low)
Min£140 Max£150pw (High)

B Mr B F Smales **Maenheere Holiday Bungalows** Maenheere Hotel, Grove Place, Falmouth, Cornwall TR11 4AU
☎Falmouth(0326)312009

Modernised conventionally built bungalows in attractive development close to harbour, each with private lawn or patio. Situated in quiet mews-like area behind hotel they comprise large sitting-room with convertible settee, twin bedroom, double room, children's bedroom with twin bunk beds, bathroom/WC and kitchen. All bedrooms have wash hand basin and an additional single bed is also available.

All year MWB out of season 1wk min, 5units, 1–9persons ◆ ◆ no dogs ◎ fridge Electric Elec metered ⨅ inclusive ☎ Iron & Ironing board [Launderette on premises] ⊙ CTV ⊕3pin square P ⊞ ⌂(300yds) ⊖ ♪(2m) ♀ 🎞(100yds) ♫(100yds)

Min£63.25 Max£69pw (Low)
Min£178.25 Max£201.25pw (High)

F Mr B F Smales **Maenheere Holiday Flats** Maenheere Hotel, Grove Place, Falmouth, Cornwall TR11 4AU
☎Falmouth(0326)312009

The flats are located in a purpose-built block behind the hotel. Accommodation consists of a twin bedroom, double bedroom with wash hand basin, large lounge with dining alcove, kitchen/breakfast room and bathroom/WC. The flats have fitted carpets and comfortable, conventional furnishings.

All year MWB out of season 1wk min, 6units, 8persons ◆ ◆ no dogs 🐕 ◎ fridge Electric Gas/Elec metered ⨅ inclusive ☎ Iron [Launderette on premises] ⊙ CTV ⊕3pin square P ⊞ ⌂(300yds) ⊖ ♪(2m) ♀ 🎞 ♫ 🛁

Min£57.50 Max£63.25pw (Low)
Min£172.50 Max£184pw (High)

F **Northbrook Holiday Flats** Melvill Road for bookings S A Higgs, Crossways, Seaview Road, Falmouth, Cornwall TR11 4EA
☎Falmouth(0326)313985

Four flats situated in property overlooking Fox Rosehill Gardens and set back from the road in attractive gardens. Flat A, on the ground floor, has one bedroom, lounge with bed-settee, kitchen and bathroom/WC. Flat B, also on the ground floor, has open plan kitchen/lounge with single bed-settee and bedroom with en suite bathroom. A door leads off to a patio

Falmouth
—
Fearnan

at the kitchen end. Flat C, on the first floor, has two bedrooms, lounge/diner with kitchen area, bathroom and WC. Flat D, is on the second floor and has one bedroom, open plan kitchen/lounge/diner with bed-settee and bathroom/WC. All the flats are well planned and maintained.

mid Mar–mid Nov MWB out of season 1wk min, 4units, 2–6persons, nc2 no pets ◎ fridge Electric Elec metered ⨅ inclusive ☎(300yds) Iron & Ironing board on premises ⊙ CTV ⊕3pin square 4P ⊞ ⌂(½m) ⊖ ♪(1m) ♀(200yds) 🎞(½m) ♫(½m) 🛁(½m)

Min£55 Max£75pw (Low)
Min£88 Max£221pw (High)

C & F Mrs B Morris **2 Stratton Place** Falmouth, Cornwall TR11 2ST
☎Falmouth(0326)314853

The two flats are located on the lower ground and top floors of a fine Georgian house, overlooking the harbour. The lower ground-floor flat has a hall, lounge/ diner, bathroom/WC, separate WC, two bedrooms and lounge. The top-floor flat is reached by a large external stairway and comprises kitchen/diner with serving hatch to lounge, two bedrooms, one with wash hand basin and bathroom/WC. Both flats offer fine views from the lounges and front bedrooms. Stratton Cottage is located to the rear of the house and has a kitchen/lounge with stone screen to one bedroom, bathroom and gallery room with single bed, reached by a ladder. All the properties have been converted with care and create an atmosphere of charm and character.

All year MWB out of season 1wk min, 8wks max, 3units, 2–4persons, nc5 no pets ◎ fridge Electric Elec metered ⨅ can be hired ☎(20yds) Iron & Ironing board in unit ⊙ CTV ⊕3pin square ⊞ ⌂(½m) ⊖ ♪(3m) ♀(30yds) 🎞(½m) ♫(½m) 🛁(½m)

Min£60 Max£80pw (Low)
Min£140 Max£150pw (High)

F Mr & Mrs N Winter **7 Stratton Place,** Falmouth, Cornwall
☎Falmouth(0326)318068

Three flats with Flat 1 having two bedrooms (one twin, one double), lounge, kitchen, bath/shower and two WCs; this flat has 20 internal steps to front door. Flat 2 has one double bedroom, lounge with convertible settee, dining room, bathroom and WC; this flat has six steps to front door. Flat 3 has two bedrooms (one double, one twin), kitchen/living area with internal spiral staircase.

All year 1wk min, 3units, 1–4persons ◎ fridge 🍴(Flat1) Electric Elec metered

⨅ inclusive Iron & Ironing board in unit CTV ⊕3pin square P ⊞ ⌂(200yds) ⊖ ♪(2m) ♀(50yds) 🎞(200yds) ♫(200yds)

Min£30 Max£45pw (Low)
Min£50 Max£150pw (High)

F Mrs G Williams **Swanpool House Holiday Flats** 21 Silverdale Road, Falmouth, Cornwall TR11 4HP
☎Falmouth(0326)313205

Swanpool House is situated in just under an acre of secluded garden in a quiet residential part of Falmouth. Consisting of six, self-contained flats comprising lounge/diner/kitchen (2 units), lounge/diner (3 units), kitchen/diner and separate lounge (1 unit), bathroom with bath, shower and WC, and offering one or two bedrooms with some having additional fold away double beds in the lounge.

All year MWB out of season 1wk min, 1mth max, 6units, 2–6persons ◆ ◆ no pets ◎ fridge night storage Elec metered ⨅ inclusive ☎(50yds) [SD & TD on premises] Iron & Ironing board in unit ⊙ CTV ⊕3pin square 6P ⊞ ⌂(¾m) pool table ⊖ ♪(1m) ♀(¾m) 🎞(1m) ♫(2m) 🛁(2m)

Details not confirmed for 1987

H & F **38 Trelawney Road** for bookings Mr & Mrs P W Grinsted, 'Suhaili', 26 Pennance Road, Falmouth, Cornwall TR11 4EB
☎Falmouth(0326)313653

A terrace house and self-contained flatlet close to town centre. The house comprises lounge/dining room, kitchen and breakfast room, bathroom/shower/WC, one double, one twin and one bunk-bedded room. The flatlet situated on the first floor of the house has its own access and comprises kitchen, bathroom/WC and bed/sitting room with convertible double couch.

All year (ex Etr & autumn school ½ term) MWB out of season 1wk min, 3mths max, 2units, 1–6persons ◆ ◆ (House) ◎(Flat) fridge Gas/Elec inclusive ⨅ inclusive ☎(House) ☎(50yds) Iron & Ironing board in unit [Launderette within 300yds] ⊙ CTV ⊕3pin square P ⊞ ⌂(75yds) ⊖ ♪(1½m) ♀(100yds) 🎞(½m) ♫(½m) 🛁(½m)

Min£55.50 Max£157.50pw (Low)
Min£84 Max£200pw (High)

FEARNAN
Tayside *Perthshire*
Map **11** NN74

B The Secretary **Boreland Riding Centre** Fearnan, Aberfeldy, Perthshire PH15 2PG
☎Kenmore(08873)212

Five modern bungalows situated on the hillside above the village and commanding magnificent views across Loch Tay. All comprise lounge/dining room, kitchen, bath/shower room/WC, one →

doubled-bedded room and one bedroom with four bunks. All are close to the main part of the farm and riding centre where there is a bar and meals are available.

Mar – Oct MWB out of season 3nights min, 5units, 1 – 6persons ◆ ◆ £5 charge for dogs ◎ fridge convectors Elec metered 🔲 can be hired ☎(200yds) WM & SD on premises [TD on premises] Iron & Ironing board in unit ☺ CTV ⊕3pin square 8P 🎞 ♨(1m) Riding, fishing, clay pigeon shooting & cycle hire

⊖ δ(3m) ☻(200yds)

Min£75 Max£140pw (Low)
Min£170 Max£220pw (High)

FENITON
Devon
Map**3** SY09

C   CC Ref 6072 ELP Sherwood for bookings Character Cottages (Holidays) Ltd, 34 Fore Street, Sidmouth, Devon EX10 8AQ ☎Sidmouth(03955)77001

A delightful white stucco cottage with thatched roof. Beamed lounge/dining area with quality furniture and canopy log fire. Large modern fully-fitted kitchen, open tread staircase to twin and double bedrooms. Bathroom/WC/wash hand basin, ground-floor twin-bedded room with adjacent cloakroom and WC. High standard throughout.

All year MWB out of season 1wk min, 6wks max, 1unit, 1 – 6persons ◆ ◎ fridge Electric & Aga Elec metered 🔲 can be hired ☎ Iron & Ironing board in unit ☺ TV ⊕3pin square P 🏠 🎞 ♨(½m)

⊖ ☻(½m)

£207pw (Low)
Min£248 Max£330pw (High)

FENNY BENTLEY
Derbyshire
Map**7** SK14

B   Drysdale
for bookings Mrs B Herridge, Bent Farm, Tissington, Ashbourne, Derbys ☎Parwich(033525)214

Fearnan
—
Fishguard

This brick-built bungalow stands just off the A515 and overlooks the surrounding countryside from the rear bedrooms and lounge. It comprises kitchen with Rayburn, WC, lounge/dining room, bathroom/ shower/WC, one double-bedded room, one twin- and one bunk-bedded room.

All year 3days min, 3mths max, 1unit, 1 – 6persons ◆ ◎ fridge ♨ Elec metered 🔲 not provided ☎(½m) ⊗ CTV ⊕3pin square 2P 🎞 ♨(2m)

⊖ δ ☻

Min£70 Max£120pw

FFESTINIOG
Gwynedd
Map**6** SH74

C   Stwlan View 8 Pant Llwyd for bookings Shaws Holidays, Y Maes, Pwllheli, Gwynedd LL53 5HA ☎Pwllheli(0758)614422

This stone-built cottage, part of a neat row of similar properties, is modestly furnished with beautiful views. It comprises lounge/ diner, kitchen, two double-bedded rooms, single bed-settee in lounge and bathroom/ WC.

All year wkd min, 6wks max, 1unit, 2 – 6persons ◆ ◎ fridge Electric & open fires Elec metered 🔲 not provided ☎(½m) Iron & Ironing board in unit CTV ⊕3pin square 1P ♨(½m)

⊖ δ(1m) ☻(½m)

Min£79 Max£124pw

FILEY
North Yorkshire
Map**8** TA18

Ch   Blue Dolphin Holiday Park
Gristhorpe Bay
for bookings Haven Holidays, PO Box 20, Truro, Cornwall TR1 2UG ☎Truro(0872)40400

A vast holiday complex situated between Filey and Scarborough with extensive

---

recreational facilities. There are three basic types of chalet available. **Moons** are terraced and sleep up to six in two bedrooms and double bed-settee in the living area. **Mist** are detached and **Charm** semi-detached and both types sleep up to four in two bedrooms.

Etr & May – Sep MWB 2days min, 1mth max, 99units, 4 – 6persons ◇ [◆ ◆] ◎ fridge ♨& electric heaters Elec metered 🔲 inclusive ☎ HCE in unit [Launderette on premises] ☺ CTV ⊕3pin square 99P 🏠 ▣&⌂ putting Fast Food restaurant, take-away food, amusement arcade

⊖ ☻ 🎞 ♫ ♨(2½m)

Min£69 Max£141pw (Low)
Min£159 Max£230pw (High)

FINDOCHTY
Grampian Banffshire
Map**15** NJ46

C   3 Station Road
for bookings Scott Holiday Homes, 8 Markethill Road, Turiff, Aberdeenshire ☎Turiff(0888)63524

A pleasant little cottage close to the harbour and comprising lounge, kitchen, bathroom and double bedroom on the ground floor and one twin and one double bedroom on the first floor reached by steep staircase.

All year MWB out of season 3days min, 1unit, 1 – 6persons ◆ ◎ fridge Electric Elec metered 🔲 not provided ☎ WM & SD in unit Iron & Ironing board in unit ☺ CTV ⊕3pin square 2P ♨(70yds)

⊖ δ(1m) ☻(3m)

Min£70 Max£140pw

FINSTOWN
See **Orkney**

FISHGUARD
Dyfed
Map**2** SM93

C   Crows Nest
for bookings Coastal Cottages of Pembrokeshire, Seaview, Abercastle, Mathry, Dyfed SA62 5HJ ☎Croesgoch(03483)7742

A delightful, comfortably furnished cottage nestling in the hillside and overlooking the Old Harbour at Lower Town and the Preseli Mountains. Accommodation comprises sitting room with french windows to the patio area, kitchen/diner, bathroom, one twin bedroom and one double bedroom with a four poster bed.

All year MWB out of season 4days min, 2mths max, 1unit, 2–6persons ◊ ◆ ◉ fridge Storage & portable heaters Elec metered ⓛinclusive ☎(300yds) Iron & Ironing board in unit ⊙ CTV ⊕3pin square 1P 🛏 ♨(400yds)
↔ ☖(400yds) 🐾(½m)
Min£65 Max£235pw

F Garden Guest Wing 6 Feidr Dylan, Pen-y-Aber
for bookings Mr A A Rees, Cerbid Quality Cottages, Solva, Haverfordwest, Dyfed ☎Croesgoch(034 83)240 or 531

Compact modern guest wing adjoining a private property, but independent. There is an attractive living room with adjoining dining section, integral kitchen and french windows leading to a patio. A wrought iron staircase leads to gallery bedroom with twin beds; a 'Z' bed is also provided. Combined shower/WC.

All year MWB out of season 2days min, 1unit, 1–3persons [◊] ◊ ◆ ◉ fridge Electric Elec inclusive microwave ⓛinclusive ☎(400yds) SD in unit Iron & Ironing board in unit ⊙ CTV ⊕3pin square P 🛏 ♨(300yds)
↔ ☖(300yds) 🐾(300yds)
Min£65 Max£130pw (Low)
Min£115 Max£190pw (High)

C Rock Cottage
for bookings Cerbid Quality Cottages, Solva, Haverfordwest, Dyfed SA62 6YE ☎Croesgoch(03483)240

A modernised and comfortable cottage in a quiet cul-de-sac, overlooking the beautiful old fishing harbour of Lower Fishguard. Accommodation comprises a large lounge/diner with open fire, fully-equipped kitchen with microwave, bathroom/WC and separate WC, one double bedroom and two twin bedrooms. There is also a garden, patio and children's play area.

Fishguard
—
Fort William

All year MWB out of season 2days min, 6wks max, 1unit, 2–6persons ◆ ◉ fridge Portable & open fires Elec inclusive ⓛinclusive ☎ WM, SD & TD in unit Iron & Ironing board in unit ⊙ CTV ⊕3pin square 2P 🛏 ♨(50yds)
↔ ☖(50yds)
Min£110 Max£225pw (Low)
Min£175 Max£395pw (High)

FLASH
Staffordshire
Map**7** SK06

F Mrs Andrews *Northfield Farm (Old Stables)* Flash, Buxton, Derbyshire ☎Buxton(0298)2543

Converted stable block incorporating two modern flats located on a working farm and pony trekking centre in what is reputedly the highest village in England. Both flats sleep six people in a twin-bedded room and one containing two pairs of bunk beds. The other accommodation comprises small kitchenette, bathroom, WC and lounge.

All year MWB out of season 1wk min, 3mths max, 2units, 1–6persons ◊ ◆ ◉ fridge storage heaters Elec inclusive ⓛinclusive ☎(75yds) ⊙ CTV ⊕3pin square 6P ♨(75yds) Horse riding & pony trekking
↔ ☖(100yds)
Details not confirmed for 1987

FORTON
Lancashire
Map**7** SD45

F Mrs P Roberts *Clevely Mill* Forton, Garstang, Lancashire PR3 1BY ☎Forton(0524)792050

This well furnished flat is adjacent to the owners property in a unique, historic converted watermill. It comprises large lounge (with extra put-u-up), modern and spacious kitchen, two twin-bedded rooms

and bathroom. The furnishings are of a high standard throughout. It overlooks a lake and is in a truly rural backwater. Fishing available.

All year MWB out of season 1day min, 3mths max, 1unit, 2–5persons ◊ ◉ fridge Electric radiators & calor gas Elec metered ⓛinclusive ☎(next door) WM & SD on premises Iron & Ironing board in unit ⊙ CTV ⊕3pin square 3P 🛏 ♨(1m)
Min£70 Max£90pw (Low)
Min£100 Max£120pw (High)

FORT WILLIAM
Highland *Inverness-shire*
Map**14** NN17

Ch Glen Nevis Holiday Cottages Glen Nevis, Fort William, Inverness-shire PH33 6SX
☎Fort William(0397)2191

Brick-built cottages situated in Glen Nevis, with splendid views of Ben Nevis. Tastefully furnished accommodation comprises two bedrooms, open plan lounge, kitchen and bathroom/WC. Beautiful situation with shopping facilities and licensed restaurant, 2½m from Fort William.

7Mar–Dec MWB out of season 2nights min, 1mth max, 12units, 1–5persons [◆ ◆] ◉ fridge Electric Elec inclusive ⓛcan be hired ☎ Iron & Ironing board in unit [Launderette on premises] ⊙ CTV ⊕3pin square P ♨
↔ ☖(¼m) 🎵(3m) 🎵(3m)
Min£82 Max£230pw

Ch Great Glen Holidays
for bookings Mr C Carver, Great Glen Holidays, Torlundy, Fort William, Inverness-shire ☎Fort William(0397)3015

Eight timber chalets in peaceful surroundings in pine woodland, with attractive outlooks especially towards Ben Nevis. The interiors are smart modern pine panelled and carpeted, with tasteful pine furnishings. Accommodation comprises open plan diner sitting room with kitchen, compact twin and double rooms and modern bathroom. →

Mar–Oct MWB out of season 1wk min, 3mths max, 8units, 4–6persons [◈] ◎ fridge Electric Elec metered ☐inclusive ☎ [Launderette] ⊙ CTV ⊕3pin square P ▥ (3m) Pony trekking

(1m) (3m) (3m) (3m)

Min£110 Max£225pw

F **Inseagan Apartments** Inseagan Holidays, Achintore Road, Fort William, Inverness-shire PH33 6RW
☎Fort William(0397)2452

Six comfortable and well-appointed purpose built holiday apartments each furnished and decorated to a high standard. They comprise one twin bedroom, lounge/diner with double bed-settee, bathroom, kitchen and balcony overlooking Loch Linnhe.

All year MWB out of season 1wk min, 6units, 1–4persons no pets ◎ fridge Elec metered ☐inclusive ☎ ⊙ CTV ⊕3pin square 6P ▥ (1½m)

(3m) (20yds) (1½m) (1½m) (1½m)

Min£105 Max£125pw (Low)
Min£155 Max£210pw (High)

FOYERS
Highland *Inverness-shire*
Map**14** NH42

***Ch* The Coach House** Foyers Hotel
for bookings Blakes Holidays, Wroxham, Norwich NR12 8DH
☎Wroxham(06053)2917

Converted and fully modernised coach house situated high above Loch Ness and adjacent to the hotel. Accommodation comprises kitchen/diner/lounge, three bedrooms and bathroom.

All year 1wk min, 1unit, 1–6persons ◈ ◆ ◎ fridge Electric Elec inclusive ☐inclusive ☎ Iron in unit ⊙ CTV ⊕3pin square 2P ▥ (½m) fishing

(50yds)

Details not confirmed for 1987

FREMINGTON
Devon
Map**2** SS53

C K J & W H Le Voir, **Muddlebridge House Holiday Cottages** Fremington, Barnstaple, Devon EX31 2NQ
☎Barnstaple(0271)76073

A unique collection of six stone cottages, reached through an ancient arch and specially developed and renovated. ***Millers*** *is a spacious three bedroomed cottage comprising open plan lounge/kitchen/diner, modern bathroom and WC, one double, one twin and one bunk-bedded room.* ***Thatchers*** *has been converted from one half of a large barn. It has a lounge/diner, kitchen, bathroom, one family bedroom with a double and single bed, one twin bedded room and a third bedroom with single and bunk bed.* ***The Forge*** *is a one bedroomed cottage with modern kitchen, bathroom, lounge/diner and three single beds.* ***Weavers*** *is a two bedroomed cottage, it has one double bedroom with additional single bed, and a twin-bedded room, a modern fitted kitchen, lounge/diner and bathroom/WC.* ***Potters****, an attractive open-plan cottage, has a lounge/diner/kitchen, bathroom and WC, one double bedroom and one with bunk beds and a single bed.* ***Wheelwrights*** *is the other half of the barn and although the layout is different the bedrooms are the same as Thatcher's cottage.*

Mar–Jan MWB 3days min, 1mth max, 6units, 3–8persons ◇ ◈ ◆ ◎ fridge Storage heaters & Electric fires Elec inclusive (storage heaters only) Elec metered ☐inclusive ☎(½m) [WM, SD & TD on premises] Iron & Ironing board in unit [Launderette on premises] ⊙ CTV ⊕3pin square P ▥ (½m) (heated)

(½m) (2½m) (2½m) (2½m) Sports centre(2½m)

Min£181 Max£130pw (Low)
Min£145 Max£320pw (High)

FRESHFORD
Avon
Map**3** ST76

F B Elliot & P Harward, **Tyning House (Flats 1 & 2)** Freshford, Bath, Avon BA3 6DR
☎Limpley Stoke(022122)3288

Two first-floor flats set in extensive grounds, with countryside adjoining, they offer comfort space and peace. Both are approached by external concrete steps (rather steep to flat 1). ***Flat 1*** *has a hall, lounge with dining area and bed-settee, kitchen, one double and one twin bedroom, bathroom/WC and a separate WC.* ***Flat 2*** *has hall, large drawing room with bed-settee and dining area, kitchen, bathroom/WC, one double and one twin bedroom. Facilities include table tennis and pony riding.*

All year MWB out of season 1wk min, 1mth max, 2units, 1–5persons [◇] ◈ ◆ fridge (Gas) Gas inclusive ☐inclusive ☎(¼m) WM, SD & TD on premises ⊙ CTV ⊕3pin square 4P ▥ (¼m)

(½m)

Min£100pw (Low)
Min£205pw (High)

FRESHWATER
See **Wight, Isle of**

FYLINGDALES
North Yorkshire
Map**8** NZ90

C **Billira Cottage**
for bookings Mr & Mrs J Thornton, 6 Flock Leys, Scalby, Scarborough, North Yorkshire YO13 0RG
☎Scarborough(0723)362682

Detached self-contained two-storey ex-gamekeeper's cottage in a secluded moorside location, containing a double-bedded room, a twin-bedded room and a single room. WC on the ground floor, separate bathroom, pleasantly restored and modernised. Sitting room and well-equipped dining kitchen plus utility room/washhouse and surrounding rough gardens. Situated halfway between Scarborough and Whitby off the A171, close to the Flask Inn.

Apr–Oct 1wk min, 1unit, 1–5persons
◈ no pets ◎ fridge Electric
Elec inclusive 🗔inclusive ☎(½m) WM,
Iron & Ironing board in unit CTV
⊕3pin square P ⚫(1m)
↩ ♨(1m) ♫(1m)
Min£100 Max£165pw (Low)
Min£185 Max£235pw (High)

GAIRLOCH
Highland Ross & Cromarty
Map14 NG87

F Mr I Ednie **Gairloch Sands
Apartments** Gairloch, Ross-shire IV21 2BL
☎Gairloch(0445)2131

*Twenty self-contained apartments
tastefully converted from former hotel
bedrooms. Accommodation consists of
either one or two twin bedrooms, lounge/
dining room with convertable sofa, kitchen
and bathroom. Each apartment has a
balcony or patio overlooking Gairloch
Bay.*

All year MWB out of season 1wk min,
20units, 1–6persons ◈ ◆ ◎ fridge
Electric Elec metered 🗔inclusive ☎
Iron & Ironing board in unit ☺ Ⓦ
CTV ⊕3pin square 50P ⚫(200yds)
Fishing & Tennis, games room
↩ δ(½m) ♨ ♫
Min£30 Max£215pw

F **Millcroft Hotel** Gairloch, Wester Ross,
Ross-shire
☎Gairloch(0445)2376

*Seven modern apartments, part of a
stone-built hotel, situated in the town and
overlooking Loch Gairloch. Each unit has
been decorated and furnished to a
modern standard and have artex walls
and pine ceilings. Most are on two levels
between the first and second floors of the
building and have two or three bedrooms.
The facilities at the hotel are available to
residents.*

All year MWB out of season 3days min,
7units, 1–6persons ◈ ◆ ◎ fridge
🍴 Elec inclusive 🗔inclusive ☎ WM
& SD on premises Iron & Ironing board in
unit CTV ⊕3pin square 10P
⚫(20yds) boat trips, fishing
↩ δ(1½m) ♨ ♫(1m) ♫(1m)
Sports centre(½m)
Min£94 Max£130pw (Low)
Min£150 Max£235pw (High)

GALPHAY
North Yorkshire
Map8 SE27

C & F **Galphay Estate** Galphay Manor,
Galphay, Ripon, North Yorkshire HG4 3NJ
☎Kirkby Malzeard(076583)205

*The properties are all situated in the
grounds of the Manor House and on or
near to the village green of an attractive
hamlet in Lower Wensleydale. Barn 1 & 2
are ground- and first-floor flats converted
from an estate building. Barn 2, on the
ground floor has a large lounge/diner,
kitchen, bathroom/WC and three
bedrooms, one of which has an en suite*

Fylingdales
—
Gartly

*bathroom/WC. Barn 1, on the first floor,
(access by external staircase) has a
spacious lounge/diner with folding beds
available if required, kitchen, bathroom/
WC and two bedrooms. Apple House is a
detached converted applestore, with small
lawned garden and holly hedge.
Accommodation comprises lounge/diner
with twin-beds, kitchen and shower/WC.
Ivy Cottage is one of a pair of semi-
detached stone-built country cottages,
with lawned garden and a small back
yard. It has a kitchen/diner and sitting
room on the ground floor and two
bedrooms and bathroom/WC on the first
floor.*

Apr–Oct 1wk min, 4wks max, 4units,
1–6persons [◇] ◈ ◆ pets by
arrangement ◎ fridge Electric
Elec metered 🗔can be hired ☎(except
Apple House) Iron & Ironing board in
unit ☺ CTV ⊕3pin square 9P 🔲
⚫(3m) ⚓Hard Table tennis
↩ ♨(100yds)
Min£80 Max£135pw (Low)
Min£115 Max£240pw (High)

GALSTON
Strathclyde *Argyllshire*
Map11 NS53

H **Auchencloigh Cottage**
for bookings Mrs J Bone, Auchencloigh
Farm, Galston, Ayrshire KA4 8NP
☎Galston(0563)820567

*A quietly situated semi-detached farm
house. Accommodation which is spacious
and comfortably furnished comprises
sitting/dining room, kitchen, bathroom
and double bedroom on ground floor, one
room with three single beds and one twin
bedroom on first floor. Located 5m south
of Galston off the B7037 towards Sorn.*

All year MWB out of season 3days min,
1unit, 1–7persons [◇] ◈ ◆ ◎
fridge Electric & coal fires Elec metered
🗔inclusive Telephone for incoming calls
in unit ☎(½m) WM in unit Iron & Ironing
board in unit ☺ CTV ⊕3pin square
5P 🔲 ⚫(3m) Fishing & Riding can be
arranged close by
↩ ♨(3m)
Min£85 Max£140pw

GARSDALE HEAD
Cumbria
Map7 SD79

C **3 Railway Cottages**
for bookings Mr Wiseman, 37 Charles
Street, Blackpool, Lancashire
☎Blackpool(0253)28936(am)&43471(pm)

*A stone-built property in a row of former
railwaymen's cottages adjacent to
Garsdale Station. There is a lounge and
kitchen on the ground floor and the first
floor has three bedrooms and a bathroom.*

---

*Modernised throughout. Ideal for touring
the Dale country.*

All year MWB out of season 3days min,
1unit, 2–6persons ◈ ◎ fridge
Electric & open fires Elec metered
🗔not provided ☎(50yds) ☺ TV
⊕3pin square 1P ⚫(50yds)
↩ ♨(2m)
Min£50 Max£140pw

GARTHMYL
Powys
Map7 SO19

Ch **Brynllwyn Luxury Cabins**
for bookings Mr W J H Black, Brynllwyn
Farm, Garthmyl, Powys
☎Berriew(068685)269

*Twelve Scandinavian-style wooden
chalets set on low density wooded hillock.
All have verandahs, cedarwood-clad walls
and are furnished to a high standard.
They vary in size and sleep up to eight
people.*

All year MWB out of season 2days min,
6wks max, 12units, 1–8persons [◇] ◈
◆ ◎ fridge 🍴 Elec metered
🗔not provided ☎(100yds) Iron &
Ironing board in unit ☺ Ⓦ CTV
⊕3pin square 8P ⚫(1m)
↩ ♨(1m)
Min£70 Max£110pw (Low)
Min£155 Max£220pw (High)

C Mr W J Black **Wain House Cottage**
Brynllwyn Farm, Garthmyl, Powys
☎Berriew(068685)269

*Recently converted barn retaining much
original character, situated at entrance to
the farm, overlooking the lake. It comprises
of lounge with woodburning stove, open
plan kitchen with breakfast bar, one
double-bedded room and shower/WC;
stairs lead to a loft, beamed, twin-bedded
room. Furnished and decorated to a high
standard.*

All year MWB out of season 2days min,
6wks max, 1unit, 1–4persons [◇] ◈
◆ ◎ fridge 🍴 Elec metered
🗔not provided ☎(½m) Iron & Ironing
board in unit ☺ Ⓦ CTV
⊕3pin square 2P ⚫(1m) Fishing
↩ ♨(1m)
Min£80pw (Low)
Min£180pw (High)

GARTLY
Grampian *Aberdeenshire*
Map15 NJ53

C **Limes & Beeches Cottages**
for bookings Mrs E Innes, Ardlair, Insch,
Aberdeenshire AB5 6YR
☎Kennethmont(04643)250

*Semi-detached stone cottages,
modernised and on roadside on the edge
of a small village, they offer lounge/diner,
kitchen, bathroom and three bedrooms,
one reached by open plan stairway.*

All year MWB 1wk min, 2units,
1–8persons ◈ ◆ ◎ fridge
Electric Elec inclusive 🗔can be hired →

🛏(200yds) SD in unit Iron & Ironing board in unit ☺ TV ⊕3pin square 4P 🔌(100yds) ⊖ 🍴(100yds)

Min£80 Max£120pw

GATE BURTON
Lincolnshire
Map**8** SK88

C   The Chateau
for bookings The Landmark Trust, Shottesbrooke, Maidenhead, Berkshire SL6 3SW
🕿Littlewick Green(062882)5925

An unusual building of brick and stone built in 1740 and restored to superb condition with a wealth of character and providing compact but good quality accommodation. Comprises modern kitchen with adjoining dining area, bathroom and WC on ground floor. On the first floor there is a comfortable lounge containing a convertible bed-settee and there are two compact single-bedded rooms. Good views of the River Trent.

All year MWB out of season 2 nights (out of season) min, 1 unit, 3 persons no pets ◎ fridge storage heaters
Elec inclusive ⬛not provided 🕿(1m) ☺ ⊕3pin square 2P 🔌(1m)
⊖ 🛁(3m) 🍴(1m)

Min£100 Max£160pw (Low)
Min£115 Max£180pw (High)

GATEHOUSE OF FLEET
Dumfries & Galloway *Kirkcudbrightshire*
Map**11** NX55

C   Drumwall
for bookings G M Thomson & Co, 27 King Street, Castle Douglas, Kirkcudbrightshire
🕿Castle Douglas(0556)2701

Detached farm cottage commanding spectacular views over the Fleet Estuary and surrounding hills. Accommodation comprises kitchen, living/dining room, bathroom and three bedrooms, two with a double bed and one with two single beds. ½m E of Gatehouse of Fleet off A75.

Mar–Nov MWB out of season 1wk min, 6mths max, 1 unit, 1–6 persons ◆ ◎ fridge Electric & open fires

---

Gartly
—
Gigha, Island of

Elec inclusive ⬛not provided 🕿(3m) TV ⊕3pin round P 🅿 🔌(2m) ⊖ 🛁(3m) 🍴(3m)

Min£85 Max£155pw

GERRICK
Cleveland
Map**8** NZ71

H   High Farm
for bookings Margrove Park Holidays, The Red House, Skelton-in-Cleveland, Saltburn-by-the-Sea, Cleveland TS12 2ET
🕿Guisborough(0287)53616

Situated in peaceful location surrounded by moorland and among farm buildings which are no longer in use, this recently renovated farmhouse comprises lounge, kitchen, dining room, three bedrooms, bathroom and WC.

Apr–Oct MWB 1wk min, 1 unit, 2–6 persons ◆ ◎ fridge Electric Elec metered ⬛not provided 🕿(2m) Iron & Ironing board in unit [CTV] ⊕3pin square 4P 🔌(2m)
⊖ 🍴(1m)

Min£80 Max£120pw

GIGHA, ISLAND OF
Strathclyde *Argyllshire*
Map**10** NR64

H   Achamore House
for bookings Mr & Mrs K L Roebuck, Gigha Hotel, Isle of Gigha, Argyll PA41 7AD
🕿Gigha(05835)254

Surrounded by the famous rhododendron and azalea gardens of Gigha; Achamore, which was rebuilt after a fire in 1892, is well maintained and graciously furnished with many antiques, oak panelling and chandeliers. The accommodation comprises a library, drawing room, sitting room, dining room and eight bedrooms (two with bathroom en suite) sleeping up to 15 people or 20 if the nursery wing is also let (see right).

All year MWB out of season 1wk min, 1 unit, 1–15 persons ◇ ◆ ◎ 🍴 fridge Electric & open fires
Elec inclusive ⬛inclusive 🕿 WM, SD & TD on premises Iron & Ironing board in unit ☺ CTV ⊕3pin square P 🔌(1m)
⊖ 🍴(¾m)

Min£550 Max£800pw

C   1 & 2 Ferry Crofts
for bookings Mr & Mrs K L Roebuck, Gigha Hotel, Isle of Gigha, Argyll PA41 7AD
🕿Gigha(05835)254

Overlooking an old jetty and the sound of Gigha, these crofts have retained the original walls but have been fully modernised internally. They provide a high standard of accommodation with open plan kitchen/lounge/diner and balcony-bedroom with twin beds. The sofa converts to a divan bed, and a camp bed is also available. The Island is reached by ferry from Tayinloan on the Mull of Kintyre.

All year MWB out of season 1wk min, 2 units, 1–5 persons ◇ ◆ 🍴 fridge Gas & Electric Gas/Electric inclusive ⬛inclusive 🕿(150yds) Iron & Ironing board in unit [Launderette within 300yds] ☺ CTV ⊕3pin square P 🔌(150yds) Fishing & Achamore gardens
⊖ 🍴(300yds)

Min£115 Max£200pw

H   Nursery Wing Achamore
for bookings Mr & Mrs K L Roebuck, Gigha Hotel, Isle of Gigha, Argyll PA41 7AD
🕿Gigha(05835)254

A wing of Achamore House, this can be let as a self-contained unit or with the connecting door opened as part of the main house. It comprises two twin-bedded rooms, one single bedroom, bathroom, living/dining room and large old fashioned nursery kitchen. Well furnished and decorated. Located 1m from ferry slip at southern end of the Island.

All year MWB out of season 1wk min, 1 unit, 1–5 persons ◇ ◆ ◎ 🍴 fridge Elec inclusive ⬛inclusive 🕿 WM, SD & TD on premises Iron & Ironing board in unit ☺ CTV ⊕3pin square P 🔌(1m)
⊖ 🍴(¾m)

Min£180 Max£300pw

Nearest & fairest of the Hebrides . . .

THE ISLE OF GIGHA (pronounced "Ghee-a") is 3 miles from Kintyre and just 2½ hrs drive from Glasgow, with a regular daily ferry service from TAYINLOAN (20 min. crossing). Splendid views, sandy beaches, peace & quiet; birds & wild flowers... The great shrub & woodland gardens of Achamore, known to experts throughout the world, are open daily to the public.
There are some cottages to let, or flats in Achamore House for larger parties; bed & breakfast at the Island's Shop/Post Office. The GIGHA HOTEL, with nine comfortable rooms, central heating and cheerful bar, is famous for good home fare and local specialities. Coffee, snacks & crafts at the old Boat House.
For ferry times, phone Whitehouse (088073) 253/4; colour brochure and all other information from: The Gigha Hotel, Dept. AA .
Isle of Gigha, Argyll Phone: Gigha (05835) 254

GILLING EAST
North Yorkshire
Map**8** SE67

C & F   Sunset Cottages & Flats
for bookings Mr R J Kelsey, Grimston
Manor Farm, Gilling East, York YO6 4HR
☎Brandsby(03475)654

Three cottages and two flats converted
from a farm granary in the rural
surroundings of the Howardian Hills. The
cottages have open plan lounge/diner/
kitchen combined and sleeping
accommodation on the first floor for up to
four people. The ground-floor flat sleeps
four in a double and bunk beds (family
room). The first-floor flat sleeps three in
one double and one single bed.

All year   MWB out of season   7days min,
6wks max, 5units, 1–4persons ◈
no pets ◎ fridge 🍴 Elec inclusive
Ⓛinclusive ☎ WM & TD on premises
⊙ CTV ⊕3pin square 10P 🆓
♨(3m)
↔ ♭ ☎(1½m)
Min£80 Max£90pw (Low)
Min£160 Max£175pw (High)

GIRVAN
Strathclyde Ayrshire
Map**10** NX19

F   52 Dalrymple Street
for bookings Mrs M M Hay, Bon Accord, 50
Dalrymple Street, Girvan, Ayrshire
KA26 9BT
☎Girvan(0465)4421

A first-floor modernised flat with own
entrance situated above shop in main
shopping centre of coastal town. The
accommodation comprises lounge/diner,
kitchen, bathroom and two bedrooms.

All year   1wk min, 1mth max, 1unit,
2–4persons ◈ no pets ◎ fridge
Electric   Elec metered Ⓛinclusive
☎(150yds) Iron & Ironing board in unit
[Launderette within 300yds] CTV ⊙
⊕3pin square ♨
↔ ♭(¾m) ♨(100yds) 🎣(100yds)
🎵(100yds) ⚽(50yds)
Min£75 Max£150pw

Gilling East
—
Glenlivet

GITTISHAM
Devon
Map**3** SY19

C   CC Ref 7561
for bookings Character Cottages
(Holidays) Ltd, 34 Fore Street, Sidmouth,
Devon EX10 8AQ
☎Sidmouth(03955)77001

Very attractive thatched cottage with many
exposed beams and enclosed garden. It
comprises lounge/diner with inglenook
fireplace, kitchen with small breakfast bar,
three bedrooms and bathroom.

All year   MWB out of season   3days min,
6wks max, 1unit, 1–6persons, nc8
no pets ◎ fridge 🍴 Elec inclusive
Ⓛnot provided ☎(½m) WM, SD & TD in
unit   Iron & Ironing board in unit ⊙
CTV ⊕3pin square 2P ♨(¾m)
↔ ♨ (3m)
Min£200 Max£300pw

GLADESTRY
Powys
Map**3** SO25

H   Wern Willa
for bookings Mrs S Meredith, Wernwilla
Farm, Gladestry, Kington, Hereford
HR5 3PW
☎Gladestry(054422)278

Located in a working farmyard this old
stone-built farmhouse comprises kitchen,
dining room, lounge, three double-bedded
rooms and bathroom/WC. Ideal for the
walker as it is close to the Offa's Dyke
footpath.

All year   MWB out of season   3days min,
3mths max, 1unit, 1–8persons ◈ ◎
fridge Electric fires   Elec metered Ⓛcan
be hired ☎(1½m) Iron & Ironing board in
unit ⊙ ⓥ CTV ⊕3pin square 3P
♨(1½m) 🐴 Pony trekking
↔ ♨ (1½m) 🎵(1½m)
Min£50 Max£125pw

GLAN CONWY
Gwynedd
Map**6** SH87

H   Mr & Mrs M Slater Cromlech Farm
Glan Conwy, Colwyn Bay, Clwyd
☎Glan Conwy(049268)274

A semi-detached farmhouse consisting of
dining room with an Aga cooker, kitchen
and lounge. On the first floor there is a
twin-bedded room with two folding single
beds and one double-bedded room.
Bathroom/WC combined.

Etr–Oct   1wk min, 1mth max, 1unit,
6persons ◈ ◆ no pets Aga fridge
Electric   Elec metered Ⓛnot provided
☎(½m) SD in unit   Iron & Ironing board
in unit ⊙ TV ⊕3pin square
P ♨(2m)
↔ ♨ (2m)
Min£70 Max£100pw

GLASGOW
Strathclyde Lanarkshire
Map**11** NS56

F   Mr S Taylor White House 12 Cleveden
Crescent, Glasgow G12 0PA
☎041-339 9375

A listed Edwardian town house in a tree-
lined crescent in the heart of the West End,
opposite small gardens and a park. The
suites are of mixed sizes and full
chambermaid service is available as well
as many other facilities.

All year   MWB   1night min, 32units,
1–4persons [◇] ◈ ◆ no pets ◎
fridge 🍴 Elec inclusive Ⓛinclusive
☎ Iron & Ironing board on premises
⊙ ⓥ CTV ⊕3pin square 🆓 ♨(½m)
↔ ♭(3m) ♨(½m) 🎵(1m) ⚽(1m)
fr£310.10

GLENLIVET
Grampian Banffshire
Map**15** NJ12

**C & Ch   Mr & Mrs G M Godfrey Glenlivet
Holiday Lodges** Glenlivet, Ballindalloch,
Banffshire AB3 9DR
☎Glenlivet(08073)209

Small holiday complex offering ten high
quality lodges and two modernised
cottages. All comprise open plan lounge/→

---

kitchen/diner and offer a choice of two or three bedrooms. Four of the lodges have sauna and a shower instead of a bath. **Gamekeepers** is the larger of the two cottages and occupies two floors. **Stag Cottage** is all on ground level and has a shower instead of bath.

Dec–Oct(Chalets) All year(Cottages) MWB out of season 1wk min, 1mth max, 12units, 1–6persons [◈ ◆] ◎ fridge Electric Elec metered ⊔inclusive ☎ Iron & Ironing board in unit [Launderette on premises] ⊖ CTV ⊕3pin square 15P ▥ ♨(3m) ⊖ ♀

Min£115 Max£170pw (Low)
Min£160 Max£270pw (High)

GLENPROSEN
Tayside *Angus*
Map15 NO36

C Braeshalloch Cottage
for bookings Mrs C Maclean, Balnaboth, Glenprosen, Kirriemuir, Angus DD8 4SA
☎Cortachy(05754)302

An 18th-century stone cottage set in small clearing and bordered by trees and river. Comprising kitchen/diner, bathroom, sitting room with bed-settee and one bedroom with a double and single bed.

Apr–Dec MWB out of season 1wk min, 1mth max, 1unit, 1–6persons [◇] ◆ ◆ ◎ fridge Electric & open fires Elec metered ⊔can be hired ☎(1½m) Iron & Ironing board in unit ⊖ ⊕3pin square 3P ♨(6m) Cycle hire, fishing, pony trekking
Min£60 Max£110pw

C East Dalairn Cottage
for bookings Mrs C Maclean, Balnaboth, Glenprosen, Kirriemuir, Angus DD8 4SA
☎Cortachy(05754)302

A pleasant semi-detached stone cottage with good views down the glen and overlooking the river. It offers kitchen/diner, sitting room with two chair beds, bathroom/WC, one double and one twin-bedded bedroom.

Apr–Oct MWB out of season 1wk min, 1mth max, 1unit, 1–6persons [◇] ◆ ◆ ◎ fridge Electric & open fires Elec metered ⊔can be hired ☎(1m) Iron & Ironing board in unit ⊕3pin square 2P ♨(6m) Cycle hire, fishing, pony trekking
Min£60 Max£110pw

C Mrs P Maclean Glentairie Cottage
Balnaboth, Glenprosan, Kirriemuir, Angus DD8 4SA
☎Cortachy(05754)302

Set in splendid isolation on an open hillside close to a small stream, this former shepherd's cottage offers a peaceful retreat. It comprises small but modern fitted kitchen, living/dining room with stone fireplace, bathroom, one double bedroom and one bunk-bedded room with additional single bed. Access is by rough track which, although accessible by car,

---

Glenlivet
—
Glenshee (Spittal of)

cannot be guaranteed during bad weather (you may have to walk).

Apr–Oct 1wk min, 1unit, 5–7persons ◈ ◆ ◎ fridge Electric & open fire Elec metered ⊔can be hired ☎(¾m) Iron & Ironing board in unit TV ⊕3pin square & ⊕3pin round 2P ♨(6m) cycles for hire
Min£80 Max£120pw

C Pitcarity Cottage
for bookings Mrs C Maclean, Balnaboth, Glenprosen, Kirriemuir, Angus DD8 4SA
☎Cortachy(05754)302

An 18th-century single-storey, stone cottage offering a pleasant but simple standard in appointments comprising kitchen/diner, sitting room with bed-settee, bathroom/WC, one twin and one double bedroom. A peaceful setting in a glen with access via unclassified road.

All year MWB out of season 1wk min, 1mth max, 1unit, 1–6persons [◇] ◆ ◆ ◎ fridge storage heaters Elec metered ⊔can be hired ☎(200yds) Iron & Ironing board in unit TV ⊕3pin square 4P ♨(6m) Cycle hire, fishing, pony trekking
Min£60 Max£110pw

F Mrs P Maclean West Wing Flat
Balnaboth, Glenprosen, Kirriemuir, Angus DD8 4SA
☎Cortachy(05754)302

A spacious self-contained 1st floor flat created out of the Georgian wing of the historic Balnaboth House, which lies in extensive grounds at the head of the Glen. The flat has been furnished and decorated to retain its original character and consists of large open-plan kitchen/diner/living room, separate lounge, three bedrooms and two bathrooms. Facilities include fishing and pony trekking, there are also cycles for hire.

All year MWB out of season 1wk min, 1unit, 7persons ◆ ◆ ◎ fridge 料& open fires Elec inclusive ⊔can be hired ☎(1m) [WM on premises] Iron & Ironing board in unit ⊖ CTV ⊕3pin square & ⊕3pin round 2P ♨(6m) ⊖ ♂(1m)

Min£155pw (Low)
Min£180pw (High)

GLENSHEE (SPITTAL OF)
Tayside *Perthshire*
Map15 NO16

C Mr S N Winton Dalmunzie Ltd (Cottages) Spittal of Glenshee, Blairgowrie, Perthshire PH10 7QG
☎Glenshee(025085)226

Eight cottages located on the Dalmunzie Estate in a secluded Highland Glen. **Glenlochsie** *is a former shepherd's cottage comprising small kitchen, lounge/*

---

dining room, bathroom and two bedrooms. **Dalmunzie** *comprises room, kitchen/diner, bathroom, one double and one twin bedroom.* **Dower** *is the largest property with lounge, dining room, kitchen, two bathrooms and two bathrooms.* **Lochsie** *has a lounge/double bedroom, dining room, small kitchen, bathroom and large porch.* **Sauchmore** *has a lounge/dining room, kitchen, bathroom and three bedrooms.* **Logie** *has a lounge, kitchen/dining area, bathroom and two bedrooms.* **Gate Lodge South** *has a kitchen/dining/lounge area, bathroom and two bedrooms.* **Gate Lodge North** *has a kitchen/dining area, lounge, bathroom and two bedrooms. The cottages are reached by a long drive off the A93 at Spittal off Glenshee.*

All year MWB out of season 2days min, 1mth max, 8units, 1–8persons [◇] ◆ ◆ ◎ fridge Night storage heaters Electric Elec metered ⊔inclusive ☎(400yds) Iron & Ironing board in unit ⊖ CTV ⊕3pin square P ▥ ♨(21m) ⊖ ♂ ♀(400yds)

Min£60 Max£160pw (Low)
Min£120 Max£288pw (High)

C Mrs Burke & Mrs Cameron **Dalnaglar Castle** Glenshee, Blairgowrie, Perthshire
☎Blacklunans(025082)232

Dalnaglar Castle is a castellated mansion of the mid-Victorian period standing on an elevated site in the heart of Glenshee, above the water meadows of the Shee Water which runs through the grounds. The three cottages are situated within and around the mansion. **Easter & Wester Calpich** *have been converted from the coach house and stables.* **Easter** *has a large living room with beamed ceiling and gallery (which can be used as additional sleeping area), kitchen, bathroom and three bedrooms.* **Wester** *has a living room with additional bedroom over it (loft access), bathroom and two bedrooms.* **Keeper's Cottage** *is a detached two-storey building offering lounge/dining room with kitchen off, two bedrooms and bathroom plus two bedrooms in the attic.* **Tower House** *is a charming cottage offering kitchen, dining hall and bedroom with a living room and bathroom on first floor.*

All year MWB out of season 2days min, 4units, 1–7persons ◆ ◎ fridge Electric & open fires Elec metered ⊔can be hired ☎(3m) Iron & Ironing board on premises ⊖ CTV ⊕3pin square P ♨(8m) Trout fishing ⊖ ♀(3m)

Min£95 Max£105pw (Low)
Min£130 Max£155pw (High)

F East Wing Dalnaglar Castle
for bookings Mrs Burke & Mrs Cameron, Dalnaglar Castle, Glenshee, Blairgowrie, Perthshire PH10 7LP
☎Blacklunans(025082)232

A spacious flat set on three floors of Dalnaglar Castle offering twelve bedrooms served by four bathrooms with

WC, five shower rooms with WC, large dining room and spacious lounge.

Allyear MWB out of season 2days min 1mth max 1unit 20–40persons] ◇ ◆ ◉ fridge Electric & open fires Elec metered ⬜can be hired 👕 Iron & Ironing board in unit ⊕ CTV ⊕3pin square 6P ⚙(7m) fishing

⊖ 🔌(3m)

Min£550 Max£900pw

GLEN TROOL

Dumfries & Galloway Kirkcudbrightshire
Map10 NX48

H Glentrool Village

for bookings Forest Holiday Bookings, Forestry Commission (Dept AA) 231 Corstorphine Road, Edinburgh, EH12 7AT ☎031-334 0303 & 031-334 2576

Six two-storey semi-detached former forestry workers' houses set in Forestry Commission village. Neat and comfortable accommodation comprising lounge/diner, kitchen, bathroom and single bedroom on the ground floor and two twin-bedded rooms on the first floor. Access is from A714 Newton Stewart/Girvan road; Bargrennan follow unclass road to Glentrool/Straiton.

Feb–10Jan MWB out of season 3days min, 1mth max, 6units, 1–5persons ◇ ◉ fridge Electric Elec inclusive ⬜not provided ☎(100yds) ⊕3pin square 11P ⚙(100yds)

⊖ 🔌(½m)

Min£66 Max£170pw

GLYNARTHEN

Dyfed
Map2 SN34

H S P Williamson College Mawr

Glynarthen, Llandysul, Dyfed SA44 6PP ☎Rhydlewis(023975)333

Comfortable farmhouse in tranquil setting affording rural views and about 5 miles from the beach at Aberporth. Accommodation comprises lounge, kitchen, dining room, four bedrooms, reached by open plan stairway and bathroom/WC. Separate outside WC by rear door.

Allyear MWB out of season 3days min, 1unit, 1–9persons ◇ ◆ ◔ fridge Electric Gas/Elec inclusive ⬜not provided ☎(100yds) Iron & Ironing board in unit [Launderette on premises] ⊕ CTV ⊕3pin square 3P 🎞 ⚙(2m) children's play area.

⊖ 🔌(2m)

Min£70 Max£215pw

Glenshee (Spittal of)
—
Goodnestone

GODOLPHIN CROSS

Cornwall
Map2 SW63

B The Oaks, 9 Forth Vean

for bookings Mr & Mrs G N F Broughton, Orchard House, 26 Wall Rd, Gwinear, Hayle Cornwall TR27 5HA ☎Leedstown(0736)850201

Detached, modern bungalow situated on a very small private site in a rural location approx 4m NW of Helston. This well-appointed property comprises of lounge with open fire, kitchen and breakfast bar and dining area, two twin-bedded rooms and one double and a bathroom/WC.

Allyear MWB out of season 1wk min, 1unit, 6persons ◇ ◉ fridge 🍴 Elec inclusive ⬜can be hired WM Iron & Ironing board in unit ⊕ CTV ⊕3pin square 1P 1🔥 🎞 ⚙(100yds)

⊖ 🔌(100yds)

Min£85 Max£225pw

GOLSPIE

Highland Sutherland
Map14 NH89

Ca Log Cabin Backies

for bookings Mr J M L Scott, Priory House, Priory Road, Tinwell, Stamford, Lincolnshire
☎Stamford(0780)63365(wknds & evenings) & 52075(office hours)

A modern, pine log cabin offering holiday accommodation in a peaceful setting, with splendid views. There are three bedrooms, lounge/diner, kitchen and bathroom.

Mar–Nov MWB out of season 1wk min, 1mth max, 1unit, 1–5persons no pets ◉ fridge Electric & open fires Elec metered ⬜not provided ☎(100yds) Iron & Ironing board in unit ⊕ TV can be hired ⊕3pin square P ⚙(1½m) ➔(1½m) 🛏(1½m)

⊖ 🍴(1½m) 🔌(1½m) 🎵(1½m)

Min£40 Max£60pw (Low)
Min£70 Max£100pw (High)

GOODNESTONE

Kent
Map5 TR25

H The Dower House

for bookings The Estate Office, Knowlton Court, Wingham, Canterbury, CT3 1PT ☎Sandwich(0304)617344

A spacious Elizabethan residence comprising two double, one single and four twin bedrooms, three bathrooms, kitchen containing an Aga & electric cooker, separate dining room, drawing room, study and garden. There are inglenook fireplaces, fine furnishings, a dishwasher machine and a deep freeze.

Allyear MWB out of season 1wk min, 6mths max 1unit 2–13persons ◇ ◉ fridge 🍴 Elec metered ⬜can be hired 👕 SD in unit Iron & Ironing board in unit ⊕ TV ⊕3pin square ⊕3pin round 5P 🎞 ⚙(2m)

⊖ 🔌

Min£125 Max£300pw

C 8 Lower Rowling

for bookings The Estate Office, Knowlton Court, Wingham, Canterbury, Kent CT3 1PT
☎Sandwich(0304)617344

Country cottage sleeping six people. Well-furnished accommodation comprises three bedrooms, sitting room, dining room, kitchen and bathroom/WC. Garage and garden.

Allyear MWB out of season 1wk min, 1unit, 1–6persons [◇] ◇ ◆ ◉ fridge Electric Elec metered ⬜can be hired ☎(1m) Iron Ironing board ⊕ TV ⊕3pin square 🔥 🎞 ⚙(1m)

⊖ 🔌(1m)

Min£65 Max£80pw (Low)
Min£95 Max£130pw (High)

C 3 & 4 Meadow Cottages Lower Rowling

for bookings The Estate Office, Knowlton Court, Wingham, Canterbury, Kent CT3 1PT
☎Sandwich(0304)617344

Two cottages with communicating door through the kitchens, can be let separately or together, each sleeping six in two twin-bedded rooms and one with a pair of bunks, bathroom, kitchen and sitting room. Well-furnished, retaining a farm cottage atmosphere.

Allyear MWB out of season 2units, 1–12persons [◇] ◇ ◆ ◉ fridge Electric Elec metered ⬜can be hired ☎(1m) Iron Ironing board ⊕ TV ⊕3pin square ⚙(1m)

⊖ 🔌(1m)

Min£60 Max£75pw (Low)
Min£90 Max£125pw (High)

C Rowling Court Cottage Rowling

for bookings The Estate Office, Knowlton Court, Wingham, Canterbury, Kent CT3 1PT
☎Sandwich(0304)617344 →

Semi-detached cottage having extensive views of countryside with driveway to garden. Accommodation comprises kitchen, dining room, sitting room, three bedrooms, one double room, one twin-bedded room, one room with bunks, and bathroom/WC.

All year MWB out of season 1wk min, 1unit, 1–6persons [◇] ◆ ◎ fridge Elec metered ⌷can be hired ☎ Iron & Ironing board in unit ⊕ TV ⊕3pin square ♨(1m)
↩ ♀

Min£65 Max£80pw (Low)
Min£95 Max£130pw (High)

C Southview No 1 Lower Rowling
for bookings The Estate Office, Knowlton Court, Wingham, Canterbury, Kent CT3 1PT
☎Sandwich(0304)617344

Farm cottage in rural setting 9m from Canterbury. Accommodation comprises five twin-bedded rooms, kitchen, dining room, sitting room and two bathrooms/WC.

All year MWB out of season 1wk min, 1unit, 1–10persons [◇] ◆ ◆ ◎ fridge Electric Elec metered ⌷can be hired ☎ Iron Ironing board ⊕ TV ⊕3pin square ▥ ♨(1m)
↩ ♀(1m)

Min£70 Max£85pw (Low)
Min£100 Max£140pw (High)

GOODRICH
Hereford & Worcester
Map**3** SO51

C Yew Tree's Coppett Hill
for bookings Mrs Smith, Old Kilns, Howle Hill, Ross-on-Wye, Herefordshire HR9 5SP
☎Ross-on-Wye(0989)62051

A two-storey 17th-century cottage located on the side of a hill. Accommodation comprises kitchen with breakfast table, lounge with two double convertible Chesterfields and small dining area, bathroom, one twin and two double bedrooms (one with a cot, one with a shower cubicle). All well decorated and maintained.

All year MWB in season 1day min, 8mths max, 1unit, 10–12persons [◇ ◆ ◆] ◎ fridge ▦ & electric fires Elec metered ⌷can be hired ☎(½m) WM & SD in unit Iron & Ironing board in unit ⊕ ⊕ CTV ⊕3pin square 3P ▥ ♨(¾m)
↩ ♀(½m) 🎵(1m) fishing
from£25pw

GOOSEHAM
Cornwall
Map**2** SS21

F Wild Goose Cottage Flats 1 & 2
for bookings Mrs W P Stuart-Bruges, Quarley Down, Cholderton, nr Salisbury, Wiltshire SP4 0DZ
☎Cholderton(098064)235

Goodnestone
—
Grantown-on-Spey

A detached stone cottage converted into two flats. The first flat is approached by an outside stairway of stone steps and comprises one double bedroom, one twin-bedded room, one bedroom with twin bunks, kitchen/diner and lounge The ground-floor flat comprises lounge with two divans, one twin-bedded room, kitchen/diner and has a lawned garden.

All year MWB out of season 4days min, 6mths max, 2units, 2–6persons ◆ ◆ fridge ▦ Elec metered ⌷not provided ◎(1m) WM in one unit SD in one unit Iron & Ironing board in unit ⊕ CTV ⊕3pin square P ♨(1m)
↩ ♀(1½m)

Min£30 Max£145pw

GRAMPOUND
Cornwall
Map**2** SW94

C Golden Keep
for bookings Mr & Mrs Perry, Golden Manor, Grampound, Cornwall TR2 4DF
☎Tregony(087253)500

Attractive furnished stone cottage set in large gardens of a beautiful hamlet. Comprises lounge/diner, kitchen, one double bedroom and one twin bedroom and bathroom/WC.

Apr–Sep MWB out of season 1wk min, 3mths max, 1unit, 1–4persons [◇] ◆ ◆ ◎ fridge Electric Elec metered ⌷inclusive ☎(2m) Iron & Ironing board in unit ⊕ CTV ⊕3pin square 2P ▥ ♨(2m)
↩ ♀(2m)

Details not confirmed for 1987

F Golden Manor Flat
for bookings Mr & Mrs D W C Perry, Golden Manor, Grampound, Truro, Cornwall TR2 4DF
☎Tregony(087 253)500

A first-floor flat in a 400-year-old Cornish stone manor house, set in peaceful hamlet. The flat is approached through the original studded manor house door. Accommodation comprises well-equipped kitchen with dining facilities, large comfortable living room with stone mullioned windows and double bed-settee, a twin bedroom and bathroom/WC.

All year MWB out of season 1wk min, 3mths max, 1unit, 1–4persons ◆ ◆ pets by arrangement ◎ fridge Night storage(inclusive) Elec metered ⌷inclusive ☎(2m) Iron & Ironing board in unit ⊕ ⊕ CTV ⊕3pin square P ▥ ♨(2m)
↩ ♀(2m)

GRANGE (in Borrowdale)
Cumbria
Map**11** NY21

C Fell View
for bookings Lakeland Holiday Cottages, Yew Tree Cottage, Ullock, Keswick, Cumbria CA12 5SP
☎Braithwaite(059682)493
or Keswick(07687)72059

Mid-terrace cottage in centre of tiny village, by the village green. Accommodation comprises cosy lounge, spacious kitchen/diner, three twin-bedded rooms, bathroom/WC and separate WC/ cloakroom.

All year 1mth max, 1unit, 2–5persons ◇ ◆ no pets ◎ fridge open & electric fires Elec inclusive ⌷inclusive ☎(30yds) WM, SD & TD in unit Iron & Ironing board in unit ⊕ CTV ⊕3pin square 1P ▥ ♨(4m)
↩ ♀(1m)

Min£96 Max£219pw

GRANGE-OVER-SANDS
Cumbria
Map**7** SD47

F Mrs M Shrigley **Granville Holiday Flats**
Granville, Methven Terrace, Kents Bank Road, Grange-over-Sands, Cumbria LA11 7DP
☎Grange-over-Sands(04484)2509

Two large, comfortable and well-equipped flats in a stone-built terraced house, on the coast road west of the town centre. Both flats have good views across Morecambe Bay and are convenient for visiting the Lake District.

All year MWB out of season 1wk min, 1mth max, 2units, 4–6persons, nc4 ◎ fridge Electric Elec metered ⌷inclusive ☎ Iron & Ironing board on premises ⊕ TV ⊕3pin square ▥ ♨(½m)
↩ ♀(300yds) 🎵(½m)

Min£60 Max£65pw (Low)
Min£70 Max£75pw (High)

GRANTOWN-ON-SPEY
Highland *Morayshire*
Map**14** NJ02

H Mr J W Walker **Dunvegan Cottage**
Dunvegan Hotel, Heathfield Road, Grantown-on-Spey, Inverness-shire
☎Grantown-on-Spey(0479)2301

Two-storey modern house next door to the hotel and with views of Crondale Hills; 5 minutes car journey from River Spey. Accommodation comprises sitting/dining room, kitchen, a single bedroom and bathroom on the ground floor with one double, one twin-bedded room on the first floor.

29Mar–Oct 7days min, 2wks max, 1unit, 1–5persons ◆ ◆ ◎ fridge ▦ Elec metered ⌷can be hired ☎ WM & SD in unit Iron & Ironing board in unit ⊕ CTV ⊕3pin square 2P ▥ ♨(1m)
↩ ♿(200yds) ♀ 🎵(1m) 🎵(½m)

Min£110 Max£160pw

H Mrs G Turnbull **Reidhaven** Woodside Avenue, Grantown-on-Spey, Morayshire PH26 3JP
☎Grantown-on-Spey(0479)2061

Spacious wing of a detached Victorian stone house standing in own ground and gardens. The house offers good standard of decor and furnishings and comprises sitting room, modern kitchen/diner, double bedroom, bunk-bedded room with WHB, twin bedroom with WHB, bathroom/WC and separate WC.

Etr – Oct 1wk min, 1mth max, 1unit, 1 – 6persons ◊ ◆ ◎ fridge
Electric Elec metered ⌷can be hired
☎20yds Iron & Ironing board in unit
⊙ TV ⊕3pin square 1P ▥
▣(200yds)
⊖⊦(½m) ☎(200yds) 🎵(200yds)
Min£60 Max£90pw (Low)
Min£100 Max£110pw (High)

H **Strathspey Lodges** South Street
for bookings Mrs C Lawson, Arnish, Market Road, Grantown-on-Spey, Morayshire PH26 3HP
☎Grantown-on-Spey(0479)2339

Five comfortable and well designed modern style houses furnished and fitted to a high standard. The ground floor comprises of lounge/dining room, kitchen, while the upper floor has three bedrooms and a bathroom.

All year MWB out of season 3days min, 1mth max, 5units, 1 – 6persons ◊ ◆
◎ fridge 🍴 & Electric fire Elec metered ⌷inclusive ☎(300yds) ⊙
CTV ⊕3pin square 8P ▥ ▣(100yds)
⊖⊦ ♪(100yds) ☎(50yds) 🎵(300yds)
🎵(300yds)
Min£90 Max£195pw (Low)
Min£142 Max£245pw (High)

GRASMERE
Cumbria
Map**11** NY30

F **Beck Allans Self-Catering Apartments**
for bookings Mr B G Yates, Beck Allans Cottage, Grasmere, Ambleside, Cumbria LA22 9SZ
☎Grasmere(09665)329

Grantown-on-Spey
—
Gresham

Six flats located in an attractive stone-built house in the heart of Grasmere Village. They vary in size sleeping 2 – 5 persons and are all very well appointed and comfortable. One flat is entirely ground-floor and RADAR approved for the disabled.

All year MWB out of season 2days min, 6units, 1 – 5persons ◊ ◆ ◎ fridge
Electric Elec metered ⌷inclusive ☎
WM TD in unit ⊙ CTV ⊕3pin square
12P ▥ ▣(300yds)
⊖⊦ ♨(50yds) ☎(½m)
Min£110 Max£190pw (Low)
Min£150 Max£275pw (High)

H **Grey Crag Barn**
for bookings Mr C V Dodgson, Butter Crags, Grasmere, Cumbria LA22 9QZ
☎Grasmere(09665)259

A charming and unusual house converted from an old barn, some of the original beams can still be seen. The ground floor consists of an enormous hall with double bed-settee and WC, off a spiral staircase to the first floor, comprising three bedrooms, spacious lounge/diner and bathroom/WC.

All year MWB out of season 3days min, 1mth max, 1unit, 2 – 8persons ◊ ◆
no pets ◎ fridge 🍴 & electric radiators Elec metered ⌷not provided
⊙ TV ⊕3pin square 6P 2🏠 ▥
▣(½m)
⊖⊦ ☎(½m)
Min£100 Max£195pw

F & H **Wood Close** How Head Lane
for bookings Mr & Mrs B E Cole, Elm Bank, Askham, Penrith, Cumbria CA10 2PF
☎Hackthorpe(09312)531

A traditional lakeland country house offering comfortable accommodation, divided into seven flats plus one house and standing in its own secluded grounds of 2½ acres on the slopes of Rydal Fell. They offer a variety of well-appointed

---

accommodation sleeping up to nine persons.

Mar – Oct & Xmas 2nights min, 1mth max, 8units, 2 – 9persons ◊ ◆ ◎ fridge
Electric Elec metered ⌷can be hired
☎ Iron & Ironing board in unit
[Launderette on premises] ⊙ CTV
⊕3pin square P ▥ ▣(½m)
⊖⊦ ☎(½m)
Details not confirmed for 1987

GRATTON DALE
Derbyshire
Map**8** SK26

B **East & West Cottages**
for bookings Mrs E Hague, Dale End Farm, Gratton Dale, Youlgrave, Bakewell, Derbyshire DE4 1LN
☎Winster(062988)453

Two tastefully converted ground-floor units with **East Cottage** *comprising open plan lounge/dining room/kitchen, with bed-settee in the lounge, three bedrooms and bathroom/WC.* **West Cottage** *is similar except for the kitchen which is separate and the central heating is solid fuel, whereas East Cottage is electric heating. Situated in the grounds of the proprietors home in the peaceful and picturesque Peak National Park.*

Etr – Oct MWB 1wkd min, 2units, 2 – 8persons [◊] ◊ ◆ ◎ fridge
🍴 & Electric Elec metered ⌷can be hired ☎(200yds) WM & Iron in unit ⊕
CTV ⊕3pin square 4P ▣(1m)
🅿Hard
⊖⊦ ☎(1m)
Min£55 Max£75pw (Low)
Min£80 Max£125pw (High)

GREAT
Placenames incorporating the word 'Great' such as Gt Malvern and Gt Yarmouth will be found under the actual placename, ie Malvern, Yarmouth

GRESHAM
Norfolk
Map**9** TG13

C & F Mrs G M Briars **Camelot House**
Gresham, Norwich, Norfolk NR11 8AD
☎Matlaske(026377)560 →

Beck Allans
Self Catering Apartments
GRASMERE ambleside cumbria LA22 9sz

Attractive mid-19th C house in the centre of Grasmere village with 6 luxury apartments sleeping 2-5 people; one entirely ground floor suitable for handicapped visitors. Ample parking; well kept garden & lawn. Tenancies from Friday to Friday from Easter — October. Tariff ranges £120—£210 (low season) and £165—£300 (high season). Off Season breaks — minimum 2 nights excluding Christmas/New Year — from £40 for 2 people. Electricity extra. Pets accepted.

Comprehensive Brochure from Resident Proprietors

Camelot House, formerly an old flintstone barn, stands in grounds of over an acre amidst surrounding fields in the village. **Ragnell** *at Camelot House is a first floor flat with galley-type kitchen, sitting room and a twin bedroom.* **Linnet** *at Camelot House is a maisonette with kitchen/dining area on ground floor twin bedroom and sitting area on first floor.*
Gringalet Cottage *is a delightful flintstone single-storey building converted from an old barn and has one bedroom with twin beds plus a single divan in the lounge.*

All year (Cottage) Mar–Oct (Flat) MWB out of season 3days min, 4mths max, 3units, 2–3persons, nc in Linnet & Ragnell ◇ ◆ no pets in Linnet & Ragnell ◉ fridge ♨ Elec inclusive ⬜not provided ☎(200yds) SD on premises Iron & Ironing board in unit ☺ CTV ⊕3pin square P 2🏠 🎞 🎱(200yds)

◒ ♨(3m) ♨(½m) 🎵(3m) 🎵(3m)
Min£75 Max£105pw (Low)
Min£103 Max£160pw (High)

GREWELTHORPE
North Yorkshire
Map**8** SE27

B Allendale
for bookings Mrs T Mould, Sunnydale Ilton Road, Grewelthorpe, Ripon, N Yorks HG4 3DF
☎Kirkby Malzeard(076583)389

Self-contained semi-detached bungalow near the village centre. Sleeping accommodation is for five in a double-bedded room, a room with three single beds and a bed-settee in the lounge. Also a kitchen and bathroom/shower with WC.

All year MWB out of season 1wk min, 3mths max, 1unit, 1–5persons ◇ ◉ fridge ♨ Elec metered ⬜can be hired ☎(150yds) WM & SD in unit Iron & Ironing board in unit ☺ ◉ TV ⊕3pin square P 🏠 🎞 🎱(150yds)

◒ ♨(150yds)

Details not confirmed for 1987

GRUINART
Strathclyde *Argyllshire*
See **Islay, Isle of**

GUERNSEY
See **Channel Islands**

GUISBOROUGH
Cleveland
Map**8** NZ61

C Old Font House Cottages 109–111
Westgate
for bookings Mrs S A Lowery, 113 Westgate, Guisborough, Cleveland TS14 6AH
☎Guisborough(0287)32866

A pair of 18th-century cottages attractively restored with beams and original features. Both have two bedrooms (one with

---

Gresham
—
Harlech

bunks), lounge/diner, bathroom/WC and kitchen. Large shared garden of ⅓ acre.

All year 1wk min, 6mths max, 2units, 1–4persons ◇ ◆ no pets ◉ fridge ♨ & gas fires Gas & Elec inclusive ⬜can be hired ☎(100yds) Iron & Ironing board on premises ☺ CTV ⊕3pin square 3P 🎱(100yds)

◒ ♨(200yds)
Min£55 Max£75pw (Low)
Min£80 Max£105pw (High)

GWINEAR
Cornwall
Map**2** SW53

C Mr & Mrs D B & J E Busfield Wall Farm
Gwinear, Hayle, Cornwall
☎Leedstown(0736)850506

Three modern cottages adjacent to the farmhouse which dates back to the 18th century. Each comprises of lounge with bed-settee, kitchen/diner, one double bedroom with additional single bed and one twin-bedded room, bathroom/WC. The farm is situated in the quiet hamlet of Wall, 3m W of Camborne.

All year MWB out of season !wk min, 1mth max, 3units, 1–6persons ◇ ◆ ◉fridge Electric Elec inclusive ⬜can be hired ☎(400yds) SD in unit Iron & Ironing board in unit ☺ CTV ⊕3pin square 3P 🎞 🎱(400yds)

◒ ♨(¾m)
Min£35 Max£95pw (Low)
Min£140 Max£185pw (High)

GWITHIAN
Cornwall
Map**2** SW54

F B R Staker Sandbank Holiday Flats
Gwithian, Hayle, Cornwall TR27 5BL
☎Falmouth(0326)311063

Located off the B3301 Gwithian to Hayle road, the flats are in two blocks of eight surrounded by lawns and shrubbery, and within walking distance of beaches. The flats have one or two bedrooms and all have bathroom/WC, kitchen/diner/lounge with convertible settee.

Apr–Nov MWB out of season 1wk min, 1mth max, 18units, 1–6persons ◇ no pets in high season ◉ fridge Electric Elec metered ⬜can be hired ☎ Iron & Ironing board on premises ☺ CTV ⊕3pin square 1P 🎱(50yds)

◒ ♨(½m) 🎵(1m) 🎵(1m) 🐾(1m)
Min£35 Max£75pw (Low)
Min£115 Max£195pw (High)

HADDISCOE
Norfolk
Map**5** TM49

C Mr & Mrs P Mummery Haddiscoe Hall
Haddiscoe, Norfolk NR14 6PE
☎Lowestoft(0502)77291

The hall stands in 32 acres, comprising paddock with prize winning Suffolk Punch horses, pastures with cattle, 8 acres of woodland and gardens and a 2 acre lake with good coarse fishing. **Rose** *and* **Honeysuckle** *cottages are semi-detached and share a large lawn; each comprises two double, one single, and one bunk bedded room, bathroom/WC, sitting/dining room and kitchen.* **Coach House** *is a bungalow with two doubles one twin bedroom, sitting/dining room with adjoining kitchenette and bathroom/WC.* **Ostlers House** *is a bungalow with one double, one twin and one bunk bedded room, bathroom/WC, kitchen/diner and large sitting room.*

Etr–Oct 3days min, 4units, 6–7persons [◇] ◆ ◉ fridge wood burning Elec metered ⬜inclusive ◉ WM, SD & TD on premises Iron & Ironing board in unit ☺ CTV ⊕3pin square P 🏠 🎱(1m) table tennis pool

◒ ♨(1m)
Min£85 Max£170pw

HALTWHISTLE
Northumberland
Map**12** NY76

C Smithy Cottage
for bookings Mrs J I Laidlow, Ald White Craig Farm, Shieldhill, Haltwhistle, Northumberland NE49 9NW
☎Haltwhistle(0498)20565

Attractive cottage recently converted from a smithy, the ground floor of which affords sitting room with convertible bed-settee and kitchen/diner. The first floor comprises one bedroom which sleeps four people and a shower room/WC.

All year MWB out of season 3nights min, 1mth max, 1unit, 4–6persons ◇ ◆ pets by arrangement ◉ fridge ♨ & wood stove Elec metered ⬜inclusive ☎(½m) [WM, SD & TD on premises] Iron & Ironing board on premises ☺ ◉ CTV ⊕3pin square 1P 🎞 🎱(½m) ➴(1½m) children's play area, cycles for hire

◒ ♨(3m) ♨(½m)
Min£50 Max£155pw

HARLECH
Gwynedd
Map**6** SH53

B Hafan & Mordan Llandanwg Caravan Park
for bookings J & P G Conolly, 10 Frampton Way, Great Barr, Birmingham B43 7UH
☎021-3608199

A pair of semi-detached bungalows overlooking Tremadog Bay, consisting of one double bedroom, one twin (with wash hand basin in Mordan only), kitchen/diner and bathroom/WC. Llandawg, 1½m SW off A496.

8Mar–25Oct 1wk min, 1mth max, 2units, 4–6persons no pets ⊚ fridge Electric Elec metered ⊡not provided ☎(10yds) Iron in unit ⊙ ⊕3pin square P ⬚

⊖ ƒ(1½m) ☻(1½m) ♫(½m)
Min£50 Max£90pw (Low)
Min£95 Max£110pw (High)

C Moel View
for bookings Mrs A Stumpp, Bron Haul, Harlech, Gwynedd LL46 2UL

Mid-terrace Welsh stone cottage comprising lounge, dining room, kitchen, bathroom/WC and three bedrooms (one double, two single).

Mar–Nov MWB out of season 1wk min, 4wks max, 1unit, 1–4persons, nc3 no pets ⊚ fridge Electric Elec metered ⊡not provided ☎ [Launderette] ⊙ ⊕3pin square 1P ▥ ⬚(½m)

⊖ ƒ(½m) ☻(½m)
Min£40 Max£70pw

HARROGATE
North Yorkshire
Map**8** SE35

F Mrs S McNamara *Abbey Lodge Apartments* 29 Ripon Road, Harrogate, North Yorkshire HG1 2JL
☎Harrogate(0423)69712

Ground, first and second-floor flats with attractive garden surrounds near the town centre. No's 1 & 3 have sleeping accommodation for four people in one double and one twin-bedded room (No 3 has extra single bed in double room). No 2 sleeps three people in a double-bedded room and a single-bedded room and an extra two if required on a bed-settee in the lounge. There is a lounge/diner and separate kitchen (kitchen/diner and lounge in No 2) and a bathroom/WC.

All year MWB 1wk min, 3mths max, 3units, 1–5persons nc10 no pets ⊚ fridge ✹ Elec metered ⊡inclusive ☎ Iron & Ironing board in unit [Launderette within 300yds] ⊙ CTV ⊕3pin square 4P ▥ ⬚(300yds)

⊖ ƒ(½m) ☻(½m) ♫(½m) ♫(1m) ☻(1½m)

Details not confirmed for 1987

Harlech
—
Harrogate

F *Ashness Apartments* St Mary's Avenue
for bookings Mr J F Spinlove, 49 St Leonards Road, Harrogate HG2 8NS
☎Harrogate(0423)885580

Four substantial terraced town houses have been converted to form these comfortable self-contained apartments close to the town centre. Each flat has a lounge, kitchen and bathroom/WC, all well furnished and fitted. Accommodation is available for up to four people in eight ground or lower ground floor flats; three people in two first floor units; four people in two second floor units, while two maisonettes each sleep up to seven people.

All year MWB 1wk min, 4wks max, 14units, 2–7persons ◊ ◆ ♂ fridge ✹ Gas & Elec inclusive ⊡inclusive ☎ Iron & Ironing board in unit [Launderette within 300yds] ⊙ CTV ⊕3pin square 14P ▥ ⬚(100yds)

⊖ ƒ(1m) ☻(150yds) ♫(500yds) ♫(500yds) ☻(800yds)
Min£95 Max£135pw (Low)
Min£145 Max£200pw (High)

C Claro, Beagle and Keepers Cottage
Follifoot
for bookings Rudding Park Holiday Cottages, Rudding Park, Follifoot, Harrogate, N Yorks HG3 1DT
☎Harrogate(0423)870439

Situated to the north of Rudding Park and in close proximity to each other the cottages have south facing gardens with woodlands to the rear. Claro comprises sitting/dining room with bed settee, kitchen and one double bedroom leading to shower/WC. Beagle comprises open plan kitchen/diner/sitting room with bed settee, one double bedroom and bathroom/WC. Keepers comprises sitting room with open fire, kitchen/diner, bed sitting room, three bedrooms and bathroom/WC.

All year MWB out of season 2days min, 6mths max, 3units, 3–9persons ◊ ◆ ⊚ fridge ♂ ✹ & open fires Gas inclusive Elec metered ⊡can be hired Pay phone can be hired WM in unit SD in (Claro, Beagle) TD in (Keepers) Iron & Ironing board in unit ⊙ CTV ⊕3pin square P ⬚(3m)

⊖ ƒ(2m) ☻(1m) ♫(3m) ☻(3m)
Min£104 Max£245pw

C Ducks Nest Farm Follifoot
for bookings Rudding Park Holiday Cottages, Rudding Park, Follifoot, Harrogate, N Yorks HG3 1DT
☎Harrogate(0423)870439

Situated to the north of Rudding Park just beyond the park wall, these properties have been sympathetically converted from farm buildings reputedly in use since the 17th century. Ducks Nest Farm Cottage comprises sitting room with open fire, dining/kitchen, utility room, cloakroom/ WC, three bedrooms and bathroom/WC. The Granary comprises sitting/dining room with open fire, kitchen, two bedrooms and bathroom/WC. The Loft a converted grain store is approached by external stone-stairs and comprises bed/ sitting room, small kitchen, shower/WC and garage.

All year MWB out of season 2days min, 6mths max, 3units, 2–7persons ◊ ◆ ⊚ fridge ♂(Farm Cottage & Granary by prior arrangement) Gas inclusive Elec metered ⊡can be hired Pay phones can be hired WM & SD in unit Iron & Ironing board in unit ⊙ CTV ⊕3pin square P ⌂(Loft) ⬚(3m)

⊖ ƒ(2m) ☻(1m) ♫(3m) ☻(3m)
Min£70 Max£225pw

F The Manager **Hospitality Inn** Prospect Place, West Park, Harrogate, North Yorkshire HG1 1LB
☎Harrogate(0423)64601

Five luxury apartments created from a row of magnificent Georgian houses each with its own private entrance. Apartments 5 & 6 are on the lower ground floor sleeping two in a double room with lounge and small dining room, kitchen and bathroom. Apartments 7, 8 & 9 also sleep two people in a twin-bedded room with lounge and →

open plan kitchen/diner and bathroom/
WC. Furnished and fitted to a very high
standard.

All year MWB 1 day min, 6mths max,
5units, 1–2persons, [◇] ✦ ◆ ◎
fridge ♨ Elec inclusive ⬜inclusive
☎ Iron & Ironing board in unit
Launderette on premises ⊕ CTV
⊕3pin square 5P ⚍(200yds)
↔ ♒(3m) ♀(40yds) 🎣(½m) ♫(½m)
🐾(½m)
£250pw

**C, H & Ch   North Lodge, Bothy &
Gardners Cottages, Teal, Heron &
Mallard Chalets** Follifoot
for bookings Rudding Park Holiday
Cottages, Rudding Park, Follifoot,
Harrogate, N Yorks HG3 1DT
☎Harrogate(0423)870439
Situated within the thirty acres of Rudding
Park. The properties offer differing types of
accommodation for various numbers of
people. **North Lodge** comprises sitting
room with single bed-settee, dining room,
kitchen, one double and one twin
bedroom and bath/WC. **Bothy Cottage**
comprises sitting room, diner/kitchen,
cloakroom/WC, utility room, two double
and one triple bedroom and bath/WC.
Gardners Cottage a detached Victorian
house comprises sitting room, diner/
kitchen, bed sitting room leading to WC,
one double and one twin bedroom and
bath/WC. **Teal, Heron** and **Mallard** are
three timber-built chalets set in a
woodland clearing beside a lily pond.
Each chalet comprises open plan kitchen/
diner/sitting room, bath/WC. Teal and
Heron have one double and one single
bedroom, Mallard has one double and
one twin bedroom plus bed-settee.

All year MWB out of season 2days min,
6mths max, 6units, 1–7persons ◇ ◆
♨(Calor in chalets only) ◎ fridge
♨(& open fires Bothy & North Lodge)
Gas inclusive Elec metered ⬜can be
hired Pay phone can be hired WM & TD
in Bothay & North Lodge WM & SD in
Gardners Iron & Ironing board in Lodge,
Gardners & Bothy Launderette within
300yds for use chalets ⊕ CTV
⊕3pin square P ⚍on campsite
⚏(at campsite)
↔ ♒(3m) ♀(1m) 🎣(3m) 🐾(3m)
Sports centre(3m)
Min£100 Max£245pw

C   Rock Cottage & Manor Cottages 1 & 2
Follifoot
for bookings Rudding Park Holiday
Cottages, Rudding Park, Follifoot,
Harrogate, N Yorks HG3 1DT
☎Harrogate(0423)870439
Situated in Follifoot village these stone
cottages have been sympathetically
renovated. **Rock Cottage** comprises sitting
room, diner/kitchen, one double and one
single bedroom, bath/WC. **Manor Cottage
1** comprises sitting room, diner/kitchen,
one double and one twin bedroom, bath/
WC. **Manor Cottage 2** comprises open
plan sitting room/kitchen/diner, one

double and one single bedroom,
bathroom/WC.

All year MWB out of season 2days min,
6mths max, 3units, 1–4persons ◇ ◆
♫(Rock Cottage) ◎(Manor Cottages)
fridge ♨ Gas inclusive Elec metered
⬜can be hired Pay phone can be hired
WM in unit SD in (Manor Cottages) TD
in unit/on premises (Rock Cottage) Iron
& Ironing board in unit ⊕ CTV
⊕3pin square 2P ⚍(30yds)
↔ ♒(2m) ♀(adjacent) 🎣(3m)
🐾(3m)
Min£104 Max£195pw

HARTINGTON
Derbyshire
Map**7** SK16

F   Mrs E Gould Croft Cottage (Flat 2) Mill
Lane, Hartington, Derbys
☎Hartington(029884)307
An old two-storey cottage built of
limestone, which has been modernised to
a high standard, situated opposite the
Charles Cotton Hotel in village centre. The
first floor is occupied by the proprietor and
the ground floor with a separate entrance
is the holiday flat. Accommodation
comprises kitchen with dining table and
chairs, lounge, bathroom with WC and a
double-bedded room.

Mar–Oct MWB 1wk min, 1mth max,
1unit, 2persons no pets ◎ Electric
Elec metered ⬜not provided
☎(500yds) ⊕3pin square 2P ⬛
⚍(500yds)
↔ ♀(300yds)
Min£25 Max£30pw (Low)
Min£35 Max£45pw (High)

C   Mews Cottage Mill Lane
for bookings Mrs P Collins, 'April Rise', 10
The Green, Cranswick, Driffield,
Humberside YO25 9QU
☎Driffield(0377)70471
Modernised two-storey cottage
comprising two bedrooms, kitchen/diner
with breakfast bar, lounge with convertible
bed-settee and bathroom/WC. It stands in
the village centre within the Peak National
Park.

All year MWB out of season 3days min,
1mth max, 1unit, 6persons ◎
fridge Storage heaters (inclusive)
Elec metered ⬜not provided
☎(300yds) SD in unit Iron in unit ⊕
◎ CTV ⊕3pin square 1P ⬛
⚍(300yds)
↔ ♀(100yds)
Min£50 Max£65pw (Low)
Min£70 Max£110pw (High)

HARTLAND
Devon
Map**2** SS22

**C   Mrs Y Heard West Titchberry Farm
(Cottage)** Hartland, Bideford, Devon
☎Hartland(02374)287
A recently modernised and extended
cottage adjoining the owners farmhouse,
with the front door of the cottage leading
from a walled garden, into lounge with
bed-settee and wood burning stove. There
is a kitchen/diner with stairs leading to
first-floor landing with two bedrooms and
bathroom/WC.

All year MWB out of season 3days min,
6mths max, 1unit, 1–7persons ◇ ◆
◆ no pets ◎ fridge Electric &
woodburning stove Elec metered ⬜can
be hired ☎(3m) SD in unit Iron
& Ironing board in unit ⊕ CTV
⊕3pin square P ⬛ ⚍(3m) Games
room
↔ ♀(3m)
Min£40 Max£155pw

HASTINGS
East Sussex
Map**5** TQ80

B, Ch & H   Combe Haven Holiday Park
Harley Shute Road, St Leonards-on-Sea
for bookings Haven Holidays, Haven
House, Quay Street, Truro, Cornwall
TR1 2UE
☎Truro(872)40400
Scotney bungalows are 34 semi-detached
properties comprising one double, one
twin and one bunk-bedded room, shower
and WC and an open plan lounge and
kitchen area. **Hastings Chalets** are single
storey and comprise one twin and one
double bedroom, bathroom and WC and
an open-plan lounge and kitchen area.
Sunset villas are two storey, link detached
and comprise one double, one twin and
one bunk bedroom, shower and WC and
lounge with kitchen area. Facilities include
sauna, solarium and hairdressing.

Etr & May–Sep MWB 1wk min,
1mth max, 82units, 2–8persons [◇
◆] Teenage groups by prior
arrangement ◎ fridge
Electric Convection Elec
inclusive (Scotney & Hastings)
Elec metered(sunset) ⬜inclusive
☎(300yds) [WM & TD on premises]
[Iron & Ironing board on premises]
[Launderette within 300yds] ⊕ CTV
⊕3pin square P ⚍(300yds) ⚏
↔ ♒(3m) ♀ 🎣 ♫ 🐾(2m)
Min£81 Max£174pw (Low)
Min£175 Max£276pw (High)

F   9 Strongs Passage The Old Town
for bookings The House of Brandon-
Bravo Ltd, Beauport Park, The Ridge,
Hastings, East Sussex TN37 7PP
☎Hastings(0424)53207 (reverse charges)
A modern ground-floor flat in an old town
300yds from beach and harbour.
Accommodation comprises lounge,
kitchen and a double-bedded room. Fitted
carpets and modern furnishings
throughout.

All year 1wk min, 3wks max, 1unit,
2persons, nc ◎ fridge ▥
Elec inclusive ⌷ not provided
☎(300yds) Iron & Ironing board in unit
[Launderette within 300yds] ⬢ CTV
⊕3pin square P ▥ ♨(300yds)
↔ ♪(3m) ♀(200yds) ♫(½m)
♬(½m) ☂(½m)
Min£97.75 Max£155.25pw

HATCH BEAUCHAMP
Somerset
Map3 ST32

C CC Ref 849
for bookings Character Cottages
(Holidays) Ltd, 34 Fore Street, Sidmouth,
Devon EX10 8AQ
☎Sidmouth(03955)77001

An attractive thatched cottage built of
Somerset stone comprising kitchen,
lounge with Parkray fire, dining room and
ground floor WC. There are three
bedrooms and bathroom/WC on the first
floor.

All year MWB out of season 1wk min,
1mth max, 1unit, 1–5persons no pets
◎ fridge Electric Elec metered
⌷ not provided ☎(½m) Iron & Ironing
board in unit ⊕ CTV ⊕3pin square
3P ▥ ♨(400yds)
↔ ♀(200yds)
Min£86 Max£129pw (Low)
Min£160 Max£198pw (High)

C CC Ref 886P
for bookings Character Cottages Ltd, 34
Fore Street, Sidmouth, Devon EX10 8AQ
☎Sidmouth(03955)77001

Detached cottage with well kept garden.
Accommodation comprises lounge, dining
room with kitchen off, one double
bedroom and one bedroom with two
children's beds plus bunk beds and
bathroom/WC.

All year MWB out of season 3days min,
2mths max, 1unit, 5persons ◈ ◆ ◎
fridge Storage heaters & fires
Elec metered ⌷ not provided
☎(100yds) Iron & Ironing board in unit
⊕ CTV ⊕3pin square 2P ▥
♨(500yds) Horse riding locally
↔ ♀(100yds)
Min£91 Max£155pw

HATFIELD
Hertfordshire
Map4 TL20

F Chantry Court Flats Woods Avenue
for bookings Mrs S Benn, Accommodation
Office, The Hatfield Polytechnic, PO Box
109, Hatfield, Hertfordshire AL10 9AB
☎Hatfield(07072)79062

Modern, well-equipped flats used during
Polytechnic summer vacation and
comprising compact kitchen units, living
room, bathroom/WC and either one or two
bedrooms. Extra beds are available in the
larger units. Clean, simple decor.

11Jul–5Sep MWB in season 1wk min,
2½mths max, 16units, 1–6persons ◈

Hastings
—
Hawes

no pets ◎ fridge ▥ Elec inclusive
⌷ inclusive ☎(20yds) Iron on
premises Ironing board in unit CTV
⊕3pin square 45P ▥ ♨(½m)
↔ ♀ ♫
Min£100 Max£125pw

HATHERLEIGH
Devon
Map2 SS50

C Motcombe Cottage 23 Bridge Street
for bookings Mrs P M Sutton, Jubilee
Cottage, Exbourne, Okehampton, Devon
EX20 3RX
☎Exbourne(083785)292

Delightfully modernised cottage in olde-
worlde village with lounge/diner
(inglenook fireplace), kitchen, two
bedrooms, one with three singles and one
with two, bathroom and WC. Enter
Hatherleigh by A386 from Okehampton,
Motcombe Cottage is on right.

Apr–Oct 1wk min, 1mth max, 1unit,
2–5persons no pets [◇] ◈ ◆
fridge Electric Elec metered ⌷ can be
hired ☎(50yds) WM & SD in unit Iron &
Ironing board in unit ⊕ TV
⊕3pin square ⊕2pin round P ▥ ♨
↔ ♀ ♫ ♬
Min£55 Max£65pw (Low)
Min£70 Max£100pw (High)

HAUGH OF URR
Dumfries & Galloway *Kirkcudbrightshire*
Map11 NX86

B Kabria
for bookings G M Thomson & Co, 27 King
Street, Castle Douglas, Kirkcudbrightshire
DG7 1AB
☎Castle Douglas(0556)2701 & 2973

Modern bungalow with its own garden
and open outlook from lounge. It is well
maintained, homely and comprises three
bedrooms, large comfortable lounge with
patio and dining area off, a spacious
kitchen and bathroom. It lies in the village
which is off A75 between Dumfries and
Castle Douglas.

Mar–Nov MWB out of season 1wk min,
1unit, 1–7persons ◈ ◎ fridge ▥ &
open fire Elec inclusive ⌷ not provided
☎(50yds) SD in unit Iron & Ironing
board in unit ⊕ CTV ⊕3pin square
⊕3pin round P ⌂ ♨(100yds)
↔ ♀(200yds)
Min£100 Max£200pw

HAVERFORDWEST
Dyfed
Map2 SM91

H Mrs G Warren **Dreenhill Farm** Dale
Road, Haverfordwest, Dyfed SA62 3XG
☎Haverfordwest(0437)4494

A wing of the farmhouse allocated for
guests, well furnished and appointed,
comprising living/dining room and kitchen
on the ground floor with two bedrooms
and bathroom on the first floor. The living
room and bedrooms overlook the lawn
and gardens to the fields. The farm lies
2½m from the centre of Haverfordwest.

All year MWB out of season 1wk min,
1unit, 1–5persons ◈ ◆ no pets
◎ fridge ▥ Elec inclusive
⌷ inclusive ☎ WM in unit TD on
premises Iron & Ironing board in unit
⊙ CTV ⊕3pin square 2P ▥
↔ ♀(200yds)
Min£70 Max£145pw

C Rogeston Cottages
for bookings Mr & Mrs J D Rees, Rogeston,
Portfield Gate, Haverfordwest, Dyfed
SA62 3LH
☎Broad Haven(043783)373

A charming conversion from farm
buildings, the cottages are equipped to a
high standard with maximum use made of
natural materials. They comprise open
plan timbered living/dining area with
kitchen, pine clad shower room with WC,
one twin-bedded room with continental
quilts plus a bed-settee in the lounge.
Each unit has a patio.

All year MWB out of season (Nov–Mar)
2nights min, 5 units, 4persons [◇] ◈
◆ no pets ◎ fridge ▥
Elec inclusive ⌷ inclusive ☎(1m) Iron
& Ironing board in unit [Launderette on
premises] ⊙ CTV ⊕3pin square
10P ▥ ♨(2m)
↔ ♀(1½m)
Min£51 Max£110pw (Low)
Min£164 Max£245pw (High)

F Old Granary Apartments
for bookings Mr & Mrs J D Rees, Rogeston,
Portfield Gate, Haverfordwest, Dyfed
SA62 3LH
☎Broad Haven(043783)373

Spacious, bright, comfortable apartments
on ground- and first-floor level. Sitting/
dining room, kitchen and three bedrooms
and bathroom/WC. Private patio with
each unit. Delightful views.

All year MWB out of season (Nov–Mar)
2nights min, 2units, 2–6persons [◇]
◈ ◆ no pets ◎ fridge ▥
Elec inclusive ⌷ inclusive ☎(1m) Iron
& Ironing board in unit [Launderette on
premises] ⊙ CTV ⊕3pin square
10P ▥ ♨(2m)
↔ ♀(1½m)
Min£57 Max£164pw (Low)
Min£189 Max£308pw (High)

HAWES
North Yorkshire
Map7 SD88

C Beckside & Dyers Cottages Dyers
Garth
for bookings Mr J N Wiseman, 37 Charles
Street, Blackpool, Lancashire
☎Blackpool(0253)28936(day)
& 43471(evening) →

Two stone-built modernised cottages situated off the main street alongside Duerley Beck in this picturesque village. **Beckside** comprises living room, kitchen/dinette and two first-floor bedrooms. **Dyers** has lounge, kitchen and one first-floor bedroom which is reached via a spiral staircase.

All year MWB out of season 2units, 2–5persons ◆ ◎ fridge Electric & open fire Elec metered ☐not provided ☎(50yds) Iron & Ironing board in unit ☉ TV ⊕3pin square 1P Beckside only ♨(50yds)

↤ ♨ (100yds)

Min£45 Max£140pw

C Brunskill Cottage
for bookings Mrs B A Stott, Shaw Ghyll Farm, Simonstone, Hawes, N Yorks DL8 3LY
☎Hawes(09697)359

Stone-built 17th-century cottage comprising one twin and one double bedroom with additional single bed. Ground floor; bathroom/WC, small living room and separate kitchen. Authentic beam ceilings. Quiet position in rural surroundings at head of Wensleydale.

All year MWB out of season 2days min (out of season) 1mth max, 1unit, 1–5persons ◆ ◆ ◎ fridge Electric Elec metered ☐can be hired ☎(500yds) SD in unit Iron & Ironing board in unit ☉ CTV ⊕3pin square P ▥ ♨(2m)

↤ ♨ (500yds) ♬(2m)

Min£65 Max£85pw (Low)
Min£88 Max£115pw (High)

C Greystones Cottage
for bookings Mrs Brenda Stott, Shaw Ghyll Farm, Simonstone, Hawes, N Yorks DL8 3LY
☎Hawes(09697)359

An attractive cottage which has been converted so that the lounge and kitchen/diner are upstairs, thus making the most of the views of Staggs Fell. The ground floor comprises two bedrooms, extra space is provided and convertible settee in the lounge. Delightfully furnished throughout to a high degree.

All year MWB out of season 1wk min, 1unit, 2–6persons ◆ ◆ ◎ fridge ╫ Elec metered ☐can be hired ☎(500yds) WM & SD in unit Iron & Ironing board in unit ☉ CTV ⊕3pin square 2P ▥ ♨(2m)

↤ ♨ (500yds)

Min£68 Max£98pw (Low)
Min£105 Max£140pw (High)

Hawes
—
Haworth

H High Shaw Farmhouse
for bookings Mrs B A Stott, Shaw Ghyll Farm, Simonstone, Hawes, N Yorks DL8 3LY
☎Hawes(09697)359

An 18th-century stone-built farmhouse which has been completely modernised, set in open countryside with views across Stags Fell. Accommodation comprises four bedrooms with various combinations of beds, kitchen, dining room and a pleasant lounge complete with piano.

All year MWB out of season 2days min, 1unit, 2–10persons ◆ ◆ ◎ fridge Electric Elec metered ☐can be hired ☎(½m) WM & SD in unit Iron & Ironing board in unit ☉ CTV ⊕3pin square 4P ▥ ♨(2m)

↤ ♨ (500yds)

Min£75 Max£110pw (Low)
Min£120 Max£180pw (High)

C Stags Fell Cottage
for bookings Mrs Brenda Stott, Shaw Ghyll Farm, High Shaw, Simonstone, Hawes, N Yorks DL8 3LY
☎Hawes(09697)359

Designed to be all on one level this cottage is ideal for disabled visitors. Accommodation comprises spacious lounge, kitchen tiled bathroom and two bedrooms, all delightfully furnished throughout.

All year MWB out of season 1wk min, 1unit, 2–5persons ◆ ◆ ♂ fridge ╫ Gas & Elec metered ☐can be hired ☎(500yds) WM & SD in unit Iron & Ironing board in unit ☉ CTV ⊕3pin square 2P ▥ ♨(2m)

↤ ♨ (500yds)

Min£68 Max£95pw (Low)
Min£98 Max£130pw (Low)

HAWKSHEAD
Cumbria
Map**7** SD39

H & F Rogerground House
for bookings Mrs I G Mackie, 2 Rowanside, Prestbury, Macclesfield, Cheshire SK10 4BE
☎Prestbury(0625)828624

In a quiet hamlet, surrounded by lovely walled gardens and orchards. A Tudor cottage, 17th-century farmhouse and converted barn provide quality holiday homes. They are comfortable and well-equipped while retaining their distinctive traditional character. Situated ⅓ mile from Hawkshead on high ground, the property enjoys fine views.

All year MWB out of season 1wk min, 6units, 2–8persons ◆ ◆ ◎ fridge ╫ Elec metered ☐not provided ☎(½m) SD on premises Drying room CTV ⊕3pin square 9P ▥ ♨(½m)

↤ ♨(½m)

Min£65 Max£180pw (Low)
Min£80 Max£245pw (High)

Ch Mrs Evans **Ramsteads Coppice** (1m E B5286) Outgate, Hawkshead, Ambleside, Cumbria LA22 0NH
☎Hawkshead(09666)583 & 051-428 2605

Six timber-clad chalets of good design in 15 acres of mature deciduous woodland, 2m N of Hawkshead. Three of the chalets have two bedrooms while the other three chalets have three bedrooms. They all have lounge, kitchen and bathroom.

Mar–Oct MWB out of season 1wk min, 6units, 2–6persons no pets ◆ ◆ Calor gas fridge Electric Gas/Elec inclusive ☐not provided ☎(½m) ☉ ⊕3pin square P 1▥ ♨(2m)

Min£82 Max£162pw

HAWORTH
West Yorkshire
Map**7** SE03

H 3 Main Street Stanbury
for bookings Mrs M Lund, Cross Farm, Stanbury, Keighley, West Yorkshire BD22 0HA

A delightful old world beamed detached cottage sympathetically modernised, situated in an attractive village surrounded by moorland. The accommodation includes lounge, cloakroom, kitchen/dining area, three bedrooms, bathroom/WC and shower room en suite. 1m W on unclass road.

Mar–Dec MWB out of season 7days min, 1mth max, 1unit, 2–6persons ◆ ◆ no pets ◎ fridge ╫ Elec metered ☐inclusive Iron & Ironing board in unit ☉ CTV ⊕3pin square 1▥ ▥ ♨(100yds)

↤ ♨ (100yds) Horse riding(2m)

Min£55 Max£80pw (Low)
Min£85 Max£110pw (High)

H 5 Stanbury
for bookings Mrs H M Holroyd, Greenacres, Moorhouse Lane, Oxenhope, Keighley, W Yorks BD22 9RY
☎Haworth(0535)42787

A solid stone-built semi-detached house with very good furnishings throughout.

There are four bedrooms, one double, two twins and one single, a bathroom and WC, lounge and kitchen.

All year MWB out of season 7days min, 1unit, 2–7persons ◊ ♦ ∂ fridge ∰ Gas/Elec metered ⬚inclusive ☎(½m) WM in unit Iron & Ironing board in unit ☺ CTV ⊕3pin square 1🏠 ⊞ ♨(200yds)
↩ ♪(2m) ☕(100yds) ♬(2m)
Min£60 Max£85pw (Low)
Min£75 Max£100pw (High)

H 55 Sun Street
for bookings Mrs Sunderland, Moor House, Oxenhope, Keighley, W Yorks
☎Haworth(0535)42421

A single fronted, two-storey, middle terraced cottage situated close to village amenities. Accommodation comprises living room leading to small rear garden, kitchen, one twin bedded and one single or bunk bedroom, as required and bathroom/WC. Ideal for touring Brontë country and dales.

All year 1wk min, 1unit, 2–4persons ◊ ♦ ◉ fridge ∰ Elec metered ⬚inclusive ☎ Iron & Ironing board in unit TV ⊕3pin square ⊞ ♨(200yds)
↩ ☕(100yds)

Details not confirmed for 1987

C 57 Sun Street
for bookings Mrs C A Ellison, 13 Hebden Bridge Road, Oxenhope, Keighley, W Yorks BD22 9OY
☎Haworth(0535)42283

One of a row of wool-workers cottages situated on the fringe of town. Accommodation comprises two bedrooms, one with bunk beds, lounge/diner, kitchen and bathroom/WC. Garden to rear.

All year MWB out of season 1wk min, 1mth max, 1unit, 1–4persons ◊ ♦ fridge Electric & gas fire Gas & Elec metered ⬚inclusive Iron & Ironing board in unit TV ⊕3pin square ⊞ ♨(500yds)
↩ ♪(2m) ☕(500yds)
Min£45 Max£65pw (Low)
Min£70 Max£90pw (High)

HAYLE
Cornwall
Map2 SW53

Ch & H Tolroy Holiday Village
for bookings Haven Leisure (ECC) Ltd, Haven House, Quay Street, Truro, Cornwall TR1 2UE
☎Truro(0872)40400

Set around walkways in grounds of a former country house are terraces of villas and brick and cedar built chalets. The villas comprise of open-plan living area, kitchen, shower room with separate WC, one double, one twin and one bunk-bedded room. The chalets have a lounge/

Haworth
—
Hebden Bridge

diner with bed-settee, kitchen area, one double and one twin bedroom and a bathroom with separate WC. The entertainment complex includes Squash Courts, Sauna, Solarium, lounge and children's bars and restaurant.

Etr–Sep MWB 3days min, 1mth max, 177units, 1–8persons [◊ ♦] no pets ◉ fridge Electric convector Elec metered ⬚inclusive ☎ [Iron on premises] Ironing board on premises [Launderette on premises] ☺ CTV ⊕3pin square P ♨ ≋(heated)
↩ ♨Hard ☕ ♫ ♬
Min£68 Max£199pw (Low)
Min£186 Max£296pw (High)

HAY-ON-WYE
Powys
Map3 SO24

C Rose Cottage Bronydd
for bookings Mrs D L Williams, Cabalva Farmhouse, Whitney-on-Wye, Herefordshire HR3 6EX
☎Clifford(04973)324

A stone-built cottage in elevated position with magnificent views across the River Wye, Black Mountains and Brecon Beacons. This recently renovated accommodation comprises lounge, dining room, kitchen, bathroom and two bedrooms (double and twin). Bronydd, 2½m N A348.

All year MWB out of season 2days min, 6wks max, 1unit, 1–5persons [◊] ◊ ♦ ◉ fridge Gas & electric fires Elec inclusive ⬚inclusive ☎(1m) Iron & Ironing board in unit ☺ CTV ⊕3pin square 3P ⊞ ♨(1m) Fishing ↩ ♪(3m) ☕(1m) ♫(1m) ♬(1m)
Details not confirmed for 1987

HAYSCASTLE
Dyfed
Map2 SW82

H Hayscastle Farm
for bookings Coastal Cottages of Pembrokeshire, Seaview, Abercastle, Mathry, Dyfed SA62 5HJ
☎Croesgoch(03483)7742

A spacious renovated farmhouse situated on a working farm in a peaceful location. It comprises large lounge with open fire, dining room, fitted kitchen, utility room with separate WC, three bedrooms with double and single beds, two twin bedrooms and one double bedroom and a large bathroom/WC.

All year MWB out of season 4days min, 2mths max, 1unit, 2–12persons ◊ ♦ pets by arrangement Gas fired Aga Cooker fridge ∰ Gas & Elec Metered ⬚inclusive ☎(1m) WM & SD in unit

---

Iron & Ironing board in unit ☺ CTV ⊕3pin square ℗ ♨(1m)
↩ ☕(1m)
Min£85 Max£395pw

HEBDEN
North Yorkshire
Map7 SE06

C, F & H Mrs J M Joy **Jerry & Bens**
Hebden, Skipton, North Yorkshire BD23 5DL
☎Grassington(0756)752369

Jerry & Bens are six converted properties on a privately-owned estate in Hebden Gill with its rocky crags, deciduous trees and picturesque waterfalls. **Cruck Rise** is situated 100yds up hill from the main building and sleeps up to six people in two bedrooms plus a bed-settee in the lounge. **High Close** is open plan with sitting area (incorporating bed-settee), kitchen, bathroom and sleeps seven to nine people. **Mamie's Cottage** sleeps 6–8 persons and comprises kitchen, sun lounge/dining room, lounge with bed-settee and wood burning stove, bathroom/WC. **Paradise End & Robin Middle** both sleep up to six people in two bedrooms plus two single bed-settees in the lounge. **Ghyll Cottage** is a large single-storey cottage of stone and timber comprising sitting room with open fire and bed-settee, galley kitchen and dining room, three bedrooms and bathroom/WC.

All year MWB out of season 1wk min, 6units, 1–9persons ◊ ◊ ◉ fridge Electric Elec metered ⬚can be hired ☎ [WM & SD on premises] Iron & Ironing board on premises CTV ⊕3pin square P ⊞(summer only) ♨(½m)
↩ ♨(1½m) ♫(1½m)
Min£46 Max£86pw (Low)
Min£80 Max£148pw (High)

HEBDEN BRIDGE
West Yorkshire
Map7 SD92

C Mrs J Soothill **Great Burlees Farm**
Hebden Bridge, West Yorkshire HX7 8PS
☎Hebden Bridge(0422)843382

Two cottages, part of a 17th-century stone-built farmhouse with beamed ceilings and mullioned windows. Each cottage has two bedrooms (one double and one twin), lounge, with extra bed space available, kitchen and bathroom. Situated on south facing hillside with views over the Pennines.

All year MWB out of season 3days min, 2units, 2–6persons ◊ ◊ no pets ◉ fridge Electric & open fires Elec metered ⬚inclusive Iron & Ironing board in unit ☺ TV ⊕3pin square 10P ⊞ ♨(1m)
↩ ♪(½m) ☕(½m) ⛏(1m)
Min£45 Max£55pw (Low)
Min£110 Max£125pw (High)

HELENSBURGH

Strathclyde *Dunbartonshire* Map**10** NS28

F   The Hill House (No.3 Flat) 8 Upper Colquhoun Street
for bookings The Landmark Trust, Shottesbrooke, Maidenhead, Berkshire SL6 3SW ☎Littlewick Green(062882)5925

No.3 Flat is on the second floor of the Hill House with access by a steep spiral staircase. Accommodation consists of kitchen/diner, the School Room – an expansive sitting room, three twin bedrooms and bathroom. The unit is spacious and full of character and furnished to a high standard featuring some of the original Charles Rennie Mackintosh furnishing.

All year   MWB out of season   2 nights min, 1 unit, 1 – 6 persons ◆ no pets ◎ fridge 🍴 & gas fire   Gas & Elec inclusive 🔲not provided ☎(1m)   Iron & Ironing board in unit ☺ ⊕3pin square ⊕3pin round   1P 🏛(1m)
↩ ♪(1½m) 🚻(1m) 🎬(1m) 🎵(1m)
Min£77 Max£165pw (Low)
Min£85 Max£175pw (High)

HELLANDBRIDGE

Cornwall Map**2** SX07

B   Bungalows 1 – 5
for bookings Mr & Mrs A Goggs, Silverstream, Hellandbridge, Bodmin, Cornwall ☎Bodmin(0208)4408

Five attractive cedar-wood bungalows in idyllic surroundings by River Camel. Accommodation comprises lounge/diner, kitchen, bathroom and separate WC, and either two or three bedrooms.

Apr – Oct   MWB out of season   1wk min, 1mth max, 5units, 1 – 6 persons [◆ ◆]
◎ fridge   Storage heaters   Electric   Elec metered 🔲can be hired ☎(1m) Iron on premises   Ironing board in unit ☺ TV ⊕3pin square   2P 🎬
🏛(1½m)   Private trout fishing ↩ 🚻(2½m)
Min£75 Max£92pw (Low)
Min£98 Max£160pw (High)
See advertisement under Bodmin

F & C   Mr & Mrs K G Jones **The Grange** Helland, Bodmin, Cornwall PL30 4PY ☎Bodmin(0208)2249

The Barn, Sycamore, Honeysuckle, Swallows Nest, Primrose & Meadow View Cottages all comprise kitchen, lounge/diner with bed-settee, bathroom/WC, one double bedroom and one with either bunk or twin beds. The Loft has lounge, kitchen/diner, shower/WC and one double bedroom. The Granary has lounge, kitchen/diner, shower/WC and one double bedroom, one double with bunk beds and a further room with bunks. Grange Flat comprises lounge, kitchen, shower/WC and a twin-bedded room. Croft Cottage has an open-plan lounge/diner with kitchen area and bed-settee, one double room, one bunk-bedded room and shower/WC.

All year (self-catering only Nov – Mar)
MWB   3days min, 1mth max, 10units

Helensburgh
—
Helstone

1 – 10 persons ◆ ◆ ◎ fridge   Electric   Elec metered 🔲inclusive ☎(50yds)   Iron & Ironing board on premises   [Launderette on premises]
☺ CTV ⊕3pin square P 🎬 🏛 ⌂ Children's play area. Games room, paddling pool, video, meals ↩ 🚻
Details not confirmed for 1987

C   Horseshoe Cottage
for bookings Mr & Mrs A Goggs, Silverstream, Hellandbridge, Bodmin, Cornwall PL30 4QR ☎Bodmin(0208)4408

Attractive stone cottage in idyllic setting on the banks of River Camel. Accommodation comprises kitchen, lounge/diner with open fire, bathroom, separate WC, one double- and one twin-bedded.

All year   MWB out of season   1wk min, 1mth max, 1 unit, 1 – 4 persons [◆ ◆]
◎ fridge 🍴(Oil & Electric)
Elec metered 🔲can be hired ☎(1m)
Iron on premises   Ironing board in unit ☺ TV ⊕3pin square   2P 🎬
🏛(1½m)   Private trout fishing
Min£75 Max£123pw (Low)
Min£144 Max£175pw (High)
See advertisement under Bodmin

HELLIFIELD

North Yorkshire Map**7** SD85

C   Rook Cottage Gisburn Road
for bookings Mrs J Richardson, 563 Gisburn Road, Blacko, Nelson, Lancashire ☎Nelson(0282)66122

An attractive old world cottage, now a listed building. All rooms are at ground level and comprise kitchen/diner, comfortable lounge, one double, one twin and one single bedroom, and modern bathroom. Located in the centre of the village.

All year   MWB   3mths max, 1unit, 2 – 5 persons ◆ ◆ ◎ fridge   Electric fires   Elec metered 🔲can be hired ☎(50yds)   Iron & Ironing board in unit ☺ CTV ⊕3pin square   2P 🎬
🏛(50yds) ↩ 🚻(50yds) 🎵(50yds)
£54pw (Low) Min£90 Max£130pw (High)

HELMSLEY

North Yorkshire Map **8** SE68

C   Bank Cottage
for bookings Mrs Armstrong, Golden Square Farm, Oswaldkirk, York, North Yorkshire YO6 5YQ ☎Ampleforth(04393)269

Charming 17th-century cottage with original fittings and having four bedrooms, lounge, kitchen and bathroom/WC. Sproxton 1½m south A170.

All year   MWB out of season   1wk min, 3wks max, 1unit, 1 – 7 persons ◆ ◎ fridge   Electric & open fires

---

Elec metered 🔲can be hired ☎(250yds)   WD & SD in unit   Iron & Ironing board in unit   CTV ⊕3pin square ⊕3pin round   2P 1🏛 🎬
🏛(1½m) ↩ 🚻(1½m)
Min£35 Max£75(Low)
Min£55 Max£140(High)

C   Mrs M Begg **Townend Farmhouse (Cottage)**, Beadlam, Nawton, Helmsley, North Yorkshire YO6 5SY
☎Helmsley(0439)71617

A modernised farm cottage with the original stone walls and beams a feature. Accommodation comprises a comfortable lounge/diner, spacious kitchen/breakfast room, one twin bedroom and one double bedroom and a modern bathroom. Situated just off the A170 three miles east of Helmsley.

All year   MWB out of season   2days min, 1unit, 4persons ◆ ◆ ◎ fridge 🍴open fires & electric heaters   Gas inclusive   Elec metered 🔲can be hired ☎(200yds)   WM & SD in unit   Iron & Ironing board in unit ☺ CTV ⊕3pin square   2P 🎬 🏛(300yds)
↩ ♪(3m) 🚻(200yds)

HELSTON

Cornwall Map**2** SW62

B   Mr G R Goodere **Greenacres Holiday Bungalows** Clodgey Lane, Helston, Cornwall TR13 8PN
☎Helston(0326)572620

Twelve semi-detached cedar and block built chalets of conventional design. Secluded site with lawns, trees and shrubs. Each contains one twin and one double bedroom, lounge/diner with kitchen area off, either a single or double studio couch, bathroom and WC. Clean and modern accommodation.

Apr – Sep   MWB   4days min, 12units, 1 – 6 persons ◆ ◆ no single sex groups ◎ fridge   Electric   Elec metered 🔲inclusive ☎ [Launderette within 300yds]   Iron & Ironing board in unit ☺ CTV ⊕3pin square P 🎬 🏛(200yds)
↩ ♪(3m) 🚻(1m) 🎬(1m) 🎵(1m)
🚻(1m)   Sports centre(1m)
Min£55 Max£125pw (Low)
Min£115 Max£200pw (High)

HELSTONE

Cornwall Map**2** SX18

C   Saddlers, Toadstools, Waggoners & Wheelers Cottages
for bookings Mr C F Ahrens, Mayrose Farm, Helstone, Camelford, Cornwall ☎Camelford(0840)213507

Waggoners has two bedrooms and lounge. Wheelers has three bedrooms, one with bunk beds and lounge with woodburning stove. Toadstools has three bedrooms, one with bunks and lounge. Saddlers has three bedrooms, one with bunks, served by an internal slate

---

staircase, and lounge. All cottages have kitchen area and bathroom.

Closed Jan   MWB out of season
3days min, 1mth max, 4units, 1 – 6persons
◇ ◆ ◎ fridge Electric
Elec metered Ⓛcan be hired ☎(½m)
Iron & Ironing board in unit ☺ CTV
☺3pin square 8P Ⅲ ♨(½m) Dinner & breakfast available on request

⊖ ♀(1m) ⌷⌹(3m) ♫(3m)

Min£50 Max£145pw (Low)
Min£185 Max£245pw (High)

See advertisement under Camelford

HEMSBY
Norfolk
Map**9** TG41

Ch   Belle Aire Chalet Site Beach Road
for bookings Mrs R Lawrence, 30 Cutcliffe Grove, Bedford MK40 4DD
☎Bedford(0234)56331

Located on a large site which is on sloping grassland 700 yards from the beach. The chalets have two or three bedrooms, sleeping up to five, with an additional convertible settee in the lounge. All have shower/WC.

Mar – Oct   MWB   3days min, 3wks max,
11units, 1 – 7persons [◇ ◆] ◎
fridge Electric Elec inclusive
Ⓛinclusive ☎ Iron on premises
[Launderette within 300yds] CTV
☺3pin square 20P ♨(200yds)

⊖ ♀(300yds) ⌷⌹(300yds) ♫(300yds)

Min£42 Max£95pw (Low)
Min£85 Max£139pw (High)

Ch   Bermuda Holiday Park
for bookings Mr W Lawrence, 30 Cutcliffe Grove, Bedford MK40 4DD
☎Bedford(0234)56331

Modern terraced cottages on a large seaside estate, 800 yards from the beach. Accommodation comprises lounge/diner with alcoved kitchen, bathroom/WC and three bedrooms, one with bunks.

Mar – Oct   MWB out of season   3days min,
3wks max, 15units, 1 – 6persons[◇ ◆]
no dogs ◎ fridge Electric
Elec metered Ⓛinclusive
☎[Launderette on premises] ☺ CTV
☺3pin square ♨ Sauna & solarium
Clubhouse

⊖ ♀ ⌷⌹ ♫

Min£42 Max£99pw (Low)
Min£82 Max£150pw (High)

Ch   Excelsior, Sundowner Holiday Park
Newport Road, Newport Beach
for bookings Hoseasons Holidays,
Sunway House, Lowestoft, Suffolk
NR32 3LT
☎Lowestoft(0502)62271

Purpose-built timber chalets, with accommodation comprising a two bunk-bedded room, double-bedded room, compact lounge/kitchen/dining room, shower and separate WC.

Apr – Sep   MWB out of season   3days min,
2units, 2 – 6persons [◇ ◆] ◎
fridge Electric Elec metered

Helstone
—
Hereford

Ⓛinclusive ☎ [Iron on premises]
[Launderette on premises] ☺ CTV
☺3pin square P ♨(200yds) ▱
⊖ ♀(½m) ⌷⌹(½m) ♫(1m)
Min£50 Max£140pw

Ch   Haiti, Sundowner Holiday Park
Newport Road, Newport Beach
for bookings Hoseasons Holidays,
Sunway House, Lowestoft, Suffolk
NR32 3LT
☎Lowestoft(0502)62271

Timber and brick-built semi-detached chalets with two twin-bedded rooms, one double, kitchen, lounge, bathroom/WC.

Apr – Sep   MWB out of season   3days min,
12units, 2 – 8persons [◇ ◆] ◎
fridge Electric Elec metered ☎ [Iron on premises] [Launderette on premises]
☺ CTV ☺3pin square P ♨(200yds)
▱
⊖ ♀(½m) ⌷⌹(½m) ♫(1m)
Min£65 Max£170pw

Ch   Hemsby Beach Chalet Centre
Beach Road
for bookings Hoseasons Holidays,
Sunway House, Lowestoft, Suffolk
NR32 3LT
☎Lowestoft(0502)62271

Spacious chalet park extending over 14 acres of lawns and only 300yds from the beach. Chalets are designed to sleep two to six people in either one or two bedrooms; all have a double studio couch in lounge area and shower/WC.

Apr – Sep   MWB out of season   3days min,
224units, 2 – 6persons [◇ ◆] ◎
fridge Electric Elec inclusive
Ⓛinclusive ☎ [Iron & Ironing board on premises] Launderette on premises
CTV ☺3pin square P ♨ ▱
⊖ ♀ ⌷⌹ ♫
Min£38 Max£156pw

Ch   Sunbeam & Sunshine, Sundowner Holiday Park Newport Road, Newport Beach
for bookings Hoseasons Holidays,
Sunway House, Lowestoft, Suffolk
NR32 3LT
☎Lowestoft(0502)62271

Timber and brick-built semi-detached chalets on a well-maintained site comprising one twin and one double-bedded room, lounge/kitchen, combined bathroom/WC and small patio area.

Apr – Sep   MWB out of season   3days min,
90units, 2 – 6persons [◇ ◆] ◎
fridge Electric Elec metered
Ⓛinclusive ☎ [Iron on premises]
[Launderette on premises] ☺ CTV
☺3pin square P ♨(200yds)
⊖ ♀(½m) ⌷⌹(½m) ♫(1m)
Min£55 Max£150pw

HEMYOCK
Devon
Map**3** ST11

H   CC Ref 684
for bookings Character Cottages
(Holidays) Ltd, 34 Fore Street, Sidmouth,
Devon EX10 8AQ
☎Sidmouth(03955)77001

An attractive modernised farmhouse in an isolated position close to Hemyock village. A high standard of furnishing. Accommodation comprises kitchen, utility room, children's playroom, dining room, lounge, shower room, two bathroom/WCs and five double bedrooms.

All year   MWB out of season   1wk min,
2mths max, 1unit, 10persons ◆ ◆
no pets ◎ fridge Electric inclusive
except heating Ⓛnot provided ☎ WM
& SD in unit   Iron & Ironing board in unit
☺ TV ☺3pin square P Ⅲ ♨(2m)
⊖ ♀(2m)
Min£108 Max£203pw (Low)
Min£243 Max£405pw (High)

HENLLAN-AMGOED
Dyfed
Map**2** SN21

H & C   Henllan Farmhouse & Y-Bwthyn
for bookings Mr & Mrs E J T Davies,
Caeremlyn Farm, Henllan-Amgoed,
Whitland, Dyfed
☎Whitland(0994)240260

Excellently converted Farmhouse comprising on the ground floor spacious lounge with beamed ceiling, open plan diner and kitchen, and separate shower/WC; on the first floor, bathroom/WC, one bunk bedded room, three double and one twin bedded room. Originally a workers cottage, Y-Bwthyn adjoins the farmhouse and comprises on the ground floor shower/WC, kitchen/diner, one twin and one double bedded room; on the first floor is a galleried lounge with stone fireplace. Farm produce is available and there are cows to milk, calves to feed and a reliable pony for young children.

All year   MWB out of season   4days min,
6wks max, 2units, 2 – 12persons [◇]
◆ ◆ ◎ & microwave oven   fridge
♨(gas) Gas/Elec metered Ⓛinclusive
☎(½m) [WM, SD & TD on premises] Iron
& Ironing board in unit ☺ ☺ CTV
☺3pin square P Ⅲ ♨(2½m)
Snooker, table tennis, rough shooting,
farm involvement
⊖ ♀(1m)
Min£117   Max£441pw

HEREFORD
Hereford & Worcester
Map**3** SO54

C   Mrs V Beaumont Poolspringe Farm
Much Birch, Hereford, Herefordshire
HR2 8JJ
☎Golden Valley(0981)540355

A recently converted 17th-century barn retaining many original oak beams and→

now incorporating four compact holiday cottages. **Rose** sleeps four, **Honeysuckle** sleeps six and **Cider Mill** and **Granery** sleeps two. All cottages have open plan kitchen/diner, lounge area and bathroom. **Stable Cottage** actually adjoins the farmhouse and comprises lounge/dining area, bathroom and kitchen on the ground floor and one double bedroom with wash hand basin and second bedroom with three single beds on the first floor. Use of pool, sauna and solarium.

All year   MWB out of season   2 days min, 6 wks max, 5 units, 1–6 persons ◇ ◆ ◎ fridge   Electric fire   Elec metered ⌷ can be hired ☎ [WM, SD & TD on premises]   Iron & Ironing board in unit ☺ CTV ⊕3pin square P ▥ ▨(1m) ⛵ Canoe, pool table, children's play area

⊖ ♨(1m) ♬(1m) ♪(1m)

Min£60 Max£160pw

H   Tupsley Court Cottage
for bookings Mrs R J Eaton, Hallaton House, 27 Hafod Road, Hereford HR1 1SG
☎Hereford(0432)55754
Situated on a farm, this modern house offers accommodation comprising of kitchen/diner, lounge, bathroom and three bedrooms. Garden area available to guests.

All year   MWB out of season   2 days min, 6 wks max, 1 unit, 1–6 persons ◇ no pets ◎ fridge ♨ Electric & open fires   Elec metered ⌷ can be hired (overseas visitors only) ☎(100yds)   Iron & Ironing board in unit   CTV ⊕3pin square 3P ▥ ▨(½m)

⊖ ♨(2m) ♨(100yds) ♬(3m) ♪(3m)

Min£60 Max£90pw

HEWISH
Avon
Map**3** ST46

C & F   Mr & Mrs S H Peatling **Doubleton Farm Cottages** Hewish, Weston-Super-Mare, Avon BS24 6RB
☎Yatton(0934)833304

Doubleton Farm is ideally situated for the resort and for touring the countryside. There is a charming rural atmosphere

Hereford
—
Holbeton

here, the farmhouse itself dating back to around 1720. The stables, hay lofts and outbuildings have recently been imaginatively converted to holiday cottages variously tailored for couples and families of all sizes. Comfortable accommodation offering lounge, kitchen or kitchen/diner, bath or shower room with WC and two or three bedrooms.

All year   1 night min, 12 units, 2–8 persons ◇ ◎ fridge   Electric   Elec metered ⌷ inclusive(ex towels) ☎(1m)   Iron & Ironing board on premises ☺ CTV ⊕3pin square 20P ▨(1m)

⊖ ♨(3m) ♨(1m) ♬(3m) ⛾(3m)

Min£40 Max£60pw (Low)
Min£89 Max£200pw (High)

HIGH LORTON
Cumbria
Map**11** NY12

C   Kirkfell Cottage
for bookings K W Burton, Kirkfell House, High Lorton, Cumbria CA13 9TX
☎Lorton(090085)689
A detached cottage in this tiny village, nestling in the Buttermere Valley. It comprises lounge, dining room, kitchen, two first-floor twin-bedded rooms, bathroom and WC.

All year   MWB out of season   2 nights min, 1 unit, 2–4 persons ◇ ◆ ◎ fridge ♨ [Elec] ⌷ inclusive   Iron & Ironing board in unit ☺ CTV ⊕3pin square P ▥ ▨(½m)

⊖ ♨(¼m)

Min£95 Max£170pw (Low)
Min£135 Max£195pw (High)

HILLBERRY
See **Man, Isle of**

HINDRINGHAM
Norfolk
Map**9** TF93

C   58 & 60 Lower Green
for bookings Mrs P Forrest, 195 East End Road, London N2 0LZ
☎01-883 8137
Semi-detached traditional brick and flint cottages partly dating from the 17th century. Accommodation comprises: **No 58** – downstairs lounge, kitchen and bathroom/WC, one twin-bedded room and one double-bedded room with wash hand basin; **No 60** – downstairs lounge, kitchen and cloakroom/WC and wash-basin, one double-bedded room, one twin-bedded room with wash hand basin, one bunk-bedded room and bathroom/WC.

Mar–Dec   MWB   3 days min, 6 mths max, 2 units, 1–6 persons [◇] ◆ ◎ fridge   Electric   heating included Elec metered ⌷ not provided ☎(¼m) ⊕3pin square P ▨(1½m)   Children's playhouse

⊖ ♨(1½m)

Min£55 Max£85pw (Low)
Min£80 Max£205pw (High)

H   The Windmill Mill Lane
for bookings Mrs P Forrest, 195 East End Road, London N2 0LZ
☎01-883 8137
A tower mill which has been carefully restored and converted so that externally it resembles a working mill without sails and has a Norfolk boat shaped cap. On the first floor there is a dining room, kitchen and cloakroom. On the second floor, a lounge, and on the third, one double bedroom and a bathroom. On the fourth floor there is one twin-bedded room, a bunk-bedded room on the fifth, and one single bedroom on the sixth. Located on outskirts of village.

Mar–Dec   MWB   3 days min, 6 mths max, 1 unit, 1–8 persons [◇] ◆ ◎ fridge   Electric   Elec metered ⌷ not provided ☎(½m) ☺ ⊕3pin square P ▨(1½m)

⊖ ♨(1½m)

Min£90 Max£165pw (Low)
Min£180 Max£315pw (High)

HOLBETON
Devon
Map**2** SX65

Pennoxstone Court Holiday Flat. Herefordshire.
Spacious, well-equipped flat in period country house and Fruit Farm in beautiful Wye Valley near Ross-on-Wye. Lovely situation and views. Many local places of interest, and Cotswolds and Welsh hills within comfortable reach. Coarse fishing. Moderate terms.
Brochure from Capt. and Mrs. J F Cockburn, Pennoxstone Court, Kings Caple, Herefordshire. Telephone Carey 284.

LAKE DISTRICT
These delightful cottages in the peaceful village of High Lorton have been carefully modernised to provide comfortable and carefree holidays. They all have central heating, fitted carpets, Colour TV, electric blankets and everything else you could possibly need. Open all year from £80 to £190 weekly.
Brochure from Marion and Keith Burton, Kirkfell House, High Lorton, Cumbria, CA13 9TX. Telephone; Lorton (090 085) 689.

C Mrs J Baskerville **Keaton Farm, (Rose Cottage)**, Holbeton, Plymouth, Devon PL8 1HL
☎Holbeton(075530)255

Semi-detached cottage joining farmhouse in quiet country setting. Comprising compact kitchen, lounge, dining room, shower/WC, two bedrooms, one double and one twin, both with WHB, plus additional cot or Z-bed. Secluded garden and private beach.

All year MWB out of season 2days min, 4wks max, 1unit, 2–5persons ◇ ◆
◆ no pets ◉ fridge night storage Elec inclusive ⬜not provided ☎(½m) WM & SD in unit Iron & Ironing board in unit ⊙ CTV ⊕3pin square 2P ⊞ ▥(2m)
⊶ ⬧ (2m)
Min£80 Max£150pw

HOLLYBUSH
Strathclyde *Ayrshire*
Map**10** NS31

H Mrs C Henderson **Holiday Homes**
Skeldon Caravans, Hollybush, Ayr, Ayrshire KA6 7EB
☎Dalrymple(029256)580

Two semi-detached cottages in a picturesque setting on the banks of the River Doon. Accommodation comprises two bedrooms (one double, one with three single beds), lounge with double bed settee, kitchenette and shower unit. Adjacent to a small caravan park and use of all its facilities are available.

Apr–Sep MWB out of season 1wk min, 2units, 1–6persons ◇ ◆ ◉
Electric Elec inclusive ⬜not provided ☎(½m) TV ⊙ ⊕3pin square P ⊞ ▥(100yds)
⊶ ⬧(¾m)
Min£70 Max£150pw

HOLNEST
Dorset
Map**3** ST60

F A J & A F Claypole **Manor Farm Country House** Holnest Park, Holnest, Sherborne, Dorset DT9 6HA
☎Holnest(096321)474

Blackmore Vale on the ground floor and Cloudcroft on the first floor both comprise lounge/diner, kitchen, two double and one twin bedroom, bathroom/WC and separate WC. Cloudcroft is reached by outside staircase and has a balcony. Grooms Cottage on the ground floor of the west wing has lounge and kitchen/diner, put-u-up in the lounge, three bedrooms and bathroom/WC. Russet on

---

Holbeton
—
Honiton

the first floor has lounge/diner, kitchen, one double bedroom with en suite bathroom and another double and twin bedded room that share a bathroom/WC. Tulip Trees on the ground floor has one double and one twin-bedded room with wash hand basin, kitchen, large lounge/dining room, with double put-u-up, bathroom/WC.

Apr–Oct 1wk min, 2mth max, 5units, 2–8persons ◇ ◆ ◉ fridge ▥
Elec metered ⬜can be hired ☎(50yds & 100yds) [Launderette on premises] Iron & Ironing board on premises ⊙
CTV ⊕3pin square 20P ⊞ ▥(2½m)
Games room
⊶ ⬧(1½m)
Min£60 Max£155pw

HOLSWORTHY
Devon
Map**2** SS30

F Mr & Mrs C Clarke **Thorne Farm**
Holsworthy, Devon EX22 7JD
☎Holsworthy(0409)253342

A tasteful conversion of 10 flats from stone farm buildings offering well-equipped and comfortable accommodation. Goldfinch is on the ground floor comprising three double bedrooms, open-plan lounge/ diner, kitchen area and bathroom, WC. Eagles Lair is on the first floor and comprises lounge, kitchen/diner, two bedrooms and bathroom/WC. Crows Nest & Dovecote are both on the first floor, with balcony, comprising lounge/kitchen/diner, two double bedrooms and bathroom/WC. Curlew, Fieldfair, Linnet, Wagtail, Woodlark & Woodpecker each have open-plan lounge, kitchen, diner, two bedrooms and bathroom/WC.

mid Mar–mid Nov MWB out of season 3days min, 1mth max, 10units, 1–6persons ◇ [◆] ◉ fridge Electric Elec metered ⬜can be hired ☎ Iron & Ironing board on premises [Launderette on premises] ⊙ CTV ⊕3pin square P ⊞ ▥ ⌒ ♨Hard Games room & 2 squash courts Nature trail & reserve
⊶ δ(1½m) ⬧
Min£57.50 Max£180pw

HOLT
Norfolk
Map**9** TG03

C 1–8 **Carpenters Cottages** Carpenters Close, Norwich Road
for bookings Mr J P Siddall, Fell Dyke Cottage, Well Street, Langham, Oakham, Leicestershire LE15 7JS
☎Oakham(0572)56515

Early 18th-century terraced cottages built in traditional flint. Accommodation comprises lounge/kitchen, double-bedded room, single-bedded room and bathroom with WC. Located on edge of town.

All year MWB out of season 6wks max, 8units, 1–6persons ◇ ◇ ◆ ◉
fridge ▥ Elec metered ⬜can be hired ☎ SD in unit Iron & Ironing board in unit [Launderette within 300yds] ⊙ CTV ⊕3pin square P ⊞ ▥(100yds)
⊶ ⬧ (100yds)
Min£70 Max£120pw (Low)
Min£115 Max£210pw (High)

C **Owl Holiday Cottages** Obelisk Plain
for bookings Mrs J L Duffield, Jacob's House, High Street, Holt, Norfolk NR25 6BH
☎Holt(0263)713549

Two superbly-equipped brick and flint cottages in a private courtyard with large lawned garden at the side. Barn Owl has bathroom, lounge/diner, kitchen and two bedrooms, one with twin beds. Tawny Owl has kitchen/diner, lounge, bathroom and two bedrooms, one with bunks.

All year MWB out of season 3days min, 1mth max, 2units, 2–6persons [◇] ◆
◆ ◉ fridge ▥ & Electric
Elec metered ⬜inclusive ☎(300yds) WM & TD in unit Iron & Ironing board in unit ⊙ ⊕ CTV ⊕3pin square 3P 3▥ ⊞ ▥(10yds) Swing & barbeques
⊶ ⬧(100yds) ♫(½) ♫(½m)
Min£95 Max£210pw

HONITON
Devon
Map**3** ST10

C **CC Ref 7564 L**
for bookings Character Cottages (Holidays) Ltd, 34 Fore Street, Sidmouth, Devon EX10 8AQ
☎Sidmouth(03955)77001

A terraced period cottage situated in the main street of the market town. It comprises lounge/diner, kitchen, one double bedroom, one single and a bathroom.

All year MWB out of season 1wk min, 1mth max, 1unit, 1–3persons ◇
no pets ◉ fridge Electric & gas fires Elec inclusive ⬜inclusive ☎(100yds)→

Iron & Ironing board in unit ☺ CTV
⊕3pin square ▥ ♨(50yds)
↔ ♪(2m) ☎(100yds)
Min£72 Max£98pw (Low)
Min£117 Max£136pw (High)

HOPE
Derbyshire
Map**7** SK18

C   Granary, Lime Loft & Stable Cottages
for bookings Mrs D M Gladstone, Laneside
Farm, Hope, Sheffield S30 2RR
☎Hope Valley(0433)20214

*Granary and Lime Loft cottages are part
of an 18th-century stone barn which has
been converted and modernised, while
The Stables Cottage also modernised,
was once, as it's name implies, a stable
building. All are grouped around a
farmyard overlooking the River Noe.
Granary sleep four people on the first floor
with bathroom/WC all with pine flooring, a
ground-floor lounge with studio couch.
The quarry tile flooring extends into the
kitchen. Lime Loft also sleeps four
persons but in ground-floor bedrooms,
there is a spacious pine floored lounge on
the first floor with extra studio couch and
kitchen. Stable Cottage sleeps up to three
with one bedroom plus bed-settee in the
lounge, dining room, bathroom/WC and
kitchen.*

Mar–Nov   MWB out of season
3days min, 3mths max, 3units,
1–6persons ◆ ◆ ♪ fridge Gas &
Electric fires Gas inclusive & Elec metered
⌷can be hired ☎(¼m) Iron & Ironing
board in unit ☺ CTV ⊕3pin square
6P ▥ ♨(¼m)
↔ ♪(¼m) ☎(¼m)
Min£70 Max£145pw

HOPTON CASTLE
Shropshire
Map**7** SO37

B   Mrs J Thomas **The Brambles**
Llanhowell Farm, Hopton Castle,
Shropshire SY7 0QG
☎Little Brampton(05887)307

*A detached modern dormer bungalow
with integral garage set in a beautiful
picturesque location. Accommodation
comprises lounge, modern kitchen/diner,
bathroom with separate WC, one double
bedroom and two twin bedrooms. Guests
can enjoy looking around the owner's
mixed farm.*

Allyear   MWB out of season   1wk min,
1unit, 6persons, ◆ ◆ ◎& oil fired
stove fridge ▥ & open fire
Elec metered ⌷can be hired ☎(1m)
WM & SD in unit Iron & Ironing board in
unit ⊕3pin square 2P 1▥
♨(3m)
↔ ☎(2½m)
Min£35 Max£55pw (Low)
Min£60 Max£85pw (High)

HORNING
Norfolk
Map**9** TG31

Honiton
—
Hunstanton

Ch   Ferry Marina Chalets Ferry Boat
Yard Ltd, Ferry Road
for bookings Blakes Holidays, Wroxham,
Norwich, Norfolk NR12 8DH
☎Wroxham(06053)2917

*Five cedar-wood Swiss/Scandinavian style
chalets in a peaceful location, within the
confines of Ferry Marina, which provides
all facilities and amenities for boating
activities. Two double bedrooms on first
floor and one twin-bedded room on
ground floor. Combined bathroom/WC on
the ground-floor and one separate WC on
first-floor. Good quality furnishings and
equipment throughout.*

Etr–Oct   MWB out of season   1wk min,
5units, 6persons [◆ ◆] ◎ fridge
Electric Elec metered ⌷inclusive
☎(200yds) ☺ CTV ⊕3pin square P
▥ ♨(50yds) ⌷ ⌷ Boats for hire
↔ ☎(100yds)
Details not confirmed for 1987

HORNS CROSS
Devon
Map**2** SS32

**B, C, F.   Drakes, Frobisher, Gilbert
Hawkins & Raleigh Cottages**
for bookings C T Johnson, Foxdown
Manor, Horns Cross, Bideford, Devon
EX39 SPJ
☎Horns Cross(02375)325 or 642

*Former outbuildings of the Manor House
have been converted into five well-
modernised and furnished apartments.
Accommodation comprises open-plan
lounge/kitchen/diner, either two or three
bedrooms all with wash hand basin and
bathroom/WC. Frobisher is particularly
suitable for disabled persons.*

Mar–Oct   MWB out of season   3day min,
1mth max, 5units, 1–6persons ◇ ◆
◆ ◎ fridge ▥ Elec inclusive
⌷inclusive ☎ Iron & Ironing board on
premises [Launderette on premises]
☺ CTV ⊕ 3pin square 12P ▥
♨(4m) ⌷(heated) ✍hard croquet,
sauna, solarium, jaccuzi, children's play
room
↔ ☎(3m)
Details not confirmed for 1987

HORTON
West Glamorgan
Map**2** SS48

B   3 Westernside Farm
for bookings Mr G R Macpherson, 75
Sketty Road, Uplands, Swansea SA2 0EN
☎Swansea(0792)298512

*A brick-built bungalow situated on a small
development of holiday homes in rural
surroundings. Accommodation comprises
open-plan lounge/diner/kitchen area, two
bedrooms (one with double and one with*

---

*twin beds) and bathroom/WC. A bed-
settee is available in the lounge.*

Mar–Oct   MWB in season 2nights min,
1unit, 2–6persons [◆ ◆] ◎ fridge
electric Elec metered ⌷can be hired
(overseas visitors only) ☎(200yds) ☺
CTV ⊕3pin square 1P ♨(200yds)
↔ ☎(1m)
Details not confirmed for 1987

HOW CAPLE
Hereford & Worcester
Map**3** SO63

F   Rugden Granary Flat
for bookings Mrs J Cross, Rugden House,
How Caple, Hereford
☎How Caple(098 986)224

*Situated on a fruit farm this first-floor flat
forms part of an old stone farm building
and comprises lounge/kitchen, bathroom
and sleeps up to six persons.*

Allyear   2nights min, 1mth max, 1unit,
1–6persons ◆ ◆ ♪ no pets ◎
fridge Gas & Electric heaters Gas/
Elec metered ⌷can be hired ☎(½m)
SD in unit Iron in unit Ironing board in
unit ☺ CTV ⊕3pin square 4P
♨(½m) ✍Hard
↔ ☎(½m)
Details not confirmed for 1987

HUCKLOW, GREAT
Derbyshire
Map**7** SK17

C   South View Cottage
for bookings Mrs M Waterhouse, Holme
Cottage, Windmill, Great Hucklow, Buxton,
Derbyshire SK17 8RE
☎Tideswell(0298)871440

*A tastefully modernised semi-detached
country cottage situated in the tiny hamlet
of Windmill in the Peak National Park. The
accommodation comprises one double-
bedded room, one small twin-bedded
room, a fully-equipped kitchen, open-plan
lounge with separate dining area.*

Allyear   MWB out of season   1wk min,
1mth max, 1unit, 1–6persons ◆ ◆
no pets ◎ fridge ▥ Elec metered
⌷can be hired ☎(½m) WM & SD in
unit Iron & Ironing board in unit CTV
2P 1▥ ♨(2m)
↔ ☎(½m)
Min£65 £Max£75pw (Low)
£95pw (High)

HUNSTANTON
Norfolk
Map**9** TF64

Ch   Manor Park Manor Road
for bookings Hoseasons Holidays,
Sunway House, Lowestoft, Suffolk
NR32 3LT
☎Lowestoft(0502)62271

*Chalets situated on a caravan site each
accommodating six persons. There are
two bedrooms (one double, the other has
twin bunk beds), lounge, kitchen and
bathroom/WC.*

Mar−Sep MWB out of season
3days min, 6wks max, 25units,
1−6persons [◆◆] ◎ fridge
Electric Elec metered Ⓛinclusive ☎
☉ CTV ㉛3pin square P ⚏(20yds)
⊇

⊖ ☎(100yds) ♫(100yds) ⚌(½m)
Min£42 Max£155pw

B Sandringham Bungalows Old
Hunstanton Road
for bookings Hoseasons Holidays,
Sunway House, Lowestoft, Suffolk
NR32 3LT
☎Lowestoft(0502)62271

*Wood & brick bungalows situated
adjacent to the Lodge Hotel, and 1m from
the sea. Accommodation comprises two
bedrooms (one double, one twin-bedded),
lounge/kitchen and bathroom/WC.*

Mar−Oct MWB out of season 3days min,
3mths max, 30units, 1−8persons [◆◆]
◎ fridge Electric Elec metered
Ⓛinclusive ☎(150yds) [Iron & Ironing
board on premises] CTV
㉛3pin square P ⚏(150yds)
⊖ ♿(¾m) ☎(100yds) ♫(1½m)
♫(1½m) ⚌(1½m)
Min£50 Max£156pw

IDEN GREEN
Kent
Map5 TQ83

C Tudor Farmhouse Cottage
for bookings Mrs A C Grant, Campion
House, Iden Green, Cranbrook, Kent
TN17 4LB
☎Cranbrook(0580)240617

*Period cottage adjoining 15th-century
Tudor farmhouse containing two
bedrooms, bathroom/WC and ground-
floor lounge and kitchen. South facing
with outstanding country views over the
Weald and sharing 1½ acres of private
garden.*

All year MWB 2days min, 1unit,
1−6persons ◆ ◆ ◆ ◎ fridge
🍴 Elec metered Ⓛinclusive ☎(¾m)
WM & SD in unit Iron & Ironing board on
premises ☉ CTV ㉛3pin square 3P
🔲 ⚏(½m) ⊇
⊖ ♿(3m) ☎(½m) ♫(2½m) ♫(2½m)
Min£50 Max£90pw (Low)
Min£103 Max£143pw (High)

ILCHESTER
Somerset
Map3 ST52

F Mrs W T C Hawkes **Flats 3 & 4** Bos
House, Limington Road, Ilchester,
Somerset BA22 8LX
☎Ilchester(0935)840507

*Two self-contained flats with own
entrance. Ground-floor flat comprises
kitchen/diner, lounge, bathroom with WC,
one double and one twin bedroom. First-
floor flat has dining unit in lounge, kitchen,
bathroom/WC, one double and one twin
bedroom.*

Hunstanton
—
Ilfracombe

All year MWB out of season 1wk min,
8wks max, 2units, 1−4persons [◇] ◆
◆ ◎ fridge Electric Elec metered
Ⓛcan be hired ☎(100yds) WM & SD on
premises [TD on premises] Iron &
Ironing board in unit ☉ CTV
㉛3pin square 🔲 ⚏(100yds)
⊖ ☎(100yds)
Min£65 Max£110pw

ILFRACOMBE
Devon
Map2 SS54

C 1 & 2 Dean Cottages
for bookings Mrs A Hookway, Dean Farm,
West Down, Ilfracombe, Devon EX30 8NT
☎Ilfracombe(0271)63915

*Attractive, whitewashed semi-detached
farm cottages with front lawn, situated
close to working farm. Both comprise
lounge, kitchen/diner, bathroom and one
with two bedrooms, the other with three.*

All year MWB out of season 4days min,
4wks max, 2units, 1−5persons ◆ ◆
no pets ◎ fridge Elec metered Ⓛcan
be hired (overseas visitors only) ☎(1m)
Iron & Ironing board in unit TV
㉛3pin square 2P 🔲 ⚏(1m)
⊖ ♿(3m) ☎(½m) ♫(3m) ♫(3m)
⚌(3m)
Details not confirmed for 1987

Ch A W Kino & D J Leishman *Golden
Coast Holiday Village*, Worth Road,
Ilfracombe, Devon
☎Ilfracombe(0271)63543

*Sixteen holiday chalets set in 1½ acres of
pleasant wooded and lawned estate
affording views of sea and cliffs.
Accommodation, equipped for six,
comprises two bedrooms (one double, one
twin-bedded), lounge/diner with
convertible double bed, kitchen, bathroom
and WC.*

15Mar−15Jan MWB out of season
2days min, 16units, 2−6persons [◇ ◆
◆] ◎ fridge Electric Elec metered
Ⓛcan be hired ☎ [Launderette on
premises] Iron & Ironing board on
premises ☉ CTV ㉛3pin square P
🔲 ⚏(on site) use of facilities adjacent
site
⊖ ♿(2m) ☎(100yds) ♫(100yds)
♫(1m) ⚌(1m)
Details not confirmed for 1987

F A R & B A Kift, *Harbour Heights* 12
Hillsborough Terrace, Ilfracombe, Devon
EX34 9NR
☎Ilfracombe(0271)64011

*Second and third floor flats within a three
storey georgian mid-terrace house. Set
well above the main Combe Martin to
Ilfracombe road with glorious views over
the harbour and Bristol Channel. They are
well-decorated throughout and comprise*

*open-plan lounge diner, kitchen area, two
double bedrooms one with additional
single bed and bathroom/WC*

May−Sep 1wk min, 4wks max, 2units,
1−5persons ◆ ◆ ◎ fridge
Electric Elec metered Ⓛinclusive
☎(200yds) Iron & Ironing board in unit
[Launderette within 300yds] ☉ CTV
㉛3pin square 2P 🔲 ⚏(200yds)
Putting
⊖ ♿(50yds) ☎(200yds)
♫(200yds) ⚌(½m)
Min£75 Max£175pw

C Mr D S Dovey **Hele Valley Holiday
Park** Hele Bay, Ilfracombe, Devon
EX34 9RD
☎Ilfracombe(0271)62460

*Two pairs of recently constructed semi-
detached houses near entrance of
caravan and camping park, in quiet area
on edge of Ilfracombe. They comprise
spacious lounge, kitchen/dining room and
stairs to first-floor with two double
bedrooms, a room with bunks and shower
room/WC.*

All year MWB out of season 3days min,
3mths max, 4units, 1−8persons [◇ ◆
◆] ◎ fridge Electric Elec metered
Ⓛinclusive ☎ Airing cupboard in unit
Iron & Ironing board in unit HCE in unit
[Launderette on premises] ☉ CTV
㉛3pin square 2P ⚏
⊖ ♿(½m) ☎(½m) ♫(½m) ♫(½m)
⚌(1m)
Min£50 Max£120pw (Low)
Min£140 Max£200pw (High)

B JFH GC46B Marlborough Road
for bookings John Fowler Holidays, Dept
58, Marlborough Road, Ilfracombe, Devon
☎Ilfracombe(0271)66666

*An end of terrace bungalow with views of
the sea. It comprises lounge/diner with
small kitchen area and breakfast bar,
bathroom with separate WC, one double
bedroom and one twin bedded room. The
bungalow is situated close to the John
Fowler Holiday Complex and facilities
include solarium, sauna, crazy golf, dance
club, bar and restaurant.*

Mar−Oct MWB out of season 1wk min,
1mth max, 1unit, 6persons [◇] ◆ ◆
◎ fridge Electric fires Elec metered
Ⓛnot provided Iron in unit Launderette
on premises ☉ TV ㉛3pin square
24P ⊇(heated) 🔲 ♫ ♫
⊖ ♿(1m) ⚌(1m)
Min£79.35 Max£205.85pw

C Sunningdale Cheglinch, West Down
for bookings Mr W A J Hewitt, Leonard
House, Sampford Peverell, Tiverton, Devon
EX16 7EL
☎Tiverton(0884)820677

*Semi-detached cottage in quiet lane with
fine views. Accommodation comprises
small lounge, dining room, kitchen and
breakfast room, two double bedrooms,
one twin and bathroom. Pleasant cottage
furniture.* →

Mar–Oct 1wk min, 4wks max, 1 unit,
1–6persons ◆ ◆ ◎ fridge
Electric Elec metered 🔲 not provided
☎(1m) WM in unit Iron & Ironing board
in unit ⊕ ⊗ TV ⊕3pin square 2P
1☒ ▥ ♨(1½m)
⊖ ♪(3m) ♀(1m) 🎵(3m) ♬(3m)
🐾(3m)

Min£70 Max£85pw (Low)
Min£100 Max£120pw (High)

INGLETON
North Yorkshire
Map7 SD67

C 1 Pemberton Cottages
for bookings Mrs M Bell, 'Langber',
Ingleton, via Carnforth, N. Yorks LA6 3DT
☎Ingleton(0468)41587

An end of terrace cottage, overlooking
open countryside, large garden with
stream to rear. Accommodation comprises
lounge, kitchen/diner, two bedrooms and
bathroom.

All year MWB out of season 1wk min,
1 unit, 2–6persons ◆ ◆ ◎ fridge
Electric Elec metered 🔲 can be hired
☎(½m) CTV ⊕3pin square 2P ▥
♨(½m)
⊖ ♪(3m) ♀(½m)

Min£58 Max£85pw (Low)
Min£98 Max£115pw (High)

INKBERROW
Hereford & Worcester
Map4 SP05

C Rose Cottage
for bookings Mr & Mrs C V Cullingford,
Bramley House, Withybed Lane,
Inkberrow, Worcs WR7 4JJ
☎Evesham(0386)792956

This detached listed cottage has great
charm and character and is set within the
conservation area of this Worcestershire
village. Accommodation comprises
kitchen/dining room, large lounge with
stone inglenook fireplace (logs supplied),
two double bedrooms on the first-floor
and two double bedrooms on the second-
floor.

Mid Mar–Nov also Xmas & New Year
MWB out of season 1 mth max, 1 unit,
1–8persons [◇] ◆ ◆ ◎ fridge
🍴 Elec metered 🔲 can be hired
☎(200yds) WM & SD in unit Iron &
Ironing board in unit ⊕ CTV
⊕3pin square 3P ▥ ♨(10yds)

Min£95 Max£125pw (Low)
Min£145 Max£185pw (High)

INVERGARRY
Highland Inverness-shire
Map14 NH30

Ch Kilfinnan Holiday Lodges Kilfinnan
for bookings Blakes' Holidays, Wroxham,
Norwich, Norfolk
☎Wroxham(060 53)2917

Ten wood lodges on W side of Loch
Lochy, 3m S off A82 by single-track road

Ilfracombe
—
Inverness

and forest track. Isolated position on the
edge of forest. Each cabin has its own
balcony and can accommodate up to
eight people.

Etr–Oct MWB out of season 10 units,
8persons [◆] no pets ◎ fridge
Electric Elec Metered 🔲 inclusive ☎
Airing cupboard HCE in unit ⊕ CTV
⊕3pin square P ♨(2½m) Fishing
Details not confirmed for 1987

INVERKIRKAIG
Highland Sutherland
Map14 NC01

Ch Mr W Hutchison Valhalla Chalets
Inverkirkaig, Lochinver, Sutherland
IV27 4LF
☎Lochinver(05714)382

Six timber-built chalets pleasantly situated
on the north shore of Loch Kirkaig. The
accommodation comprises open plan
kitchen/diner/lounge with pull-down
settees, one double and one twin bedroom
and bathroom with shower/WC. Located
3m from Lochinver.

Mar–Oct MWB in season 3days min,
5wks max, 6units, 1–6persons ◆ ◆
no pets ◎ fridge 🍴 🔲 inclusive
☎(50yds) [WM & TD on premises] Iron
& Ironing board on premises ⊕ CTV
⊕3pin square 20P ♨(2½m)
⊖ ♀(2½m)

Min£103.50 Max£237pw (Low)
Min£264.50 Max£423pw (High)

INVERMORISTON
Highland Inverness-shire
Map14 NH41

**C Altruadh, Farm, Farmburn & Levishie
Cottages**
for bookings Estate Office, Glenmoriston
Estates Ltd, Glenmoriston, Inverness
IV3 6YA
☎Glenmoriston(0320)51202

Four individual cottages at varying
locations in an 8m section of
Glenmoriston. Although beautiful, the
locations are often isolated, making a car
a necessity. Each cottage provides
suitable accommodation for the sporting
enthusiast and tourist alike. Sleeping up to
8 people, the cottages offer privacy and
peacefulness.

8Mar–Oct MWB 1–2wks min, 4units,
1–8persons [◆] No tents or caravans
◎ fridge Night storage & Electric
Elec metered 🔲 can be hired ☎(½m)
Iron & Ironing board in unit CTV
⊕3pin square P ♨(¾m) Fishing
⊖ ♀(¾m)

Min£85 Max£98pw (Low)
Min£196 Max£216pw (High)

**Ch Bhlaraidh, Dalcattaig, Eagle Lodge
& Sian Drochit Chalets**
for bookings Estate Office, Glenmoriston
Estates Ltd, Glenmoriston, Inverness
IV3 6YA
☎Glenmoriston(0320)51202

Bhlaraidh, Dalcattaig, Eagle Lodge and
Sian Drochit Chalets are four groups of
chalets situated in pleasant wooded
locations within the estate grounds.
Bhlaraidh and **Dalcattaig** are identical in
style also situated 3 miles apart, two have
three bedrooms, the other 10 have two.
Sian Drochit is comprised of eight two-
bedroomed chalets. All comprise living
room with double divan bed, and kitchen/
diner, plus bathroom/WC. **Eagle Lodge**
comprises open plan kitchen/lounge/diner
with two single convertible beds, two
bedrooms, one accessed by step-ladder,
and bathroom.

8Mar–Oct MWB 1–2wk min, 21units,
1–8persons [◆] No tents or caravans
◎ fridge Night storage & Electric
Elec metered 🔲 can be hired ☎(½m)
Iron & Ironing board in unit CTV in
Bhlaraidh, Dalcattaig & Eagle Lodge (CTV
can be hired in Sian Drochit)
⊕3pin square P ♨(½m) Fishing
⊖ ♀(½m)

Min£72 Max£94pw (Low)
Min£161 Max£196pw (High)

B Sian Drochit Bungalow
for bookings Estate Office, Glenmoriston
Estates Ltd, Glenmoriston, Inverness
IV3 6YA
☎Glenmoriston(0320)51202

Comfortable, modern bungalow near a
river bank and about one mile from the
village. Accommodation comprises
kitchen/diner, lounge with two convertible
single beds, three bedrooms, one with
bunks and a bathroom.

8Mar–Oct MWB 1wk min, 1 unit,
1–10persons [◆ ◆] ◎ fridge Night
storage & Electric Elec metered 🔲 can
be hired ☎(1m) Iron & Ironing board in
unit ⊕ CTV ⊕3pin square 2P
♨(1m) Fishing
⊖ ♀(1m)

Min£95 Max£106pw (Low)
Min£166 Max£235pw (High)

INVERNESS
Highland Inverness-shire
Map14 NH64

B Fuinary Cottage 10A Culduthel Road
for bookings Scottish Highland Holiday
Homes, Wester Altaurie, Abriachan,
Inverness-shire
☎Dochgarroch(046386)247

Traditional detached bungalow situated in
its own garden, 10 minutes' walk from the
town centre. It comprises sitting room with
views across the town, small dining room,
kitchen, bathroom/WC and three
bedrooms, one with bunk beds. Street
parking only but no restrictions.

May–Sep MWB out of season 1wk min,
1 unit, 1–6persons ◎ fridge 🍴

Elec metered ⬜ not provided ☎ Iron &
Ironing board in unit TV ⊕3pin round
🎇(½m) ♨(½m)
↔ ♪(3m) ♀(100yds) 🎵(½m)
🎵(½m) 🍴(½m)

Min£90 Max£140pw

IPSTONES
Staffordshire
Map7 SK05

C Clough Head Farm
for bookings Mrs Leeson, Crow Gutter
Farm, Ipstones, Staff ST10 2ND
☎Ipstones(053871)428

*A cottage approximately 150 years old
situated on a farm with pleasant rural
views, in a quiet picturesque area ½m SE of
Ipstones village. It comprises lounge/diner,
kitchen, bathroom and WC, one large
family bedroom, one twin-bedded room.*

Etr–Oct MWB out of season 1wk min,
1mth max, 1unit, 2–5persons ◇ ◎
fridge 🍴 Electric & open fires
⬜ not provided ☎(½m) CTV
⊕3pin square 6P ♨(½m)
↔ ♪ ♀(½m)

Min£70 Max£110pw

F Mrs J Brindley Glenwood House Farm
Ipstones, Stoke-on-Trent, Staffordshire
ST10 2JP
☎Ipstones(053871)294

*A former sandstone outbuilding adjacent
to the farmyard, has been converted into
two ground-floor flats. Each has a kitchen,
compact lounge, two bedrooms, Flat 1
with double bed and bunk beds, Flat 2
with twin beds and a single bed. Both have
shower and WC. The farm lies at the end of
a ½m track just ¾m W of Ipstones on the
Cheddleton road.*

Mar–Nov, MWB out of season
2nights min, 1mth max, 2units,

Inverness
—
Islay, Isle of

1–6persons ◇ ◆ ◎ fridge
Electric Elec metered ⬜ can be hired
(overseas visitors only) ☎(1½m) WM &
SD on premises [Iron & Ironing board on
premises] ⊙ CTV ⊕3pin square P
🎇 ♨(1½m) Games room, children's
play area 🏌Hard
↔ ♀(1½m)

Min£65 Max£70pw (Low)
Min£95 Max£100pw (High)

IRONBRIDGE
Shropshire
See **Telford**

ISLANDS
An explanation is given at the
commencement of the gazetteer section,
page 21.

ISLAY, ISLE OF
Strathclyde *Argyllshire*
Map10 NR

BOWMORE
Map10 NR35

F The Inns The Square
for bookings Mrs Fay MacNeill, 19 Elder
Crescent, Bowmore, Isle of Islay,
Argyllshire
☎Bowmore(049681)532

*A former inn situated beside the harbour
wall and overlooking Loch Indaal,
renovated and converted into four modern
flats. Each flat has lounge/diner and
kitchen and the three two-bedroomed flats
have a bathroom while the one
bedroomed flat has a shower.*

All year MWB out of season 3nights min,
4units, 1–4persons [◇] ◇ ◆ ◎
fridge 🍴 Elec metered ⬜ inclusive
☎(100yds) WM in unit Iron & Ironing
board on premises CTV ⊕3pin square
4P 🎇 ♨(15yds)
↔ ♪(25yds)

Min£60 Max£76pw (Low)
Min£120 Max£170pw (High)

GRUINART
Map10 NR26

B 2 Bola-na-Traigh
for bookings Mr & Mrs G A Archibald,
'Craigens', Gruinart, Isle of Islay,
Argyllshire
☎Port Charlotte(049685)256

*Modern, white painted, small bungalow
comprising three bedrooms, bathroom/
WC plus additional WC, kitchen/diner and
lounge. Located to the west of Islay,
100yds from the owners dairy farm and
overlooking a roost for wintering flocks of
Barnacle geese; otters can also be seen
close by.*

All year MWB out of season 2nights min,
1unit, 1–6persons ◇ ◆ ◎ fridge
Electric Elec inclusive ⬜ can be hired
☎(4m) Airing cupboard in unit Iron in
unit HCE in unit ⊙ TV
⊕3pin square 2P ♨(4m)

Min£103.50 Max£143.75pw

PORT CHARLOTTE
Map10 NR25

H An Cala House
for bookings Lady Wilson, Cala Na Ruadh,
Port Charlotte, Islay, Argyll PA48 7TS
☎Port Charlotte(049685)289

*A two-storey white-fronted house on
seafront looking across Loch Indaal.
Simply furnished with gloss-painted walls →*

and linoleum flooring with rugs; the accommodation comprises of a large kitchen/diner with oil-fired stove, separate sitting room with piano and book collection, scullery, bathroom, one double bedroom and two twin bedrooms, one with additional single bed.

All year   MWB out of season   1wk min, 1mth max, 1unit, 1–8persons   fridge Open fire & Electric   Elec metered ⃞not provided   ☎(200yds)   Iron & Ironing boad in unit   ⊕3pin square   P ⚌(200yds)

↤ 🚿(200yds)   ♫(200yds) high season only

Min£75 Max£85pw (Low)
Min£110 Max£125pw (High)

F   The Annexe An Cala
for bookings Lady Wilson, Cala Na Ruadh, Port Charlotte, Islay, Argyll PA48 7TS
☎Port Charlotte(049685)289

Small unit, comprising a bedsitting room, separate bathroom leading off from a small scullery and kitchenette. Simply but pleasantly furnished. Bed-settees, bookcase, attractive picture window. Pleasantly situated in fishing village.

All year   MWB out of season   1wk min, 1mth max, 1unit, 1–2persons   fridge Electric   Elec metered   ⃞not provided ☎(200yds)   ⊕3pin square   P ⚌(200yds)

↤ 🚿(200yds)   ♫(200yds)

Min£55 Max£80pw

F   The Flat An Cala
for bookings Lady Wilson, Cala Na Ruadh, Port Charlotte, Islay, Argyll PA48 7TS
☎Port Charlotte(049685)289

First-floor flat on seafront of small fishing village. It is simply furnished with vinyl flooring with rugs and gloss-painted walls; accommodation comprises living room with piano, book collection and open fire, kitchen/dining room and double bedroom on first floor. A steep staircase leads to two large attic bedrooms with five single beds one with a table tennis table double as a playroom. Double-glazing throughout.

All year   MWB out of season   1wk min, 1mth max, 1unit, 1–8persons   fridge Open fires, Storage heaters & Electric Elec metered   ⃞not provided ☎(200yds)   Iron & Ironing board in unit ⊕3pin square   P ⚌(200yds) Table tennis

↤ 🚿(200yds)   ♫(200yds)

Min£75 Max£85pw (Low)
Min£110 Max£125pw (High)

ISLE OF ARRAN Strathclyde
Map**10**
See Arran, Isle of

ISLE OF BARRA Western Isles
Inverness-shire
Map**13**
See Barra, Isle of

ISLE OF BUTE Strathclyde
Map**10**
See Bute, Isle of

ISLE OF COLL Strathclyde
Argyllshire
Map**13**
See Coll, Isle of

ISLE OF COLONSAY Strathclyde
Argyllshire
Map**10**
See Colonsay, Isle of

ISLE OF ISLAY Strathclyde
Argyllshire
Map**10**
See Islay, Isle of

ISLE OF MAN
Map**6**
See Man, Isle of

ISLE OF MULL Strathclyde
Argyllshire
Map**10 & 13**
See Mull, Isle of

ISLE OF WIGHT
Map**4**
See Wight, Isle of

ISLE OF SKYE Highland
Inverness-shire
See Skye, Isle of

ISLE ORNSAY Highland
Inverness-shire
See Skye, Isle of

IVYBRIDGE
Devon
Map**2** SX65

C   CC Ref 407L (2 & 3)
for bookings Character Cottages Ltd, 34 Fore Street Sidmouth, Devon EX10 8AQ
☎Sidmouth(03955)77001

Mid and end terrace cottages with their own gardens and comprising lounge area with log burning stove step up to kitchen/dining area, one double and one bunk bedded room and bathroom with shower.

Mar–Oct   MWB out of season   3days min. 2mths max, 2units, 2–4persons   ◆ no pets   fridge   🍳   Elec metered ⃞inclusive   ☎(¾m)   Iron & Ironing board in unit   [Launderette on premises]   ⊙ CTV   ⊕3pin square   ▥   ⚌(½m)   ⅋   δ

↤   δ(3m)   🚿(½m)

Min£122 Max£215pw

C   CC Ref 407L (4)
for bookings Character Cottages Ltd, 34 Fore Street, Sidmouth, Devon EX10 8AQ
☎Sidmouth(03955)77001

Split level stone built barn conversion with patio area beside the river. Comprises lounge/dining area, bathroom, WC, double, twin and bunk bedded room.

Mar–Oct   MWB out of season   3days min, 2mths max, 1unit, 6persons   ◆   no pets 🍳   fridge   storage heaters Elec metered   ⃞inclusive   ☎(¾m)   Iron & Ironing board in unit   [Launderette on premises]   ⊙   CTV   ⊕3pin square 2P ▥   ⚌(½m)   ♫(by request)   trout fishing

↤   δ(3m)   🚿(½m)

Min£183 Max£290pw

C   CC Ref 407L (5)
for bookings Character Cottages Ltd, 34 Fore Street, Sidmouth, Devon EX10 8AQ
☎Sidmouth(03955)77001

Detached stone built cottage with enclosed garden and views over the river. Accommodation comprises kitchen/diner, utility room with WC off, lounge with open fire place, four bedrooms two with double beds, one twin-bedded and one with bunk beds and two bathrooms with WC.

Mar–Oct   MWB out of season   3days min, 2mths max, 1unit, 8persons   ◆   no pets 🍳Rayburn   fridge   storage heaters Elec metered   ⃞inclusive   ☎(1m)   WM, SD & TD in unit   Iron & Ironing board in unit   ⊙   CTV   ⊕3pin square   2P 1🔥 ▥   ⚌(½m)   ♫(on request)   Trout fishing

↤   δ(3m)   🚿(¾m)

Min£210 Max£395pw

C & F   Mr & Mrs C J Hardman Filham House Filham, Ivybridge, Devon PL21 0LR
☎Plymouth(0752)892503

A tasteful self-catering complex located in the converted stables and outbuildings of Filham House, an idyllic setting by a 13th-century monastery site with lakes, beautiful lawns and gardens. Accommodation comprises lounge/diner in four units (lounge/kitchen/diner in two units), separate kitchen bath or shower room/WC and between one and three bedrooms, sleeping up to seven people in the larger units. All are well-furnished and equipped and full of character and charm.

Apr–Sep   1night min, 6wks max, 6units, 1–7persons   [◇]   ◆   1 pet per unit 🍳   fridge   🍴in 1 unit   Electric fires Elec inclusive   ⃞can be hired   ☎   WM on premises   Iron & Ironing board in unit ⊙   CTV   ⊕3pin square   20P   ▥ ⚌(½m)

↤   🚿(3m)   ♫(3m)

Min£65 Max£115pw (Low)
Min£125 Max£250pw (High)

IWERNE COURTNEY
Dorset
Map**3** ST81

C   Fairfield Cottage
for bookings Heart of England Cottages, The Market Place, Fairford, Gloucestershire GL7 4AB
☎Cirencester(0285)713295

End cottage of terrace of three in the village, adjacent to church.

Accommodation comprises kitchen/diner, lounge with open fire, one single room with wash hand basin on the ground floor and one double and one single bedroom on the first floor and bathroom/WC. Older, traditional furnishings throughout. Small garden with rustic table and chairs.

Apr–Oct MWB out of season 1wk min, 6mths max, 1unit, 2–4persons ◆ ◆
◉ fridge storage heaters & electric fires Elec metered ⌷ can be hired ☎ Iron & Ironing board in unit TV
⊕3pin square 2P ▥ ♨(250yds)
⊖ ♀(250yds)
Min£75 Max£135pw

JACOBSTOWE
Devon
Map2 SS50

C 9 The Village
for bookings Mr I H Greenslade, Swan Cottage, Okehampton, Devon
☎Exbourne(083785)357

A partly thatched end of terrace cottage; approximately 200-years-old, it is pleasantly furnished and has lounge/diner, kitchen, bathroom and a double bedroom with a brass bed. On entering the village the cottage is next to the church.

All year MWB out of season 1wk min, 3wks max, 1unit, 2persons ◆ ♪
fridge Electric & wood burning stove Gas/Elec inclusive ⌷ can be hired
☎(200yds) SD, Iron & Ironing board in unit ⊕ ⊗ TV ⊕3pin square 1P
♨(1m)
⊖ ♀(1m)
Min£65 Max£75pw (Low)
Min£80 Max£110pw (High)

JEDBURGH
Borders Roxburghshire
Map12 NT62

C Stable Cottage Knowesouth Farm
for bookings Blakes Holidays, Wroxham, Norwich, Norfolk NR12 8DH
☎Wroxham(06053)2917

Single-storey conversion in farm courtyard, offering two bedrooms, (one with twin beds one with a double and a single), lounge with dining table, kitchen and bathroom. Nicely furnished and well equipped. Situated 3m from Jedburgh off A968.

Apr–Oct MWB out of season 1wk min, 1unit, 5persons ◆ ◉ fridge Electric Elec metered ⌷ can be hired ☎(1m)
WM & SD on premises Iron & ironing board on premises ⊕ CTV
⊕3pin square 2P ♨(3¼m)

Details not confirmed for 1987

JORDANSTON
Dyfed
Map2 SM93

C Tan-Lan
for bookings Coastal Cottages of Pembrokeshire, Seaview, Abercastle.
Mathry, Dyfed SA62 5HJ
☎Croesgoch(03483)7742

Iwerne Courtney
—
Kendal

A delightfully restored cottage providing comfortable accommodation and within easy reach of North Pembrokeshire. It comprises a large lounge with open fire, kitchen/diner, bathroom with separate WC, two twin bedrooms and one double room.

All year MWB out of season 4days min, 2mths max, 1unit, 4–6persons ◆ ◆
◉ fridge storage, open & portable fires Elec metered ⌷ inclusive ☎(2m)
WM & SD in unit Iron & Ironing board in unit ⊕ CTV ⊕3pin square 2P ▥
♨(3m)
⊖ ♀(3m)
Min£70 Max£275pw

KEESTON
Dyfed
Map2 SM82

B The Bungalows
for bookings Mr & Mrs C Grundy, Keeston Hall, Keeston, Haverfordwest, Dyfed SA62 6EH
☎Camrose(0437)710482

Two-bedroomed bungalows, all have fully-equipped kitchens, spacious living room with dining area, bathroom and WC.

Apr–Oct MWB out of season 3nights min, 8units, 1–6persons [◇]
◆ ◆ fridge Electric Elec metered ⌷ inclusive ☎(25yds) SD in unit Iron & Ironing board in unit (Laundry facilities available) ⊕ TV
⊕3pin square P ▥ ♨ ⌲
⊖ ♀(1m) ♬(2m)
Min£65 Max£163pw (Low)
Min£233 Max£260pw (High)

C Keeston Hall
for bookings Mr & Mrs C Grundy, Keeston Hall, Keeston, Haverfordwest, Dyfed SA62 6EH
☎Camrose(0437)710482

Four character cottages in the heart of the Pembrokeshire countryside overlooking the village green and on the edge of the national park. Keeston Hall stands in tastefully-landscaped grounds with lawns and mature trees. All have lounge, bathroom/WC and kitchen, one with kitchen/diner and either two or three bedrooms.

Apr Oct MWB out of season 3days min, 4units, 1–7persons [◇] ◆ ◆ ◉
fridge Electric Elec metered
⌷ inclusive ☎(50yds) SD in unit Iron & Ironing board in unit (Laundry facilities available) ⊕ CTV ⊕3pin square P
▥ ♨ ⌲
⊖ ♀(1m) ♬(2m)
Min£61 Max£302pw

KELSO
Borders Roxburghshire
Map12 NT73

F Mr P Halley **Maxmill Park** Kelso, Roxburghshire TD5 8DQ
☎Kelso(0573)24468

A group of eleven flats forming two extensions within the gardens of owner's house, all are modern, decorated and equipped to a high standard. **Tweed flats** are three ground-floor flats where accommodation comprises open plan lounge/diner/kitchen (with Baby Belling cooker), small double-bedded room and bathroom; an additional bed-settee is available in each flat. **Teviot flats** offer two ground and two first floor flats, comprising kitchen, lounge with dining area, bathroom, a twin bedroom and double bedroom with bunks, both bedrooms have WHB. The four **Bowmont flats** comprise double and single bedrooms, shower room and open-plan lounge/diner/ kitchen. Access is from the B6352.

All year MWB out of season 3days min, 11units, 2–8persons ◇ ◆ ◆ ◉
fridge ▥ℐ Elec metered ⌷ inclusive
☎ WM, SD, TD on premises, Iron & Ironing board in unit ⊕ CTV
⊕3pin square P ▥ ♨(1m) ⌑
⊖ ♪(2m) ♟(1m)
Min£60 Max£200pw

KENDAL
Cumbria
Map7 SD59

C Garth Cottage 36 Castle Garth
for bookings Mrs E Steele, 53 Burton Road, Kendal, Cumbria LA97 7JA
☎Kendal(0539)23400

Stone-built end-terraced cottage set in a quiet area on the N side of town. The accommodation comprises two bedrooms, one room with a double and single bed and the other with twin beds. Extra folding bedspace is also available in lounge. There are two lounges, kitchen/ diner and modern bathroom and WC.

All year MWB out of season 1wk min, 1unit, 2–5persons ◆ no pets ◉
fridge Electric & gas fires Gas/ Elec metered ⌷ can be hired
☎(400yds) Iron & Ironing board in unit [Launderette within 300yds] ⊕ CTV
⊕3pin square P ▥ ♨(200yds)
⊖ ♪(1½m) ♀(200yds) ♬(½m)
♬(½m) ♟(½m)
Min£45 Max£85pw (Low)
Min£75 Max£90pw (High)

Ch & F Plumgarths Holiday Flats
Plumgarths
for bookings Jonathan & Fidelia Somervell, Crook, Kendal, Cumbria LA8 8LE
☎Staveley(0539)821325

A 17th-century country house carefully converted into six spacious flats of character, and a wooden chalet, situated in 3 acres of gardens. Accommodation varies in size sleeping from two to seven →

people. Plumgarths is situated on the B5284, 200yds from the junction with the A591.

All year MWB out of season 3days min, 3mths max, 7units, 2–7persons [◈ ◆] no cats ◎ fridge 🍴 Electric & open fire Elec metered Ⓛcan be hired ☎ [WM & TD on premises] Iron & Ironing board in unit ⊙ CTV ⊕3pin square 30P 🎬 ♨(2m)
⊖ ♀(100yds) 🎔(2m) 🎵(2m) 🎪(2m) Sports centre(2m)

Min£72 Max£98pw (Low)
Min£147 Max£235pw (High)

KENNETHMONT
Grampian *Aberdeenshire*
Map**15** NJ52

C I Yonderton of Auchlyne
for bookings Mrs E Innes, Ardlair, Insch, Aberdeenshire AB5 6YR
☎Kennethmont(04643)250

Semi-detached cottage on farm of same name, comprising large kitchen with dining area, lounge (with two single beds, used as seating during the day), a double and a twin bedroom and bathroom.

Apr–Oct MWB 1wk min 1unit 4–6persons ◈ ◆ ◎ fridge Electric fires Elec inclusive Ⓛcan be hired ☎(1½m) SD in unit Iron & Ironing board in unit ⊙ CTV ⊕3pin square 2P ♨(1½m)
⊖ ♀(1½m)

Min£75 Max£105pw (Low)
Min£95 Max£110pw (High)

KENTISBEARE
Devon
Map**3** ST00

B CC Ref 682
for bookings Character Cottages

Kendal
—
Keswick

(Holidays) Ltd, 34 Fore Street, Sidmouth, Devon EX10 8AQ
☎Sidmouth(039 55)77001

A detached brick-built bungalow with a lawned garden. Accommodation comprises two twin-bedded rooms, one double-bedded room, kitchen, dining room and lounge. Approach on M5 and leave motorway at junction 28.

All year MWB out of season 1wk min, 6mths max, 1unit, 2–6persons ◈ ◎ fridge Open fire Elec metered Ⓛcan be hired Iron & Ironing board in unit TV ⊕3pin square P ♨(1½m)
⊖ ♀(1½m) 🎔(1½m)

Min£54 Max£79pw (Low)
Min£112 Max£142pw (High)

KESSINGLAND
Suffolk
Map**5** TM58

Ch Sea View Chalet Park Kessingland Beach, Green Lane
for bookings Hoseasons Holidays, Sunway House, Lowestoft, Suffolk NR32 3LT
☎Lowestoft(0502)62271

Well-equipped and furnished chalets on site overlooking the sea. Accommodation comprises three bedrooms, one double, two singles, lounge and kitchen. Divan in lounge converts to sleep two extra people. Leave A12 signposted Kessingland Beach, turn left into Green Lane upon entering village.

Apr–Sep MWB out of season 1wk min, 3wks max, 39units, 1–6persons [◈ ◆] ◎ fridge Electric Elec metered Ⓛinclusive ☎(½m) CTV ⊕3pin square P 🎬 ♨(½m)
⊖ ♀(½m)

Min£50 Max£140pw

KESWICK
Cumbria
Map**11** NY22
See map 11 for details of other establishments in the vicinity.

F Mr & Mrs J B Wivell Greycote (Flat)
Eleventrees, Keswick, Cumbria CA12 4LW
☎Keswick(07687)72400

Comfortable first-floor flat with balcony on two sides situated one mile from town centre with views of surrounding hills. Accommodation comprises lounge, kitchen, bathroom and three bedrooms.

All year 1wk min, 1unit, 2–5persons ◈ ◆ ◎ fridge Electric Elec metered Ⓛinclusive ☎(200yds) SD & TD in unit Iron & Ironing board in unit ⊙ ⊛ CTV ⊕3pin square 2P 🎬 ♨(½m)
⊖ 💰(3m) ♀(½m) 🎔(1m)

Max£100pw (Low)
Max£150pw (High)

B Lakeland Rise
for bookings Lakeland Cottage Holidays, Yew Tree Cottage, Ullock, Keswick, Cumbria CA12 5SP
☎Braithwaite(059682)493
or Keswick(07687)72059

A modern bungalow situated on the fringe of the town with views over the fells. Accommodation comprises lounge, kitchen, bathroom/WC and two bedrooms.

All year 1mth max, 1unit, 2–4persons ◈ ◆ no pets ◎ fridge 🍴 Elec inclusive Ⓛinclusive ☎(½m) Iron

---

The Bungalow, Threlkeld, Nr Keswick.
Two top class bungalows & cottage, overlooking the village. Fully equipped, central heating and double glazing. An ideal centre for walking, climbing or touring. Golf course & pony trekking nearby. Sleep 5/6. Prices fully inclusive i.e. no meters. Open all year round. **Enquiries to: Mr & Mrs Sunley, The Bungalow, Sunnyside, Threlkeld, Keswick, Cumbria CA12 4SD or Tel (059683) 679.** *See gazetteer under Threlkeld*

Between Kendal and Windermere
Open All Year
6 Spacious Flats — Garden Chalet
Sleep 2-7
Central Heating, C.T.V.,
3 acres secluded grounds.
Jonathan and Fidelia Somervell,
Crook, Kendal, Cumbria LA8 8LE
Tel: Staveley (0539) 821325 evenings

For full details see under:
Kendal.
Founder Member Cumbria and Lakeland
Self-Caterers' Association.

Plumgarths Holiday Flats

130

& Ironing board in unit ⊖ CTV
⊕3pin square 2P ▥ ♨(¼m)
⊖⊖ ♪(3m) ♀(½m) ⬛(½m)
Min£84 Max£183pw

H Sandholm 3 The Heads
for bookings Lakeland Holiday Cottages,
Yew Tree Cottage, Ullock, Keswick,
Cumbria CA12 5SP
☎Braithwaite(059682)493
or Keswick(07687)72059

Large three-storey house with superb
views of the fells. Accommodation
comprises four bedrooms, lounge, dining
room and spacious kitchen.

All year 1mth max, 1unit, 2–12persons
◈ ◆ ♫ fridge ♨♨ Elec inclusive
ⓛinclusive ☎(¼m) Iron & Ironing board
in unit ⊖ CTV ⊕3pin square 2P ▥
♨(¼m)
⊖⊖ ♪(3m) ♀(¼m) ⬛(½m)
Min£102 Max£264pw

C Shalom 5 High Hill
for bookings Lakeland Cottage Holidays,
Yew Tree Cottage, Ullock, Keswick,
Cumbria CA12 5SP
☎Braithwaite(059682)493
or Keswick(07687)72059

A charming 18th-century town cottage
recently renovated to retain its character.
Accommodation comprises beamed
lounge, kitchen, two bedrooms and
bathroom/WC.

All year MWB out of season 3nights min,
1mth max, 1unit, 3–4persons ◈ ◆
♫ fridge Gas fires storage heaters Gas
& Elec inclusive ⓛinclusive ☎(¼m)
WM, SD, TD in unit Airing cupboard, Iron
& Ironing board in unit HCE in unit ⊖
CTV ⊕3pin square 1P ▥ ♨(¼m)
⊖⊖ ♪(3m) ♀(½m) ⬛(½m)
Min£63 Max£159pw

F Mr D A Naylor **Underscar Apartments**
Underscar Country House Hotel,
Applethwaite, Keswick, Cumbria
CA12 4PH
☎Keswick(07687)72469

Five very comfortable units in the grounds
of a country house hotel, situated in the
fells overlooking Derwentwater and
surrounding countryside. Four are on
ground level, three offer two bedrooms,
one offers one double bedroom and the
fifth is on two levels and has two
bedrooms. Extremely comfortable and
tastefully appointed apartments. The hotel
facilities, including meals, are available in
season.

All year MWB 3days min, 4wks max,
5units, 2–6persons ◈ ◆ ♫ fridge
♨♨ Gas & Elec inclusive ⓛinclusive
☎ [WM, SD & TD on premises] Iron &
Ironing board available ⊖ CTV
⊕3pin square 10P ▥ ♨(1½m)
⊖⊖ ♪(3m) ♀(1m) ♫(1m) ⬛(1m)
Min£100 Max£250pw (Low)
Min£120 Max£400pw (High)

KETTLESBASTON
Suffolk
Map**5** TL95

C Water Hall
for bookings Suffolk Holiday Cottages, 1
Lower Road, Glemsford, Sudbury, Suffolk
CO10 7QU
☎Glemsford(0787)281577

A flint-built cottage located in a peaceful
country lane adjacent to the River Brett.
Accommodation comprises kitchen, with

---

dishwasher, utility room, dining room,
lounge and shower/wc on the ground
floor. Upstairs, there are three bedrooms
(one double, one twin, two single) and
bathroom/WC. It has a large enclosed
garden bordered by the river so care must
be taken with young children.

All year MWB 1wk min, 1unit,
1–6persons ◈ ◆ ⓜ fridge
Storage heaters Elec metered ⓛcan be
hired ☎ WM, SD & TD in unit Iron &
Ironing board in unit ⊗ CTV
⊕3pin square 3P ♨(1½m) Games
room, piano
⊖⊖ ♀(1½m)
Min£70 Max£75pw (Low)
Min£155 Max£210pw (High)

KETTLEWELL
North Yorkshire
Map**7** SD97

C Maypole Cottage
for bookings Mrs C Harker, Knocklong,
The Green, Kettlewell, North Yorkshire
☎Kettlewell(075676)202

An attractive stone-built converted barn
situated in the heart of Kettlewell,
surrounded by beautiful scenery and close
to the river. The cottage has sitting room,
kitchen/diner and three good-sized
bedrooms. Ideal location for touring the
Dales.

All year MWB out of season 1wk min,
1mth max, 1unit, 2–6persons ◈ ⓜ
fridge Electric Elec metered
ⓛnot provided ☎(100yds) WM, SD &
TD in unit Iron & Ironing board in unit
⊖ CTV ⊕3pin square 1P ▥
♨(100yds)
⊖⊖ ♀(100yds)
Min£35 Max£70pw (Low)
Min£80 Max£120pw (High)

131

KEYHAVEN
Hampshire
Map4 SZ39

C Mr B Trehearne **Fishers Mead Cottages** Keyhaven, Lymington, Hants SO4 0TP
☎Lymington(0590)42047

These cottages are situated near the sea in a quiet location about 1m E of Milford-on-Sea. The well furnished accommodation comprises lounge/diner with two divans, two bedrooms, kitchen, bathroom and WC.

All year MWB out of season 1wk min, 5wks max, 2units, 1–6persons ◇ [◆]
◆ ⌀ fridge ♨ Gas/Elec inclusive
⌷ can be hired ☎(150yds) ⊖ TV
⊕3pin square P ▥ ♨(1m) ➙
⊖ ⚇ (150yds)

Min£70 Max£110pw (Low)
Min£142 Max£218pw (High)

F Mr B Trehearne **Fishers Mead Flats** Keyhaven, Lymington, Hants SO4 0TP
☎Lymington(0590)42047

Terraced ground-floor flats in quiet rural surroundings. Three flats with one bedroom and a bed-sitting room, kitchen/diner, bathroom and WC.

All year MWB out of season 1wk min, 5wks max, 3units, 1–5persons ◇ [◆]
◆ ⌀ fridge ♨ Gas/Elec inclusive
⌷ can be hired ☎(150yds) ⊖ TV
⊕3pin square 10P ▥ ♨(1m) ➙
⊖ ⚇ (150yds)

Min£60 Max£82pw (Low)
Min£131 Max£172pw (High)

KILGETTY
Dyfed
Map2 SN10

B **Rhoslyn** Ash Park
for bookings Powell's Cottage Holidays High Street, Saundersfoot, Dyfed
☎Saundersfoot(0834)812791

Modern, detached bungalow in quiet cul-de-sac. Comprising lounge/dining area and kitchen, three bedrooms, bathroom and WC. Off A477 at Kilgetty, 2½m from Saundersfoot and 5½m from Tenby.

May–Sep MWB out of season 1wk min, 4wks max, 1unit, 2–5persons [◇] ◆

Keyhaven
—
Killiecrankie

◎ fridge Electric Elec inclusive ⌷ can be hired ☎(100yds) Iron & Ironing board in unit CTV ⊕3pin square 2P ▥ ♨(100yds)
⊖ ⚇ (200yds) ♫(2m) ♪(2m)
Min£81 Max£180pw

KILKHAMPTON
Cornwall
Map2 SS21

B & C **No 1 & 2 Mill House, No 2 Hawkers Cottage, Chapel Cottage, Ford Cottage & The Carpenters Shop** Coombe for bookings The Landmark Trust, Shottesbrooke, Maidenhead, Berkshire SL6 3SW
☎Littlewick Green(062882)5925

A group of six properties built round a ford on a shallow, fast-running stream and situated in a wooded valley, ¼ mile from the sea. They include four thatched cottages, a converted carpets workshop and Mission Hall and offer two-three bedrooms with either twin, single or bunk beds, sleeping between 2-6 people. All well-furnished and containing a number of country antiques and situated in a glorious position in secluded hamlet. 3¼ miles from Kilkhampton on unclass road towards coast.

All year MWB out of season 3days min, 4wks max, 6units, 1–6persons ◆ no pets (ex dogs) ◎ fridge Night storage & open fire Elec inclusive
⌷ not provided ☎(½m) Iron & Ironing board in unit ⊙ ⊕3pin square 2P ▥(every 2 days) ♨(5m)
⊖ ⚇ (3m)

Min£133 Max£320pw (Low)
Min£165 Max£320pw (High)

C **Grenville & Stowe Cottages**
Houndapitt Farm Holiday Cottages
for bookings Mrs D H W Heard, 61 Kings Hill, Bude, Cornwall
☎Bude(0288)2756

Originally Houndapitt farmhouse, now tastefully converted into two self-catering cottages. Grenville has a large kitchen with Aga cooker, lounge, dining room and sleeps up to nine persons. Stowe has a ground-floor bathroom, kitchen, lounge, dining room, three bedrooms sleeping up to seven persons and a small front garden. Stibb ¾m W unclass road towards Sandy Mouth.

All year MWB out of season 3days min, 4wks max, 2units, 2–9persons [◇] ◆
◆ ◎ fridge Electric Elec inclusive
⌷ can be hired ☎(100yds) WM & SD on premises ⊙ CTV ⊕3pin square P ♨(100yds)
⊖ ♂(3m) ⚇ (100yds) 🐾(3m)

Details not confirmed for 1987

C **1–8 Houndapitt Farm Cottages**
for bookings Mrs D H W Heard, 61 Kings Hill, Bude, Cornwall
☎Bude(0288)2756

Eight cottages converted from farm buildings all with lounge/kitchen/diner and shower room/WC. Three of the cottages have one double bedroom and one twin, whilst the other five have two double and one twin room. Many of the rooms afford sea views. Stibb 1¼m W unclass road towards Sandy Mouth.

Feb–Dec MWB out of season 3days min, 4wks max, 8units, 2–7persons [◇] ◆ ◆ ◎ fridge Electric Elec inclusive ⌷ can be hired ☎(100yds) WM & SD on premises ⊙ CTV ⊕3pin square P ♨(100yds) Games room Fishing Horse riding
⊖ ⚇ (100yds) ♫(2m) ♪(2m)

Details not confirmed for 1987

KILLIECRANKIE
Tayside *Perthshire*
Map14 NN96

Ch Mrs E P Stephen **Old Faskally Chalets** Killiecrankie, Pitlochry, Perthshire PH16 5LR
☎Pitlochry(0796)3436

Situated 4 miles N of Pitlochry, these recently constructed chalets are pleasantly sited amongst conifers and comprise lounge/dining room with double

bed-settee, two bedrooms, one twin, one double-bedded and an open kitchen area.
All year MWB out of season 3days min, 5units, 1–6persons [◆ ◆] ◎
fridge Electric Elec inclusive
▣inclusive ☎(¼m) WM & TD on premises Iron & Ironing board on premises ⊙ CTV ⊕3pin square 12P ▥ ♨(¼m)
↤ ♪(3m) ♚(¼m)
Min£95 Max£126pw (Low)
Min£165 Max£215pw (High)

KILLINGTON
Cumbria
Map**7** SD69

C Mr & Mrs C M Kevan **Upper Ghyll Style Cottage** Killington, Sedbergh, Cumbria LA10 5EH
☎Sedbergh(0587)20628

17th-century stone-built cottage overlooking terraced gardens with good views of Howgill Fells and comprising lounge, kitchen, bathroom and two bedrooms.
All year MWB out of season 1wk min, 1unit, 2–6persons ◆ ◆ ◎ fridge
▮ Elec metered ▣can be hired
☎(500yds) WM in unit Iron & Ironing board in unit ⊙ CTV ⊕3pin square 2P ♨(3m)
↤ ♪(3m) ♚(3m)
Min£50 Max£80pw (Low)
Min£100 Max£140pw (High)

KILMELFORD
Strathclyde *Argyllshire*
Map**10** NM81

C *Ardenstur Cottages*
for bookings Woodside Park Estates, Park Avenue, Hartlepool TS26 0EA
☎Hartlepool(0429)67266

Detached stone building forming three modernised self-contained cottages, in a sheltered hillside position. Each comprises lounge/diner with open-plan kitchenette, one twin bedroom and a bathroom in two cottages, the other having a shower. Situated off the A816 at the head of Loch Melford.
All year MWB out of season 1wk min, 5wks max, 3units, 1–6persons [◇] ◆ ◎ fridge Electric & open fires
Elec metered ▣inclusive ☎(3m) Iron & Ironing board in unit ⊙ ⊕3pin square P ♨(3m) Fishing, sailing & deer stalking
↤ ♚(3m)
Details not confirmed for 1987

C **Steading Cottage**
for bookings Woodside Park Estates, Park Avenue, Hartlepool, Cleveland TS26 0EA
☎Hartlepool(0429)67266

A terraced cottage forming part of a stone building beside Melfort Farm, Loch Melfort. On the ground floor is the sitting room, kitchen/diner and shower room/WC, and on the first floor two twin bedrooms.

Killiecrankie
—
Kilninver

All year MWB out of season 1wk min, 5wks max, 1unit, 1–4persons ◆ ◎
fridge Electric & open fires
Elec metered ▣inclusive ☎(2m) Iron & Ironing board in unit ⊙ ⊕3pin square 2P ▥ ♨(2m)
↤ ♚(2m)

H **Top Ardenstur**
for bookings Woodside Park Estates, Park Avenue, Hartlepool, Cleveland TS26 0EA
☎Hartlepool(0429)67266

A quietly situated detached stone house with super views over Loch Melfort. It is comfortably furnished and comprises open plan lounge/diner/kitchenette, WC and one twin bedroom downstairs, and upstairs a bathroom and two twin bedrooms one of which is accessed from the other.
All year MWB out of season 1wk min, 5wks max, 1unit, 1–6persons ◆ ◎
fridge Electric & open fire Elec metered
▣inclusive ☎(3m) Iron & Ironing board in unit ⊙ ⊕3pin square 4P ▥
♨(3m)
↤ ♚(3m)

KILMORY
Strathclyde *Argyllshire*
Map**10** NR77

B **Holiday Homes at Kilmory**
for bookings Castle Sween Bay (Holidays) Ltd Estate Office, Ellary, Lochgilphead, Argyll PA31 8PB
☎Ormsary(08803)232 or 209 & Achnamara(054685)223

Five modern chalet-style bungalows in an isolated location, with magnificent views overlooking the Sound and Isle of Jura. Accommodation comprises three bedrooms, lounge, kitchen, bathroom and verandah. All units are fitted to a good standard. Windsurfing boards and cycles for hire. Fishing.
All year MWB out of season 2nights min, 5units, 1–6persons ◆ ◎ fridge
Electric Elec metered ▣not provided
☎(½m) TV ⊕3pin square P ♨(2½m)
Min£103 Max£204pw

KILNINVER
Strathclyde *Argyllshire*
Map**10** NM82

C **Alpein Cottage**
for bookings D R Kilpatrick, Kilninver, Oban, Argyll PA34 4UT
☎Kilninver(08526)272 (before 9pm)

Single-storey cottage beautifully situated on a 1000-acre estate, overlooking loch towards the Island of Mull, 8m S of Oban off A816 road signed Kilninver/Easdale. The accommodation consists of two bedrooms, lounge/dining room, kitchen and bathroom. There is also a garage with a table tennis table.

20Mar–10Nov 1wk min, 1unit, 1–4persons ◆ ◆ ◎ fridge
Electric Elec inclusive ▣not provided
☎ SD, TD, Iron & Ironing board in unit
CTV ⊕3pin square 2P ▥ ♨(8m)
Loch fishing & boat free
Min£120 Max£220pw

C **Dairy Cottage**
for bookings D R Kilpatrick, Kilninver, Oban, Argyll PA34 4UT
☎Kilninver(08526)272 (before 9pm)

An estate cottage with views across the fields to the sea loch. Accommodation comprises two bedrooms (one double bed, folding single bed and two bunk beds), living room with convertible settee, kitchen, bathroom/WC. The barn has been converted into a games room.

20Mar–10Nov 1wk min, 1unit, 1–6persons ◆ ◆ ◎ fridge
Electric Elec inclusive ▣not provided
☎(75yds) SD, TD, Iron & Ironing board in unit CTV ⊕3pin square P ▥
♨(8m) Loch fishing & boat free
Min£120 Max£220pw

H **Home Farm**
for bookings D R Kilpatrick, Kilninver, Oban, Argyll PA34 4UT
☎Kilninver(08526)272 (before 9pm)

Modern detached house built on a hillside in the 1000-acre estate grounds offering splendid views northwards towards Island of Mull, 8m S of Oban on A816. Accommodation comprises sitting room, dining room, kitchen, four bedrooms, one double, one twin, one family room and a single-bedded room. There is also a bed-settee in the sitting room, a separate games room and bathroom/WC plus additional WC.

20Mar–10Nov 1wk min, 1unit, 1–9persons ◆ ◎ fridge
Electric Elec inclusive ▣not provided
☎ SD & TD in unit Iron & Ironing board in unit CTV ⊕3pin square 6P ▥
♨(8m) Loch fishing & boat free
Min£140 Max£280pw

H **The Old Kirk**
for bookings D R Kilpatrick, Kilninver, Oban, Argyll PA34 4UT
☎Kilninver(08526)272 (before 9pm)

18th-century kirk on part of the 1000-acre Kilninver Estate converted into a holiday home with pine-panelled interior, situated on a rocky knoll with fine views across Loch Feochan. Accommodation comprises open plan kitchen/living area, three twin bedrooms, bathroom/WC. A children's games room has been built into the loft, with two beds and one folding bed.

20Mar–10Nov 1wk min, 1unit, 1–9persons ◆ ◆ ◎ fridge
Electric Elec inclusive ▣not provided
☎(200yds) SD & TD in unit Iron & Ironing board in unit ⊙ CTV
⊕3pin square P ▥ ♨(8m) Loch fishing & boat free
Min£140 Max£280pw

H The Old Manse
for bookings D R Kilpatrick, Kilninver, Oban, Argyll PA34 4UT
☎Kilninver(08526)272

A former manse fully modernised and delightfully situated within the grounds of Kilninver Estate which is set on a hillside with views of the islands of Kerrera and Mull. Accommodation comprises kitchen/diner/lounge, with convertible bed, two bedrooms and bathroom.

20Mar–10Nov 1wk min, 1unit, 1–6persons ⬗ ◆ ◎ fridge Electric Elec inclusive 🄻not provided ☎(½m) SD & TD in unit Iron & Ironing board in unit ⊙ CTV ⊕3pin square P 🅼 ⛟(8m) Games room Loch fishing & boat free

Min£120 Max£220pw

KINGHAM
Oxfordshire
Map**4** SP22

***H & C* Yew Tree Cottage, The Lodge and The Coach House**
for bookings Mrs V Metcalfe, Pegasus, West End, Kingham, Oxford OX7 6YL
☎Kingham(060871)8071

Converted from a Georgian country house, two houses and one cottage of imposing proportions. ***Yew Tree Cottage*** *has open plan kitchen, lounge, dining areas, one double, one twin and one single bedroom.* ***The Lodge*** *has separate lounge, combined kitchen/dining area, one double,.one twin and one single bedroom.* ***The Coach House*** *stone-built about 250 years ago, has four bedrooms, one with en suite bathroom, bathroom and separate WC, lounge/dining room, kitchen/breakfast room and playroom/music room. All are elegant, spacious with quality equipment.* **Southern England Holiday Home of the Year – see page 10.**

Allyear MWB out of season 3days min, 1mth max, 3units 1–8persons [◇] ⬗ ◆ ◎ fridge 🔥 Elec inclusive 🄻inclusive ☎(100yds) WM & SD in unit TD in 1 unit Iron & Ironing board in unit ⊙ Ⓦ CTV ⊕3pin square 20P 🅼 ⛟(100yds) Hard

⊖ 🍷 🎵 ♫

Min£95 Max£180pw (Low)
Min£150 Max£260pw (High)

KINGSBRIDGE
Devon
Map**3** SX74

C Little Melbury 126 Church Street
for bookings Mr L Thackstone, Melbury Hotel, Devon Road, Salcombe, Devon TQ8 8HJ
☎Salcombe(054884)2883

Situated in the old part of town, close to church, shops and estuary, this modernised and tastefully appointed cottage comprises three bedrooms, lounge, with double put-u-up, kitchen/diner and bathroom/WC all on first floor level.

Etr–Sep MWB out of season 1wk min, 1mth max, 1unit, 2–8persons ⬗ no pets ◎ fridge Electric Elec metered 🄻not provided ☎(100yds) Iron & Ironing board in unit [Launderette within 300yds] ⊙ CTV ⊕3pin square 3🏠 🅼 ⛟(100yds)

⊖ 🍷(10yds) 🎵(200yds) 🎥(¼m)

Min£100 Max£210pw

C Mrs J Lambert **Stanbrook Court** 114 Fore Street, Kingsbridge, Devon TQ7 1AW
☎Kingsbridge(0548)6959

Quiet 'inner courtyard' setting at rear of Georgian Stanbrook Court. Accommodation comprises on the ground floor, two bedrooms (one double, the other with one single, two bunks and single put-u-up) and bathroom/WC. The first floor consists of kitchen and combined lounge/diner. Comfortable and tastefully appointed in a central position in Kingsbridge.

Mar–Sep 3days min, 4wks max, 1unit, 2–6persons ⬗ ◆ no pets ◎ fridge Electric fires & radiators Elec metered 🄻inclusive ☎(100yds) [WM, SD & TD on premises] Iron & Ironing board in unit ⊙ CTV ⊕3pin square 🅼 ⛟(100yds)

⊖ 🍷(200yds) 🎵(½m) ♫(½m) 🎥(½m)

Min£80 Max£150pw (Low)
Min£145 Max£240pw (High)

KING'S CAPLE
Hereford & Worcester
Map**3** SO52

F Captain & Mrs J F Cockburn
Pennoxstone Court King's Caple, Herefordshire HR1 4TX
☎Cary(043270)284

A first-floor flat in a Georgian mansion on a fruit farm. The accommodation comprises a kitchen/diner, bathroom, two bedrooms and a lounge which can also serve as an additional bedroom. There are extensive grounds open to guests. Situated about ¾m W of the village.

Etr–Oct 1wk min, 4wks max, 1unit, 1–7persons ⬗ ◆ ◎ fridge Electric Elec metered 🄻can be hired ☎(½m) Iron & Ironing board in unit ⊙ CTV ⊕3pin square P 🅼 ⛟(5½m) Fishing

⊖ 🍷(¾m)

Details not confirmed for 1987

See advertisement under Hereford.

KING'S NYMPTON
Devon
Map**3** SS61

C Mrs S D Francis **Collacott Farm Luxury Cottages** Kings Nympton, Umberleigh, Devon
☎South Molton(07695)2491

Four terraced two-storey cottages ***(Kings, The Shippon, The Linney and Pond)*** *recently converted from period-stone barns. Accommodation comprises lounge, kitchen/diner, two/three bedrooms and bathroom/WC in each cottage. All tastefully furnished and decorated.*

Apr–Jan MWB out of season 2days min 1mth max, 4units, 1–8persons [◇] ⬗ ◆ ◎ fridge 🔥 & woodburner Elec metered (heating only) 🄻inclusive ☎(1m) Iron & Ironing board in unit [Launderette on premises] ⊙ CTV ⊕3pin square 12P ⛟(1m) ⛵

⊖ ⛳(3m) 🍷(1m)

Min£80 Max£141pw (Low)
Min£117 Max£295pw (High)

H Sletchcott
for bookings Mrs W P Stuart-Bruges,
Quarley Down, Cholderton, Nr Salisbury,
Wiltshire SP4 0DZ
☎Cholderton(098 064)235

*Farmhouse of historical interest set in 3
acres of gardens and orchard. Study,
drawing room, kitchen/diner, one
bedroom all on ground floor. On the first
floor there are four bedrooms, all with oak
beams and bathroom. Special features are
inglenook fireplaces and an old bread
oven. Electricity paid to caretaker. Leave
A377 at King's Nympton railway station
onto B3226. Turn right in 1m to King's
Nympton.*

All year MWB out of season 4days min,
6mths max, 1unit, 2–10persons [◇]
◆ ◆ ⊚ fridge Storage heaters
�827not provided ☎(1½m) WM & SD in
unit Iron & Ironing board in unit ☺ ⊛
CTV ⊕3pin square P 🏠(1½m)
⊕ 🍺(1½m)

Min£55 Max£130pw (Low)
Min£160 Max£275pw (High)

KINGSTON DEVERILL
Wiltshire
Map**3** ST83

**C Mr R A Brown Kingston House
Holiday Cottages** Kingston Deverill,
Warminster, Wiltshire BA12 7HE
☎Maiden Bradley(09853)448

*Five skilfully converted adjoining cottages
in grounds of Kingston House. Foxlinch
and Badgers Mount are one-bedroomed,
whilst Rylands, Hatherwood and
Churchfields have two bedrooms each. All
cottages are well-appointed with lounge/
diner, kitchen and bathroom/WC.*

All year MWB out of season 3days min,
6mths max, 5units, 1–4persons [◇] ◆
◆ (Pets charged for) ⊚ fridge
Electric Elec metered ⎿inclusive ☎
Iron & Ironing board on premises
[Launderette on premises] ☺ CTV
⊕3pin square 5P 🏠(250yds)
🔥(heated)
⊕ 🍺(3m)

King's Nympton
—
Kingswear

Min£80 Max££140pw (Low)
Min£170 Max£270pw (High)

F Mrs R A Brown Kingston House (Flats)
Kingston Deverill, Warminster, Wilts
BA12 7HE
☎Maiden Bradley(09853)448

*Ground- and first-floor flats in a large
stone-built country house dating from the
17th century and standing in 2½ acres of
grounds. Ground floor comprises two
bedrooms (both with a double and single
bed), lounge/diner, large kitchen and
bathroom/WC. One of the first-floor flats
comprise kitchen/lounge/diner,
bathroom/WC and two bedrooms (both
with double and single bed). The other has
kitchen/diner, lounge, bathroom/WC and
two bedrooms (one twin-bedded and one
with a double and single bed).*

All year MWB out of season 1wk min,
6mths max, 3units, 1–6persons [◇]
[◇] ◆ ⊚ fridge Electric
Elec metered ⎿inclusive ☎
[Launderette on premises] ☺ CTV
⊕3pin square 3P 🏠(200yds)
🔥(heated)
⊕ 🍺(3m)

Min£98 Max£145pw (Low)
Min£210 Max£272pw (High)

C Rose Cottage
for bookings Mrs R A Brown, Kingston
House, Kingston Deverill, Warminster,
Wilts BA12 7HE
☎Maiden Bradley(09853)448

*Self-contained cottage with own entrance
attached to country house in 2½ acres of
gardens. Accommodation comprises
kitchen/diner, lounge and bathroom/WC.
Two first-floor bedrooms each with a
double and single bed.*

All year MWB out of season 1wk min,
6mths max, 1unit, 1–6persons [◇]
[◇] ◆ ⊚ fridge Electric
Elec metered ⎿inclusive ☎ Iron &
Ironing board in unit [Launderette on
premises] ☺ ⊛ CTV ⊕3pin square
3P 🏠(200yds)

⊕ 🍺(3m) 🔥(heated)
Min£103 Max£150pw (Low)
Min£218 Max£275pw (High)

KINGSTON UPON THAMES
Greater London
Map**4** TQ16

F Hotel Antoinette Ltd 26 Beaufort Road
Kingston upon Thames, Surrey KT1 2TQ
☎01-546 1044

*Two flats situated near an excellent
shopping centre, and with good train
services to London. Accommodation
comprises either one or two bedrooms
(twin-bedded), lounge, kitchen and
bathroom.*

All year 1night min, 8mths max, 2units,
1–6persons [◇] ◆ ◆ ⬭ ⊚
fridge 🍴 Gas/Elec inclusive
⎿inclusive ☎ Iron & Ironing board in
unit ☺ CTV can be hired
⊕3pin square P 📺 🏠(100yds)
⊕ 🍺(½m) 🎵(½m) ♫(½m) 🍺(½m)

KINGSWEAR
Devon
Map**3** SX85

C Brittania Cottage
for bookings Mr & Mrs J A Hutching, 2
Longford House, Priory Street, Kingswear,
Dartmouth, Devon TQ6 0AB
☎Kingswear(080425)389

*This detached riverside cottage was once
occupied by the keeper of the railway
crossing. The accommodation now
converted and well furnished comprises
lounge, open plan dining room/kitchen,
three bedrooms one with a double and
single bed, one twin-bedded and one with
double bed and folding bed, bathroom,
shower and WC. Large lawns with flower
beds and garden seating.*

All year MWB out of season 3days min,
1unit, 1–7persons ◆ ◆ ⊚ fridge
Storage & convector heaters
Elec metered ⎿can be hired ☎ Iron &
Ironing board in unit ☺ CTV
⊕3pin square 3P 📺 🏠(1m)
⊕ 🍺(¼m)
Min£170 Max£300pw

C **Longford Cottage Mews**
for bookings Mr & Mrs J A Hutching, 2
Longford House, Priory Street, Kingswear,
Dartmouth, Devon TQ6 0AB
☎Kingswear(080425)389

*Once a coach house and stabling, this
modernised character property is situated
just yards from the river.* **Curlew Cottage**
*all ground floor consists lounge/diner with
door to patio garden, kitchenette, a
double and a twin bedroom and separate
bath/WC.* **Fulmar Cottage** *has a first floor
lounge with a double and single put-u-up,
kitchen/diner, ground-floor bedroom with
one twin and two bunk beds, first-floor
bedroom with a double and single bed
and modern bathroom.*

All year   MWB out of season   3 days min,
2 units, 1–10 persons ◇ ♣ ◎ fridge
Storage & convector heaters
Elec metered ⌷can be hired
☎(20yds)   SD in unit   Iron & Ironing
board in unit   [Launderette within
300yds] ⊙ CTV ⊕3pin square 1P
⚐(½m)

↭ ⚑(½m)

Min£70 Max£130pw (Low)
Min£120 Max£190pw (High)

KINLOCHARD
Central *Perthshire*
Map**11** NN40

F **Forest Hills Estate** Kinlochard,
Aberfoyle, Perthshire
☎Kinlochard(08777)277

*Part of a multi-ownership/time share
development complex in the grounds of a
hotel overlooking Loch Ard. All units have
been furnished and equipped to the
highest standards, and comprise large
lounge/diner with drop down double bed,
modern kitchen area, large balcony, and
two twin-bedded rooms. Each property
has a bathroom/WC with whirlpool and
sauna, a second bathroom/WC, and a
shower room/WC with heated cabinet.*

All year   3 nights min, 47 units,
1–6 persons ◇ [♣ ♠] ◎ fridge
🍴 Elec metered ⌷inclusive ☎ Iron &
Ironing board in unit ⊕ ❀ CTV
⊕3pin square P ⚐(½m) ⫸ water
sports 🏊Hard 𝄢

↭ ⚑(200yds) 🎵(200yds)
Min£300 Max£580pw

KINLOCHEWE
Highland *Ross & Cromarty*
Map**14** NH06

B **Cairn Shiel** Tarridon Road
for bookings Mr C V Dodgson, Butter
Crags, Grasmere, Cumbria LA22 9QZ
☎Grasmere(09665)259

Kingswear
—
Kinlochleven

*Spacious and comfortable modern
bungalow located within the northern
boundary of the spectacular Beinn Eighe
nature reserve. The accommodation
comprises of open plan lounge/dining
room, two twin-bedded rooms, one family
bedroom, kitchen, bathroom and
cloakroom/WC. Located on the Torridon
road, ½m from the village.*

Mid Mar–mid Nov   MWB out of season
1 wk min, 4 wks max, 1 unit, 1–7 persons
◇ no pets ◎ fridge Electric
Elec metered ⌷not provided ☎(½m)
Iron & Ironing board in unit ⊙
⊕3pin square 3P ⚐(½m)

↭ ⚑(½m)

Min£110 Max£160pw

KINLOCHLAGGAN
Highland *inverness-shire*
Map**14** NN58

H & C   G A D Chalmer **Ardverikie Estate
Ltd** Estate Office, Kinlochlaggan,
Newtonmore PH20 1BY
☎Laggan(05284)300

*Set in a 35,000-acre estate in secluded
highland setting the five stone-built
houses offer modernised facilities in
traditional buildings of character ranging
from a turreted Victorian Gate Lodge
sleeping 3–4, to a large farmhouse
sleeping 10–16. Access from A86 Spean
Bridge/Newtonmore Road approximately
15m south of Newtonmore.*

All year   MWB out of season   3 days min,
4 wks max, 5 units, 3–16 persons ◇
◑ or ◎ fridge Gas/electric/oil or open
fire heating Gas & Elec inclusive ⌷can
be hired ☎ Iron & Ironing board in unit
⊕ CTV in some units ⊕3pin square
P ⛾ ⚐(6m)

Min£60 Max£340pw

KINLOCHLEVEN
Highland *Argyllshire*
Map**14** NN16

Ca **Log Cabin**
for bookings Mr Paul Bush, Mamore
Lodge, Kinlochleven, Argyll PA40 4QH
☎Kinlochleven(08554)213

*Log cabin of modern design situated on a
hillside within the grounds of Mamore
Lodge and commands a spectacular view
over the town some 800ft below. The cabin
is on one level and offers lounge/diner/*

---

*kitchen, two twin-bedded rooms and
shower/WC. Access is by a 1m drive from
the B863 on the North Lochside road just
out of Kinlochleven.*

All year   MWB out of season   1 day min,
3 mths max, 1 unit, 2–6 persons [◇] ◆
♣ Dogs charged for ◎ fridge
Elec metered ⌷inclusive ☎(330yds)
[Launderette on premises] ⊙ CTV
⊕3pin square 2P ⛾ ⚐(2m) Games
room, fishing
↭ ⚑

Min£99 Max£260pw

H **Mamore Farmhouse**
for bookings Mr Paul Bush, Mamore
Lodge, Kinlochleven, Argyll PA40 4QH
☎Kinlochleven(08554)213

*The farmhouse is situated in the grounds
of Mamore Lodge and comprises large
lounge/diner, kitchen, four bedrooms and
WC all on ground floor level plus two
separate showers and one bathroom all
with WCs on lower ground floor. Access is
by a 1m drive from the B863 on the North
Lochside Road just out of Kinlochleven.*

All year   MWB out of season   1 day min,
3 mths max, 1 unit, 2–8 persons [◇] ◆
♣ Dogs charged for ◎ fridge
Electric   Elec metered ⌷inclusive
☎(330yds)   Iron & Ironing board in unit
[Launderette on premises] ⊙ CTV
⊕3pin square 3P ⛾ ⚐(2m) Games
room, fishing
↭ ⚑

Min£99 Max£260pw

F Mr Paul Bush **Mamore Lodge (Flats)**
Kinlochleven, Argyll PA40 4QH
☎Kinlochleven(08554)213

*Large, white-painted shooting lodge
dating from 1902 standing 800ft above sea
level in 45,000-acre estate. Magnificent
views. The house has been converted into
two ground-floor and three first-floor flats
and offers good standard in décor and
modern furniture. Three of the flats have
three bedrooms sleeping six and two have
accommodation to sleep eight. The house
is situated on a steep hillside with a 1m
drive from the B863 on the North Lochside
Road just out of Kinlochleven.*

All year   MWB out of season   1 day min,
5 units, 6–8 persons [◇] ◆ ♣
Dogs charged for ◎ fridge
Elec metered ⌷inclusive ☎ Iron &
Ironing board on premises [Launderette
on premises] ⊙ CTV ⊕3pin square
50P ⛾ ⚐(1m) Games room, fishing
↭ ⚑ 🎵(1m) 🎵(1m) 🐾(1m)

Min£99 Max£260pw

KINLOCH RANNOCH
Tayside *Perthshire*
Map**14** NN65

F   Loch Rannoch Estate Kinloch
Rannoch, Pitlochry, Perthshire
☎Kinloch Rannoch(08822)201

*Multi ownership/time share units, built on
a hillside overlooking Loch Rannoch and
offering the facilities of the adjacent hotel.
Accommodation comprises either one, two
or three bedrooms and one, two or three
bathrooms and WC's. All have lounge/
diner, with drop down double bed, kitchen
and balcony with French doors and patio
furniture. In house video system available
and some units have a sauna.*

All year   3 nights min, 85 units,
1–8 persons   ◇ [◈ ◆] ◎ fridge
🍴 [Elec] Ⓛinclusive ☎ Iron &
Ironing board in unit [Launderette within
300yds] ⊕ ⓥ CTV ⊕3pin square
P ♨(½m) ⅋ dry ski slope, squash
court, gymnasium/solarium, marina,
nature trail

⊕ ⬛(200yds) 🎏(200yds)
Min£195 Max£580pw

KINNERTON
Powys
Map**3** SO26

C   Corner House
for bookings Mrs R L Jones, Upper House,
Kinnerton, Presteigne, Powys LD8 2PE
☎Whitton(05476)207

*Attractive black and white/stone cottage
in peaceful hamlet 2 miles west of Offa's
Dyke, comfortably furnished, offering
accommodation comprising lounge with
open fire, kitchen/diner, two bedrooms
and bathroom. It has an attractive garden.
Farm produce and logs available.*

All year   MWB out of season   3 days min,
1 unit, 1–6 persons   ◇ ◆ ◎ fridge
🍴 Elec metered Ⓛnot provided
☎(100yds) Iron & Ironing board in unit
⊕ CTV ⊕3pin square 3P ♨(2¼m)

Min£30 Max£50pw (Low)
Min£70 Max£100pw (High)

KIPPFORD
Dumfries & Galloway *Kirkcudbrightshire*
Map**11** NX85

Ch   Mr & Mrs McLellan River View Park
Kippford, Dalbeattie, Kirkcudbrightshire
DG5 4LG
☎Kippford(055662)204
*Small complex of Norwegian-style
timbered lodges set well apart on
landscaped hillside overlooking the Urr
estuary and one mile from Kippford. Each*

Kinloch Rannoch
—
Kirkbymoorside

*lodge comprises open-plan lounge/
dining/kitchen area and either two or
three bedrooms.*

Closed 15 Jan–15 Feb & 15 Nov–15 Dec
MWB out of season   3 days min, 4 wks max,
6 units, 2–7 persons   [◇] ◈ ◆ ◎
fridge 🍴 Elec metered Ⓛcan be
hired ☎(1m) [WM, SD & TD on
premises] Iron & Ironing board ⊙
CTV ⊕3pin square 12P 🔟 ♨(½m)

⊕ ♊ ⬛(1m)
Min£100 Max£170pw (Low)
Min£160 Max£255pw (High)

KIRBY HILL
North Yorkshire
Map**12** NZ10

F   Old Grammar School
for bookings The Landmark Trust,
Shottesbrooke Park, Maidenhead,
Berkshire SL6 3SW
☎Littlewick Green(062882)5925
*Converted 16-century grammar school
adjacent to village church.
Accommodation is on first and second
floors above the small community hall and
includes sitting room, combined
bathroom/WC, two twin-bedded rooms
plus a folding bed for a fifth person.*

All year   MWB out of season   1 day min,
3 wks max, 1 unit, 1–5 persons   ◎ fridge
Electric Elec inclusive Ⓛinclusive
☎(50yds) Iron & Ironing board in unit
⊙ ⊕3pin square 🔟 ♨(½m)

⊕ ⬛(50yds)
Min£133 Max£260pw (Low)
Min£165 Max£260pw (High)

KIRKBY MALHAM
North Yorkshire
Map**7** SD86

C   Glen Cottage
for bookings Mrs J Richardson, 563
Gisburn Road, Blacko, Nelson, Lancashire
☎Nelson(0282)66122
*A pretty little 17th century cottage
comprising a fitted kitchen with dining
area, comfortable lounge, two twin-
bedded rooms and bathroom. Situated in
the centre of the village.*

All year   MWB   3 mths max, 1 unit,
2–4 persons   ◈ ◆ ◎ fridge
Electric fires Elec metered Ⓛcan be
hired ☎(50yds) Iron & Ironing board in
unit ⊙ CTV ⊕3pin square 1P 🔟
♨(5m)

⊕ ⬛(50yds)
£54pw (Low)
Min£80 Max£119pw (High)

C & F   Mr & Mrs G Durham *Scalegill*
Kirkby Malham, Skipton, N Yorks
BD23 4BN
☎Airton(07293)293

*Scalegill consists of a water mill converted
into five modern flats and a row of three
stone-built cottages which were previously
for the mill workers. They are of varying
sizes sleeping from two to six people. Set in
5¼ acres of secluded grounds to the east
of the village.*

All year   MWB out of season   3 days min,
3 wks max, 8 units, 2–6 persons   ◆ no
pets (in flats) ◎ fridge 🍴
Elec metered ☎ Iron & Ironing
board on premises ⊙ CTV
⊕3pin square 12P 🔟 ♨(2m) Fishing

⊕ ⬛(1m)

Details not confirmed for 1987

KIRKBYMOORSIDE
North Yorkshire
Map**8** SE68

H   Glenmorven Gillamoor
for bookings Mr Griffiths, Country &
Coastal Self Catering Holidays, 9 Birdgate,
Pickering, North Yorkshire
☎Pickering(0751)75058

*A detached house on the edge of the
village near the North York moors,
situated in a large unspoilt garden with all
round views. The sleeping
accommodation is for eight people in four
bedrooms, one of which has bathroom en
suite; large living room, kitchen, dining
room and cloakroom/WC.*

All year   MWB out of season   1 day min,
3 mths max, 1 unit, 1–8 persons   [◇] ◈
◆] ◎ fridge Elec metered Ⓛcan
be hired ☎(150yds) ⊙ CTV
⊕3pin square 2P 🔟 ♨(2m)

⊕ ♊(2m) ⬛(150yds)
Min£50 Max£300pw

C   Town Farm Cottage
for bookings Mr Griffiths, Country &
Coastal Self Catering Holidays, 9 Birdgate,
Pickering, North Yorkshire
☎Pickering(0751)75058

*An 18th-century converted farmhouse with
original beams and small garden. The
accommodation sleeps up to nine people
in four bedrooms, with living room, dining
room, kitchen and two bedrooms.*

All year   MWB out of season   1 day min,
3 mths max, 1 unit, 1–9 persons   [◇] ◈
◆ ♩ fridge 🍴 Gas/Elec metered →

L can be hired ☎(50yds) ⊕ CTV
⊕3pin square P Ⅲ ♨(50yds)
⊖ ♪(½m) ♨(50yds)
Min£50 Max£200pw

KIRKBY-ON-BAIN
Lincolnshire
Map**8** TF26

H Clements Farmhouse
for bookings Mrs K J Laughton, Wellsyke
Farm, Kirkby on Bain, Woodhall Spa,
Lincolnshire LN10 6YU
☎Woodhall Spa(0526)52151
*Former farmhouse in peaceful rural
location, with adequate accommodation
consisting of lounge, dining room, kitchen,
bathroom and four/five bedrooms.*

All year MWB out of season 1wk min,
1unit, 8persons ◆ ◆ no pets ◎
fridge Electric & open fires
Elec metered L not provided ☎(1m)
Iron & Ironing board in unit TV
⊕3pin square 6P 2🏠 ♨(1m)
⊖ ♪(3m) ♨(1m) 🐾(3m)

Details not confirmed for 1987

KIRKCUDBRIGHT
Dumfries & Galloway *Kirkcudbrightshire*
Map**11** NX65

H Bomble Glen Farm House
for bookings G M Thomson & Co, 27 King
Street, Castle Douglas, Kirkcudbrightshire
DG7 1AB
☎Castle Douglas(0556)2701 & 2973
*Modernised farmhouse tastefully
furnished with many period and antique
pieces. The spacious accommodation
offers kitchen, dining room, sitting room,
sun lounge, four bedrooms and two
bathrooms. Situated in a lovely setting
within its own grounds by the side of a
burn, amidst farm land 3m E of
Kirkcudbright.*

Mar–Nov 1wk min, 1unit, 1–8persons
◎ fridge Electric & open fires
Elec inclusive L not provided WM & SD
in unit Iron & Ironing board in unit ⊙
TV ⊕3pin square P ♨(3m) Games
room, fishing
Min£125 Max£275pw

Kirkbymoorside
—
Kirkhill

C Cumstoun Cottage Cumstoun House
for bookings G M Thomson & Co, 27 King
Street, Castle Douglas, Kirkcudbrightshire
DG7 1AB
☎Castle Douglas(0556)2701 & 2973
*A wing of Cumstoun House which has
recently been converted to provide one
double bedroom, one twin-bedded room,
kitchen, bathroom, WC and living/dining
room with a view.*

Mar–Nov 1wk min, 1unit, 1–4persons
◆ ◎ fridge 🔥 & wood burning
stove Elec inclusive L not provided
Iron & Ironing board in unit ⊙ CTV
⊕3pin square P ♨(2m) ⚓Hard
Dinghy & canoe available
⊖ ♪(3m) ♨(2m)
Min£85 Max£155pw

KIRKHILL
Highland *Inverness-shire*
Map**14** NH54

C Mr M Fraser Garden Cottage Reelig
House, Kirkhill, Inverness-shire IV5 7PR
☎Drumchardine(046383)208
*A stone-built cottage with wood clad
extension in an original farmyard type
situation. The interior is largely wood
panelled in original materials, it comprises
lounge and sitting room with polished
wood floors, open fire and studio-couch,
kitchen/diner, bathroom, one single
bedroom and one double bedroom with
additional single bed. Facilities include
games room and fishing.*

All year MWB out of season 1wk min,
1unit, 6persons [◆ ◆] ◎ fridge
Elec metered L can be hired ☎ Iron &
Ironing board in unit [Launderette on
premises] ⊙ CTV ⊕3pin square 6P
Ⅲ ♨(5m)
⊖ ♨(2m)
Min£80 Max£116pw (Low)
Min£123 Max£175pw (High)

F Garden Flat
for bookings Mr M R Fraser, Reelig House,
Kirkhill, Inverness-shire IV5 7PR
☎Drumchardine(046383)208
*A conversion of a farm building providing
a large hallway, kitchen, living room and
three bedrooms. The estate is reached by
an unclass road leading from A862.*

Apr–Oct MWB out of season 1wk min,
1unit, 1–7persons [◆ ◆] ◎ fridge
Electric Elec metered L can be hired
☎ Iron & Ironing board in unit
[Launderette on premises] ⊙ CTV
⊕3pin square P Ⅲ ♨(5m)
putting green, Fishing, Croquet, Games
room
⊖ ♨(2m)
Min£87 Max£122pw (Low)
Min£130 Max£185pw (High)

C Gate Lodge
for bookings Mr M R Fraser, Reelig House,
Kirkhill, Inverness-shire IV5 7PR
☎Drumchardine(046383)208
*Stone-built cottage standing at estate
entrance by hump backed bridge ¼m from
A862. It contains a kitchen/diner, living
room and two twin-bedded rooms.*

All year MWB out of season 1wk min,
1unit, 1–4persons [◆ ◆] ◎ fridge
Electric Elec metered L can be hired
☎ Iron & Ironing board in unit
[Launderette on premises] ⊙ CTV
⊕3pin square P Ⅲ ♨(5m) putting
green, Fishing, Croquet, Games room
⊖ ♨(2m)
Min£80 Max£116pw (Low)
Min£123 Max£175pw (High)

C Hardies Byre
for bookings Mr M R Fraser, Reelig House,
Kirkhill, Inverness-shire IV5 7PR
☎Drumchardine(046383)208
*A converted stone-built byre standing in
estate woodlands. It contains lounge/
dining room, kitchen and three bedrooms.*

All year MWB out of season 1wk min,
1unit, 1–5persons [◆ ◆] ◎ fridge
Electric Elec metered L can be hired
☎ Iron & Ironing board in unit
[Launderette on premises] ⊙ CTV
⊕3pin square P Ⅲ ♨(5m)

putting green, Fishing, croquet, games room

⊖ ☎(2m)

Min£87 Max£122pw (Low)
Min£130 Max£185pw (High)

C Mill House
for bookings Mr M R Fraser, Reelig House, Kirkhill, Inverness-shire IV5 7PR
☎Drumchardine(046383)208

A modernised stone-built cottage standing in estate woodlands. It contains kitchen, dining room, sitting room and three bedrooms. The estate is reached by unclass road leading from A862.

All year MWB out of season 1wk min, 1unit, 1–5persons [◆ ◆] ⑨ fridge Electric Elec metered Ⓛcan be hired ☎ Iron & Ironing board in unit [Launderette on premises] ⊕ CTV ⨁3pin square P Ⓜ ♨(5m) putting green, Fishing, croquet, games room

⊖ ☎(2m)

Min£87 Max£122pw (Low)
Min£130 Max£185pw (High)

Ch Reelig Glen Chalets
for bookings Mr M R Fraser, Reelig House, Kirkhill, Inverness-shire IV5 7PR
☎Drumchardine(046 383)208

Twelve cedar wood chalets all having pleasant views. They are either two or three-bedroomed, some with open plan kitchen/sitting room. The estate is reached by unclass road leading from A862.

Apr–Oct MWB out of season 1wk min, 12units, 1–5persons [◆ ◆] ⑨ fridge Electric Elec metered Ⓛcan be hired ☎ Iron & Ironing board in unit [Launderette on premises] ⊕ CTV ⨁3pin square P Ⓜ ♨(5m) Fishing, croquet, games room

⊖ ☎(2m)

Min£80 Max£122pw (Low)
Min£123 Max£185pw (High)

KIRKOSWALD
Cumbria
Map**12** NY54

C Mr R Massingham Crossfield Farm
Kirkoswald, Cumbria CA11 9NQ
☎Lazonby(076883)711

Red sandstone farm buildings have been tastefully converted into six charming cottages. Set in attractive surroundings with two trout lakes in the grounds and lots of domesticated farm animals. Four of the cottages have a combined lounge/diner/kitchen, one double bedroom and a modern bathroom, all have sheltered balconies. The other two cottages are

---

Kirkhill
—
Kniveton

larger, one has a double and a twin bedroom, the other a double and a triple bedroom, they feature oak beams and flag floors. All are well-furnished and comfortable. There is a children's play area, fishing and a picnic area by the river.

All year MWB out of season 2days min, 6units, 2–5persons [◇] ◆ ◆ ⑨ fridge Elec metered Ⓛcan be hired ☎ [WM & SD on premises] Iron & Ironing board on premises ⊕ ⑩ CTV ⨁3pin square 30P Ⓜ ♨(2m)

⊖ ☎(½m)

Min£65 Max£189pw

KIRKPATRICK DURHAM
Dumfries & Galloway Kirkcudbrightshire
Map**11** NX87

B Walton Park Farm Cottage
for bookings G M Thomson & Co, 27 King Street, Castle Douglas, Kirkcudbrightshire DG7 1AB
☎Castle Douglas(0556)2701 & 2973

Modern, fully-furnished bungalow on quiet farmland near the River Urr. It has two double-bedded rooms, each with a single and double bed, a twin-bedded room, kitchen, bathroom and a living room. Situated just off the B784 towards Corsock.

All year MWB out of season 1wk min, 6mths max, 1unit, 1–8persons ◆ no pets ⑨ fridge Open & electric fires Elec inclusive Ⓛnot provided ☎(2m) WM & SD in unit Ironing board in unit TV ⨁3pin square P Ⓜ ♨(2m) Fishing in private loch and use of boat

Min£85 Max£155pw

KIRKTON MANOR
Borders Peeblesshire
Map**11** NT23

C Glenrath Farm Cottages
for bookings Mrs J P Campbell, Glenrath Farm, Kirkton Manor, Peebles
☎Kirkton Manor(072 14)221

Situated in rolling-border hill country approximately 6½m from Peebles. The three stone and stone cottages, built 30 years ago, form a part of a large farm complex. They are well decorated and pleasantly furnished and sited close to the main farm buildings. The cottages have small garden areas and stand in tree-studded surroundings. Electricity charged separately.

All year MWB out of season 1wk min, 1mth max, 3units, 2–8persons ◆ ◆ ⑨ fridge Electric storage Electric metered Ⓛcan be hired ☎(4m) Ironing board in unit ⊕(2units) CTV ⨁3pin square P ♨(7m) Fishing

Min£58 Max£110pw (Low)
Min£110 Max£155pw (High)

KNIGHTON
Powys
Map**7** SO27
See **Llangunllo**
See also advertisement on page 140

KNIGHTON-ON-TEME
Hereford & Worcester
Map**7** SO67

H Church Farm House
for bookings Mrs C Hurst, Peters Place, Gorst Hill, Rock, Kidderminster, Worcestershire
☎Rock(0299)266216

Large, Georgian farmhouse that has been converted into two apartments. Both comprise kitchen, lounge/dining room, two bedrooms (one double, one twin) and bathroom/WC. A remote, peaceful location.

All year MWB out of season 3days min 2mths max 2units 1–5persons no pets ⑨ fridge Open fires & calor gas Elec inclusive Ⓛcan be hired ☎ WM & SD in unit Iron in unit ⊕ TV ⨁3pin square 4P Ⓜ ♨(¾m)

⊖ ☎(1m)

Details not confirmed for 1987

KNIVETON
Derbyshire
Map**8** SK25

H Merryfields Farm
for bookings Mrs E J Harrison, Little Park Farm, Okeover, Ashbourne, Derbyshire
☎Thorpe Cloud(033529)341

A detached pebbledash and tiled farmhouse just 100yds off the B5035 Ashbourne/Wirksworth road (signposted Kniveton Wood). The accommodation consists of two double bedrooms and one twin-bedded, kitchen, dining room, lounge, bathroom/WC and separate WC. Places of interest in the north Staffordshire and Derbyshire border accessible, but own transport is a necessity.

Apr–Oct 1wk min, 3wks max, 1unit, 1–6persons, nc2 ⑨ fridge Electric & coal fires Elec metered Ⓛnot provided ☎(½m) TV ⨁3pin square P ♨(2m)

⊖ ☎(½m)

Min£65 Max£100pw

KNOCK
Highland *Inverness-shire*
See **Skye, Isle of**

LAIRG
Highland *Sutherland*
Map**14** NC50

F   The Hotel Apartment
for bookings Sutherland Arms Hotel, Lairg,
Sutherland IV27 4AT
☎Lairg(0549)2291
A first-floor apartment in the hotel and
with separate entrance to rear. Two
bedrooms, one double and one twin
bedded, lounge/diner with bed-settee
kitchen and bathroom.

Mid Apr−Oct   1wk min, 1 unit,
2−6 persons ◈ ◆ ◎ fridge
Electric   Elec metered   ⌷ inclusive
☎(in hotel)   Iron & Ironing board in unit
⊕ ⊛ CTV ⊕3 pin square P
♨(200yds)   fishing, deer stalking,
pony trekking

⊖ 🍷
£85pw (Low)
Min£145 Max£205pw (High)

C   The Cottage
for bookings Sutherland Arms Hotel, Lairg,
Sutherland IV27 4AT
☎Lairg(0549)2291
Single-storey cottage in grounds of hotel
with views over Loch Shin. Two bedrooms,
one twin and one double-bedded, lounge/

Knock
—
Lambley

diner with convertible settee, well
equipped kitchen and modern bathroom.

All year   1wk min, 1 unit, 2−6 persons ◈
◆ ◎ fridge   Electric   Elec metered
⌷ inclusive ☎(75yds)   Iron & Ironing
board in unit ⊕ CTV ⊕3 pin square
P ♨(200yds)   Fishing, deer stalking,
pony trekking

⊖ 🍷(75yds)
£85pw (Low)
Min£145 Max£205pw (High)

F   Garden Cottages
for bookings Sutherland Arms Hotel, Lairg,
Sutherland IV27 4AT
☎Lairg(0549)2291
Tastefully converted apartments with one
or two bedroomed accommodation,
lounge/diner, kitchen and bathroom, all
furnished to a good standard. Located in
hotel grounds.

All year   1wk min, 4 units, 2−6 persons
◈ ◆ ◎ fridge   Electric
Elec metered   ⌷ inclusive ☎(50yds)
Iron & Ironing board in unit ⊕ CTV
⊕3 pin square P ♨(200yds)   Fishing,
deer stalking & pony trekking

⊖ 🍷(50yds)

Min£70 Max£85pw (Low)
Min£190 Max£205pw (High)

LALEHAM
Surrey
Map**4** TQ06

H Mr D J Patmore **Burway House** Ferry
Lane, Laleham on Thames, Middlesex
TW18 1SP
☎Staines(0784)57773

Set in secluded, mature, walled garden,
overlooking a park and a few yards from
the Thames is this self contained unit in
the owners Tudor style house. It has a
large double bedroom, bathroom/WC,
lounge with double bed-settee, kitchen
and a separate WC.

All year   MWB out of season   3 days min,
7 wks max, 1 unit, 4 persons [◇] ◈ ◆
no pets ◎ fridge   ⌷ can be hired ☎
Iron & Ironing board on premises ⊕
⊛ CTV ⊕3 pin square 1P ♨(50yds)
⊖ ♪(1m) 🍷(100yds) 🐾(2m)

Min£100 Max£125pw (Low)
Min£130 Max£150pw (High)

LAMBLEY
Northumberland
Map**12** NY65

C   Bracken Cottage & Meadow View
for bookings Mrs M Dawson, Park
Burnfoot Farm, Featherstone, Haltwhistle,
Northumberland
☎Haltwhistle(0498)20378

Two pleasant little cottages in a terrace of four, in a lovely setting with magnificent views of the surrounding countryside, with their own well maintained little gardens. Both cottages have one double and one twin bedroom, bathroom, separate kitchen and combined lounge and dining room.

Etr–Oct MWB out of season 2days min, 1mth max, 2units, 4persons [◇] ◈
◆ ◎ fridge open fires Elec metered
Ⓛcan be hired ☎(200yds) Iron in unit
☉ TV ⊕3pin square 2P ▧(1m)

⊖ ♨ (2m)
Min£45 Max£110pw

LAMLASH
Strathclyde *Buteshire*
See **Arran, Isle of**

LANDSHIPPING
Dyfed
Map**2** SN01

H Woodhouse Grange
for bookings Powell's Cottage Holidays, 55 High Street, Saundersfoot, Dyfed
☎Saundersfoot(0834)812791

An interesting 17th-century farmhouse standing in extensive grounds alongside the estuary of the River Cleddau where small boats can be launched and 1m S of Landshipping Quay. The Landshipping Pottery is situated in the grounds and visitors are welcome. There are five bedrooms, several with good views, a drawing room, sitting room, dining room, kitchen, conservatory and garden.

May–Sep MWB out of season 1wk min, 6wks max, 1unit, 2–10persons ◇ ◆
no pets ◎ fridge ▥ Elec inclusive
Ⓛcan be hired WM in unit Iron &
Ironing board in unit ☉ CTV
⊕3pin square P ▧(1½m) Fishing

⊖ ♨(1m)
Min£165 Max£351pw

LANGDALE, GREAT
Cumbria
May**11** NY30

Ch Coniston, Grasmere & Ullswater
for bookings The Langdale Partnership, Great Langdale, Ambleside, Cumbria
LA22 9JD
☎Langdale(09667)302

Norwegian alpine lodges in the wooded Langdale Estate, offering superb luxury accommodation of sumptuous lounge/diner with high quality furnishings and a pull-down bed, also extremely well-fitted kitchen. **Coniston & Grasmere** have these facilities as well as two bedrooms, one with an en-suite whirlpool bathroom and separate hydro-massage shower. **Ullswater**, the largest sized lodge, has an additional bedroom to the above.

All year 7nights min, 38units, 2–8persons [◇] ◈ ◆ no pets ◎
fridge ▥ Elec metered Ⓛinclusive
☎ Iron & Ironing board in unit ☉ ⊕
CTV ⊕3pin square 100P ▧(½m)

Lambley
—
Lazonby

▨ Sauna, solarium, gym, spa bath, squash courts

⊖ ♨ 🎵

Details not confirmed for 1987

LANREATH
Cornwall
Map**2** SX15

F Mr R W Potts **The Old Rectory**
Lanreath, Looe, Cornwall PL13 2NU
☎Lanreath(0503)20247

Seven well converted and attractively furnished flats in large rectory on outskirts of village. Two flats on ground floor, comprising kitchen, lounge/diner, one twin and one double bedroom with inter-connecting bathroom. Four flats on first floor, comprising kitchen, lounge/diner with either one or two double bedrooms, bathroom and WC. One flat on second floor, comprising kitchen, lounge/diner with twin sofa bed, two twin-bedded rooms and bathroom/WC.

All year MWB out of season 1wk min, 1mth max, 7units, 1–6persons ◇ ◈
no pets ◎ fridge Storage heaters
Elec metered Ⓛcan be hired
☎(200yds) [WM, SD & TD on premises]
Iron & Ironing board on premises ☉
CTV ⊕3pin square 10P ▥
▧(400yds) ⌒ Croquet lawn

⊖ ♨ (200yds)
Min£60 Max£160pw (Low)
Min£100 Max£215pw (High)

LAUNCESTON
Cornwall
Map**2** SX38

B & C Mrs J A Chapman **Higher Bamham Farm** Launceston, Cornwall
PL15 9LD
☎Launceston(0566)2141

One bungalow and four cottages converted from stone and cob farm buildings, all well-equipped and tastefully furnished. Each comprise either open-plan lounge/diner with kitchen area or separate kitchen, one, two or three bedrooms and bathroom/WC or shower/WC. The one bedroom cottage also has a bed-settee in the lounge. Private fishing is available to guests.

Etr–Oct MWB out of season 1wk min, 1mth max, 5units, 4–8persons ◇ ◆
no pets ◎ fridge Electric
Elec metered Ⓛcan be hired ☎(½m)
Iron & Ironing board on premises ☉
CTV ⊕3pin square P ▥ ▧(1m) ▨
Solarium

⊖ ♨(1½m) ♨(1m) 🎵(1m) ♩(1m)
Min£40 Max£80pw (Low)
Min£120 Max£270pw (High)

C **Primrose Cottage** Langore
for bookings Mrs K Riley, Bywater, Westbridge Road, Launceston, Cornwall
PL15 8HS
☎Launceston(0566)3216

Detached stone and cob cottage situated in a small village and would make an ideal touring base. Accommodation comprises, hallway, lounge with polished flag stone floor and exposed beams, kitchen/dining area, bathroom, one double bedroom and one bunk-bedded room.

All year MWB out of season 2days min, 1mth max, 1unit, 4persons ◇ ◆
no pets ◎ fridge ▥ & solid fuel
Elec metered Ⓛinclusive ☎(½m) WM &
SD in unit Iron & Ironing board in unit
CTV ⊕3pin square 1P ▥ ▧(1m)

⊖ ♨(1m) ♨ (2m)
Min£75 Max£145pw

H Mr & Mrs Graham-Jones **Tredidon** St Thomas, Launceston, Cornwall PL15 8SJ
☎Pipers Pool(056686)288

This self-contained wing of a beautiful period farmhouse with attractive gardens, amidst rural surroundings on a 200-acre farm. The very spacious accommodation consists of a large entrance hall, living room, master bedroom, three double bedrooms, one single bedroom with adjoining bathroom and WC on each floor. There are many interesting features including a parliament clock set above the Georgian stairway, a barrel ceiling in the master bedroom, which is of stately home proportions. Provides an opportunity to experience gracious living at moderate cost.

Mar–Sep MWB out of season 1wk min, 1mth max, 1unit, 1–9persons ◇ ◈
◆ no pets ◎ fridge Electric & log
fires Elec inclusive Ⓛnot provided ☎
WM in unit Iron & Ironing board in unit
☉ CTV ⊕3pin square P ▥ ▧(3m)
Fishing & games room

⊖ ♨(3m)
Details not confirmed for 1987

LAZONBY
Cumbria
Map**12** NY53

C **Eden Grove Holiday Cottages**
for bookings Mrs E P Bell, The Post Office, Lazonby, Penrith, Cumbria CA10 1BX
☎Lazonby(076883)242 & 437

A row of late 19th-century cottages in the village. Each has a lounge/diner, spacious kitchen and three bedrooms. Two cottages have two twin- and one single-bedded rooms, the other two have one double, one twin and one room with bunk-beds. Bedrooms and bathrooms are all on the first floor.

All year MWB out of season 5days min, 6mths max, 4units, 5–6persons ◇ ◆
no pets ◎ fridge/freezer ▥
Elec metered Ⓛnot provided ☎(½m)
WM Iron & Ironing board in unit ☉
CTV ⊕3pin square P ▥ ▧(½m) →

141

⊖ ♀(¼m)

Min£55 Max£80pw (Low)
Min£90 Max£130pw (High)

LEA
Hereford & Worcester
Map**3** SO62

C   Castle End Cottage
for bookings Captain M R Lowe, Castle
End, Lea, Ross-on-Wye, Herefordshire
☎Lea(098981)276

*A stone-built cottage comprising kitchen/
dining room, bathroom/WC, lounge, two
singles and one double bedroom. It is
simply but comfortably furnished and
guests have use of garden.*

Apr–Oct 2days min, 4wks max, 1unit,
1–4persons [◇] ◆ ◆ ⓦ fridge
Electric & open fires   Elec metered
Ⓛnot provided ☎(½m) Iron & Ironing
board in unit TV ⊕3pin square P 🎦
🎿(½m) ⌂ ⚲Hard

⊖ ♀(½m)

Min£40 Max£85pw

LEADBURN
Borders *Peeblesshire*
Map**11** NT25

H   Easter Deans Farmhouse
for bookings Mrs J P Campbell, Glenrath
Farm, Kirkton Manor, Peebles,
Peeblesshire
☎Kirkton Manor(07214)221

*This farmhouse is on the last farm in
Tweeddale and is only 12 miles from
Edinburgh, with Peebles 9 miles to the
south. It is 1 mile off the A703 and ideally
situated for touring the Borders. The
accommodation includes large kitchen,
two lounges, three bedrooms and
bathroom.*

May–Oct MWB out of season 1wk min,
1mth max, 1unit, 2–8persons ◆ ⓦ
fridge   Electric & open fires
Elec metered Ⓛcan be hired ☎(1½m)
Iron & Ironing board in unit ⊕ CTV
3pin square 3P 🎿(4m)

⊖ ♀(1½m)

Min£100 Max£150pw (Low)
Min£175 Max£230pw (High)

Lazonby
—
Leckmelm

LEAMINGTON SPA (ROYAL)
Warwickshire
Map**4** SP36

F   Ettington House 13 Radford Road
for bookings Mrs Reader, 4 Offchurch
Lane, Radford Semele, Leamington Spa,
Warwickshire CV31 1TN
☎Leamington Spa(0926)24801

*Early 19th-century house at southern edge
of town divided into ground, first and
second-floor flats and a maisonette. The
flats sleep up to three persons and
comprise kitchen, lounge/diner with bed-
settee, bathroom/WC and one twin-
bedded bedroom. The maisonette sleeps
up to five and comprises lounge/diner,
kitchen, bathroom, WC and three
bedrooms, all with wash hand basins. Car
not essential.*

Apr–Oct MWB 1wk min, 1mth max,
4units, 1–5persons, nc5yrs no pets ⓦ
fridge   Electric   Elec metered Ⓛinclusive
(except towels which can be hired) ☎
Iron & Ironing board in unit [Launderette
within 300yds] ⊙ ⓥ CTV
⊕3pin square 4P 🎦 🎿(100yds)

⊖ δ(½m) ♀(200yds) 🎣(½m)
♬(½m) ⛵(½m)

Min£65 Max£170pw

LECKMELM
Highlands *Ross & Cromarty*
Map**14** NH19

B   The Bungalow
for bookings The Manager, Leckmelm
Holiday Cottages, Loch Broom, Garve,
Ross-shire IV23 2RL
☎Ullapool(0854)2471

*Comfortable modern bungalow situated
on edge of chalet complex with extensive
views of Loch Broom. The
accommodation comprises kitchen/diner,
lounge, two bedrooms sleeping up to five
people, bathroom and WC. Direct access
from the A835.*

All year MWB out of season 3days min,
4wks max, 1unit, 1–5persons [◆ ◆]
ⓦ fridge 🍳 & coal fire Elec metered
Ⓛcan be hired ☎(½m) Iron & Ironing
board in unit [Launderette on premises]
CTV ⊕3pin square 4P 🎦 🎿(3m)
Fishing, shooting & rowing boat available

⊖ ♀(200yds)

Min£70 Max£85pw(Low)
Min£130 Max£160pw(High)

Ca   The Cabin
for bookings The Manager, Leckmelm
Holiday Cottages, Leckmelm, Loch Broom,
Garve, Ross-shire IV23 2RL
☎Ullapool(0854)2471

*Wood-built cabin commanding fine views
of Loch Broom. Accommodation consists
of kitchen, lounge/dining room, double
bedroom, single bedroom and a third
bedroom containing bunks. 3½m E of
Ullapool on the A835.*

May–Oct MWB out of season
3days min, 4wks max, 1unit, 1–5persons
[◆] ⓦ fridge Electric Elec metered
Ⓛcan be hired ☎ [WM & SD on
premises] Iron & Ironing board in unit
⊙ CTV ⊕3pin square P 🎿(3½m)
Fishing, shooting & rowing boat available

⊖ ♀

Min£65 Max£80pw (Low)
Min£120 Max£150pw (High)

C   Campbeltown Cottages
for bookings The Manager, Leckmelm
Holiday Cottages, Loch Broom, Garve,
Ross-shire IV23 2RL
☎Ullapool(0854)2471

*Substantial stone building housing six
cottages, all containing kitchen, living/
dining room, twin- or double-bedded room
and a bedroom with full-size bunks. Set
some 300yds from A835 3mE of Ullapool.*

All year MWB out of season 3days min,
4wks max, 6units, 1–4persons ◆ ◆
ⓦ fridge 🍳 coal fires Elec metered
Ⓛcan be hired ☎(½m) [WM & SD on
site] Iron & Ironing board in unit ⊙
⊕3pin square P 🎿(3m) Fishing,
shooting & rowing boat available

⊖ ♀(½m)

Min£60 Max£70pw (Low)
Min£90 Max£110pw (High)

C Lochside Cottages
for bookings The Manager, Leckmelm
Holiday Cottages, Loch Broom, Garve,
Ross-shire IV23 2RL
☎Ullapool(0854)2471

*Attractive modern cottages on the slope of
Loch Broom adjacent to the Leckmelm
Farm. Two of the units are semi-detached
and all contain kitchens, sitting/dining
rooms, double or twin bedrooms. 300yds
from main A835.*

Allyear MWB out of season–3days min,
4wks max, 3units, 1–4persons ◆ ◆
◎ fridge 🍴 coal fire Elec metered
Ⓛcan be hired � [WM & SD on site]
Iron & Ironing board in unit ◎
⊕3pin square P ⚓(3m) Fishing,
shooting & rowing boat available

⟿ ☕(¾m)

Min£65 Max£80pw (Low)
Min£120 Max£150pw (High)

LEEK
Staffordshire
Map**7** SJ95

C Lowe Hill Cottages No 1 & No 2
for bookings Mrs C M Pickford, Lowe Hill
Farm, Ashbourne Road, Leek,
Staffordshire
☎Leek(0538)383035

*Two cottages in a row of three stone-built
terraced cottages (approximately 200-
years-old), in fairly peaceful location. ¾m S
of Leek just off A523. Both cottages have
been tastefully modernised and have
simple but clean décor. No 1 comprises
kitchen/diner, lounge with exposed ceiling
beam and natural stonework. Upstairs
there is a family bedroom, a small double
bedroom and bathroom/WC. No 2
comprises lounge/diner/kitchen on
ground-floor, the small kitchen area has a
breakfast bar. One double bedroom and
bathroom/WC on first floor.*

Allyear MWB out of season 2days min,
2units, 6persons ◆ (No 1) no pets
No 2 ◎ fridge Electric & open fires
Elec metered Ⓛcan be hired �(¼m)
Iron & Ironing board in No 1 TV
⊕3pin square P 📺 ⚓(¼m)
⟿ 🜨(2m) ☕(¼m) 🎦(1m) 🎵(1m)
🐾(1¼m)
Min£45 Max£110pw

LELANT
Cornwall
Map**2** SW53

Ch St Ives Holiday Village
for bookings Haven Holidays, PO Box 20,
Truro, Cornwall TR1 2UG
☎Truro(0872)40400

*This Holiday Village consists of stone and
cedar-clad chalets each with two
bedrooms, lounge/kitchen, bathroom and
WC. The chalets are well-furnished and
well-sited in woodland.*

Etr–Sep MWB 2days min, 300units,
2–6persons [◇ ◈] ◆ no pets ◎
fridge Electric Elec metered
Ⓛinclusive � [Iron & Ironing board on
premises] [Launderette on premises]
☉ ☯ CTV ⊕3pin square
⊕2pin round 300P ⚓ ☒ restaurant.
sauna, bar & disco on site
⟿ 🜨(3m)
Min£59 Max£151pw (Low)
Min£136 Max£244pw (High)

LENDALFOOT
Strathclyde *Ayrshire*
Map**10** NX19

C Gull Cottage
for bookings Mrs M M Hay, Bon Accord, 50
Dalrymple Street, Girvan, Ayrshire
KA26 9BT
☎Girvan(0465)4421

*Modernised stone cottage comprising
attractive beamed split-level lounge/diner
with open stairway leading to two twin-
bedded rooms. Modern kitchen and
bathroom on ground floor. Located on the
foreshore with splendid views over Firth of
Clyde and Ailsa Craig.*

Allyear 1wk min, 1mth max, 1unit,
2–4persons ◆ ◎ fridge Electric
Elec metered Ⓛnot provided
�(150yds) Iron & Ironing board in unit
☉ CTV ⊕3pin square 3P ⚓(150yds)
Min£75 Max£160pw

LENTRAN
Highland *Inverness-shire*
Map**14** NH54

Ch Pine Chalets Newton Hill
for bookings Mr A Chisholm, 'Fernlea',
Kirkhill, Inverness, Inverness-shire
☎Drumchardine(046383)619

*Five wooden chalets set on a hillside
offering splendid views of the Beauly Firth
and the Black Isle. Units comprise kitchen,
living/dining room with two convertible
beds, two double or twin bedrooms, and
bathroom. Situated 8m W of Inverness on
an unclass road off the A862 at the village
of Inchmore.*

Mar–Oct MWB out of season 1wk min,
5units, 1–6persons ◆ ◆ ◎ fridge
Electric Elec metered Ⓛinclusive
�(1m) WM in 2 units Iron & Ironing
board in unit ☉ CTV ⊕3pin square
12P 📺 ⚓(5m)
⟿ ☕(1m) Childrens' play area
Min£90 Max£120pw (Low)
Min£140 Max£165pw (High)

LEOMINSTER
Hereford & Worcester
Map**3** SO45

**F & C Ashton Court Farm, Kiln Cottages
& Granary Cottages**
for bookings Mrs P Edwards, Ashton Court
Farm, Ashton, Leominster, Herefordshire
☎Brimfield(058472)245

*Four flats, two of which form part of a
farmhouse, the other two have been
converted from an old hop kiln. The first
two comprise lounge, two bedrooms and
sleep from two to ten people. The other
two flats are on the ground-floor and first-
floor with the 1st floor flat reached by an
outside staircase. Both sleep two people,
comprising double wall bed, kitchen and
bathroom/WC. The two cottages have
been tastefully converted from a half
timbered granary and approached by a
short flight of steps. Both comprise
kitchen/diner, sitting room with exposed
timbers a bathroom and two bedrooms.
Ashton 3m NE A49.*

Allyear MWB in season 2nights min,
1mth max, 6units, 1–10persons ◆ ◆
◎ fridge 🍴 Elec metered Ⓛcan be →

---

hired ☎(½m) Laundry room Iron & Ironing board in unit ☺ CTV ⊕3pin square P ▥ ♨(2m)

↩ ♨(2m)

Min£45 Max£60pw (Low)
Min£75 Max£110pw (High)

H   The Hollies Hyde Ash, Ivington
for bookings Mrs M O Wood, Little Dilwyn, Dilwyn, Herefordshire
☎Ivington(056888)279

A fully modernised country cottage in a quiet setting with garden and lawn. The accommodation comprises three bedrooms on the first floor and large kitchen, dining room, lounge and bathroom/WC on the ground floor.

Mar−Nov   3days min, 2wks max, 1unit, 1−6persons ◈ ◆   no pets ◎
fridge   Electric & open fires (fuel provided)   Elec metered ▢ provided ☎(½m)   WM & SD in unit   Iron & Ironing board in unit ☺ CTV   Freezer ⊕3pin square   4P ♨(3m)

↩ ♨(3m)

£65 (Low)
Min£80 Max£95pw (High)

LESNEWTH
Cornwall
Map**2** SX19

C   Courtyard Cottages
for bookings Mr & Mrs A Tomkinson, The Courtyard Farm, Lesnewth, Boscastle, Cornwall
☎Otterham Station(08406)256

These cottages are conversions from old farm and mill buildings some 200 years old, built of Cornish stone and slate round an attractive courtyard. There are seven cottages of varying sizes, most of which have panoramic views to the sea. Follow B3266 from Boscastle towards Camelford, turn left after Tredorh farm, follow signs to Lesnewth. Courtyard Farm is near church.

All year   MWB out of season   Wknd min, 1mth max, 7units, 2−8persons [◇] ◈ ◆   no pets ◎   fridge   Electric (heating free)   Elec metered ▢ can be hired ☎ [WM, SD & TD on premises]   Iron & Ironing board in unit ☺ CTV ⊕3pin square ⊕2pin round P ▥ ♨(2½m)   Games room, badminton court

---

Leominster
—
Lintrathen

↩ ♞ riding

Min£35 Max£60pw (Low)
Min£195 Max£315pw (High)

See advertisement under Boscastle

LEWES
East Sussex
Map**5** TQ41

F   19A Cliffe High Street
for bookings Mrs S J Chapple, 44 Hill Brow, Hove, E Sussex BN3 6QH
☎Brighton(0273)507381

First-floor flat in late 18th-century building comprising lounge/diner, separate kitchen, bathroom, WC and three bedrooms. Located half a mile from the castle.

Jun−Sep   1wk min, 3mths max, 1unit, 1−6persons ◈ ◆   no pets ◎
fridge   Electric   Elec metered ▢ inclusive except tea towels ☎(100yds)   Iron & Ironing board in unit [Launderette within 300yds] ☺   TV ⊕3pin square ♨(60yds)

↩ ♨(1m)
Min£95 Max£135pw

C   Leigh Cottage, 37 Southover High Street Southover
for bookings Mrs B M Cheeseman, High Barn, Piddinghoe, Newhaven, East Sussex BN9 9AW
☎Newhaven(0273)514484

A terraced three-storeyed cottage, comprising a twin and two single bedrooms, bathroom/WC, sitting room and kitchen/diner with direct access to garden patio.

All year   MWB out of season   4wks max, 1unit, 1−4persons, nc   no pets ◔ ◎
fridge ♨♨ Gas & Elec metered ▢ can be hired ☎(100yds)   Iron & Ironing board in unit ☺ CTV ⊕3pin square ▥ ♨(150yds)

↩ ♞
Min£75 Max£120pw (Low)
Min£150 Max£175pw (High)

LIFTON
Devon
Map**2** SX38

F   Wortham Manor
for bookings The Landmark Trust, Shottesbrooke, Maidenhead, Berkshire SL6 3SW
☎Littlewick Green(062882)5925

A large medieval manor house which dates back to the 15th century, set in its own grounds. The Hall has a lounge with polished wood floor, open fire place with beautiful carved wood surround, stone mullioned windows, kitchen/dining area, spiral stone staircase, two twin bedrooms and one single bedroom and bathroom/WC. The old Solar is a first floor apartment with kitchen/dining area, lounge with wooden floors, feature open stone fireplace and antique furniture, bathroom, two twin bedrooms and one single with a four poster bed. Miss Burgess Rooms is a ground floor apartment with kitchen, bathroom, one twin bedded room, large lounge with open fire and stone mullioned windows. All of the apartments have been furnished to suit the period of the manor.

All year   MWB out of season   2days min, 5wks max, 3units, 2−5persons ◈ ◎
fridge ♨♨ Elec inclusive ▢ not provided ☎(1m)   Iron & Ironing board in unit ☺ ⊕3pin square 6P ▥ ♨(1½m)

↩ ♨(1½m)

Min£100 Max£235pw (Low)
Min£110 Max£240pw (High)

LINTRATHEN
Tayside Angus
Map**15** NO25

Ch   Loanhead Chalet
for bookings Mrs M E Houston, Lintrathen Lodge, Kirriemuir, Angus DD8 5JJ
☎Lintrathen(05756)228

Modern single-storey chalet in elevated country location with panoramic views. Compact and secluded with two bedrooms, lounge/diner, kitchen and bathroom. On the outskirts of the village and reached via B951 Kirriemuir/Glenisla Road.

All year   MWB out of season   1wk min, 1mth max, 1unit, 1−6persons ◈ ◆

© fridge Electric Elec inclusive
ⓛinclusive ☎(1m) WM & SD in unit
Iron & Ironing board in unit ⊕ CTV
⊕3pin square 2P 🏠(2m)
£90 (Low)
Min£110 Max£150pw (High)

LISKEARD
Cornwall
Map2 SX26

Ca Deer Park Forest Cabins
for bookings Forest Holidays, Forestry
Commission, (Dept AA) 231 Corstorphine
Road, Edinburgh EH12 7AT
☎031-334 2576 or 0303
A beautiful and well run lakeside complex
offering peace and tranquillity. There are
45 log cabins all with open plan lounge,
dining and kitchen area and shower
room/WC. Twenty-nine units have one
double bedroom and one three-bunk-
bedded room plus roof play area. Sixteen
units have one double- and one two-
bunked bedrooms with further sleeping
area in lounge.

Feb–Dec MWB out of season
3days min, 6wks max, 45units,
1–6persons ◆ © fridge
Elec metered ⓛinclusive ☎ Iron &
Ironing board on premises [Launderette
on premises] ⊕ ⊕3pin square 45P
🛏 🏠(1m) table tennis
↔ ♀(2m)
Min£78 Max£240pw

LITTLEHAMPTON
West Sussex
Map4 TQ00

Ch Mr J A Sinclair Canadian Village
Rope Walk, Littlehampton, W Sussex
BN17 5DE
☎Littlehampton(0903)713816
Eighteen modern, one-, two- or three-
bedroomed bungalows with lounge/diner,
kitchen, bathroom and WC. Near to golf
course, 12 minutes walk from beach and
town centre. On the west bank of the River
Arun off the A259.

All year MWB 18units, 1–6persons ◆
◆ no pets © fridge Electric
Elec metered ⓛcan be hired ☎ Iron &
Ironing board in unit ⊕ CTV
⊕3pin square P 🛏 🏠(600yds)
↔ ♪ ♀(300yds) 🎵(1m) 🐾(1m)
Min£35 Max£70pw (Low)
Min£65 Max£190pw (High)

LITTLE HAVEN
Dyfed
See **WALWYNS CASTLE**

LITTLE HEREFORD
Hereford & Worcester
Map7 SO56

**C Mr & Mrs H W Porter Mistletoe Bough
Holiday Cottages** Little Hereford, Ludlow,
Shropshire SY8 4LQ
☎Brimfield(058472)311

Early 18th-century black and white
timbered barn, restored and converted

Lintrathen
—
Llanarthney

into two three-bedroomed and two two-
bedroomed cottages of great charm. All
have a large lounge, kitchen, bathroom,
and are furnished and decorated to a high
standard. 3 miles west of Tenbury off the
A456 Kidderminster/ Leominster road.

Mar–Oct & Xmas MWB out of season
3days min, 3wks max, 4units, 1–6persons,
nc5 © fridge Elec inclusive
ⓛinclusive ☎(½m) Iron & Ironing board
on premises ⊕ CTV ⊕3pin square
8P 3🛏 🛏
↔ ♀(½m)
Min£120 Max£175pw

LITTLE SALKELD
Cumbria
Map12 NY53

C & F Salkeld Hall Little Salkeld, Penrith,
Cumbria CA10 1NN
☎Langwathby(076881)618
An interesting historic building, part
medieval and converted in a way that
preserves many unusual features whilst
creating space and comfort. The Old
Nursery flat sleeps up to nine in three
bedrooms, one with bunks and a foldaway
bed in the lounge. The Willow Rooms and
Pepper Rooms flats sleep up to five in one
bedroom and foldaway bed in the
lounges. The Coach House and Hayloft
cottages both sleep up to six in two
bedrooms, one in the Hayloft with bunks,
and foldaway bed in the lounges.

All year MWB out of season 2nights min,
6mths max, 5units, 2–9persons [◇] ◆
◆ no pets © 🐾 Elec inclusive
ⓛcan be hired ☎ Iron & Ironing board
on premises (in unit in Cottages) ⊕ TV
can be hired in Penrith ⊕3pin square
12P 🛏 🏠(1½m)
↔ ♀(1½m)
Min£123 Max£313pw (Low)
Min£179 Max£377pw (High)

LITTLETHORPE
North Yorkshire
Map8 SE36

C Abbeydale Self Catering The Lodge
Littlethorpe Hall, Littlethorpe, Ripon, North
Yorkshire
☎Ripon(0765)5133 or York(0904)707211
A Victorian neo-Gothic gate lodge in
delightful surroundings accommodating
up to six people in three bedrooms. There
is a ground-floor bathroom/WC, kitchen,
living room and dining room.

All year 1night min, 4mths max, 1unit,
1–6persons ◆ © fridge 🐾
Elec metered ⓛinclusive ☎(½m) Iron &
Ironing board in unit ⊕ CTV
⊕3pin square 2P 🛏 🏠(1½m) 🖼
↔ ♪(3m) ♀(1½m)
Min£50pw (Low)
Min£60 Max£220pw (High)

Suffolk
Map5 TL94

C Vine Cottage
for bookings Suffolk Holiday Cottages, 1
Lower Road, Glemsford, Sudbury, Suffolk
CO10 7QU
☎Glemsford(0787)281577
The cottage is a half-timbered part of the
15th-century Wood Hall and has its own
private garden. Accommodation
comprises a sitting room with wood block
floor and open fireplace, kitchen, two twin-
bedded rooms and bathroom/WC. It has
many exposed beams and joists and an
oak front door.

All year MWB out of season 1wk min,
1unit, 1–5persons ◆ ◆ © fridge
Storage heaters Elec metered ⓛcan be
hired ☎ WM & SD in unit Iron &
Ironing board in unit ⊕ ⊕ CTV
⊕3pin square 3P 🏠(½m) Dishwasher
↔ ♀(30yds)
Min£64 Max£69pw (Low)
Min£140 Max£155pw (High)

LIZARD
Cornwall
Map2 SW71

**F Mr K Williams Penmenner House
Hotel** The Lizard, Cornwall TR12 7NR
☎The Lizard(0326)290370
Three flats attached to the hotel with No's
1 & 3 on the first floor and No 2 on the
ground floor. Each comprise open plan
lounge/kitchen/diner, bathroom/WC with
flats 1 & 2 having three bedrooms and flat
3 having two. Superb sea views from the
grounds.

Apr–Oct MWB out of season 1wk min,
4wks max, 3units, 1–6persons [◇] ◆
◆ © fridge Electric (night storage)
Elec metered ⓛnot provided
↔(20yds) Iron & Ironing board in unit
⊕ CTV ⊕3pin square P 🛏 🏠(½m)
putting green
↔ ♀(½m) 🎵(½m)
Min£70 Max£80pw (Low)

LLANARTHNEY
Dyfed
Map2 SN52

C Tower Hill Lodge
for bookings Landmark Trust,
Shottesbrooke, Maidenhead, Berkshire
SL6 3SW
☎Littlewick Green(062882)5925
An early 19th-century house looking
south over beautiful countryside in a
remote location. It comprises a lounge
with open fire, kitchen/diner, two
bedrooms (one twin and one triple with
additional single folding bed) and
bathroom/WC. This cottage is personally
furnished in keeping with its origin and
promotes charm and cosiness
throughout.

All year MWB out of season
wknd(winter) min, 1unit, 1–6persons ◆
no cats © fridge night storage →

145

Elec inclusive ⬜ not provided ☎(2m)
Iron & Ironing board in unit ⊙
⊕3pin square ⬛(2m)
⊖ ☎(2m)

Min£120 Max£230pw (Low)
Min£150 Max£245pw (High)

LLANBEDROG
Gwynedd
Map**6** SH33

B Hyfrydle, Mynytho
for bookings Mrs N A Overton, 7 Oak Drive,
Seisdon, Wolverhampton
☎Wolverhampton(0902)893855

A modernised stone cottage, set in a quiet
situation overlooking Abersoch and its
islands. All accommodation is on the
ground floor and comprises lounge with
inglenook fireplace, kitchen/diner,
bathroom/WC, two twin bedrooms
and one double bedroom.

All year   MWB out of season   3days min,
1mth max, 1unit, 2–6persons ◊ @
fridge portable heater Elec inclusive
⬜ not provided ☎(½m) SD in unit Iron
in unit CTV ⊕3pin square 4P ▦
⬛(½m)
⊖ δ(3m) ☎(3m)
Min£75 Max£240pw

H Tanrhiwiau 2 Ladbrooke, Mynytho
for bookings Mrs N A Overton, 7 Oak Drive,
Seisdon, Wolverhampton WV5 7ET
☎Wombourne(0902)893855

Modern detached house in elevated
position with good sea views. It comprises
lounge, dining room, kitchen on ground
floor and three bedrooms, plus bathroom
and WC on first floor. There is a
convertible settee in the lounge which
makes a single bed if required. 2m W
B4413.

All year MWB out of season 2day min,
6wks max, 1unit, 2–7persons ◊ @
fridge ☯ Elec inclusive
⬜ not provided ☎(200yds) SD in unit
Iron in unit ⊙ ◉ CTV
⊕3pin square 1P 1⌂ ▦ ⬛(200yds)
⊖ ☎(2m)
Min£75 Max£240pw

LLANBERIS
Gwynedd
Map**6** SH56

C Pen-y-Bryn & Ty-Cerrig Rallt Goch
for bookings Mrs J B Eaton, Gwynt-y-
Mynydd, Bryn Gwyn, Tan-y-Coed, Llanrug,
Gwynedd LL55 4RG
☎Caernarfon(0286)4481

Two compact stone cottages overlooking
the village and Llyn Padarn. **Pen-y-Bryn**

Llanarthney
—
Llandudno

comprises large lounge/diner, bathroom/
WC, kitchen and two bedrooms. **Ty-Cerrig**
comprises lounge, small dining room,
kitchen, bathroom/WC and two bedrooms,
one with bunks. Sheltered garden to rear
with garden furniture.

All year   MWB out of season   3days min,
6wks max, 2units, 2–7persons ◊ ◈
◆ ⌀(Ty-Cerrig) ◉(Pen-y-Bryn)
fridge ☯(Pen-y-Bryn) Gas & Electric
(Ty-Cerrig) Gas & Elec metered ⬜ can
be hired ☎(300yds) SD in unit Iron &
Ironing board in unit ⊙ CTV
⊕3pin square 2P ▦ ⬛(300yds)
Swimming, wind surfing & fishing in lake
200yds
⊖ ☎(150yds) 🎵(150yds)
Details not confirmed for 1987

LLANDEGFAN
Gwynedd
Map**6** SH57

C Pant Howel Cottage
for bookings Menai Holidays, Old Port
Office, Port Penrhyn, Bangor, Gwynedd
LL57 3HN
☎Bangor(0248)351055 or 362254

A converted farm cottage in a rural
situation with secluded lawns. All
accommodation is on the ground floor:
one double and one three bedded room;
lounge/diner; kitchen and bath/WC.

Jun–Sep 3days min, 6wks max, 1unit,
5persons ◈ ◆ fridge Elec &
open fires Elec metered ⬜ not provided
☎(1½m) Iron & Ironing board in unit
CTV ⊕3pin square 2P ⬛(2¼m)
⊖ ☎(1m) 🎵(2½m)
Min£120 Max£130pw (Low)
Min£150 Max£170pw (High)

LLANDEILO
Dyfed
Map**2** SN62

C The Maerdy Cottages Taliaris
for bookings Mrs M E Jones, Dan-y-Cefn,
Manordeilo, Llandeilo, Dyfed SA19 7BD
☎Llandovery(0550)777448
or Fakenham(0328)51155

Granary carefully converted and
modernised, comprises bath/shower/WC,
one double and one twin bedded room
(two extra single beds available) on the
ground floor and kitchen/diner, large
lounge with unique open fireplace on the
first floor. **The Cottage** part of a 17th-

---

century stone farmhouse with original
beams and fireplaces. Comprises bath/
WC, kitchen/diner, lounge on ground-floor
and one double and one twin-bedded –
room on first floor. **The Farmhouse**, the
other part of the original farmhouse
comprises kitchen/diner with Aga cooker,
lounge, second lounge with put-u-up on
ground floor and one double, two twin
bedded rooms and bath/shower/WC on
first floor. Three miles north of Llandeilo
on B4302.

All year MWB out of season 2days min,
6wks max, 3units, 2–8persons ◊ ◈
◆ ◉ fridge ☯(Granary) Storage/
open/wall heaters (The Farmhouse & The
Cottage) Gas/Elec metered ⬜ inclusive
☎(½m) WM, SD & TD on premises Iron &
Ironing board in unit ⊙ CTV
⊕3pin square P ▦ ⬛(3m)
⊖ ☎(3m) 🎵(3m) 🎵(3m)
Min£50 Max£145pw (Low)
Min£95 Max£310pw (High)

LLANDUDNO
Gwynedd
Map**6** SH78

F Conway Court Vaughan Street, for
bookings Mr A Robinson, Delamere, Bryn
Gosol Road, Llandudno LL30 1NT
☎Llandudno(0492)83884

Six self-contained holiday flats in the town
centre, fifty yards from promenade. Four of
the flats have two bedrooms sleeping six,
two have one bedroom sleeping three, all
have lounge with bed-settee or pull-down
bed, bathroom/WC and kitchen/diner.

All year MWB out of season 1wk min,
4wks max, 6units, 2–8persons ◊ ◆
◉ fridge Electric Elec metered
⬜ inclusive ☎ TD, Iron & Ironing
board in unit [Launderette within
300yds] ⊙ CTV ⊕3pin square
⬛(30yds)
⊖ δ(2m) ☎(20yds) 🎵(½m) 🎵(½m)
🌂(½m)
Min£75 Max£105pw (Low)
Min£135 Max£205pw (High)

F Mrs D O'Sullivan **Grove House** 118
Upper Mostyn Street, Llandudno,
Gwynedd
☎Llandudno(0492)75942

Seven compact flats contained in a three-
storey house, near to shops and sea. Units
have kitchen/diners or lounge/diners, bath
or shower room with WC and one
bedroom.

All year (ex Xmas) MWB out of season
3days min, 5wks max, 7units, 1–3persons,
nc6yrs no pets ◉ fridge Electric
Elec metered ⬜ inclusive ☎
[Launderette within 300yds] ⊙ CTV

⊕3pin square ⚓(30yds) Hair dryer available

↭ ♪(1m) ♀(30yds) ♬(150yds) ♬(150yds) ▓-(100yds)

Min£55 Max£75pw (Low)
Min£60 Max£145pw (High)

H 19 Victoria Street
for bookings Mr V Thomieson, Fairhaven Hotel, Promenade, Llandudno, Gwynedd
☎Llandudno(0492)76123

Three-storey modernised end of terrace property with kitchen and dining room on the ground floor, three bedrooms, two with wash hand basins, lounge and bathroom on the first floor and a further bedroom on the second floor.

Mar–Nov MWB 1wk min, 1mth max, 1unit, 1–9persons ◆ ◆ ♦ fridge
Electric & gas Gas/Elec metered
⬜inclusive ☎(20yds) Iron & Ironing board in unit [Launderette within 300yds] ☺ ⚈ CTV ⊕3pin square 2P ⚓(110yds)

↭ ♪(½m) ♀(20yds) ♬(100yds) ♬(½m) ▓-(1m)

Min£90 Max£130pw (Low)
Min£150 Max£175pw (High)

H Waters Edge West Parade, West Shore
for bookings Mr E J Carter, The Pines, Brockencote, Chaddesley Corbett, Kidderminster, Worcs.
☎Chaddesley Corbett(056283)210

A detached house overlooking the bay on the west shore. It comprises lounge, kitchen/diner and WC on the ground floor and WC, bathroom and three bedrooms on the first floor. Situated ¾m from the town centre.

Mar–Nov 1wk min, 3wks max, 1unit, 4–8persons ◆ no pets ♦ fridge
♥ Gas inclusive Elec metered
⬜not provided SD in unit [Launderette within 300yds] ☺ CTV ⊕3pin square P ⚈ ⚓(300yds)

↭ ♪(½m) ♀(300yds) ♬(¾m) ▓-(¾m)

Min£120 Max£155pw (Low)
Min£165 Max£230pw (High)

LLANDUDNO JUNCTION
Gwynedd
Map**6** SH87

C Castle Keep & Gwyrfai Cottages
Glan Conwy Corner
for bookings Mr A E Mardon, Gateway Cottages, 5 Prestwick Drive, Liverpool L237XB
☎051-924 6996

Architect-designed conversion of a typical Welsh cottage style house. **Castle Keep**

Llandudno
—
Llandyssul

comprises open plan lounge/kitchen, three bedrooms, one double and two twin-bedded and bathroom/WC. **Gwyrfai** has lounge, kitchen, two bedrooms with twin beds and bathroom/WC. Both have superb views across the River Conwy and large gardens.

All year MWB out of season 2units, 4–6persons no pets ♦ fridge ♥
Gas/Elec metered ⬜not provided
☎(¼m) CTV ⊕3pin square P ⚓(¼m)

↭ ♪ ♀(½m) ♬(3m)

Min£60 Max£90pw (Low)
Min£100 Max£155pw (High)

LLANDWROG
Gwynedd
Map**6** SH45

C 1 & 2 Tyn-y-Maes Y. Fron
for bookings Rev E Plaxton, St Johns Vicarage, Belmont Rise, Belmont, Sutton, Surrey SM2 6EA
☎01-642 2363

Stone-built cottages comprising lounge, dining room, fitted kitchen and bathroom/WC. One has two double-bedded rooms and a loft-bedroom, suitable for children, with two single beds. The other has one double-bedded room and another room with two single beds.

All year MWB out of season 1wk min, 4wks max, 2units, 2–6persons ◇ ◆
♦ fridge ♥ Electric & open fires
Elec metered ⬜not provided ☎in unit
WM & SD in unit Iron & Ironing board in unit ☺ CTV ⊕3pin square P ⚈
⚓(¼m)

Min£35 Max£85pw (Low)
Min£75 Max£125pw (High)

LLANDYFRYDOG
Gwynedd
Map**6** SH48

C Ty Refail Capel Parc
for bookings Mrs M A Riley, 34 Redland Crescent, Chorlton-cum-Hardy, Manchester M21 2DL
☎061-881 8045

Small traditional farmhouse with own gardens comprising kitchen/diner, play room, lounge and bathroom/shower/WC. There are two bedrooms on the ground floor and one on the first.

Etr–Oct 1wk min, 4wks max, 1unit, 1–8persons [◇] ◆ ◆ ♦ fridge

---

Electric Elec metered ⬜not provided
Iron & Ironing board on premises ⚈
TV ⊕3pin square 4P ▥ ⚓(2m)
Games room

↭ ♀(2m)

Min£80 Max£125pw (Low)
Max£150pw (High)

LLANDYGWYDD
Dyfed
Map**2** SN24

C Church Cottage
for bookings Landmark Trust, Shottesbrooke, Maidenhead, Berkshire SL6 3SW
☎Littlewick Green(062882)5925

This small early Victorian cottage built of Cilgerran slate has charm and character and promotes the very quiet rural setting. Accommodation comprises a cosy lounge/dining room furnished in period styling with beamed ceiling and open fire, well-equipped kitchen, two charming, cosy bedrooms (one double, one twin) and pine clad bath/shower room/WC.

All year MWB out of season 1wk min 1unit 1–4persons ◆ ◆ ♦ fridge
storage heaters Elec metered ⬜not provided ☎(¾m) Iron & Ironing board in unit ☺ ⊕3pin square 1P 1⚈ ⚓(¾m)

↭ ♀(2m)

Min£154 Max£265pw (Low)
Min£175 Max£265pw (High)

LLANDYSSUL
Dyfed
Map**2** SN44

C Mrs E Lewis, Cwm-Meudwy Country Cottages, Llandyssul, Dyfed SA44 4JW
☎Llandyssul(055932)2302

Three delightful character cottages in peaceful, rural location offering high standards of accommodation. **Derwen, Bedwen and Onnen** all comprise cosy lounge, kitchen/diner, two bedrooms (one double and either 1 twin or bunk beds with an additional single bed) and either combined or separate bathroom, WC. All contain a mixture of modern and antique yet retain the character with old stone walls, timber and open log fires.

All year MWB out of season 1wk min 3–4wks max 3units 1–6persons ◆
♦ (pets out of season only) ♦ fridge
Electric & open fires Elec inclusive
⬜inclusive ☎(½m) Iron & Ironing board on premises [Launderette on premises]
☺ CTV ⊕3pin square 2P ▥
⚓(½m) Games & utility room

↭ ♀(½m) ♬(½m) →

147

Min£90 Max£125pw (Low)
Min£195 Max£250pw (High)

C Mr & Mrs B P Davies **Tivy-Side Country Cottages** Gilfachwen-Uchaf, Llandyssul, Dyfed
☎Llandyssul(055932)2230

*Small complex of cottages converted from farm outbuildings in peaceful valley of River Teifi. Surrounding a large courtyard, three cottages are split level **Gwill** having lounge, kitchen/diner and two bedrooms. **Cerdin** has open plan kitchen/lounge and two bedrooms, **Towy** has a lounge, kitchen/diner, three bedrooms and a balcony. The other three cottages are single-storey having lounge, kitchen/diner, **Clettwr** and **Twelly** have three bedrooms and **Teifi** two bedrooms; all cottages have bathroom.*

Etr Nov MWB out of season 1day min, 6units, 1–7persons [◇] ◆ ◆ ◉ fridge Electric Elecmetered Ⓛcan be hired ☎ Iron & Ironing board in unit [Launderette on premises] ☺ CTV ⊕3pin square 2P Ⅲ ♨(½m) Games room & playing area
↦ ♀(½m) ♫(½m) ♬(½m)
Min£90 Max£165pw (Low)
Min£165 Max£180pw (High)

LLANFAIRFECHAN
Gwynedd
Map6 SH67

B **Bungalows 1, 2, 3 & 4**
for bookings Mrs E Kenyon, Moelwyn Newydd, Parc Drive, Off Park Crescent, Llanfairfechan, Gwynedd
☎Llanfairfechan(0248)680056

Four modern brick-built bungalows situated in quiet position off main road. They each comprise good sized lounge/diner with small open-plan kitchen leading off, shower/WC and two bedrooms, except No 4 which has an additional double-bedded room.

Allyear MWB out of season 4days min, 4wks max, 4units, 2–6persons ◆ ◆ no pets ◉ fridge Electric Elecmetered Ⓛinclusive ☎(50yds) Iron & Ironing board on premises [Launderette within 300yds] ☺ CTV ⊕3pin square P ☺(100yds)

Llandyssul
—
Llanferres

↦ ♂(½m) ♀(50yds) ♫(100yds)
Min£55 Max£100pw (Low)
Min£90 Max£140pw (High)

C & Ch **Chalets 1 & 2, Cottages 1, 2, 3 & 4** Queens Court
for bookings Mrs E Kenyon, Moelwyn Newydd, Parc Drive, Off Park Crescent, Llanfairfechan, Gwynedd
☎Llanfairfechan(0248)680056

Two wood built chalets and four stone built cottages. All units have lounge/diner with bed-settee, kitchenette or separate kitchen, bathroom/WC except No 1 cottage and chalets which have a lounge with bed-settee, kitchen/diner and Bathroom/WC.

Allyear MWB out of season 4days min, 6units, 2–6persons ◆ ◆ ◉ fridge Electric Elecmetered Ⓛinclusive (except towels) ☎ Iron & Ironing board on premises [Launderette within 300yds] TV P Ⅲ ♨(½m)
↦ ♂(100yds)
Min£40 Max£85pw (Low)
Min£72 Max£120pw (High)

F **Yenton Holiday Flats** Promenade
for bookings Terry Allix, The Yenton, Promenade, Llanfairfechan, Gwynedd
☎Llanfairfechan(0248)680075

Semi-detached double fronted house on the promenade facing the beach which provides five flats with lounge/diner, shower and WC (Flats 3 & 5 have baths) combined and sleeping accommodation for four, a 'Z'-bed is available for the lounge.

May–Sep MWB out of season 1wk min, 5units, 2–4persons [◇] ◆ ◆ ◉ fridge Electric Elecmetered Ⓛinclusive ☎ [Launderette within 300yds] TV ⊕3pin square Ⅲ ♨(300yds)
↦ ♂(½m) ♀(200yds) ♫(200yds) ♬(200yds)
Min£75 Max£90pw (Low)
Min£105 Max£125pw (High)

LLANFAIR WATERDINE
Shropshire
Map7 SO27

C **Myrtle Cottage**
for bookings Mrs A Gwilt, Rose Villa, Llanfair Waterdine, Knighton, Powys
☎Knighton(0547)528511

Semi-detached, stone-built cottage next to the post office. Accommodation comprises lounge, bathroom/WC and kitchen/diner on the ground floor and two twin-bedded rooms and one double bedroom on the first floor. Wood-burning stove. Situated in centre of small country village.

Allyear MWB out of season 1wk min, 1mth max, 1unit, 6persons [◇] ◆ ◉ fridge Electric Elecmetered Ⓛinclusive ☎ SD in unit Iron & Ironing board in unit TV ⊕3pin square P ♨ ☺ Fishing
↦ ♀(10yds)
Min£68 Max£80pw (Low)
Min£80 Max£92pw (High)

H Mrs J M Morgan **Selley Hall** Llanfair Waterdine, Knighton, Powys LD7 1TR
☎Knighton(0547)528429

A wing of a farmhouse comprising a separate lounge, kitchen/diner, two double-bedded rooms, one twin-bedded room, bathroom and WC. There is also a bed-settee in the lounge.

Allyear MWB out of season 1wk min, 1mth max, 1unit, 1–6persons [◇] no pets ◉ fridge Electric Elecmetered Ⓛnot provided ☎(3½m) SD in unit Iron & Ironing board in unit ☺ TV ⊕3pin square P Ⅲ ♨(3½m)
↦ ♀(2m)
Min£45 Max£85pw

LLANFERRES
Clwyd
Map7 SJ16

C Mr & Mrs Brierley-Jones **Pont-y-Mwynwr** Llanferres, Mold, Clwyd CH7 5LU
☎Llanferres(035285)226

Modernised country cottage in lovely setting on River Alyn, comprising lounge/diner, bathroom/WC, kitchen and three bedrooms. 2m of fishing available.

THE YENTON
Promenade, Llanfairfechan, Gwynedd
Telephone: (0248) 680075

Enjoy a happy and carefree holiday or short stay in the comfort of a modern, centrally heated sea front flat, close to Llandudno and Anglesey. Send for your colour brochure now.

Proprietors: Barbara & Terry Allix

All year MWB out of season 2 days min,
6wks max, 1unit, 2–8 persons ◇ ◆
◆ no pets ◎ fridge ♨ & Electric &
open fires (fuel charged for)
Elec metered 🅛 can be hired ☎(1m)
Iron & Ironing board in unit ⊖ Ⓥ
CTV ⊕3pin square 4P ▥ ♨(2m)
⊖ ⬤(1m)
£75 (Low)
Min£100 Max£160pw (High)

LLANFIHANGEL-Y-PENNANT
Gwynedd
Map**6** SH60

H Nantcaw Fawr
for bookings Mrs M Jones, Tynybryn,
Llanfihangel, Tywyn, Gwynedd LL36 9TN
☎Abergynolwyn(065477)277

*Large stone farmhouse in elevated and
isolated position on River Cader nestling
in the Cader Idris mountains. It comprises
large beamed lounge with stone fire place,
sitting room, kitchen/diner and two utility
rooms. There are four bedrooms sleeping
up to ten persons and a bathroom/WC.
Well furnished and decorated.*

All year MWB out of season wknd min,
6wks max, 1unit, 2–10persons ◆ ◎
fridge Electric & log fires (logs free)
Elec metered 🅛 can be hired ☎(1m)
Iron & Ironing board in unit ⊖
⊕3pin square 5P ♨(2m)
⊖ ⬤(2m)
Min£60 Max£215pw

See advertisement under Tywyn

LLANGARRON
Hereford & Worcester
Map**3** SO52

C Langstone Cottage
for bookings Mrs P Amos, Oaklands,
Llangarron, Ross-on-Wye, Herefordshire
HR9 6NZ
☎Llangarron(098984)277

*A stone-built semi-detached, two-storey
cottage overlooking the surrounding
countryside; the ground floor comprises
the kitchen, bathroom, dining room, and
lounge. The first floor has two double
bedrooms and one room with three single
beds.*

Llanferres
—
Llangunllo

All year MWB out of season 3 days min,
8mths max, 1unit, 1–7persons ◆ ◆
◎ fridge ♨ Elec metered 🅛 can be
hired ☎(1m) WM & SD in unit Iron &
Ironing board on premises TV
⊕3pin square P ♨(1m)
⊖ ⬤(1½m)
Details not confirmed for 1987

C Owls Nest Cottage & The Barn House
for bookings Mrs P Amos, Oaklands,
Llangarron, Ross-on-Wye, Herefordshire
HR9 6NZ
☎Llangarron(098984)277

*Recently re-built stone cottages adjoining
farmland. Both comprise WC, kitchen,
lounge and dining room on the ground
floor and one double, one twin, one single
bedroom and bathroom on first floor.*

All year MWB out of season 3 days min,
8mths max, 2units, 1–6persons ◆ ◆
◎ fridge ♨ Elec metered 🅛 can be
hired ☎(400yds) WM & SD in unit Iron
& Ironing board in unit ⊖ TV
⊕3pin square P ♨ ▥ ♨(700yds)
⊖ ⬤(1m)
Details not confirmed for 1987

LLANGORSE
Powys
Map**3** SO12

C P J & E A Sheppard The Old Stables
Trefinon Farm, Llangorse, Powys LD3 0P8
☎Llangorse(087484)607

*Six well appointed cottage units converted
from former stable block. Units 1 to 4 have
one bedroom each, 5 and 6 have two, all
with extra sleeping facilities in the lounge,
kitchen, and separate shower or bathroom
with WC.*

All year MWB out of season 1wk min,
6units, 2–7persons [◇] ◆ ◆ Pets
charged for ◎ fridge wood stoves
Elec metered 🅛 can be hired ☎ SD on
premises [TD on premises] Iron &
Ironing board on premises ⊖ CTV

⊕3pin square P ▥ ♨(2m) Games
room, barbeque
⊖ ⬤(2m)
Min£57.50 Max£100pw (Low)
Min£115 Max£160pw (High)

LLANGROVE
Hereford & Worcester
Map**3** SO51

C The Elms
for bookings Mrs P Amos, Oaklands,
Llangarron, Ross-on-Wye, Herefordshire
☎Llangarron(098984)277

*Detached cottage recently modernised to
a high standard. There is a large rear
garden and patio. Accommodation
comprises kitchen, dining room, lounge,
and WC on the ground floor, and one
single bedroom, one twin, and a double
bedroom with combined bathroom on the
first floor.*

All year MWB out of season 3 days min,
8mths max, 1unit, 1–6persons ◆ ◆
◎ fridge ♨ Elec metered 🅛 can be
hired ☎(½m) WM & SD in unit Iron &
Ironing board in unit ⊖ [CTV]
⊕3pin square 4P ▥ ♨(¼m)
⊖ ⬤(¼m)
Details not confirmed for 1987

LLANGUNLLO
Powys
Map**7** SO27

F Mrs G E Morgan Cefnsuran
Llangunllo, Knighton, Powys LD7 1SL
☎Llangunllo(054781)219

*Self-contained wing of an old farmhouse,
situated in its own grounds. Lounge/diner,
separate kitchen, large bathroom/WC,
family room, one double and one small
room with bunk beds. 4½m W of Knighton
turn N from Llandrindod road.*

All year MWB out of season wknd min,
1mth max, 1unit, 8persons ◇ ◆ ◆
no pets ◎ fridge ♨ Elec metered
🅛 can be hired WM in unit Iron &
Ironing board in unit TV ⊕3pin square
P ♨(1½m) Games room
Min£60 Max£70pw (Low)
Min£90 Max£110pw (High)

H   Upper Baily Farm
for bookings Mrs S Williams, White
Anthony Bungalow, Knighton, Powys
☎Knighton(0547)528405

Self-contained spacious and recently
modernised two-storey farmhouse
situated in beautiful open countryside.
Accommodation comprises a cosy open-
fired lounge with double bed-settee,
separate beamed ceiling kitchen/dining
room, utility room, three bedrooms (one
double, one twin with bunk beds, one
double with bunk beds) and bath/shower
with WC.

All year   MWB out of season   1wk min,
1unit, 1–12persons ◊ ♦ no pets ◉
fridge ▥, Electric & open fire
Elec metered ⬜ can be hired ☎(1m)
WM & SD in unit   Iron & Ironing board in
unit ⊕ TV ⊕3pin square   3P   1☗
♨(1m)
↩ ♪(3m)   ☻(1m)
Min£50 Max£70pw (Low)
Min£105 Max£130pw (High)

See advertisement under Knighton

LLANGWNNADL
Gwynedd
Map**6** SH23

H   Mrs M Williams Glanrafon Fawr
Llangwnnadl, Pwllheli, Gwynedd
LL53 8NU
☎Tudweiliog(075887)661

Located in the middle of the Lleyn
Peninsula, this completely modernised
farmhouse is well furnished and comprises
lounge, kitchen/diner, two double
bedrooms, one twin-bedded room and
bathroom/WC.

Etr–Sep   1wk min, 3wks max, 1unit,
2–6persons ◊ ♦ ◉ fridge
Electric   Elec inclusive ⬜ can be hired
☎(½m)   WM & SD on premises   Iron &
Ironing board in unit ⊕ CTV
⊕3pin square   3P   ▥   ♨(½m)
↩ ☻(3m)

Details not confirmed for 1987

C   Rhos-y-Grug
for bookings Mrs N A Overton, Woodcroft,
7 Oak Drive, Seisdon, Wolverhampton
WV5 7ET
☎Wombourne(0902)893855

Detached cottage set in ½-acre of lawns
and gardens situated off main
Nefyn–Aberdaron road. The
accommodation comprises lounge,
kitchen/diner, bathroom/WC, laundry
room and study on the ground floor and
three bedrooms on the first floor. There is
also an outside WC.

All year   MWB out of season   2days min,
6wks max, 1unit, 2–8persons ◊ ◉
fridge   Storage & portable gas   Gas/
Elec inclusive ☎(10yds)   WM & SD in
unit   Iron & Ironing board in unit ⊕
CTV ⊕3pin square   2P   1☗   ▥
♨(400yds)   Children's swing & climbing
frame

Llangunllo
—
Llanrug

↩ ☻(3m)
Min£75 Max£240pw

C   Mrs A Griffith Tŷcam 1 & 2
Llangwnnadl, Pwllheli, Gwynedd
☎Tudweiliog(075887)627

Farmhouse situated in the Lleyn
Peninsular, divided into two compact
units, both with lounge, kitchen/diner,
bathroom/WC and two bedrooms.

All year   MWB out of season   2days min,
6wks max, 2units, 2–6persons ◊ ◈
♦ ◉ fridge   electric   Elec metered
⬜ not provided ☎(½m)   Iron & Ironing
board in unit ⊕ TV ⊕3pin square
5P   ▥   ♨(½m)

Details not confirmed for 1987

LLANGYNIDR
Powys
Map**3** SO11

F   Mrs P James Flats 1 & 2 Penlan, Forge
Road, Llangynidr, Crickhowell, Powys
☎Bwlch(0874)730461

Modern, ground- and first-floor flats with
lovely views of river, countryside and
mountains beyond. Both are comfortable
and well maintained with the ground-floor
flat sleeping two persons and the first-floor
flat sleeping four.

Mar–Oct   MWB out of season   2units,
2–4persons [◊] ◈ ♦ ◉ fridge
Electric   Elec metered ⬜ inclusive
☎(100yds)   SD & TD in unit   Iron &
Ironing board in unit ⊕ ◐ CTV
⊕3pin square   2P   ♨(100yds)
↩ ☻(½m)
Min£80 Max£105pw (Low)
Min£125 Max£155pw (High)

LLANON
Dyfed
Map**6** SN56

C   Trefin Self Catering Cottage
for bookings D J Pugh, Isfryn, Llanrhystyd,
Dyfed SY23 5DW
☎Llanon(09748)362

Renovated cottage situated in the village
and within walking distance of the beach.
It comprises kitchen/breakfast room,
lounge and one double bedroom with
shower/WC en suite. An open tread
staircase leads to the first floor and two
twin-bedded rooms and a bathroom/WC.

All year   MWB out of season   3days min,
1unit, 1–6persons [◊] ◈ ♦ ◉
fridge ▥ & open fire   Elec metered
⬜ not provided ☎(100yds)   Iron &
Ironing board in unit ⊕ CTV
⊕3pin square   1P   ▥   ♨(15yds)
↩ ☻(100yds)
£50pw (Low)
£180pw (High)

C & H   Ty Gwartheg & Maes Gwyn
for bookings Coastal Cottages of
Pembrokeshire, Seaview, Abercastle,
Mathry, Dyfed SA62 5HJ
☎Croesgoch(03483)7742

Maes Gwyn is a spacious Victorian
farmhouse in a peaceful rural situation
with sea views from St David's Head to
Strumble Head. It comprises a lounge with
open fire, kitchen/breakfast room, utility
room, dining room/reading room,
bathroom, separate shower room/WC, two
double, one twin and two single
bedrooms. **Ty Gwartheg** is a converted
hayshed adjoining Maes Gwyn.
Accommodation is compact and
comfortable, comprising lounge with open
fire and bow window, kitchen/diner,
shower room, one double and one twin
bedroom and also a studio couch. Both
properties have a lawned area for children
to play.

All year   MWB out of season   4days min,
2mths max, 2units, 2–8persons ◊ ♦
◉ fridge   Storage , open & portable
fires   Elec metered ⬜ inclusive ☎(½m)
WM & SD in unit   Ironing & Ironing board
in unit ⊕ CTV ⊕3pin square   2P   ▥
♨(½m)
↩ ☻(½m)
Min£65 Max£340pw

LLANRUG
Gwynedd
Map**6** SH56

F The Secretary **Bryn Bras Castle**
Llanrug, Caernarfon, Gwynedd LL55 4RE
☎Llanberis(0286)870210

These nine charming flats are located
within the imposing castellated walls,
turrets and towers of Bryn Bras Castle.
This 19th-century building stands amidst
graceful gardens and woodlands, pools
and statuary, on the foothills of Snowdon,
covering a total of 32 acres.
Accommodation ranges from three one-
bedroomed flats sleeping two to five
persons, four two-bedroomed flats
sleeping four to five persons and two four-
bedroomed flats sleeping five to six. Each
flat has its own unique character and all
are tastefully furnished and decorated.
The Flat Tower has a four-poster bed.

All year   MWB out of season   2nights min,
1mth max, 9units, 1–6persons ◊ [♦]
◉ fridge   Electric   Elec metered
⬜ not provided ☎ TV ⊕3pin square
20P   ▥   ♨(½m)
↩ ☻(½m)
Min£86 Max£109pw (Low)
Min£92 Max£259pw (High)

See advertisement under Caernarfon

C & F   Bryn Gwyn Cottage & Gwel Elidir
Bryn Gwyn Terrace
for bookings Mrs J B Eaton, Gwynt-y-
Mynydd, Bryn Gwyn Terrace, Llanrug,
Caernarfon, Gwynedd
☎Caernarfon(0286)4481

Bryn Gwyn is an attractive stone and
rendered terraced cottage with a small
garden to the front and side.

Accommodation comprises open plan kitchen/diner/lounge, bathroom, one double bedroom and one with bunks and a single bed. ***Gwel Elidir*** *is a ground-floor flat comprising kitchen, sitting/dining room with bed-settee, bathroom and one twin bedroom.*

Allyear MWB out of season 3days min, 6wks max, 2units, 1–5persons [◇ ◈ ◆] ◎ fridge Storage & bottle gas Elec inclusive (Gwel Elidir) Elec metered (Bryn Gwyn) 🄻can be hired ☎(300yds)– SD in unit Iron & Ironing board in unit ⊙ CTV ⊕3pin square 4P ▣ 🛒(½m)

⊖ 🍷(½m)

Min£48 Max£145pw

B **4 & 5 Craig-y-Dinas**
for bookings Mrs W Williams, 2 Craig-y-Dinas, Llanrug, Gwynedd
☎Llanberis(0286)870643 or Pwllheli(0758)612854

Two semi-detached white painted bungalows each having small hall, kitchen, lounge/diner, one double bedroom and one twin-bedded room. Bathroom with coloured suite. Patio area with small rockery garden. Good views of Snowdon. Along A4086 from Llanberis, right on entering Llanrug over two hump backed bridges, turn right.

Allyear MWB out of season 1wk min, 6wks max, 2units, 4persons ◈ ◆ ◊(no5) ◎(no4) fridge Electric & open fire Elec metered 🄻can be hired ☎(½m) ⊙ CTV ⊕3pin square 2P ▣ 🛒(½m)

⊖ ⛳(3m) 🍷(½m) 🎞(3m)

Min£30 Max£140pw

B **Starling Cottage** Ffordd Glanmoel
for bookings Menai Holidays, Old Port Office, Port Penrhyn, Banger LL57 3HN
☎Bangor(0248)362254 or 351055

Detached modern bungalow in residential area with secluded lawns. Accommodation comprises kitchen, utility room, bath/WC, dining room, lounge with stone fireplace and three bedrooms, one double, one twin and one with bunk beds.

Allyear MWB out of season 3days min, 6wks max, 1unit, 2–6persons ◊ fridge ▥ Gas & Elec metered 🄻can be hired ☎(200yds) WM, SD & TD in unit Iron & Ironing board in unit ⊙ CTV ⊕3pin square 3P ▣ 🛒(200yds)

⊖ 🍷(½m)

Min£130 Max£210pw

LLANSANTFFRAID YM MECHAIN
Powys
Map**7** SJ21

C **Tan-y-Bryn** Deytheur
for bookings Mrs M E Jones, Glanvyrnwy Farm, Llansantffraid ym Mechain, Powys
☎Llansantffraid(069181)258

Modernised detached cottage situated 1m off B4393 opposite Glanvyrnwy Farm and comprising lounge, kitchen/diner, three bedrooms sleeping up to eight, a bathroom/WC and separate WC.

Llanrug — Llanystumdwy

Allyear MWB 1wk min, 2wks max, 1unit, 8persons ◈ ◆ ◎ fridge Electric & log fires Elec metered 🄻not provided ☎(1m) WM in unit Iron & Ironing board in unit CTV ⊕3pin square P 🛒(1m)

Min£85 Max£100pw (Low)
Min£95 Max£130pw (High)

LLANSTEPHAN
Dyfed
Map**2** SN31

Ch **Elmrise Park Holiday Village**
for bookings Hoseasons Holidays, Sunways House, Lowestoft, Suffolk NR32 3LT
☎Lowestoft(0502)62281

Situated on elevated terraces, each well-decorated cedar wood chalet has two or three bedrooms, lounge and kitchen/dining area.

Mid-Mar Oct MWB out of season 3days min, 4mths max, 95units, 2–8persons [◇ ◈ ◆] ◎ fridge Electric Elec inclusive 🄻inclusive ☎ Iron & Ironing board in unit [Launderette on premises] ⊙ CTV ⊕3pin square P 🛒 ≏ [horse riding]

⊖ 🍷 ♫

Min£60 Max£230pw

LLANTEG
Dyfed
Map**2** SN11

H **Garness Farm**
for bookings Powell's Cottage Holidays, 55 High Street, Saundersfoot, Dyfed
☎Saundersfoot(0834)812791

One split-level unit in a large house, situated in 26 acres of pastureland within view of the sea. Comprising lounge, dining area, kitchen, one double and one twin bedroom.

May–Sep MWB out of season 1wk min, 6wks max, 1unit, 2–4persons ◇ ◈ ◆ no pets ◎ fridge ▥ Elec inclusive 🄻provided Iron & Ironing board in unit ⊙ Ⓥ(1unit) CTV ⊕3pin square P 🛒(2m)

⊖ 🍷(¾m)

Min£111 Max£237pw

LLANWRTYD WELLS
Powys
Map**3** SN84

C Mr & Mrs K H Walters **Cwmirfon Lodge Cottages** Cwmirfon Lodge, Llanwrtyd Wells, Powys LD5 4TN
☎Llanwrtyd Wells(05913)217

In a tranquil setting of 3 acres of grounds, these former outbuildings have been skilfully converted to provide well-appointed cottages with fine views, ***Woodpecker & Buzzard*** *have one double and one twin-bedded room, sitting room, with bed/settee, kitchen and dining area, bathroom and balcony.* ***Kite*** *has one double and one single bedroom, sitting room/diner, bathroom and balcony.* ***Nuthatch*** *has one twin-bedded room and one room with two tier bunk, kitchen, sitting room/diner, shower room, balcony.* ***Cockloft*** *has one twin-bedded room with stairs to bathroom, kitchen and sitting room/diner.*

Mar–Nov MWB out of season 3days min, 1mth max, 5units, 2–6persons ◈ ◆ in Nuthatch, Woodpecker & Buzzard no pets ◎ fridge ▥ Elec metered 🄻inclusive ☎(2m) Launderette on premises ⊙ ⊕3pin square P ▣ 🛒(3m)

⊖ 🍷(3m)

Min£36 Max£158pw (Low)

C & F **Kite I & II, Nant Garreg & Raven Barn**
for bookings Mrs C Johnson, Trallwm, Forest Lodge, Abergwesyn, Llanwrtyd Wells, Powys LD5 4TS
☎Llanwrtyd Wells(05913)229

Kite I & II *and* ***Nant Garreg*** *are three delightful cottages each with cosy lounge/diner, with beamed ceilings and kitchenette off, two bedrooms (four singles in Kite I, one double and two singles in Kite II & Nant Garreg) and bathroom/WC.* ***Raven*** *is a small rustic-styled flat which is a conversion of an 18th-century barn and is similar in content to Kite I & II but with one double- and two single beds.*

Allyear MWB out of season 1day min, 4wks max, 4units, 1–6persons [◇] ◈ ◆ no pets ◎ fridge Electric & open/woodburning fires Elec inclusive 🄻inclusive ☎(1½m) Iron & Ironing board in unit ⊙ ⊕3pin square P ▣ 🛒(1½m) Fishing, barbeque

Min£70 Max£130pw (Low)
Min£120 Max£180pw (High)

LLANYSTUMDWY
Gwynedd
Map**6** SH43

Ca **The Ranch**
for bookings Shaws Holidays Y Maes, Pwllheli, Gwynedd LL53 5HA
☎Pwllheli(0758)614422

Four comfortably furnished detached cedar log-cabins, part of about twenty similar privately owned properties situated in peaceful surroundings. Accommodation comprises lounge/diner, kitchen, one double and one twin-bedded room plus a double bed-settee in lounge and bathroom/WC (one unit has shower/WC).

Allyear MWB out of season wknd min, 6wks max, 4units, 2–6persons ◈ ◆ no pets in 1 unit ◎ fridge Electric Elec inclusive in 1unit Elec metered 🄻not provided ☎(100yds) Iron & Ironing board in unit ⊙ CTV ⊕3pin square 2P 🛒(1m) Fishing, horse riding, restaurant

⊖ ⛳(2m) 🍷(2m)

Min£100 Max£192pw

H Tyddyn Du
for bookings Shaws Holidays, Y Maes,
Pwllheli, Gwynedd LL53 5HA
☎Pwllheli(0758)614422

Large 19th-century farmhouse offering
comfortable, spacious accommodation
for up to eight people. It comprises a large
kitchen/diner, utility room, lounge, one
bunk-bedded room and WC on the
ground floor and three bedrooms; two
double (one with shower) and one twin,
and bathroom/WC on the first floor.
Private fishing available and thirteen acre
nature reserve nearby.

All year MWB out of season wknd min,
6wks max, 1 unit, 2−8persons ◈ no
pets ◎ fridge ﷽ Elec metered
Ⓛnot provided ☎(1½m) Iron & Ironing
board in unit ⊙ CTV ㉛3pin square
4P ♨(1½m) Fishing

⟷ ♒(3m) ♟(1½m)

Min£89 Max£224pw

LLWYNCELYN
Dyfed
Map2 SN45

B, C & F Mr Banks **Gilfach-y-Halen**
Holiday Farm Estates Llwyncelyn,
Aberaeron, Dyfed SA46 0HN
☎Llanarth(0545)580288

Holiday Farm Estate is situated on the
coast amidst unspoilt countryside and
comprising forty-eight detached
bungalows to sleep four persons; six

Llanystumdwy
—
Llwyndafydd

modern, well appointed apartments and a
delightful character bijou-cottage,
sleeping two persons. All are comfortably
furnished and decorated. Club house and
bar on site and convenient for beaches.

Etr−Oct MWB out of season
3nights min, 55units, 1−4persons ◈
◆ ◎ fridge Electric Elec metered
Ⓛinclusive ☎ Iron & Ironing board on
premises [Launderette on premises]
⊙ CTV ㉛3pin square P ▥
♨(1½m) Stables, playground
⟷ ♟

Details not confirmed for 1987

LLWYNDAFYDD
Dyfed
Map2 SN35

C Mr & Mrs M Headley **Neuadd Farm**
Holiday Cottages Llwyndafydd,
Llandyssul, Dyfed SA44 6BT
☎New Quay(0545)560324

Set in thirty two acres of undulating grass
and woodlands. These nine luxurious
holiday cottages overlook the beautiful
Cwm Tydu valley and lie a short distance
from nearby beaches. They have been
artistically converted from old farm

buildings and form a most attractive south
facing courtyard. The cottages are
comfortably furnished and vary in size
sleeping from two to eight people. The
extensive estate which even has its own
rabbit warren where children are invited to
play, has its own lake, swimming pool and
adventure playground, Malcolm and
Karen Headley are always available to
tend their guests' needs to ensure a happy
holiday for all.

All year MWB out of season 9units,
2−8persons [◇] ◈ ◆ ◎ fridge
﷽ Elec inclusive Ⓛinclusive (except
towels) ☎ WM, SD & TD on premises
Iron & Ironing board in unit ⊙ CTV
㉛3pin square P ▥ ♨(500yds)
⌂Heated Barbecue facilities
⟷ ♟(500yds)

Min£110 Max£165pw (Low)
Min£160 Max£450pw (High)

C Mr & Mrs Kelly **Ty Hen Farm**
Llwyndafydd Near New Quay, Llandyssul,
Dyfed
☎New Quay(0545)560346

Terrace of three cottages overlooking the
farmyard. **Granary** cottage has open plan
lounge/dining area, kitchenette and
bedroom with bathroom leading off.
Stable & **Grain Mill** cottage complete the
group and consists of lounge, kitchen/
diner, shower room with WC and two
bedrooms. Nearby in a separate terrace
are **Stackyard** cottage comprising open

plan lounge/kitchen/diner, spiral stairs to first floor with bath/WC, one double, one twin and one single bedroom also extra bed available. Interconnecting or for separate let are **Hay & Dairy** cottage. Hay on first floor and Dairy on ground floor are suitable for the disabled, they are bedsits with double bed, shower/WC, kitchen area and breakfast bar. Small restaurant on site.

All year MWB out of season 6units, 2–6persons [◇] ◆ ◆ ◉
🦆(Grain Mill) fridge Electric & wood stoves ⊡inclusive ☎ [WM, SD & TD on premises] Iron & Ironing board in unit ⊕ CTV ⊕3pin square P ▥ 🏔(1m) Children's play area, patio
⊖ ☏(2m)
Min£60 Max£200pw

LLWYNGWRIL
Gwynedd
Map**6** SH50

B Golwg-y-Bae
for bookings Mrs M A Bareham, The Hill Cottage, Bausley, Crew Green, Shrewsbury, Shropshire SY5 9BP
☎Halfway House(074378)320

Recently constructed bungalow set down 14 steps from A493 with extensive views over Cardigan Bay. Accommodation comprises lounge with kitchen off, one twin, one double-bedded room and shower/WC.

Mar–Nov MWB out of season 2days min, 6wks max, 1unit, 1–4persons ◆ ◆ ◉ fridge 🍴 Elec metered ⊡not provided ☎(½m) Iron & Ironing board in unit ⊕ TV ⊕3pin square 2P ⊖ ☏(1m)
Min£90 Max£130pw

C Beudy, Helm, Ysgubor & Ystabl Cottages Plas-y-Nant
for bookings Mrs M J S Pugh, Henblas, Llwyngwril, Gwynedd
☎Fairbourne(0341)250350

Four cottages which have been converted from stone farm buildings, situated on the Cardigan Bay coast. **Beudy** and **Ystabl** both on the ground floor, sleep four people in two bedrooms and comprise lounge, kitchen and shower room. **Helm** and **Ysgubor** sleep up to eight in two bedrooms, and a bed settee in lounge, kitchen and bathroom. All have original pine beams, pine furnishings and panoramic sea views. Winner of 1984 Prince of Wales Award for Cottages.

All year MWB out of season 2days min, 1mth max, 4units, 2–8persons ◆ ◆

Llwyndafydd
—
Loddiswell

no pets ◉ fridge Electric Elec metered ⊡inclusive ☎(300yds) WM, SD & TD on premises Iron & Ironing board in unit ⊕ CTV ⊕3pin square 10P 🏔(350yds)
⊖ ☏(400yds)
Min£80 Max£100pw (Low)
Min£139.15 Max£164.45pw (High)

LOCHEAD
Strathclyde Argyllshire
Map**10** NR77

C, Ch Holiday Homes at Lochead
for bookings Castle Sween Bay (Holidays) Ltd, Estate Office, Ellary, Lochgilphead, Argyll PA31 8PB
☎Ormsary(08803)232 & 209 or Achnamara(054685)223

Four wooden chalets overlooking the tidal shore of Loch Caolisport. Three units comprise two double bedrooms, one with bunk beds, living room with convertible settee, kitchenette, shower/WC. The fourth chalet is more spacious. Also available is Lochead cottage with three double bedrooms, living room, kitchen and bathroom. Only 2m from Ellary holiday homes.

All year MWB out of season 2nights min, 5units, 1–6persons ◆ ◉ fridge Electric Elec metered ⊡not provided ☎(1m) TV ⊕3pin square P ▥ 🏔(12m) Windsurfing, Fishing cyles for hire
Min£82 Max£90pw (Low)
Min£156 Max£170pw (High)

LOCHEARNHEAD
Central Perthshire
Map**11** NN52

Ch Mrs C Borland **Lochearn Lodges**
Lochearnhead, Perthshire FK19 8PT
☎Lochearnhead(05673)211

Six pleasantly furnished wooden chalets well spaced on hillside above the village with magnificent views south over Loch Earn. Ideally situated just off the A85, a good base for touring, fishing, watersports and hill walking.

All year MWB out of season 1wk min, 1mth max, 6units, 1–6persons ◆ ◆
no camping gas or paraffin on premises ◉ fridge Electric Elec metered ⊡inclusive except towels ☎(½m) [WM, SD & TD] on premises Iron & Ironing

---

board in unit ⊕ CTV ⊕3pin square 12P 🏔(¼m)
⊖ ☏(50yds) 🎵(50yds)
Min£80 Max£110pw (Low)
Min£120 Max£220pw (High)

LOCHINVER
Highland Sutherland
Map**14** NC02

Ch Lochinver Holiday Lodges 33
Strathan, Lochinver, Sutherland IV27 4LR
☎Lochinver(05714)282

Scandinavian lodges with double glazed doors and windows set in secluded bay with tree lined back-drop and splendid sea views. Accommodation comprises modern lounge/diner, kitchen, one double and one twin bedroom, modern bathroom. All lodges have balconies. Located 1½m from Lochinver on the unclass scenic coast route, signed Ullapool.

All year 1wk min, 5wks max, 7units, 1–6persons ◆ no pets ◉ fridge 🍴 Elec metered ⊡inclusive ☎ Iron & Ironing board on premises [Launderette on premises] ⊕ CTV ⊕3pin square 14P 🏔(1½m) Sea & Loch fishing
⊖ ☏(1½m) 🎵(1½m)
Min£205.60 Max£450pw

LODDISWELL
Devon
Map**3** SX74

F D E Pethybridge **Reads Farm**
Loddiswell, Kingsbridge, Devon TQ7 4RT
☎Kingsbridge(0548)550317

A flat on two floors, part of an old farmhouse consisting of two bedrooms, one with double bed and the other with double bed plus two single beds, bathroom with WC, on first floor, and kitchen/lounge/diner on the ground floor. It has its own entrance from small private garden with fine views of Avon Valley. Turn left in Loddiswell travelling S.

All year MWB out of season 1wk min, 4wks max, 1unit, 1–6persons ◆ ◆ ◉ fridge Electric Elec metered ⊡not provided ☎(½m) Iron & Ironing board in unit ⊕ CTV ⊕3pin square 3P 🏔(½m) 🌊(heated)
⊖ ☏(½m)
£60pw Max£150pw

F & B Mr & Mrs B Clayton **Woolston House** Loddiswell, Kingsbridge, Devon TQ7 4DU
☎Kingsbridge(0548)550341

Georgian Mansion in 30 acres of parkland in peaceful countryside between Dartmoor and the coast. with six flats and one →

bungalow. *Three flats are in the main house.* **Garden** *sleeps up to four and is a ground-floor apartment suitable for the disabled. Accommodation comprises two bedrooms, one with wash hand basin, kitchen/diner and lounge with bay window and door to private lawn.* **Cloudsmoor** *also sleeps four and is reached by an outside staircase and is similar to Garden but with separate WC and bathroom.* **Penthouse** *sleeps six and covers the whole second floor and reached by an outside staircase. Accommodation comprises three bedrooms, one with wash hand basin, lounge with dining area and kitchen. The other three flats have been tastefully converted from outbuildings.* **Coach House** *sleeps six and is the ground floor of the stable block and has three bedrooms, one with wash hand basin, overlooking the courtyard, lounge/diner, sun terrace and kitchen.* **Stable Corner** *sleeps eight and is on the first floor of the stable block with level entrance from its own garden and has four bedrooms overlooking the courtyard, living room/ kitchen with views and additional shower room/WC.* **Swallows,** *which sleeps six, is on the first floor but entered on the level from the side drive. Accommodation comprises three bedrooms, one with bunks and one with wash hand basin, kitchen/diner and lounge.* **The bungalow Old Dairy** *sleeps six in spacious accommodation with its own garden. There are four bedrooms, two of which are connected singles, lounge with door to garden, kitchen/diner and separate WC. All units have bathroom/WC with shower.*

Allyear MWB 2days min, 5mths max, 7units, 2–8persons [◇] ◆ no pets ◎ fridge Elecmetered ⎣inclusive ☎ WM on premises SD in unit TD on premises Iron & Ironing board in unit ⊙ CTV ⊕3pinsquare P ▥ ▩(1m) ▤(heated) ✎Hard private bar, meal service

Min£85 Max£145pw (Low)
Min£147 Max£348pw (High)

LOGIE-COLDSTONE
Grampian *Aberdeenshire*
Map**15** NJ40

C   Redburn
for bookings Holiday Dept/6, Estate Office, Dinnet, Aberdeenshire AB3 5LL
☎Dinnet(033985)341

A former gamekeeper's cottage in isolated setting on Heatherclad hillside with superb views south across Dee Valley. It comprises lounge/dining room, kitchen and twin bedroom on ground floor and

Loddiswell
—
London

upstairs a double room, twin room and bathroom. It is reached by way of a mile-long unmetalled track leading off unclassified road, approx 3m N of A93.

Mar–25Oct 1wkmin, 1mthmax, 1unit, 1–6persons ◇ ◆ nopets ◎ fridge Electricfires Elecinclusive ⎣can be hired ☎(3m) CTV ⊕3pinsquare P ▩(3m)
⊖ ☎ (3m)
Min£120 Max£135pw

LONDON
Greater London
Map**4**
Places within the London postal area are listed below in postal district order commencing North, then South West and West. Other places within the county of London are listed under their respective place names and are keyed to maps **4 & 5**.

NW11 Golders Green

F   21 Bigwood Court Bigwood Road
for bookings J Ballantine, Brick Hill Cottage, Hook Norton, Banbury, Oxford OX15 5QA
☎Hook Norton(0608)730071

Well appointed ground-floor apartment in quiet residential area of Hampstead Garden Suburb. Compact accommodation in good decorative order, consisting small lounge, kitchen, bathroom and two bedrooms.

Allyear MWB 1wkmin, 1mthmax, 1unit, 4persons, nc12 nopets ◔ fridge ▥ Gas/Elecinclusive ⎣inclusive ☎ Iron & Ironing board in unit [Launderette within 300yds] ⊙ ☯ CTV ⊕3pinsquare ▥ ▩(600yds)
⊖ δ(½m) ☎(½m) ▤(½m) ▤(½m) ✖(½m)
Min£130 Max£190pw

SW1 Westminster, Chelsea, Kensington, Victoria.

F   4 Lower Sloane Street
for bookings Mrs H Hoyer, 42 Lower Sloane Street, London SW1 W8BP
☎01-730 5766 Telex Basil G 895 1859

Five luxurious flats with very comfortable amenities in residential area near Sloane Square. All flats have lounge, kitchen and bathroom with the larger flats having two bathrooms.

Allyear MWB 2wksmin, 5units, 1–7persons ◇ ◎ fridge ▥ Elecmetered ⎣inclusive ☎ Iron & Ironing board in unit [Launderette within 300yds] ⊙ CTV ⊕3pinsquare ▥ ▩(100yds)
⊖ ☎(100yds) ▤(100yds)
▤(500yds) ✖(500yds)
Min£266 Max£560pw (Low)
Min£280 Max£588pw (High)

F   11 Sloane Gardens
for bookings Mrs H Hoyer, 42 Lower Sloane Street, London SW1 W8BP
☎01-730 5766 Telex Basil G 895 1859

A four-storey block of flats set in a residential area; one maisonette has three bedrooms and two bathrooms, two flats with two bedrooms and one with one bedroom. All have separate lounge, kitchen and bathroom. Well maintained with fitted carpets throughout.

Allyear MWB 2wksmin, 5units, 1–6persons ◇ ◎ fridge ▥ Elecmetered ⎣inclusive ☎ Iron & Ironing board in unit [Launderette within 300yds] ⊙ CTV ⊕3pinsquare ▥ ▩(300yds)
⊖ ☎(¼m) ▤(¼m) ▤(¼m) ✖(¼m)
Min£266 Max£560pw (Low)
Min£280 Max£588pw (High)

SW7 South Kensington

F   Mr M Raphael 45 Ennismore Gardens Knightsbridge SW7 1AQ ☎01-584 4123

In a quiet street within walking distance of Knightsbridge and Hyde Park. A Victorian terraced house divided into ten flats with lift to all floors. All are cleaned daily and consist of lounge/bedroom, kitchen/diner and bathroom.

Allyear MWB 1wkmin, 6mthsmax, 10units, 2persons nopets ◎ fridge ▥ Elecinclusive ⎣inclusive ☎ Iron & Ironing board in unit ⊙ CTV ⊕3pinsquare ▥ ▩(200yds)
⊖ ☎(100yds) ▤(1m) ▤(3m) ✖(1m)
Min£220 Max£230pw (Low)
Min£255 Max£265pw (High)

W8 Kensington

F   18–19 Prince of Wales Terrace Kensington
for bookings Clearlake Hotel Apartments, 18–20 Prince of Wales Terrace, Kensington, London W8 5PQ
☎01-937 3274

Thirteen flats in a quiet street off Kensington High Street. Five large family apartments with one, two or three bedrooms sleeping up to seven people.

Eight studio flats with bedroom/lounge areas, separate kitchen/diners and bath or shower room. The sizes of units vary but all are well-equipped.

All year MWB 1day min, 3mths max, 13units, 1–7persons [◇] ◎ fridge ♨ Elec inclusive ⌷ inclusive ☎ Iron & Ironing board in unit ◔ ◑ CTV ⊕3pin square ⊞ ♣(200yds) bar on premises
⊖ ☐(50yds) ♫(200yds) ☷(500yds)
Min£245 Max£777pw

W13 West Ealing

F Ealing Tourist Flats
for bookings Mr W G Smith, 1 Park Road East, Uxbridge, Middx UB10 0AQ
☎Uxbridge(0895)33365
Large Edwardian house containing two studio flats with large living area, kitchen, separate shower and WC, two flats with double bedroom, lounge, kitchen, shower and WC. The other two flats in an annexe have lounge, two bedrooms, kitchen and bathroom. Central London is a 20-minute underground ride away.
All year MWB 1wk min, 3mths max, 6units, 2–7persons ◇ no pets ⌀ ◎ fridge ♨ Electric Gas/ Elec metered ⌷ inclusive ☎ HCE [Launderette] ◔ CTV ⊕3pin square ⊞ ♣Hard
⊖ ☐(300yds) ♫(¼m) ☷(¼m)
Min£85 Max£269pw (Low)
Min£115 Max£269pw (High)

LONGBOROUGH
Gloucestershire
Map4 SP12

C The Bothy & Garden Cottages Windy Ridge
for bookings Longborough Properties Ltd, The Cruck, Longborough, Moreton-in-Marsh, Glos GL56 0QL
☎Cotswold(0451)30327 (9am–5pm weekdays)
A pair of cottages unobtrusively set in attractive gardens both compact and on one floor. They comprise one twin-bedded room, cosy sitting room, kitchen and combined bathroom/WC.
All year MWB 2days min, 2units, 2persons ◇ ♦ ◎ fridge ♨ Elec metered ⌷ inclusive ☎ Iron & Ironing board in unit [Launderette on premises] ◔ CTV ⊕3pin square P ⊞ ♣(½m) ⌂ ♣Hard
⊖ ☐(200yds)
Min£132.25 Max£184pw

C Crook Cottage Windy Ridge
for bookings Longborough Properties Ltd, The Cruck, Longborough, Moreton-in-Marsh, Glos GL56 0QL
☎Cotswold(0451)30327 (9am–5pm weekdays)
Situated on the fringe of the Windy Ridge estate this cottage is a traditional country home with its own garden. The ground floor comprises cloakroom/WC, kitchen,

---

London
—
Longnor

dining room and sitting room with open fire and three bedrooms plus bathroom on the first floor.
All year MWB 2days min, 1unit, 1–6persons ◇ ♦ ◎ fridge ♨ Elec metered ⌷ inclusive ☎(200yds) WM in unit Iron & Ironing board in unit ◔ CTV ⊕3pin square P ⊞ ♣(½m) ⌂ ♣Hard
⊖ ☐(200yds)
Min£184 Max£299pw

C The Gatehouse Windy Ridge
for bookings Longborough Properties Ltd, The Cruck, Longborough, Moreton-in-Marsh, Glos GL56 0QL
☎Cotswold(0451)30327 (9am–5pm weekdays)
A compact but well-fitted cottage in garden surroundings with extensive views. The accommodation, all on the ground floor, comprises two bedrooms, sitting/dining room, kitchen and bathroom.
All year MWB 2days min, 1unit, 1–4persons ◇ ♦ ◎ fridge ♨ Elec metered ⌷ inclusive ☎(200yds) WM in unit Iron & Ironing board in unit ◔ CTV ⊕3pin square P ⊞ ♣(½m) ⌂ ♣Hard
⊖ ☐(200yds)
Min£172.50 Max£287.75pw

F Stable Flat Windy Ridge
for bookings Longborough Properties Ltd, The Cruck, Longborough, Moreton-in-Marsh, Glos GL56 0QL
☎Cotswold(0451)30327
A first-floor flat, with entrance behind reception, in a thatched cottage. It comprises fitted kitchen with dining area, bathroom, attractive comfortable lounge, one single and one twin-bedded room.
All year MWB 2days min, 1unit.
1–3persons ◇ ♦ no pets ◎ fridge ♨ Elec metered ⌷ inclusive ☎(30yds) WM & SD on premises Iron & Ironing board in unit ◔ TV ⊕3pin square 1P ⊞ ♣(1m) ⌂ ♣Hard
⊖ ☐(¼m)

C Timbers Windy Ridge
for bookings Longborough Properties Ltd, The Cruck, Longborough, Moreton-in-Marsh, Glos GL56 0QL
☎Cotswold(0451)30327 (9am–5pm weekdays)
A most attractive cottage, with its own garden, comprising two bedrooms, bathroom, kitchen and sitting room with dining facilities, all on one floor.
All year MWB 2days min, 1unit, 1–4persons ◇ ♦ ◎ fridge ♨ Elec metered ⌷ inclusive ☎(50yds) WM in unit Iron & Ironing board in unit

---

◔ CTV ⊕3pin square P ⊞ ♣(½m) ⌂ ♣Hard
⊖ ☐(200yds)
Min£172.50 Max£287.75pw

C Windy Ridge Cottage
for bookings Longborough Properties Ltd, The Cruck, Longborough, Moreton-in-Marsh, Glos GL56 0QL
☎Cotswold(0451)30327 (9am–5pm weekdays)
A very attractive cottage with its own garden within Windy Ridge estate with views of the Cotswolds. Very well appointed and most comfortable. Spacious sitting room with open fire, dining room, fully fitted kitchen, utility room, three bedrooms, a double, a twin, and a further double-bedded room with two additional bunk beds. Bathrooms ground- and first-floor.
All year MWB 2days min, 1unit, 1–8persons ◇ ♦ ◎ fridge ♨ Elec metered ⌷ inclusive ☎(50yds) WM in unit Iron & Ironing board in unit ◔ CTV ⊕3pin square P ⊞ ♣(½m) ⌂ ♣Hard
⊖ ☐(200yds)
Min£195.50 Max£327.75pw

LONGNOR
Shropshire
Map7 SO49

C Lawley Cottage
for bookings Mr & Mrs T W E Corbett, Home Farm, Leebotwood, Church Stretton, Shropshire
☎Dorrington(074373)628
A detached modernised stone cottage enjoying superb views across to the Long Mynd and is set in a third-acre of garden and orchard. It comprises lounge/kitchen with dining facilities on ground floor and one double, two single bedrooms on first floor. Also two fold down beds.
20May–Oct 1wk min, 1mth max, 1unit, 1–6persons ◎ fridge Electric & open fires Elec metered ⌷ not provided ☎ ◔ CTV ⊕3pin square 4P
Min£150 Max£180pw

LONGNOR
Staffordshire
Map7 SK06

C Brund Mill Cottage
for bookings Mrs J Humphries, Brund Mill, Sheen, Longnor, Buxton, Derbys
☎Hartington(029884)383
A stone-built detached cottage with a fully modernised interior, the accommodation comprises of downstairs kitchen/dining room and a lounge with open fire and upstairs, two bedrooms, one with twin beds, one with two single beds and bathroom/WC. 3m S of B5053.
All year except Xmas & New Year 2nights min, 3mths max, 1unit, 1–4persons ◇ ♦ ◎ fridge Electric (night storage) Elec metered ⌷ not provided ☎(1m) ◑ ⊕3pin square 2☗ P ♣(1m) Fishing →

155

⊖ ♀(1¼m)
Min£70 Max£80pw (Low)
Min£90 Max£105pw (High)

C 4 & 5 Chapel Street
for bookings Mrs J Humphries, Brund Mill, Sheen, Longnor, Buxton, Derbyshire
☎Hartington(029884)383

Two terraced cottages converted into one, fully modernised throughout, the downstairs accommodation has a lounge/ dining room, separate kitchen. Upstairs is a bathroom/WC, one single bedroom, one twin bedroom and a bedroom with two single beds. 3m S of B5053.

All year except Xmas and New Year
2nights min, 3mths max, 1unit,
1–4persons ◆ ◎ fridge Electric
(night storage) Elec metered
L not provided ☎(200yds) ⊗
⊕3pin square ⌁(25yds)

⊖ ♀(50yds)
Min£70 Max£80pw (Low)
Min£90 Max£105pw (High)

F No 7 Chapel Street
for bookings Mrs J Humphries, Brund Mill, Sheen, Longnor, Buxton, Derbys
☎Hartington(029884)383

Located above a tea room in the centre of this quiet village; a modernised flat comprising of lounge/diner, open-plan kitchen, bathroom/WC and three bedrooms, two twin-bedded rooms and one with a single bed. 3m S of B5053.

All year except Xmas & New Year
2night min, 3mths max, 1unit, 1–5persons
◆ ◆ ◎ fridge Electric
Elec metered L not provided ☎ ⊗
⊕3pin square 6P ⌁(25yds)

⊖ ♀(50yds)
Min£70 Max£80pw (Low)
Min£90 Max£105pw (High)

LONGSLEDDALE
Cumbria
Map7 NY40
H Mrs J Farmer **The Coach House**
Capplebarrow House, Longsleddale, Kendal, Cumbria LA8 9BB
☎Selside(053983)686

Situated in a peaceful valley with excellent views of the surrounding fells, especially

---

Longor
—
Looe

from the lounge, this stone-built property was once a coach house and has been tastefully modernised to offer very comfortable accommodation. It sleeps up to five people, two in a twin-bedded room on the ground floor, the rest in convertible settee's in the first-floor lounge.

All year MWB out of season 3days min, 1mth max, 1unit, 2–4persons ◆ ◆
◆ ◎ fridge Electric & solid fuel fires
Elec inclusive L inclusive ☎(200yds)
WM, SD & TD on premises Iron in unit
Ironing board on premises ⊖ CTV
⊕3pin square 2P ⌁(6m)

Details not confirmed for 1987

C Mrs H Andrews **Stockdale Cottage**
Longsleddale, Kendal, Cumbria LA8 9BE
☎Selside(053983)210

Single-storey stone-built converted barn situated next to owners house, in isolated position close to the valley head. Pleasantly appointed, offering two bedrooms, open-plan lounge, kitchen area, and shower room. Set in beautiful fells to the north of Kendal.

All year MWB out of season 1day min, 1unit, 2–4persons ◆ ◆ ◎ fridge
Electric Elec metered L inclusive
☎(1½m) Iron & Ironing board on
premises ⊖ ⊕3pin square 1P Ⅲ
⌁(10m)

Min£56 Max£85pw

LOOE
Cornwall
Map2 SX25

F Bay, Blyth & Pilchard Cottages East Looe
for bookings Mrs A Lean, Trelean, West Looe Hill, Looe, Cornwall PL13 2HW
☎Looe(05036)2530

Five holiday homes converted from a 400-year-old harbour warehouse and fish store. Units with modern interiors, consist of two bedrooms (one double and one twin-bedded), lounge, and convertible

---

settee, dining area, kitchenette and bathroom.

All year 1wk min, 1mth max, 5units, 6persons ◆ ◆ ◑ fridge Electric
Gas/Elec metered L can be hired
☎(100yds) Iron in unit [Launderette within 300yds) ⊖ CTV ⊕3pin square
Ⅲ ⌁(100yds)

⊖ ♀(¼m) ♫(¼m) ♪(¼m)
Min£60 Max£120

B Fernbank Kellow
for bookings Mr & Mrs S G Emmons, Beechwood, The Coombe, Streatley, Berkshire
☎Goring-on-Thames(0491)872395

Modern bungalow in a superb position with lovely sea views; well furnished and decorated comprising two twin-bedded rooms, one double, bathroom/WC, kitchen and L-shaped lounge/diner.

All year MWB out of season 1wk min, 3mths max, 1unit, 1–6persons ◆
no pets ◎ Electric Elec metered
L not provided ☎(300yds) Iron in unit
[Launderette within 300yds)
⊕3pin square 2P 1⌁ Ⅲ ⌁(300yds)

⊖ ♪(2m) ♀(300yds) ♫(300yds)
♪(300yds)
Min£45 Max£155pw (Low)
Min£160 Max£205pw (High)

F B, G & M Sampson **Lemain Garden Apartments** Portuan Road, West Looe, Cornwall PL13 2DR
☎Looe(05036)2073 or
Widegates(05034)649

Eight self-contained flats within a stone-built detached house overlooking the sea. There are one, two and three bedroomed units all with varying sized kitchen/dining area, and lounge, some with bath/WC or shower/WC en-suite and others with balconies also.

All year MWB out of season 3days min, 8units, 1–10persons ◆ ◆ ◆ ◎
fridge ⅋ & Electric Elec metered
L can be hired ☎ in each unit Iron & Ironing board in unit Launderette on premises ⊖ CTV ⊕3pin square 16P
Ⅲ ⌁(150yds)

⊖ ♪(3m) ♀(100yds) ♫(1m) ♪(1m)

Min£58 Max£110pw (Low)
Min£154 Max£260pw (High)

F   Stonerock Holiday Flats Portuan
Road, Hannafore
for bookings Mr & Mrs R M C Hore, Green
Borders, Marine Drive, Looe, Cornwall
PL13 2DH
☎Looe(05036)2928

*Once a hotel, now converted into nine
well-maintained flats with one, two and
three bedrooms. Close to shops and about
150yds from Hannafore Beach and the
western seafront.*

All year MWB out of season 1wk min,
1mth max, 9units, 2−9persons [◆]
no cats ◎ fridge Electric
Elec metered L̲can be hired
☎(150yds) Iron & Ironing board in unit
☉ CTV ⊕3pin square ⊕2pin round
🏠 ♨(½m) ⅙ putting green
⊖ ⬚ ▣ ♫

Min£38 Max£70pw (Low)
Min£53 Max£180pw (High)

C   Tiree & Tyrina Lower Chapel Street
for bookings Mrs J P M Stevens, 25 Station
Road, Keyham, Plymouth, Devon
☎Plymouth(0752)563532

Tiree and *Tyrina* are a pair of 17th-
century fishermens cottages. Both
comprise lounge/diner, kitchen, two twin-
bedded rooms and bathroom/WC, with
Tiree having brass beds and *Tyrina* an
inglenook fireplace.

mid Mar−mid Nov 1wk min, 3wks max,
2units, 1−4persons ◇ ◆ no pets ◎
fridge Electric (Heating free early/late
season) Elec metered L̲can be hired
☎(50yds) SD in unit Iron & Ironing
board in unit [Launderette 300yds] ☉
TV ⊕3pin square ⚏(50yds)
⊖ ♪(3m) ♨(20yds) ▣(50yds)
♫(50yds) ♫(50yds)

Min£50 Max£80pw (Low)
Min£98 Max£158pw (High)

Ch & F   Treble 'B' Holiday Centre Ltd
Polperro Road, Looe, Cornwall
☎Looe(05036)2425

*Two chalets and six flats adjacent to a
large camping park, near to beach. The
chalets are well-decorated and modestly
furnished, one is cedarwood, the other*

Looe
—
Ludgvan

*block-built. The flats are concrete-built
with stucco finish, well appointed,
furnished and have access to all the
facilities of the holiday centre.*

3May−26Sep MWB out of season
2nights min, 8units, 2−6persons [◆
◆] no pets ◎ fridge Electric
Elec metered L̲can be hired
☎(60yds) [Launderette] [CTV]
⊕3pin square P ⚏(60yds)

Min£50 Max£80pw (Low)
Min£135 Max£265pw (High)

F   Up-Aloft The Quay, West Looe
for bookings Mrs A Lean, Trelean, West
Looe Hill, Looe, Cornwall PL13 2HW
☎Looe(05036)2530

*Self-contained flat with magnificent views
of the harbour and East Looe.
Accommodation comprises three
bedrooms (two double and one twin-
bedded), lounge with double studio
couch, kitchen and bathroom. Parking
opposite in car park.*

All year 1wk min, 1mth max, 1unit,
8persons ◆ ◆ ◎ fridge Electric
Elec metered L̲can be hired
☎(50yds) Iron & Ironing board in unit
☉ CTV ⊕3pin square ▥ ⚏(50yds)
⊖ ♨(½m) ▣(½m) ♫(½m)

Min£85 Max£160

LOWESTOFT
Suffolk
Map**5** TM59

Ch   Broadland Chalets Oulton Broad
for bookings Hoseasons Holidays,
Sunway House, Lowestoft, Suffolk
NR32 3LT
☎Lowestoft(0502)62271

*Delightful brick-built chalets situated by
the southern shore of Oulton Broad, 2½m
from Lowestoft. There is a private yacht
harbour where motor launches may be
hired and boats moored for a small fee.
The chalets vary in size with* **Broadsedge**
sleeping for six to eight persons in three

---

bedrooms plus studio couch in lounge.
Broadshaven *sleeps four to five people in
two bedrooms plus single divan in living
room.* **Broadside** *sleeps two to four people
in one double bedroom plus studio couch
in lounge.* **Broadsmead** *sleeps four to six
people in two bedrooms plus studio couch
which converts into a double or two single
beds.* **Broadrest** *sleeps from three to five
people in two bedrooms plus double put-
u-up in lounge. All have kitchen,
bathroom/WC and are equipped to a high
standard.*

Apr−Sep MWB out of season 2days min,
1mth max, 60units, 2−8persons [◆
◆] no pets ◎ fridge Electric
Elec metered L̲inclusive ☎(½m) [Iron
& Ironing board on premises] ☉
⊕3pin square P 🏠 ⚏ Fishing,
Children's Play area
⊖ ♪(2m) ♨(½m) ▣(½m) ⊠(2m)

Min£50 Max£170pw

LUDGVAN
Cornwall
Map**2** SW53

**B, C, F, H   Mr & Mrs Richards Nanceddan
Farm** Ludgvan, Penzance, Cornwall
TR20 8AW
☎Penzance(0736)740238 or 740293

*Fully-equipped modern holiday homes
situated on working farm and holiday
complex conveniently positioned within
easy reach of many famous beauty spots
surrounding the Cornish peninsula.
Location midway between St Ives and
Penzance approx 1m off A30 and 2¼m
from sea.*

Mar−Oct MWB in season 1wk min,
15units, 1−8persons ◆ no pets ◎
fridge Electric Elec metered L̲can be
hired ☎(on site) [Iron & Ironing board
on premises] [Launderette on premises]
☉ CTV ⊕3pin square 2P 1🏠 ▥
⚏(on site)
⊖ ♪(3m) ♨(½m) ▣(3m) ♫(3m)
⊠(3m)

Min£60 Max£100pw (Low)
Min£115 Max£215pw (High)

See advertisement under St Ives

C Mr D Edwards **Little Rosevidney Farm Cottages** Ludgvan, Penzance, Cornwall TR20 9BX
☎Penzance(0736)740642

Three stone cottages, converted from farm buildings to a high standard. Accommodation comprises open plan lounge/kitchen/diner with double bed-settee, one twin and one double bedroom, bathroom and WC. Weekly barbeque during the summer months in gardens. Off A30 midway between the Hayle and Marazion By-passes.

Mar–2Jan MWB out of season 3days min, 1mth max, 3units, 1–6persons [◇] ◈ ◆ ◎ fridge Electric fires & storage heaters Elec metered Ⓛcan be hired ☎(1m) Iron & Ironing board in unit ☉ CTV ⊕3pin square 10P ▥ ⚎(1½m) ✿grass
⊖ ⚌ (1½m) ♫(3m)
Min£60 Max£95pw (Low)
Min£110 Max£220pw (High)

LUING, Isle of
Strathclyde *Argyllshire*
Map**10** NM71

F Miss A Stone **Cluain Flats** Cullipool, Isle of Luing, Oban, Argyll
☎Luing(08524)209

Two comfortable holiday flats in a Victorian, stone-built house with superb views over Firth of Lorn and the islands of the Inner Hebrides. Each flat has two twin-bedded rooms and extra beds are provided in the sitting room. Each has kitchen/dining room and modern bathroom. Deep freeze in each unit.

Mar–Nov MWB in season 1wk min, 6mths max, 2units, 4–8persons ◈ ◎ fridge ▥ Elec metered Ⓛinclusive ☎(½m) SD on premises Iron & Ironing board in unit ☉ TV ⊕3pin square P ▥ ⚎(100yds)
Min£65 Max£85pw (Low)
Min£90 Max£140pw (High)

LULLINGTON
Derbyshire
Map**8** SK21

C **Aubretia Cottage**
for bookings Mrs R A Cooper, The Grange, Lullington, Burton-on-Trent, Staffordshire DE12 8ED
☎Clifton Campville(082786)219

Refurbished semi-detached cottage located in this small Derbyshire village, with accommodation comprising lounge, kitchen/diner, two bedrooms and bathroom.

All year MWB out of season 3days min, 1mth max, 1unit, 1–2persons ◔ fridge ▥ open and Electric fires Gas inclusive Elec metered Ⓛinclusive ☎(100yds) Iron & Ironing board ☉ ⊘ CTV ⊕3pin square 2P ▥ ⚎(100yds)
⊖ ⚌ (100yds)
Min£35 Max£80pw (Low)

Ludgvan
—
Lundy, Isle of

LUMPHANAN
Grampian *Aberdeenshire*
Map**15** NJ50

C **St Finans Barn**
for bookings Mrs T M Collier, 32 Graham Park Rd, Gosforth, Newcastle upon Tyne NE3 4BH
☎(091)285 3651

Modernised stone-built cottage on the outskirts of Lumphanann ½m north of village on A980. Open-plan living room/kitchen and three bedrooms all on ground floor.

All year MWB out of season 1wk min, 1unit, 1–8persons ◎ fridge ▥ Elec metered Ⓛnot provided ☎(½m) Iron & Ironing board in unit ☉ TV can be hired ⊕3pin square 4P ▥ ⚎(½m)
⊖ ♪(2m) ⚌(½m)
Min£70 Max£145pw (Low)

LUNDY, ISLE OF
Devon
Map**2** SS14

C **Bramble Villas**
for booking The Landmark Trust, Shottesbrooke, Maidenhead, Berkshire SL6 3SW
☎Littlewick Green(062882)5925

A pair of semi-detached cedar wood bungalows with stream running through the garden. Comprises compact kitchen, comfortable lounge with dining area, two twin-bedded rooms and bathroom/WC.

All year MWB out of season 3days min, 4wks max, 2units, 1–4persons ◈ ◆ no pets ◔ fridge Night storage Gas & Elec inclusive Ⓛcan be hired ☉ ⊕3pin square ⚎(½m)
⊖ ⚌ (½m)
Min£66 Max£130pw (Low)
Min£90 Max£175pw (High)

B & C **Castle Keep North, Castle Keep South & The New House**
for bookings The Landmark Trust, Shottesbrooke, Maidenhead, Berkshire SL6 3SW
☎Littlewick Green(062882)5925

Two recently restored Victorian stone cottages within the Castle Keep and a newly constructed granite dwelling in period style offering accommodation in two to three bedrooms sleeping up to six people. Castle Keep North has a lounge/diner, compact kitchen and shower room/WC. Castle Keep South comprises spacious lounge, kitchen/diner, shower room and separate WC. The New House has lounge/diner, pine-fitted kitchen, bathroom/WC and an extra WC.

All year MWB out of season 3days min, 4wks max, 3units, 1–5persons ◈ ◆ no pets ◔ fridge ▥(New House) storage heaters Gas & Elec inclusive

---

Ⓛcan be hired ☉ ⊕3pin square ⚎(½m)
⊖ ⚌ (½m)
Min£72 Max£144pw (Low)
Min£115 Max£240pw (High)

C & H **Old House North, Old House South & The Square Cottage**
for bookings The Landmark Trust, Shottesbrooke, Maidenhead, Berkshire SL6 3SW
☎Littlewick Green(062882)5925

Two granite houses and a cottage formerly part of original Manor farmhouse, recently modernised to a high standard. Old House North comprises pine-fitted kitchen, lounge/dining room with open fire, one twin-bedded room and bathroom/WC. Old House South offers kitchen/diner, lounge, verandah, two twin- and one single-bedded rooms, bathroom/WC and separate WC/wash hand basin. Square Cottage has lounge/diner, pine fitted kitchen, one twin- and one single-bedded room, and bathroom/WC.

All year MWB out of season 3days min, 4wks max, 3units, 1–5persons ◈ ◆ no pets ◔ fridge ▥ Gas & Elec inclusive Ⓛcan be hired ☉ ⊕3pin square ⚎(100yds)
⊖ ⚌ (100yds)
Min£48 Max£138pw (Low)
Min£60 Max£230pw (High)

B **Hanmers**
for bookings The Landmark Trust, Shottesbrooke, Maidenhead, Berkshire SL6 3SW
☎Littlewick Green(062882)5925

Detached timber-clad and lined bungalow comprising compact sitting room, galley-type kitchen, dining room (with extra bed), two bedrooms (one twin, one with bunk beds) and shower room/WC. Splendid views and this property has additional gas lighting.

All year MWB out of season 3days min 4wks max, 1unit, 1–5persons ◈ ◆ no pets ◔ fridge night storage Gas & Elec inclusive Ⓛcan be hired ☉ ⊕3pin square ⚎(½m)
⊖ ⚌ (½m)
Min£84 Max£126pw (Low)
Min£115 Max£210pw (High)

F **Old Light**
for bookings The Landmark Trust, Shottesbrooke, Maidenhead, Berkshire SL6 3SW
☎Littlewick Green(062882)5925

Converted from former lighthouse keeper's quarters on the west side of the island, comprising compact pine-fitted kitchen, sitting room/dining area, three bedrooms (one twin, two with bunks), and shower room/WC. The lighthouse is locked for safety reasons, but key always available.

All year MWB out of season 3days min 4wks max, 1unit, 1–6persons ◈ ◆ no pets ◔ fridge night storage Gas & Elec inclusive Ⓛcan be hired ☉ ⊕3pin square ⚎(½m)

⊖ ⚲(½m)
Min£90 Max£162pw (Low)
Min£120 Max£270pw (High)

LUPPITT
Devon
Map**3** ST10

C Mr & Mrs E Chapman **'Pulshays'**
Luppitt, Honiton, Devon EX14 0JU
☎Luppitt(040489)326

Situated in peaceful country setting and isolation these delightful modern fitted bungalow cottages have been created from existing barn outbuildings and comprise open plan kitchen/diner/lounge with double bed-settee, two twin-bedded rooms and bathroom/WC. Properties adjoin workshop for making musical instruments and spinning wheel instruction is offered.

Mar–Jan MWB out of season 1wk min, 4wks max, 3units, 2–6persons [◇ ◆] no pets ◎ fridge night storage Elec metered Ⓛinclusive ☎(2m) [WM on premises] Iron & Ironing board on premises ⊙ CTV ⊕3pin square 6P ▥ ♨(3m)

⊖ ⚲(2m) 🎜(2m)
Min£60 Max£160pw

LUSTLEIGH
Devon
Map**3** SX78

C **Becka, Fingle & Holne Cottages** East Wray, Barton Court
for bookings Mrs V J Procter, Alston Farm, Alston Lane, Churston Ferrers, Brixham, Devon TQ5 0HT
☎Churston Ferrers(0803)845388

These three converted old barn buildings offer well-maintained and comfortably furnished accommodation. Becka and Fingle have two bedrooms, kitchen/diner and lounge, while Holne has three bedrooms, lounge/diner and a kitchen. All have modern bathroom/WC.

4Apr–31Oct MWB out of season 3nights min, 1mth max, 3units, 1–6persons [◇] ◎ fridge Electric Elec metered Ⓛcan be hired ☎(1m) Iron & Ironing board in unit ⊙ CTV ⊕3pin square 3P ▥ ♨(1m)

⊖ ♪(2m) ⚲(1m) 🎜(2m)
Min£60 Max£75pw (Low)
Min£125 Max£140pw (High)

C **CC Ref 4095**
for bookings Character Cottages (Holidays) Ltd, 34 Fore Street, Sidmouth, Devon EX10 8AQ
☎Sidmouth(03955)77001

Converted linney in the grounds of Lussacombe. Accommodation comprises lounge/dining area with inglenook fireplace, stone pillars and exposed wooden beams, kitchen with small eating area, stairs to one double and two twin bedrooms and bathroom. All well furnished and decorated.

Lundy, Isle of
—
Lynton

All year MWB out of season 2days min, 8wks max, 1unit, 6persons, nc8years no pets ◎ fridge 🔥& elec fires Elec metered Ⓛnot provided ☎(1m) WM & TD in unit Iron & Ironing board in unit ⊙ CTV ⊕3pin square 2P ♨(1m)

⊖ ♪(2m) ⚲(1m)
Min£108 Max£243pw

LYME REGIS
Devon
See **Uplyme**

LYMPSTONE
Devon
Map**3** SX98

C **CC Ref 658**
for bookings Character Cottages (Holidays) Ltd, 34 Fore Street, Sidmouth, Devon EX10 8AQ
☎Sidmouth(03955)77001

Well-built fisherman's cottage overlooking water front on River Exe with views of Haldon Hills from sun parlour. Accommodation comprises two twin-bedded rooms, lounge/kitchen/diner, and a library; all tastefully furnished. Leave A376 at Sadler's Arms and proceed to far end of village to rivers edge.

Apr–Oct MWB out of season 1wk min, 6mths max, 1unit, 2–4persons no pets ◎ fridge Electric Elec inclusive Ⓛnot provided ☎(100yds) Iron & Ironing board in unit ⊙ TV ⊕3pin square ⊕2pin round ▥ ♨(100yds)

⊖ ⚲
Min£155pw (Low)
Min£168 Max211pw (High)

C **CC Ref 6030 L**
for bookings Character Cottages (Holidays) Ltd, 34 Fore Street, Sidmouth, Devon EX10 8AQ
☎Sidmouth(03955)77001

Double terraced cottage, on River Exe, with three bedrooms (one twin and two single beds), lounge, dining room, kitchen, bathroom and WC. Leave A376 at Sadlers Arms Inn, proceed through village to Globe Inn, cottage opposite.

Jul–Sep 1wk min, 6mths max, 1unit, 2–4persons [◇] ◆ no pets ♪ fridge Electric Gas inclusive Elec metered Ⓛcan be hired ☎(½m) Iron & Ironing board in unit ⊙ TV ⊕3pin square ⊕2pin round ▥ ♨

⊖ ⚲
Min£140 Max£180pw

LYNDON
Leicestershire
Map**4** SK90

H **Honeysuckle Cottage** 5 Church Road
for bookings Sir John Conant Bt, Lyndon Hall, Oakham, Leics LE15 8TU
☎Manton(057285)275

Semi-detached house in quiet and attractive country village. It has its own small garden area. Downstairs there is a lounge, kitchen/dining area and upstairs two twin-bedded rooms and a bathroom with WC and wash basin.

All year 3days min, 4mths max, 1unit, 1–4persons [◇] ◆ ◆ no pets ◎ fridge 🔥 Elec metered Ⓛcan be hired ☎(25yds) TV ⊕3pin square P ▥ ♨(1¾m) ▣ ◡Hard

⊖ ⚲(1½m)
Min£45 (Low)
Min£70 Max£95pw (High)

C **Rose Cottage** 12 Post Office Lane
for bookings Sir John Conant Bt, Lyndon Hall, Oakham, Leics LE15 8TU
☎Manton(057285)275

Attractive, stone-built cottage standing in its own grounds at end of cul-de-sac in quiet country village. Upstairs there is one twin-bedded room, and a double room, downstairs there are a sitting, kitchen/dining area and bathroom with WC and wash basin.

All year 3days min, 4mths max, 1unit, 1–4persons [◇] ◆ no pets ◎ fridge 🔥 Elec metered Ⓛcan be hired ☎(75yds) ⊕ TV ⊕3pin square P ▣ ▥ ♨(1¾m) ▣ ◡Hard

⊖ ⚲(½m)
Min£45 (Low)
Min£75 Max£100pw (High)

LYNTON
Devon
Map**3** SS74

F Mrs P I Harris **Oaklands** Lynbridge, Lynton, Devon EX35 6AX
☎Lynton(0598)52344

Ground- and first-floor flat on end of owners Victorian stone house on edge of village. Both comprise kitchen/diner with modern fitted units and comfortable lounge. First-floor flat contains one bedroom with a double and twin beds and a separate double bedded room and shower room/WC. Ground-floor flat has only one bedroom with a double and twin beds, bathroom/WC. Located between Lynton and Lynbridge.

Mar–Oct MWB out of season 1wk min, 4wks max, 2units, 1–6persons ◆ ◆ ◎ fridge 🔥 (night storage ground-floor flat) Elec metered Ⓛcan be hired ☎ SD on premises Iron & Ironing board in unit ⊙ CTV ⊕3pin square 2P ▥ ♨(½m)

⊖ ⚲(½m)
Min£70 Max£85pw (Low)
Min£95 Max£145pw (High)

See advertisement on page 160

LYONSHALL
Hereford & Worcester
Map**3** SO35

C Offa's Cottage
for bookings Mrs M A Eckley, The Holme,
Lyonshall, Kington, Herefordshire HR5 3JP
☎Lyonshall(05448)216

*A modernised, 17th-century stone-built
cottage built on Offa's Dyke. There are
three bedrooms, a double on the ground
floor, two doubles upstairs with two double
children's bunk beds, a lounge, dining
room, kitchen and bathroom. Situated at
the end of a drive, surrounded by rich
farmland and with views across to Radnor
Forest, own transport is essential.*

All year 2 days min, 1 mth max, 1 unit,
1–8 persons ◆ ◆ ◎ fridge Electric
& open fire Elec metered
⌑not provided ☎(¾m) Iron & Ironing
board in unit TV ⊕3 pin square P ⊖
ẟ(3m) ⚲(1m) ⚐(¾m)

Min£50 Max£70pw (Low)
Min£100 Max£110pw (High)

LYTHAM ST ANNES
Lancashire
Map**7** SD32

F E & D Bitar Argyll Holiday Flats 336
Clifton Drive North, Lytham St Annes,
Lancashire FY8 2PB
☎St Annes(0253)721810

*Tall, semi-detached, stone-fronted house,
containing four well-designed and
spacious flats. Standing to the N of St
Anne's Square opposite Ashton Park and
gardens, the flats are conveniently placed
for the town's amenities, with the beach
and pier only a short walk away.*

All year MWB out of season 1 wk min,
4 units, 2–7 persons ◆ ◆ ◎ fridge
⚱ Electric Elec metered ⌑inclusive
☎(on premises) Airing cupboard in unit
HCE in unit CTV ⊕3 pin square P ⊞
⚐(100yds) ⚘Grass
⊖ ⚲(100yds) ♫(3m) ♪(3m)
⚐(½m)

Min£50 Max£170pw

F Mrs Hyra Towle Belgrave House 4
Victoria Road, Lytham St Annes,
Lancashire FY8 1LE
☎St Annes(0253)727967

Lyonshall
—
Lytham St Annes

*A semi-detached house converted into
three flats, situated close to the sea. Each
flat consists of lounge, dining room,
kitchen, shower/WC and sleeps up to six
persons.*

Apr–Oct 1 wk min, 3 units, 2–6 persons
no pets ◎ fridge Electric
Elec metered ⌑inclusive ☎ ⊙ CTV
⊕3 pin square 4P ⊞ ⚐(50yds)
⊖ ẟ(1m) ⚲(400yds) ♪(400yds)
♫(400yds) ⚐(½m)

Details not confirmed for 1987

F Mr D Whitehead Berri Court 20 North
Promenade, Lytham St Annes, Lancashire
FY8 2NQ
☎St Annes(0253)723392

*Nine holiday apartments situated in a
large house overlooking the sea. They are
all self-contained but the WC for flat 6 is
adjacent although for the sole use of the
occupants. One apartment is known as
the Mews Cottage and it has its own
entrance to the rear of the main building.
The units are within easy reach of all
amenities.*

All year MWB out of season 2 days min,
9 units, 2–8 persons [◆ ◆] no pets in
5 units only ◎ fridge Electric
Elec metered ⌑inclusive except tea
towels ☎ [TD on premises] ⊙ CTV
⊕3 pin square 10P ⚐(300yds)
⊖ ẟ(½m) ⚲(100yds) ♪(100yds)
♫(100yds) ⚐(300yds)

Min£46 Max£161pw (Low)
Min£80.50 Max£230pw (High)

F Claremont Court Flats 43 South
Promenade
for bookings Lindum Hotel, 63–67 South
Promenade, Lytham St Annes, Lancashire
☎St Annes(0253)721534/722516

*Six flats within a three-storey house on the
seafront and overlooking gardens. Each
flat has lounge, with convertible settee,
kitchen, bathroom and one bedroom with
two single beds.*

May–Oct 1 wk min, 5 mths max, 6 units,
2–4 persons [◆ ◆] no pets ◎
fridge ⚱ Elec charged ⌑can be
hired ☎(50yds) Iron & Ironing board in
unit [Launderette within 300yds] ⊙
CTV ⊕3 pin square 6P ⊞ ⚐(½m)
⊖ ẟ(½m) ⚲(50yds) ♪(50yds)
♫(50yds) ⚐(½m)

Min£80 Max£85pw (Low)
Min£115 Max£120pw (High)

F Heyesleigh Court 373 Clifton Drive
North
for bookings Mrs I Thompson, 200 Clifton
Drive South, Lytham St Annes, Lancashire
☎Lytham(0253)735028

*Five spacious self-contained flats, situated
within a semi-detached house, close to
shops and within walking distance of
beach. There is one flat on the ground
floor sleeping up to eight persons; two on
the first floor and two on the second floor
each sleeping up to six in various
combinations including bed-settees in
lounge.*

All year MWB out of season 1 wk min,
5 units, 2–8 persons ◆ ◆ ◎ fridge
⚱ Elec metered ⌑can be hired
☎(300yds) Iron & Ironing board on
premises CTV ⊕3 pin square 5P ⊞
⚐(300yds)
⊖ ẟ(1m) ⚲(200yds) ♪(200yds)
♫(200yds) ⚐(200yds)

Min£75 Max£150pw (Low)
Min£120 Max£200pw (High)

F Mrs J Hughes Silverdale Holiday Flats
381 Clifton Drive North, Lytham St Annes,
Lancashire FY8 2PA
☎St Annes(0253)724928

*Four fully-equipped flats located within a
large house situated on the main
Blackpool road, convenient for shops, sea
and amenities. They sleep from two to six
people in double or family bedrooms, plus
additional sleeping facilities in lounges.*

24May–27Sep MWB out of season
1 wk min, 6 mths max, 4 units, 2–6 persons
◆ ◆ ◎ fridge Electric
Elec metered ⌑inclusive ☎(400yds)
⊙ CTV ⊕3 pin square 4P ⊞
⚐(400yds)

⊕ ♿(½m) ♨(400yds) 🎵(400yds)
🎵(½m) 🛁(400yds)
Min£75 Max£120pw (Low)
Min£105 Max£150pw (High)

F F R & M T Hoyle **Trevelyn House** 23
Fairhaven Road, Lytham St Annes,
Lancashire
☎St Annes(0253)727871

*A large three-storey, semi-detached, brick-
built house situated in a quiet side road
just off the Promenade. Five self-
contained units, all with one or two
bedrooms with extra bed space within the
lounges (wall beds). Proprietor lives on
premises.*

All year MWB out of season 1wk min,
5units, 2–6persons ◆ ◆ ◎ fridge
🍴 Elec metered ⬛inclusive Iron in
unit Ironing board on premises
[Launderette within 300yds] ☺ CTV
⊕3pin square P 📺 ♨(200yds) ⌓
Putting

⊕ ♿(½m) ♨(400yds) 🎵(400yds)
🎵(200yds) 🛁(½m)
Min£58 Max£68pw (Low)
Min£78 Max£125pw (High)

MALBOROUGH
Devon
Map**3** SX73

F Mrs W Harder **'West Soar'** Soar Mill
Cove, Malborough, Kingsbridge, Devon
TQ7 3DS
☎Kingsbridge(0548)561334

*Originally a barn and now tastefully
modernised and furnished, all on the first
floor giving superb views of the cove. It
comprises kitchen, lounge/diner,
bathroom/WC, two bedrooms (one
double, one twin) plus double bed-settee
in the lounge. There is a balcony which
leads directly to rising ground laid to lawn.*

28Mar – Oct MWB out of season
1wk min, 3wks max, 1unit, 2–6persons
[◆ ◆] no pets ◎ fridge 🍴
Elec inclusive ⬛inclusive ☎(300yds)
WM & SD in unit Iron & Ironing board in
unit ☺ CTV ⊕3pin square 2P 📺
♨(2¼m)

⊕ ♨(2¼m)
Min£75 Max£100pw (Low)
Min£135 Max£190pw (High)

MALHAM
North Yorkshire
Map**7** SD96

C & F **Gordale Court**
for bookings Mr R Robinson, The Buck
Inn, Malham, Skipton, North Yorkshire
☎Airton(07293)317

*Modernised stone-built cottages and
apartments set around a courtyard in the
centre of the village. The three cottages
Ostler, Tally-Ho! and **Stirrup** have one
bedroom with double and single bed. The
flats **Anvil** and the **Stable** have three
bedrooms, one double, one twin and one
with bunks. All are well furnished to a
modern standard. Located at the rear of
the Buck Inn, in beautiful countryside,*

*ideal for walking and exploring the
Yorkshire Dales.*

All year MWB out of season 5units,
2–6persons ◆ ◆ ◎ fridge Electric
& storage Elec metered ⬛can be hired
☎(20yds) Iron & Ironing board on
premises ☺ TV ⊕3pin square 5P
📺 ♨(50yds)

⊕ ♨(20yds)
Min£53 Max£78pw (Low)
Min£75 Max£152pw (High)

MALTON
North Yorkshire
Map**8** SE77

F Mrs J Floris **Florios Holiday Flats** 11
Yorkersgate, Malton, North Yorkshire
YO17 6AA
☎Malton(0653)5006

*Four very comfortable modern flats in the
upper floors of a listed 18th century
building in town centre. Flat A sleeps four
in a double bedded room and on bed-
settee in the lounge. Flat B and C sleep
four in one twin-bedded room and bed-
settee in the lounge. Flat D sleeps six in
three twin-bedded rooms. All have
bathroom facilities and kitchen diners with
combined lounges.*

All year MWB 2days min, 1mth max,
4units, 2–6persons ◆ ◆ no pets
◎ fridge 🍴 Elec inclusive
⬛inclusive ☎(20yds) WM, SD & TD on
premises Iron & Ironing board on
premises Launderette within 300yds ☺
CTV ⊕3pin square No parking at
premises 📺 ♨

⊕ ♿(1m) ♨(20yds) 🎵(20yds)
Sports centre(1m)
Min£40 Max£95pw (Low)
Min£125 Max£190pw (High)

MALVERN
Hereford & Worcester
Map**3** SO74

C & F Mrs J Wright **Butlers, Coachmans
& Ostlers** Westwood House, Park Road,
West Malvern, Malvern, Worcestershire
WR14 3DS
☎Malvern(06845)66997

Butlers *is a well-equipped garden flat with
exceptional views of Herefordshire
countryside. Accommodation consists of
diner/kitchen, lounge, double bedroom,
bathroom, use of garden.* **Coachmans**
and **Ostlers** *are two cottages converted
from the original coach house and consist
of lounge, kitchen/diner and lobby area
on ground floor. On the first floor*
Coachmans *has one twin-bedded room
and one double bunk bedroom,* **Ostlers**
*has one double-bedded room and one
twin-bedded room. Both have shower
room/WC.*

All year MWB out of season 3days min,
6wks max, 3units, 1–4persons [◇]
no pets ◎ fridge 🍴 Elec inclusive
⬛inclusive ☎(300yds) WM in unit
(Coachmans & Ostlers) Iron & Ironing
board in unit HCE in unit ☺ CTV
⊕3pin square P ♨(400yds)

⊕ ♨(100yds) 🛁(3m)
Min£95 Max£155pw (Low)
Min£165 Max£215pw (High)

C Mr & Mrs M G Allen **Hartlands**
Evendine Lane, Colwall, Malvern,
Worcestershire WR13 6DT
☎Colwall(0684)40658

*A modernised 17th-century thatched
cottage with a large garden, orchard and
brook. The stone-built cider house and
outbuildings, also sheep and chickens,
give it a farm-like atmosphere. It is situated
3m SW of town on B4218 on the sunny,
west slopes of the Malvern Hills and is a
good centre for walking and touring.*

All year MWB out of season
1night – wknds min, 4wks max, 1unit,
1–4persons ◇ ◆ ◎ fridge
Electric Elec metered ⬛can be hired
☎(½m) WM & SD in unit Iron & Ironing
board in unit ☺ 📺 CTV
⊕3pin square P 📺 ♨(½m)

⊕ ♨(½m)
Min£50 Max£80pw (Low)
Min£90 Max£140pw (High)

C Mr & Mrs P T Williams **Whitewells
Farm** Ridgeway Cross, Malvern,
Worcestershire WR13 5JS
☎Ridgeway Cross(088684)607

*An award winning conversion of farm
buildings including: a hop kiln, milking
parlour, stables, hayloft, stone workshop
and pigs cot now provides seven cottages
differing in size and character and
featuring beams, posts, half cruck trusses
and even circular rooms. All are equipped
to a high standard of comfort and one
cottage has been designed specifically
with the disabled in mind.*

All year MWB 3days min, 7units,
2–6persons [◇] ◆ ◆ ◎ fridge
storage heating Elec inclusive
⬛inclusive ☎ Iron & Ironing board in
unit [Launderette on premises] ☺
CTV ⊕3pin square 8P 📺 ♨(½m)

⊕ ♨(1m)

See advertisement on page 162

MAMHEAD
Devon
Map**3** SX98

B **CC Ref 404 P**
for bookings Character Cottages
(Holidays) Ltd, 34 Fore Street, Sidmouth,
Devon EX10 8AQ
☎Sidmouth(03955)77001

*Spacious detached bungalow in open
country facing S. Entrance hall, large
lounge with picture windows giving fine
views, sun room with extra bed, large well-
equipped kitchen with bright décor, and
two large bedrooms with wash hand →*

161

basin. One double and one twin bedded. Modern bathroom/WC and separate WC.

All year MWB out of season 1wk min, 1mth max, 1unit, 2–6persons ◆ ◎ fridge ♨ Elec inclusive 🔲not provided ☎ Iron & Ironing board in unit ⊙ TV ⊕3pin square ⊕2pin round P ♨(2½m)

⊖ 🚻(2½m)

Min£80 Max£117pw (Low)
Min£157 Max£194pw (High)

MAN, ISLE OF
Map6 SC

DOUGLAS
Map6 SC37

F Mr & Mrs C D Scully **Griffindale House** Brunswick Road, Douglas, Isle of Man
☎Douglas(0624)73203

Seven flats located in a detached house with new extension to the rear. The accommodation is of modern design and five flats have one bedroom with double bed, shower room and WC. Extra childs bed is available. Two flats have two bedrooms one double one twin.

All year MWB out of season 1wk min, 7units, 2–4persons ◆ ◆ ◎ fridge Electric Elec metered 🔲inclusive ☎ Iron & Ironing board on premises [Launderette on premises] ⊙ CTV ⊕3pin square P ▣ ▥ ♨(100yds) ➥Hard/grass

⊖ 🚻(100yds) 🎵(300yds) ♫(½m) 🚻(½m)

Min£60 Max£75pw (Low)
Min£120 Max£140pw (High)

F Mrs A Dawson **Havelock Holiday Flats** 13 Mount Havelock, Douglas, Isle of Man
☎Douglas(0624)27270 or 25148

Four flats within a terraced property in Upper Douglas with three having views of the bay also three comprise of twin-bedded rooms with convertible beds in the lounge, the other has only a convertible bed. All have kitchen, bathroom and lounge.

All year MWB out of season 1wk min, 4units, 2–4persons ◆ no pets ◎ fridge Electric Elec metered

---

Mamhead
—
Man, Isle of

🔲inclusive ☎ Iron & Ironing board in unit [Launderette on premises] ⊙ CTV ⊕3pin square ♨(20yds)

⊖ ♫(1m) 🚻(100yds) 🎵(100yds) ♫(100yds) 🚻(½m)

C & H Mr R W Knight **Laureston Manor Town and Country Cottages** Ballaquale Road, Douglas, Isle of Man
☎Douglas(0624)22737

Mews type cottages set in 5 acres of manor house grounds. There are four converted outbuildings furnished to a high standard. **Deaks Cottage, Woodcroft Rose Cottage** and **Westacre** have two or three bedrooms, lounge, dining area, fitted kitchen and bathroom/WC. **West Wing** is part of the main house and has one bedroom, lounge with double bed-settee (as does Woodcroft). Close to town centre.

All year MWB out of season 1wk min, 6mths max, 5units, 2–8persons [◇] ◆ ◆ no pets ◎ fridge ♨(3units) Electric/Gas fires Gas/Elec metered 🔲inclusive Telephone in all units ☎(½m) Iron & Ironing board in unit ⊙ CTV ⊕3pin square 8P ▥ ♨(300yds)

⊖ ♫(1½m) 🚻(½m) 🎵(½m) ♫(½m) 🚻(1m)

Min£50 Max£80pw (Low)
Min£89 Max£245pw (High)

C Rentachalet **Silverburn Cottages** Little Switzerland Holiday Village, Douglas, Isle of Man
☎Douglas(0624)24515

A complex of well-appointed cottages sleeping up to seven in comfort. They incorporate lounge/dining area adjacent to kitchen and a well furnished bathroom, two bedrooms plus fold-away beds in lounge.

All year MWB out of season 3days min, 1mth max, 62units, 2–7persons ◆ ◆ no pets ◇ fridge ♨ Gas inclusive 🔲inclusive ☎ Iron & Ironing board on premises [Launderette on premises]

⊙ CTV ⊕3pin square 70P ♨(100yds)

⊖ ♫(2m) 🚻(500yds) ♫(1m) 🚻(1m)

Details not confirmed for 1987

Ch Rentachalet **Sulby Glen Chalets** Little Switzerland Holiday Village, Douglas, Isle of Man
☎Douglas(0624)24515

Spacious chalets incorporating lounge with comfortable seating and dining area, two bedrooms and bathroom/WC. Extra bed space is available in the lounge on fold-down singles.

23Mar–28Sep MWB out of season 3days min, 1mth max, 45units, 2–7persons ◆ ◆ no pets ◇ fridge Electric Gas inclusive 🔲inclusive ☎ Iron & Ironing board on premises [Launderette on premises] ⊙ CTV ⊕3pin square 50P ♨(300yds)

⊖ ♫(2m) 🚻(500yds) ♫(1m) 🚻(1m)

Details not confirmed for 1987

F Mr & Mrs G S & J P Shimmin **3 Tennis Road** Douglas, Isle of Man
☎Douglas(0624)75469

Large flats situated in a detached house in pleasant residential area. The five flats have two bedrooms (one with double bed and one with double and single beds) plus studio bed in lounge. The house is adequately furnished and close to shops.

All year MWB 7days min, 5units, 2–6persons ◆ ◆ 1 ◇ 4 ◎ fridge Electric Gas/Elec metered 🔲inclusive ☎(100yds) [WM & SD on premises] Iron & Ironing board on premises ⊙ CTV ⊕3pin square 9P ▥ ♨(100yds)

⊖ 🚻(100yds) 🎵(½m) ♫(½m) 🚻(½m)

Min£60 Max£100pw (Low)
Min£120 Max£175pw (High)

HILLBERRY (near Douglas)
Map6 SC37

C Bwanne, **The Farm Cottage** Lower Sulby Farm
for bookings Mr P Know, Clearview, Lower Sulby Farm, Abbeylands, Isle of Man
☎Douglas(0624)22737

Two original Victorian farm workers cottages now extensively modernised and made into one unit. There are four bedrooms, one twin, one with bunks and two doubles. Extra bed space is available in lounge on convertible settee. There are two bathrooms a separate dining room and modern kitchen. Situated on a working Manx Farm in rural surroundings yet close enough to the resort of Douglas.

All year MWB out of season 1wk min, 1unit, 10persons [◆ ◆] ◎ fridge Electric & open Elec metered Ⓛinclusive ☎(1m) WM & SD in unit Iron & Ironing board in unit ⊕ ⍉ CTV ⊕3pin square 4P ♨(2m)
⊖ ♪(4m)
Min£55 Max£75pw (Low)
Min£105 Max£215pw (High)

B & F Meadowview Bungalow & The Apartment
for bookings Glen Dhoo Camping Site, Hillberry, Onchan, Isle of Man
☎Douglas(0624)21254

The Apartment is situated above the camp site shop in a converted stone building central to all camp site facilities. It comprises lounge, dining room, kitchen, shower/WC and two twin bedded rooms plus studio couch in lounge. Meadowview bungalow situated near the main building on the camping site in rural surroundings comprises lounge, kitchen, two twin-bedded rooms, shower/WC and studio couch in lounge. Guests can use camp site facilities.

All year MWB out of season 2units, 1–6persons ◆ ◆ ◎ fridge Electric Elec metered Ⓛinclusive ☎ Iron & Ironing board in unit [Launderette within 300yds] ⊕ CTV ⊕3pin square 2P ⅿ ♨ Games room
⊖ ☎(1m) ♀(1m) ♬(2½m) ♪(2½m)
☎-(2½m)
Min£40 Max£90pw (Low)
£130pw (High)

ONCHAN
Map6 SC37

C Mr C V Walters The Cottages Groudle Glen, Onchan, Douglas, Isle of Man
☎Douglas(0624)23075

A village of 38 modern cottages set in a pleasant glen leading to a small cove. All are well furnished and each has three bedrooms (one with double bed, one with two singles and one with two bunks).

All year MWB out of season 1wk min, 38units, 2–6persons ◇ [◆] [◆] no pets ◎ fridge ☎(12units) Electric Elec metered Ⓛinclusive ☎ Iron on premises TV [CTV]
⊕3pin square P ⅿ ♨
⊖ ☎(1m) ♀(1m) ♬(3m) ♪(3m)
☎-(3m)
Min£72 Max£150pw (Low)
Min£160 Max£230pw (High)

MANESTY
Cumbria
Map11 NY21

C Manesty Holiday Cottages
for bookings A T & C A Leyland, Youdale Knot, Manesty, Keswick, Cumbria CA12 5UG
☎Borrowdale(059684)216

Traditional Lakeland farmhouse and adjacent barn recently converted and refurbished to form four spacious cottages designed and equipped to provide convenient holiday accommodation, offering between one and four bedrooms, lounge, dining room, kitchen, and bathroom/WC. Situated in the Borrowdale valley in attractive rural setting, 5m S of Keswick. Ideal centre for walking.

All year MWB out of season 1night min, 1mth max, 4units, 2–7persons ◆ ◆ no pets ◎ fridge Electric Elec metered Ⓛprovided ☎(¾m) Iron & Ironing board in unit ⊕ CTV
⊕3pin square 7P ⅿ ♨(5m)
⊖ ♀(3m)
Min£66 Max£121pw (Low)
Min£109 Max£252pw (High)

MANORBIER
Dyfed
Map2 SS09

C Coach House Tarr Farm
for booking Powell's Cottage Holidays, 55 High Street, Saundersfoot, Dyfed
☎Saundersfoot(0834)812791

Retaining the old arched entrance of the Coach House, this semi-detached cottage with character is set in the grounds of a farm. It has an open plan lounge with dining area and kitchen. There are two bedrooms on the first floor.

May–Aug MWB out of season 1wk min, 6wks max, 1unit, 2–4persons ◇ ◆ ◆ no pets ⌀ fridge Electric Gas/ Elec inclusive Ⓛprovided (overseas visitors only) Iron in unit ⊕ TV
⊕3pin square P ⅿ ♨(150yds)
⊖ ♀(150yds)
Min£93 Max£210pw

C Coachmans Cottage Sunnyhill Farm
for bookings Powell's Cottage Holidays, 55 High Street, Saundersfoot, Dyfed
☎Saundersfoot(0834)812791

Renovated detached cottage, two bedrooms, lounge, kitchen/diner, bathroom and WC. 2½ from Manorbier beach.

May–Sep MWB out of season 1wk min, 1unit, 5persons [◆] ◆ ◎ fridge ♨♨ Elec metered Ⓛnot provided ☎(30yds) Iron & Ironing board in unit CTV ⊕3pin square P ♨(1½m)
⊖ ♀(1½m)
Min£81 Max£180pw

C Tarr Cottage Tarr Farm
for bookings Powell's Cottage Holidays, 55 High Street, Saundersfoot, Dyfed
☎Saundersfoot(0834)812791

A newly adapted semi-detached cottage within the grounds of a farm. The accommodation consists of an open plan lounge with dining area and kitchen. There are two bedrooms.

May–Sep MWB out of season 1wk min, 6wks max, 1unit, 2–4persons ◇ ◆ ◆ no pets ⌀ fridge Electric Gas/ Elec inclusive Ⓛnot provided (overseas visitors only) Iron in unit ⊕ CTV
⊕3pin square P ⅿ ♨(150yds)
⊖ ♀(150yds)
Min£93 Max£210pw

MARAZION
Cornwall
Map2 SW53

F Clipper, Coach House, Schooner & Gun Room Flats
for bookings C Oats, Lynmere, 8 Trungle, Paul, Penzance, Cornwall TR19 6UG
☎Penzance(0736)731878 & 788238

The Coach House and Schooner flats have two bedrooms each, whilst Clipper and Gun Room flats offer one bedroomed accommodation. Each unit has lounge, kitchen, dining area and bathroom, some also with balconies.

All year MWB out of season 1wk min, 16units, 1–8persons ◇ ◆ ◎ fridge Electric Elec metered Ⓛinclusive ☎ Iron & Ironing board on premises CTV
⊕3pin square 10P ⅿ ♨(200yds)
⊖ ☎(2m) ♀(200yds) ♬(1m)
♪(1m) ☎-(1m)
Min£55 Max£105pw (Low)
Min£140 Max£255pw (High)

MARDEN
Hereford & Worcester
Map3 SO54

H Kingsfield Farm
for bookings Mrs D Pritchett, Hermitage Farm, Canon Pyon, Hereford HR4 8NN
☎Hereford(0432)760217

A well-modernised farmhouse containing two self-contained adjoining units, (sleeping eight in total) retaining old beams and fireplaces and set in peaceful surroundings overlooking open farmland and wooded countryside. Both comprise lounge/kitchen/diner, bathroom and two bedrooms (one double, one single); one unit has extra double bed increasing sleeping accommodation from three to five.

Mar–Oct (also winter long lets) MWB out of season 3days min, 6mths max, 2units, 1–5persons ◆ ◆ no pets ◎ fridge log burning stove electric radiators Elec metered Ⓛcan be hired ☎(2m) SD in unit Iron & Ironing board in unit ⊕ CTV ⊕3pin square P ♨(2m)
⊖ ♀(2m)
Min£50 Max£94pw

MARGATE
Kent
Map**5** TR37

F Mr & Mrs Mather **39 Prices Avenue**
Cliftonville, Margate, Kent CT9 2NT

Two flats on the ground floor of a Victorian house occupying a corner position ¼m from seafront. Both flats have lounge, dining room, kitchen and bathroom/WC, with two bedrooms in one flat and one in the other. The proprietor's flat is on the first floor.

Apr–Oct 3days min, 3mths max, 2units, 2–6persons ◊ ◉ fridge Electric Elec metered Ⓛcan be hired ☎(100yds) Iron & Ironing board in unit [Launderette within 300yds] ☉ TV ⊕3pin square Ⅲ ♨(100yds)

↩ ♀(200yds) ♫(½m) ♫(½m) ☏(½m)

Min£45 Max£80pw (Low)
Min£55 Max£110pw (High)

MARNHULL
Dorset
Map**3** ST71

C & F Mr & Mrs R G Gorton **Walton Elm House** Marnhull, Sturminster Newton, Dorset DT10 1QG
☎Marnhull(0258)820553

*A country residence of the late 19th century of which the outbuilding and cottages have been converted into seven self-catering units. **The Flat** which is on the first floor and reached by an outside staircase comprises sitting room with divider, kitchen, bathroom/WC and two bedrooms. **Lodge Cottage** is a two-storey, three-bedroomed property with living room, open-plan kitchen, bathroom and WC. A 'put-u-up' is also available. **Pavilion** is a two-bedroomed cottage with living room, open-plan kitchen, bathroom/WC, and an additional 'put-u-up'. **Pool Cottages** all comprise living room (with single bed-settee), open plan kitchen, shower/WC and one double bedroom. **Wing Cottage** has ground floor accommodation with three double bedrooms (plus bed-settee), living room, kitchen and bathroom/WC.*

Allyear MWB out of season 1wk min, 6mths max, 7units, 2–6persons, nc10 no pets Aga cooker in Lodge & Wing Cottage ◉ fridge ♨ Elec inclusive Ⓛcan be hired ☎ Iron & Ironing board on premises [Launderette on premises] ☉ TV ⊕3pin square P Ⅲ ♨ ⌂ [♨] Recreation rooms, croquet [billiards] putting green

↩ ♀(1m)

Min£70 Max£140pw (Low)
Min£105 Max£185pw (High)

B Mrs G Espley **Yewhouse Farm**
Marnhull, Sturminster Newton, Dorset
☎Marnhull(0258)820412

Two attractive Swedish-style detached bungalows. Both are well appointed throughout with comfortable furnishings and comprise large lounge/diner with modern recessed kitchen, shower/WC,

---

one double and one twin bedded room, own patio and small garden. On unclassified road off B3092 at Marnhull.

Allyear MWB out of season 1day min, 1mth max, 2units, 5persons ◊ ◆ no pets ◉ fridge Wood burning stove & electric convector Elec metered Ⓛinclusive ☎(½m) WM & TD in unit Iron & Ironing board in unit ☉ CTV ⊕3pin square 4P ♨(½m)

↩ ♀(½m)

Min£75 Max£165pw

MASHAM
North Yorkshire
Map**8** SE28

F Mrs A Close **Old Hall** Jervaulx Abbey, Ripon, North Yorkshire HG4 4PH
☎Bedale(0677)60313

Abbey, Penhill & Witton cottages at Jervaulx Abbey, recently restored from pre-Victorian stabling. All at first-floor level each with its own entrance from a courtyard. They comprise sitting/dining room with wood burning stove, electric heating, kitchen, bathroom/WC. The sleeping arrangements vary with ***Abbey*** having two twin bedrooms both with en-suite bath, ***Penhill*** one double bedroom ***Witton*** two doubles and one twin bedroom. 3m NW A6108.

Allyear 1wk min, 3mths max, 3units, 1–6persons ◊ ◆ ◉ fridge Electric Elec metered Ⓛcan be hired ☎(2m) WM & SD on premises Iron & Ironing board in unit ☉ CTV ⊕3pin square Stabling available P Ⅲ ♨(4m)

↩ ♀(2m)

Min£75 Max£100pw (Low)
Min£120 Max£135pw (High)

F **The Coach House**
for bookings Mrs J Airton, Sunnyside, Red Lane, Masham, Ripon, N Yorkshire HG4 4HH
☎Ripon(0765)89327

First-floor accommodation in a converted stone-built coach house and stable, within the grounds of Sunnyside House. Restored to a good standard with one double-bedded room and another with three single beds, lounge/diner and well-fitted kitchen. Semi-rural and wooded surroundings near the village centre.

Allyear MWB out of season 3days min, 1unit, 1–5persons ◊ ◆ no pets ◉ fridge ♨ Elec inclusive Ⓛinclusive ☎(300yds) Iron in unit Ironing board in unit [Launderette on premises] ☉ CTV ⊕3pin square 2P Ⅲ ♨(200yds) Pony trekking, fishing & bowling green

↩ ♪ ♀(400yds) ♫(400yds)

Min£150 Max£180pw (Low)
Min£125 Max£140pw (High)

Ch **Hedmark & Telemark**
for bookings Charlcot River Holidays, Charlcot, Ripon, North Yorkshire HG4 4AE
☎Ripon(0765)89025

Two Norwegian-style chalets in rural surroundings, of wooden construction with pine decor and furniture. They comprise kitchen/dining room, lounge, two bedrooms, one with twin beds, one with bunks, and a combined bathroom/WC.

Mar–Dec MWB out of season 1wk min, 4wks max, 2units, 1–4persons no pets ◉ fridge Electric Elec inclusive Ⓛinclusive ☎(1m) Iron & Ironing board on premises TV can be hired ⊕3pin square 2P Ⅲ ♨(3½m)

↩ ♀(2½m)

Min£70 Max£75pw (Low)
Min£100 Max£130pw (High)

F **Nelson House** Market Square
for bookings Mrs J Airton, Sunnyside, Red Lane, Masham, Ripon, N Yorkshire HG4 4HH
☎Ripon(0765)89327

A self contained flat, within a three-storey stone-built converted 18th-century public house. The accommodation has a separate entrance, and consists of two bedrooms, lounge/kitchenette and bathroom/shower/WC.

Allyear MWB out of season 3days min, 1unit, 2–6persons ◊ ◆ no pets ◉ fridge ♨ Elec inclusive Ⓛinclusive ☎(60yds) Iron & Ironing board in unit ☉ CTV ⊕3pin square Ⅲ ♨(50yds) Fishing, pony trekking, bowling green

↩ ♪(1m) ♀(60yds)

Min£30 Max£70pw (Low)
Min£80 Max£125pw (High)

C **Sunnyside Cottage**
for bookings Mrs J Airton, Sunnyside, Red Lane, Masham, Ripon, N Yorkshire HG4 4HH
☎Ripon(0765)89327

Detached cottage situated on the outskirts of the town not far from the small local brewery. Ground floor comprises lounge, dining room and kitchen. First floor comprises one twin-bedded room, one family room with double and single bed, one double-bedded room, bathroom and WC.

Allyear MWB out of season 3days min, 3mths max, 1unit 1–8persons [◊] ◊ no pets ◉ fridge ♨ & gas fire Gas/ Elec inclusive Ⓛinclusive ☎(400yds) WM, Iron & Ironing board in unit [Launderette on premises] ☉ CTV ⊕3pin square 1P Ⅲ ♨(200yds) Fishing, pony trekking & bowling green

↩ ♪ ♀(400yds) ♫(400yds)

Min£60 Max£100pw (Low)
Min£135 Max£160pw (High)

MATLOCK
Derbyshire
Map**8** SK36

F Mrs L M Briddon **Bridge Cottage Flat**
Bridge Cottage, Two Dales, Matlock,
Derbyshire
☎Matlock(0629)732221

Compact ground-floor flat situated in a
17th-century cottage, and comprising
kitchen/diner, shower/WC, lounge and
bedroom with exposed ceiling beams. Two
Dales 2½ miles N off A6, then B5057
towards Chesterfield.

Allyear 1wk min, 3mths max, 1unit,
2persons ◑ fridge Gasfire Ⓛcan be
hired ☎(25yds) Iron & Ironing board in
unit ☉ CTV ⊕3pin square 1P 🅼
🛁(200yds)
⊖ ♪(3m) ☕(15yds) 🦮(3m)
Min£69 Max£103.50pw

C Brook Cottage Brookside
for bookings Mrs L M Briddon, Bridge
Cottage, Two Dales, Matlock, Derbyshire
☎Matlock(0629)732221

Tastefully modernised and well kept 17th-
century terraced cottage, affording
kitchen/diner, lounge with beamed ceiling,
two bedrooms and bathroom. Two Dales
2½ miles N off A6, then B5057 towards
Chesterfield.

Allyear 1wk min, 3mths max, 1unit,
4persons [◇] ◑ ◆ ◔ fridge 🍴
Ⓛcan be hired ☎(30yds) Iron & Ironing
board in unit ☉ CTV ⊕3pin square
1P 🅼 🛁(300yds)
⊖ ♪(3m) ☕(25yds) 🦮(3m)
Min£92 Max£132.25pw

H Chesterfield House Chesterfield Road
for bookings Mrs L M Briddon, Bridge
Cottage, Two Dales, Matlock, Derbyshire
☎Matlock(0629)732221

A hairdressers salon occupies the front
part of this 1930's semi-detached house,
which otherwise offers accommodation of
kitchen/diner, lounge, three bedrooms
and bathroom/WC. Two Dales 2½ miles N
off A6, then B5057 towards Chesterfield.

Allyear 1wk min, 3mths max, 1unit,
6persons [◇] ◑ ◆ ◔ fridge 🍴
Ⓛcan be hired ☎(200yds) Iron in unit
☉ CTV ⊕3pin square 🅼 🛁(50yds)
⊖ ♪ ☕(½m) 🦮(3m)
Min£115 Max£155.25pw

C Corner Cottage Chesterfield Road
for bookings Mrs L M Briddon, Bridge
Cottage, Two Dales, Matlock, Derbyshire
☎Matlock(0629)732221

Tastefully modernised terraced cottage
with kitchen/diner, comfortable lounge
with beamed ceiling, three bedrooms and
modern bathroom. Two Dales 2½ miles N
off A6, then B5057 towards Chesterfield.

Allyear 1wk min, 3mths max, 1unit,
6persons [◇] ◑ ◆ ◎ fridge 🍴
Ⓛcan be hired ☎(100yds) Iron &
Ironing board in unit ☉ CTV
⊕3pin square 🅼 🛁(300yds)
⊖ ♪(3m) ☕(15yds) 🦮(3m)
Min£100 Max£126.50pw (Low)
Min£115 Max£161pw (High)

Matlock
—
Menai Bridge

C 10 North Street Cromford
for bookings The Landmark Trust,
Shottesbrooke, Maidenhead, Berkshire
SL6 3SG
☎Littewick Green(062882)5925

One of a row of terraced houses built in
gritstone by Richard Arkwright in 1771 to
house his millworkers. The
accommodation has two twin-bedded
rooms, one on 1st floor and one on
second floor (steep narrow stairs). On the
ground floor there is a modern kitchen/
diner, bathroom/WC and cosy lounge.
Small garden at rear. Cromford 2½ miles S
off A6.

Allyear MWB out of season 1night min,
3wks max, 1unit, 4persons ◑ ◔
fridge 🍴& open fires Gasinclusive
Ⓛnot provided ☎(½m) Iron & Ironing
board in unit ☉ ⊕3pin square 🅼
🛁(300yds)
⊖ ♪(3m) ☕(300yds) 🎵(2m)
🎵(2m) 🦮(3m)
Min£60 Max£130pw (Low)
Min£70 Max£150pw (High)

MAWGAN PORTH
Cornwall
Map**2** SW86

F Europa Court International
for bookings Mr N Maine-Tucker, 2
Gwendroc House, Barrack Lane, Truro,
Cornwall TR1 2DS
☎Truro(0872)73137

Two-storey block of luxury holiday villas,
with either patio or balcony, in a protected
position overlooking Mawgan Porth
beach. Accommodation comprises two
bedrooms (one double and one two/three-
bedded), lounge with one double
convertible settee, kitchen/diner and
bathroom/WC.

Mar–Nov MWB out of season 1wk min,
9mths max, 18units, 2–7persons ◑ ◆
nopets ◎ fridge Electric Heating
inclusive (Sep–May) Elecmetered
Ⓛinclusive ☎ Launderette on
premises ☉ CTV ⊕3pin square P
🅼 🛁(100yds) ⌂ [🐾] putting
Sauna, solarium
⊖ ☕(100yds) 🎵(½m)
Min£71 Max£114pw (Low)
Min£149 Max£249pw (High)

B & F Trevarrian Court
for bookings Mrs P A Eastlake, Treago
Farm, Crantock, Newquay, Cornwall
TR8 5QS
☎Newquay(0637)830277

Two bungalows and six flats set around a
courtyard approximately 4 miles along the
coast road from Newquay. The bungalows
comprise kitchen, diner/lounge with
double put-u-up, one twin and one double
bedroom, bathroom and WC. The flats
comprise open plan lounge/dining area

with kitchen, bathroom and WC. One flat
has a double and two twin bedrooms,
whilst the rest have a double, a twin room,
and a double put-u-up in the lounge.

Etr–Nov MWB out of season 3days min,
6wks max, 8units, 6persons ◑ ◎
fridge Storage heating Elec metered
Ⓛinclusive (duvets) ☎(30yds) Iron &
Ironing board in unit ☉ CTV
⊕3pin square P 🅼 🛁(½m)
⊖ ☕(100yds)
Min£60 Max£210pw

MEIGLE
Tayside Perthshire
Map**11** NO24

Ch Mr A J G Brown **Kings of Kinloch
Holiday Lodges** Meigle, Blairgowrie,
Perthshire PH12 8QX
☎Meigle(08284)273

Small, complex of the five modern Finnish
timbered lodges, individually sited in tree-
studded setting in the grounds of a
country hotel. Each has large living room
with open plan kitchen, a twin-bedded
room and a bedroom with four bunk beds.
There is also a verandah.

Allyear MWB out of season 1wk min,
3wks max, 5units, 1–6persons ◑ ◆
◎ fridge Electric Elecmetered
Ⓛinclusive ☎ Iron & Ironing board on
premises ☉ CTV ⊕3pin square 2P
🅼 🛁(1m)
⊖ ♪(3m) ☕(100yds)
Min£110 Max£130pw (Low)
Min£145 Max£200pw (High)

MELLON UDRIGLE
Highland Ross & Cromarty
Map**14** NG89

Ch Ceol Na Mara Lodges
for bookings M E Tew, Ceol Na Mara Ltd,
South Kenwood, Kenton, Exeter, Devon
☎Starcross(0626)891672

Five timber framed lodges set on edge of a
fir wood only yards from the sea and
beach; commanding superb coastal and
mountain views. Mellon Udrigle is a small
hamlet set in quiet location 3 miles off
A832. Dinghy with each lodge.

21Mar–7Nov 1wk min, 5units,
1–6persons ◑ ◎ fridge 🍴
Elec metered Ⓛcan be hired ☎(½m)
Iron & Ironing board in unit ☉ TV
⊕3pin square P 🛁(3m) Sauna, sailing
dinghy
⊖ ☕(3m)
Min£57.50 Max£110pw (Low)
Min£120 Max£210pw (High)

See advertisement under Aultbea

MENAI BRIDGE
Gwynedd
Map**6** SH57

H 23 Pen Lon
for bookings Menai Holidays, Old Port
Office, Port Penrhyn Bangor, Gwynedd
LL57 3HN
☎Bangor(0248)362254 or 351055 →

A modern detached house situated one mile from town centre. Ground floor comprises lounge/diner, one single and one twin-bedded room, bathroom/WC and kitchen. First floor comprises two twin-bedded rooms and WC.

All year   MWB out of season   3days min, 6wks max, 1unit, 7persons   no pets   ⊚   fridge   ⊯   Elec metered   └┘can be hired   ☎(½m)   WM & SD in unit   Iron & Ironing board in unit   ⊙   CTV   ⊕3pin square   1P   1☎   ▥   ♨(1m)
⊙≀   ♀(1m)

Min£110 Max£160pw (Low)
Min£150 Max£200pw (High)

H   Treetops Mount Street
for bookings Menai Holidays, Old Port Office, Port Penrhyn, Bangor, Gwynedd LL57 3HN
☎Bangor(0248)362254 or 351055

Semi-detached house in quiet residential area. Accommodation comprises one twin and one double bedroom, bathroom/WC on ground floor and one single bedroom, lounge/diner and kitchen on first floor. Views over Menai Straits and Snowdonia.

All year   MWB out of season   3days min, 6wks max, 1unit, 5persons   no pets   ⊚   fridge   ⊯(Gas)   Gas & Elec metered   └┘can be hired   ☎(400yds))   WM & SD in unit   Iron & Ironing board in unit   TV   ⊕3pin square   P   1☎   ▥   ♨(400yds)
⊙≀   ♀(½m)

Min£120 Max£140pw (Low)
Min£150 Max£170pw (High)

MEMBURY
Devon
Map**3** ST20

C   CC Ref 7524L (1&2) Lea Hill Farm
for bookings Character Cottages (Holidays) Ltd, 34 Fore Street, Sidmouth, Devon EX10 8AQ
☎Sidmouth(03955)77001

Two cottages tastefully converted from a 14th-century barn, situated in the grounds of a country hotel. One of the cottages sleep up to six people, the other up to four and they both comprise open plan lounge/diner with kitchen area and bathroom/WC.

All year   MWB out of season   3days min, 6wks max, 2units, 1–6persons   [◇]   ◆   no pets   ⊚   fridge   ⊯   Elec metered   └┘can be hired   ☎   SD in unit   Iron & Ironing board in unit   HCE in unit   ⊙   CTV   ⊕3pin square   P   ▥   ♨(½m)
⊙≀

Min£100 Max£125pw (Low)
Min£144 Max£227pw (High)

MEMUS
Tayside Angus
Map**15** NO45

H   Midtown Farm House Glenquiech
for bookings Mrs M Fleming, Strone Farm, Memus, Forfar DD8 3UA
☎Cortachy(05754)245

Small former farmhouse in isolated but attractive setting high into the hillside. It

---

offers modest accommodation comprising kitchen/scullery, living/dining room, sitting room and bathroom and two bedrooms. Ideal for quiet walking holidays.

All year   MWB out of season   1wk min, 1mth max, 1unit, 1–8persons   ◇   ◆   ◆   fridge   Electric   Elec metered   └┘inclusive   ☎(1½m)   WM in unit   SD in unit   Iron & Ironing board in unit   TV   ⊕3pin round   2P   ♨(2½m)

Details not confirmed for 1987

MEVAGISSEY
Cornwall
Map**2** SX04

C   Coach House, Dormer Cottage and Goose Cottage
for bookings Mr & Mrs J L Owens, Mevagissey House, Vicarage Hill, Mevagissey, Cornwall
☎Mevagissey(0726)842427

Three cottages in the grounds of Mevagissey House with views over village and harbour. Coach House above garages has lounge/diner, kitchen, bath and WC, one double and one bunk-bedded room. Goose Cottage, a ground-floor flat, has kitchen with breakfast bar, lounge and one double en-suite bedroom. Dormer Cottage, a first-floor flat, has kitchen, lounge/diner and one en-suite double room. All cottages have a sofa bed in the lounge.

Mar–Dec   MWB out of season   2days min, 3wks max, 3units, 2–6persons   [◇]   ◆   ◆   fridge   electric convectors   Elec inclusive   └┘inclusive   ☎   Iron & Ironing board in unit   [Launderette on premises]   ⊙   CTV   ⊕3pin square   P   ▥   ♨(½m)
⊙≀   ♀(½m)

Min£70 Max£210pw

MILFORD-ON-SEA
Hampshire
Map**4** SZ29

C   20, 21 & 22 Windmill Close
for bookings Mrs M E Perham, Danescourt, 14 Kivernell Road, Milford-on-Sea, Lymington, Hampshire SO4 0PQ
☎Lymington(0590)43516

Three mid-terrace, two-storey Georgian style cottage/town houses in quiet residential area, half a mile from village centre. They comprise lounge/diner, kitchen and three bedrooms, plus bathroom/WC.

Apr–Oct   1wk min, 4wks max, 3units, 1–5persons   ◇   ◆   ⊚   fridge   ⊯   Elec inclusive (summer)   Elec metered (winter)   └┘inclusive   ☎   WM & SD in unit   Iron & Ironing board in unit   ⊙   ⊗   CTV   ⊕3pin square   3P   3☎   ▥   ♨(½m)
⊙≀   ♪(3m)   ♀(½m)

Min£85 Max£125pw (Low)
Min£130 Max£240pw (High)

MILLERS DALE
Derbyshire
Map**7** SK17

C   The Dale House & Miller's Dale Cottage
for bookings Mrs A Lewis, 3 Curzon Terrace, Litton Mill, Miller's Dale, Buxton, Derbyshire SK17 8SR
☎Tideswell(0298)871564

Two adjoining properties situated amidst magnificent walking country. The Dale House was once a small country pub and has retained the bar area in the kitchen. The other ground floor rooms are the dining room and lounge. Upstairs are three bedrooms and bathroom/WC. At the rear there is a flagged patio and small split-level lawn. Miller's Dale Cottage is stone-built and three-storeyed and comprises kitchen/diner on the ground floor, lounge on the first-floor and two bedrooms and bathroom/WC on the second-floor. There is a small split-level patio garden at the rear.

All year   MWB out of season   1wk min, 3mths max, 2units, 1–6persons   ◇   ◆   no pets   ⊚   fridge   Electric   Elec metered   └┘inclusive   ☎(400yds)   Iron & Ironing board in unit   ⊙   ⊗   TV   ⊕3pin square   4P   ♨(3m)
⊙≀   ♀(400yds)   ♫(3m)

Min£73 Max£89pw (Low)
Min£93 Max£109pw (High)

MILTON ABBAS
Dorset
Map**3** ST80

C   Mrs V Davey Little Hewish Farm
Milton Abbas, Blandford, Dorset DT11 0LH
☎Milton Abbas(0258)880326

Three adjoining farm cottages situated on an arable farm. Each have large well-appointed kitchen/lounge/diner, bathroom and WC. Carters Cottage has two double and one twin-bedded room; Shepherds Cottage one twin and one double bedroom and Keepers Cottage one single and two double bedrooms. All soundly furnished in traditional style and located on Milborne St Andrews road one mile from attractive village of Milton Abbas.

All year   MWB out of season   3days min, 4wks max, 3units, 2–6persons   ◇   ◆   no pets   ⊚   fridge   Electric & night storage   Elec metered   └┘can be hired   ☎(1½m)   SD in unit   Iron & Ironing board in unit   ⊙   TV   ⊕3pin square   8P   ♨(1½m)
⊙≀   ♀(1½m)

Min£55 Max£70pw (Low)
Min£70 Max£135pw (High)

MINCHINHAMPTON
Gloucestershire
Map**3** SO80

C The Cottage Peaches Barton
for bookings Mrs Somers, Peaches Barton, Peaches Farm, Minchinhampton, Stroud, Gloucestershire
☎Brimscombe(0453)886303

Restored cottage in quiet peaceful setting. Accommodation comprises lounge with double bed-settee (or two singles), kitchen/diner, one twin bedroom and one with two bunks, bathroom and WC; small garden.

Allyear MWB out of season 3days min, 1mth max, 1unit, 6persons ◆ ◆ no pets ◎ fridge night storage heaters Elec inclusive ☐not provided ☎(½m) WM on premises Iron & Ironing board in unit ⊙ TV can be hired ⊕3pin square P 🛒(1m) Hard (by arrangement) Horse riding (children only) stables under construction

⊖ δ(Adjacent) 🍷(1m)

Min£86 Max£140pw

MINEHEAD
Somerset
See **Blue Anchor & Wheddon Cross**

MINIONS
Cornwall
Map**2** SX27

F Mrs P M Hart **Cheesewring Farm** Minions, Liskeard, Cornwall
☎Liskeard(0579)62200

Detached stone-built barn modernised and converted to a one-bedroomed flat with lounge/diner, kitchen, bathroom and WC. Steps to entrance hall. Good views of Kit Hill and Tamar Valley. Leave Liskeard by B3254, continue to Upton Cross, turn left, sharp right before Minions village.

Apr–Oct MWB out of season wkd min, 1mth max, 1unit, 2–4persons [◇] ◆ ◆ ◎ fridge Electric Elec metered ☐not provided ⊙ TV ⊕3pin square P 🛒(1m)

⊖ 🍷(1m) 🎵(1m)

MINSTER LOVELL
Oxfordshire
Map**5** SP31

C Hill Grove Cottage
for bookings Mrs K Brown, Hill Grove Farm, Minster Lovell, Oxford OX8 5NA
☎Witney(0993)3120

Small cotswold stone-built cottage with modern furnishing and facilities. Accommodation comprises three bedrooms, lounge, dining room, kitchen breakfast room, bathroom and WC.

Allyear 1wk min, 2mths max, 1unit, 2–6persons [◇] ◆ ◆ no pets ◎ fridge 🔥 Elec metered ☐inclusive ☎(18yds) WM & SD in unit Iron & Ironing board in unit ⊙ CTV ⊙3pin square P 🅼 🛒(1m) coarse fishing

⊖ 🍷(1¼m) Sports centre(1¼m)

Min£120 Max£140pw
Min£160 Max£170pw

Minchinhampton — Morecambe

MOELFRE
Gwynedd
Map**6** SH58

H Aber Farm
for bookings Menai Holidays, Old Port Office, Port Penrhyn, Bangor LL57 3HN
☎Bangor(0248)362254 or 351055

Detached modernised farmhouse with views of Lligwy Bay. Accommodation comprises lounge, dining room and kitchen with dining area on the ground floor. One double room, two twin-bedded rooms and bathroom/WC on first floor.

Apr–Oct MWB out of season 3days min, 6wks max, 1unit, 2–6persons ◆ ◆ ◎ fridge Storage heaters & open fires Elec metered ☐can be hired ☎(1m) TD in unit Iron & Ironing board in unit CTV ⊙3pin square 3P 🛒(1m)

⊖ 🍷(1m)

Min£115 Max£130pw (Low)
Min£145 Max£175pw (High)

MOFFAT
Dumfries & Galloway *Dumfriesshire*
Map**11** NT00

F Mrs B Raw **Holmfield** Beechgrove, Moffat, Dumfriesshire
☎Moffat(0683)20228

Occupying part of a private house the flats offer one- or two-bedroomed accommodation, with lounge/diner, kitchen area, and bath or shower room.

Whit–Sep MWB in season 1night min, 2units, 2–4persons ◆ ◎ fridge Electric Elec inclusive ☐can be hired ☎(¾m) Iron & Ironing board on premises CTV can be hired ⊕3pin square 4P 🅼 🛒(¾m)

⊖ δ(2m) 🍷(¾m) 🎵(¾m) 🎵(¾m)

fr£100

B MacAdam & Telford Beechwood Country House Hotel
for bookings G M Thomson & Co, 27 King Street, Castle Douglas, Kirkcudbrightshire DG7 1AB
☎Castle Douglas(0556)2701 or 2973

Two high quality semi-detached bungalows in the gardens of the hotel to which guests are welcome to use the facilities. Accommodation comprises lounge/diner, kitchen, shower/WC and three bedrooms, one in MacAdam having en-suite shower/WC.

Mar–Nov 1wk min, 2units, 1–6persons [◇] ◆ ◆ ◐ fridge 🔥 Gas & Elec inclusive ☐inclusive ☎(¼m) Iron & Ironing board in unit ⊙ CTV ⊕3pin square 4P 🅼 🛒(¼m)

⊖ δ(1m) 🍷(¼m) 🎵(¼m)

Min£95 Max£190pw

MOLD
Clwyd
Map**7** SJ26

B The Firs
for bookings Mrs L Dowling, 23 Gleneagles Road, Great Sutton, South Wirral L66 4NF
☎(051)339 5316

Two modern bungalows specially adapted for the disabled, comprising lounge/diner, bathroom/WC, kitchen and two bedrooms. There is also an additional disabled persons bathroom.

Allyear 2units, 1–6persons ◐ fridge 🔥 Gas/Elec metered ☐not provided ☎ Iron & Ironing board in unit ⊙ ⊛ CTV ⊕3pin square 3P 🅼 🛒(200yds) Patio with barbeque

⊖ δ(3m) 🍷(200yds) 🎵(1m)
Sports centre(½m)

MONTGOMERY
Powys
Map**7** SO29

H Castle Terrace
for bookings Mrs J N Corfield, Castle Terrace House, Montgomery, Powys
☎Montgomery(068681)481

Three-storey terraced house built in the mid-17th century, situated on a hillside with panoramic views. First floor comprises one double and one single room. The second floor comprises one single room, one double bedroom and bathroom/WC. The living room and kitchen are on the ground floor.

Jun–Oct 3days min, 4wks max, 1unit, 2–7persons [◇] ◆ ◆ no pets ◎ fridge Electric Elec metered ☐can be hired ☎(50yds) WM & SD in unit Iron & Ironing board in unit ⊙ CTV ⊕3pin square 3P 🛒(50yds)

⊖ 🍷(50yds)

Details not confirmed for 1987

MORECAMBE
Lancashire
Map**7** SD46

F The Anchorage 19 Clarence Street
for bookings Mrs M Woodcock, 99 Regent Road, Morecambe, Lancashire LA3 1AF
☎Morecambe(0524)413466

Detached stone-built house divided into double-bedded flats. Good quality accommodation, very reasonably priced. One minute's walk from promenade.

Etr–19Oct 1wk min, 2wks max, 3units, 2–4persons, nc6 no pets ◎ fridge Electric Elec metered ☐inclusive ☎(200yds) [Launderette within 300yds] ⊙ TV ⊕3pin square 🛒(30yds)

⊖ 🍷(100yds) 🎵(250yds) 🎵(250yds) 🎥(½m)

Min£54 Max£60pw (Low)
Min£56 Max£70pw (High)

MORETONHAMPSTED
Devon
Map**3** SX78

C Prof & Mrs S Lander **Saxon Cottage**
Cross Tree House, Moretonhampsted,
Devon TQ13 8NL
☎Moretonhampsted(0647)40726
Period cottage in the wing of Cross Tree
house. Comprises entrance to wood-
panelled hallway, kitchen/diner with
original cobbled floor and wooden walls
dating back to Saxon times. Stairs to
landing with twin bedroom, lounge with
studio couch sleeping two, through
lounge to bathroom/WC, through
bathroom to further twin-bedded room.

All year MWB out of season 3 days min,
1mth max, 1 unit, 4−5persons, nc5yrs ⌀
fridge 🍳 Gas/Elec metered Ⓛcan be
hired ☎(½m) [WM, SD & TD on
premises] Iron & Ironing board on
premises ⊕ CTV ⊕3pin round Ⅲ
🏠(½m)
⊖ 🔔(1m) 🔔(200yds)
Min£80 Max£165pw

MORFA BYCHAN
Gwynedd
Map**6** SH53

B **50 Cefn-y-Gader Estate** Beach Road
for bookings Shaws Holidays, Y Maes,
Pwllheli, Gwynedd LL53 5HA
☎Pwllheli(0758)614422
Modern detached bungalow, ½m from the
sea and commanding good views.
Accommodation comprises kitchen, large
lounge/diner, four bedrooms (one double,
one bunk and two twin-bedded) and
bathroom/WC. Good comfortable
accommodation.

All year wknd min, 6wks max, 1unit,
2−8persons ◆ no pets ◎ fridge
🍳 Elec metered Ⓛnot provided
☎(½m) Iron & Ironing board in unit ⊕
CTV ⊕3pin square 2P 🏠(½m)
⊖ 🔔(1m) 🔔(½m) 🎵(3m) 🐾(3m)
Min£74 Max£224pw

MORTEHOE
Devon
Map**2** SS44

C **Priors Cottage**
for bookings Mr & Mrs J A Notley, Leacroft,
9 Willoway Lane, Braunton, Devon
EX33 1AS
☎Braunton(0271)813885
Cottage converted from an old chapel,
retaining the original pine-block flooring
throughout most of the ground-floor area.
There are three bedrooms (two double
beds, one twin-bedded), lounge, dining
room, kitchen and bathroom/WC plus a
separate WC. There are good views of the
sea and National Trust hills beyond
Mortehoe.

Etr−Oct 1wk min, 4wks max, 1unit,
1−6persons ◆ ◆ ⌀ fridge 🍳
Gas inclusive Elec metered
Ⓛnot provided ☎(100yds) Iron &

Moretonhampsted
—
Muir of Ord

Ironing board in unit ⊕ CTV
⊕3pin square 1P 1🏠 Ⅲ 🏠(200yds)
⊖ 🔔(100yds) 🎵(1½m) 🎵(1½m)
🐾(1½m)
Details not confirmed for 1987

MOSSDALE
Dumfries & Galloway *Kirkcudbrightshire*
Map**11** NX67

H **Airds of Kells Cottage** Airds of Kells
Farm
for bookings G M Thomson & Co, 27 King
Street, Castle Douglas, Kirkcudbrightshire
DG7 1AB
☎Castle Douglas(0556)2701 & 2973
Neatly decorated former keepers house
situated on its own in a peaceful setting
with access through farm and gated field
(Wellies useful!). The accommodation
comprises dining room, sitting room with
bed-settee, kitchen, bathroom and two
twin bedrooms which are on the first floor.
The farm lies 1m E of Mossdale.

Mar−Nov 1wk min, 6mths max, 1unit,
1−6persons ◆ ◎ fridge Electric
Elec metered Ⓛnot provided ☎(1m)
TV ⊕3pin square P Ⅲ 🏠(1m)
Min£90 Max£160pw

B **Bellevue** Airds of Kells
for bookings G M Thomson & Co, 27 King
Street, Castle Douglas, Kirkcudbrightshire
DG7 1AB
☎Castle Douglas(0556)2701 & 2973
Attractive, neat bungalow set amidst
farmland with panoramic views. It
comprises a comfortable lounge/dining
room, kitchen, bathroom and three
bedrooms. Located ½m E of Mossdale.

Mar−Nov 1wk min, 6mths max, 1unit,
1−6persons ◆ no pets Oil fired
cooker fridge Electric & open fires
Elec inclusive Ⓛnot provided ☎(½m)
WM in unit Iron & Ironing board in unit
CTV ⊕3pin square P 🏠(½m) Fishing
Min£90 Max£170pw

B **Drumwhill**
for bookings G M Thomson & Co, 27 King
Street, Castle Douglas, Kirkcudbrightshire
DG7 1AB
☎Castle Douglas(0556)2701 & 2973
Self-contained wing of a modern newly-
built house at the head of Woodhall Loch.
The accommodation which is all on the
ground floor, comprises two twin- and one
single-bedded room, sitting room, diner,
kitchen with breakfast table, bathroom
and utility room. Access via A762 N from
Laurieston for 2½m. Take left turn for
Slogarie then next left.

Mar−Nov 1wk min, 1unit, 1−5persons,
nc3 no pets ◎ fridge 🍳 & open fires
Elec inclusive Ⓛnot provided ☎(2m)

Iron & Ironing board in unit ⊕ TV
⊕3pin square P 🏠 🏠(2m)
⊖ 🔔(3m)
Min£85 Max£155pw

MOULTON, GREAT
Norfolk
Map**5** TM19

F Mrs J Musgrave **Laurels Farm** Great
Moulton, Norwich, Norfolk NR15 2HN
☎Tivetshall(037977)304
The flat is situated within a charming
farmhouse, built in the 16th and 17th
centuries, retaining all its old features but
with modern conveniences. It comprises
two bedrooms (one double, one twin),
large kitchen/living room with two 'store
away' single beds and a bathroom/WC.

All year except Xmas MWB 2days min,
3wks max, 1unit, 4−6persons [◇] ◆
◆ ◎ fridge 🍳 Elec inclusive
Ⓛmust be hired ☎ WM & SD in unit
⊕ ⊕ CTV ⊕3pin square 6P
🏠(½m) garden games room and licensed
bar in house
⊖ 🔔(½m)
Min£70 Max£85pw (Low)
Min£85 Max£100pw (High)

See advertisement under Norwich

MOUSEHOLE
Cornwall
Map**2** SW42

F K J & L J Best **Old Coastguard**
Apartments Mousehole, Cornwall
TR19 6PR
☎Penzance(0736)731222
Flat 1 on the second floor comprises
bedroom with four poster and en suite
shower/WC, family bedroom with three
single beds, kitchen/diner, lounge and
WC. Flat 2 comprises kitchen/diner, one
twin bedroom, lounge, shower and WC.
Flat 3 on the first floor comprises lounge,
kitchen/diner, double bedroom with
additional twin beds, shower and WC. Flat 4
on the ground floor comprises lounge/
diner, kitchen, double bedroom, shower
and WC.

All year MWB out of season 2days min,
1mth max, 4units, 2−6persons ◆ ◆
no pets ◎ fridge Storage & Electric
fires Elec metered Ⓛcan be hired ☎
Iron & Ironing board on premises ⊕
CTV ⊕3pin square 4P 🏠(100yds)
⊖ 🔔(on premises) 🎵(on premises)

MUIR OF ORD
Highland *Ross & Cromarty*
Map**14** NH55

H Mrs A B G Fraser **Gilchrist Farm** Muir
of Ord, Ross-shire IV6 7RS
☎Muir of Ord(0463)870243
A white semi-detached house standing in
the farmyard. 1½m outside Muir of Ord off
A832. There is a kitchen, living/dining
room, two double- and one twin-bedded
room.'

168

Apr–Oct 1wk min, 4wks max, 1unit,
1–7persons ◆ ⊚ fridge Electric &
open fires Elec metered 🔲 inclusive
🚰(1½m) WM & SD in unit Iron & Ironing
board in unit TV ⊕3pin square P 🔟
♨(1½m) Pony trekking, boating
⊖ ♦(1½m) ☎(1½m) 𝄞(1½m)
Min£55 Max£80pw (Low)
Min£85 Max£115pw (High)

C Croft Ardnagrask
for bookings Mrs McLean, 43 Riccarton
Mains Road, Currie, Midlothian EH14 5NF
☎(031)449 2448

Detached country cottage in peaceful
setting, amidst open farmland with fine
views across the Beauly Firth.
Accommodation comprises kitchen,
sitting/dining room, bathroom and one
double bedroom on the ground floor,
whilst the first floor has a double and a
twin bedroom.

Apr–Oct 1wk min, 1unit, 1–6persons
◆ ⊚ fridge Electric Elec metered
🔲 not provided ☎ WM in unit Iron &
Ironing board in unit TV ⊕3pin square
7P ♨(1m)
⊖ ♦(2m) ♥(1m)
Min£45 Max£49pw (Low)
Min£90 Max£94 (High)

MULL, ISLE OF
Strathclyde *Argyllshire*
Map**10 & 13** NM

CARSAIG
Map**10** NM52

C Mrs A McLean **Pier Cottage** Carsaig,
Pennyghael, Isle of Mull, Argyll, PA70 6HD
☎Pennyghael(06814)216

A little cottage in a superb location, nicely
furnished, well-fitted and full of character.
Accommodation consists of kitchen/diner,
scullery area, lounge, sun-porch with bed-
settee, two bedrooms (one double, one
twin) and a bathroom. Situated beside a
rocky shore with commanding views of
Scarba, Jura and Colonsay. Owner lives in
the adjacent cottage.

May–mid Nov MWB out of season
1wk min, 1unit, 5persons ◇ ♦ ⊚
fridge 🍲& log burner Elec metered

Muir of Ord
—
Mullion

🔲 not provided ☎ Iron & Ironing board
in unit ⊕ ⊕3pin square 2P 🔟
♨(4m) sea fishing
Min£120 Max£130pw (Low)
Min£150 Max£180pw (High)

DERVAIG
Map**13** NM45

Ch Mr J G King **Glen Houses** Dervaig,
Isle of Mull, Argyll PA75 6QJ
☎Dervaig(06884)270 & Tobermory(0688)
2422

Ten modern wood-framed chalets with
Skye chip rendering and concrete tile
roofs set on a terraced site. Each offers an
open-plan lounge/dining room/kitchen
with twin convertible settee, two bedrooms
with twin or bunk beds, and a modern
bathroom. Three chalets are fitted with low
level cookers and oven for the disabled.
Good views, ½m from Dervaig on unclass
road to Salen.

Mar–Oct MWB out of season 3days min,
5wks max, 10units, 1–5persons [◇] ◆
♦ £12 charge for dogs ⊚ fridge
Electric Elec metered 🔲 inclusive
☎(½m) ⊖ CTV can be hired
⊕3pin square P 🔟 ♨(½m) Trout
fishing, sea fishing, pony trekking &
birdwatching play area with sandpit
Min£70 Max£115pw (Low)
Min£140 Max£180pw (High)

SALEN
Map**10** NM54

C & H Killiechronan Holiday Cottages
for bookings Highland Estates Ltd, 18
Maxwell Place, Stirling FK8 1JU
☎Stirling(0786)62519

The Farmhouse and Farmsteading
Cottages are built round a courtyard
situated in an elevated position with fine
views of Lochna Keal. **The Farmhouse** is
detached and has three twin bedrooms.
The former Farmsteadings have been
converted into modern cottages with

Stables having one twin bedroom, *Bothy,*
Mill Cottage, Granary and *Bull* having
two twin rooms and *Byre* having three
twin bedrooms. The three other cottages
are in a quiet wooded setting. *Burnside*
has one twin bedroom, *West Steading* two
twin bedrooms and *East Steading* three
twin bedrooms. Killiechronan is located
approximately 3 miles from Salen on the
Ulva Ferry road.

All year MWB out of season 1wk min (in
season) 3days min (out of season)
10units, 2–6persons ◇ ♦ ⊚ fridge
electric(coal fire 2units) Elec metered
🔲 inclusive ☎ Iron & Ironing board in
unit [Launderette on premises] ⊖
⊕3pin square P ♨(3m) games room
with pool table, fishing, deer park, cycle
hire
⊖ ♥(3m)
Min£34 Max£150pw

TOBERMORY
Map**13** NM55

Ca Normand Enterprises (Heanish)
Heanish, Tobermory, Isle of Mull, Argyll
PA75 6PP
☎Tobermory(0688)2097

Ten large log cabins beside the
proprietors house in residential area. The
cabins are arranged in pairs, connected
by a double carport. Each has two small
bedrooms, one with bunks and wash hand
basin and one which can have either
bunks or a double bed. There is a
spacious living room with two divan beds,
and a large kitchen.

All year MWB out of season 1wk min,
10units, 1–6persons [◇] ◆ ♦ ⊚
fridge Electric Elec metered
🔲 inclusive ☎(½m) Iron & Ironing board
on premises [Launderette on premises]
⊖ CTV ⊕3pin square P ♨(½m)
⊖ ♦(400yds) ♥(200yds) 𝄞(½m)
Min£65 Max£190pw

MULLION
Cornwall
Map**2** SW61

C J O & L N Jaine Ltd **Trenance Farm**
Mullion, Helston, Cornwall
☎Mullion(0326)240639 →

Trenance is a coastal farm situated midway between the village of Mullion and Mullion Cove. The single and two storey cottages, some modern and some part of the farmhouse (parts of which date back to the 12th century), vary in accommodation sleeping between four to eight people. All offer comfortable well-equipped accommodation of character.

All year MWB out of season 10units, 1–8persons ◈ ◆ ◉ fridge Electric Elec metered Ⓛcan be hired ☎(½m) Iron & Ironing board in unit ⊙ CTV ⊕3pin square P Ⅲ ▨(½m)

◒ ♌(2m) ♟(1m) ♫(2m)

Min£35 Max£140pw (Low)
Min£173 Max£225pw (High)

B Pedn-y-ke Holiday Bungalows
for bookings Mr L R Francis, Polurrian Hotel Ltd, Mullion, Helston, Cornwall
☎Mullion(0326)240421

Six purpose built bungalows located approx 100yds from hotel and situated with their own small private rear gardens. Each comprises one double- and one twin-bedded room, lounge/diner, kitchenette and bathroom/WC. Full use of hotel amenities.

Apr–Oct MWB 3days min, 6units, 1–6persons [◇] ◈ ◆ ◉ fridge Electric Elec metered Ⓛinclusive Telephone each unit Iron & Ironing board on premises [Launderette on premises] ⊙ CTV ⊕3pin square P 🏠 Ⅲ ▨(½m) ▭ ⌒ ⚑Hard putting, billiards, solarium, sauna, spa bath, squash

◒ ♌(2m) ♟ ♫

Min£95 Max£245pw (Low)
Min£335 Max£385pw (High)

See advertisement on page 169

MUMBLES
West Glamorgan
Map2 SS68

F Highcliff Court
for bookings Langland Court Hotel, Langland Court Road, Langland Bay, Mumbles, Swansea, W Glamorgan
☎Swansea(0792)61545

Spacious purpose-built flats with balcony and good sea views. Large sitting/dining room, kitchen, one twin and one double bedroom, shower/bathroom and separate WC.

All year MWB out of season 2units, 4–6persons [◈] ◆ ◔ fridge ♨ Elec inclusive Ⓛinclusive ☎(50yds) Iron & Ironing board in unit [Launderette on premises] ⊙ CTV ⊕3pin square P 🏠 Ⅲ ▨(½m) ⚑Hard(300yds)

Mullion
—
Narberth

◒ ♌ ♟(50yds) ♫ ♫
Details not confirmed for 1987

B 19 Limeslade Drive
for bookings Mr & Mrs B & M Davies, Bar Marc Holiday Properties, 7A Redcliffe, Caswell Bay, Swansea, W Glamorgan SA3 3BT
☎Swansea(0792)69169

Modern brick-built bungalow with large lounge, two bedrooms (double and twin), kitchen and bathroom/WC.

Feb–Nov MWB out of season 1wk min, 3mths max, 1unit, 2–4persons ◈ ◉ fridge Electric Elec-metered Ⓛnot provided ☎(½m) ⊙ CTV ⊕3pin square P Ⅲ ▨(½m)

◒ ♟(1m) 🐾(3m)

Max£72pw (Low)
Max£149pw (High)

B 10 Sealands Drive
for bookings Mr & Mrs B & M Davies, Bar Marc Holiday Properties, 7A Redcliffe, Caswell Bay, Swansea, W Glamorgan SA3 3BT
☎Swansea(0792)69169

Modern brick-built bungalows with large lounge, two bedrooms (double and twin), kitchen and bathroom/WC.

Feb–Nov MWB out of season 1wk min, 3mths max, 1unit, 2–4persons ◈ ◉ fridge Electric Elec metered Ⓛnot provided ☎(½m) ⊙ CTV ⊕3pin square P Ⅲ ▨(½m)

◒ ♟(1m) 🐾(3m)

Max£72pw (Low)
Max£149pw (High)

B 11 Sealands Drive
for bookings Mr & Mrs B & M Davies, Bar Marc Holiday Properties, 7A Redcliffe, Caswell Bay, Swansea, W Glamorgan SA3 3BT
☎Swansea(0792)69169

Brick-built bungalow sleeping up to four persons and comprises large lounge, two bedrooms (one double and one twin), kitchen and bathroom/WC.

Feb–Nov MWB out of season 1wk min, 3mths max, 1unit, 2–4persons ◈ ◉ fridge Electric Elec metered Ⓛnot provided ☎(½m) CTV

◒ ♟(1m) 🐾(3m)

Max£72pw (Low)
Max£149pw (High)

F Woodridge Court
for bookings Langland Court Hotel, Langland Court Road, Langland Bay, Mumbles, Swansea, W Glamorgan
☎Swansea(0792)61545

Ten purpose-built units and a Penthouse Flat each with a balcony with sea view. Spacious lounge/diner, kitchenette, shower/WC and one small double bedroom, plus convertible bed-settee in the lounge. The Penthouse has a large double bedroom with en suite bathroom and a small twin-bedded room plus shower room/WC.

All year MWB out of season 6 units 2–6persons [◈] ◆ ◉ fridge ♨ Elec inclusive Ⓛinclusive ☎ Iron & Ironing board in unit [Launderette on premises] ⊙ CTV ⊕3pin square P 🏠 Ⅲ ▨(½m) ⚑Hard(300yds)

◒ ♌ ♟(50yds) ♫ ♫
Details not confirmed for 1987

NANTLLE
Gwynedd
Map6 SH55

C & H Dol Gwydion, Plas Bach, Dol Wennol & Dol Pebin Baladeulyn
for bookings Mr H D Roberts, Gwynant, 31 Cefn Coed Road, Cyncoed, Cardiff CF2 6AP
☎Cardiff(0222)751879 or Penygroes(0286)880676

Three cottages and one house near Nantlle Lake with good mountain views. The three cottages all comprise two bedrooms, bathroom/WC, one with kitchen, the other two kitchen/diner and two have bed-settee's in the lounge. **Dol Pebin**, *the house, comprises lounge/diner, TV lounge and another separate lounge, kitchen, three bedrooms, bathroom and WC.*

All year (except Xmas & New Year) MWB 1wk min, 4wks max, 4units, 4–6persons ◈ ◉ fridge Electric Elec metered Ⓛnot provided ☎(in Dol Wennol & Dol Pebin) Iron & Ironing board in unit ⊙ CTV ⊕3pin square P 🏠 Ⅲ ▨(½m) Fishing

Min£80 Max£100pw (Low)
Min£120 Max£195pw (High)

NARBERTH
Dyfed
Map2 SN11

H Burwood Lodge
for bookings Powell's Cottage Holidays, 55 High Street, Saundersfoot, Dyfed
☎Saundersfoot(0834)812791

SNOWDONIA
Choice of 4 delightfully situated cottages by Nantlle Lake, comfortable, warm and well furnished. Bathroom, TV and some with views over the lake to Snowdon. Swimming, fishing and boating from own fields. Riding centre 4 miles. Central for beaches and National Park, Caernafon 8 miles.
Rates: to sleep 4,5,6, £90–£195 according to season.
SAE to H D Roberts, Baladeulyn, Nantlle, Gwynedd LL54 6BW or tel. 0286 880 676 or 0222 751879
H D Roberts, Gwynant, 31 Cefn Coed Road, Cyncoed, Cardiff CF2 6AP

A luxurious house with garden in rural setting. Well furnished and carpeted, comprising large lounge, dining room, breakfast room, luxury fitted kitchen including dishwashing machine and micro-wave oven. There are four bedrooms, one double, one twin and two single-bedded, bathroom/WC and shower plus a separate WC.

May–Sep MWB out of season 1wk min, 1unit, 6persons [♢] ◈ ◆ no pets ◉ fridge ♨ Elec inclusive ⌧ not provided Iron & Ironing board in unit ⊖ TV & CTV ⊕3pin square 2P � ♒(4m)

Min£117 Max£258pw

H   Glanrhyd Farm Lampeter Velfrey
for bookings Powell's Cottage Holidays, 55 High Street, Saundersfoot, Dyfed
☎Saundersfoot(0834)812791

Farmhouse situated within 50 acres of pasture land. Accommodation comprises comfortably furnished lounge, dining room, well-equipped kitchen, study/ playroom, bathroom with WC plus an additional shower/WC outside, three double bedrooms with wash basins and two twin-bedded rooms.

May–Sep MWB out of season 1wk min, 6wks max, 1unit, 2–10persons [♢] ◈ ◆ fridge Electric Elec inclusive ⌧ not provided ☎(1m) Iron & Ironing board in unit ⊖ TV ⊕3pin square 6P ⑆ ♒(4m)

⊖ ♀(1m)

Min£123 Max£276pw

C   Mews Cottage Upper Coxhill Farm
for bookings Powell's Cottage Holidays, 55 High Street, Saundersfoot, Dyfed
☎Saundersfoot(0834)812791

Cottage in rural setting adjacent to farm. Accommodation comprises lounge/diner, kitchen, two double bedrooms one with additional single bed, and bathroom/ shower and WC. Small lawned garden.

May–Sep MWB out of season 1wk min, 6wks max, 1unit, 2–3persons ◆ ◉ fridge ♨ Elec metered ⌧ not provided ☎(1m) Iron in unit ⊖ TV ⊕3pin square 4P ⑆ ♒(½m)

⊖ ♀(½m)

Min£75 Max£168pw

NETHY BRIDGE
Highland *Inverness-shire*
Map**14** NJ02

C   Mrs Valery Dean Badanfhuarain
Nethy Bridge, Inverness-shire
☎Nethybridge(047982)642 or
Fortrose(0381)20802

Small cottage with fenced garden in woodland setting, with views of the Cairngorms. Accommodation comprises living room, kitchen and three bedrooms, which sleep up to five people. Riding, tennis & fishing are all close by.

All year MWB out of season, 1unit, 1–5persons ◈ ◆ ◉ fridge Electric Elec inclusive ⌧ not provided

---

Narberth
—
Nethy Bridge

☎(½m) Iron & Ironing board in unit ⊖ TV ⊕3pin square P ♒(½m)

⊖ ♀(1m) ♫(1m)

Min£80 Max£170pw

H   Byna & Creggan The Causar
for bookings Mr & Mrs J B Patrick, 1 Chapelton Place, Forres, Moray
☎Forres(0309)72505

Two modern bungalow-type houses containing kitchen, lounge, one twin-bedded room, a room with bunks and a double room.

Closed Nov MWB out of season 2nights min, 2units, 1–6persons [♦] ◉ fridge Elec metered ⌧ can be hired ☎(150yds) Iron & Ironing board in unit Laundry room ⊖ CTV ⊕3pin square P ♒(100yds)

⊖ ♪(400yds) ♀(400yds)

Min£105 Max£140pw (Low)
Min£145 Max£215pw (High)

H   Derrald Dell Road
for bookings Mr & Mrs J B Patrick, 1 Chapelton Place, Forres, Moray
☎Forres(0309)72505

This bungalow-type house has kitchen, lounge, a twin-bedded room, a double room, and a room with bunks.

Closed Nov MWB out of season 2nights min, 1unit, 1–6persons [♦] ◉ fridge Elec metered ⌧ can be hired ☎(300yds) Iron & Ironing board in unit Laundry room ⊖ CTV ⊕3pin square P ♒(900yds)

⊖ ♪(900yds) ♀(200yds)

Min£90 Max£140pw (Low)
Min£145 Max£185pw (High)

C   East Dell, Little Dell, South Dell & West Dell
for bookings Mr & Mrs J Fleming, Dell of Abernethy, Nethy Bridge, Inverness-shire PH25 3DL
☎Nethybridge(047982)643

Modernised cottages located within the wings of Dell Lodge, a Georgian house dating from 1775. West Dell and South Dell have three twin bedrooms, living room/diner, bathroom and kitchenette. Little Dell has two bedrooms, sitting room with diner/kitchenette and bathroom. East Dell comprises open plan sitting room/ kitchenette/diner, bathroom and two bedrooms. All have good standard of décor and fittings.

All year MWB out of season 2days min, 4wks max, 4units, 1–7persons ◆ ◉ fridge Electric Elec inclusive (summer only) ⌧ inclusive ☎(½m) WM & TD on premises Iron & Ironing board on premises ⊖ CTV ⊕3pin square P ⑆ ♒(1m) ☜ Riding stables, fishing

⊖ ♪(1m) ♀(½m) ♫(1m)

Min£86 Max£154pw (Low)
Min£120 Max£215pw (High)

C & F   Juniper Cottage & Stables Cottage Tulloch Road
for bookings Mr & Mrs J B Patrick, 1 Chapelton Place, Forres, Morayshire IV36 ONL
☎Forres(0309)72505

Juniper Cottage is a two-storey dwelling situated in a quiet and pleasant part of the village. Accommodation comprises lounge, kitchen/diner, utility room/ bathroom and two bedrooms on the ground floor and another bathroom plus two bedrooms on the first floor. *Stables Cottage* is a converted hayloft above a disused stable at the rear of Juniper Cottage. It has timber clad interior and comprises kitchen/diner, bathroom, lounge with convertible couch and one bedroom, with skylight window.

Closed Nov MWB out of season 2nights min, 2units, 1–10persons [♦] ◉ fridge Electric Elec metered ⌧ can be hired ☎(400yds) WM in unit (Juniper) Iron & Ironing board in unit Laundry room ⊖ CTV ⊕3pin square 5P ♒(400yds)

⊖ ♪(½m) ♀(½m)

Min£70 Max£80pw (Low)
Min£95 Max£130pw (High)

C   Near Dell & Far Dell
for bookings Mr & Mrs J Fleming, Dell of Abernethy, Nethy Bridge, Inverness-shire PH25 3DL
☎Nethybridge(047982)643

Modern cottages located in the 2½ acres of tree-studded grounds of Dell Lodge, on the outskirts of Nethy Bridge. They are well decorated and furnished. *Near Dell* having three twin bedrooms, sitting room, kitchen/dining room and bathroom and *Far Dell* two twin bedrooms, one single bedroom with double bunk, living room/ diner, kitchenette and bathroom. They are set in a secluded spot with views of the mountains.

All year MWB out of season 1wk min, 4wks max, 2units, 2–8persons ◆ ◉ fridge Electric Elec included (in summer only) ⌧ included ☎(½m) WM & TD on premises Iron & Ironing board on premises ⊖ CTV ⊕3pin square P ⑆ ♒(1m) ☜ Pony trekking, bowling green, fishing

⊖ ♪(1m) ♀(½m) ♫(1m)

Min£86 Max£154pw (Low)
Min£120 Max£225pw (High)

H   Old Smithy The Causar
for bookings Mr & Mrs J B Patrick, 1 Chapelton Place, Forres, Moray
☎Forres(0309)72505

Converted blacksmith's shop with many original features maintained. It contains open plan living/dining/kitchen area and four bedrooms sleeping up to nine, bathroom and shower room. Open fire, logs and peat available. Secluded garden with access to river bank. →

Closed Nov   MWB out of season
2nights min, 1unit, 1–9persons   [◆]   ◎
fridge   Electric & log fires   Elec metered
Ⓛ can be hired   ☎(150yds)   SD in unit
Iron & Ironing board in unit
Laundry room   ⊙   CTV   ⊕3pin square
3P   ♨(100yds)
⊖   ♪(400yds)   ♀(400yds)
Min£120 Max£150pw (Low)
Min£160 Max£260pw (High)

H   Straanmore Dell Road
for bookings Mr & Mrs J B Patrick, 1
Chapelton Place, Forres, Moray
☎Forres(0309)72505

*Modern house with garden in a quiet
village location. Dell Road runs off B970
and is close to the River Nethy. It contains
kitchen, lounge, two twin-bedded rooms,
bathroom, shower room/WC and a room
with two sets of bunks.*

Closed Nov   MWB out of season
2nights min, 1unit, 1–8persons   [◆]   ◎
fridge   Electric & open fires
Elec metered   Ⓛ can be hired
☎(300yds)   SD in unit   Iron & Ironing
board in unit   Laundry room   ⊙   CTV
⊕3pin square   P   ♨(300yds)
⊖   ♪(900yds)   ♀(400yds)
Min£100 Max£140pw (Low)
Min£145 Max£220pw (High)

NETLEY MARSH
Hampshire
Map**4** SU31

F   Holiday Flat
for bookings Mrs J Puttock, The Old
Vicarage, Netley Marsh, Southampton,
Hants SO4 2GX
☎Southampton(0703)869444

*A first-floor self-contained flat within a
wing of the Old Vicarage comprising
kitchen/diner, lounge, one twin-bedded
and one double-bedded room, shower/
WC.*

All year   1wk min, 3mths max, 1unit,
1–6persons   [◇]   ◆   ◎   fridge   ♨
Gas   Elec metered   Ⓛ not provided
☎(200yds)   WM & SD in unit   Iron &
Ironing board in unit   ⊙   ⊛   CTV
⊕3pin square   2P   Ⅲ   Badminton
⊖   ♪(3m)   ♀(200yds)   𝄞(2m)   ♬(2m)
Min£85 Max£120pw

NEVERN
Dyfed
Map**2** SN03

C   The Ivy
for bookings Coastal Cottages of
Pembrokeshire, Seaview, Abercastle,
Mathry, Dyfed SA62 5HJ
☎Croesgoch(03483)7742

*A charming secluded cottage set in a
delightful garden in the centre of this small
village. It is comfortably furnished and
comprises lounge/diner with log burner
and a separate French anthracite stove,
kitchen, bathroom and two twin
bedrooms.*

All year   MWB out of season   2days min,
6wks max, 1unit, 2–4persons   ◇   ◆

Nethy Bridge
—
Newmilns

pets by arrangement   ◎   fridge
Storage, log & portably fires
Elec metered   Ⓛ inclusive   ☎(100yds)
Iron & Ironing board in unit   ⊙   CTV
⊕3pin square   2P   Ⅲ   ♨(4m)
⊖   ♀(100yds)
Min£65 Max£235pw

NEW FOREST
Hampshire
Map**4**
For details of AA-listed self-catering
establishments in this area see **Ashurst,
Netley Marsh** and **Woodlands**

NEW GALLOWAY
Dumfries & Galloway *Kirkcudbrightshire*
Map**11** NX67

H.   Makkevet Bor
for bookings G M Thomson & Co, 27 King
Street, Castle Douglas, Kirkcudbrightshire
DG7 1AB
☎Castle Douglas(0556)2701 & 2973

*Spacious newly built three-storey house
with garden standing back from the main
street, it has a living room, kitchen/dining
room, utility room, and bedrooms sleeping
up to 10 people.*

Mar–Nov   MWB out of season   1wk min,
1unit, 1–10persons   ◇   ◎   fridge   ♨ &
open fire   Elec inclusive   Ⓛ not provided
☎(200yds)   WM & SD in unit   Iron &
Ironing board in unit   CTV
⊕3pin square   P   Ⅲ   ♨(100yds)
⊖   ♪(100yds)   ♀(100yds)
Min£120 Max£250pw

NEWHAVEN
East Sussex
Map**5** TQ40

F   The Granary
for bookings Mrs B M Cheeseman, High
Barn, Piddinghoe, Newhaven, East Sussex
BN9 9AW
☎Newhaven(0273)514484

*A modern ground-floor flat comprising
large lounge, dining room with access to a
small garden terrace, kitchen, one twin
and one single bedroom and separate
bathroom and WC. Well maintained,
comfortable accommodation. 1m N
unclassified road.*

All year   MWB out of season   4wks max,
1unit, 1–4persons, nc   no pets   ◎
fridge   ♨   Elec metered   Ⓛ can be
hired   ☎(100yds)   [WM & SD on
premises]   Iron & Ironing board in unit
⊙   CTV   ⊕3pin square   1P   Ⅲ
♨(1½m)
⊖   ♀(100yds)
Min£75 Max£100pw (Low)
Min£130 Max£165pw (High)

NEWICK
East Sussex
Map**5** TQ42

B   Netherall Cottage
for bookings Mrs P Welfare, 1 Netherall
Cottages, Fletching Common, Newick,
Lewes, E Sussex
☎Newick(082572)2713

*Small bungalow set at the rear of cottages
in quiet rural surroundings.
Accommodation is one double bedroom,
small lounge with bed-settee, kitchen/
diner and bathroom. 1¼m from the village.*

All year   MWB out of season   1wk min,
1mth max, 1unit, 1–4persons   ◇   ◆
◎   ♨   Elec metered   Ⓛ inclusive   Iron &
Ironing board in unit   ⊙   TV
⊕3pin square   ⊕2pin round   3P   Ⅲ
♨(1½m)   ⌁
⊖   ♪(2m)   ♀(1m)   𝄞(1m)   ♬(1m)
Min£65 Max£80pw (Low)
Min£90 Max£125pw (High)

C   2 Netherall Cottages
for bookings Mrs P Welfare, 1 Netherall
Cottages, Fletching Common, Newick,
Lewes, E Sussex
☎Newick(082572)2713

*Late Victorian semi-detached cottage with
modern extension, accommodation
includes two double-bedded rooms, one
twin and one single, large lounge,
separate dining room, kitchen, two
bathrooms and WCs. Garden includes
heated pool. 1m from Newick village.*

All year   MWB out of season   1wk min,
1mth max, 1unit, 1–8persons   ◇   ◆
◆   no pets   ◎   fridge   ♨
Elec metered   Ⓛ inclusive   ☎   WM, SD &
TD in unit   Iron & Ironing board in unit
⊙   ⊛   CTV   ⊕3pin square   P   🔥   Ⅲ
♨(1m)   ⌁
⊖   ♪(2m)   ♀(1m)
Min£85 Max£115pw (Low)
Min£155 Max£190pw (High)

NEWLANDS
Cumbria
Map**11** NY22

H   The Old Vicarage Littletown
for bookings Lakeland Cottage Holidays,
Yew Tree Cottage, Ullock, Keswick,
Cumbria CA12 5SP
☎Braithwaite(059682)493
or Keswick(07687)72059

*Spacious 18th-century house with lovely
views and walled gardens, affording
farmhouse kitchen, cloakroom, lounge,
dining room, three bedrooms (one double,
two twin) and bathroom.*

All year   1mth max, 1unit, 2–6persons
◇   ◆   no pets   ◎   fridge   ♨
Elec inclusive   Ⓛ inclusive   ☎(1m)   WM
& SD in unit   Iron & Ironing board in unit
⊙   CTV   ⊕3pin square   3P   Ⅲ   ♨(3m)
⊖   ♀(2m)
Min£114 Max£318pw

NEWMILNS
Strathclyde *Ayrshire*
Map**11** NS53

C Gilbank
for bookings Mrs Hodge, Loudoun Mains,
Newmilns, Ayrshire KA16 9LG
☎Darvel(0560)21246

Set high on a hillside with good views of
the valley, this farm cottage has been
recently renovated to give two well-
appointed units (a connecting door will
also permit the cottage to be let as one
unit). The larger unit is all on ground-floor
level with two bedrooms, small kitchenette,
bathroom with sunken bath and lounge/
diner, the smaller unit is similar but one
bedroom is on the first floor and lounge/
diner includes kitchen area.

All year MWB out of season 2 days min,
6 wks max, 2 units, 1–4 persons [◇] ◎
fridge 🍴 Elec metered 🔌 inclusive
🛁 ⊙ CTV ⊕3 pin square 4P
🔥(1½m)
⊖ 𝄞(2m) 🔔(1½m) 🎬(1½m) 🎵(1½m)
Min£50 Max£69pw (Low)
Min£150 Max£170pw (High)

NEW MILTON
Hampshire
Map4 SZ29

Ch Bashley Park Ltd Sway Road, New
Milton, Hampshire BH25 5QR
☎New Milton(0425)612340

Twenty-five chalets with modern
furnishings, part of a large holiday
complex with chalets and static and
touring caravans. In open rural

Newmilns
—
Newport

surroundings on the fringe of the New
Forest 12 m E of Bournemouth on the
B3055.

Mar–Oct 1 wk min, 1 mth max, 25 units,
2–6 persons [◆ ◆] ◎ fridge
Electric Elec metered 🔌not provided
☎(10yds) [Iron on premises] Ironing
board on premises [Launderette within
300yds] CTV ⊕3 pin square P 📺
🔥 🍴 ☞Hard Licensed clubroom,
Restaurant putting 🎬 🎵
games room
Min£70 Max£210pw

NEWPORT
Dyfed
Map2 SN03

C Ffynnon Dofn
for bookings Coastal Cottages of
Pembrokeshire, Seaview, Abercastle,
Mathry, Dyfed SA62 5HJ
☎Croesgoch(03483)7742

A small stone farmhouse quietly situated,
only a few minutes from the sea with
superb views. Accommodation comprises
sitting room with wood burning stove,
kitchen/dining room, bathroom, one
double and two twin bedrooms. There is
also a well tended garden.

All year MWB out of season 2 days min,
6 wks max, 1 unit, 2–6 persons ◇ ◆
◎ fridge 🍴 Gas & Elec metered
🔌inclusive ☎(2m) WM & SD in unit
Iron & Ironing board in unit ⊙ CTV
⊕3 pin square 4P 📺 🔥(2m)
⊖ 𝄞(1m) 🔔(2m)
Min£70 Max£275pw

F Seaview 1 Mount Pleasant Terrace
for bookings Miss Davies, Gwynfi House,
Market Street, Newport, Dyfed
☎Newport(0239)820 246

Converted property close to town centre,
comprising one ground-floor and one
first-floor flat with seaviews. **Ground-
floor flat** sleeps up to six people in two
double bedrooms (one with wash hand
basin) and a kitchen and shower/WC. There
is a kitchen and shower/WC. **First-floor
flat** sleeps up to ten in three bedrooms
(one with wash hand basin) plus bed-
settee in lounge, kitchen, separate WC
and bathroom.

All year MWB out of season 2 units,
1–10 persons [◇] ◆ ◆ ◎ fridge
Electric storage heaters Elec metered
🔌can be hired ☎(½m) WM in first-floor
flat only Iron & Ironing board on
premises [Launderette within 300yds]
⊙ CTV ⊕3 pin square P 📺 🔥(½m)
⊖ 𝄞(3m) 🔔(½m) 🎬(1m) 🎵(1m)
Min£45 Max£110pw (Low)
Min£125 Max£250pw (High)

C & H Taibach Farmhouse & Cottage
for bookings Coastal Cottages of
Pembrokeshire, Seaview, Abercastle,
Mathry, Dyfed SA62 5HJ
☎Croesgoch(03483)7742

*A charming stone farmhouse and stable
cottage, beautifully renovated to provide
comfortable accommodation, in a
peaceful, picturesque situation close to
the sandy beach. The farmhouse
comprises a lounge with open fire,
kitchen/diner, bathroom, one double and
two twin bedrooms and a small patio. The
cottage comprises a shower room/WC,
kitchen/diner, open-plan lounge with
woodburner and a spiral staircase to the
gallery double bedroom. It also has a patio
area.*

All year MWB ut of season 2days min,
6wks max, 2units, 2–6persons ◆ ◆
no pets ◉ fridge Storage heaters
Elec inclusive ⓛinclusive ☎(2m) Iron
& Ironing board in unit ⊙ CTV
⊕3pin square P ♨(2m)
↩ ♀ (2m)
Min£55 Max£275pw

NEWQUAY
Cornwall
Map**2** SW86

F The Anchorage Porthway, Porth
for bookings Mrs P S Schofield, High Cove
Farm, Trenance, Mawgan Porth,
Newquay, Cornwall TR8 4B2
☎St Mawgan(0637)860567

*Four modern apartments within small
complex of flats, positioned in secluded
cul-de-sac approx 300yds from Porth
Beach. Each comprises of one double-
bedded and one twin-bedded room,
lounge/diner with double bed-settee,
kitchen and bathroom/WC.*

All year MWB out of season 1wk min,
4units, 1–6persons ◆ no pets ◉
fridge ♨ Electric Elec metered ⓛcan
be hired ☎(400yds) [SD in unit] Iron &
Ironing board on premises ⊙ CTV
⊕3pin square 1P 1♨ ▥ ♨(300yds)
↩ ♀(½m) ♫(½m) ♪(½m) ☎-(½m)
Min£45 Max£210pw

H The Barn
for bookings Mrs J Schofield, Hendra Paul
Farm, St Columb Minor, Newquay,
Cornwall
☎Newquay(0637)874695

*Converted from its former farm use to its
present condition of a lovely open beamed
four bedroomed house. The
accommodation comprises of a large
living/dining room, one four poster
bedroom and washbasin, one four poster
bedroom, together with single bed and
washbasin, a further two bedrooms off the
sitting room, one with a four poster double
bed and the other containing twin beds.
Shower room and WC available. Steps
from sitting room lead to garden. This
character property offers accommodation
in a picturesque rural setting. Located off
the A3059 St Columb Major to Newquay
road approx 3m NE of Newquay.*

Newport
—
Newquay

All year MWB out of season 1wk min,
1unit, 1–8persons ◆ ◆ ◉ fridge
Electric Elec metered ⓛcan be hired
☎ WM & SD in unit Iron & Ironing board
in unit ⊙ CTV ⊕3pin square 2P ▥
♨(2m) ✈ ▱
↩ ♀ (2m) ♫(3m) ♪(3m)
Min£70 Max£400pw

H 61 & 65 Mount Wise
for bookings Mrs R B Richards,
Goonhoskyn, Summercourt, Newquay,
Cornwall
☎Mitchell(087251)226

*Two cosy terraced houses with
accommodation comprising lounge,
dining room, kitchen, three bedrooms,
bathroom and WC, also some rooms have
sea views. All equipped and furnished to a
high standard.*

All year MWB out of season 3days min,
1mth max, 2units, 2–5persons ◆ ◆
no pets ⌀ fridge/freezer Gas fires &
storage heaters Gas/Elec metered
ⓛinclusive ☎(500yds) Iron & Ironing
board in unit ⊙ CTV ⊕3pin square
2P ♨(100yds)
↩ ♪ (1m) ♀ (100yds) ♫(100yds)
♪(100yds) ☎-(500yds)
Min£45 Max£185pw

F The Orchard Porth Way
for bookings Mrs J L M Rickard, Poldistra,
7 Riverside Avenue, Pentire, Newquay,
Cornwall TR7 1PL
☎Newquay(06373)3412

*Attractive three-storey, purpose-built flats
with modern furnishings. In residential
area 170yds from Porth Beach.*

All year MWB out of season 3days min,
1mth max, 6units, 2–6persons ◆ ◉
fridge ♨ Elec metered ⓛcan be
hired ☎(100yds) Iron & Ironing board in
unit CTV ⊕3pin square P ♨ ▥
♨(100yds)
↩ ♀ ♫ ♪ ☎-
Details not confirmed for 1987

F Porthcova Holiday Flats Beach Road,
Porth (2m E B3276)
for bookings Mrs J Schofield, Hendra Paul
Farm, St Columb Minor, Newquay,
Cornwall
☎Newquay(0637)874695

*Sited in their own grounds each with its
own garage, approx 150yds from Porth
Beach. Each apartment comprises of one
double and one twin-bedded room,
lounge with double bed-settee separate
kitchenette and modern bathroom/WC.
2m E B3276.*

All year MWB out of season 1wk min,
3units, 1–6persons ◆ ◆ ◉ fridge
Electric Elec metered ⓛcan be hired
☎(150yds) SD for hire, Iron & Ironing
board in unit ⊙ CTV ⊕3pin square
1P 1♨ ▥ ♨(500yds)

↩ ♪ (3m) ♀ (200yds) ♫(2m)
♪(2m) ☎-(2m)
Min£45 Max£160pw (Low)
Min£170 Max£225pw (High)

H 3 & 4 Seymour Avenue
for bookings Mrs R B Richards,
Goonhoskyn, Summercourt, Newquay,
Cornwall
☎Mitchell(087251)226

*Close to the town centre, these two well
kept terraced houses offer lounge, dining
room, kitchen, three bedrooms and
shower/WC.*

All year MWB out of season 3days min,
1mth max, 2units, 2–5persons ◆ ◆
no pets ⌀ fridge/freezer Gas fires &
storage heaters Gas/Elec metered
ⓛinclusive ☎(200yds) Iron & Ironing
board in unit [Launderette within
300yds] ⊙ CTV ⊕3pin square 2P
♨(50yds)
↩ ♪ (1m) ♀ (100yds) ♫(100yds)
♪(100yds) ☎-(500yds)
Min£45 Max£180pw

F 1–6 Tides Reach Porthway, Porth
for bookings A & P Eastlake, Treago Farm,
Crantock, Newquay, Cornwall
☎Crantock(0637)830277

*Spacious purpose built flats and
maisonettes situated two hundred yards
from Porth beach. The two flats and four
maisonettes all afford the same
accommodation of open-plan kitchen/
diner/lounge with wall bed, one double
and one twin-bedded room, bathroom
and WC.*

All year MWB out of season 1wk min,
3mth max, 6units, 2–6persons ◆ ◆
◉ fridge Elec Elec metered
ⓛcan be hired ☎(100yds) Iron &
Ironing board in unit ⊙ CTV
⊕3pin square 6P 6♨ ▥ ♨(200yds)
↩ ♪ (2½m) ♀ (70yds) ♫(½m)
♪(½m) ☎-(1m) Sports centre(1m)
Min£50 Max£60pw (Low)
Min£200 Max£210pw (High)

**F Mr & Mrs A Wiseman Trevanson Court
Holiday Flats** 121 Mount Wise, Newquay,
Cornwall
☎Newquay(0637)874625

*Six flats located on the ground, first and
second floors of this detached house, set
in 1-acre of secluded gardens. They sleep
one to eight people have either lounge/
kitchen/diner or separate lounge, some
with double bed-settee, bathroom, WC or
shower, WC.*

All year MWB 3days min, 1mth max,
6units, 1–8persons ◇ ◆ ◆ ◉
fridge ♨ & Electric Elec metered
ⓛcan be hired ☎(50yds) Iron & Ironing
board in unit [Launderette within
300yds] ⊙ CTV ⊕3pin square 14P
▥ ♨(400yds) ▱(heated)
↩ ♪ (500yds) ♀ (100yds) ♫(½m)
♪(½m) ☎-(½m)
Min£50 Max£250pw

H Treverrick Gummows Shop
for bookings Mrs R B Richards,
Goonhoskyn, Summercourt, Newquay,
Cornwall TR8 4PP
☎Mitchell(087251)226

A remote stone farmhouse, fully renovated to a high standard, situated ½m from the owners farm, down a not-too rough track. Accommodation comprises spacious lounge, well-fitted kitchen, dining room, study, two double bedrooms with WHB, twin bedroom and also a single bedroom and bathroom/WC/shower.

All year MWB out of season 4 days min,
3 wks max, 1 unit, 1–7 persons ◆ ◆
no pets, no weaponary, no single sex
groups ◎ fridge night storage &
electric fires Elec metered ⊡ inclusive
☎(1½m) WM & SD in unit Iron & Ironing
board in unit ⊙ CTV ⊕3 pin square
3P ♨(1½m)

↔ ♀(1½m)
Min£60 Max£280pw

NEW QUAY
Dyfed
Map2 SN35

C Mr & Mrs J S White **Nanternis Farm Cottage** Nanternis, New Quay, Dyfed
SA45 9RP
☎New Quay(0545)560181

Carefully converted stone-built stable providing compact but comfortable accommodation all on one floor, conservatory, lounge/diner, open plan kitchen, shower with separate WC, one twin-bedded room and one with bunk beds.

All year MWB out of season 2 days min,
6 wks max, 1 unit, 2–6 persons [◇] ◆
◆ ◎ fridge storage heaters & wood
burner Elec inclusive ⊡ inclusive
☎(100yds) SD on premises Iron &
Ironing board in unit ⊙ CTV
⊕3 pin square P ▥ ♨(1½m)

↔ ♀(1m) ♫(1½m) ☙(2½m)
Min£90 Max£210pw

Ch Woodlands Holiday Village
for bookings Haven Holidays, P.O. Box 20,
Truro, Cornwall TR1 2UG
☎Truro(0872)40400

Newquay
—
Newtonmore

A chalet village located in a wooded valley amongst the rolling countryside of West Wales and only 2½ miles from the sea. **Oak** *chalet sleeps four with one double and one twin bedroom, open-plan lounge/ diner, kitchenette and bathroom/WC.* **Palm** *chalet also sleeps four and accommodation is identical to Oak.* **Beechwood** *chalet is slightly more spacious and sleeps six. It has one double, one twin and one bunk-bedded room, lounge, fully fitted kitchen with dining area and bathroom/WC.*

Apr–Sep MWB out of season 3 days min,
11 units, 1–6 persons ◆ ◆ ◎
fridge Electric fire Elec metered
⊡ inclusive ☎ [WM, SD & TD on premises] Iron & Ironing board on premises [Launderette on premises]
⊙ CTV ⊕3 pin square 1P ♨ ⌖

↔ ♀ ♫ ♫ ☙(2m)
Min£59 Max£152pw (Low)
Min£125 Max£248pw (High)

NEWTON
Cambridge
Map5 TL45

H & C 3, 4 & 5 Coach House Lane and 1 Whittlesford Road
for bookings Mr & Mrs Short, The Queens
Head, Newton, Cambridge CB2 5PG
☎Cambridge(0223)870436

These three terrace cottages are set in the quiet village of Newton, handily placed for the city of Cambridge. The cottages are traditional in style, built between 1650 and 1800, they are simply furnished and well maintained and have access to rear communal garden. The house, more modern in style and furnishing, dating back to 1830's is more spacious and has small garden/courtyard.

mid Mar–mid Oct 1 wk min, 4 units,
2–4 persons [◇] ◆ ◎ fridge solid
fuel & electric heating Elec metered
⊡ can be hired ☎(400yds) WM & SD
Iron & Ironing board in unit

⊙(cottages) CTV ⊕3 pin square ▥
♨(500yds)
↔ ♀(400yds)
Min£60pw (Low)
Min£75pw (High)

NEWTON ABBOT
Devon
Map3 SX87

C CC Ref 460L
for bookings Character Cottages
(Holidays) Ltd, 34 Fore Street, Sidmouth,
Devon EX10 8AQ
☎Sidmouth(03955)77001

Olde worlde thatched cottage of character with beamed sitting room and fireplace (wood burning stove), fitted kitchen/diner, two bedrooms and a bathroom/WC.

End Jun–end Sep 1 wk min, 1 mth max,
1 unit, 1–4 persons ◆ no pets ◎
fridge Electric Elec metered ⊡ can be
hired ☎ Iron & Ironing board in unit
TV ⊕3 pin square 2P ▥ ♨(2m)

↔ δ(3m) ♀(2m) ♫(3m) ♫(3m)
Min£150 Max£179pw

NEWTONMORE
Highland *Inverness-shire*
Map14 NN79

B Ballathie Station Road
for bookings Mr A G T Troup, 32 Fowgay
Drive, Solihull, West Midlands B91 3PH
☎Solihull(021)7053950

Situated in a quiet street close to the centre of the village, a modern bungalow in its own grounds. Accommodation comprises of lounge with bed-settee, kitchen/diner and three double bedrooms.

All year MWB out of season 3 nights min,
1 unit, 1–8 persons ◆ ◎ fridge
Night storage Elec metered ⊡ can be
hired ☎ WM & TD, Iron & Ironing board
in unit ⊙ CTV ⊕3 pin square 3P ▥
♨(½m)

↔ δ(½m) ♀(½m) ♫(½m)
Min£80 Max£100pw (Low)
Min£110 Max£150pw (High)

C Mrs E MacPherson **Glentruim Cottages** Glentruim, Newtonmore,
Inverness-shire
☎Newtonmore(05403)221 →

GLENTRUIM ESTATE

Glentruim is a private estate close to the A9 in the very centre of the Highlands. It is an ideal place for those who wish to see as much as possible of the Highlands. For those who prefer a quieter holiday, Glentruim offers traditional Highland buildings, formerly occupied by estate staff which are comfortable, well equipped and situated in private woods and farmland. Fishing is included and other recreations available include swimming, riding, canoeing, gliding, skiing, sailing and golf. Phone Newtonmore 221.

These simple old fashioned stone-built cottages were originally occupied by staff from the castle estate. They vary in size and have traditional décor and furnishings. Situated in a quiet tree-studded location in extensive estate grounds 3m S of Newtonmore. The rivers Spey and Truim are a short distance away.

All year MWB out of season 1wk min, 3mths max, 3units, 2–8persons ◆ ◆
◎ fridge Electric & open fires
Elec metered ⬒ not provided
☎(100yds) TV ⊕3pin square P
🛁(3m) Fishing
⊖ ♨(3m) 🎵(3m)
Min£80 Max£100pw (Low)
Min£95 Max£135pw (High)

NEWTON POPPLEFORD
Devon
Map**3** SY08

C   CC Ref 7664
for bookings Character Cottages Ltd, 34 Fore Street, Sidmouth, Devon EX10 8AQ
☎Sidmouth(03955)77001

Thatched cottage quietly situated in the grounds of a country house, approximately 4 miles from Sidmouth. Accommodation comprises spacious circular lounge, dining room, kitchen, bathroom, one double and one twin bedded room.

All year 1wk min, 2mths max, 1unit, 4persons, nc7yrs no pets ◎ fridge
storage & electric fires Elec metered
⬒ inclusive Iron & Ironing board in unit
⊙ CTV ⊕3pin square 2P 🛁(2m)
⊖ ♨(2m)
Min£84 Max£181pw

NEWTON STEWART
Dumfries & Galloway *Wigtownshire*
Map**10** NX46

Newtonmore
—
Oakford

C   Cairnhouse Farm Cottage
for bookings G M Thomson & Co, 27 King Street, Castle Douglas, Kirkcudbrightshire DG7 1AB
☎Castle Douglas(0556)2701 or 2973

Modernised cottage in farmyard near to the main house. Accommodation comprises lounge, kitchen/diner, two bedrooms and bathroom. Owners are amenable to tenants and children taking an interest in the farm in a sensible manner.

Mar–Nov 1wk min, 1unit, 1–6persons
◆ ◎ fridge ᨏ Elec inclusive
⬒ not provided ☎(1m) WM in unit Iron
in unit ⊙ CTV ⊕3pin square 2P
1🛏 🛁(4m) Trout loch
⊖ δ(3m) ♨(3m)
Min£90 Max£170pw

Ch Mr & Mrs I S Lowth **Conifers Leisure Park** Newton Stewart, Wigtownshire DG8 6AN
☎Newton Stewart(0671)2107

Twenty-four timber chalets of Finnish design in an elevated position in a pine wood. High standard of furnishings. Secluded position, although there is an hotel conveniently situated in the same grounds. 1m E of Newton Stewart off A75.

All year MWB out of season 2days min, 24units, 1–6persons ◆ ◆ ◎ fridge
Electric Elec inclusive ⬒ can be hired
☎ Iron & Ironing board on premises
⊙ CTV ⊕3pin square 50P 🆖
🛁(1m) Salmon & sea trout fishing (free), golf (free)
⊖ δ(adjacent) ♨(½m)

Min£87 Max£115pw (Low)
Min£125 Max£237pw (High)

NITON
Map**4** See **Wight, Isle of**

NORTH CREAKE
Norfolk
Map**9** TF83

C   12 & 14 Burnham Road
for bookings Dr H Salmon, 1 Corwell Lane, Hillingdon, Uxbridge, Middlesex UB8 3DD
☎01-573-0085

*In a row of flint faced cottages on the B1355, offering a useful base for touring west Norfolk. No **12** has a sitting room with bed settee, well equipped kitchen/diner, ground-floor bathroom/WC and upstairs a double and single bedded room with an additional single bed in the wide landing. There is also a nice lawned garden at the rear. No **14** is similar but slightly smaller, the bathroom is upstairs and there is one double bedroom and a small room with bunk beds.*

All year MWB out of season 3days min, 1mth max, 2units, 4–5persons ◆ ◎
fridge Electric storage & fires
Elec inclusive ⬒ not provided
☎(100yds) Iron & Ironing board in unit
CTV can be hired ⊕3pin square 3P
🆖 🛁(100yds)
⊖ ♨(100yds)
Min£40 Max£90pw

NORWICH
Norfolk
See **Moulton, Great**

OAKFORD
Dyfed
Map**2** SN45

C Keith & Wendy Langley **Oakford Country Cottages** Oakford, Llanarth, Dyfed SA7 0RL
☎Llanarth(0545)580696

Barn Owl, Cobnut, Oak Apple, Pear Tree and *Coach House* cottages are all equipped and maintained to a very high standard. Each has a well-designed open plan living room, kitchen and bathroom. Sleeping accommodation varies, *Oak Apple Cottage* and the *Coach House* having three bedrooms, the others have two. They have all retained their individual charm and are tastefully furnished to suit their character.

All year MWB out of season 2 days min, 5 units, 2–6 persons ◇ ◈ ◆ no pets ◎ fridge Electric & open fires Elec inclusive ⊡ inclusive (except towels) ☎(½m) Laundry room Iron & Ironing board in unit ⊖ CTV ⊕3pin square P �📺 ♨(½m) Barbecue area

⊖ ♀(1m)

Min £124 Max £162 pw (Low)
Min £248 Max £379 pw (High)

OAKHAM
Leicestershire
Map**4** SK80
See also **Braunston**

Oakford
—
Oban

C **Birch Cottage**
for bookings Mrs R S C Abel-Smith, Old Hall Cottage, 36 Burley Road, Langham, Oakham, Leicestershire LE15 7JE
☎Oakham(0572)2964(evenings)

Two-storey stone-built cottage overlooking the village 14th-century church. On the ground floor there is a lounge with simple, clean décor, and a kitchen which provides basic requirements, dining area. Upstairs there is a bathroom/WC with washbasin, one double room, one twin and one with full-size bunks. 2m NW on A606.

All year wknd min, 2 mths max, 1 unit, 8 persons ◈ ◎ fridge Gas & Electric fires Gas/Elec metered ⊡ not provided ☎(150yds) ⊖ TV ⊕3pin square P 📺 ♨(150yds)

⊖ ♀(200yds) 🎵(200yds) ♬(2m)
🎣(2m)

Details not confirmed for 1987

F **The Old Hall (Garden Flat)**
for bookings Mrs R S C Abel-Smith, Old Hall Cottage, 36 Burley Road, Langham, Oakham, Leicestershire LE15 7JE
☎Oakham(0572)2964(evenings)

This garden flat, all on one level, is a modernised wing of the Old Hall comprising of lounge, dining room, kitchen, bathroom/WC, one double bedroom, a single bedroom and a child's room. 2m NW on A606

All year wknds min, 6 mths max, 1 unit, 1–4 persons ◇ ◈ ⌀ fridge 🍴 Gas/Elec metered ⊡ can be hired ☎ Iron & Ironing board in unit CTV ⊕3pin square 4P 📺 ♨(150yds)

⊖ ♀(200yds) 🎵(2m) ♬(2m)
🎣(2m)

Details not confirmed for 1987

OBAN
Strathclyde *Argyllshire*
Map**10** NM82

B **Braes of Ganavan** Ganavan
for bookings Highland Hideaways, 5/7 Stafford Street, Oban PA34 5NJ
☎Oban(0631)62056 or 63901

Modern single-floor bungalow in superb hillside position with own garden. It comprises two twin-bedded rooms, one double and one single bedroom, bathroom/WC, separate WC, kitchen and large lounge with splendid sea views. 2m along unclass road beside Oban Bay.

Etr–Mid Oct 1wk min, 3mths max, 1 unit, 1–7 persons no pets fridge Electric Elec inclusive ⊡ not provided ☎(500yds) Iron & Ironing board in unit →

⊕ CTV ⊕3pin square P ⌂
⚿(500yds)
⊕ ♪(2¼m) ☕(2m) 🎵(2m) 🎶(2m)
🛏(2m)

Min£126 Max£267pw

Ch Mr S Woodman **Cologin Chalets**
Cologin Homes Ltd, Lerags, Oban, Argyll
PA34 4SE
☎Oban(0631)64501

*Modern timber clad bungalows, fourteen
detached and four semi-detached, located
in small glen south of Oban amidst
highland scenery. Two properties are
specially designed to suit disabled. The
fourteen detached bungalows comprise
one twin-, one double-bedded room,
kitchen/lounge/diner (with sofa bed) and
bathroom. The other four comprise one
twin-bedded room, shower/WC and
lounge/diner/kitchen, with additional sofa
bed in the lounge. There is a bar with all
day buffet, games room and farm animals
on site. Along unclassified road from
junction with A816, 2m S of Oban.*

All year MWB out of season 1day min,
5wks max, 18units, 1−7persons [◇]
◆ ◆ ◉ fridge Electric or 🍳
🆑can be hired ☎ Iron & Ironing board
on premises [Launderette on premises]
⊕ CTV ⊕3pin square P ⚿
Bicycles, fishing & boating
⊕ ♪(3m) ☕ 🎵 🎶(3m) 🛏(3m)

Min£75 Max£160pw (Low)
Min£145 Max£225pw (High)

F Mr I Nicholson **Esplanade Court**
Corran Esplanade, Oban, Argyll
☎Oban(0631)62067

*Purpose-built flats of good standard. Each
flat has at least one room overlooking
Oban Bay to the Islands of Kerrera and
Mull. The esplanade is right in the heart of
the town, but private parking is available.*

5Apr−1Nov MWB out of season
1wk min, 1mth max, 14units, 1−7persons
◆ ◆ no pets ◉ fridge 🍳
Elec metered 🆑inclusive ☎ [WM & TD
on premises] Iron & Ironing board on
premises ⊕ CTV ⊕3pin square P
⚿(100yds)
⊕ ♪(½m) ☕ 🎵 🎶 🛏

Min£103 Max£207pw (Low)
Min£195 Max£240pw (High)

F Hamilton House Holiday Flats
Dunollie Road
for bookings Mrs Connelly, Hamilton
House, Dunollie Road, Oban PA34 5PJ
☎Oban(0631)62384

*Purpose-built modern flats with tasteful
furnishings and sea views, affording*

Oban
—
Onich

*lounge/diner, kitchen, bathroom and two
bedrooms.*

All year MWB out of season 3days min,
6wks max, 2units, 2−6persons ◇ ◆
◉ fridge 🍳 Elec metered
🆑inclusive ☎(150yds) WM & SD in
unit Iron & Ironing board in unit ⊕
CTV ⊕3pin square P ⚿(100yds)
⊕ ♪(1½m) ☕ (150yds) 🎵(150yds)
🎶(150yds) 🛏(200yds)

Min£80 Max£140pw (Low)
Min£170 Max£200pw (High)

Ch Mr & Mrs D Wren **Lag-na-Keil
Chalets (Oban) Ltd** Lerags, Oban, Argyll
PA34 4SE
☎Oban(0631)62746

*Four different types of chalet, all with
either bath or shower and separate or
open plan kitchen/living room as required.
Pleasant situation on sloping ground with
picturesque views of hills and Loch
Feochan in the distance. Reached by
heading south of Oban along the A816 for
2m, then turning right (signposted Lerags)
along a single track road for 1½m.*

Mar−Oct MWB out of season 1wk min,
4wks max, 19units, 1−6persons ◇ ◉
fridge Electric Elec metered 🆑can be
hired ☎ [Launderette] Iron & Ironing
board on premises ⊕ CTV
⊕3pin square P 📺 ⚿ (limited on
site)
⊕ ☕(½m) 🎵(3m)

Min£67.75 Max£143.75pw (Low)
Min£103.50 Max£195.50pw (High)

F Mrs M MacDonald **Mingulay Holiday
Apartments** Laurel Crescent, Oban, Argyll
☎Oban(0631)62627

*Self-contained flats forming a modern
extension to the owners house with views
over hilly countryside. They sleep up to six
in two bedrooms plus a convertible settee
in the lounge/diner.*

All year MWB out of season 1wk min,
2units, 1−6persons ◆ ◉ fridge
Electric Elec metered 🆑inclusive
(except for towels) ☎(½m) Iron & Ironing
board in unit ⊕ CTV ⊕3pin square
P 📺 ⚿(½m)
⊕ ♪(½m) ☕(½m) 🎵(½m) 🎶(½m)
🛏(½m)

Min£50 Max£115pw (Low)
Min£145 Max£180pw (High)

B & F David Hutchison **Soroba House
Hotel** Oban, Argyllshire
☎Oban(0631)62628

*Located about a mile from town centre on
A816 Lochgilphead road. Soroba House is
set on the hillside overlooking the town.
The ten semi-detached bungalows
comprise two bedrooms, lounge/diner,
kitchen, bath/WC and additional sofa-bed
in the lounge. The four flats comprise one
bedroom, lounge/diner, kitchen,
bathroom/WC and an additional sofa bed
in the lounge. Both units are well-
appointed with Scandanavian furnishings.*

All year MWB 1day min, 14units,
1−6persons [◆ ◆] ◉ fridge
Electric Elec metered 🆑inclusive ☎
Iron & ironing board on premises
[Launderette on premises] ⊕ ⊛ CTV
⊕3pin square P ⚿(½m) 🚶Hard
putting
⊕ ♪(1m) ☕ 🎵 🎶(1m) 🛏(1m)

Min£136 Max£190pw (Low)
Min£185 Max£265pw (High)

OLD RADNOR
Powys
Map**3** SO25

H **Stockwell Farm**
for bookings Landmark Trust,
Shottesbrooke, Maidenhead, Berkshire
SL6 3SG
☎Littlewick Green(062882)5925

*A 17th-century stone and timber-framed
farmhouse still retaining its charm and
character and affording beautiful views
across the rolling Welsh countryside. It
comprises spacious, beamed dining room,
small well-equipped kitchen, utility room
and cosy, open-fired lounge with separate
small study. A spiral staircase leads to
three character twin-bedded rooms,
bathroom and WC. Rustically located in
the sleepy village of Old Radnor,
convenient for touring.*

All year MWB out of season 2days min
3wks max, 1unit, 1−6persons ◆ ◆
no cats ◉ fridge night storage
Elec inclusive 🆑not provided
☎(100yds) Iron & Ironing board in unit
⊕ ⊕3pin square 1🅿 ⚿(2½m)
⊕ ♪(3m) ⚿ (100yds) 🎵(3m)

Min£145 Max£265pw (Low)
Min£160 Max£265pw (High)

ONCHAN
See **Man, Isle of**

ONICH
Highland *Inverness-shire*
Map**14** NN06

Ardrhu Cottages

**Ardrhu House, Onich,
Inverness-shire
Telephone:
Onich (08553) 228**

Comfortable cottages in delightful setting on the shores of Loch
Leven with fine views. Eight comprising double and twin bedroom,
four have three bedrooms and one has four bedrooms. Accommodation is of a high standard, all have lounge with single bed-settee,
kitchen/ diner and bathroom. A wide range of facilities are available
on site including boating, windsurfing, solarium and sauna.

C Mr D M Button **Ardrhu Cottages**
Ardrhu House, Onich, Inverness-shire
☎Onich(08553)228

Comfortable cottages in delightful setting on the shores of Loch Leven with fine views. Eight comprise a double and twin bedroom, four have three bedrooms and one has four bedrooms. Accommodation is of a high standard, all comprise lounge with single bed-settee, kitchen/diner and bathroom. A wide range of facilities are available on site including beach, boating, tennis, coach house with private bar, solarium and sauna.

All year MWB out of season 1 day min, 13units, 1–8persons [◇] ◈ ◆ ◎
fridge Electric Elec metered
Ⓛinclusive ☎ Iron & Ironing board on premises [Launderette on premises]
☺ CTV ⊕3pin square 20P ♨(½m)
✍Hard ♨

◑ ♀ 📻(1m) 🎵(2m)
Min£70 Max£120pw (Low)
Min£180 Max£245pw (High)

C Cuilcheanna Holiday Cottages
for bookings Mr A Dewar, Cuilcheanna House, Onich, Inverness-shire PH33 6SD
☎Onich(08553)226

Three modern chalet cottages situated on a 100-acre farm, in elevated position overlooking Loch Linnhe and the Glencoe mountains. Accommodation is of a high standard and comprises of open plan sitting room/diner and fold away double bed, two bedrooms and a bathroom. Access is from the A82 at the N end of the village.

All year MWB out of season 2 days min, 3units, 1–6persons ◈ ◆ ◎ fridge
Electric Elec metered Ⓛinclusive
☎(½m) Iron & Ironing board in unit
[Launderette on premises] ☺ TV
⊕3pin square 8P 📺 ♨(½m)

◑ ♀ (¾m)
Min£90 Max£115pw (Low)
Min£140 Max£215pw (High)

Ch Mr & Mrs King **Loch Leven Chalets**
Onich, Fort William, Inverness-shire
PH33 6SA
☎Onich(08553)272

Seven timber chalets with extensive views of Glencoe Mountains. Accommodation in each unit comprises open plan lounge/diner/kitchen, two bedrooms and bathroom.

All year MWB out of season 3 days min, 7units, 1–6persons [◇ ◆] ◎
fridge Electric Elec metered
Ⓛinclusive ☎(4m) Iron & Ironing board in unit ☺ CTV ⊕3pin square 9P 📺
♨(5m)
Min£137 Max£240pw

ORKNEY
Map**16**

FINSTOWN
Orkney
Map**16** HY31

Onich
—
Ottery St Mary

B, F & H Orkney Self Catering
for bookings Mrs K Reid, Boathouse, Finstown, Orkney
☎Finstown(085676)397

Located right off A965 entering Finstown from Kirkwall, a neatly-planned crescent of five bungalows, two flats and an upside-down 'boathouse' (roof is an upturned boat) set between the road and sea. All provide a high standard of facilities.

All year MWB out of season 1 wk min, 8units, 1–8persons ◇ ◎ fridge
Electric Elec metered Ⓛinclusive
☎(100yds) [WM on premises] ☺ CTV
⊕3pin square P 📺 ♨(100yds)
Fishing
Details not confirmed for 1987

ORPHIR
Orkney
Map**16** HY30

H Waterslap
for bookings Mrs V Pirie, Orakirk, Orphir, Orkney KW17 2RE
☎Orphir(085681)328 (Evenings)
Stromness(0856)850177 (Daytime)

Modern four-bedroomed house set in close proximity to the A964, and 8m from Stromness which it faces to the W across Holy Sound. The house is well maintained with a spacious and comfortable living room. Transport is recommended. Ideally located for sea and countryside.

Closed Feb MWB out of season
1 wk min(winter), 2wks min(summer), 1unit, 1–8persons ◇ no pets ◎ fridge
Electric Elec metered Ⓛnot provided
☎(4m) Iron & Ironing board in unit ◐
CTV ⊕3pin square P 📺 ♨(3m)
Min £85 Max£115pw

STENNESS
Orkney
Map**16** HY31

H Blackbraes
for bookings Mrs V Pirie, Orakirk, Orphir, Orkney KW17 2RE
☎Orphir(085681)328
(Evenings)Stromness(0856)850177
(Daytime)

Detached two-storey stone house formerly a farm set in an isolated position off A964 2m S of the junction with the Stromness–Finstown road. Comprises large kitchen/dining area, lounge, two double bedrooms, two twin-bedded rooms and a bathroom.

Closed Feb 2wks min(summer), 1wk min(winter), 1unit, 1–8persons ◇
no pets ◎ fridge Electric
Elec metered Ⓛnot provided ☎(1m)
WM in unit Iron & Ironing board in unit
◐ CTV ⊕3pin square P 📺 ♨(2m)

◑ ♀ (2m) 📻(2m)

£85pw (Low)
£115pw (High)

ORMSARY
Strathclyde *Argyllshire*
Map**10** NR77

Ch Camas Log Cabins
for bookings Mrs C Winnard, Lithgows Ltd, Estate Office, Ormsary, PO Box 7, Lochgilphead, Argyll PA31 8JH
☎Ormsary(08803)222

Modern timber-framed cabins lying together in natural surroundings, overlooking Loch Coalisport. Accommodation comprises three bedrooms (one double, one twin and one room with bunk beds), living room, open plan fitted kitchen and bathroom.

All year MWB out of season 1 wk min, 6wks max, 13units, 1–6persons ◇ ◎
fridge Electric Elec inclusive
Ⓛprovided ☎(2½m) SD in unit ☺
CTV ⊕3pin square P ♨(12m)
putting
Details not confirmed for 1987

ORPHIR
See **Orkney**

ORSETT
Essex
Map**5** TQ68

C The Cottages
for bookings Mrs M A Wordley, Lorkin's Farm, Orsett, Essex RM16 3EL
☎Grays Thurrock(0375)891439

Two attractive cottages located in a quiet area of Orsett village, whose proximity to London is convenient. One cottage has a double a twin and a single room, while the other has a double room and a twin-bedded room with put-u-up. Both have cosy well appointed lounges, bathrooms and modern well equipped kitchen with dining tables. They also have small well kept gardens

All year MWB wknd min, 7mths max, 2units, 1–6persons [◇] ◈ ◆
no pets ◙ or ◎ fridge ◎ Gas/
Elec inclusive Ⓛinclusive ☎
WM (both units) & SD in one unit Iron & Ironing board in unit ◐ ☺ CTV
⊕3pin square 4P 📺 ♨(310yds)

◑ ♂(1m) ♀ (50yds) 📻(3m) 🎵(3m)
🐎(3m) riding, fishing (bowling green & tennis court 300yds)
Min£140 Max£185pw

OTTERY ST MARY
Devon
Map**3** SY19

H CC Ref 757L
for bookings Character Cottages (Holidays) Ltd, 34 Fore Street, Sidmouth, Devon EX10 8AQ
☎Sidmouth(03955)77001

Modern terraced house on small attractive estate. Accommodation is comprised of lounge/diner, fully-equipped separate kitchen, bathroom/WC, and two bedrooms →

(one with a double bed and the other having bunk beds).

End Mar–End Sep MWB out of season 1wk min, 4wks max, 1unit, 1–6persons ◆ no pets ◎ fridge ♨ Elec inclusive ⌷ can be hired ☎(500yds) WM Iron & Ironing board in unit ⊙ TV ⊕3pin square 1P 1⌂ ▥ ⌸(½m)
⊖ ☏(½m) ♫(1m) ♬(1m)
Min£117 Max£226pw (High)

C CC Ref 7667L
for bookings Character Cottages Ltd, 34 Fore Street, Sidmouth, Devon EX10 8AQ ☎Sidmouth(03955)77001

Terraced cottage situated in the centre of the village. Accommodation comprises lounge/diner with two feature fireplaces, small kitchen, bathroom, a single and a double bedroom.

All year 1wk min, 2mths max, 1unit, 3persons no pets ◎ fridge storage & electric fires Elec metered ⌷inclusive phone in unit Iron & Ironing board in unit ⊙ CTV ⊕3pin square ▥ ⌸(20yds) video in unit
⊖ ☏ (50yds) Sports centre(1m)
Min£71 Max£149pw

OWLPEN
Gloucestershire
Map**3** ST79

C The Court House
for bookings Mr & Mrs N Mander, Owlpen Manor, Owlpen, Dursley, Gloucestershire GL11 5BZ
☎Dursley(0453)860261

A charming building, fundamentally Stuart period, situated within the Manor estate. Ground floor includes small kitchen, bathroom and dining area leading to garden. The living room and a double-bedded room are on the first floor. On the top floor under the eaves there are two cosy bedrooms, one with a single bed (or two childs beds) leading through to a larger room with a double bed. Comfortably furnished.

All year MWB 2nights min, 1unit, 3–6persons ◇ ◆ ● ◎ fridge ♨ Elec inclusive ⌷inclusive ☎ Iron

---

Ottery St Mary
—
Owlpen

& Ironing board in unit ⊙ ⊛ CTV ⊕3pin square 2P ⌸(1m)
⊖ ☏(2m) ☏(1m)
Min£125 Max£200pw (Low)
Min£225 Max£300pw (High)

H Grist Mill
for bookings Mr & Mrs N Mander, Owlpen Manor, Owlpen, Dursley, Gloucestershire GL11 5BZ
☎Dursley(0453)860261

A listed building which provides essentially modern accommodation of unrivalled character and charm, features of the working mill have been retained. Open plan dining/living room, pine fitted kitchen, on the first floor there is a double-bedded room with four poster bed and a twin-bedded room, bathroom and WC. The second floor is reached by narrow stairs giving access to a large open area with a double and two single beds and a further bathroom and WC. The mill has its own drive and garden and offers seclusion, and quiet.

All year MWB 2nights min, 1unit, 4–9persons ◇ ◆ ● no pets ∅ fridge ♨ Gas/Elec inclusive ⌷inclusive ☎ Iron & Ironing board in unit ⊙ ⊛ CTV ⊕3pin square P ⌸(1m)
⊖ ☏(3m) ☏(1m)
Min£150 Max£250pw (Low)
Min£310 Max£410pw (High)

H Manor Farm
for bookings Mr & Mrs N Mander, Owlpen Manor, Owlpen, Dursley, Gloucestershire GL11 5BZ
☎Dursley(0453)860261

Modern house comfortably furnished, comprising living/dining room with open fireplace, kitchen, one double and one twin-bedded room, and shower room with WC. The main bedroom has a mahogany Hepplewhite four poster.

All year MWB 2nights min, 1unit, 2–4persons [◇] ◆ ● ◎ fridge ♨ Elec inclusive ⌷inclusive ☎ WM in unit Iron & Ironing board in unit ⊙ ⊛ CTV ⊕3pin square P ⌸(1m)
⊖ ☏(3m) ☏(1m)
Min£125 Max£200pw (Low)
Min£225 Max£300pw (High)

C Marling's End Cottage
for bookings Mr & Mrs N Mander, Owlpen Manor, Owlpen, Dursley, Gloucestershire GL11 5BZ
☎Dursley(0453)860261

Attractive cottage in pleasant valley setting. Accommodation consists of comfortable sitting room, dining room, kitchen, cloakroom/WC, double and twin bedrooms with a smaller room containing bunk beds and bathroom/WC.

All year MWB 2nights min, 1unit, 2–6persons [◇] ◆ ● ◎ fridge ♨ Elec inclusive ⌷inclusive ☎ Iron & Ironing board in unit ⊙ ⊛ CTV ⊕3pin square 2P ⌸(½m)
⊖ ☏(2m) ☏(1m)
Min£140 Max£240pw (Low)
Min£275 Max£375pw (High)

H Overcourt
for bookings Mr & Mrs N Mander, Owlpen Manor, Owlpen, Dursley, Gloucestershire GL11 5BZ
☎Dursley(0453)860261

*Adjoining Manor Farm this very comfortable, attractive cottage comprises sitting room, kitchen, bathroom/WC and three bedrooms, one of which is a small child's room. This can be let in conjunction with **Manor Farm** to sleep up to nine people.*

All year MWB 2nights min, 1unit, 2–5persons [◇] ◆ ● ◎ fridge ♨ Elec inclusive ⌷inclusive ☎ WM, SD in unit Iron & Ironing board in unit ⊙ ⊛ CTV ⊕3pin square 2P ⌸(1m)
⊖ ☏(2m) ☏(1m)
Min£125 Max£200pw (Low)
Min£225 Max£300pw (High)

C Peter's Nest
for bookings Mr & Mrs N Mander, Owlpen Manor, Dursley, Gloucestershire GL11 5BZ
☎Dursley(0453)860261

A small but very charming cottage for two comprising kitchen, living room with dining and sitting areas, and a bathroom. Upstairs under the eaves, with lowish ceilings, is the double bedroom. A small private garden.

All year   MWB   2 nights min, 1 unit, 2 persons ◎ fridge 🍴 Elec inclusive � 🛁 Iron & Ironing board in unit ☺ ⊛ CTV ⊕3 pin square 2P 🎵 ⚙(1m)

⊖ 𝄞(2m) ⚊(1m)

Min£120 Max£195pw

C   Summerfield Cottage
for bookings Mr & Mrs N Mander, Owlpen Manor, Owlpen, Dursley, Gloucestershire GL11 5BZ
☎Dursley(0453)860261

A small charming cottage with open views, situated a few minutes from the Manor House Estate. Accommodation includes sitting room, double bedroom, kitchen and bathroom, patio sitting area.

All year   MWB   2 nights min, 1 unit, 2 persons ◇ ◈ ◆ ◎ fridge 🍴 Elec inclusive ⌐inclusive 🛁 Iron & Ironing board in unit ☺ ⊛ CTV ⊕3 pin square 2P ⚙(1m)

⊖ 𝄞(2m) ⚊(1m)

Min£120 Max£195pw

C   Tithe Barn
for bookings Mr & Mrs N Mander, Owlpen Manor, Owlpen, Dursley, Gloucestershire GL11 5BZ
☎Dursley(0453)860261

The smallest cottage at Owlpen, this character cottage apartment forms part of a Grade 1-listed Tithe barn, with massive oak cruck beams and trusses. Stairs lead up through the minstrels' gallery to the open-plan studio with kitchen/dining area, and a large double bed and bathroom.

All year   MWB   2 nights min, 1 unit, 2 persons ◎ fridge 🍴 Elec inclusive ⌐inclusive 🛁 Iron & Ironing board in unit ☺ ⊛ CTV ⊕3 pin square 2P 🎵 ⚙(1m)

⊖ 𝄞(2m) ⚊(1m)

Min£100 Max£165pw

H   Woodwells
for bookings Mr & Mrs N Mander, Owlpen Manor, Owlpen, Dursley, Gloucestershire GL11 5BZ
☎Dursley(0453)860261

A comfortable stone-built farmhouse offering seclusion in beech woods. It comprises attractive dining room, pretty Victorian sitting room, farmhouse style kitchen, utility room and one twin-bedded room. The first floor has two double bedrooms, one with Victorian brass bed and a bathroom/shower.

All year   MWB   2 nights min, 1 unit, 2–6 persons ◇ ◈ ◆ ◎ fridge, freezer, dishwasher 🍴 Elec inclusive ⌐inclusive 🛁 WM in unit Iron & Ironing board in unit ☺ ⊛ CTV ⊕3 pin square 2P 🎵 ⚙(1m)

⊖ 𝄞(2m) ⚊(1m)

Owlpen
—
Padstow

Min£150 Max£250pw (Low)
Min£310 Max£410pw (High)

OXENHOPE
West Yorkshire
Map**7** SE03

C   2 Mouldgreave Cottage
for bookings Mrs Mackrell, Mouldgreave, Oxenhope, Keighley, W Yorkshire BD22 9RT
☎Haworth(0535)42325

A very attractive stone-built 18th-century semi-detached cottage with modern furnishings throughout, yet retaining its original charm. Set in pleasant rural position in the heart of Brönte country, close to the owners house. The accommodation comprises two bedrooms sleeping up to five persons, lounge, kitchen and bathroom.

All year   MWB   out of season   1 wk min, 1 unit, 2–5 persons ◇ ⬦ fridge Gas & electric fires Gas & Elec metered ⌐inclusive SD, Iron & Ironing board in unit CTV ⊕3 pin square 1P 🎵 ⚙(1½m)

£75pw (Low)
£90pw (High)

OXFORD
Oxfordshire
Map**4** SP50

F   Morrell Hall John Garne Way, Marston
for bookings Mr P Ledger, Head of Catering & Conference Services, Oxford Polytechnic, Gipsy Lane, Headington, Oxford.
☎Oxford(0865)64777 ext 626

Located one and a half miles from city centre, in eleven acres of grounds. The six split level flats comprise 'L' shaped open plan kitchen/diner/lounge area, bath with shower, WC, one twin bedroom, and upstairs four single bedrooms. Designed as student accommodation these units are functional rather than luxurious.

mid Jul–mid Sep also Xmas & Etr vacations   1 wk min   2 mth max   6 units 1–6 persons [◇] ◇ no pets   1 adult to each party ◎ fridge 🍴 Elec inclusive ⌐inclusive ☎(20yd) [WM & TD on premises] Iron & Ironing board in unit ☺ CTV can be hired ⊕3 pin square P 🎵 ⚙(½m)

⊖ 𝄞 ⚊ 🎵 🎵 ⚙

Min£135 Max£165pw

F   Mr & Mrs R B Naylor Northfield House
106 Banbury Road, Oxford OX2 6JU
☎Oxford(0865)54222

Situated one mile from the town centre this three-storey Victorian house has been converted into ten compact studio flats. Each apartment comprises a bed-sitting room, bathroom and kitchenette.

All year   MWB   3 days min, 1 mth max, 10 units, 2–4 persons ◇ ◆ no pets ◎ fridge Convector heaters Elec inclusive ⌐inclusive 🛁 Iron & Ironing board on premises ☺ TV ⊕3 pin square 6P 🎵 ⚙(½m)

⊖ 𝄞(1½m) ⚊(½m) 🎵(1¼m)
Sports centre(½m)

£150pw

OXWICH
West Glamorgan
Map**2** SS58

Ch   No 40 Oxwich Leisure Park
for bookings Mr A C & Mrs H M Williams, 2a Heol Maespica, Lower Cwmtwrch, Swansea, Glamorgan
☎Upper Cwmtwrch(0639)830847

A small bungalow chalet situated within a large holiday complex on the Gower Peninsular. Accommodation comprises two double bedrooms, small lounge/diner with double bed-settee, kitchen and bathroom/WC.

Mar–Oct   1 wk min, 1 unit, 6 persons ◇ ◆ ◎ fridge Electric fires Elec metered ⌐not provided ☎(50yds) ☺ CTV ⊕3 pin square 1P ⚙

⊖ ⚊ 🎵(½m)

Min£43 Max£158pw

PADSTOW
Cornwall
Map**2** SW97

C   Martinette & St Martins Trevone
for bookings Mrs S Edwards, 76 Somerset Place, Stoke, Plymouth, Devon
☎Plymouth(0752)563594

Two cottages in small terrace with orchard to rear, **Martinette** *comprises kitchen/ diner, lounge, bathroom/WC, with large twin bedroom on the first floor.* **St Martins** *has kitchen/diner, lounge and two double bedrooms and bathroom/WC. 300yds from beach. Turning to Trevone off A39 coast road, Padstow–Newquay.*

Mar–Nov   1 wk min, 2 units, 2–4 persons ◇ ◎ fridge Electric Elec metered ⌐not provided ☎(15yds) Iron & Ironing board in unit ☺ TV can be hired ⊕3 pin square 2P 🎵 ⚙(15yds)

⊖ 𝄞(2m) ⚊(100yds)
Min£50 Max£180pw (Low)

F   Raintree House, Flats 1, 2 & 3 Windmill
for bookings Mr & Mrs K S Rawlins, Whistlers, Treyarnon Bay, Padstow, Cornwall PL28 8JR
☎Padstow(0841)520358

Occupying a detached house which stands in half an acre of grounds, flats 1 and 2 both offer two bedroomed accommodation, lounge, diner, kitchen and bathroom/WC. Flat number 3 has a kitchen/diner, separate lounge, two bedrooms and a bathroom/WC, some bedrooms have wash hand basins.

Mar–Oct   MWB   out of season   1 wk min, 1 mth max   3 units   1–6 persons ◇ ◆ →

181

⊘ ◎ fridge ⊞ Gas & Elec metered
L can be hired ☎ WM, SD & TD on premises Iron & Ironing board in unit
⊙ CTV ⊕3pin square 6P ▥ ♨(¼m)
⊖ ⛳(3m) 🍷(¼m) 🎥(2m)
Min£63 Max£142pw

PAIGNTON
Devon
Map**3** SX86

F Mr & Mrs A L Wilson ***Ashdene*** Cliff Park Road, Paignton, Devon
☎Paignton(0803)558397

Six flats located on ground and first floor of this detached modern villa-style property. Each comprises lounge/diner, bathroom/WC, kitchen, large bedroom with double and bunk beds. Flats 4 and 5 have two bedrooms.

Allyear MWB out of season 2days min, 5mths max, 6units, 2–4persons ◇ [◆] ◎ fridge Electric Elec metered L can be hired ☎(400yds) Iron & Ironing board in unit ⊙ CTV ⊕3pin square 10P ▥ ♨(400yds)
⊖ ⛳(2m) 🍷(200yds) ♫(1½m) ♫(1½m) 🎥(1½m)
Details not confirmed for 1987

C **Barcombe Cottages** 6B Old Torquay Road
for bookings Mr & Mrs G S J Monckton, The Mill House, Manaton, Newton Abbot, Devon TQ13 9UH
☎Manaton(064722)232

Fine 17th-century terraced cottages in central location within short walking distance of seafront. ***Rose Cottage, Fig Tree & The Oaks*** *each sleep six people,* ***Lavender*** *sleeps five and* ***The Willows*** *sleeps four. They all have lounge, kitchen/ diner and bathroom/WC except for Rose which has shower/WC.*

Allyear MWB out of season 3days min, 4wks max, 5units, 2–8persons ◆ ◆ ◎ fridge Electric L can be hired ☎(150yds) [Launderette on premises] ⊙ CTV ⊕3pin square 8P ▥ ♨(25yds)
⊖ ⛳(2m) 🍷(25yds) ♫(200yds) ♫(200yds) 🎥(1m)
Min£70 Max£115pw (Low)
Min£195 Max£300pw (High)

F Mr & Mrs Fullalove ***Bel-Air Apartments*** 14A Cleveland Road, Paignton, Devon TQ4 6EL
☎Paignton(0803)524209

Purpose-built modern apartments in select area a short distance from the beach and enjoying sea views overlooking Torbay. The flats have lounge/diner separate kitchen, and bathroom/WC. They vary in size having one to three bedrooms, and some flats also have a double studio couch in the lounge.

Apr–Oct 1wk min, 4wks max, 7units 2–12persons [◇ ◆ ◆] No single sex groups ◎ fridge Electric fires Elec metered L can be hired ☎ Iron & Ironing board in unit [Launderette on premises] ⊙ CTV ⊕3pin square 14P ▥ ♨(250yds) ⌓(heated) Pool table
⊖ ⛳(3m) 🍷(250yds) ♫(250yds) ♫(500yds) 🎥(¼m)
Details not confirmed for 1987

F Miss A W Owens ***Casa Marina*** 2 Keysfield Road, Paignton, Devon TQ4 6EP
☎Paignton(0803)558334

Flats located in a skilfully converted Victorian house in a pleasant residential area which climbs up from the promenade and seafront. They are of varied design, five having shower units and the remainder baths. The furnishings are comfortable and modern and all units have fitted carpets and bright décor.

Allyear MWB out of season 9units, 1–6persons ◆ ◆ no pets fridge Electric Elec metered L can be hired ☎ Iron & Ironing board on premises ⊙ CTV ⊕3pin square P ▥ ♨(400yds)
⊖ 🍷 ♫ ♫ 🎥
Details not confirmed for 1987

F Mr & Mrs T S Gabbott **Cranmore Lodge** 45 Marine Drive, Paignton, Devon TQ3 2NS
☎Paignton(0803)556278

Cranmore Lodge is a detached property standing in ½ acre of ground on the seafront. There are seven apartments which sleep up to five people with a lounge and bed-settee, bedroom (except flat 5 which has two bedrooms), kitchen area and bathroom with WC.

Etr–Oct MWB out of season 3days min, 1mth max, 7units, 2–5persons, nc8 no pets ◎ fridge Electric Elec metered L provided (for overseas visitors only) ☎(80yds) [Launderette within 300yds] ⊙ CTV ⊕3pin square P ▥ ♨(250yds)
⊖ 🍷(250yds) ♫(¼m) ♫(½m) 🎥(¾m)
Min£68 Max£179pw (Low)
Min£114 Max£236pw (High)

F Mrs S M Dixon **Redlands** (Flat 1), 18 Broadsands Park Road, Paignton, Devon TQ4 6JG
☎Churston(0803)842236

First-floor self-contained flat with its own entrance off communal stairs, with two double bedrooms, kitchen/dinette, lounge with double bed-settee, shower room and separate WC. Going W on A379 Paignton-Brixham road, turn left near the end of the dual carriageway into Broadsands Park Road, Redlands is on the right.

Allyear MWB out of season 3days min, 3wks max, 1unit, 2–6persons ◆ ◆ no pets ◎ fridge Electric Elec metered L inclusive ☎(½m) Iron & Ironing board in unit ⊙ TV ⊕3pin square P ▥ ♨(½m)
⊖ ⛳(1m) 🍷(1m) ♫(2m) ♫(2m) 🎥(2m)
Min£50 Max£90pw (Low)
Min£120 Max£190pw (High)

F Mrs S Leishman **South Eden Holiday Flats (1, 2, 3, 4, 6 & 7)** 14 Belle Vue Road, Paignton, Devon TQ4 6ER
☎Paignton(0803)558364

A town villa set in its own grounds converted into compact, self-contained flats. They can accommodate between 2–8 persons in one bedroom which has combinations of double, twins, bunks, single and Z-beds, plus a convertible bed-settee in the lounge, and all have either bath/shower room/WC or separate WC. Short walking distance from sea front.

Allyear MWB in season 3days min, 1mth max, 6units, 2–8persons ◇ ◆ ◆ ◎ fridge Electric Fires Elec metered L can be hired ☎(300yds) [WM & TD on premises] Iron & Ironing board on premises ⊙ CTV ⊕3pin square 6P ▥ ♨(200yds)
⊖ ⛳(2m) 🍷(200yds) ♫(200yds) ♫(300yds) 🎥(500yds)
Min£42 Max£84pw (Low)
Min£105 Max£196pw (High)

Ch South Sands Holidays, Type A & B
for bookings I F & J L Glover, South Sands Holidays, Goodrington Beach Holiday Estate, Cliff Park Road, Paignton, Devon
☎Torquay(0803)22517

Types A & B are purpose-built chalets built in a square around a car park. Accommodation for up to six persons comprising living room with double bed-settee, two bedrooms (one double and one twin), kitchen and bathroom. All 16 units are situated within 500yds of beautifully laid-out recreation grounds and a few seconds' walk from the beach.

Mar–Oct MWB out of season 2days min, 16units, 2–6persons [◇] [◆ ◆] no pets ⊘ fridge Electric & gas fires Gas & Elec charged L can be hired Iron & Ironing board on premises [Launderette within 200yds] ⊙ CTV ⊕3pin square P ♨(20yds)
⊖ ⛳(1m) 🍷(¼m) ♫(¼m) ♫(¼m) 🎥(1½m)
Details not confirmed for 1987

Ch South Sands Holidays, Type C & D
for bookings I F & J L Glover, South Sands Holidays, Goodrington Beach Holiday Estate, Cliff Park Road, Paignton, Devon
☎Torquay(0803)22517

Types C & D have sitting room with bed-settee, three bedrooms (one double, one twin and one with bunk beds), kitchen and bathroom or shower, in each unit. There are 14 units.

Mar–Oct MWB out of season 2days min, 14units, 2–8persons [◇] [◆ ◆] no pets ⊘ fridge Electric & Gas fires Gas & Elec charged L can be hired ☎ Iron & Ironing board on premises [Launderette within 300yds] ⊙ CTV ⊕3pin square P ♨(20yds)

◑ δ(1m) ♨(½m) 𝄞(½m) ♪(½m)
🛁(1½m)

Details not confirmed for 1987

B South Sands Holidays, Type E
for bookings I F & J L Glover, South Sands Holidays, Goodrington Beach Holiday Estate, Cliff Park Road, Paignton, Devon ☎Torquay(0803)22517

Type E sleeps up to six persons in two bedrooms (one double and one twin) and double settee in living room. Each of the seven units also contains a small kitchen, bathroom and sun balcony.

Mar–Oct MWB out of season 2days min, 7units, 2–6persons [◇] [◆ ◆]
no pets ◔ fridge Electric & gas fires Gas & Elec charged ⌷can be hired ☎ Iron & Ironing board on premises [Launderette within 300yds] ⊕ CTV ⊕3pin square P ▰(20yds)

◑ δ(1m) ♨(½m) 𝄞(½m) ♪(½m)
🛁(1½m)

Details not confirmed for 1987

F Tregarth Flats 2 & 3
for bookings Mrs J L Jackman, Tregarth, Cliff Park Road, Goodrington, Paignton, Devon TQ4 6NB
☎Paignton(0803)550382

A chalet bungalow 'Tregarth', built in 1927, converted into two units. Accommodation comprises two bedrooms, lounge/kitchen, bathroom and WC. Five other units in grounds, three not up to required standards.

Apr–Oct MWB out of season 1wk min, 4wks max, 2units, 2–6persons ◇ [◆ ◆] ⑥ fridge Electric Elec metered
⌷can be hired ☎(150yds) SD on premises iron & Ironing board in unit
⊕ CTV ⊕3pin square P 📺 ▰(100yds)

◑ ♨(100yds) 𝄞(½m) ♪(½m) 🛁(1m)

Min£55 Max£135pw (Low)
Min£152 Max£199pw (High)

B, Ch Tregarth Holiday Bungalow & Family Chalet
for bookings Mrs J L Jackman, Tregarth, Cliff Park Road, Goodrington, Paignton, Devon TQ4 6NB
☎Paignton(0803)550382

Paignton
—
Parkham

Two units in the grounds of 'Tregarth', sleeping five and six persons respectively. Accommodation in the recently built bungalow comprises kitchen, living room with convertible couch (double), bedroom with one double and one single bed and bathroom/WC. The chalet comprises living room/kitchen with studio couch, two bedrooms (one double and one single bed in each room) and shower/WC.

May–Oct MWB out of season 1wk min, 4wks max, 2units, 2–6persons ◇ ◆
◔(1unit) ⑥(1unit) fridge Electric Gas/Elec metered ⌷can be hired ☎(150yds) SD on premises Iron & Ironing board in unit ⊕ CTV ⊕3pin square P 📺 ▰(100yds)

◑ ♨(100yds) 𝄞(½m) ♪(½m) 🛁(1m)

Min60 Max£129pw (Low)
Min£152 Max£179pw (High)

PARAN
Dyfed
Map2 SM82

H Paran House Near Solva
for bookings Coastal Cottages of Pembrokeshire, Seaview, Abercastle, Mathry, Dyfed SA62 5HJ
☎Croesgoch(03483)7742

A spacious detached farmhouse modernised to provide comfortable accommodation. It comprises outside WC, lounge with open fire, dining room, kitchen, children's playroom, one double bedroom, one bunk bedroom, and two double bedrooms with additional single beds, bathroom and separate WC.

Allyear MWB out of season 4days min, 6wks max, 1unit, 2–10persons ◇ ◆
pets by arrangement ⑥ fridge 🍴
Elec metered ⌷inclusive ☎(2m) WM &
SD in unit Iron & Ironing board in unit
⊕ CTV ⊕3pin square 3P 1🎣
▰(3m)

◑ ♨(3m)

Min£85 Max£370pw

PARKHAM
Devon
Map2 SS42

C CC Ref 507 ELP
for bookings Character Cottages (Holidays) Ltd, 34 Fore Street, Sidmouth, Devon EX10 8AQ
☎Sidmouth(03955)77001

Originally a granary, now converted to a delightful studio cottage. Steps lead to modern living room with picture window and through modern room divider to attractive kitchen. A flight of stairs leads down to two bedrooms, one with double bed and one with bunks, and shower room with WC.

Allyear MWB out of season 1wk min, 1mth max, 1unit, 2–4persons ◆ ⑥
fridge Electric Elec metered ⌷can be hired ☎ Iron & Ironing board in unit
⊕ TV ⊕3pin square ⊕2pin round
P 📺 ▰(½m)

Min£52 Max£73pw (Low)
Min£94 Max£133pw (High)

B, C & F Rose, Ivy, Fig Tree, Penhaven Cottage & The Stables
for bookings Mr & Mrs A K Wade, Penhaven Country House, Parkham, Bideford, Devon EX39 5PL
☎Horns Cross(02375)711 or 388

Three cottages, one flat and one bungalow situated in the grounds of Penhaven Country House Hotel. All units are well-furnished and equipped and three have open fires in the living area. They have between two and four bedrooms accommodating four to eight persons. The facilities at the hotel are available for use.

Allyear MWB out of season 1wk min, 4wks max, 5units, 1–8persons ◇ ◆
◆ ⑥ fridge 🍴(Fig Tree) Electric or open fires Elec metered ⌷can be hired
☎(100yds) WM in unit Iron & Ironing board in unit ⊕ CTV ⊕3pin square
2P 📺 ▰(½m) dishwasher, play area, video system

◑ ♨

Min£95 Max£245pw (Low)
Min£175 Max£310pw (High)

PARTON
Dumfries & Galloway *Kirkcudbrightshire*
Map**11** NX66

H Nether Ervie Farmhouse
for bookings G M Thomson & Co. 27 King
Street, Castle Douglas, Kirkcudbrightshire
☎Castle Douglas(0556)2701 or 2973

*Former farmhouse still surrounded by
working steadings, situated in elevated
position above Loch Ken. It consists of
sitting room, dining room, kitchen &
bathroom, and upstairs four bedrooms
and a box room. 10m N of Castle Douglas
on A713.*

Mar−Nov MWB out of season 1wk min,
6mths max, 1unit, 1−7persons ◆ ⊚
fridge Rayburn, Electric & open fires
Elec inclusive ⊡not provided ☎(3m)
SD in unit TV ⊕3pin round P ♨(3m)
Boat available
Min£90 Max£170pw

─────────────────────

PATHLOW
Warwickshire
Map**4** SP15

H Hardwick Rise
for bookings T E Tunnicliffe, 27 Meadow
Sweet Road, Stratford-upon-Avon,
Warwickshire CU37 7RH
☎Stratford-upon-Avon(0789)293518

*Pair of semi-detached houses in peaceful
countryside setting, offering spacious
accommodation of lounge/diner, kitchen,
bathroom, three bedrooms & outside WC.*

All year MWB out of season 7days min,
8mths max, 2units, 1−6persons ◆ ⊚
fridge ♨ Elec metered ⊡inclusive
☎ Iron & Ironing board in unit ⊙ TV
⊕3pin square 3P 🎬 ♨(1½m)
⊖ ♪(3m) ⏲(1m)
Min£80 Max£160pw (High)

─────────────────────

PEASENHALL
Suffolk
Map**5** TM36

C New Inn Cottage
for bookings The Landmark Trust,.
Shottesbrooke, Maidenhead, Berks
SL6 3SW
☎Littlewick Green(062 882)5925

*The end cottage of a delightfully restored
former 15th-century inn, with walled rear
garden and parking, situated in attractive
village. The cottage is equipped with
period furniture and sleeps six in three
bedrooms.*

All year MWB out of season 1day min,
3wks max, 1unit, 1−5persons ◆ ⊚
fridge ♨ Elec inclusive
⊡not provided ☎(400yds) Iron &
Ironing board in unit ⊙ ⊕3pin square
P 🎬 ♨
⊖ ⏲(½m)
Min£120 Max£205pw (Low)
Min£140 Max£225pw (High)

─────────────────────

Parton
—
Pelynt

C Peasenhall High End
for bookings The Landmark Trust,
Shottesbrooke, Maidenhead, Berks
SL6 3SW
☎Littlewick Green(062 882)5925

*Fully-restored period cottage with
entrance of the Wool Hall, which formed
part of a 15th-century inn. Equipped with
period furniture, the cottage has two first-
floor bedrooms (sleeps four) and
attractive sitting room, separate kitchen/
diner and well-fitted bathroom.*

All year MWB out of season 1day min,
3wks max, 1unit, 1−4persons ◆ ⊚
fridge Elec inclusive ⊡not provided
☎(400yds) Iron & Ironing board in unit
⊙ ⊕3pin square P 🎬 ♨
⊖ ⏲(½m)
Min£110 Max£190pw (Low)
Min£135 Max£190pw (High)

C Peasenhall Low End
for bookings The Landmark Trust,
Shottesbrooke, Maidenhead, Berks
SL6 3SW
☎Littlewick Green(062 882)5925

*Attractive cottage equipped with fine
furniture, but with all modern facilities.
Accommodation comprises two first-floor
bedrooms to sleep four and ground-floor
sitting room plus kitchen/diner.*

All year MWB out of season 1day min,
3wks max, 1unit, 1−4persons ◆ ⊚
fridge ♨ Elec inclusive
⊡not provided ☎(400yds) Iron &
Ironing board in unit ⊙ ⊕3pin square
P 🎬 ♨
⊖ ⏲(½m)
Min£110 Max£200pw (Low)
Min£120 Max£190pw (High)

─────────────────────

PELYNT
Cornwall
Map**2** SX25

**C Mr A E Collins Cartole Farm
(Cottages)** Pelynt, Looe, Cornwall
PL13 2QH
☎Lanreath(0503)20486

*Seven self-contained cottages converted
from old barns with mellow stone walls
and slate roofs and designed to retain
their traditional Cornish character.
Modern style furnishings; the cottages
offer one or two bedrooms (duvets
provided), lounge/dining room, kitchen
(some open plan) and laundry room is
provided on site.*

All year MWB out of season 3days min,
1mth max, 7units, 1−6persons [◇] ◆
◆ ⊚ fridge Electric fires
Elec metered ⊡inclusive ☎(1m) WM,
SD & TD on premises Iron & Ironing
board in unit ⊙ CTV [Launderette on
premises] ⊕3pin square 7P 🎬
♨(1m)
⊖ ⏲(1m)

─────────────────────

Min£90 Max£180pw (Low)
Min£120 Max£265pw (High)

C 1 & 2 Jasmin Cottages The Green
for bookings Mrs J W M Collings, Brook
Cottage, Longcombe Lane, Polperro,
Cornwall PL13 2PL
☎Polperro(0503)72274

*Previously the village carpenters, these
stone-built cottages are adjacent to the
village green and have oak beams.
Accommodation in No 1 includes lounge,
kitchen/diner, combined bathroom/WC, a
bedroom with a double and single bed
and another upstairs room with double
bed. No 2 comprises a lounge/dining room
with kitchen area, one family bedroom
with one double and single divan,
bathroom/WC.*

All year MWB out of season 1wk min,
1mth max, 2units, 2−5persons [◇] ◆
◆ ⊚ fridge Electric Elec metered
⊡can be hired ☎(200yds) Iron &
Ironing board in unit ⊙ CTV
⊕3pin square 🎬 P ♨(100yds)
⊖ ♪(2m) ⏲(½m) 🎵(3m) ♫(3m)
Min£65 Max£185pw

**C John Joliff, Pendower Farm Tremaine
Green** Pelynt, Looe, Cornwall PL13 2LS
☎Lanreath(0503)20333

*Tremaine Green is a hamlet of local
stone-built cottages with slated roofs in
the traditional Cornish style, grouped
around a green providing a 'country
village' atmosphere. Situated in a
sheltered south-facing valley with a
streamlet running through which later
becomes the Polperro river, and located
within 3 acres of grounds, approached by
a private drive. The cottages each have a
small garden with terrace furniture and
have been given a distinctive character,
each devoted to a craft from a bygone
age, such as Blacksmiths cottage, Millers
and Carpenters, etc, with artefacts
denoting same.
Blacksmiths has two double bedrooms
(one with three divans), Cobblers and
Gamekeepers have two bedrooms (with
four poster), Farmhouse comprises three
bedrooms (one with antique four poster
bed). Mariners and Carpenters have one
bedroom, each with antique beds.
Housekeepers and Millers have one
bedroom each (with a half tester), while
Ploughmans has three bedrooms, one
with a four poster bed. All comprise
bathroom/WC, kitchen or kitchen/diner
and lounge or lounge/diner.*

All year MWB out of season 1wk min,
6mths max, 9units, 1−6persons [◇] ◆
◆ ⊚ fridge Electric Elec metered
⊡inclusive (except towels & tea towels)
☎(50yds) Dishwasher(in Farmhouse)
Iron & Ironing board in unit [Launderette
on premises] ⊙ CTV ⊕3pin square
P 🏠 🎬 ♨(1m) ⏱Hard
putting green
⊖ ⏲(1m) 🎵(1m) ♫(1m)
Min£80 Max£400pw

See advertisement under Looe

─────────────────────

PENCOYD
Hereford & Worcester
Map**3** SO52

C **1 The Ark**
for bookings Mrs A Bevan, Lenaston,
Harewood End, Hereford HR2 8NQ
☎Harewood End(098987)218

*A semi-detached 18th-century stone
cottage with a small rear garden. The
accommodation comprises lounge/dining
room, kitchen, bathroom/WC and a twin-
bedded room. The first floor consists of a
double bedroom and a single.*

Etr–Oct MWB out of season 1wk min,
3wks max, 1 unit, 1–5 persons ◈ ◎
fridge Electric Elec metered
⊡ not provided ☎(¾m) Iron & Ironing
board in unit ⊕ CTV ⊕3pin square
2P 1🏠 ♨(2m)

⊖ ♀ 🎬(2m) 🎵(2m)

Min£60pw (Low)
Min£100pw (High)

PENDINE
Dyfed
Map**2** SN20

F **Brook Mill**
for bookings Powell's Cottage Holidays,
55 High Street, Saundersfoot, Dyfed
☎Saundersfoot(0834)812791

*On ground floor part of a modern split-
level bungalow offering woodland and sea
views. Accommodation comprises lounge,
dining/kitchen, bathroom/WC and two
bedrooms sleeping up to six people. Patio
and garden.*

May–Aug MWB out of season 1wk min,
4wks max, 1 unit, 2–6 persons [◇] ◈
◆ ◎ fridge Elec inclusive
⊡ inclusive ☎ Iron & Ironing board in
unit ⊕ CTV ⊕3pin square P 🛅
♨(1m)

⊖ ♀(1m) 🎵(2m)
Min£171 Max£390pw

PENNAL
Gwynedd
Map**6** SH70

Ch **Cedar Wood Lodges**
for bookings Llugwy Estates Ltd, Pennal,
Machynlleth, Powys
☎Pennal(065475)228

*Cedar wood chalets set on high ground in
rural surroundings overlooking the valley.
Accommodation comprises kitchen/diner,
lounge, two or three bedrooms.*

Mar–Oct MWB out of season 1wk min,
3wks max, 6 units, 4–8 persons [◇ ◈
◆] ◎ fridge Electric Elec included
⊡ inclusive ☎ Iron & Ironing board on
premises ⊕ CTV ⊕3pin square 14P
♨(1½m) Fishing & shooting

⊖ ♀(400yds) 🎬(3m)

Min£60 Max£80pw (Low)
Min£150 Max£230pw (High)

B, F & H The General Manager **Plas
Talgarth Estate** Pennal, Machynlleth,
Powys SY20 9JY
☎Pennal(065475)631

Pencoyd
—
Penzance

*Ten luxury bungalows, 14 flats, 8 luxury
apartments and 15 houses of
exceptionally high standard, very clean
and spacious. Located within the
Snowdonia National Park, enjoying
magnificent views in all directions and
overlooking the Dyfi Valley.*

All year 2 nights min, 6wks max, 47 units,
1–8 persons ◇ ◈ ◆ ◎ fridge
🍴 Elec metered ⊡ inclusive
☎(200yds) Iron & Ironing board on
premises [Launderette on premises]
⊕ ⊗ CTV ⊕3pin square 100P 🛅
♨(½m) 🖂 ✆Hard Sauna, Solarium &
Whirlpool bath

⊖ ♿(3m) ♀ 🎬(2m)

Min£195 Max£550pw

See advertisement on page 186

PENRHYNDEUDRAETH (for Portmeirion
Village)
Gwynedd
Map**6** SH63

B, C & F Portmeirion Ltd **Portmeirion
Village** Penrhyndeudraeth, Gwynedd
LL48 6ER
☎Porthmadog(0766)770228

*Two bungalows, 12 cottages and six flats
of individual character situated within the
grounds of the famous Portmeirion.
Italianate village, created by Sir Clough
Williams-Ellis. The buildings are scattered
upon the rocky tree studded hills which
are covered with azaleas, hydrangeas and
rhododendrons. Portmeirion was used to
film the television series 'The Prisoner' and
is also renowned for the Portmeirion
Pottery. Angel, Belvedere and Toll House
sleep up to six people. Battery Cottage
and Cliff House both sleep up to five
people. Dolphin, Gate House, Mermaid
and White Horses sleep up to four people.
Chantry and Government House sleep up
to eight people. Villa Winch Nos 1 & 2 are
flats with No 1 in the ground floor and No 2
on the second floor, both sleep up to three
people. Telfords Tower, a cottage, also
sleeps three people. Chantry Row Nos 1 &
2 are semi-detached bungalows sleeping
one to two people. Upper Arches and
Lower Trinity are first-floor flats and
Upper Trinity a second-floor flat sleeping
two to three people. Unicorn is a ground-
floor flat sleeping up to four people. All
have combinations of either lounge or
lounge/diner, kitchen, or kitchen/diner,
bathroom/WC's or shower/WC's plus extra
WC's and bathrooms in the larger units.*

All year MWB out of season 1wk min,
6wks max, 20 units, 1–8 persons [◇]
◆ ◎ fridge 🍴 & Electric
Elec inclusive ⊡ can be hired ☎ Iron &
Ironing board in unit ⊕ CTV
⊕3pin square P 🛅 ♨(½m) 🖂
✆Hard

⊖ ♿(3m) ♀(100yds)

Min£120 Max£260pw (Low)
Min£205 Max£385pw (High)

PENSFORD
Avon
Map**3** ST66

B & C **Bungalows 4–7 & The Cottage**
for bookings Mr & Mrs C Smart, Leigh
Farm, Pensford, Bristol BS18 4BA
☎Compton Dando(07618)281

*Four simply-appointed bungalows
converted from former farm buildings and
a spacious character cottage both
offering economical holiday
accommodation. The bungalows
comprise open-plan kitchen, lounge/diner,
one or two bedrooms (double or twin
beds) and shower room/WC. The Cottage
offers beamed sitting/dining room, large
kitchen, three bedrooms (two doubles, one
twin), bathroom and toilet. The farm has a
Welsh pony mare for the children to ride.*

All year MWB 3 nights min, 5 units
2–6 persons [◇ ◈] dogs only
(charged) ◎ fridge Electric fires & gas
convector (cottage only) Elec metered
⊡ can be hired ☎ TV & CTV (in
cottage) ⊕3pin square 10P 🛅
♨(½m)

⊖ ♀(¾m) 🐾(4m)

Min£55 Max£115pw (Low)
Min£100 Max£210pw (High)

PENTON
Cumbria
Map**12** NY47

B Mr & Mrs J E Newton **Liddel Park**
Penton, Carlisle, Cumbria
☎Nicholforest(022877)317

*Formerly a block of brick-built stables now
converted into three terraced bungalows
with courtyard at rear. Modernised and
equipped to a very high standard. Two
units have one twin-bedded room and a
double room while the third has two twins.
In addition each has two single foldaway
beds. Set in very quiet rural surroundings
in an area used by the Forestry
Commission, with views of Scottish hills.*

All year 3 units, 8 persons [◇] ◈ ◎
fridge 🍴 Elec inclusive ⊡ inclusive
☎(½m) [WM, SD & TD on premises] Iron
& Ironing board in unit ⊕ CTV
⊕3pin square P 🛅 ♨(½m)

⊖ ♀(1m) 🎬(1m)

Min£65 Max£120pw

PENZANCE
Cornwall
Map**2** SW43

H **CC Ref 313 ELP**
for bookings Character Cottages
(Holidays) Ltd, 34 Fore Street, Sidmouth,
Devon EX10 8AQ
☎Sidmouth(03955)77001

*Comfortable terraced house on the
seafront with views of St Michael's Mount.
It comprises sitting room with sea view,
dining room, well-equipped kitchen/
breakfast room and three bedrooms (one →*

185

Plas Talgarth
COUNTRY CLUB ★★★

Situated in its own grounds of 50 acres overlooking the River Dovey within the Snowdonia National Park in one of the most beautiful parts of Wales. Close to Aberdovey with its sandy beaches, yachting, windsurfing, canoeing, golf, fishing and pony trekking.

Plas Talgarth blends a sense of peace and tranquility with recreational facilities of international standard.

FACILITIES INCLUDE . . . . . .
A comprehensive range of activities to suit every age and mood. Indoor and outdoor heated swimming pool, tennis and squash courts, fun-run/ trim trail, childrens' adventure playground, barbecue area and pitch & putt golf course. Laundrette. Excellent restaurant and cocktail bar together with intimate informal Bistro and friendly medieval farmhouse bar. Unique Health and Beauty Spa run in conjunction with Champneys of Tring includes beauty therapy rooms, saunas, solarium, whirlpool, steam rooms, gymnasium, underwater message bath and hairdressing salon.

Accommodation ranges from charming bungalows and split level villas to lager apartments with their own saunas and whirlpool baths. Accommodation from two to eight persons. All available to rent of Timeshare purchase.

BARRATT MULTI-OWNERSHIP & HOTELS LIMITED
Plas Talgarth Estate, Pennal, Nr.Machynlleth, Powys SY20 9JY
Telephone:(065475) 631

One of the world's great Timeshare Resorts

with bunk beds, two with divans), bathroom and WC.

Apr–Oct 1wk min, 1mth max, 1unit, 2–6persons ◇ no pets ⊚ Electric Elec metered ⌷can be hired ☎(100yds) WM on premises Iron & Ironing board in unit [Launderette within 300yds] ⊕ TV ⊕3pin square ⊕2pin round ♨ ⋒ ⚏ ✒
⊖ ♨(200yds) ♫(200yds)
♫(200yds) ☕(200yds)
Min£171 Max£266pw

F   Carne House Newlyn
for bookings Mrs J M McGrath, The Old Vicarage, Bath Road, Littlewick Green, Berkshire SL6 3QP
☎Littlewick Green(062 882)5989

Two flats with the first-floor flat containing two twin-bedded rooms, open-plan kitchen with breakfast bar to lounge, luxury bathroom with shower, bath & WC, whilst the ground floor has one twin-bedded room, lounge and dining room, kitchen, separate bathroom and WC and garage. Each have one double bedroom with wash hand basin and are exceptionally appointed with quality furnishings.

All year 1wk min, 6wks max, 2units, 1–6persons [◆ ◆] ⊚ fridge Electric Elec metered ⌷can be hired ☎(100yds) Iron & Ironing board in unit [Launderette within 150yds] ⊕ CTV ⊕3pin square 3P 1♨ ⋒
⚏(200yds) ✒Hard Bowls & riding
⊖ ♨(200yds) ♫(½m) ♫(½m) ☕(½m)
Min£65 Max£90pw (Low)
Min£100 Max£185pw (High)

F   Egyptian House Chapel Street
for bookings The Landmark Trust, Shottesbrooke, Maidenhead, Berkshire SL6 3SG
☎Littlewick Green(062882)5925

Three flats above the National Trust Shop in a character street. All approached via a spiral staircase from a central entrance (difficult for elderly). Each comprises hall leading to bathroom/WC, fitted kitchen, small bedroom with single bed or twin bunk beds, lounge/diner with a further twin bedroom leading off. All well-

Penzance
—
Perranporth

appointed, decorated and furnished in period style.

All year MWB out of season 1wk min, 3wks max, 3units, 1–4persons ◇ no pets ⊚ fridge ⋘ Elec inclusive ⌷not provided ☎(160yds) Iron & Ironing board in unit ⊕ ⊕3pin square ⚏(50yds)
⊖ ♨(10yds) ♫(200yds) ♫(200yds)
☕(300yds)
Min£55 Max£215pw (Low)
Min£90 Max£215pw (High)

B   19–20 Park Bungalows Kenegie Manor, Gulval
for bookings Mr & Mrs H E Betham, Bowness Holidays, 38 South Canterbury Road, Canterbury, Kent CT1 3LJ
☎Canterbury(0227)69803

Purpose built semi-detached bungalows built on traditional lines in a courtyard garden setting. Accommodation comprises lounge/diner with double bed-settee, galley kitchen off, two bedrooms, one double and one twin bedded and shower/WC.

Mar–Oct & Xmas 1wk min, 1mth max, 2units, 1–6persons [◆ ◆] ⊚ fridge Convector heaters Elec metered ⌷can be hired ☎ Iron & Ironing board in unit ⊕ CTV(metered) ⊕3pin square 2P per unit ⚏(½m) ⌅ Hotel facilities
⊖ ♨(on site) ♫(on site) ♫(on site)
Min£120 Max£185pw (Low)
Min£195 Max£250pw (High)

F   Tremayne Holiday Flats C & D Alexandra Road
for bookings M & R O'Brien, St Dorothy's Nurseries, Crowlas, Penzance, Cornwall
☎Penzance(0736)740334

Two flats situated in a late Victorian terraced house. **Flat C** *is on the second floor and consists of one twin- and one double-bedded room, small lounge, kitchenette, bathroom and WC.* **Flat D** *is on the ground floor with one double-*

bedded room and one single bed in lounge, small kitchen, shower and WC.

All year MWB out of season 1wk min, 2mths max, 2units, 2–4persons ◆ ◆ no pets ⊚ fridge Electric Elec metered ⌷inclusive ☎(150yds) ⊕ CTV ⊕3pin square ⋒ ⚏(400yds)
⊖ ♨(¼m) ♫(¼m) ♫(¼m) ☕(¼m)
Min£55 Max£65pw (Low)
Min£100 Max£155pw (High)

PERRANPORTH
Cornwall
Map2 SW75

C   4 Eureka Vale
for bookings Mrs J A Cuthill, Claremont, 27 St Georges Hill, Perranporth, Cornwall TR6 0JS
☎Perranporth(087257)3624

Pleasant old world terraced cottage of character situated in quiet position 100yds from beach with secluded garden. The accommodation comprises lounge with bay window, dining room, kitchen. There are two bedrooms on the first floor and an attic childrens' bedroom with sea views, the shower and WC are also on the first floor.

All year MWB out of season 6wks max, 1unit, 2–8persons ◆ no pets ⊚ fridge Electric Elec metered ⌷can be hired ☎(100yds) Iron & Ironing board in unit ⊕ TV ⊕3pin square 2P ⚏(100yds)
⊖ ♪(500yds) ✒(600yds) ♨(300yds)
♫(600yds) ♫(600yds)
Min£90 Max£155pw (Low)
Max£215pw (High)

F   Heron Court Flats The Gounce, Beach Road
for bookings Burrells Enterprises Ltd, The Gables, Newquay Road, Perranporth, Cornwall TR6 0BX
☎Truro(0872)572168 & 572823

Set around a courtyard, 150yds from the beach are these first-floor development purpose-built flats. Each flat consists of lounge/diner, fitted kitchen, bathroom with WC; bedrooms range from one double room to two double rooms and a twin bedroom with additional single bed. →

PARK BUNGALOWS, Kenegie Manor, Gulval, between Penzance and St Ives
Grouped round a garden courtyard in the extensive grounds of a country house hotel 1½ miles from Penzance. They sleep 4-6 persons on double, twin and convertible beds. Col TV. Access to all hotel amenities including swimming and children's pools, bars, restaurant and carvery. An indoor heated pool is planned for 1987. Nearest sandy beach 1 mile. St Michael's Mount and Marazion beach 3 miles. St Ives (5 beaches) 6 miles. Land's End 10 miles.
Colour brochure Penzance Holidays (TG),
38 South Canterbury Road, Canterbury, Kent.
Telephone: (0227) 69803.

All year MWB out of season 3days min,
6units, 1–7persons [◆ ◆] no pets, no
single sex groups ◎ fridge Electric
Elec metered ⬛can be hired
☎(50yds) Iron & Ironing board in unit
☉ CTV ⊕3pin square 6P
🏠(charge) Ⅲ ▟(50yds)
↔ ♪(1m) ♀(50yds) 🎦(200yds)
♬(100yds)

Min£70 Max£120pw (Low)
Max£85 Max£240pw (High)

B,Ch Mr C P Banfield **Leycroft**
Perrancombe, Perranporth, Cornwall
TR6 0JQ
☎Perranporth(0872)573044

*Twenty bungalows and ten chalets
constructed of wood located in a small
holiday park within a very picturesque
valley. Each has two bedrooms, lounge
with bed-settee, kitchen/diner, and
bathroom/WC. They sleep from one to
eight persons.*

29Mar–20Oct MWB out of season
1wk min, 3mths max, 30units, 1–8persons
◆ ◆ no pets (high season) ◎
fridge Electric Elec metered ⬛for hire
☎ Iron & Ironing board on premises
Launderette on premises ☉ CTV
⊕3pin square P Ⅲ ▟
↔ ♪(2m) ♀ 🎦(2m) ♬(2m)
Min£45 Max£65pw (Low)
Min£145 Max£200pw (High)

F Marine Court Holiday Flats
for bookings R T & S Rilstone, 22 Pentreve,
Wheal Leisure, Perranporth, Cornwall
TR6 0EY
☎Truro(0872)572157

*Ten purpose-built holiday flats comprising
two double-bedded rooms (one with
additional bunks), open plan lounge, with
bed-settee, kitchen and separate
bathroom and WC.*

All year MWB out of season 3mths max,
10units, 2–7persons ◆ [◆] ◎
fridge Electric Elec metered ⬛can be
hired ☎(50yds) Iron & Ironing board in
unit [Launderette within 30yds] ☉
CTV ⊕3pin square P Ⅲ ▟(20yds)
↔ ♪(½m) ♀(50yds) 🎦(50yds)
♬(50yds)
Min£50 Max£79pw (Low)
Min£90 Max£249pw (High)

B St Pirans Bungalow The Gounce,
Beach Road
for bookings Burrell Enterprises Ltd., The
Gables, Newquay Road, Perranporth,
Cornwall TR6 0BX
☎Truro(0872)572186 & 572823

*A semi-detached, pebble-dashed
bungalow with its own small enclosed
garden. It has a spacious lounge/diner,
tiled kitchen, two double bedrooms and
bathroom/WC.*

Etr–Oct MWB out of season 3days min,
3mths max, 1unit, 1–4persons [◆ ◆]
no pets, no single sex groups ◎ fridge
Electric Elec metered ⬛can be hired
☎(50yds) Iron & Ironing board in unit
☉ CTV ⊕3pin square 1P Ⅲ
▟(50yds)

Perranporth
—
Pipers Pool

↔ ♪(1m) ♀(50yds) 🎦(200yds)
♬(100yds)

Min£85 Max£110pw (Low)
Min£120 Max£220pw (High)

F St Piran Flats The Gounce, Beach
Road
for bookings Burrell Enterprises Ltd, The
Gables, Newquay Road, Perranporth,
Cornwall TR6 0BX
☎Truro(0872)572186 & 572823

*A semi-detached house divided into four
flats, two ground-floor and two first-floor
with lounge/diner, fitted kitchen, two
double bedrooms and bathroom/WC. Also
two first-floor flats above shops opening
on to a verandah, they comprise open
plan lounge/diner, kitchen area, one
double bedroom and bathroom/WC.*

Etr–Oct MWB out of season 3days min,
3mths max, 6units, 1–4persons [◆ ◆]
no pets, no single sex groups ◎ fridge
Electric Elec metered ⬛can be hired
☎(50yds) Iron & Ironing board in unit
CTV ⊕3pin square 1P Ⅲ ▟(50yds)
↔ ♪(1m) ♀(50yds) 🎦(200yds)
♬(100yds)

Min£70 Max£90pw (Low)
Min£85 Max£185pw (High)

F Mrs S Rilstone Seathrift Seaside Flat
22 Pentreve, Wheal Leisure, Perranporth,
Cornwall TR6 0EY
☎Truro(0872)572157

*Well-appointed first-floor flat with own side
entrance comprising lounge, kitchen/
diner, four bedrooms; 2 double (one with
en suite bathroom); one twin and one with
two bunk beds, all with wash hand basins.
There is also a separate bathroom/WC
and shower room. Central position and
only 75yds from the beach.*

All year MWB out of season 3days min,
3mths max, 1unit, 4–10persons ◆
no pets family groups only ◎ fridge
🍴 Elec metered ⬛can be hired
☎(50yds) Iron & Ironing board in unit
[Launderette within 300yds] ☉ CTV
⊕3pin square 2P 🏠 Ⅲ ▟(10yds)
↔ ♪(½m) ♀(50yds) 🎦(50yds)
♬(50yds)
Min£75 Max£106pw (Low)
Min£175 Max£387pw (High)

F Seaway 10a Beach Road
for bookings Burrells Enterprises Ltd., The
Gables, Newquay Road, Perranporth,
Cornwall TR6 0BX
☎Truro(0872)572186 & 572823

*A first-floor flat above Beach Road shop,
recently modernised to a good standard. It
comprises kitchen/breakfast room,
lounge, one double and one twin bedroom
and bathroom/WC.*

Etr–Oct MWB out of season 3days min,
3mths max, 1unit, 1–4persons [◆ ◆]
no pets, no single sex groups ◎ fridge

Electric Elec metered ⬛can be hired
☎(50yds) Iron & Ironing board in unit
☉ CTV ⊕3pin square 1P Ⅲ
▟(50yds)
↔ ♪(1m) ♀(50yds) 🎦(200yds)
♬(100yds)

Min£80 Max£95pw (Low)
Min£100 Max£190pw (High)

PICKERING
North Yorkshire
Map**8** SE78

C 92 Westgate
for bookings Mrs V Montague, 32 Potter
Hill, Pickering, North Yorkshire YO18 8AA
☎Pickering(0751)73904

*19th-century stone-built terrace cottage
on the A170 road, a short walk from the
town centre. It is Grade III listed and has
original beams and sash windows. The
sleeping accommodation is on the first
floor with two bedrooms, access for one is
through the other, the rest of the
accommodation is ground-floor level
comprising sitting room, kitchen/diner and
shower/WC. There is a small flower
garden.*

Etr–Late Oct 1wk min, 2wks max, 1unit,
1–4persons, nc no pets ◎ fridge Gas
& open fires Elec inclusive Gas metered
⬛not provided ☎(300yds) Iron &
Ironing board in unit ☉ ⓦ TV
⊕3pin square 🏠(300yds) ▟(150yds)
↔ ♀(½m) 🎦(½m)
Min£66 Max£111pw

PINWHERRY
Strathclyde *Ayrshire*
Map**10** NX18

C Carlenrig Poundland
for bookings Mrs A Shankland, 'Talberg',
Burnfoot Farm, Colmonell, Girvan,
Ayrshire
☎Colmonell(046588)265 & 220

*A semi-detached white-painted country
cottage, attractive garden, at the rear of
the house. And comprises kitchen, lounge
and dining room, three bedrooms and
bathroom. Well maintained with good
standard of décor and furnishings.*

All year MWB out of season 3days min
Low season 1unit, 1–6persons ◆ ◆
◎ fridge Electric & storage heaters
Elec metered ⬛can be hired ☎(1m)
WM & SD in unit Iron & Ironing board in
unit ☉ CTV ⊕3pin square 2P 1🏠
▟(2m) Fishing
↔ ♀(2m) 🎦(3m) ♬(3m)
Min£55 Max£70pw (Low)
Min£80 Max£110pw (High)

PIPERS POOL
Cornwall
Map**2** SX28

C CC Ref 3051
for bookings Character Cottages
(Holidays) Ltd, 34 Fore Street, Sidmouth,
Devon EX10 8AQ
☎Sidmouth(03955)77001

Cottage adjoining Coombe House and surrounded by open countryside. Accommodation comprises lounge/dining area with open stone fireplace and exposed beams, small kitchen off, one ground-floor bedroom with bunks, spiral wrought iron staircase to double-bedded room, small double room and shower room.

All year MWB out of season 2 days min, 8 wks max, 1 unit, 6 persons [◇] ◈ ◆
no pets ◎   fridge 🍴 & log fires
Elec inclusive ⌁ not provided ☎(2m)
Iron & Ironing board in unit ⊙ CTV
⊕3 pin square 2P 🎞 ♨(5m)
Min£84 Max£181 pw

PITLOCHRY
Tayside *Perthshire*
Map**14** NN95

C April Cottage 111 East Moulin Road
for bookings Mrs E Egglishaw, Bruach Mhor, 54 West Moulin Road, Pitlochry, Perthshire PH16 5EQ
☎Pitlochry(0796)2084

On the eastern outskirts of this popular holiday town, this detached white painted and modernised cottage sits in its own small garden. Accommodation comprises lounge/dining room, kitchen, one bedroom (one double, one single bed) and bathroom.

All year MWB out of season 3 mths max, 1 unit, 1–3 persons ◆ no pets ◎
fridge Panel heating Elec metered
⌁ can be hired ☎(100yds) ⊙ CTV
⊕3 pin square 2P 🎞 ♨(¾m)
⊖ ♪(1m) ☎(400yds) 🎵(400yds)
🎯(¾m)
Min£75 Max£85pw (Low)
Min£100 Max£115pw (High)

F 15 Cloichard Place
for bookings Mrs E Egglishaw, Bruach Mhor, 54 West Moulin Road, Pitlochry, Perthshire PH16 5EQ
☎Pitlochry(0796)2084

Situated behind the main street in the centre of town this first-floor flat comprises kitchen/dining room, sitting room, one double bedroom, off which are two single bedrooms, and shower room.

All year MWB out of season 3 mths max, 1 unit, 1–4 persons ◆ no pets ◎
fridge Panel heating Elec metered
⌁ can be hired ☎(200yds) ⊙ CTV
⊕3 pin square 2P 🎞 ♨(100yds)
⊖ ♪(½m) ☎(100yds) 🎵(100yds)
🎯(¾m)
Min£90 Max£100pw (Low)
Min£115 Max£130pw (High)

PITTENWEEM
Fife
Map**11** NO50

Ch J W Duncan **Grangemuir Woodland Park** Pittenweem, Anstruther, Fife KY10 2RB
☎Anstruther(0333)311213

Pipers Pool
—
Plymouth

Finnish pine chalets with verandahs in secluded setting offering well-appointed accommodation of modern lounge/diner/kitchen, three bedrooms and bathroom.

1 Apr–3 Nov MWB out of season 2 nights min, 2 mths max, 15 units, 1–6 persons [◈ ◆] no pets ◎
fridge Electric Elec metered
⌁ inclusive ☎(50yds) Iron & Ironing board in unit [Launderette on premises]
⊙ CTV ⊕3 pin square 30P 🎞
♨(50yds) Games room Nature trail
⊖ ♪(2m) ♀(50yds) 🎞(2m) 🎵(2m)
Min£75 Max£245pw

PLAITFORD
Hampshire
Map**4** SU21

F Mrs J M Brindle **1 Bridgefoot Cottage** Sherfield English Road, Plaitford, Romsey, Hampshire
☎West Wellow(0794)23197

A modern, well maintained garden flat offering combined lounge/diner ktichen, one double-bedded room, shower and WC. Quietly located close to the New Forest, Winchester, Salisbury and Southampton.

All year MWB out of season 1 wk min, 28 days max, 1 unit, 2 persons ◇ ◈ ◆
no pets ◎   fridge 🍴 Elec inclusive
⌁ inclusive WM & SD in unit TD on premises Iron & Ironing board in unit
⊙ ⊗ CTV ⊕3 pin square 2P 🎞
♨(2m)
⊖ ♪(3m) ♀(½m)
Details not confirmed for 1987

PLUMMERS PLAIN
West Sussex
Map**4** TQ22

B Silver Crest
for bookings Mrs S M Passfield, Plummers Plain, Horsham, West Sussex
☎Lower Beeding(040376)285

Brick-built bungalow in own grounds, set in a peaceful and remote but not isolated position. It is on the edge of St Leonards Forest. Accommodation comprises lounge/dining area with polished wooden floor, kitchen, bathroom/WC, laundry room and a conservatory. There are three bedrooms sleeping up to six people.

All year MWB out of season 1 day min, 1 unit, 6 persons ◇ ◈ ◆ fridge 🍴 Elec metered ⌁ can be hired
☎(600yds) [WM & SD in unit] Iron & Ironing board in unit ⊙ TV
⊕3 pin square 2P 1🎙 🎞 ♨(500yds)
⊖ ♪(1m) ♀(1m) 🎞(3m)
Min£70 Max£135pw

PLYMOUTH
Devon
Map**2** SX45
F Breckon House, 20 Connaught Avenue, Mutley
for bookings Mr & Mrs Broad-Kemp, Denrut Properties, 38 Vapron Road, Mannamead, Plymouth, Devon PL3 5NN
☎Plymouth(0752)669066

Three select apartments in a Victorian terraced residence approximately one mile from the city centre. Each unit is self-contained and comprises a lounge/diner, kitchen, bathroom, one has a double bedroom, one two twin rooms and the third two twins and a single bedroom. All are air-conditioned, well decorated and furnished.

All year MWB 3 days min, 3 mths max, 3 units, 2–5 persons [◇] ◆ no pets
◎   fridge Storage heaters
Elec inclusive ⌁ inclusive ☎ SD in unit Iron & Ironing board in unit ⊙
CTV ⊕3 pin square 3P 🎞 ♨(100yds)
⊖ ♀(100yds) 🎞(1m) 🎵(1m)
🎯(1m) Sports centre(1m)
Min£181 Max£381pw

F 13, 15, 17 & 19 Buckley Quarry, Park Road, Plymstock
for bookings Mr & Mrs Broadkemp, Denrut Properties Ltd, 38 Vapron Road, Mannamead, Plymouth, Devon PL3 5NN
☎Plymouth(0752)669066

Situated in quiet residential road 5 miles from city centre. **15** *&* **17** *are on ground floor* **13** *&* **19** *are on first floor. All flats comprise lounge/diner, large twin-bedded room plus bed settee.*

All year MWB 3 days min, 3 mths max, 4 units, 3 persons [◇] ◈ ◆ ◎
fridge 🍴 Elec inclusive ⌁ inclusive
☎ SD in unit Iron & Ironing board in unit ⊙ CTV ⊕3 pin square 🎞
⊖ ♪(2m) ♀(½m)
Min£100 Max£120pw

F Hoeside Flats 1A, 2A & 3A 10 Athenaeum Street, The Hoe
for bookings Mrs D L Seymour, 170 Beacon Park Road, Beacon Park, Plymouth PL22QS
☎Plymouth(0752)563504

Three maisonettes, each set on two floors, conveniently situated within walking distance of Plymouth Hoe. **Flat 1A** *comprises two twin-bedded rooms, lounge, kitchen with breakfast bar and fridge and combined bathroom/WC. High chairs are provided in flat.* **Flat 2A** *has one twin-bedded room, lounge, kitchen, with fridge and breakfast bar, and combined bathroom.* **Flat 3A** *consists of one double bedroom, one twin and bunk-bedded room, lounge, modern fitted kitchen with breakfast bar and fridge.*

All year 1 wk min, 1 mth max, 3 units, 2–8 persons ◆ ◎ Electric
Elec metered ⌁ inclusive ☎ Iron & Ironing board in unit [Launderette within 300yds] ⊙ CTV ⊕3 pin square →

⊕2pin round　P　🛁(10yds)　⌐
🏌Hard/grass　putting

⦿ 💈 🎰 🎵 🐴

Min£60 Max£120pw (Low)
Min£110 Max£145pw (High)

F 41 & 41A Kimbra Pasley Street, Stoke
for bookings Mr & Mrs Broad-Kemp, 38
Vapron Road, Mannamead, Plymouth,
Devon PL3 5NN
☎Plymouth(0752)669066

*Near the centre of Plymouth in quiet
residential area. 41 is a ground floor flat,
with hallway lounge/dining room, kitchen,
bathroom with WC and two twin-bedded
rooms. 41A on first floor is similar but also
has a childrens cabin bedded room and a
small off lounge.*

All year　MWB　3days min, 3mths max,
2units, 4–5persons　[◇]　◆　◆　⦿
fridge　🍴　Elec inclusive　🔲inclusive
🎗 SD in unit　Iron & Ironingboard in
unit　[Launderette within 300yds]　☉
CTV　⊕3pin square　🔲　🛁(½m)

⦿ 💈(½m)　🎵(2m)　🎵(2m)　🐴(2m)
Sports centre(1m)

Min£120 Max£150pw

F Kobe House 14a Alexandra Road,
Mutley
for bookings Mr & Mrs Broad-Kemp,
Denrut Properties, 38 Vapron Road,
Mannamead, Plymouth, Devon PL3 5NN
☎Plymouth(0752)669066

*Close to the city centre, three select
apartments in a Victorian corner house.
Each is self-contained and comprises
lounge/diner, kitchen, bathroom, two of
the flats are ground floor, with one twin
bedroom, the third flat is on the first floor
and has two twin bedrooms. All three have
air-conditioning and are well equipped.*

All year　MWB　3days min, 3mths max,
3units, 2–4persons　[◇]　◆　no pets
⦿　fridge　storage heaters
Elec inclusive　🔲inclusive　🎗 SD in
unit　Iron & Ironing board in unit　☉
CTV　⊕3pin square　P　🔲　🛁(100yds)

⦿ 💈(100yds)　🎵(1m)　🎵(1m)
🐴(1m)　Sports centre(1m)

Min£181 Max£315pw

POLPERRO
Cornwall
Map**2** SX25

C Beville Cottage The Coombes
for bookings Mrs N J Blake, Sunways, the
Coombes, Polperro, Cornwall
☎Polperro(0503)72485

*Old terraced cottage comprising lounge/
diner, kitchen, two double bedrooms (one
with an additional single bed) and
bathroom. Parking by arrangement.*

All year　MWB out of season　1wk min,
2wks max, 1unit, 1–5persons, nc7
no pets　⦿　fridge　Electric
Elec metered　🔲not provided　☉ CTV
⊕3pin square　🔲　🛁(100yds)

⦿ 💈

Min£48 Max£98pw (Low)
Min£155 Max£172pw (High)

Plymouth
—
Polzeath

C Bwthyn Cernywaidd Little Laney
for bookings Mrs N J Blake, Sunways, The
Coombes, Polperro, Cornwall
☎Polperro(0503)72485

*Old terraced cottage extensively
modernised with open staircase, lounge,
dining room, kitchen, two double
bedrooms, a single bedroom and
bathroom. Close to harbour. Car parking
by arrangement.*

All year　MWB out of season　1wk min,
2wks max, 1unit, 5persons, nc7　no pets
⦿　fridge　Electric　Elec metered
🔲not provided　🎗(300yds)　Iron &
Ironing board in unit　☉　🐝　CTV
⊕3pin sqaure　🔲　🛁(100yds)

⦿ 💈 (300yds)

Min£45 Max£98pw (Low)
Min£158 Max£178pw (High)

C Crumplehorn Cottages 1 & 2
for bookings Mrs W J M Collings, Brook
Cottage, Longcombe Lane, Polperro,
Cornwall PL13 2PL
☎Polperro(0503)72274

*Two stone-built cottages in a terrace of
three situated at the entrance of this
Cornish fishing village. One has lounge/
diner with kitchen area, bathroom and
WC, and one family bedroom sleeping
three. The other cottage has a kitchen/
diner, lounge with open fireplace, two
bedrooms, bathroom and WC.*

All year　MWB out of season　1wk min,
1mth max, 2units, 2–5persons　◆　⦿
fridge　Electric (1unit)　Elec metered
🔲can be hired　🎗 Iron & Ironing board
in unit　☉ 🐝(1unit)　CTV
⊕3pin square　⊕2pin round　P　🔲
🛁(100yds)

⦿ 💈(3m)　💈 🎵(½m)　🎵(½m)

Min£65 Max£200pw

C Hael-a-Gwynt Little Laney
for bookings Miss L G Blake, Sunways,
The Coombes, Polperro, Cornwall
☎Polperro(0503)72485

*Well modernised old terraced cottage with
two double bedrooms, lounge/diner,
kitchenette and bathroom. Car parking by
arrangement. Close to harbour.*

All year　MWB out of season　1wk min,
2wks max, 1unit, 2–4persons, nc7
no pets　⦿　fridge　Electric
Elec metered　🔲not provided
🎗(300yds)　Iron & Ironing board in unit
☉ CTV　⊕3pin square　🔲　🛁(100yds)

⦿ 💈 (300yds)

Min£48 Max£98pw (Low)
Min£155 Max£172pw(High)

H Seabreeze Cottage 88 Carey Park
for bookings W J M & G Collings, Brook
Cottage, Longcombe Lane, Polperro,
Cornwall PL13 2PL
☎Polperro(0503)72274

*A modern detached house, situated at the
entrance to Polperro and comprising
entrance hall with open tread staircase,
modern kitchen, lounge/diner, one double,
one twin bedroom and a bunk-bedded
room, bathroom and separate WC.
Modern, well-equipped accommodation.*

All year　MWB out of season　2nights min
3mths max　1unit　2–6persons　[◇]
◆　◆　⦿　fridge　🍴　Elec metered
🔲inclusive　Iron & Ironing board in unit
☉ CTV　⊕3pin square　1P　1🏠　🔲
🛁(300yds)

⦿ 💈(3m)　💈 (300yds)　🎵(300yds)
🎵(300yds)

Min£80 Max£225pw

B Sunny Harbour Cottage The
Coombes
for bookings WJM & G Collings, Brook
Cottage, Longcombe Lane, Polperro,
Cornwall, PL13 2PL
☎Polperro(0503)72274

*A detached bungalow, approached by a
stone bridge over the Pol, with
accommodation comprising lounge, well-
equipped kitchen/diner, two double
bedrooms, one with extra single bed,
bathroom and WC. Good standard of
decor and furnishing throughout.*

All year　MWB out of season　2nights min
3mths max　1unit　2–5persons　[◇]
◆　◆　⦿　fridge　Electric fires
Elec metered　🔲can be hired
🎗(300yds)　Iron & Ironing board in unit
☉ CTV　⊕3pin square　1P　🔲
🛁(100yds)

⦿ 💈(3m)　💈 (½m)　🎵(½m)

Min£75 Max£105pw(Low)
Min£105 Max£200pw (High)

POLZEATH
Cornwall
Map**2** SW97

F & B Mr & Mrs T. Wheatman **Polzeath
Holiday Cottage & Apartments** Polzeath,
Wadebridge, Cornwall
☎Trebetherick(020 886)2371

*A former hotel converted into nine flats,
most with good coastal views. All flats
have lounge/diner with incorporated
kitchen, bathroom/WC. Sleeping
accommodation varies. The detached
white bungalow is adjacent to the flats
and comprises, lounge/diner with bed-
settee, two double bedded rooms one with
bunks both with wash basin, well
equipped kitchen, bathroom and WC.
Both the flats and bungalow are well
furnished and decorated and only a short
distance from beach.*

Mar–Dec　MWB out of season
3days min　1mth max　10units
1–8persons　◆　◆　no pets in flats
⦿　fridge　Electric　Elec metered
🔲not provided　🎗 Iron & Ironing board
on premises　[Launderette on premises]
☉ CTV in bungalow　CTV in flats
⊕3pin square　P　🔲　🛁(300yds)

⦿ 💈(2½m)　💈

Min£45 Max£160pw (Low)
Min£135 Max£220pw (High)

F F M W & A E Rhodes **Westward**
Polzeath, Cornwall PL27 6TQ
☎Trebetherick(020886)3235

Fourteen purpose-built flats built in 1970 on two floors, the first-floor units open onto a verandah. Each property comprises a lounge/diner with bed-settee, and kitchen leading off, one double- and one twin-bedded room, and bathroom/WC, and are well decorated throughout.

Allyear MWB out of season 3days min, 4wks max, 14units, 1–6persons ◈ ♦no pets ◎ fridge Electric Elec metered 🄻not provided ☎ [WM & TD on premises] Iron & Ironing board on premises ⊙ CTV 🅼 ⛴(400yds)

⊖ ♂(2½m) ♀(50yds)

Min£84 Max£210pw

PONTSHAEN
Dyfed
Map**2** SN45

C A D & L A Nunn **Castell Howell**
Pontshaen, Llandysul, Dyfed SA44 4UA
☎Pontshaen(054 555)209

A group of well equipped cottages in a rural setting offering a full range of leisure facilities. The cottages are about 200 years old with thick stone walls and slate roofs and have been converted from genuine Welsh farm outbuildings.

Allyear MWB 1day min, 6wks max, 10units, 2–7persons [◇] ◈ ♦ ◎ fridge 🔥 Elec inclusive Gas metered 🄻inclusive ☎(100yds) [Launderette on premises] ⊙ CTV ⊕3pin square P 🅼 ⛴(1½m) 🏊heated squash court, table tennis, restaurant, licensed bar

Min£90 Max£335pw

POOLE
Dorset
Map**4** SZ09

F **Aern House** 93 Tatnam Road
for bookings Mrs P Broad, 63 Springdale Road, Broadstone, Dorset BH18 9BN
☎Broadstone(0202)698957

An individually designed purpose-built block of two flats in a quiet residential area. Each fully-equipped unit has one or two twin-bedded rooms, hall, lounge, kitchen and bathroom/WC. Tatnam Road lies off the A349 Wimborne Road.

Allyear MWB out of season 2days min, 1mth max, 2units, 2–4persons ◈ ♦ no pets ◎ fridge Electric Elec metered 🄻inclusive ☎(¼m) Iron & Ironing board in unit [Launderette within 300yds] ⊙ ⊕3pin square 🏠 🅼 ⛴(¼m)

⊖ ♂(2m) ♀(¼m) 🎵(¼m) ♫(¼m) 🎥(½m)

Min£66 Max£150pw (Low)
Min£110 Max£196pw (High)

F **28 Banks Road**
for bookings Mrs J W Philips, 7 Brownsea Road, Sandbanks, Poole, Dorset BH13 7QW
☎Poole(0202)708600

Two flats in modern style house, situated on approach road to ferry departure point and, within walking distance of beach. Both flats have two twin bedded rooms and two double bedded rooms (one double has en suite shower/WC), bath/WC. ***Flat 1*** *on ground floor has large kitchen/diner, lounge plus sun lounge and patio.* ***Flat 2*** *on first floor has large lounge with dining area and small kitchen.*

Allyear 1wk min, 3wks max, 2units, 2–8persons ◈ [♦] no pets ⌀ fridge 🔥 Gas & Elec charged 🄻can be hired ☎ SD in unit Iron & Ironing board in unit CTV ⊕3pin square 6P 🅼 ⛴(150yds)

⊖ ♂(2m) ♀(250yds) 🎵(250yds) ♫(250yds)

Min£100 Max£180pw (Low)
Min£330 Max£400pw (High)

B **8 Brownsea Road** Sandbanks
for bookings Mrs J W Philips, 7 Brownsea Road, Sandbanks, Poole, Dorset BH13 7QW
☎Poole(0202)708600

A detached bungalow with rear garden and small front garden. In quiet road close to Sandbank beaches. Comprises good size kitchen, large dining room, lounge, one double, one twin, and one bunk-bedded room, bathroom/WC plus separate WC.

Allyear 1wk min, 3wks max, 1unit, 2–6persons ◈ [♦] no pets ⌀ fridge 🔥 Gas & Elec charged 🄻can be hired ☎ SD in unit Iron & Ironing board in unit [CTV] ⊕3pin square 2P 1🏠 🅼 ⛴(¼m)

⊖ ♂(2m) ♀(250yds) 🎵(250yds) ♫(250yds)

Min£100 Max£160pw (Low)
Min£330 Max£375pw (High)

H **25, 27 & 29 Longfleet Road**
for bookings Mr M Clayton, 5 Arran Mews, Crosslands Avenue, Ealing, London W5 3QH
☎01-993-2095

Early 20th-century terraced houses containing three bedrooms, kitchen, bathroom, lounge/diner in ***Nos 25*** *and* ***27****; separate lounge and dining rooms in* ***No 29****. Close to town centre.*

Allyear 1wk min, 8mths max, 3units, 2–10persons ◈ ♦ ◎ fridge Electric Elec metered 🄻can be hired ☎(150yds) Iron & Ironing board in unit CTV ⊕3pin square 3P 🅼 ⛴(200yds)

⊖ ♂(2m) ♀(200yds) 🎵(¾m) ♫(¾m) 🎥(200yds)

Min£90 Max£120pw (Low)
Min£250 Max£295pw (High)

F **31, 33 & 35 Longfleet Road**
for bookings Mr M Clayton, 5 Arran Mews, Crosslands Avenue, Ealing, London W5 3QH
☎01-993 2095

Dating from the early 1900's ***No31*** *contains two flats, each having lounge/diner, bathroom, kitchen and two bedrooms.* ***No 33*** *offers three flats, one with two bedrooms and two with one bedroom, also lounge/diner, small kitchen and bathroom. Finally,* ***No 35*** *houses a neat one-bedroomed flat with lounge, kitchen and shower/WC.*

Allyear MWB out of season 1wk min, 8mths max, 6units, 2–6persons ◈ ♦ ◎ fridge Electric Elec metered 🄻can be hired ☎ Iron & Ironing board in unit ⊙ CTV ⊕3pin square 6P 🅼 ⛴(200yds)

⊖ ♂(2m) ♀(200yds) 🎵(¾m) ♫(¾m) 🎥(200yds)

Min£75 Max£100pw (Low)
Min£110 Max£195pw (High)

F **71 Panorama Road (Flat A & B)**
for bookings Mrs J W Philips, 7 Brownsea Road, Sandbanks, Poole, Dorset BH13 7QW
☎Poole(0202)708600

The flats are part of a detached bungalow, close to beaches and ferry. ***Flat A*** *has a simple lounge/diner/kitchen area, one bedroom with double and single bed with shower/WC en suite.* ***Flat B*** *has large kitchen/diner, good size lounge, two twin bedded rooms, one room with double bed, single bed and shower/WC.*

Allyear 1wk min, 3wks max, 2units, 2–7persons ◈ [♦] no pets ⌀ fridge Elec/storage heaters Gas & Elec charged 🄻can be hired ☎Flat B SD in unit Iron & Ironing board in unit CTV ⊕3pin square P 🅼 ⛴(¼m)

⊖ ♂(2m) ♀(250yds) 🎵(250yds) ♫(250yds)

Min£60 Max£150pw (Low)
Min£180 Max£350pw (High)

PORT APPIN
Strathclyde *Argyllshire*
Map**14** NM94

C **Spring Cottage**
for bookings D E Hutchison, Kinlochlaich House, Appin, Argyll PA38 4BD
☎Appin(063173)342

Set in its own, rough garden which runs down to the shore of Loch Creran offering magnificent views over Loch Linnhe to Lismore, Morven and Mull. Accommodation comprises lounge/diner, kitchen, one twin-bedded room, one double-bedded room, one bunk-bedded room and bathroom. Situated 1m S of Port Appin on an unclass road.

Apr–Oct 1wk min, 5wks max, 1unit, 1–8persons ◈ no pets ◎ fridge Electric Elec inclusive 🄻not provided ☎(1m) SD in unit Iron in unit ⊙ ⊕3pin square P ⛴(1m)

⊖ ♀(1m)

Min£90pw (Low)
Min£225pw (High)

PORT CHARLOTTE
Strathclyde *Argyllshire*
See **Islay, Isle of**

PORT DINORWIC
Gwynedd
Map**6** SH56

F **23 Ffordd Garnedd** Port Dinorwic
for bookings R D Vellacott, Lineridge
House, Chollacott Lane, Tavistock
PL19 9DD.
☎Tavistock(0822)3225

*Modern, well-equipped second-floor flat
overlooking Menai Straits. It comprises
large lounge/diner with kitchenette, three
bedrooms (one double, one twin, one with
bunk beds), bathroom/WC. Located on a
new marina development.*

All year 1wk min, 6wks max, 1unit,
2–6persons ◆ no pets ◎ fridge
portable & storage heaters [Elec]
☎(½m) WM & SD in unit Iron & Ironing
board in unit ⊙ ⊗ CTV
⊕3pin square 2P ▥ ▱(½m) Slipway
& mooring facilities
↔ ♨(½m)
Min£37.50 Max£95pw (Low)
Min£125 Max£155pw (High)

F **61 Ffordd Garnedd**
for bookings Mrs W M Gillibrand, Crud-y-
Gwynt, Tal-y-coe, Tregarth, Bangor,
Gwynedd LL57 4AE.
☎Bangor(0248)600916

*61 Ffordd Garnedd is a first-floor flat and
has three bedrooms, one double bedded,
one twin-bedded and one with two bunk
beds, bathroom/WC and lounge/diner
with open plan kitchen.*

All year 1wk min, 6wks max, 1unit,
1–6persons [◇] ◆ ◆ no pets ◎
fridge Electric Elec metered ⊔can be
hired ☎ Iron & Ironing board in unit
[Launderette within 300yds] ⊙ CTV
⊕3pin square 2P ▥ ▱(¼m)
↔ ♨(½m)
Min£75 Max£83pw (Low)
Min£114 Max£152pw (High)

PORTHALLOW
Cornwall
Map**2** SW82

F Mr A R Peters **Gallentreath
Selfcatering Holiday Flats,** Porthallow, St
Keverne, Helston, Cornwall
☎St Keverne(0326)280400

*Six modern purpose built holiday flats,
situated adjacent to the proprietors
guesthouse. Two of the flats have one
double bedroom and one with bunks the
other four flats have one double, one twin
and a pull down double bed in the lounge.
They all have kitchen/diner/lounge and
either bathroom or shower and WC.*

All year MWB out of season 3days min,
6wks max, 6units, 1–6persons ◆ ◆
◎ fridge Elec metered ⊔can be
hired ☎(200yds) [WM, SD & TD on

premises] Iron & Ironing board on
premises ⊙ CTV ⊕3pin square 6P
▥ ▱(200yds)
↔ ♨(200yds)
Min£85 Max£110pw (Low)
Min£130 Max£175pw (High)

PORTHGAIN
Dyfed
Map**2** SM83

H **Kiln House**
for bookings Coastal Cottages of
Pembrokeshire, Seaview, Abercastle,
Mathry, Dyfed SA62 5HJ
☎Croesgoch(03483)7742

*A beautifully situated house built almost
above an old time kiln and right by the
small harbour. It has good sea views from
most rooms and comprises sitting room
with open fire, kitchen/diner with oil fired
Aga cooker, utility room with WC,
bathroom, two double bedrooms, one twin
bedroom and one with bunks.*

All year MWB out of season 4days min,
2mths max, 1unit, 4–8persons ◆ ◆
Aga, oil fired fridge open & electric
heaters Oil inclusive Elec metered
⊔can be hired ☎(50yds) WM & SD in
unit Iron & Ironing board in unit ⊙
CTV ⊕3pin square 2P 1▥ ▥
▱(1m)
↔ ♨(100yds)
Min£85 Max£370pw

PORTHLEVEN
Cornwall
Map**2** SW62

F **Harbourside Holiday Flats (1–4)**
for bookings Mrs E M Stoyles, 1 Rock
Road, The Lidden, Penzance, Cornwall
TR18 4PS
☎Penzance(0736)62834

*Former Cornish cannery converted into
flats adjacent to harbour, in the heart of
the village. Flats 1 & 3 on the first floor
have one double and one twin bedded
room plus foldaway bed, lounge/diner,
kitchen, bathroom and WC. Flat 2 & 4 on
the second floor have a double bedroom,
twin bedroom, (also a foldaway single bed
in flat 2), lounge/diner, kitchen, bathroom
and WC.*

All year MWB out of season 1wk min,
4units, 1–5persons no pets ◎ fridge
Electric Elec metered ⊔can be hired
☎(100yds) Iron & Ironing board in unit
[Launderette within 300yds] ⊙ CTV
⊕3pin square 1P ▥ ▱(100yds)
↔ ♨(50yds) 🎵(2m) 🎵(2m) ⛟
Min£70 Max£145pw

PORT ISAAC
Cornwall
Map**2** SW98

H CC Ref 314E
for bookings Character Cottages
(Holidays) Ltd, 34 Fore Street, Sidmouth,
Deon EX10 8AQ
☎Sidmouth(03955)77001

*Georgian-type house in secluded position
with good views and terraced garden.
Accommodation includes 'L' shaped living
room with bow window, three bedrooms
(one double, one twin, one single) all
newly furnished, modern bathroom and
toilet facilities.*

Mar–Aug 1wk min, 1mth max, 1unit,
2–5persons ◆ ◎ fridge ▦
Elec inclusive ⊔can be hired
☎(200yds) Iron & Ironing board in unit
⊙ TV ⊕3pin square ⊕2pin round
P ▥ ▥ ▱
↔ ♨
Min£104 Max£233pw

B & H Mr & ,Mrs J H P Symons **Damson
& Rose Cottage,** Trevathan Farm, St
Endellion, Port Isaac, Cornwall PL29 3TT
☎Bodmin(0208)880248

*Damson Cottage is a single storey stone
and slate former stable converted in 1984,
and set in ¼ acre of private garden. It
comprises a spacious living room, kitchen
area, one double and one twin bedroom
and bathroom/WC. Rose Cottage is a 17th
century stone and slate farmhouse with
good views from all windows. The lounge
has a rustic slate fireplace and there is
also a double bed settee, kitchen dining
room, separate WC and upstairs there is
one double, one twin and one bunk-
bedded room and the bathroom.*

All year MWB out of season 2days min,
1mth max, 2units, 2–8persons ◇ ◆
◆ fridge Electric, open &
log burner Elec metered ⊔can be
hired ☎(½m) WM in unit TD in unit
(Rose Cottage) Iron & Ironing board in
unit ⊙ CTV ⊕3pin square 4P ▥
▱(1½m) ♨Hard
↔ ♨(2m)
Min£35 Max£80pw (Low)
Min£92 Max£218pw (High)

PORTKNOCKIE
Grampian *Banffshire*
Map**15** NJ56

C **30 Church Street**
for bookings Scott Holiday Homes, 8
Markethill Road, Turriff, Aberdeenshire
☎Turriff(0888)63524

*Attractively modernised cottage on main
street of little fishing village.
Accommodation comprises one double
and one triple bedroom, lounge, kitchen/
dining room and bathroom.*

All year MWB out of season 3days min,
1unit, 1–5persons ◆ ◎ fridge
Electric Elec metered ⊔not provided
☎(200yds) WM & SD in unit Iron &
Ironing board in unit ⊙ CTV
⊕3pin square 2P ▱(200yds)
↔ δ(1m) ♨(600yds)
Min£70 Max£140pw

C No 1 Cliff Terrace
for bookings Scott Holiday Homes, 8
Markethill Road, Turriff, Aberdeenshire
☎Turriff(0888)63524

*Modernised stone cottage in quiet street
which overlooks the harbour of fishing
village. The cottage offers lounge, small
kitchen, two bedrooms and bathroom.*

All year MWB out of season 3days min,
1unit, 1–5persons ◆ ◆ ◎ fridge
Electric Elec metered ⌷not provided
☎(200yds) WM & SD in unit Iron &
Ironing board in unit ☉ CTV
⊕3pin square 2P 🔊(500yds)
↮ ♪(1½m) ☕(500yds)

Min£70 Max£140pw

H Cormorant & Gannet 23/25 Pulteney
Street
for bookings Blantyre Holiday Homes Ltd,
West Bauds, Findochty, Buckie, Moray
AB5 2ED
☎Buckie(0542)31773

*Two semi-detached houses both of which
offer comfortable accommodation of living
room (with bed-settee), modern kitchen,
bathroom, twin- and double-bedded
rooms. In quiet street above harbour.
Pulteney Street runs parallel to main street,
off A92.*

End Mar–end Oct MWB out of season
1wk min, 3wks max, 2unit, 1–6persons
[◇] [◆] [◆] ◎ fridge Electric
Elec metered ⌷can be hired
☎(300yds) Iron & Ironing board in unit
☉ CTV ⊕3pin square 🔊(300yds)
↮ ♪(2m) ☕(200yds)

Min£64pw (Low)
Min£145pw (High)

C Curlew 40 Church Street
for bookings Blantyre Holiday Homes Ltd,
West Bauds, Findochty, Buckie, Banffshire
AB5 2EB
☎Buckie(0542)31773

*Tasteful conversion of an old fisherman's
cottage situated in main street of village.
Accommodation comprises dining room,
modern open plan kitchen, lounge with
wood burning stove, a double and a twin
bedroom and bathroom. A neat, attractive
holiday home.*

Etr–Oct MWB out of season 1wk min,
3wks max, 1unit, 4–6persons [◆ ◆]
◎ fridge Electric & wood burning
stove Elec metered ⌷can be hired
☎(10yds) Iron & Ironing board in unit
☉ CTV ⊕3pin square 2P 🔟
🔊(300yds)
↮ ♪(2m) ☕(200yds)

Min£64 Max£145pw

C 12 & 14 Pulteney Street
for bookings Scott Holiday Homes, 8
Markethill Road, Turriff, Aberdeenshire
☎Turriff(0888)63524

*Two adjoining modernised cottages in
quiet street. The smaller property
comprises lounge, double and triple
bedrooms, kitchen/diner. The larger
property has lounge, dining room, kitchen,
shower room (no bath), double bedroom*

Portknockie
—
Portsmouth & Southsea

*on the ground-floor and double and twin
bedrooms on the first floor*

All year MWB out of season 3day min,
2units, 1–8persons ◆ ◎ fridge
Electric Elec metered ⌷not provided
☎ WM & SD in unit Iron & Ironing board
in unit ☉ CTV ⊕3pin square 2P
🔊(200yds)
↮ ♪(1m) ☕(600yds)

Min£70 Max£155pw

PORTMEIRION
Gwynedd
See **Penrhyndeudraeth**

PORT OF MENTEITH
Central *Perthshire*
Map**11** NN50

Ch Mrs J Nairn **Lochend Chalets**
Lochend House, Port of Menteith, Kippen,
Stirlingshire FK8 3JZ
☎Port of Menteith(087 75)268

*Attractive cedar wood and 'A' frame
chalets situated on the banks of the Lake
of Menteith with its island priory where
Mary, Queen of Scots was once held. Most
of the chalets have a view of the lake
through foliage. They comprise open-plan
kitchen, dining/lounge area and all have
verandahs. On the B8034.*

All year (Chalets), 29Mar–8Nov (Cabins)
MWB out of season 6mths max, 14units,
1–7persons [◇] ◆ no pets ◎
fridge Electric Elec metered
⌷inclusive ☎ [SD & TD on premises]
Iron & Ironing board on premises ◎
CTV ⊕3pin square 30P 🔟 🔊(5m)
Games room, boating & fishing
↮ ☕(1m)

Min£80 Max£150pw (Low)
Min£115 Max£290pw (High)

PORTPATRICK
Dumfries & Galloway *Wigtownshire*
Map**10** NX05

C, F & H Mrs E S Orr Ewing **Dunskey
Estate Holiday Houses** Portpatrick,
Stranraer, Wigtownshire
☎Portpatrick(077681)211

*Three cottages and a flat are all estate
properties and access, whilst not difficult,
is by unmetalled roads or tracks.
Auchtriemakain sits on the side of a hill
overlooking wooded glens and the Irish
Channel. The accommodation is for six
people. **Craigbowie** is a small cottage
adjacent to Dunskey House, it sleeps six in
a double, twin and bunk-bedded rooms
and has a sheltered wooded garden. **Glen
Cottage** is situated above two small bays
at the foot of Dunskey Glen amid unique
surroundings, it sleeps up to five people
and is ideal for families who like the
seclusion of the countryside as well as the
sea. **Home Farm Flat**, a self-contained*

---

*ground-floor flat adjoins the farmhouse
and looks into the attractive, but not
always tidy, farmyard (the buildings are
listed), and it sleeps two to three people.*

Apr–Sep 1wk min, 4units, 1–8persons
[◇] ◆ ◆ no pets in Craigbouie
◙ (Craigbouie & Glen Cottage) ◎
fridge 🐴 or Electric & open fires
Gas inclusive Elec metered
⌷can be hired ☎(1m) Iron & Ironing
board in unit TV available
⊕3pin square ⊕3pin round (Glen
Cottage) 8P 🔟 🔊(1m) Loch fishing,
Shooting in season Pony trekking
Gardens
↮ ♪(1m) ☕(1m)

Min£75 Max£185pw

PORTREE
Highland Inverness-shire
See **Skye, Isle of**

PORTSMOUTH & SOUTHSEA
Hampshire
Map**4** SZ69

**F Aucklands (Flats 1, 3, 4, 6, 9, 12, 13,
16, 18 & 19)**
for bookings 17 Auckland Road East,
Southsea, Portsmouth, Hampshire
PO5 2HA
☎Portsmouth(0705)756554 & 255362

*Well decorated and furnished flats (10 out
of 19 recommended) of varying sizes in
large Georgian house situated in a quiet
residential road close to all amenities.
Most have a modern kitchen with
breakfast bar and lounge area with
bedroom (Except two flats which have
either one or two bedrooms) and shower
room with WC. There are also two
apartments sleeping three people.*

All year MWB 1day min, 6mths max,
10units, 1–4persons ◆ ◎ fridge
Electric Elec metered ⌷inclusive ☎
Iron & Ironing board in unit [Launderette
within 300yds] ☉ TV ⊕3pin square
8P 5🏠 🔟 🔊(100yds)
↮ (1m & 3m) ♪ ☕(200yds)
🎵(200yds) ♪(200yds) 🍴(2m)

Min£60 Max£100pw (Low)
Min£80 Max£140pw (High)

F Craneswater 19 Craneswater Park
for bookings 17 Auckland Road East,
Southsea, Hampshire PO5 2HA
☎Portsmouth(0705)756554 & 255362

*Skilfully modernised Edwardian mansion
comprising a combination of studio and
one and two bedroomed flats, all with
compact showers, kitchen and lounge
areas. (Ten out of twelve units only listed).*

All year MWB 10units, 1–4persons ◆
◆ ◎ fridge electric Elec metered
⌷inclusive ☎ SD on premises Iron &
Ironing board in unit [Launderette within
300yds] ☉ CTV ⊕3pin square 7P
3🏠 🔟 🔊(400yds)
↮ ♪(3m) ☕(½m) 🎵(1m) ♪(1m)
🍴(1m)

Min£60 Max£100pw (Low)
Min£80 Max£140pw (High)

193

PORTSOY
Grampian *Banffshire*
Map**15** NJ56

F **54 Church Street**
for bookings Scott Holiday Homes, 8
Market Hill Road, Turriff, Aberdeenshire
AB5 7AZ
☎Turriff(0888)63524

*The upper section of a two storey house
with its own entrance to the rear, set en-
route to the harbour area. The flat
comprises lounge, modern kitchen with
dining facilities, two bedrooms and a
bathroom. There is also a grassy garden.*

All year MWB out of season 1wk min,
1unit, 4–5persons ◆ ⑩ fridge
Storage & Electric fires Elec metered
⎣not provided ☎(600yds) WM in unit
Iron & Ironing board in unit ☉ CTV
⊕3pin square P ♨(600yds)

↔ ♀(600yds)
Min£70 Max£140pw

PORTWAY
Hereford & Worcester
Map**3** SO44

H **No 2 Hermitage Cottage**
for bookings Mrs D Pritchett, Hermitage
Farm, Canon Pyon, Hereford, HR4 8NN
☎Hereford(0432)760217

*Semi-detached cottage situated on
tarmac driveway to the Hermitage Fruit
Farm, with views over adjacent fields and
orchards. Accommodation comprises a
lounge, open-plan kitchen/diner on
ground floor, one double and one twin
bedded room and bathroom on the first
floor.*

Mar–Oct MWB out of season
3nights min, 6mths max, 1unit,
1–4persons ◆ ❖ no pets ⑩
fridge oil-filled radiators & electric fires,
open fireplace Elec metered ⎣can be
hired ☎(1m) SD in unit Iron & Ironing
board in unit ☉ CTV ⊕3pin square
2P ♨(1½m)

↔ ♂(3m) ♀(1m)
Min£60 Max£104pw

B **Woodside**
for bookings Mrs D Pritchett, Hermitage
Farm, Canon Pyon, Hereford HR4 8NN
☎Hereford(0432)760217

*Spacious detached bungalow set in ¼ acre
of garden. Accommodation comprises a
large kitchen/diner, lounge, three
bedrooms (one double, one twin and one
single) and a bathroom.*

Mar–Oct MWB out of season 3days min,
6mths max, 1unit, 1–6persons ◆ ❖
no pets ⑩ fridge coal fire,
electric radiators Elec metered ⎣can be
hired ☎(½m) SD in unit Iron & Ironing
board in unit ☉ CTV ⊕3pin square
2P 1♨ ♨(2m)

↔ ♀(¼m)
Min£70 Max£112pw

PORT WILLIAM
Dumfries & Galloway *Wigtownshire*
Map**10** NX24

Portsoy
—
Powburn

See also **Eirig**

H **The Old Place of Monreith**
for bookings The Landmark Trust,
Shottesbrooke, Maidenhead, Berkshire
SL6 3SW
☎Littlewick Green(062882)5925

*This most attractive, comfortable recently
renovated 16th-century tower stands in a
lovely secluded Galloway location.
Comprising small sitting room, large
kitchen/dining room and two twin
bedrooms on first and second floors.
Reported to be haunted. High standards
throughout.*

All year MWB out of season 3wks max
1unit 1–8persons ◆ no cats ⑩
fridge ♨♨ Elec inclusive
⎣not provided ☎(2m) Iron & Ironing
board in unit ☉ ⊕3pin square 4P
1♨ ♨(5m)

Min£196 Max£330pw (Low)
Min£235 Max£345pw (High)

C **47 & 49 South Street**
for bookings Mrs F E Shaw, Blew House
Farm, Finghall, Leyburn, North Yorkshire
DL8 5ND
☎Bedale(0677)50374

*A pair of semi-detached two-storey
traditional style cottages with shared
garden to rear. Situated on the main street
on the edge of this coastal village. Each
comprises sitting room, living/dining room
and three bedrooms. No 47 has kitchen
and bathroom, whereas No 49 has a
shower room leading off a small kitchen.*

All year (No 49) & Mar–Nov (No 47)
1wk min, 2units, 1–6persons [◇] ◆
⑩ fridge Electric fires Elec inclusive
⎣can be hired (provided for overseas
visitors) ☎(No 47) ☎(100yds)
WM & SD in unit Airing cupboard
in No 47 only Iron & Ironing board
in unit HCE in unit ☉ CTV
⊕3pin square 2P No 49 only 🛏
♨(200yds)

↔ ♂♨(2m) ♀(200yds)
Details not confirmed for 1987

PORTWRINKLE
Cornwall
Map**2** SX35

C, F & H **Whitsand Bay Hotel**
Portwrinkle, Torpoint, Cornwall PL11 3BU
☎St Germans(0503)30276

*Accommodation comprises three cottages
three houses and three flats which are
located in the grounds of the hotel. They
are spacious and well furnished, have
ample wardrobe space and good décor.
The grounds are surrounded by an 18
hole golf course. There are panoramic sea
and cliff views with distant views of the
Eddystone lighthouse. The amenities of
the adjacent hotel are available.*

All year MWB out of season 1wk min,
6mths max, 9units, 2–8persons [◇ ❖
◆] ⑩ fridge Electric Elec metered
⎣can be hired ☎ CTV Launderette
within 300yds ☉ ⊕3pin square
⊕2pin round P 🛏 ♨(200yds) 🖼
↔ ♂ ♀

Min£69 Max£103.50pw (Low)
Min£138 Max£253pw (High)

POUNDSTOCK
Cornwall
Map**2** SX29

B **Cancleave**
for bookings Mr & Mrs A Cummins,
Mineshop, St Gennys, Bude, Cornwall
EX23 0NR
☎St Gennys(08403)338

*A solitary bungalow on cliff road between
Widemouth Bay and Crackington Haven.
Leave A39 at Box's shop for Widemouth
Bay. Turn left following the cliff road to 1m
W of Millook Haven. It is then on the right.
Accommodation includes two double
rooms, one with twin beds, a room with
bunks and Z-bed, a lounge/dining room,
kitchen and combined bathroom and WC.*

All year MWB out of season 1wk min,
6wks max, 1unit, 2–9persons ◆ ⑩
fridge night storage heaters
Elec metered ⎣can be hired ☎(2m)
Iron & Ironing board in unit CTV
⊕3pin square 2P ♨(3½m)

↔ ♀(3½m)
Min£63 Max£89pw (Low)
Min£124 Max£215pw (High)

H **JFH P6C**
for bookings John Fowler Holidays, Dept
58, Marlborough Road, Ilfracombe, Devon,
EX34 8PF
☎Ilfracombe(0271)66666

*A farmhouse situated in rural Cornwall. It
comprises lounge, dining room with
rayburn, kitchen, ground-floor, bathroom
and upstairs a family bedroom, one
double bedroom and also a single, all with
low ceilings. Stream fishing is available.*

Mar–Oct MWB out of season 1wk min,
1mth max, 1unit, 6persons [◇] ◆ ◆
⑩ fridge Electric & open fires (charge
for logs) Elec metered ⎣not provided
☎(1½m) Iron & Ironing board in unit
☉ CTV(metered) ⊕3pin square 4P
♨(1½m)

↔ ♂(3m) ♀(1½m) 🎵(3m) 🎵(3m)
Sports centre(3m)
Min£67.85 Max£182.85pw

POWBURN
Northumberland
Map**12** NU01

C & F **Breamish Valley Cottages**
for bookings Mr & Mrs A Hardie, Branton,
Powburn, Alnwick, Northumberland
NE66 4LW
☎Powburn(066578)263

*Two charming stone-built cottages and a
ground- and first-floor flat built around an
old courtyard setting. One of the cottages*

is single storey, the other with ground-floor bedrooms and first-floor open plan living room/kitchen. Both offer two bedrooms, bathroom/WC and additional single folding bed. The flats have open plan living room/kitchen, bathroom/WC and separate WC. There are three bedrooms plus single folding bed available.

All year MWB out of season 2nights min, 1mth max, 4units, 4–7persons [◇] ◈ ◆ ◉ fridge ♨ & wood burning stove Elec inclusive 🅛can be hired ☎ WM & SD on premises Iron & Ironing board in unit ⊕ CTV ⊕3pin square 8P 🎬 ♿(1m) Pottery shop & demonstrations, cycle hire, games room, children's outdoor play area. Freezer facilities.

⟊ 🍴(1m)
Min£84 Max£110pw (Low)
Min£155 Max£208pw (High)

PRESTATYN
Clwyd
Map**6** SJ08

Ca Presthaven Sands Holiday Park
for bookings Haven Holidays, P.O. Box 20, Quay Street, Truro, Cornwall TR1 2UG
☎Truro(0872)40400

Well furnished, compact log cabins within a large Holiday Park complex. All have open plan lounge/kitchen/diner with double bed-settee, one double, one bunk-bedded room or one twin-bedded room and bathroom/WC. Numerous leisure facilities available, including restaurant, sauna, solarium and private beach.

Etr–Sep MWB in season 2days min, 62units, 2–6persons [◇ ◈ ◆] ◉ fridge Portable heaters Elec metered 🅛inclusive ☎ [Launderette on premises] ⊕ CTV ⊕3pin square P ♿ ⬜& 🏊 ⚑Hard putting green ⟊ 🍴 📻 🎵

Min£85 Max£135pw (Low)
Min£160 Max£221pw (High)

PRIMROSE VALLEY
North Yorkshire
Map**8** TA17

Powburn
—
Pwllheli

Ch 5 The Paddock
for bookings Mrs J Nicholson, Edelweiss, North Drive, Bramhope, Leeds LS16 9DF
☎Leeds(0532)673487

A detached cedar chalet on the edge of a holiday village complex, of which all facilities are available. The accommodation comprises three bedrooms (one double and two single), living room, kitchen and bathroom. The chalet has a small lawned garden and is a few minutes walk from the beach (Primrose Valley), also approx two miles from Filey and six miles from Scarborough.

Mar–Oct 1wk min, 3mths max, 1unit, 1–4persons ◈ ◉ fridge Electric Elec metered 🅛can be hired ☎(200yds) Iron, Ironing board in unit [Launderette on premises] ⊕ CTV ⊕3pin square 1P ♿(200yds) ▦
⟊ ♪(2m) 🍴(200yds) 📻(200yds) 🎵(200yds) ☕(200yds)
Min£45 Max£140pw

PUDSEY
West Yorkshire
Map**8** SE23

H Calverley Old Hall Woodhall Road
for bookings Landmark Trust, Shottesbrooke Park, Maidenhead, Berkshire SL6 3SW
☎Littlewick Green(062882)5925

Wing of a traditional stone-built mansion house dating from Tudor/Elizabethan period, and beautifully restored. Accommodation comprises large lounge, kitchen, three bedrooms, bathroom with WC and separate WC.

All year MWB out of season 1wk min, 1unit, 1–6persons no pets ◉ fridge ♨ & open fire Elec inclusive 🅛inclusive ☎(300yds) Iron & Ironing board in unit [Launderette within 300yds] ⊕ ⊕3pin square 🎬 ♿(100yds)
⟊ ♪(2m) 🍴(200yds)

Min£112 Max£170pw (Low)
Min£120 Max£180pw (High)

PURLEY
Greater London
Map**4** TQ36

F 163–165 Brighton Road
for bookings Gillian Mitchell, London Country Apartments, Ravenscroft, Coulsdon Lane, Coulsdon, Surrey CR3 3QG
☎01-660 8167

Nine well-converted flats situated on A23 London–Brighton road. There are three different types of unit, one or two bedrooms with lounge, kitchen, bathroom, plus studio units which have combined bedroom/lounge, kitchen, bath or shower. Five of the units have automatic washing machines. All units have an inclusive weekly laundry/cleaning service.

All year MWB out of season 1wk min, 6mths max, 9units, 1–7persons [◇] ◈ ◆ pets by arrangement ⚬ fridge ♨ Gas/Elec metered 🅛inclusive ☎ Iron & Ironing board in unit ⊕ CTV ⊕3pin square 9P 🎬 ♿(½m)
⟊ ♪(1m) 🍴(300yds) 📻(300yds) 🎵(300yds) ☕(1m)
Min£105 Max£310pw

PWLLHELI
Gwynedd
Map**6** SH33

C & F Mrs J E Ellis **Gwynfryn Farm**
Pwllheli, Gwynedd LL53 5UF
☎Pwllheli(0758)612536

Converted farm buildings house the six units available, **Cwellyn, Dinas, Gwynant, Mymbyr** and **Padarn** and **Tegid**, offering two to four bedroomed accommodation with lounge/diner, kitchen and bathroom/WC. Also available is a three bedroomed apartment offering family accommodation of kitchen/diner, lounge and shower room/WC. The owners are happy for families to roam freely on this working organic farm. Fresh farm milk and free range eggs are available. There is also a games room for family use.

All year MWB out of season 2days min, 6wks max, 7units, 1–8persons [◇] ◈→

◆ pets by arrangement ◎ fridge
Storage heaters, electric & open fires
storage heating inclusive Elec metered
🅛 can be hired ☎(½m) [Launderette on
premises] ⊙ CTV ⊕3pin square
10P 🎬 ♨(1m)
⟷ ♪(1¼m) ♨(1m) 🎵(2m) 🐕(1m)
Min£51.75 Max£115pw (Low)
Min£132 Max£213pw (High)

H 31 Min-y-Mor Promenade
for bookings Shaws Holidays, Y Maes,
Pwllheli, Gwynedd LL53 5HA
☎Pwllheli(0758)613835 or 614422

*Modern town house with beautiful views of
Cardigan Bay. Accommodation comprises
lounge with balcony and dining area,
kitchen, utility/washroom, two double
bedrooms, one bunk-bedded room plus
double bed-settee in lounge and
bathroom/WC. Good comfortable
property on the sea-front.*

All year wknd min, 6wks max, 1unit,
2–8persons ◇ ◆ no pets ◎
fridge ♨ Elec metered
🅛 not provided ☎(½m) WM in unit Iron
& Ironing board in unit ⊙ CTV
⊕3pin square 1P 1🎬 ♨(300yds)
⟷ ♪(1m) ♨(300yds) 🐕(½m)
Min£45 Max£235pw

RAFFORD
Grampian *Morayshire*
Map**15** NJ05

Ch Mrs Du Boulay **Tulloch Holiday
Lodges** Rafford, Forres, Moray IV36 0RU
☎Forres(0309)73311

*A group of four attractive cedar wood
lodges lying in a peaceful setting amidst
Birchwood, off B9010, 4m S of Forres.
Each contains an open plan kitchen/
dining area, lounge with convertible
settee, two bedrooms and a modern
bathroom. Frozen food dishes are
available from Mrs Du Boulay.*

Apr–Dec MWB out of season
3nights min, 3wks max, 4units,
1–5persons [◇] ◇ ◆ ◎ fridge
♨ Elec metered 🅛 inclusive ◎ Iron &
Ironing board on premises ⊙ CTV
⊕3pin square P 🎬 ♨(4m) Tourist
Information Hut
Min£65 Max£195pw

Pwllheli
—
Rathillet

RASHFIELD
Strathclyde *Argyll*
Map**10** NS18

Ca Mrs Amy Bryden **Lamont Country
Highland Lodges** Rashfield, Dunoon,
Argyll PA23 8QT
☎Kilmun(036984)205

*These log cabins are attractively situated
in the Benmore National Forest Park area
of Argyll. Two sizes are available and all
are well-equipped. The larger cabin has
three bedrooms (the smaller two) and the
kitchen is separate from the living/dining
room area. All the cabins have sofa beds
which provide alternative sleeping in the
lounge area. Free golf at 18-hole course 6
miles from site can be arranged.*

All year MWB out of season 1night min,
28days max, 18units, 1–8persons ◇
◆ ◎ fridge Panel & storage
heating Elec metered 🅛 inclusive ☎
WM, SD & TD in unit Iron & Ironing
board in unit ⊙ CTV ⊕3pin square
2P 🎬 ♨(1m) Dishwasher, fridge-
freezer
⟷ ♨(1m)
Min£96 Max£155pw (Low)
Min£265 Max£295pw (High)

RATFORD BRIDGE
Dyfed
Map**2** SM81

C Mr & Mrs T A Poole **Solbury Mountain
Farm Cottages** Tiers Cross, Ratford
Bridge, Haverfordwest, Dyfed SA62 3SB
☎Haverfordwest(0437)5368

*Five attractive cottages located within
farm complex, the décor and furnishings
are of a good standard; they vary in size
sleeping up to five persons.*

All year MWB out of season 3days min,
5units, 2–5persons ◇ ◇ ◆
no pets ◎ fridge Electric & open fires
Elec inclusive (Heating) Elec metered
🅛 inclusive ☎(1m) Iron & Ironing board

---

on premises Launderette on premises
⊙ CTV ⊕3pin square 8P ♨(1m)
⟷ ♪(3m) ♨(1m) 🐕(3m)
Min£55 Max£265pw

RATHILLET
Fife
Map**11** NO32

C Cedar Cottage
for bookings Mr & Mrs A H B Wedderburn,
Mountquhanie Holiday Homes, Cupar,
Fife KY15 4QJ
☎Gauldry(082624)252 due to change to
(038236)252

*A modern timber cottage set in gardens
within an extensive estate and affording
excellent views. Accommodation
comprises two bedrooms, sleeping up to
six, lounge/diner, kitchen, bathroom/WC
and separate WC, all on ground level.*

All year MWB out of season 1wk min,
1mth max, 1unit, 2–6persons [◇] ◆
◆ ◎ fridge 🍴 Elec metered 🅛 can
be hired Iron & Ironing board in unit
[Launderette on premises] ⊙ CTV
⊕3pin square 2P 1🎬 ♨(3m)
🏌Hard Putting green Shooting &
fishing
⟷ ♨(3m)
Min£65 Max£160pw

H Creich Farmhouse
for bookings Mr & Mrs A H B Wedderburn,
Mountquhanie Holiday Homes, Cupar,
Fife KY15 4QJ
☎Gauldry(082624)252 due to change to
(038236)252

*A traditional Scottish lowland, stone
farmhouse standing back off the road. It
offers five first-floor bedrooms (one
double, four twins), sitting room, dining
room, large modernised kitchen and two
bathrooms.*

All year MWB out of season 1wk min,
1mth max, 1unit, 2–10persons ◇ ◎
fridge 🍴 Elec metered 🅛 can be
hired ☎ WM & TD in unit Iron &
Ironing board in unit CTV
⊕3pin square P 🎬 ♨(5m) 🏌
Pigeon shooting & fishing
Min£70 Max£190pw

196

F Dairy House
for bookings Mr & Mrs A H B Wedderburn,
Mountquhanie Holiday Homes, Cupar,
Fife KY15 4QJ
☎Gauldry(082624)252 due to change to
(038236)252
*Converted and modernised ground-floor
flat situated in a large mansion which
stands in an extensive estate. It comprises
four bedrooms (one with en suite
bathroom/WC) sleeping up to eight
people, sitting room, kitchen/diner and
bathroom. 1¼m NW of Rathillet.*

Allyear MWB out of season 1wk min,
1mth max, 1unit, 2–8persons ◆ ◎
fridge 🍳 Elec metered 📺can be
hired ☎ Iron & Ironing board in unit
[Launderette on premises] ⊕ CTV
⊕3pin square P Ⅲ ♨(5m) ⚓Hard
Pigeon shooting & agate hunting
↔ ♨(3m)
Min£70 Max£180pw

C Drumnod Cottages
for bookings Mr & Mrs A H B Wedderburn,
Mountquhanie Holiday Homes, Cupar,
Fife KY15 4QJ
☎Gauldry(082624)252 due to change to
(038236)252
*Two converted semi-detached stone farm
cottages on hill position commanding
good views, each consisting of two bunk-
bedded rooms (one also has bunk beds),
combined sitting room/lounge, kitchen
and bathroom. Via A914 to Rathillet then
turn left and drive for 1m.*

Allyear MWB out of season 1wk min,
1mth max, 2units, 2–6persons ◆ ◎
fridge 🍳 (log fired stove) Elec metered
📺can be hired ☎ Iron & Ironing board
in unit ⊕ CTV ⊕3pin square P Ⅲ

Rathillet
—
Redruth

♨(5½m) ⚓Hard Pigeon shooting &
agate hunting
↔ ♨(3m)
Min£55 Max£125pw

C Foresters Cottage
for bookings Mr & Mrs A H B Wedderburn,
Mountquhanie Holiday Homes, Cupar,
Fife KY15 4QJ
☎Gauldry(082624)252 due to change to
(038236)252
*A modernised 18th-century stone cottage
in rural setting and with good enclosed
garden. It offers quality throughout
comprising modern lounge, kitchen/dining
area, three twin bedrooms on ground floor
plus two large attic single bedrooms,
bathroom and separate shower room.*

Allyear MWB out of season 1wk min,
1mth max, 1unit, 1–8persons [◇] ◆
◆•◎ fridge 🍳 Elec metered 📺can
be hired ☎ Iron & Ironing board in unit
[Launderette on premises] ⊕ CTV
⊕3pin square 4P ♨(3m) ⚓Hard
putting Shooting, fishing
↔ ♨(3m)
Min£70 Max£170pw

F Gillespie House
for bookings Mr & Mrs A H B Wedderburn,
Mountquhanie Holiday Homes, Cupar,
Fife KY15 4QJ
☎Gauldry(082624)252 due to change to
(038236)252
*Converted and modernised ground-floor
flat in a large mansion standing in an
extensive estate. It comprises three twin-
bedded rooms, sitting/dining room,*

*kitchen and bathroom with bidet. 1m down
a left turn from Rathillet and A914.*

Allyear MWB out of season 1wk min,
1mth max, 1unit, 2–6persons ◆ ◎
fridge 🍳 Elec metered 📺can be
hired ☎ Iron & Ironing board in unit
[Launderette on premises] ⊕ CTV
⊕3pin square P Ⅲ ♨(5m) ⚓Hard
Pigeon shooting & agate hunting
↔ ♨(3m)
Min£65 Max£160pw

H The Lodge
for bookings Mr & Mrs A H B Wedderburn,
Mountquhanie Holiday Homes, Cupar,
Fife KY15 4QJ
☎Gauldry(082624)252 due to change to
(038236)252
*Stone lodge standing at a minor entrance
to the Mountquhanie Estate. The Lodge
offers three twin-bedded rooms, sitting/
dining room, kitchen and bathroom. Via
A914 to Rathillet, then turn left for 1m.*

Allyear MWB out of season 1wk min,
1mth max, 1unit, 2–6persons ◆ ◎
fridge 🍳 Elec metered 📺can be
hired ☎ Iron & Ironing board in unit
[Launderette within 300yds] ⊕ CTV
⊕3pin square P Ⅲ ♨(5m) ⚓Hard
Pigeon shooting & agate hunting
↔ ♨(3m)
Min£65 Max£160pw

REDRUTH
Cornwall
Map**2** SW64

C Mrs S J Y Woodward **Rayle Farm
Holiday Cottages** Bridge, Illogan, Redruth,
Cornwall
☎Portreath(0209)842245
*Six delightful stone-built cottages, which
stand around a courtyard on Rayle Farm.
Recently converted, they maintain a lot of →*

character, while being comfortably
furnished and equipped. One of the units
has an original inglenook fireplace with
clay oven. They can accommodate up to
four people (one unit six people) and are
located in peaceful surroundings.

10Apr–1Nov MWB out of season
3days min, 4wks max, 6units, 1–6persons
[◇] ◆ ◆ ◎ fridge Electric fires
Elec metered Ⓛcan be hired
☎(300yds) Laundry room Iron & Ironing
board in unit ☺ CTV ⊕3pin square
12P �🎠 ♨(300yds) Table tennis,
barbecue

⊕ ⍭(¼m)

Min£65 Max£145pw (Low)
Min£155 Max£245pw (High)

RESTRONGUET
Cornwall
Map**2** SW83

H Marlow
for bookings Mr P Watson, Restronguet,
Falmouth, Cornwall TR11 5ST
☎Falmouth(0326)72722

Semi-detached house with access to
moorings for boats. There is a tastefully
decorated lounge, modern kitchen, dining
room, cloakroom with shower and WC,
three good sized bedrooms and combined
bathroom/WC. Lawn and well kept
gardens.

All year MWB out of season 1unit,
1–7persons [◆] ◎ fridge ◎
Elec metered Ⓛnot provided ☎ WM &
SD in unit Iron & Ironing board in unit
☺ CTV ⊕3pin square P ♨(1m)

⊕ ⍭(100yds)

Min£100 Max£240pw (Low)
Min£255 Max£460pw (High)

H Oyster Shell Nos 1 & 2
for bookings Mr P Watson, Restronguet,
Falmouth, Cornwall TR11 5ST
☎Falmouth(0326)72722

Two semi-detached houses with lawned
garden overlooking Fal Estuary and
private beach. No 1 has a kitchen, lounge/
diner, and bathroom with bath, shower/
WC. No 2 has a kitchen, lounge and dining
room and a bathroom/shower/WC on the
ground floor. Upstairs in each house there
are three bedrooms, one double-, one
twin-bedded and a family room. Both
houses have a bathroom/WC upstairs.

All year MWB out of season 2units,
1–8persons [◆] ◎ fridge Electric
Elec metered Ⓛnot provided ☎ WM &
SD in unit Iron & Ironing board in unit
☺ CTV ⊕3pin square P ♨(1m)

⊕ ⍭(100yds)

Min£100 Max£220pw (Low)
Min£240 Max£465pw (High)

RHANDIRMWYN
Dyfed
Map**3** SN74

C Mrs I T Williams Gelly Farm Cottage
Galltybere, Rhandirmwyn, Llandovery,
Dyfed SA20 0PH
☎Rhandirmwyn(05506)218

Redruth
—
Roadhead

Situated near the head of the valley this
small old Welsh farm cottage has a
peaceful setting. Downstairs there is a
lounge, dining room, kitchen, bathroom/
shower with WC and a double bedroom.
Upstairs a bedroom with bunks and a
single bed, also a room with double bed
and cot.

All year MWB 1wk min, 1unit,
2–8persons ◆ ◆ no pets ◎
fridge Electric & open fires
Elec metered Ⓛnot provided ☎(⅓m)
Iron & Ironing board in unit ☺
⊕3pin square P 🎠 ♨(2m) Pony
trekking, fishing

⊕ ⍭(2m)

Min£50 Max£120pw

RHOSGADFAN
Gwynedd
Map**6** SH55

C & H Hen Gapel
for bookings Shaws Holidays, Y Maes,
Pwllheli, Gwynedd LL53 5HA
☎Pwllheli(0758)613835 or 614422

Three properties with excellent views over
the Menai Straits and Anglesey in a
remote, elevated position. Parc Drea is a
stone-built house and comprises lounge/
diner, kitchen, three double rooms (one
with cot), one twin room, bathroom/WC
and shower room/WC. Tryfan & Carreg
are a pair of terraced cottages comprising
kitchen/diner, lounge with double bed-
settee, one double bedroom and one twin-
bedded room (Tryfan has one bunk-
bedded room) and bathroom/WC.

All year MWB wknd min, 6wks max,
3units, 2–8persons ◆ ◎ fridge
Storage & electric heaters Elec metered
Ⓛnot provided ☎(1m) ☺ CTV
⊕3pin square P ♨(1m)

⊕ ⍭(2m)

Min£99 Max£179pw

RHYD-DHU
Gwynedd
Map**6** SH55

H Bron Eifion
for bookings Messrs Johnson & Davies,
218 Clive Road, London SE21 8BS
☎01-6702756

Modernised semi-detached house at the
foot of Snowdon comprising lounge,
dining room, kitchen, three bedrooms and
bathroom/WC.

All year MWB out of season 1wk min,
6wks max, 1unit, 2–6persons ◆
no pets ◎ fridge Storage heaters
Elec metered Ⓛnot provided
☎(100yds) Iron & Ironing board in unit
☺ ⊕3pin square ♨(200yds)

⊕ ⍭(150yds)

Min£35 Max£65pw (Low)
Min£90 Max£140pw (High)

RICHMOND
North Yorkshire
Map**7** NZ10

H The Culloden Tower
for bookings Landmark Trust,
Shottesbrooke Park, Maidenhead,
Berkshire SL6 3SW
☎Littlewick Green(062882)5925

Built in 1746 to commemorate the defeat of
the Jacobite rebellion, now expertly
converted into two bedroomed
accommodation with Gothic lounge,
kitchen and separate bathroom/WC.
Situated in parkland adjoining the River
Swale.

All year MWB out of season 1wk min,
1unit, 1–4persons ◆ no pets ◎
fridge ✸ Elec inclusive ☎(300yds)
Iron & Ironing board in unit ☺
⊕3pin square ⊕3pin round 4P
♨(½m)

⊕ δ(2m) ⍭(½m) 🎵(½m)

Min£70 Max£255pw (Low)
Min£190 Max£270pw (High)

RIPE
East Sussex
Map**5** TQ51

C Mrs K P Garner Brooklands Cottage
Ripe, Lewes, East Sussex BN8 6AR
☎Ripe(032183)310

A peacefully situated secluded 18th-
century cottage and garden. Comprising
an L' shaped sitting/dining room, kitchen,
three bedrooms (two singles, one twin),
bathroom/WC and separate WC.

Jul–Sep 1wk min, 20wks max, 1unit,
1–6persons ◆ pets charged ◎
fridge Wood burning stove
Elec metered Ⓛcan be hired ☎ Iron &
Ironing board in unit ☺ TV CTV can be
hired ⊕3pin square 2P ♨(100yds)

⊕ ⍭

Max£132pw

ROADHEAD
Cumbria
Map**12** NY57

F Mrs P Copeland Bailey Mill Bailey,
Newcastleton, Roxburghshire
☎Roadhead(06978)617

18th-century grain mill, nestling beside a
stream, extended and converted into a
modern house, part of which contains four
flats. Granary and Store have a shower
room/WC, Mill has an invalid bath facility,
and Loft has a galley bedroom feature. All
units are similar having lounge/dining/
kitchen area, apart from the features
mentioned.

All year MWB 1day min, 3wks max,
4units, 4–6persons [◇] ◆ ☺
fridge ✸ Elec inclusive ☎ [Iron &
Ironing board on premises] Launderette
on premises ☺ CTV ⊕3pin square
6P 🎠 ♨(3m) Games room, gym,
sauna & solarium

198

Ə♀(3m)
Min£68 Max98pw (Low)
Min£118 Max198pw (High)
C Kinkry Hill Lodge
for bookings Mrs M Phillips, The Square,
Roadhead, Carlisle, Cumbria CA6 6NE
☎Roadhead(06978)254 or 227

*A traditional Cumbrian long house
offering simple good value family
accommodation. It has an attractive little
front garden and also there is nearby
fishing and pony trekking. There is a large
combined sitting and dining room, kitchen
with larder, one family bedroom, one
double and also a twin room.*

All year MWB out of season 3days min,
1mth max, 1unit, 8persons ◊ ◎
fridge open fires Elec metered ⎍can
be hired ☎(20yds) WM & SD in unit
Iron & Ironing board in unit ⊙ ⊛
CTV ⊕3pin square 6P 📺 ♨(50yds)
Ə♀(2½m)
Min£50 Max£70pw (Low)
Min£75 Max£120pw (High)

ROCKCLIFFE
Dumfries & Galloway *Kirkcudbrightshire*
Map**11** NX85

H Boreland of Colvend Farm House
for bookings G M Thomson & Co, 27 King
Street, Castle Douglas, Kirkcudbrightshire
DG7 1AB
☎Castle Douglas(0556)2701 or 2973

*White faced stone-built two-storey
farmhouse with spacious accommodation
of large kitchen/dining room, two sitting
rooms, two bathrooms, utility room,
spacious hall and three bedrooms,
sleeping six people. Good views.*

All year MWB out of season 1wk min,
1mth max, 1unit, 1–6persons ◊
no pets ◎ fridge Electric & open fires
Elec inclusive ⎍not provided ☎(1m)
Iron & Ironing board in unit TV
⊕3pin round P 📺 ♨(1m)
Ə ♪(1½m) ♀(2m)
Min£75 Max£125pw

ROSEDALE ABBEY
North Yorkshire
Map**8** SE79

Roadhead
—
Ross-on-Wye

C 1 School Row Cottages Rosedale
East, Pickering
for bookings Mr Gill, Bank Villa, Masham,
Ripon, North Yorkshire HG4 4DB
☎Ripon(0765)89605

*A stone-built end of terrace cottage, about
100 years old, situated at the head of the
valley with all round rural views. The
sleeping arrangements are for up to five
people in two bedrooms plus single bed-
settee in the lounge. There is a good-sized
kitchen in utility room off and a bathroom/
WC. 1½m N of village.*

Apr–Oct 1wk min, 1unit,1–5persons ◎
◎ fridge Electric & solid fuel
Elec inclusive ⎍not provided ☎(1½m)
WM in unit Iron & Ironing board in unit
⊙ TV ⊕3pin square 3P ♨(1½m)
Ə ♀(1½m)
Min£80 Max£130pw

ROSS-ON-WYE
Hereford & Worcester
Map**3** SO52

H The Gate House 5 Church Street
for bookings Mr & Mrs Watson, 15A Alton
Street, Ross-on-Wye, Herefordshire
HR9 5NN
☎Ross-on-Wye(0989)62302

*Town cottage with good central location
and small rear courtyard garden.
Accommodation comprises kitchen/diner,
lounge with french windows opening to
the garden, two bedrooms (one triple, one
twin bedded), bathroom/WC plus a
separate wash hand basin.*

May–Sep 3days min, 4wks max, 1unit,
1–5persons [◊] ◎ fridge Storage
heater & electric fires Elec metered
⎍can be hired ☎(150yds) Iron &
Ironing board in unit [Launderette within
300yds] ⊙ CTV ⊕3pin square 3P
📺 ♨(20yds)
Ə ♪(3m) ♀(20yds) 🎵(200yds)
🎵(200yds) 🐾(200yds)
Min£70 Max£105pw

C Great Howle Farm Cottage Howle Hill
for bookings Heart of England Cottages,
The Barrel & Basket, The Market Place,
Fairford, Gloucestershire GL7 4AB
☎Cirencester(0285)713295

*The cottage is attached to the farm
buildings and comprises of hall,
bathroom/WC, kitchen, living/dining room,
one double bedroom, one twin and one
single bedroom. All on the ground floor.*

All year MWB out of season 3days min,
6mths max, 1unit, 1–5persons ◎
fridge Electric Elec inclusive ⎍can be
hired (overseas visitors only) ☎ Iron &
Ironing board in unit ⊙ CTV
⊕3pin square 4P ♨(3m)
Ə ♀(½m) 🎵(3m) ♪(3m) 🐾(3m)
Min£95 Max£135pw

C Hildersley Farm Cottage
for bookings Mrs D Boynton, Hildersley
Farm, Ross-on-Wye, Herefordshire
HR9 7NW
☎Ross-on-Wye(0989)62095

*A low, single-storey cottage of stone and
tile behind the main farmhouse. The farm
is situated on the A40 Gloucester–Ross-
on-Wye road. Smaller than average, the
accommodation consists of a kitchen,
utility room, lounge/dining room, two
bedrooms (the double room can only be
reached by passing through the twin-
bedded room), and bathroom/WC.*

All year MWB out of season 3days min,
4wks max, 1unit, 1–4persons ◊
no pets ⚲ fridge Electric & coal fires
Gas/Elec metered ⎍not provided
☎(½m) ⊕3pin square 2P 📺 ♨(1m)
Ə ♀(1m) 🎵(1m) ♪(1m) 🐾(1m)
Min£50 Max£60pw

C Howle Green Lodge Howle Hill
for bookings Heart of England Cottages,
The Barrel & Basket, The Market Place,
Fairford, Gloucestershire GL7 4AB
☎Cirencester(0285)713295

*Modernised semi-detached stone cottage,
situated 680ft above sea-level and offering
excellent views across the surrounding
countryside. The accommodation
comprises a ground-floor with entrance
hall, cloakroom/WC, large kitchen,
laundry room, bathroom with WC and →*

shower, dining room and large lounge with divan bed. Upstairs there are three bedrooms, two double, one with bathroom en-suite, and one with twin beds, sun lounge with divan bed and a bathroom/ WC. Dishwasher and freezer.

All year MWB out of season 3days min, 6mths max, 1 unit, 1–8 persons ◎ fridge Electric Elec inclusive Ⓛ can be hired (overseas visitors only) ☎ WM & SD in unit Iron & Ironing board in unit ☉ CTV ⊕3pin square 5P Ⅲ ♨(½m) ↩ ♀(½m) ♫(3m) ♪(3m) ☠(3m)

H   Ms H I Smith Old Kilns Howle Hill, Ross-on-Wye, Herefordshire HR9 5SP
☎Ross-on-Wye(0989)62051

The accommodation is located in one half of a neat, roughcast house and consists of two double bedrooms, lounge/diner with convertible settee, kitchen and bathroom/ WC. Two folding beds available on request. Furnishings are new. Very nice accommodation. It is situated some 3mW of Ross-on-Wye near the Crown public house and opposite the tiny village church. Six and a half acres of grounds with garden furniture and a barbecue.

All year MWB out of season 1 night min, 1 unit, 1–6 persons [◇ ◆] ◆ ◎ fridge Electric Elec metered Ⓛ can be hired ☎ WM [SD on premises] [TD on premises] Iron & Ironing board in unit ☉ ◎ CTV ⊕3pin square P Ⅲ ♨(1½m) ↩ ♀(200yds) ♫(2m) ☠ Barbecue
From £20pw

C   The Vineyard Howle Hill (2m S)
for bookings Heart of England Cottages, The Barrel & Basket, The Market Place, Fairford Gloucestershire GL7 4AB
☎Cirencester(0285)713295

The cottage is an old farmhouse converted throughout. Good views of the surrounding countryside. Downstairs is a large kitchen, cloakroom/WC, dining room, sitting room, sun lounge and bathroom with WC. On the first floor there is one room with a double and two single beds, and the second bedroom has twin beds. Each has a dressing room and fitted wardrobes.

All year MWB out of season 3days min, 6mths max, 1 unit, 1–6 persons ◎ fridge Electric Elec inclusive Ⓛ can be hired (overseas visitors only) ☎ Iron & Ironing board in unit ☉ CTV ⊕3pin square 4P 1♨ Ⅲ ♨(½m) ↩ ♀(½m) ♫(3m) ♪(3m) ☠(3m)
Min£125 Max£185pw

ROSTHWAITE
Cumbria
Map**11** NY21

B   Castle How
for bookings Lakeland Cottage Holidays, Yew Tree Cottage, Ullock, Keswick, Cumbria CA12 5SP
☎Braithwaite(059682)493 or Keswick(07687)72059

Ross-on-Wye
—
Ruan Minor

A traditional Lakeland stone building recently converted and extended to offer a cosy living room, kitchen, bathroom, WC and two double bedrooms and one single. Situated in the heart of the valley in an attractive village.

All year 1 mth max, 1 unit, 2–5 persons ◇ ◆ no pets ◎ fridge Storage heaters & open fires Elec inclusive Ⓛ inclusive ☎(50yds) WM & SD in unit Iron & Ironing board in unit ☉ CTV ⊕3pin square 1P Ⅲ ♨(50yds) ↩ ♀(300yds)
Min£102 Max£252pw

F   Kiln How Apartments
for bookings Mr & Mrs P Graham, Randlehow, Mockerkin, Cockermouth, Cumbria
☎Lamplugh(0946)861018

An attractive farmhouse built in 1725 in a delightful situation, converted into five self-contained flats. Each flat has a living room, kitchen area and bathroom. Two flats have a double bedroom and a bed-settee in the lounge, the largest flat has two double and two single bedrooms and a bed-settee and the remaining two flats both sleep six, one with a double, a twin bedroom and bed-settee and the other with a family room and a bed settee.

All year MWB out of season 2days min, 3mth max, 5 units, 2–8 persons ◇ no pets ◎ fridge Storage heaters Elec metered Ⓛ not provided ☎(300yds) Iron & Ironing board on premises CTV ⊕3pin square 8P ♨(300yds) ↩ ♀(300yds)
Min£48 Max£80pw (Low)
Min£90 Max£170pw (High)

See advertisement under Borrowdale

ROTHESAY
Strathclyde *Buteshire*
See **Bute, Isle of**

ROWSLEY
Derbyshire
Map**8** SK26

F   Greystones Church Lane
for bookings Mr G M Gillson, Manager, The Peacock Hotel, Rowsley, Matlock, Derbyshire DE4 2EB
☎Matlock(0629)733518

Ground-floor flat in a detached Victorian house, overlooking the countryside; comprising two bedrooms (only one with wash hand basin), shower room/WC, lounge/diner and kitchen. Pleasant garden to rear.

All year 1 wk min, 1 unit, 4 persons ◇ ◆ ◎ fridge ♨ Elec inclusive Ⓛ inclusive ☎ Iron & Ironing board in

---

unit ☉ CTV ⊕3pin square Ⅲ ♨(½m) ↩ δ(3m) ♀(½m)
Min£98 Max£132pw

C   Rose Cottage Church Lane
for bookings Mr G M Gillson, Manager, The Peacock Hotel, Rowsley, Matlock, Derbyshire DE4 2EB
☎Matlock(0629)733518

An old stone cottage with pleasant garden and good rural views. It has been extensively modernised to provide good comfortable accommodation comprising beamed lounge with fireplace, small kitchen, dining room, two bedrooms (one double, one twin) and bathroom/WC. Situated at the edge of the pleasant and peaceful village.

All year 1 wk min, 3 wks max, 1 unit, 4 persons ◇ ◆ ◎ fridge ♨ Elec inclusive Ⓛ inclusive ☎(½m) Iron & Ironing board in unit ☉ CTV ⊕3pin square 3P Ⅲ ♨(½m) ↩ δ(3m) ♀(½m)
Min£121 Max£155pw

ROY BRIDGE
Highland *Inverness-shire*
Map**14** NN28

Ch   Mr W A McCallum Bunroy Holiday Chalets Roy Bridge, Inverness-shire PH31 4AG
☎Spean Bridge(039781)332

Secluded and well laid out site of mainly level grass and birch trees. The A-frame, detached timber chalets are very compact with effective décor and fittings. Views over grassland to River Spean and the Nevis range of mountains with Ben Nevis just screened by Aonach Mhor.

Apr–mid Oct MWB out of season 1 wk min, 1 mth max, 8 units, 2–4 persons ◎ fridge Electric Elec metered Ⓛ not provided ☎(400yds) ☉ CTV ⊕3pin square P Ⅲ ♨(500yds) Trout fishing ↩ ♀(500yds) ♫(500yds)
Min£75 Max£105pw

RUAN MINOR
Cornwall
Map**2** SW71

B   Mullion Holiday Park
for bookings Haven Leisure ECC Ltd., Haven House, Quay Street, Truro, Cornwall TR1 2UE
☎Truro(0872)40400

Terraces of bungalows on a large static holiday park, each furnished in modern style. There are two types of bungalow, Type A comprises a lounge/diner, kitchen area, shower room with WC, one double and one twin-bedded room. Type B has a lounge/diner with bed-settee, kitchen area, bathroom with separate WC, one double and one twin bedroom.

3 May–Sep MWB 3days min, 1 mth max, 54 units 1–6 persons [◇ ◆ ◆] no

pets ⓦ fridge Electric convectors
Elec metered Ⓛinclusive ☎ [Iron on
premises] Ironing board on premises
[Launderette on premises] ⊙ CTV
⊕3pin square 54P ▦ ◢(heated)

⊖ 🕾 ♬ ♬

Min£62 Max£128pw (Low)
Min£136 Max Max£218pw (High)

_____

RUDYARD
Staffordshire
Map7 SJ95

C Reacliffe Cottage
for bookings Mrs C J Gee, Reacliffe Farm,
Rudyard, Leek, Staffordshire
☎Rudyard(053833)276

*A self-contained two-storey unit adjoining
the proprietor's stone-built farmhouse. In a
rural setting approx 1m from Rudyard. It
comprises one family bedroom, one
double room, lounge with convertible
settee, kitchen/diner and a modern
bathroom/WC with shower.*

May–Sep 1wk min, 1unit, 6persons ◇
◆ fridge 🍴 & Elec fires Gas/
Elec metered Ⓛcan be hired ☎(1m)
WM Iron & Ironing board in unit ⊙
CTV ⊕3pin square P ▦ ▦(1m)
⊖ 🕾(1m) ♬(1m) ♬(1m) 🐾(3m)
Min£70 Max£90pw

_____

RUMFORD
Cornwall
Map2 SW87

C Mr & Mrs Farmanfamai **St Ervan
Country House** St Ervan, Rumford,
Wadebridge, Cornwall PL27 7TA
☎Rumford(0841)540255

*A former rectory situated in four acres. The
cottages arranged around the courtyard
once served the rectory as Coach House,
Stables and Bakery and have been
converted into luxurious self-catering
cottages.* **Coach House, Stable** and
Cloam Cottages *each consist of one
double-bedded room, one twin and one
double bed-settee in the lounge, separate
fitted kitchen and modern bathroom/WC.
The* **Coach** *and* **Stable** *are situated on two
floors, whereas* **Cloam Cottage** *is a
ground-floor residence. Use of adjoining
hotel facilities including lounge bar.*

_____

Ruan Minor
—
St Andrews

All year MWB out of season 1wk min,
1mth max, 3units, 1–6persons ◇ ◆
ⓦ fridge Electric Elec metered Ⓛcan
be hired ☎ Iron & Ironing board on
premises [Launderette on premises]
⊙ CTV ⊕3pin square 2P ▦ ▦(½m)
⊖ 𝄢(3m) 🕾 ♬(3m) ♬(3m)
Min£75 Max£115pw (Low)
Min£160 Max£215pw (High)

_____

RUTHERNBRIDGE
Cornwall
Map2 SX06

B D J & M A Bluett **Ruthern Valley
Holidays** Ruthernbridge, Bodmin,
Cornwall
☎Bodmin(0208)831395

*Twelve detached cedar-built bungalows
set amidst woodland and gardens. They
comprise lounge, with put-u-up sofa,
kitchen/diner, and bathroom/WC. Nine of
the properties have one double- and one
twin-bedded room, the remaining three
have two double bedrooms.*

Mar–Dec MWB in season 1wk min,
1mth max, 12units, 4–6persons [◇ ◆
◆] ⓦ fridge Electric Elec metered
Ⓛnot provided ☎(½m) Iron & Ironing
board on premises ⊙ CTV
⊕3pin square P ▦ ▦ Children's
play area
⊖ 🕾(3m)
Min£70 Max£175pw

_____

RYDE
See **Wight, Isle of**

_____

SADDELL
Strathclyde *Argyll*
Map10 NR73

C Cul Na Syth
for bookings The Landmark Trust,
Shottesbrooke, Maidenhead, Berkshire
SL6 3SW
☎Littlewick Green(062882)5925

_____

*This former estate cottage is situated close
to the shore and has superb views of the
Isle of Arran. Interior is timber clad and
accommodation consists of kitchen/diner,
lounge, two twin bedrooms and
bathroom/WC. Clean, tidy and well
maintained.*

All year 1wk min, 3wks max, 1unit,
1–4persons ⓦ fridge Electric & open
fires Elec inclusive Ⓛnot provided
☎(½m) Iron & Ironing board in unit ⊙
⊕3pin square 2P ▦(6m)
Min£84 Max£220pw (Low)
Min£150 Max£235pw (High)

_____

SAGESTON
Dyfed
Map2 SN00

H Ashleigh House
for bookings Powell's Cottage Holidays, 55
High Street, Saundersfoot, Dyfed
☎Saundersfoot(0834)812791

*This is a large detached stone house with
five bedrooms, a lounge, separate dining
room, breakfast room and kitchen. A
child's bed is also available.*

May–Sep MWB out of season 1wk min,
2wks max, 1unit, 2–11persons ◇ ⓦ
fridge Electric Elec inclusive
Ⓛnot provided ☎ Iron & Ironing board
in unit ⊙ CTV ⊕3pin square P ▦
▦(1m)
⊖ 🕾(50yds) ♬(3m) 🐾(3m)
Details not confirmed for 1987

_____

ST ANDREWS
Fife
Map12 NO51

H 4 & 5 Abbotsford Place
for bookings Mr & Mrs Wedderburn,
Mountquhanie Holiday Homes, Cupar,
Fife KY15 4QJ
☎Gauldry(082624)252 due to change to
(038236)252

*Two stone-terraced houses set in quiet
mews close to shops, beach and golf
courses. Both offer well-equipped kitchen,
dining room and shower/WC on the
ground floor, one bedroom, lounge and
bathroom on the first floor and two
bedrooms on the second floor. Well
decorated and furnished houses.* →

_____

All year MWB out of season 1wk min, 4wks max, 2units, 1–6persons [◇] ◈
◆ ◔ fridge ♨ Gas & Elec metered Ⓛcan be hired ☎ WM, SD & TD in unit Iron & Ironing board in unit ☉ CTV ⊕3pin square 2P ▲(100yds)

⊖ ♪(400yds) ☻(400yds) 📁(400yds) ☏(400yds)

Min£80 Max£190pw

F Albany Park St Mary's Street
for bookings The Bursar of Residences, College Gate, St Andrews, Fife KY16 9AJ
☏St Andrews(0334)76161(Ext 547)

A student housing complex by the shore, south of the harbour. The 44 units are in blocks of 4–8 and consist of a kitchen/ dinette, six single rooms, WC, lounge and shower/WC. Recently built and well maintained, they are ideal for families and sailing enthusiasts because of their position.

27Jun–12Sep 1wk min, 3mths max, 44units, 1–6persons no pets ◉ fridge ♨ Elec metered (hot water free) Ⓛinclusive ☎(100yds) Iron & Ironing board in unit [Launderette within 300yds] ☉ TV can be hired ⊕3pin square 100P ▥ ▲(200yds)

⊖ ♀(1m) 📁(1m) ♫(1m) ☻(1m)

Min£95 Max£115pw (Low)
£155pw (High)

C & H Mrs N Harper **Dron Court** South Dron, St Andrews, Fife KY16 9YA
☏St Andrews(0334)870835

Conversion of farm buildings into a small complex of cottages and houses surrounding a landscaped courtyard. The properties range from one to four bedrooms with lounge/dining area/open plan kitchen. Some bedrooms have wash basins and some have bathrooms. Each unit has its own character and all are furnished and equipped to high standard.

All year MWB out of season 1wk min, 6wks max, 9units, 1–9persons ◆ ◈
◉ fridge ♨ Elec metered Ⓛcan be hired ☎ WM & SD in unit [TD on premises] Iron & Ironing board in unit ☉ ◉ [CTV] ⊕3pin square 20P ▲(½m) Club room, video, dancing

⊖ ♪(3m) ♀(½m) 📁(3m) ♫(3m)

Details not confirmed for 1987

St Andrews
—
St Austell

H Fife Park Strathkinness High Road
for bookings The Bursar of Residences, College Gate, St Andrews, Fife KY16 9AJ
☏St Andrews(0334)76161(Ext547)

Student accommodation in a pleasant, quiet area of the west end of town. There are 42 units. The two-storey houses each consist of six single bedrooms and a kitchen/dining area, shower and WC. No lounge.

27Jun–12Sep 1wk min, 3mths max, 42units, 1–6persons no pets ◉ fridge Electric Elec metered (except hot water) Ⓛinclusive ☎(100yds) Iron & Ironing board in unit [Launderette within 300yds] TVcan be hired ⊕3pin square 100P ▥ ▲(1m)

⊖ ♀(1½m) 📁(1½m) ♫(1½m) ☻(1½m)

Min£90 Max£105pw (Low)
£140pw (High)

F 133 South Street
for bookings Mrs S D Room, Woodriffe, 44 Buchanan Gardens, St Andrews, Fife KY16 9LX
☏St Andrews(0334)72253

Four flats located in one of the main shopping streets. Three flats sleeping two to four persons in one double-bedded room and one twin-bedded room, lounge/ dining area, modern kitchen and bathroom. The one remaining flat sleeps two to six persons in one double- and two twin-bedded rooms also with lounge/ dining area, modern kitchen and bathroom.

20Jun–30Oct MWB out of season 1wk min, 3wks max, 4units, 2–6persons ◇ ◈ ◆ no pets ◉ fridge Electric Elec inclusive Ⓛinclusive ☎coin operated in each flat WM & TD on premises Iron & Ironing board in unit ☉ CTV ⊕3pin square ▲

⊖ ♪(¼m) ♀(100yds) 📁(¼m) ♫(100yds) ☻(400yds)

Min£90 Max£120pw (Low)
Min£140pw Max£180pw (High)

ST ANTHONY IN ROSELAND
Cornwall
Map**2** SW83

H Barton Farm House & Barton Bothy
Place Estate
for bookings Mrs N Grant-Dalton, Place House, St Anthony-in-Roseland, Truro, Cornwall
☏Portscatho(087258)447

Two semi-detached stone-built houses both comprising lounge with open log fires and well-equipped kitchen/diner. **Barton farmhouse** has cloak room, laundry room, games room and four double bedrooms (one with bathroom en suite), bathroom and WC. **Barton Bothy** offers two bedrooms (one double, one twin), bathroom and WC and has a large private garden. Both located within ½m of two beaches.

All year MWB 3days min, 1mth max, 2units, 1–8persons [◇] ◈ ◆ ◉
fridge ♨ & log fires Elec inclusive Ⓛinclusive ☎(½m) WM & SD in Farmhouse Iron & Ironing board in unit ☉ CTV ⊕3pin square P ▲(3m) Dishwasher

⊖ ♀(3m)

Min£175 Max£425pw

C Cellars Cottage Place Estate
for bookings Mrs N Grant-Dalton, Place House, St-Anthony-in-Roseland, Portscatho, Truro, Cornwall
☏Portscatho(087 258)447

Luxury stone-built cottage of character in a secluded position on the edge of a sandy beach, opposite the famous fishing village of St Mawes. Accommodation consists of four bedrooms, all of which have sea views, a pine-panelled sitting room with log fires, and two bathrooms.

All year MWB 1wk min, 1unit, 8persons ◇ ◈ ◆ ◔ fridge ♨ Gas/ Elec inclusive Ⓛinclusive ☎(½m) WM Iron & Ironing board in unit ☉ CTV ⊕3pin square 4P ▲(3m)

Min£250 Max£590pw

ST AUSTELL
Cornwall
Map**2** SX05

B, C & Ch Mr & Mrs A A Milln **Bosinver Farm & Holiday Centre** St Austell, Cornwall
☎St Austell(0726)72128

A well screened complex of three cottages and fourteeen bungalows set in 35 acres of wooded meadowland. All units are comfortable and well-equipped; the number of persons accommodated in each unit is dependent on which accommodation is selected. For further information contact booking address.

All year(3units) Etr−Oct(14units) MWB out of season 1wk min, 17units, 2−8persons [◈] [◆] ◎ fridge Electric & solid fuel Elec metered 🔲 can be hired ☎ [WM TD] Iron & Ironing board on premises [Launderette on premises] ⊕3pin square P 🎴 ♨(½m) ⌓ ⚑ putting green Children's play area, sauna, solarium and games room

↩ ♪(½m) ♀(1m) 🎵(1½m) 🐾(1½m)

Min£30 Max£150pw (Low)
Min£100 Max£220pw (High)

B & Ch Mr & Mrs J C Moorman **St Margarets Holiday Park** Polgooth, St Austell, Cornwall PL26 7AX
☎St Austell(0726)74283

Eight bungalows and seven chalets built of cedarwood and set in 5 acres of wooded parkland. They all have lounge/ diner, kitchen, shower/WC or bath/WC, and various sleeping accommodation including some with bed-settee's. Two of the bungalows have a bedroom with WC and wash hand basin and doors wide enough for a wheelchair. 2m SW St Austell off A390.

Mar−Nov MWB out of season 3days min, 1mth max, 15units, 1−6persons [◇ ◈ ◆] ◎ fridge Electric Elec metered 🔲 can be hired ☎ Iron & Ironing board on premises [Launderette on premises] TV ⊕3pin square P 🎴 ♨(400yds)

↩ ♪(500yds) ♀(500yds) 🎵(3m) 🎵(3m) 🐾(2m)

Min£40 Max£90pw (Low)
Min£110 Max£205pw (High)

St Austell
—
St Breward

ST BREWARD
Cornwall
Map**2** SX17

C   Butterwell, Goosehill, Otterbridge, Jingles, Snappers & Linney
for bookings Mr & Mrs Hall, Penrose Burden, St Breward, Bodmin, Cornwall PL30 4LZ
☎Bodmin(0208)850277 or 850617

Six single-storey cottages converted from former farm buildings to a high standard. They comprise open plan lounge/kitchen/ dining area with wood burning stove, one double (four poster bed in Butterwell, Goosehill and Otterbridge), one twin- bedded room, bath/shower room/WC. Designed for the disabled and meals can be ordered.

All year MWB out of season 1wk min, 3wks max, 6units, 1−5persons [◇] ◈ ◆ no cats ◎ fridge night storage, electric fires & log burner Elec metered 🔲inclusive ☎(½m) [WM, SD & TD on premises] Iron & Ironing board in unit ⊕ CTV ⊕3pin square P 🎴 ♨(1m)

↩ ♀(1m)

Details not confirmed for 1987

F   Glenview Flats 1−5
for bookings S A McLeod, Dunvegan Holidays, Ryland, St Breward, Bodmin, Cornwall
☎Bodmin(0208)850528

Five flats in a converted old house with fine views across Bodmin Moor. Two split level flats, one comprising kitchen/diner, lounge, one double and one twin bedroom, bathroom with WC, the other is on two floors with bathroom and WC, open plan lounge/kitchen/diner and double bedroom. Two further flats, one with lounge/diner, one double and one three-bedded room, bathroom and WC, other flat sleeps up to six persons. Also an attic flat comprising lounge, kitchen/diner, one single, one double and one three-bedded room, plus bathroom and WC.

All year MWB out of season 3days min, 3mths max, 5units, 1−6persons [◇] ◆ ◆ ◎ fridge Electric Elec metered 🔲not provided ☎(100yds) [WM, SD & TD on premises] Iron & Ironing board on premises ⊕ TV ⊕3pin square P 🎴 ♨(100yds)

↩ ♀(1m)

Min£66 Max£195pw

C   2 & 3 Mount Pleasant
for bookings S A McLeod, Dunvegan Holidays, Ryland, St Breward, Bodmin, Cornwall
☎Bodmin(0208)850528

Two adjacent cottages close to centre of small village on Bodmin Moor. Pleasantly furnished, each comprising open plan lounge/kitchen/diner with open fire, one double bedroom, bathroom and WC.

All year MWB out of season 3days min, 3mths max, 2units ◇ ◈ ◆ ◎ fridge Electric & open fires Elec metered 🔲not provided ☎(150yds) [WM, SD & TD on premises] Iron & Ironing boad in unit ⊕ TV ⊕3pin square P 🎴 ♨(150yds)

↩ ♀(1m)

Min£55 Max£125pw

C   Wenford Bridge & Troutstream
for bookings Mr & Mrs Hall, Penrose Burden, St Breward, Bodmin, Cornwall PL30 4LZ
☎Bodmin(0208)850277 or 850617

Two traditional stone and slate cottages, detached in own gardens at quiet road junction. Both comprise open plan living room/diner/kitchen with log burning stove in lounge. **Wenford Bridge**, *has two double rooms, one with en suite bath/ shower/WC and one with four poster bed, one twin-bedded room and bathroom/WC.* **Troutstream** *offers two bedrooms, one twin with adjacent bath/shower/WC and a four poster double room. Suitable for disabled.*

All year MWB out of season 1wk min, 3wks max, 2units, 1−6persons [◇] ◆ ◆ no cats ◎ fridge Ceiling heating & electric fires Elec metered 🔲inclusive ☎(Wenford Bridge) ☎(½m) Iron & →

Ironing board in unit ⊙ CTV
⊕3pin square 4P 🔲 ♨(½m) fishing
↔ 🚻(½m)
Details not confirmed for 1987

ST BRIDES
Dyfed
Map2 SM81

F St Brides Castle St Bride's Haven,
Haverfordwest, Dyfed SA62 3AL
☎Dale(06465)321

The imposing turreted Castle of St Brides
is situated on the south west of St Brides
Bay, in its own parkland and surrounded
by woods and lawns. Right on the coast it
has unrivalled views and is ideal for family
holidays. It has undergone extensive
conversion and renovation work providing
finely appointed studios, and one or two
bedroom apartments with every modern
convenience. They are comfortably
furnished and each has lounge/diner, with
bed-settee, kitchen and bathroom.

Mar Oct MWB out of season 3days min,
15units, 4–12persons ◆ ◆ no pets
◎ fridge Storage heaters
🔳not provided ☎ [WM, SD & TD on
premises] Iron & Ironing board on
premises [Launderette on premises]
⊙ CTV ⊕3pin square 30P 🔲
♨(2m)
↔ 🚻 🎵(2m) Sports centre2m)
Min£59 Max£110pw (Low)
Min£99 Max£210pw (High)

St Breward
—
St Davids

ST CLEARS
Dyfed
Map2 SN21

B Hillston
for bookings Mr & Mrs E J T Davies,
Caeremlyn, Farm, Henllan-Amgoed,
Whitland, Dyfed
☎Whitland(0994)240260

A dormer bungalow set in lawns and
gardens. Ground floor has two lounges
and a sun lounge, dining room, kitchen
with microwave, separate WC and one
double bedroom. First floor has bath/WC,
one twin and one double room.

All year MWB out of season 4days min,
6wks max, 1unit, 2–6persons [◇] ◆
◆ ◎ fridge 🍴 Elec inclusive
🔳inclusive ☎(200yds) WM, SD & TD in
unit Iron & Ironing board in unit ⊙ 📺
CTV ⊕3pin square P 1🔥 🔲
♨(200yds)
↔ 🚻(200yds)
Min£135 Max£297pw

ST DAVIDS
Dyfed
Map2 SM72

B Penberry
for bookings Coastal Cottages of
Pembrokeshire, Seaview, Abercastle,
Mathry, Dyfed SA62 5HJ
☎Croesgoch(03483)7742

A modern detached bungalow on a farm
setting, but well away from the working
area. It is positioned at the foot of
Penberry Hill and about 2 miles from
Whitesands Bay. Accommodation
comprises a spacious lounge with Parkray
fire for central heating, dining room,
kitchen, utility room with shower/WC, one
double, one twin and bunk-bedded room
and bathroom/WC.

All year MWB out of season 4days min,
2mths max, 1unit, 2–6persons ◆ ◆
◎ fridge 🍴(Parkray) Elec metered
🔳inclusive ☎(2m) WM & SD in unit
Iron & Ironing board in unit ⊙ CTV
⊕3pin square 2P 🔲 ♨(2m)
↔ ♪(2m) 🚻(2m)
Min£75 Max£320pw

C Mr P Trier St Davids Studio Cottages
c/o Warpool Court Hotel, St Davids, Dyfed
SA62 6BN
☎St Davids(0437)720300

Delightful, rural location of high quality
character cottages converted from former
stable block quadrangle in spacious
grounds of small country home estate.
Each cottage is furnished and equipped to
a high standard with pine furniture,
modern facilities yet retaining their

St Bride's Castle nestles in 100 acres of woods and
parkland overlooking St Bride's Bay adjoining coastal
footpath in the Pembrokeshire National Park. Minutes
from beach and coves. Lovely coastal walks, wildlife,
island bird sanctuaries nearby. A range of elegant
award winning s/c apartments, fitted kitchens, tiled
bathrooms, comfortable lounges, colour TV. Bar,
children's playroom, pool, table tennis, badminton,
adventure playground, laundry, drying room. Lawns
and woods offer safe ideal location for children in a
setting renowned for peace and beauty.

ST BRIDE'S CASTLE, ST BRIDES, LITTLE HAVEN, DYFED, SA62 3AL
Tel: (064 65) 321

individual charm and character. Each is fractionally different in internal size and shape (some are split-level) sleeping between four or six persons. Ideal for family holiday and located overlooking the beautiful Solva Valley. Use of indoor swimming pool at nearby hotel.

All year MWB out of seson 3nights min, 8units, 1–6persons [◇] ◈ ◆ ⊚ fridge 🍳 Elec metered 🔲inclusive 📺 WM, SD & TD in unit Iron and Ironing board in unit ⊙ CTV ⊕3pin square P 📶 ▲ ⤴Hard games room, playground, dishwasher

↩ 🛏(3m) 🍽(2m) 🎵(2m) 🎵(3m)

St Davids

Min£115 Max£240pw (Low)
Min£275 Max£340pw (High)

C   15 Tower Hill
for bookings Landmark Trust,
Shottesbrooke, Maidenhead, Berkshire
SL6 3SW
📞Littlewick Green(062882)5925

Comfortable character family cottage which exudes warmth and charm in its

---

style and furnishings. It comprises, two twin-bedded rooms and one bunk-bedded room, separate bathroom and WC, kitchen and large living room. Situated in the heart of St Davids with views of the cathedral and well located for beaches and touring.

All year MWB out of season 1day min, 3wks max, 1unit, 1–6persons ◈ ◆ 🥄 fridge 🍳 Gas & Elec inclusive 🔲not provided 📞(150yds) Iron & Ironing board in unit ⊕3pin square 📶 ▲(300yds)
↩ 🛏(1m) 🍽(200yds) 🎵(200yds)
Min£147 Max£250pw (Low)
Min£170 Max£270pw (High)

ST ERTH
Cornwall
Map**2** SW53

C Honeysuckle Cottage 14 Chenhalls
Close
for bookings Mr & Mrs G N Broughton,
Orchard House, 26 Wall Road, Gwinear,
Hayle, Cornwall TR27 5HA
☎Leedstown(0736)850201

*Modern terraced cottage on a small
private site in a rural and attractive
position. It is well appointed and furnished
comprising one double-bedded room, one
twin bedded and one bunk bedded on the
first floor. There is a spacious lounge
which has an open fire, kitchen/diner,
bathroom/WC and extra WC downstairs.
Quality furnishings and décor.*

All year   MWB out of season   1wk min,
1unit, 6persons ◆ ◎ fridge   Electric
Elec inclusive Ⓛcan be hired ☎(1m)
WM in unit   Iron & Ironing board in unit
☉ CTV ⊕3pin square 1P 1🛋 ▥
🛏(1m)

↤) ☒(½m)

Min£70 Max£195pw

ST FLORENCE
Dyfed
Map**2** SN00

C Ranch Cottage East Tarr Farm
for bookings Powell's Cottage Holidays, 55
High Street, Saundersfoot, Dyfed
☎Saundersfoot(0834)812791

*Detached stone-built cottage in the
grounds of a riding school, comprising
lounge/diner with kitchen area, bath/WC
and sleeping accommodation for five.*

May–Aug   MWB out of season   1wk min,
4wks max, 1unit, 2–5persons [◇] ◆
◆ ◎ fridge   Electric   Elec metered
Ⓛcan be hired ☎(50yds) Iron & Ironing
board in unit ☉ TV ⊕3pin square P
🛏(¾m)

↤) ♪(2½m) ☒(¾m) ♫(2½m) ♫(2½m)
🎺(2½m)

Min£93 Max£210pw

ST GENNYS
Cornwall
Map**2** SX19

Ca Mineshop Lodges
for bookings Mr & Mrs A Cummins,
Mineshop Holiday Cottages, Mineshop, St
Gennys, Bude, Cornwall EX23 0NR
☎St Gennys(08403)338

*Canadian cedar wood lodges situated in a
peaceful wooded valley 1½m E of
Crackington Haven by road and 1m by*

St Erth
—
St Gennys

*footpath. They have open-plan living
rooms with wall beds, one double
bedroom and one with two bunk beds,
kitchenette, bathroom and WC. The
furnishings are modern and comfortable
and the décor of good standard.*

Etr–Oct   MWB out of season   1wk min,
6wks max, 6units, 1–6persons ◆ ◎
fridge   Elec metered Ⓛcan be hired
Iron & Ironing board on premises   laundry
room on premises   CTV ⊕3pin square
P ▥ 🛏(1½m)

↤) ☒(1½m)

Min£53 Max£70pw (Low)
Min£97 Max£160pw (High)

C Old Shippon
for bookings Mr & Mrs A Cummins,
Mineshop Holiday Cottages, Mineshop, St
Gennys, Bude, Cornwall EX23 0NR
☎St Gennys(08403)338

*Part stone and part white-washed one-
storey cottage overlooking a stream and
woodland in a peaceful valley. The
accommodation comprises one double
and two twin bedrooms, open-plan living
area with bed-settee, kitchenette,
bathroom and WC. French door leads to a
stone-paved patio.*

All year   MWB out of season   1wk min,
6wks max, 1unit, 1–8persons ◆ ◎
fridge   night storage heaters
Elec metered Ⓛcan be hired ☎(2m)
Iron & Ironing board on premises   laundry
room on premises   CTV ⊕3pin square
2P ▥ 🛏(1½m)

↤) ☒(½m)

Min£58 Max£85pw (Low)
Min£118 Max£197pw (High)

C Old Smithy
for bookings Mr & Mrs A Cummins,
Mineshop Holiday Cottages, Mineshop, St
Gennys, Bude, Cornwall EX23 0NR
☎St Gennys(08403)338

*One-storey cottage converted from the old
blacksmith's shop standing on the banks
of a stream, in a peaceful wooded valley.
Accommodation consists of one double
bedroom and one with two bunk beds,
open-plan living area with studio couch,
kitchenette, bathroom and WC. A patio
paved in traditional 'blue' Cornish slate,
and private lawn with the original
blacksmith's granite water trough still in
place are additional features.*

All year   MWB out of season   1wk min,
6wks max, 1unit, 1–6persons ◆ ◎
fridge   night storage heater
Elec metered Ⓛcan be hired ☎(2m)
Iron & Ironing board on premises   laundry
room on premises   CTV ⊕3pin square
P ▥ 🛏(1½m)

↤) ☒(1½m)

Min£55 Max£75pw (Low)
Min£106 Max£165pw (High)

B Strawberry Cottage
for bookings Mr & Mrs N P Cummins,
Mineshop, St Gennys, Bude, Cornwall
EX23 0NR
☎St Gennys(08403)338

*Modern bungalow cut into the hillside in a
wooded valley setting. The
accommodation comprises good size
lounge; well equipped kitchen, bathroom,
three bedrooms: one double, one twin and
one double with bunk beds.*

Mar–Dec   MWB out of season   1wk min,
1mth max, 1unit, 8persons ◆ ◆ ◎
fridge   electric heaters   Elec metered
Ⓛcan be hired   Iron & Ironing board in
unit   [Launderette on premises]   ☉
CTV ⊕3pin square 2P ▥ 🛏(2m)

↤) ☒(2m) ♫(2m) ♫(2m)

Min£65 Max£88pw (Low)
Min£95 Max£206pw (High)

**H & C Trelay Farmhouse, Little Trelay
& The Old Stable**
for bookings Mr & Mrs A Cummins,
Mineshop Holiday Cottages, St Gennys,
Bude, Cornwall EX23 0NR
☎St Gennys(08403)338

*Victorian stone and slate farmhouse with
Little Trelay forming the rear portion. The
Farmhouse is well furnished with spacious
lounge with open fire, kitchen/diner, two
double and two twin-bedded rooms and
two bathroom/WC's. **Little Trelay** is
smaller comprising spacious lounge/diner
with kitchen area, one double and one
twin-bedded room and bathroom/WC. **Old
Stable** has two double and one twin-
bedded room, one bunk bedded room, a
spacious lounge/diner with kitchen
leading off, bathroom/WC and a separate
WC.*

All year   MWB out of season   1wk min,
6wks max, 3units, 1–8persons ◆ ◎
fridge   night storage   Elec metered
Ⓛcan be hired ☎(1m) [WM & TD on
premises] Iron & Ironing board in unit
☉ CTV ⊕3pin square P 🛏(1m)
dishwasher (farmhouse)

↤) ☒(½m)

Min£55 Max£146pw (Low)
Min£111 Max£268pw (High)

Villa Cottages Cannalidgey Farm, St Issey, Wadebridge, Cornwall
Situated in a small hamlet, 6 miles from coast and Padstow, with excellent
sandy beaches in the area. Fully equipped and carpeted except Kitchen.
Colour television, sleeps 5, no pets. Beautiful countryside all round. Shops
1½ miles with main shops 5 miles.
**For bookings Mrs E.D. Old, Roscullion Farm, St Issey,
Wadebridge, Cornwall. Telephone: (0841) 540212.**

ST ISSEY
Cornwall
Map2 SW97

C No' 1 & 2 Villa Cottages Cannalidgey
for bookings Mrs E D Old, Roscullion, Little
Petherick, Wadebridge, Cornwall,
PL27 7RX
☎Padstow(0841)540212
*Two spacious stone-built Cornish
cottages in a rural setting, but near a
working farm.* **No. 1** *comprises kitchen,
large dining room with ornate alcoves,
lounge with open fire, ground-floor
bathroom and upstairs one double
bedroom with additional single bed and
one twin bedroom.* **No. 2** *has a large
lounge/dining room, kitchen, bathroom,
open wooded staircase to double
bedroom with additional single bed and
twin bedroom.*

All year MWB out of season 2 days min,
1 mth max, 2 units, 5 persons ◆ ◆
no pets ◎ fridge solid fuel & Electric
Elec metered Ⓛcan be hired ☎(1½m)
Iron & Ironing board in unit ⊙ CTV
⊕3 pin square 4P ♨(1½m)
⊖ ♀(¾m)

Min£50 Max£135pw

ST IVES
Cornwall
Map2 SW54

St Issey
—
St Ives

F Ayr Bank (Flats 1, 2 & Maisonette)
for bookings Mr R D Baragwanath, Cliff
Bungalow, Higher Ayr, St Ives, Cornwall
TR26 1EB
☎Penzance(0736)795855

*A large house divided into a ground-floor
flat, second-floor flat and a maisonette.
The flats sleep up to four and comprise
lounge/diner with two single divans, twin
bedded room, kitchen and bathroom. The
maisonette sleeps up to six and comprises
lounge with two single divans, one double
room, one twin bedded room, kitchen/
diner, bathroom and WC.*

All year MWB out of season 4 days min,
1 mth max, 3 units, 1–6 persons [◇] ◆
◆ no pets ◎ fridge Storage heaters
& electric fires Elec inclusive
Ⓛinclusive ☎(150yds) Iron & Ironing
board in unit [Launderette within
300yds] ⊙ CTV ⊕3 pin square P
♨(200yds)
⊖ δ(1m) ♀(400yds) 🎵(400yds)
🎵(400yds) 🐾(¼m)

Min£68 Max£155pw (Low)
Min£160 Max£265pw (High)

Ch Ayr Holiday Park
for bookings Mr R D Baragwanath, Ayr
Holiday Park, St Ives, Cornwall TR26 1EJ
☎Penzance(0736)795855

*There are 16 units, each accommodating
4–6 persons. Twelve are compact Western
Red Cedar timber chalets with a lounge,
kitchen, two bedrooms, bathroom and a
separate WC. The remainder are
traditionally-built, single-storey holiday
homes giving extra comfort and space,
with a sitting room, kitchen, two bedrooms
and a bathroom. The location gives
magnificent views over Porthmeor Beach
and the north Cornish coastline. Three
sandy beaches, the harbour and the town
are all within 1m of the Park.*

Apr–Oct MWB in season 1 wk min,
16 units, 4–6 persons ◆ ◆ ◎ fridge
Electric Elec inclusive Ⓛprovided on
request ☎(on site) [Iron] [Launderette
on premises] ⊙ CTV ⊕3 pin square
P ♨
⊖ δ(1m) ♀(½m) 🎵(½m) 🎵(½m)
🐾(½m)

Min£68 Max£150pw (Low)
Min£130 Max£243pw (High)

F 19 Ayr Terrace (Flats 1 & 2)
for bookings R D Baragwanath, Cliff
Bungalow, Higher Ayr, St Ives, Cornwall
TR26 1EB
☎Penzance(0736)795855 →

Two flats, one first floor and one ground floor, situated within an end of terrace, double-fronted house, next to Ayr Holiday Park. The ground-floor flat comprises lounge, kitchen/diner, two bedrooms (one twin and one double-bedded with additional single bed) and bathroom/WC. The first-floor flat comprises lounge/diner, compact kitchen, one bunk-bedded room and one double room with additional single bed, and bathroom/WC. Garden shared by both flats.

All year MWB out of season 4days min, 1mth max, 2units, 1–5persons [◇] ◆
◆ no pets ◎ fridge Storage heaters & electric fires Elec inclusive
⌴inclusive ☎(150yds) Iron & Ironing board in unit [Launderette within 300yds] ⊙ CTV ⊕3pin square P ♨(200yds)
↔ δ(1m) ♀(400yds) ♫(400yds) ♫(400yds) 🦞(½m)
Min£72 Max£130pw (Low)
Min£180 Max£235pw (High)

F Mr & Mrs J Blackburn **Berachah Holiday Flats** Wheal Whidden, Carbis Bay, St Ives, Cornwall TR26 2QX
☎Penzance(0736)795966
Three holiday flats situated in one wing of the owner's house. Magnificent views through garden of sea and coastline. Flat A comprises lounge, dining room, kitchen, one double and one triple (1 double & 1 single) bedroom, separate bathroom and WC on first floor. Flat B is on ground floor comprising lounge, kitchen, one double and one twin bedroom, bathroom with WC. Access to Carbis Bay Beach through Carbis Valley. Flat C is on ground floor and comprises open plan lounge/kitchen/diner, double bedroom with bathroom en suite

All year MWB out of season 1wk min, 2mths max, 3units, 1–5persons ◆
no pets ◎ fridge Electric
Elec metered ⌴not provided ☎ Iron in unit Ironing board on premises ⊙
CTV ⊕3pin square 1P 🅣 ♨(200yds)
↔ δ(1m) ♀(1m) ♫(½m) ♫(1m)
🦞(1½m)
Min£40 Max£180pw

C *Carnstabba Holiday Cottages*
Carnstabba Farm, Steeple Lane
for bookings Mr & Mrs Blackburn, Berachah, Wheal Whidden, Carbis Bay, St Ives, Cornwall TR26 2QX
☎Penzance(0736)795966
Two recently constructed cottages in rural surroundings just outside St Ives. Accommodation consists of lounge, two bedrooms, kitchen, bathroom and WC. Elevated position overlooking St Ives and Carbis Bay.

Mar–Oct MWB out of season 1wk min, 2mths max, 2units, 1–6persons ◆
no pets ◎ fridge Electric
Elec metered ⌴not provided
☎(20yds) CTV ⊕3pin square P 🅣
♨(½m)

St Ives

↔ δ(2m) ♀ ♫(½m) ♫(½m) 🦞(½m)
Details not confirmed for 1987

B Mr & Mrs Williams **Casa Bella Holiday Apartments** Hain Walk, St Ives, Cornwall
☎Penzance(0736)795427
Modern property situated in a commanding position overlooking St Ives Bay. Two-bedroomed (one double, one twin-bedded room which has separate area with bunk beds), lounge, kitchen/dining room, bathroom/WC. Private patio with sun beds. Adjacent to B3306 Carbis Bay to St Ives road approx ½m from town centre.

All year 3mths max, 1unit, 1–6persons ◆ ♦ fridge 🍴 Electric
Elec metered ⌴inclusive ☎(200yds) SD, Iron & Ironing board in unit ⊙ CTV ⊕3pin square P 🅣 ♨(250yds)
↔ δ(2m) ♫(½m) ♫(1m) 🦞(½m)
Barbeque & Patio

Min£65 Max£285pw

H **Hayeswood & Rocky Close** Higher Ayr
for bookings Mr R D Baragwanath, Ayr Holiday Park, St Ives, Cornwall TR26 1EJ
☎Penzance(0736)795855
Two houses of individual character, each standing in own grounds of ¼-acre with views of St Ives and Porthmeor Beach. Hayeswood is somewhat more spacious than Rocky Close and each enjoys private, quiet surroundings. Lots of character; comfortable furnishings.

All year MWB out of season 1wk min, 2units, 8persons ◆ ♦ no pets
◎ (Rocky Close) ♦ (Hayeswood)
fridge Electric 🍴Hayeswood
Elec inclusive ⌴inclusive ⊙ SD on premises Iron & Ironing board in unit [Launderette on premises] ⊙ CTV ⊕3pin square P ♨
↔ ♀(½m) ♫(½m) ♫(½m) 🦞(½m)
Min£140 Max£225pw (Low)
Min£230 Max£350pw (High)

B *Holiday Bungalow* Polwithen Drive, Carbis Bay
for bookings Mr & Mrs J Blackburn, Berachah, Wheal Whidden, Carbis Bay, St Ives, Cornwall TR26 2QX
☎Penzance(0736)795966
One modern bungalow situated at Carbis Bay approx 1½m from St Ives. The bungalow has lounge/dining area, two double bedrooms (one with additional single bed), kitchen, bathroom and WC.

All year MWB out of season 1wk min, 2mths max, 1unit, 1–5persons ◆
no pets ◎ fridge Electric
Elec metered ⌴not provided ☎(1m) Iron & Ironing board in unit ⊙ CTV ⊕3pin square P ♨(½m)

↔ δ(1m) ♫(1m) ♫(1m) 🦞(1m)
Details not confirmed for 1987

C **2 & 3 The Old Chapel** Halsetown
for bookings Mrs S Osborne, Polmanter Farm, Halsetown, St Ives, Cornwall
☎StIves(0736)795640
Two spacious well-equipped cottages converted from the village chapel. Both offer lounge/diner, modern fitted kitchen, one family bedroom with double and two single beds, one twin bedroom and bathroom/WC. They are comfortably furnished, still maintaining some of the original character of the building.

All year MWB out of season 3days min, 3wks max, 2units, 1–6persons ◆
no pets ◎ fridge Storage heaters
Elec metered ⌴not provided ☎(50yds) Iron & Ironing board in unit [Launderette within 300yds] ⊙ CTV ⊕3pin square 5P ♨(20yds) ⌷
↔ δ(3m) ♀(100yds) ♫(1½m) ♫(1½m) 🦞(½m)
Min£50 Max£175pw

H **Primrose Cottage**
for bookings R D Baragwanath, Cliff Bungalow, Higher Ayr, St Ives, Cornwall TR26 1EB
☎Penzance(0736)795855
A pebble-dashed former farm cottage now fully modernised and comprising kitchen/diner, lounge, three bedrooms (double, twin and bunk-bedded) and bathroom/WC.

All year MWB in season 4days min, 1mth max, 1unit, 1–6persons [◇] ◆
◆ no pets ◔ fridge Storage heaters & electric fires Elec inclusive
⌴incusive ☎(150yds) Iron & Ironing board in unit [Launderette within 300yds] ⊙ CTV ⊕3pin square 1P ♨(50yds)
↔ δ(1m) ♀(400yds) ♫(400yds) ♫(400yds) 🦞(½m)
Min£96 Max£170pw (Low)
Min£200 Max£275pw (High)

F S B Rains **Rockliff Holiday Flats** (No's 2, 3, 4, 5 & 6) Island Road, St Ives, Cornwall TR26 1NS
☎Penzance(0736)797165
A former net factory, converted to flats, situated in the old part of town. All flats have lounge, kitchen and bathroom/WC. Two have family bedrooms and three have one double and one family bedroom. Modern in style and décor. Drying cabinets in units.

All year MWB out of season 1wk min, 5units, 2–6persons ◆ ♦ ◎ fridge
Electric Elec metered ⌴can be hired
☎(100yds) Iron & Ironing board in unit [Launderette within 300yds] ⊙ TV ⊕3pin square 🅣 ♨(50yds)
↔ δ(3m) ♀(½m) ♫(½m) ♫(½m) 🦞(½m)
Min£42.50 Max£75pw (Low)
Min£65 Max£204pw (High)

F G M & C H Roberts **Talland House** St Ives, Cornwall TR26 2EH
☎Penzance(0736)796368

Built in 1850 and standing in its own grounds and well kept gardens, with glorious views over Porthminster beach, it was once the childhood home of novelist Virginia Woolf. Now five self-contained flats, each has a living room, kitchen area and bathroom/WC. Flats 1, 2 & 3 each have one double and one twin bedroom, flat 4 has two double bedrooms and flat 5 two doubles and a twin room.

22Mar–Oct MWB out of season 3days min, 5units, 4–6persons ◇ [◇ ◆] no pets ◎ fridge Electric Elec metered Ⓛcan be hired ☎(100yds) Iron & Ironing board on premises [Launderette within 300yds] ⊙ CTV ⊕3pin square P ▥ ▰(½m)
⊖ ♪(300yds) ♨(100yds) ♫(½m) ♬(100yds) 🐾(½m)
Min£75 Max£150pw (Low)
Min£205 Max£265pw (High)

B & F Mrs J Osborne **Trevalgan Farm Holiday Homes** St Ives, Cornwall TR26 3BJ
☎Penzance(0736)796433

Three flats and four bungalows which were once barns, grouped around a farmyard, have been tastefully converted into holiday homes. Boconnoc, Trelissick and Trelowarren have two bedrooms, Lanhydrock and Trewithen have three bedrooms, Trelawne and Trerice each have one bedroom. Trelowarren, Trewithen, Trerice and Trelawne have shower room/WC, the remaining units have bathroom/WC. All properties have been decorated and furnished to a high standard.

Feb–Dec MWB out of season 3days min, 4wks max, 7units, 2–7persons [◇] ◆ ◆ no pets ◎ fridge Electric Elec metered ☎(20yds) [SD on premises TD on premises] Iron & Ironing board in unit ⊙ CTV ⊕3pin square 11P ▥ ▰(1½m)
⊖ ♪(3m) ♨(1½m) ♫(2m) ♬(2m) 🐾(2m)
Min£50 Max£100pw (Low)
Min£125 Max£200pw (High)

F Mr & Mrs F L Andrews **Tremorna** Wheal Margery, St Ives, Cornwall TR26 2RH
☎Penzance(0736)795267

Five flats with fine views over Carbis Bay, converted from a large house. Horizon and Vista have double bedrooms en suite, and lead off the lounge/dining room. Horizon has a separate twin bunk room and Vista a children's twin room. Ground Floor has a double bedsitting room and separate child's room with one bed. View has a double and bedsitting room, both with balconies. Panorama has two double rooms. All except View have separate kitchen, it has a large kitchen/diner. Garden available with swings.

All year 1wk min, 4wks max, 5units, 1–5persons ◆ Family groups only

St Ives
—
St Nicholas

◎ fridge Night storage Elec metered Ⓛcan be hired ☎ SD on premises [TD on premises] Iron & Ironing board in unit ⊙ [TV] ⊕3pin square ⊕3pin round 5P ▥ ▰(½m)
⊖ ♪(½m) ♨(½m) ♫(1m) ♬(1½m) 🐾(1m)
Min£45 Max£139pw (Low)
Min£159 Max£184pw (High)

ST JUST
Cornwall
Map2 SW33

C *The Cottage* Tremythek, Higher Bosavern
for bookings Summer Cottages, Northernhay House, The Grove, Dorchester, Dorset DT1 1UL
☎Dorchester(0305)67545

Cornish stone cottage in open countryside, having two bedrooms, bathroom/WC and attractive open plan kitchen/lounge/diner.

Early Apr–late Sep 1wk min, 4wks max, 1unit, 1–4persons, nc6yrs ◎ fridge Electric Elec metered Ⓛcan be hired ☎(¾m) Iron & Ironing board in unit ⊙ TV ⊕3pin square 1P ▰(½m)
⊖ ♨(¾m)

Details not confirmed for 1987

ST KEVERNE
Cornwall
Map2 SW72

C & H St James Court Holiday Cottages *for bookings* F J H & A E Bray, Tregowris Farmhouse, Tregowris, St Keverne, Helston, Cornwall TR12 6PT
☎St Keverne(0326)280459

Small complex of character cottages in rural location approx 1½m NW of St Keverne village. Cottages 1, 2 & 7 sleep up to four, Cottage 6 is for two adults plus small child and Cottages 3, 4, & 5 sleep up to seven people.

Wk before Etr–Oct MWB in season 1wk min, 7units, 1–7persons ◆ ◆ ◎ fridge Electric Elec metered Ⓛnot provided ☎ Iron & Ironing board in unit ⊙ CTV ⊕3pin square P ▰(1½m)
⊖ ♨(2m)
Min£55 Max£120pw (Low)
Min£95 Max£170pw (High)

ST KEYNE
Cornwall
Map2 SX26

C & F Mr & Mrs P Cummins, **Badham Farm**, St Keyne, Liskeard, Cornwall PL14 4RW
☎Liskeard(0579)43572

Tastefully converted traditional Cornish farm buildings offering two apartments

sleeping four to six and one Coach-house to sleep two and one Stable to sleep eight. All well furnished and equipped. Situated in lovely quiet Looe Valley.

Mar–Dec MWB out of season 2days min, 3mths max, 4units, 1–8persons [◇] ◆ no pets ◎ fridge Storage heaters Elec inclusive Ⓛinclusive ☎in Farmhouse Iron & Ironing board in unit [Launderette on premises] ⊙ CTV ⊕3pin square 5P ▥ ▰(1m) Coarse fishing, play area, games room putting green
⊖ ♪(3m) ♨(3m) ♫(3m)
Min£60 Max£264pw

ST LAWRENCE
See **Wight, Isle of**

ST NEWLYN EAST
Cornwall
Map2 SW85

C 12 & 12A Station Road
for bookings Mrs F Gibbs, 24 St Michaels Road, Ponsanooth, Truro, Cornwall
☎Truro(0872)864279

A pair of semi-detached cottages located in the village of St Newlyn East about 5 miles from Newquay. No 12 comprises a small lounge with adjacent kitchen/diner and one twin-bedded room on the ground-floor and two bedrooms, one double, one twin-bedded on the first-floor, bathroom and WC. No 12A comprises three bedrooms, one double, one twin-bedded with additional twin-bedded room leading directly off (ideal for children's room). There is also a dining room, lounge and kitchen, bathroom and WC. Use of small gardens at rear.

May–Sep 1wk min, 2units, 1–6persons ◆ ◎ fridge Electric Elec metered Ⓛinclusive ☎(400yds) WM in unit Iron & Ironing board in unit ⊙ TV ⊕3pin square 2P ▰(400yds)
⊖ ♨(400yds)
Min£55 Max£140pw

ST NICHOLAS
Dyfed
Map2 SM93

C Parsonage Cottage
for bookings Coastal Cottages of Pembrokeshire, Seaview, Abercastle, Mathry, Dyfed SA62 5HJ
☎Croesgoch(03483)7742

A peacefully situated detached farm cottage with views of the sea and coastline to St David's Head. It is located at the end of a small private lane and comprises lounge, kitchen/diner, bathroom, one double, one twin and one double bedroom with additional single bed.

All year MWB out of season 4days min, 2mths max, 1unit, 2–7persons ◆ ◆ ◎ fridge Storage & portable heaters Elec metered Ⓛinclusive ☎(¼m) WM & SD in unit Iron & Ironing board in unit ⊙ CTV ⊕3pin square 2P ▰(¼m)
⊖ ♨(2m)
Min£70 Max£275pw

209

ST PETER PORT
Guernsey
See **Channel Islands**

ST SAVIOUR'S
Guernsey
See **Channel Islands**

SALCOMBE
Devon
Map**3** SX73
Also see East Portlemouth

C Melbury Cottage
for bookings Mr L Thackstone, Melbury
Hotel, Devon Road, Salcombe, Devon
☎Salcombe(054 884)2883

*Detached, stone-built former coach house
in elevated position within hotel grounds.
Accommodation comprises lounge
kitchen/dining room and bathroom/WC.
Two first-floor bedrooms, one of which has
sea views.*

All year MWB out of season 1wk min,
1mth max, 1unit, 2–6persons ◆
no pets ⊚ fridge Electric
Elec metered ⊔ can be hired ☎ SD in
unit Iron & Ironing board in unit ⊕ TV
⊕3pin square 2P ▥ ♨(300yds)
↔ ⬤ ⊡(½m)
Min£100 Max£210pw

SALEN
Highland *Argyllshire*
Map**13** NM66

Ch Mrs D H McEwan **Tigh-na-Creagan**
(Chalets) Salen, Acharacle, Argyllshire
PH36 4JN
☎Salen(096 785)270 (summer) &
Chelmsford(0245)421106 (winter)

*Two Scandinavian pine chalets standing
in 1¼ acres of trees and shrub-studded
land with views over Loch Sunart. Each
comprises two twin-bedded rooms, open
plan lounge (with double convertible)/
diner/kitchen and bathroom.*

May–Oct 1wk min, 3wks max, 2units,
2–6persons ◈ ◆ ⊚ fridge
Electric Elec metered ⊔ inclusive
☎(½m) Iron & Ironing board on
premises ⊖ ⊕3pin square 4P
♨(½m) Fishing & boating
↔ ⬤ (½m)
Min£90 Max£160pw

F Mrs D H McEwan **Tigh-na-Creagan**
(Flat) Salen, Acharacle, Argyllshire
PH36 4JN
☎Salen(096 785)270 (summer) &
Chelmsford(0245)421106 (winter)

---

*Flat with balcony adjoining owner's house,
situated on edge of Loch Sunart, with
good views. Accommodation comprises
twin bedroom, lounge/diner/kitchen and
bathroom. From Salen follow Kilchoan
road, B8007 for ½m.*

May–Oct 1wk min, 3wks max, 1unit,
2persons, nc no pets ◑ fridge
Electric Gas/Elec inclusive ⊔ inclusive
☎(½m) Iron & Ironing board on
premises ⊖ ⊕3pin square 1P
♨(½m) Fishing & boating
↔ ⬤ (½m)
£98pw

SALPERTON
Gloucestershire
Map**4** SP02

C Corner Cottage No 13 Salperton
for bookings Mrs Denley, 5 Salperton,
Cheltenham, Gloucestershire
☎Guiting Power(04515)529

*A tiny, attractive semi-detached cottage in
a Cotswold country hamlet comprising
small kitchen, lounge, one double
bedroom and bathroom.*

All year MWB 3days min, 8mths max,
1unit, 2persons [◈ ◆] ⊚ fridge
Electric & parkray Elec metered
⊔ inclusive ☎(200yds) Iron & Ironing
board in unit CTV ⊕3pin square 1P
▥ ♨(2m)
↔ ⬤ (2m)
Min£57.50 Max£102.25pw

DEVON'S SOUTHERNMOST HOTEL
Super Self Catering Apartments

Gara Rock

Telephone: Salcombe 2342
See entry under
East Portlemouth

Selected 1981 by The Consumers
Association as one of THE SIX BEST IN
EUROPE in the Good Hotel Guide.

A Family Hotel, run by a family, endeavouring to provide every amenity
for parents and children, use of all amenities included, offering more than
a Self Catering Holiday.

Open Easter to end of October, Self Catering open March to November.

Surrounded by National Trust Land with Sandy beaches beneath.
Amenities include:-
Outdoor heated Swimming Pool, Tennis Court, Childrens Adventure
Playground, Games Room and Garden Games.

Ideal for the Getaway weekend out of season.

SAMPFORD SPINEY
Devon
Map**2** SX57

C   Coachman's Cottage
for bookings Mr H J C Cornish,
Stoneycroft, Sampford Spiney, Yelverton,
Devon PL20 6LF
☎Yelverton(0822)852280

A single-storey stone-built cottage, set in
Dartmoor National Park and having fine
views of surrounding countryside. It
comprises kitchen, lounge/diner, shower
room/WC, and two bedrooms. One
bedroom has a double bed, and the other
has full size bunk beds.

All year   MWB out of season   1wk min,
1mth max, 1unit, 4persons   ◎ fridge
Electric   Elec metered   ⊑not provided
☎(2m)   Iron & Ironing board in unit   ⊕
TV   ⊕3pin square   2P   ▒(3m)
⊖ ♪(3m)   ☻(3m)
Min£45 Max£55pw (Low)
Min£75 Max£90pw (High)

SANDYHILLS
Dumfries & Galloway Kirkcudbrightshire
Map**11** NX85

Ch   Barend Farm
for bookings Barend Properties Ltd, 15
Barend, Sandyhills, Dalbeattie DG5 4NU
☎Southwick(038778)663

Two-storey Scandinavian-style timbered
chalets. Facilities and décor of very high
standard. The chalets are in an elevated
position overlooking a man-made loch.

All year   MWB   3days min, 4wks max,
20units, 2–12persons   [◇]   [◆ ◆]
♪ fridge   ♨Gas inclusive
⊑inclusive   ☎ Iron & Ironing board on
premises   [Launderette on premises]
⊕ CTV   ⊕3pin square   P   ▒(½m)
Riding school, pony trekking, bar,
restaurant and fly fishing
⊖ ♪(½m)   ♀
Min£110 Max£185pw (Low)
Min£210 Max£265pw (High)

SANDY LANE
Wiltshire
Map**3** ST96

C   CC Ref 807 EP
for bookings Character Cottages
(Holidays) Ltd, 34 Fore Street, Sidmouth,
Devon EX10 8AQ
☎Sidmouth(039 55)77001

A detached stone-built thatched cottage
with magnificent views over the Wiltshire
Downs. The completely modernised
interior comprises kitchen/dining room,
living room, bath/shower, two WC's and
three bedrooms.

All year   1wk min, 3mths max, 1unit,
2–4persons   ◇ ◆ ♪ fridge
Electric   Gas inclusive in summer
⊑not provided   ☎(1m)   ⊕ TV
⊕3pin square   P   ▒(5m)
⊖ ♀(1m)
Min£79 Max£113pw (Low)
Min£129 Max£182pw (High)

Sampford Spiney
—
Saundersfoot

C   CC Ref 808 EP
for bookings Character Cottages
(Holidays) Ltd, 34 Fore Street, Sidmouth,
Devon EX10 8AQ
☎Sidmouth(03955)77001

A picturesque, modernised thatched
cottage set in a hamlet of similar cottages,
with accommodation comprising kitchen/
dining room, two bedrooms, bathroom/
WC.

All year   1wk min, 3mths max, 1unit,
4persons   ◇ ◆ ♪ fridge   Electric
Gas/Elec inclusive in summer
⊑not provided   ☎(½m)   ⊕ TV
⊕3pin square   P   ▒(5m)
⊖ ♀(1m)
Min£87 Max£125pw (Low)
Min£142 Max£229pw (High)

C   CC Ref 809 EP
for bookings Character Cottages
(Holidays) Ltd, 34 Fore Street, Sidmouth,
Devon EX10 8AQ
☎Sidmouth(039 55)77001

Detached cottage comprising lounge,
kitchen/diner, three bedrooms (two
double, one single), bathroom/WC. Within
an all-thatched hamlet in peaceful country
setting.

All year   1wk min, 3mths max, 1unit,
2–5persons   ◇ no cats   ◎ fridge
Electric   Elec inclusive   ⊑not provided
Iron & Ironing board in unit   ⊕ TV
⊕3pin square   P   ▥   ▒(3m)
⊖ ♪(3m)   ♀(½m)   ♫(3m)
Min£62 Max£93pw (Low)
Min£112 Max£169pw (High)

SAUNDERSFOOT
Dyfed
Map**2** SN10

C & F   Mr & Mrs Streatfield **Baytrees**
Sandy Hill Road, Saundersfoot, Dyfed
SA69 9HW
☎Saundersfoot(0834)812219

Holiday cottage and flat in a pleasant
peaceful location enjoying good sea and
country views. The cottage is an annexe to
the main house and offers
accommodation of kitchen, lounge/diner,
two bedrooms (one double, and one
double with single bed), bathroom/WC.
The flat consists of kitchen, bathroom/WC,
lounge/diner and three bedrooms. (2
double-bedded and one twin-bedded.
Additional single in one of the double
rooms).

Mid Mar–mid Nov   MWB out of season
2days min, 3wks max, 2units, 1–7persons
[◇]   ◆ ◆ ◎ fridge   Electric &
convectors   Elec metered   ⊑can be
hired   ☎(70yds)   Iron & Ironing board in
unit   ⊕ CTV   ⊕3pin square   P   ▥
▒(½m)

⊖ ♪(3m)   ♀(½m)   ♫(½m)   ♫(½m)
☻(3m)
Min£45 Max£105pw (Low)
Min£95 Max£165pw (High)

B   Valley Close Bungalows Valley Road
for bookings Saundersvale Holiday Estate
Ltd, Valley Road, Saundersfoot, Dyfed
SA69 9BT
☎Saundersfoot(0834)812310

Group of eight semi-detached bungalows
with compact family accommodation.
Each unit comprises lounge with studio
couch (forming a double bed), kitchen/
dining room (one family bedroom (one
double and bunk beds) and bathroom/
WC. Larger families can be
accommodated by use of adjoining doors
to next unit.

All year   MWB out of season   ◇ ◆
◆ ◎ fridge   Electric   Elec inclusive
⊑can be hired   ☎(300yds)   Iron &
Ironing board in unit   [Launderette within
300yds]   ⊕ TV   ⊕3pin square   P
▒(300yds)
Min£50 Max£265pw

H   Valley Grove Villas Valley Road
for bookings Saundersvale Holiday Estate
Ltd, Valley Road, Saundersfoot, Dyfed
SA69 9BT
☎Saundersfoot(0834)812310

Ten compact villas, each with patio.
Modern accommodation comprises two
bedrooms (one double and one twin),
sitting/dining room with double bed-
settee, kitchen and bathroom/WC.

All year   MWB out of season   2nights min,
10units, 2–6persons   [◇]   ◆ ◎
fridge   Electric   Elec inclusive   ⊑can be
hired   ☎(200yds)   Iron & Ironing board in
unit   [Launderette within 300yds]   ⊕
CTV   ⊕3pin square   P   ▒(200yds)
⊖ ♀(200yds)
Min£50 Max£265pw

F   Waters Edge The Strand
for bookings Mrs J Griffiths, Sea Breeze,
The Strand, Saundersfoot, Dyfed SA69 9EX
☎Saundersfoot(0834)812617

Spacious well-maintained units available
on four levels with good views and direct
access to the beach. Flats have one or two
bedrooms and some also have sofa beds
and all flats have balcony. Magnificent
views from the higher floors.

Mar–Dec   MWB out of season
2nights min,. 12units, 2–6persons   ◆
◎ fridge   Electric   Elec inclusive   ⊑can
be hired (overseas visitors only)
☎(300yds)   Iron in unit   [Launderette
within 300yds]   ⊕ CTV   ⊕3pin square
14P   ▥   ▒
⊖ ♪(3m)   ♀(100yds)   ♫(100yds)
♫(100yds)   ☻(3m)
Min£72 Max£86pw (Low)
Min£248 Max£308pw (High)

See advertisement on page 212

Powell's Cottage Holidays 55 High Street,
Sandersfoot, Dyfed
☎Saundersfoot(0834)812791 →

The following properties are operated by Powell's.

H Alandale

for bookings see 'Powell's Cottage Holidays' for address.
☎Saundersfoot(0834)812791

Situated in a secluded position in woods and comprising lounge, diner, kitchen, bathroom/WC and three bedrooms sleeping seven people.

1wk min, 1unit, 7persons ◎ fridge
Ⓛnot provided ☎(50yds) Iron & Ironing board in unit CTV ⊕3pin square 2P
🅼 ♨(200yds)
↔ ♪(3m) ♣(150yds) 🎵(500yds)
🎵(500yds) ♞(500yds)

Min£135 Max£276pw

B Bishop-Dene

for bookings see 'Powell's Cottage Holidays' for address
☎Saundersfoot(0834)812791

A detached bungalow with fish pond in the garden, a short walk from Glen Beach. Comprises lounge,dining room, kitchen, bathroom/WC and two bedrooms with double and single bed in each.

1wk min, 1unit, 2–6persons ◇ no pets
◎ fridge electric fires Elec inclusive
☎(50yds) Iron & Ironing board in unit
CTV ⊕3pin square 3P 🅼 ♨(½m)
↔ ♪(3m) ♣(½m) 🎵(½m) 🎵(½m)
♞(3m)

Min£99 Max£222pw

B Gaythorne

for bookings see 'Powell's Cottage Holidays' for address
☎Saundersfoot(0834)812791

Situated within walking distance of the harbour and comprising lounge, dining room, kitchen, two double and one twin bedded room and bathroom, WC.

1wk min, 1unit, 2–6persons ◇ no pets
◎ fridge electric fires Elec inclusive
☎(100yds) Iron & Ironing board in unit
TV ⊕3pin square 2P 🅼 ♨(100yds)
↔ ♪(3m) ♣(½m) 🎵(½m) 🎵(½m)
♞(3m)

Min£99 Max£222pw

Saundersfoot

F Grosvenor Flat

for bookings see 'Powell's Cottage Holidays' for address
☎Saundersfoot(0834)812791

A first floor flat overlooking harbour and beach, comprising lounge. kitchen/diner bathroom/WC, separate WC, three double and one twin bedded room.

1wk min, 1unit, 2–8persons ◇ no pets
◎ fridge electric fires Elec inclusive
☎(50yds) Iron & Ironing board in unit
⊙ CTV ⊕3pin square 🅼
♨(adjacent)
↔ ♣(adjacent) 🎵(½m) 🎵(½m)
♞(3m)

Min£135 Max£297pw

H Joquita

for bookings see 'Powell's Cottage Holidays' for address
☎Saundersfoot(0834)812791

Large detached house close to beach with sea views. Accommodation comprises lounge, dining room, kitchen and three bedrooms (one double, one twin bedded and one with a double and single bed). There is a bathroom/WC and separate shower room.

May–Aug MWB out of season 1wk min,
1unit, 6–7persons no pets ◎ fridge
♨ Elec inclusive Ⓛinclusive Iron &
Ironing board in unit CTV
Min£165 Max£351pw

H Kantara

for bookings see 'Powell's Cottage Holidays' for address
☎Saundersfoot(0834)812791

An attractive modern detached house in an elevated position in a quiet cul-de-sac only a few minutes' walk from the harbour. Accommodation comprises a kitchen, dining room and lounge on the ground floor and two double bedrooms, one bedroom with two bunk beds and a bathroom/WC on the first floor.

May–Aug 1wk min, 6wks max, 1unit,
2–6persons ◇ ◆ ◎ fridge
Electric fires Elec inclusive Ⓛinclusive
☎(½m) Iron & Ironing board in unit ⊙
CTV ⊕3pin square 2P 🅼 ♨(½m)
↔ ♣(½m) 🎵(½m) 🎵(½m)
Min£99 Max£222pw

B La Rocque

for bookings see 'Powell's Cottage Holidays' for address
☎Saundersfoot(0834)812791

A modern bungalow comprising lounge, kitchen/diner, bathroom/WC, three bedrooms, one double, one double plus single and one single.

1wk min, 1unit, 6persons ◇ no pets
◎ fridge ♨ Elec inclusive ☎(50yds)
Iron & Ironing board in unit ⊙ CTV
⊕3pin square 1P 🅼 ♨(½m)
↔ ♪(3m) ♣(½m) 🎵(½m) 🎵(½m)
♞(3m)

Min£99 Max£222pw

H Mariners Reach

for bookings see 'Powell's Cottage Holidays' for address
☎Saundersfoot(0834)812791

Located beside sandy beach with extensive sea and harbour views. Accommodation comprises, lounge, dining area, kitchen, bathroom/WC, two double bedrooms one with en-suite bathroom and separate shower, one twin-bedded room plus bunks, one single room, balcony and sun terrace.

1wk min, 1unit, 7–9persons ◇ ◆
no pets ◎ fridge ♨ Elec inclusive
☎(300yds) WM in unit Iron & Ironing
board in unit ⊙ CTV ⊕3pin square
2P 🅼 ♨(300yds)
↔ ♪(1½m) ♣(½m) 🎵(½m) 🎵(½m)
Min£252 Max£570pw

B Peace Haven

for bookings see 'Powell's Cottage Holidays' for address
☎Saundersfoot(0834)812791

A split-level bungalow of unusual design overlooking village. There is a pleasant patio and small terraced garden. Accommodation comprises kitchen, spacious lounge/diner, two double

bedrooms, one twin-bedded room, one room with bunk beds and bathroom/WC with shower. There is an additional WC outside.

May–Aug MWB out of season 1wk min, 1unit, 1–8persons ◈ ◆ no pets ◎ fridge ▦ Elec inclusive ▣ can be hired ☎(½m) Iron & Ironing board in unit TV ⊕3pin square 3P ▥ ⛟(½m)

⊖ δ(2½m) ♀(½m) ▣♫(½m) ▣(2½m)

Min£123 Max£276pw

***H* Rainbow House**
for bookings see 'Powell's Cottage Holidays' for address
☎Saundersfoot(0834)812791

A detached house comprising lounge dining area, kitchen, bathroom/WC, separate WC, two double and two twin-bedded rooms and terraced garden.

1wk min, 1unit, 8persons ◈ ◆ no pets ◎ fridge storage heaters & electric fires Elec inclusive ☎(150yds) Iron & Ironing board in unit ⊙ CTV ⊕3pin square 2P ▥ ⛟(¼m)

⊖ ♀(¼m) ▣♫(¼m) ♫(¼m)

Min£135 Max£297pw

***B & F* Rainbow Vale**
for bookings see 'Powell's Cottage Holidays' for address
☎Saundersfoot(0834)812791

Situated in lawns and gardens 100yds from Glen Beach. ***The Bungalow*** *comprises lounge with dining alcove, kitchen, bathroom with bidet and WC, four bedrooms three with double beds one with twin beds and playroom with cloakroom.* ***Vale Nook*** *is a flat comprising lounge, kitchen, bathroom/WC, one twin and one double bedroom.* ***Sun Vale*** *and* ***Sea Vale*** *a ground and first-floor flat comprising lounge, dining area, kitchen, bathroom/WC, three bedrooms, two double and one twin.*

1wk min, 4units, 4–8persons ◈(in Bungalow, Sun Vale & Sea Vale) no pets ◎ fridge ▦ Elec inclusive ▣ inclusive (The Bungalow) ☎ (The Bungalow) Iron & Ironing board in unit Launderette on premises CTV ⊕3pin square P ▥ ⛟(½m)

⊖ ♀(½m) ▣♫(½m) ♫(½m)

Min£111 Max£570pw

***H* Ravenwood**
for bookings see 'Powell's Cottage Holidays' for address
☎Saundersfoot(0834)812791

A renovated farmhouse 2½miles from village beach. The accommodation comprises lounge, kitchen/dining area, bathroom/WC, three bedrooms one double, one twin and one family room with a double and bunk beds.

1wk min, 1unit, 6–8persons ◈ no pets ◎ fridge electric Elec inclusive Iron & Ironing board in unit ⊙ CTV ⊕3pin square 2P ▥ ⛟(20yds)

⊖ δ(3m) ♀(20yds) ▣♫(3m) ♫(3m) ▣(3m)

Min£111 Max£237pw

Saundersfoot — Scarborough

***H* Rob Roy**
for bookings see 'Powell's Cottage Holidays' for address
☎Saundersfoot(0834)812791

A detached house comprising lounge, kitchen/diner, bathroom/WC, three bedrooms one double, one twin and one with bunk beds.

1wk min, 1unit, 6persons ◈ ◌ fridge storage heaters Gas/Elec inclusive ☎(¼m) Iron & Ironing board in unit CTV ⊕3pin square 1P 1⌂ ▥ ⛟(¼m)

⊖ δ(2½m) ♀(½m) ▣♫(½m) ♫(½m) ▣(2½m)

Min£99 Max£222pw

***H* Tel-Quel**
for bookings see 'Powell's Cottage Holidays' for address
☎Saundersfoot(0834)812791

Split level house overlooking the sea comprising lounge/diner, kitchen, three double bedrooms, bathroom/WC, shower/WC and cloakroom/WC.

1wk min, 1unit, 2–6persons ◈ no pets ◎ fridge ▦ Elec inclusive ☎(¼m) Iron & Ironing board in unit ⊙ CTV ⊕3pin square 1P 1⌂ ▥ ⛟(½m)

⊖ δ(3m) ♀(½m) ▣♫(1m) ♫(1m) ▣(3m)

Min£165 Max£351pw

***F* Three Guys**
for bookings see 'Powell's Cottage Holidays' for address
☎Saundersfoot(0834)812791

Modern ground-floor flat 750 yds from the beach, comprising lounge/diner, kitchen bathroom and separate WC, two double bedded rooms and one twin-bedded room.

1wk min, 1unit, 6–7persons ◈ no pets ◎ fridge ▦ Elec inclusive ☎(¼m) Iron & Ironing board in unit ⊙ CTV ⊕3pin square 1P ▥ ⛟(¼m)

⊖ δ(1½m) ♀(¼m) ▣♫(¼m) ♫(¼m)

Min£93 Max£210pw

***B* Ty-Newydd**
for bookings see 'Powell's Cottage Holidays' for address
☎Saundersfoot(0834)812791

A detached bungalow with sea views comprising lounge/diner, kitchen shower/WC, two double bedrooms one with additional single bed.

1wk min, 1unit, 5persons ◈ no pets ◎ fridge ▦ Elec inclusive ☎(200yds) Iron & Ironing board in unit ⊙ CTV ⊕3pin square 1P ▥ ⛟(1m)

⊖ δ(3m) ♀(1m) ▣♫(1m) ♫(1m) ▣(3m)

Min£93 Max£210pw

***F* Verbena & Leewick**
for bookings see 'Powell's Cottage Holidays' for address
☎Saundersfoot(0834)812791

Two flats located above shops and overlooking the sea. ***Verbena*** *comprises lounge/diner, kitchen, bath/WC, two double, one twin and one bunk-bedded room.* ***Leewick*** *comprises lounge, kitchen/diner, bathroom, WC, two double and one bunk-bedded room.*

1wk min, 2units, 2–8persons ◈ ◌(Verbena) ◎(Leewick) fridge ▦ Gas/Elec inclusive ☎(50yds) Iron & Ironing board in unit ⊙ CTV ⊕3pin square ▥ ⛟(adjacent)

⊖ ♀(adjacent) ▣♫(½m) ♫(½m) ▣(3m)

Min£99 Max£237pw

***B* Westville**
for bookings see 'Powell's Cottage Holidays' for address
☎Saundersfoot(0834)812791

A modern bungalow comprising, lounge/dining area, kitchen, bathroom/WC, cloakroom, two double bedded rooms one of which also has bunk beds and one twin-bedded room.

1wk min, 1unit, 8persons ◈ no pets ◌ fridge ▦ Gas/Elec inclusive ☎(¼m) Iron & Ironing board in unit CTV ⊕3pin square 1P ▥ ⛟(½m)

⊖ δ(2½m) ♀(½m) ▣♫(½m) ♫(½m) ▣(2½m)

Min£111 Max£237pw

***H* White Oaks**
for bookings see 'Powell's Cottage Holidays' for address
☎Saundersfoot(0834)812791

A detached house on the cliff top overlooking the sea, comprising, lounge, dining room, kitchen, cloakroom, four bedrooms, one double, two twins and one bunk bedded and bathroom WC.

1wk min, 1unit, 8persons ◈ no pets ◌ fridge ▦ Gas/Elec inclusive ☎(½m) Iron & Ironing board in unit CTV ⊕3pin square 3P ▥ ⛟(500yds)

⊖ δ(3m) ♀(150yds) ▣♫(150yds) ♫(150yds) ▣(3m)

Min£171 Max£390pw

SCARBOROUGH
North Yorkshire
Map**8** TA08

***F* Albion Flats** 16 Albion Road
for bookings Mr & Mrs Shearer, 83 Cornelian Drive, Scarborough, North Yorkshire YO11 3AL
☎Scarborough(0723)363659

Occupying part of a large Edwardian terraced house near South Cliffs, each unit has a lounge, kitchen and bathroom/WC, and sleeping accommodation for up to eight persons depending on the flat size.

All year MWB out of season 1wk min, 6units, 1–8persons [◇] ◈ ◆ ◌ fridge Electric Gas & Elec metered →

Ⓛinclusive except towels ☎(200yds)
Iron & Ironing board in unit [Launderette
within 300yds] Ⓖ [CTV]
Ⓔ3pin square ♨(250yds)
Ⓔ ♪(1½m) ♀(50yds) ♫(1m)
♫(1m) ☂(½m)
Min£85 Max£120pw (Low)
Min£160 Max£190pw (High)

F Fraser Court Holiday Flats 1–5
Grosvenor Road
for bookings Mr Griffiths, Country &
Coastal Self Catering Holidays, 9 Birdgate,
Pickering, North Yorkshire
☎Pickering(0751)75058

Five flats situated within a pair of
converted Victorian houses overlooking
Valley Gardens. The flats sleep up to six
people in a combination of beds with the
larger bedrooms having wash hand basin.
They all comprise spacious lounge/dining
room, kitchen and bathroom/WC. The flats
are located on the ground, first and
second floors.

All year MWB out of season 1day min,
3mths max, 5units, 1–6persons [◇] ◆
◆ ⊚ fridge Electric Elec metered
Ⓛcan be hired ☎(50yds) Ⓖ CTV
Ⓔ3pin square ⅢⅢ ♨(100yds)
Ⓔ ♪(2m) ♀(50yds) ♫(½m) ♫(½m)
☂(½m)

Min£40 Max£200pw

F 49 Grosvenor Road
for bookings Mrs G Wittering, 54 Deepdale
Avenue, Scarborough YO11 2UF
☎Scarborough(0723)366256

Seven self-contained flats in a large
detached house near the town centre.
Four share a common entrance and three
have their own individual entrances. Good
fittings and furnishings, generally
spacious and well appointed.

May–Oct MWB out of season 1wk min,
2mths max, 7units, 4–6persons ◇ ◆
⊚ fridge Electric Elec metered
Ⓛinclusive ☎ [WM, SD & TD on
premises] [Iron on premises] Ironing
board on premises Ⓖ CTV
Ⓔ3pin square ♨(400yds)
Ⓔ ♀(400yds) ♫(800yds) ☂(600yds)
Min£69 Max£150pw (Low)
Min£104 Max£200pw (High)

F 12 Scalby Mills Road
for bookings Mrs Sellars, 10 Scalby Mills
Road, Scarborough, North Yorkshire
YO12 6RW
☎Scarborough(0723)374509 & 373022

A first-floor flat in a converted semi-
detached house in residential area
overlooking golf course. The sleeping
arrangements are up to six people plus
dining room/lounge, kitchen and
bathroom/WC. Two miles from town centre
and near to beach.

All year MWB 1wk min, 3mths max, 1unit,
1–6persons ◇ ◆ ⊚ fridge
Electric Elec metered Ⓛinclusive
☎(200yds) TD Iron & Ironing board in
unit [Launderette] CTV
Ⓔ3pin square 1P ⅢⅢ ♨(200yds)

Ⓔ ♪(½m) ♀(100yds) ♫(2m)
♫(2m) ☂(2m)
Min£70 Max£185pw

H 14 Scalby Mills Road
for bookings Mrs S R Sellars, 10 Scalby
Mills Road, Scarborough, North Yorkshire
YO12 6RW
☎Scarborough(0723)374509 & 373022

A semi-detached house in a residential
area, 2m from the town centre,
overlooking golf course. It sleeps up to six
people in three bedrooms plus a bed-
settee in the lounge, with dining room,
kitchen, bathroom/WC and shower plus
separate WC.

All year MWB 1wk min, 3mths max, 1unit,
1–7persons ◇ ◆ ⊚ fridge Electric
& gas fires Elec metered Ⓛinclusive
☎(200yds) TD, WM, SD in unit Iron &
Ironing board in unit [Launderette within
300yds] CTV
Ⓔ 3pin square 2P ⅢⅢ ♨(200yds)
Ⓔ ♪(½m) ♀(100yds) ♫(2m)
♫(2m) ☂(2m)
Min£80 Max£200pw

F 54 Scalby Mills Road
for bookings Mr A A Squire, 54 Falsgrave
Road, Scarborough, N Yorkshire
☎Scarborough(0723)360542 (day) &
374220 (evening)

Large semi-detached house divided into
two flats. Conveniently situated for north
beach, on the outskirts of town,
overlooking golf course. Good, clean
standard.

All year MWB out of season 1wk min,
2wks max, 2units, 1–6persons ◇ ◆
no pets ⊚ fridge ☃(1 flat only)
Electric Elec metered Ⓛinclusive
☎(300yds) Iron & Ironing board in unit
Ⓖ CTV P ♨(300yds)
Ⓔ ♪ ♀(100yds) ♫(1½m) ♫(1½m)
☂(2m) ☒ ⌒(1m)
Min£50 Max£60pw (Low)
Min£120 Max£195pw (High)

F 11 Valley Bridge Parade
for bookings Mrs G Wittering, 54 Deepdale
Avenue, Scarborough, N Yorkshire
YO11 2UF
☎Scarborough(0723)366256

Four self-contained flats each occupying
a single floor of the five-storeyed town
house overlooking Valley Bridge close to
the central shopping area. First-class
fittings and furnishings. Well-appointed
and well managed

May–Oct MWB out of season 1wk min,
2mths max, 4units, 4persons ◇ ◆ ⊚
fridge Electric Elec metered
Ⓛinclusive ☎(40yds) Iron & Ironing
board in unit Ⓖ CTV Ⓔ3pin square
♨(100yds)
Ⓔ ♀(300yds) ♫(500yds)
♫(500yds) ☂(300yds)

Min£71 Max£97pw (Low)
Min£104 Max£132pw (High)

F 15 Victoria Park
for bookings Mr A A Squire, 54 Falsgrave
Road, Scarborough, N Yorkshire
☎Scarborough(0723)360542 (day) &
374220 (evening)

Large semi-detached house divided into
one ground-floor and one first-floor flat
with separate entrances. Situated in town
in the heart of North Beach holiday
facilities and overlooking Peasholm Park,
close to cricket ground.

Etr–Oct MWB out of season 1wk min,
2wks max, 2units, 1–6persons ◇ ◆
no pets ⊚ fridge Electric
Elec metered Ⓛinclusive ☎(30yds)
WM, TD, Iron & Ironing board in unit Ⓖ
CTV Ⓔ3pin square P ⅢⅢ ♨(30yds)
Ⓔ ♪(1m) ☒ ⌒(300yds) ♀(50yds)
♫(100yds) ♫(2m) ☂(100yds)
Min£50 Max£60pw (Low)
Min£120 Max£195pw (High)

SCILLY, ISLES OF
No map
St Mary's

F Mr Gregory Moonrakers Holiday Flats
Garrison Lane, St Mary's, Isles of Scilly
TR21 0JF
☎Scillonia(0720)22717

Six self-contained flats comfortably
furnished and well-equipped in an
attractive detached building adjacent to
the Garrison Gateway in an elevated
position overlooking town harbour and
sea views over numerous rocky islets.

Mar–8Nov MWB 1wk min, 1mth max,
6units, 1–6persons, nc3 no pets ⊚
fridge Electric Elec metered
Ⓛinclusive ☎(100yds) Iron & Ironing
board in unit Ⓖ CTV Ⓔ3pin square
P ⅢⅢ ♨(200yds)
Ⓔ ♀(100yds)
Min£70.15 Max£154.10pw (Low)
Min£178.25 Max£296.70pw (High)

SCORTON
Lancashire
Map**7** SD44

**F The Manager Six Arches Caravan
Park** Scorton, Garstang, Preston,
Lancashire PR3 1AL
☎Forton(0524)791683

A block of six brick-built flats within the
caravan park, on the banks of the River
Wyre with good views of the Beacon Fells.
The flats are of modern design with good
furnishings. They are reached by turning E
off the A6 by the Little Chef N of Garstang
and continuing under the six arches from
which the site gets its name.

Spring Bank Hol–Oct MWB out of
season 7days min, 6units, 2–6persons
[◇] ◆ ⊚ fridge Electric
Elec metered Ⓛcan be hired
☎(50yds) [Iron & Ironing board on
premises] [Launderette on premises]
Ⓖ CTV Ⓔ3pin square P ⅢⅢ ♨ ⌒
Ⓔ ♀ ♫

214

Min£50 Max£70pw (Low)
Min£85 Max£110pw (High)

SCOURIE
Highland *Sutherland*
Map**14** NC14

B   Cnoclochan
for bookings Mr & Mrs J M Williams, Sutton
Abinger, Dorking, Surrey RH5 6PS
☎Dorking(0306)730331
*A spacious modern bungalow comprising
a large living room, kitchen/diner, utility
room, bathroom, one twin-bedded and
one double room (with shower/WC) and
one room with bunks and a single bed. ½m
from village.*

15Apr–Sep   1wk min, 1unit, 1–7persons
◎   fridge   Electric & open fire
Elec metered   ⌷not provided   ☎(½m)
TD in unit   Iron in unit   ⊕
⊕3pin square   3P   ♨(½m)   freezer
⇔   ⚲(½m)
Min£80 Max£130pw

SCRATBY
Norfolk
Map**9** TG51

Ch & H   Beach Road Chalet Park Beach
Road
for bookings Hoseasons Holidays,
Sunway House, Lowestoft, Suffolk
NR32 3LT
☎Lowestoft(0502)62271
*Mayfair are 46 purpose-built brick/timber
semi-detached chalets with small patios.
Carlton are 14 two-storey semi-detached
houses of modern design. The chalets
sleep from two to six and have combined
lounge/kitchen and a bathroom/WC. The
houses sleep from two to eight people and
comprise lounge/dining room, kitchen and
bathroom/WC.*

Apr–Sep   MWB out of season   4days min,
60units, 2–8persons   [◈   ◆]   ◎
fridge   ♨   Electric   Elec metered
⌷inclusive   ☎(½m)   [Iron on premises]
⊕   CTV   ⊕3pin square   P   ⌂(200yds)
⚘   Children's play area
⇔   ⚲(300yds)   ♬(300yds)   ♫(300yds)
Min£45 Max£160pw

Ch & H   Summerfields Holiday Park
Beach Road
for bookings Hoseasons Holidays,
Sunway House, Lowestoft, Suffolk
NR32 3LT
☎Lowestoft(0502)62271

*Summercrest, Summershore and
Summertide are 11 purpose-built brick
and timber chalets sleeping 2–6 people.
They comprise lounge/kitchen/dining
room and either bath or shower/WC.
Summerspray and Summerwave are
two-storey brick-built houses, with
Summerspray comprising 34 units
sleeping from 2–7 people, combined
lounge/kitchen and bathroom/WC.
Summerwave comprises 4 units sleeping
2–5 people and has lounge/kitchen/
dining room and shower/WC. All are set*

Scorton
—
Seaton

*within a well-maintained grassed site with
concrete roads.*

Apr–Sep   MWB out of season   4days min,
49units, 2–7persons   [◇   ◈   ◆]   ◎
fridge   Electric   Elec metered
⌷inclusive   ☎(200yds)   Iron on
premises   ⊕   CTV   ⊕3pin square   P
♨   Children's room   [♬]   ♫
Min£40 Max£155pw

SCURLAGE
West Glamorgan
Map**2** SS48

Ch   Georgian Lodge Holiday Homes
for bookings Hoseasons Holidays,
Sunway House, Lowestoft, Suffolk
NR32 3LT
☎Lowestoft(0502)62281
*Each of the chalets is laid out adjoining
the hotel and comprises lounge with bed-
settee, kitchen and bathroom. Modern
furnishings and good décor.*

Apr–Sep   MWB out of season   1wk min,
47 units, 4–6persons   [◈]   [◆]
no pets   ◎   fridge   Electric
Elec metered   ⌷inclusive   ☎   [Iron &
Ironing board on premises]   [Launderette
on premises]   ⊕   CTV   ⊕3pin square
P   ⌂   ♨   ⌑   putting green ⇔   ⚲   ♫
Min£72 Max£222pw

B   Gower Holiday Village Gower
for bookings Haven Leisure EEC Ltd,
Haven House, Quay Street, Truro,
Cornwall TR1 2UE
☎Truro(0872)40400
*There are three different types of
bungalows in this holiday village.
Countryman comprises open plan lounge/
diner, kitchenette, bathroom/WC, one
double bedroom and one with twin beds.
Penrice is a three bedroomed bungalow,
one double, one twin and one with bunks,
it has a spacious lounge, open plan dining
area, kitchentte and bathroom/WC.
Georgian has one double and one single
bedroom, spacious lounge, open plan
kitchen/dining area and bathroom/WC.*

Etr & May–Sep   MWB in season
1day min, 63units, 1–6persons   ◇
[◈ ◆]   no pets   ◎   fridge
Storage heaters   Elec metered
⌷inclusive   ☎   [WM, SD & TD on
premises]   [Iron on premises]   Ironing
board on premises   [Launderette within
300yds]   ⊕   CTV   ⊕3pin square   P
⌂   ♨   ⌑
⇔   ⚲   ♬   ♫
Min£72 Max£172pw (Low)
Min£158 Max£244pw (High)

SEATOLLER
Cumbria
Map**11** NY21

C   Scale Force Cottage
for bookings Lakeland Cottage Holidays,
Yew Tree Cottage, Ullock, Keswick,
Cumbria CA12 5SP
☎Braithwaite(059682)493 or
Keswick(07687)72059
*A mid terrace cottage standing at the
southern end of the valley above the
hamlet of Seatoller. It comprises a cottage
style lounge which is open to the dining
area and kitchen. The first-floor offers two
double bedrooms and one twin; the
bathroom and WC are on the ground floor.*

All year   1mth max, 1unit, 2–6persons
◇   ◈   ◆   no pets   ◎   fridge   Electric
& solid fuel   Elec inclusive   ⌷inclusive
☎(300yds)   WM & SD in unit   Iron &
Ironing board in unit   ⊕   CTV
⊕3pin square   2P   ⌂   ♨(1m)
⇔   ⚲(1m)
Min£102 Max£264pw

SEATON
Devon
Map**3** SY28

**Ch   Chalet 6, Tower Country Chalet
Park**
for bookings Mrs T Ash, The Robins,
Leighswood Road, Aldridge, Walsall,
Staffordshire WS9 8AH
☎Aldridge(0922)52574
*Set in a complex of similar properties, the
chalet comprises lounge with double put-
u-up, open plan kitchen, separate
bathroom/WC, one double and a twin
bedroom suitable for children.*

Mar–Nov   MWB out of season   1wk min,
6wks max, 1unit, 6persons   ◈   ◆   ◎
fridge   electric fire   Elec metered   ⌷can
be hired   ☎(on site)   Iron & Ironing board
in unit   ⊕   CTV   ⊕3pin square   1P
♨(on site)
⇔   ♪(2m)   ⚲(300yds)   ♬(2m)
Min£60 Max£100pw (Low)
Min£110 Max£130pw (High)

**Ch   Tower Country Chalet Park Nos 24,
25, 26 & 29**
for bookings Mr & Mrs W Froom, Middle
Mill Farm, Lyme Regis, Dorset DT7 3UB
☎Lyme Regis(02974)2722
*Four well-furnished cedarwood chalets
in small chalet park. Wood-panelled
interiors comprising open plan kitchen,
lounge/diner, bathroom, one double and
one twin bedroom, also sofa bed in
lounge. On main Sidmouth–Seaton road.
One mile from beach.*

Mar–Nov   MWB out of season   1wk min,
6wks max, 4units, 1–6persons   ◈   ◎
fridge   Electric   Elec metered
⌷not provided   ☎   Iron & Ironing board
in unit   ⊕   CTV   ⊕3pin square   1P   ⌂
♨
⇔   ♪(3m)   ⚲(300yds)   ♬(2m)
Details not confirmed for 1987

B   Mr E P Fox West Ridge (Bungalow)
Harepath Hill, Seaton, Devon
☎Seaton(0297)22398   →

Spacious bungalow set in 1½ acres of beautiful grounds, with commanding views of the Axe Valley and sea. Bungalow comprises of a lounge with two bed-settees, kitchen/diner, bedroom with one double and a single bed, plus bathroom and WC. An extra cot can be provided.

28Mar–31Oct MWB out of season
1wk min, 1mth max, 1unit, 5persons ◇
◆ ◆ ◒ fridge ▥ Aga Gas/
Elec inclusive Ⓛcan be hired ☎(½m)
Iron & Ironing board in unit ⊙ CTV
⊕3pin square 2P ▥ ♨(½m)
⊖ ♪(1½m) ⚲(½m) ♫(1m) ♬(1m)
Min£95 Max£195pw

SEAVIEW
See **Wight, Isle of**

SEDBERGH
Cumbria
Map**7** SD69

H   13 Queen's Drive
for bookings D H Smith, Southfield, 4 Hailey Lane, Hertford, Hertfordshire SG13 7NX
☎Hoddesdon(0992)465185

A modern house situated in a quiet cul-de-sac just within the western limits of this small market town. There are three bedrooms sleeping up to four adults plus bunk beds for up to four children and the kitchen and living rooms are on the first floor.

26Apr–24Oct MWB out of season 1unit,
6–8persons ◆ ◆ no pets ⓢ
fridge freezer Elec metered
Ⓛnot provided ☎(½m) TD & SD in unit
Iron & Ironing board in unit ⊙
⊕3pin square 1♨ ▥ ♨(1m) ⚲
⊖ ♪(2m) ⚲(1m)
Min£75 Max£125pw

SEDGEBERROW
Hereford & Worcester
Map**4** SP03

C   Forge Cottage
for bookings Mrs D Stow, Lower Portway Farm Sedgeberrow, Evesham, Worcestershire
☎Evesham(0386)881298

Modernised 200-year-old cottage with many rooms having the original beamed ceilings. It has a secluded lawned garden adjoining a plum orchard to the rear and side. Accommodation comprises of sitting room, dining room, kitchen and two bedrooms plus bathroom upstairs.

Apr–Oct 1wk min, 3mths max, 1unit,
1–4persons ◆ ◆ no pets ⓢ
fridge Electric Elec inclusive
Ⓛinclusive ☎(200yds) WM & SD in unit Iron & Ironing board in unit CTV
⊕3pin square 2P ♨(50yds) ⚯Grass Fishing
⊖ ⚲(100yds) ♫(3m) ♬(3m)
⚲(3m)
Min£110 Max£140pw (Low)
Min£155 Max£170pw (High)
See advertisement under Broadway

Seaton
—
Sheffield

F   Hall Farm Flats
for bookings Mrs D Stow, Lower Portway Farm, Sedgeberrow, Evesham, Worcestershire
☎Evesham(0386)881298

This large Georgian house has recently been converted to modern flats each having its own entrance. The accommodation varies slightly, depending on the number of occupants but all contain lounges, kitchens and bathroom/ WC's.

Apr–Oct 1wk min, 3mths max, 5units,
1–6persons ◆ ◆ no pets ⓢ
fridge Electric Elec metered Ⓛcan be hired ☎ Iron & Ironing board in unit [Launderette on premises] CTV
⊕3pin square 8P ♨(50yds) ⚯Grass putting green Fishing
⊖ ⚲(100yds) ♫(3m) ♬(3m)
⚲(3m)
Min£45 Max£75pw (Low)
Min£95 Max£120pw (High)
See advertisement under Broadway

H   Manor House
for bookings Mrs D Stow, Lower Portway Farm, Sedgeberrow, Evesham, Worcestershire
☎Evesham(0386)881298

This stone-built detached manor house stands in its own garden with lawns to front and rear. The house dates from 1572 and most of its rooms are beamed. All accommodation is on the ground floor (upstairs is closed off) and comprises large lounge with stone fireplace, kitchen, dining room, two bedrooms and bathroom/WC.

Apr–Oct 1wk min, 3mths max, 1unit,
1–6persons ◆ ◆ no pets ⓢ
fridge Electric Elec inclusive
Ⓛinclusive ☎(½m) WM & SD in unit Iron & Ironing board in unit HCE in unit CTV ⊕3pin square 3P 1♨
♨(60yds) ⚯Grass Fishing
⊖ ⚲(60yds) ♫(3m) ♬(3m) ⚲(3m)
Min£120 Max£165pw (Low)
Min£180 Max£205pw (High)
See advertisement under Broadway

SENNEN
Cornwall
Map**2** SW32

C   Mr A J Loutit **Tregiffian Cottages**
Tregiffian Hotel, Sennen, Cornwall, TR19 7BE
☎Sennen(073687)408

Four units within small complex of converted stone cottages in grounds of small hotel plus two studio flats within the hotel. Granary Cottage is on the first floor and comprises one twin-bedded room, one double, with two single wall-beds in the lounge. There is a separate kitchen

---

and bathroom/WC. Wain Cottage has one twin-bedded room, a small double bedroom, lounge, kitchen and bathroom/ WC on ground floor. Forge Cottage comprises two twin-bedded rooms, one double wall-bed in the lounge, separate kitchen and bathroom/WC. Barn Cottage has one twin-bedded room and one double, lounge, kitchen and bathroom/ WC. The purpose-built studio flats each have a small kitchen, a bedroom/lounge with a double wall-bed, bathroom/WC and comfortable furnishings.

Mar–Oct(cottages) All year(flats) MWB out of season 1wk min, 1mth max(flats)
6units, 1–6persons ◇ ◆ ◆ ◒
fridge Electric ▥(flat) Elec metered (inclusive in flats) Ⓛcan be hired (inclusive in flats) ☎ [WM on premises] SD on premises Iron & Ironing board on premises ⊙ ⊙ CTV ⊕3pin square 20P ▥ ♨(2m) ⚲
Min£51.75 Max£75pw (Low)
Min£150 Max£209pw (High)

SHALDON
Devon
See **Teignmouth**

SHANKLIN
See **Wight, Isle of**

SHEBBEAR
Devon
Map**2** SS40

B   JFH C6C
for bookings John Fowler Holidays, Dept 58, Marlborough Road, Ilfracombe, Devon EX34 8PF
☎Ilfracombe(0271)66666

A large bungalow offering spacious accommodation with a large entrance hall, two double bedrooms and one twin, bathroom, lounge/diner with open fireplace and kitchen with fitted units. There is also an outside WC.

Mar–Oct MWB out of season 1wk min,
1mth max, 1unit, 6persons ◆ no pets
ⓢ Electric Elec metered
Ⓛnot provided ☎(½m) WM & SD in unit Iron & Ironing board in unit ⓢ
CTV ⊕3pin square 2P 1♨ ♨(1½m)
⊖ ⚲(1½m)
Min£67.85 Max£182.85pw

SHEFFIELD
South Yorkshire
Map**8** SK38

F   Mrs V King **Charnwood Apartments**
The Mews, 8 Kenwood Bank, Sheffield S7 1NU
☎Sheffield(0742)57289

Nineteen purpose-built apartments in four separate buildings, situated in a pleasant urban area, 1½m from the city centre. All comprise lounge, kitchen, bathroom/ shower/WC, with either one, two or three bedrooms sleeping from two to eight persons. Twice weekly cleaning included in rent.

216

All year MWB 1 day min, 12 wks max, 19 units, 2–8 persons [◇ ◈ ◆] no pets 🍴 fridge 🎵 Gas & Elec metered ⬛ inclusive 🔺 Iron & Ironing board on premises ☺ CTV ⊕ 3 pin square P ♨

Details not confirmed for 1987

F Flat 1, 2, 3 & 4 Highfield Residence
Totley Site, Totley Hall Lane
for bookings Holiday Lettings, Sheffield City Polytechnic, 36 Collegiate Crescent, Sheffield S10 2BP
☎ Sheffield(0742)665274
Situated in a wing of the Polytechnic Hall of Residence, these flats are on the ground, first, second and third floors and the accommodation comprises lounge/diner, kitchen, bathroom and number of bedrooms ranging from one to five. Surrounded by gardens and rural views.

17 Jul–18 Sep MWB in season 1 wk min, 10 wks max, 4 units, 1–6 persons ◇ ◆
no pets 🍴 or ◎ fridge Gas or Elec fires Gas & Elec inclusive ⬛ inclusive ☎ (400yds) WM, SD & TD in unit(some) Iron & Ironing board in unit [Launderette on premises] ⊕ 3 pin square P ♨ (400yds)

↔ 𝄐(2m) ♟(400yds) ♫(400yds) ♫(2m) ⚓ Hard

Min£90 Max£100pw

Sheffield
—
Sherford

F Norfolk Park Student Residencies 200
Norfolk Park
for bookings Holiday Lettings, Sheffield City Polytechnic, 36 Collegiate Crescent, Sheffield S10 2BP
☎ Sheffield (0742)665274
Architect-designed apartments in a small hillside complex beside Norfolk Park. Four to six bedroomed units are available, all with lounge/diner, kitchen, bathroom and separate WC.

17 Jul–18 Sep MWB in season 1 wk min, 10 wks max, 27 units, 1–6 persons ◇ ◆
no pets ◎ fridge Electric
Elec inclusive ⬛ inclusive Iron & Ironing board in unit [Launderette on premises]
⊕ 3 pin square 50P 📺 ♨ (½m)

↔ 𝄐(½m) ♟(1m) ♫(1m) ⚓(1m)
Min£90 Max£100pw

SHEFFIELD GREEN
East Sussex
Map 5 TQ42

B Laramie
for bookings Mrs P Welfare, 1 Netherall Cottages, Fletching Common, Lewes, East Sussex
☎ Newick(082572)2713

Small modern bungalow in beautifully wooded countryside, 1m from Fletching and Newick village. Accommodation comprises three bedrooms (one of which has bunk beds), lounge/diner, kitchen, bathroom and WC.

All year MWB out of season 1 wk min, 4 wks max, 1 unit, 1–6 persons ◇ ◆
◎ fridge 🎵 Elec metered
⬛ inclusive ☎ (100yds) SD in unit Iron & Ironing board in unit ☺ CTV
⊕ 3 pin square P ♨ (1½m)

↔ 𝄐 (2½m)
Min£85 Max£115pw (Low)
Min£120 Max£170pw (High)

SHERBORNE
Dorset
See **Thornford**
See advertisement on page 218

SHERFORD
Devon
Map 3 SX74

C & F Mrs J Levy **Stancombe** Sherford, Kingsbridge, Devon TQ7 2BE
☎ Frogmore(054853)634
Farm complex conversion in quiet unspoilt countryside. Each unit comprises lounge/diner/kitchen with double convertible settee in lounge, bathroom/WC and one or two bedrooms with twin beds. Situated along Dartmouth road (A379) from Kingsbridge, 1½m beyond Frogmore. Sun terrace and paddling pool. →

All year MWB out of season 3 days min,
4 wks max, 7 units, 2–6 persons [◇] ◆
◆ no pets ⓦ fridge night storage
Elec inclusive Ⓛinclusive ☎ Iron &
Ironing board on premises [Launderette
on premises] ⊖ CTV ⊕3pin square
3P ⊞ ♨(2m) ▣ ⅃♥Hard snooker
room, sauna, table tennis, badminton,
solarium, mini-gymnasium,
adventure playground

⊖ ♀(2m) ♫(3m) ☗(3m)

Min£112 Max£155pw (Low)
Min£225 Max£432pw (High)

SHERSTON
Wiltshire
Map3 ST88

C Link Cottage Cliff Road
for bookings Summer Cottages,
Northernhay House, The Grove,
Dorchester, Dorset DT1 1UL
☎Dorchester(0305)67545

Grade 2 listed property with great
character, dating from the 18th century.
Accommodation comprises lounge/diner,
with exposed stone walls, and inglenook,
neat kitchen and one bedroom which
opens onto a patio.

All year MWB out of season 2 nights min,
1 unit, 2–6 persons [◇] ◆ no pets
ⓦ fridge Storage heaters & open fire
Elec metered Ⓛcan be hired
☎(200yds) WM & SD in unit Iron &
Ironing board in unit ⊖ CTV
⊕3pin square ⊞ ♨(200yds)

⊖ δ(2m) ♀(200yds)

Details not confirmed for 1987

SHETLAND
Map16

WHITENESS
Map16 HU34

Ch Mrs D Morrison **Westings Chalets**
Wormadale, Whiteness, Shetland Isles
☎Gott(059 584)292

Three 'A' frame chalets on elevated hillside
site with superb loch views.
Accommodation comprises ground-floor
lounge/diner with double and single
convertible bed-settees, a very small
kitchenette and shower/WC. A spiral
staircase leads to first floor which is one
long narrow attic room with three single
beds. Located just off A971 at Wormadale
at head of Whiteness Voe.

All year MWB out of season 3 days min,
3 units, 1–6 persons ◇ [◆◆] ⓦ
fridge Electric Elec metered
Ⓛinclusive ☎ SD & TD on premises
Iron & Ironing board on premises ⊖

Sherford
—
Shona, Isle of

⊛ CTV ⊕3pin square P ♨(¾m)
Pony trekking & fishing

⊖ δ(3½m)

Min£110 Max£168pw (Low)
Min£140 Max£252pw (High)

SHIELDAIG
Highland Ross & Cromarty
Map14 NG87

Ch **4 Alltandubh**
for bookings Mrs R L Wright, Manninagh,
Mold Road, Bodfari, Clwyd LL16 4DS
☎Bodfari(0745)75363

A comfortably furnished, well-equipped
chalet. Set on a hillside amidst pine trees
and overlooking a sheltered bay.
Accommodation comprises kitchen with
dining area, lounge and three bedrooms.

All year MWB out of season 1 wk min,
3 wks max, 1 unit, 1–5 persons ◆ ⚿
fridge ♨electric & gas fires Gas & Elec
inclusive Ⓛinclusive ☎metered WM,
SD & TD in unit Iron & Ironing board in
unit ⊖ CTV ⊕3pin square 2P
♨(2m) dinghy on sea loch, fishing

⊖ ♀(2m)

Min£200 Max£250pw

SHILBOTTLE
Northumberland
Map12 NU10

B, C, Ch Village Farm
for bookings Mrs J C Stoker, Shilbottle
Town Foot Farm, Alnwick,Northumberland
NE66 2HG
☎Shilbottle(066575)245

Small farm complex comprising six units.
One is a detached stone bungalow with
lounge, kitchen, three bedrooms (one
double, one twin and one with bunk beds)
and bathroom. Two are semi-detached
cottages, converted from the original
farmhouse. The ground floors have
lounge (with bed-settees) and kitchen.
Upstairs are two bedrooms, one with
bunks, the other with twin beds in one
cottage and a double bed in the other.
Two units are Norwegian Pine Chalets
both with lounge/diner, kitchenette,
bathroom/WC and three bedrooms, one
with double bed and two with bunks.
There is also a slightly larger Danish
chalet with double- and twin-bedded
rooms.

All year MWB out of season 2 nights min,
1 mth max, 6 units, 1–7 persons [◇] ◆
◆ ⚿ (in chalets) ⓦ (bungalows and
cottages) fridge Electric & open fires
Gas/Elec inclusive in chalets
Elec metered Ⓛnot provided ☎ ⊖
CTV ⊕2pin square 5P ⟐ ♨(200yds)
⊖ δ(3m) ♀(300yds) ☗(3m)

Min£60 Max£120pw (Low)
Min£88 Max£228pw (High)

SHILLINGSTONE
Dorset
Map3 ST81

B 1, 2 & 3 Newmans Drove Bere Marsh
Farm
for bookings Mrs A W Hughes, East Farm,
Hammoon, Sturminster Newton, Dorset
DT10 2DB
☎Child Okeford(0258)860339 or 860284

Attractive conversion of old farm buildings
resulting in three bungalow-style
properties. All units have two bedrooms,
kitchen, lounge and bathroom/WC except
No 3 which has a large shower room/WC
with facilities for the disabled and direct
access, via a ramp, from the garage.

All year MWB out of season 1 wk min,
4 wks max, 3 units, 2–6 persons ◇ [◆
◆] no pets ⓦ fridge Storage heaters
& electric Elec metered Ⓛcan be hired
☎(¾m) SD on premises Iron & Ironing
board in unit ⊖ CTV ⊕3pin square
4P 1⟐ ♨(¾m)

⊖ ♀(½m)

Details not confirmed for 1987

SHONA, ISLE OF
Highland Argyll
Map13 NM67

**C White Cottage, Lower Double
Cottage & Timber Cottage**
for bookings Eilean Shona Management
Ltd, Island of Shona, Acharacle, Argyll
PH36 4LR
☎Salen(096785)249

Shona is a small island lying off the shore
of Loch Moidart a few miles NW of
Acharacle. These three former estate
cottages are homely and comprise
kitchen, sitting/dining room, one double
bedroom, a twin-bedded room and
bathroom. The owners operate a boat
service and the remoteness of Shona has
special appeal to those seeking peace
and quiet. No vehicles on the island.

All year MWB out of season 1 wk min,
3 units, 1–4 persons ◆ ◆ ⚿ fridge
wood stove (White Cottage) open fires
(Lower Double Cottage & Timber
Cottage) Gas inclusive Elec metered

Ⓛinclusive ☎ ⊕3pin square ⚎(4m using ferry) ⚑Hard table tennis, boating
Min£80 Max£165pw

SHREWSBURY
Shropshire
See **Bicton**

SHUCKNALL
Hereford & Worcester
Map**3** SO54

C 2 Quarry Cottages
for bookings Mr & Mrs E V Sadler, 60 East Road, Stoney Hill, Bromsgrove, Worcester B60 2NS
☎Bromsgrove(0527)73734

Five miles from Hereford on A4103 Worcester road. This modernised 16th-century stone-faced cottage has ¼ acre of "rough" garden with fine views of the surrounding Herefordshire countryside. Accommodation consists of kitchen, bathroom and separate WC, dining room and lounge on the ground floor, and one double-, one single- and one twin-bedded room on the first-floor.

Allyear MWB out of season 2days min, 3wks max, 1unit, 5persons ◆ ◎ fridge Electric Elec metered Ⓛnot provided ☎(½m) Iron in unit CTV ⊕3pin square P ⚎(2m)
⊖ 🕾(1m)
Min£53 Max£125pw

SIDMOUTH
Devon
Map**3** SY18

B CC Ref 608 EL
for bookings Character Cottages (Holidays) Ltd, 34 Fore Street, Sidmouth, Devon EX10 8AQ
☎Sidmouth(039 55)77001

Contemporary bungalow in rural surroundings. Accommodation comprises attractive living room with picture windows, well-equipped kitchen, three good-sized bedrooms, one with wash hand basin, modern bathroom and WC. High quality furniture and fittings throughout.

Shona, Isle of
—
Sidmouth

Allyear MWB out of season 1wk min, 6mths max, 1unit, 5persons, nc no pets ◎ fridge 🕮 Elec inclusive Ⓛcan be hired ☎(300yds) WM in unit Iron & Ironing board in unit ⊖ TV ⊕3pin square ⊕2pin round 🏠 🕾 ⚎(2m)
⊖ 🕾(2m) 🎞(2m) 🎵(2m) 🕿(2m)
Min£75 Max£119pw (Low)
Min£155 Max£211pw (High)

H CC Ref 705L
for bookings Character Cottages (Holidays) Ltd, 34 Fore Street, Sidmouth, Devon EX10 8AQ
☎Sidmouth(039 55)77001

Luxury country residence in an elevated position with fabulous views over Sidmouth and the coast, just five minutes' drive from the town and beach. Accommodation consists of modern, fitted kitchen, good-sized lounge, dining room, further lounge with TV, laundry room, two twin rooms, one singe- and one double-bedded room, separate WC and bathroom with wash basin. All furnished to a high standard.

Allyear MWB out of season 1wk min, 6wks max, 1unit, 1–8persons ◆ no pets ◎ fridge 🕮 Elec inclusive Ⓛcan be hired ☎ WM in unit Iron & Ironing board in unit ⊖ CTV ⊕3pin square P 🏠 🕾 ⚎(½m)
⊖ 🕾(1m) 🕾(½m) 🎞(½m) 🎵(½m) 🕿(½m)
Min£155 Max£335pw (Low)
Min£348 Max£490pw (High)

F & C CC Ref 7678
for bookings Character Cottage Ltd, 34 Fore Street, Sidmouth, Devon EX10 8AQ
☎Sidmouth(03955)77001

Farmhouse flat comprises kitchen/diner, one double bedroom with en-suite bathroom, one twin room, bathroom, spacious lounge/diner with garden view. First-floor flat has lounge/diner, kitchen, bathroom, one double bedroom and one

---

bedroom with three single beds. The cottage comprises spacious lounge/diner, small kitchen, bathroom, one family bedroom and one bedroom with three single beds.

Allyear MWB out of season 3days min, 2mths max, 3units, 4–6persons, nc [◇] ◆ ◆ ◎ fridge 🕮& electric fires Elec metered Ⓛinclusive ☎(2m) Iron & Ironing board in unit ⊖ CTV ⊕3pin square 2P 🕾 ⚎(2m)
⊖ 🕾(3m) 🕾(2m)
Min£87 Max£217pw

C CC Ref 7681 Sidford
for bookings Character Cottages Ltd, 34 Fore Street, Sidmouth, Devon EX10 8AQ
☎Sidmouth(03955)77001

A terraced cottage in the centre of Sidford, comprising split level lounge, character dining room, kitchen, one double, one twin and one bunk bedded room, bath and WC, also a small yard and pretty garden.

Allyear MWB out of season 3days min, 2mths max, 1unit, 4–6persons ◆ no pets ◎ fridge Storage heaters & electric fires Elec metered Ⓛnot provided ☎(100yds) SD in unit Iron & Ironing board in unit ⊖ CTV ⊕3pin square 🕾 ⚎(100yds)
⊖ 🕾(2m) 🕾(½m) 🕿(2m)
Min£84 Max£188pw

Ch Stoneleigh Country Holidays
for bookings Mr & Mrs Salter, Stoneleigh, Weston, Sidmouth, Devon
☎Sidmouth(03955)3619

Modern purpose-built bungalows with all modern conveniences, set in a quiet position with sea views. All units are comfortably equipped and furnished with shower/WC and open-plan kitchen extending into lounge/dining area. Bedroom accommodation varies – sleeping up to nine persons.

Mar–Oct MWB in season 3days min, 1mth max, 40units, 2–9persons [◆ ◆] ◎ fridge Electric Elec metered Ⓛnot provided ☎ [WM & TD on premises] ⊖ CTV ⊕3pin square P 🕾 ⚎ ⚑Grass Putting, Swimming pool, Licensed club
⊖ 🕾(3m) 🕾(2m) 🕿(3m) →

Min£40 Max£78pw (Low)
Min£115 Max£175pw (High)

F   Willoughby House Peak Hill
for bookings Mrs G Bennett, Holly Cottage,
Wiggaton, Ottery St Mary, Devon EX11 1PY
☎Ottery St Mary(040481)4931

*Six flats in a detached flint stone house,
situated on high ground with fine views of
the sea and countryside. Each flat has two
bedrooms with single, twin or three-
bedded rooms, a large kitchen, lounge
and bathroom/WC.*

All year   MWB out of season   1wk min,
3mths max, 6units, 3–5persons ◊ ◆
◔ & ◎   fridge   ♨(part)& Electric fires
Gas & Elec metered   ⌁can be hired   ☎
Iron & Ironing board in unit   CTV
⊕3pin square 6P 3🏠 ▥ ♨(½m)
⊖   δ(1m)   ♘(600yds)   ♫(½m) ☺(½m)
Min£59 Max£72pw (Low)
Min£140 Max£185pw (High)

SILECROFT
Cumbria
Map**6** SD18

C   The Cottage Kellet Farm
for bookings Mrs S Mansergh, Kellett
Farm, Silecroft, Millom, Cumbria LA18 4NU
☎Millom(0657)2727

*A small 17th-century cottage which has
been converted and modernised. Located
near the village centre and beach, set in
pleasant rural surroundings. Good base
for touring the Lake District.*

Etr–Sep   MWB out of season   2days min,
6mths max, 1unit, 1–4persons ◊ ◆
no pets ◎   fridge   Electric & coal
Elec metered   ⌁can be hired
☎(30yds)   WM in unit   Iron & Ironing
board in unit   CTV   ⊕3pin square P
▥ ♨(100yds)
⊖   δ   ☺(100yds)   ♫(3m) ♫(3m)
☺(3m)
Min£70 Max£80pw (Low)
£100pw (High)

H   Newstead House
for bookings Mrs S Mansergh, Kellet Farm,
Silecroft, Millom, Cumbria LA18 4NU
☎Millom(0657)2727

*Situated on a quiet road between Silecroft
and the beach, this recently converted
Victorian semi-detached house of three*

Sidmouth
—
Skegness

*storeys stands in open countryside. There
are five bedrooms, all of a good size, and
sleeping a total of eight persons. On the
ground-floor there is a sitting room and
kitchen/diner.*

Etr–Oct   MWB out of season   1wk min,
1mth max, 1unit, 2–8persons ◊ ◆
no pets ◎   fridge   Electric & open fires
Elec metered   ⌁can be hired
☎(50yds)   WM in unit   Iron & Ironing
board in unit   CTV   ⊕3pin square P
▥ ♨(½m)
⊖   δ(100yds)   ♘(½m)
Min£70 Max£95pw (Low)
Min£110 Max£130pw (High)

SILLOTH
Cumbria
Map**11** NY15

F   Stanwix Park Holiday Centre Silloth,
Cumbria
☎Silloth(0965)31671

*Modern purpose-built apartments on
ground- and first-floor. Centrally situated
in the holiday complex which lies on the
fringe of Silloth, close to Solway coast. All
are compact, comfortable and well
appointed.*

All year   MWB   1night min, 8wks max,
28units, 2–8persons   no pets ◔ ◎
fridge   ♨   Gas/Elec inclusive
⌁inclusive   ☎(50yds)   WM, SD & TD on
premises   [Iron & Ironing board on
premises]   [Launderette on premises]
⊙   CTV   ⊕3pin square 28P ▥
♨(200yds) ⚲ putting
⊖   δ(½m)   ♘ ♫ ♫
Min£36 Max£90pw (Low)
Min£147 Max£237pw (High)

SKEGNESS
Lincolnshire
Map**9** TF56

Ch   Bahama, Miami & San Diego
Garden City Bungalow Park, Roman Bank,
Skegness, Lincolnshire
☎Skegness(0754)67201

---

*Situated in a quiet estate about two
minutes from the sea. Bahama chalets are
brick-built and comprise two bedrooms
(one double and one twin), lounge,
kitchen/diner and bathroom/WC. Miami
chalets are cedarwood and offer similar
accommodation to Bahama. San Diego
are smaller, flat-roofed cedarwood chalets
and comprise a double and a twin
bedroom, lounge with kitchenette recess
and bathroom/WC.*

All year   MWB out of season   2days min,
1mth max, 21units, 1–6persons [◊ ◆]
no pets   no single-sex groups ◎
fridge   Electric   ☎   [Iron & Ironing board
on premises]   ⊙   CTV   ⊕3pin square
P ♨(150yds)
⊖   δ(½m)   ♘(200yds)   ♫(1½m)
♫(1½m) ☺(1½m)
Min£30 Max£45pw (Low)
Min£150 Max£195pw (High)

**F   Mr & Mrs M Clark Merrie Mead
Apartments** 143 Drummond Road,
Skegness, Lincolnshire PE25 3BS
☎Skegness(0754)4368

*Modern two-bedroomed purpose-built
apartments. Designed to sleep six
(including put-up in lounge/diner) they
are conveniently situated for shops and
beach and have direct access to the
beach via the lawned garden. Resident
owner.*

All year   MWB out of season   3days min,
1mth max, 3units, 1–6persons [◆]
[◆]   no pets ◎   fridge   Electric
Elec metered   ⌁can be hired   ☎   WM,
TD & SD   Iron & Ironing board in unit
CTV   ⊕3pin square P 🏠 ▥
♨(220yds)
⊖   δ(½m)   ♘(200yds)   ♫(200yds)
♫(½m) ☺(½m)
Min£45 Max£100pw (Low)
Min£80 Max£145pw (High)

**F   Mr & Mrs M Clark Merrie Mead
Apartments**
143 Drummond Road, Skegness,
Lincolnshire PE25 3BS
☎Skegness(0754)4368

*A large house converted into four
spacious self-contained apartments with
lawned rear garden and direct access to
the beach. Equipped to sleep up to nine,
the apartments are of varying size,*

comfortably furnished and in a quiet
location. Resident owner.

Allyear MWB out of season 3daysmin,
1mth max, 4units, 2–9persons [◆]
[◆] no pets ∅ fridge Gas Gas/
Elec metered 🅛 can be hired ☎ WM,
TD & SD Iron & Ironing board on
premises CTV ⊕3pin square 🏠 🖾
🏊(200yds) ☺ P
⊕ ♪(½m) ♨(200yds) 🎵(200yds)
🎵(½m) 🐾(½m)

Min£45 Max£100pw (Low)
Min£80 Max£195pw (High)

SKELTON
North Yorkshire
Map**8** SE55

H Wide Open Farm
for bookings G W Proctor, Moor Park,
Skelton Lane, Wiggington, York YO3 8RF
☎York(0904)769280

Early Victorian farmhouse in a secluded
country position four miles from York.
Comprising three bedrooms (one double,
one twin-bedded and one with three single
beds), hall, sitting room, dining room,
kitchen, bathroom/WC plus downstairs
cloakroom and WC.

Allyear MWB out of season 1wkmin,
1mth max, 1unit, 1–8persons [◇] ◆
⑨ fridge 🍴& electric fires Elec
metered 🅛can be hired ☎(1½m) Iron
& Ironing board in unit ☺ CTV
⊕3pin square 6P 🏊(1m)
⊕ ♨(1m)
£70pw (Low)
Min£100 Max£120pw(High)

SKIPNESS
Strathclyde Argyllshire
Map**10** NR95

F Araneigh Upper
for bookings Mrs S A Oakes, Creggan,
Skipness, Argyll PA29 6YG
☎Skipness(08806)225

The upper flat of a large stone house
reached by an external stone staircase.
Accommodation comprises kitchenette,
dining room, lounge, bathroom, WC, one
double and one single bedroom. Fronted
by lawn.

Allyear MWB out of season 1wkmin,
6mths max, 1unit, 1–4persons [◆] ⑨
fridge Electric & open fires Elec inclusive
(in summer) Elec metered (in winter)
🅛can be hired (overseas visitors only)
☎(200yds) Iron & Ironing board in unit
⊕3pin square P 🏊(300yds) Dinghy
provided (Apr–Oct) outboard for hire

Min£50 Max£180pw

C East & West High Claonaig
for bookings Mrs S A Oakes, Creggan,
Skipness, Tarbert, Argyll PA29 6YG
☎Skipness(088 06)225

Two identical stone cottages in an
elevated position, which are reached by a
rough track and command magnificent
views towards Arran. Fresh white plaster

Skegness
—
Skye, Isle of

walls and modern furnishings are
provided in the lounge, there is a large
kitchen/diner, and three bedrooms
upstairs.

Allyear MWB out of season 1wkmin,
(1wk min winter) 6wksmax, 2units,
1–6persons [◆] ⑨ fridge Electric &
coal Electric inclusive high season &
metered low season 🅛can be hired for
overseas visitors ☎(200yds) Iron &
Ironing board in unit ⊕3pin square P
🏊(2m) Dinghy (Apr–Sep) & fishing
available

Min£55 Max£212pw

C Glenreasdell Cottage
for bookings Mrs S A Oakes, Creggan,
Skipness, Tarbert, Argyll PA29 6YG
☎Skipness(08806)225

A semi-detached cottage quietly situated
4½m from Skipness village. The unit is
compact and modestly furnished.
Accommodation consists lounge/diner,
kitchen, bathroom on ground floor and
two bedrooms on first floor.

Allyear MWB out of season 1wkmin,
6wksmax, 1unit, 1–4persons [◆] ⑨
fridge Electric & coal fires Elec inclusive
(high season & metered in low) 🅛can be
hired for overseas visitors ☎(1½m) Iron
& Ironing board in unit ⊕3pin square
P 🏊(1½m) Dinghy (Apr–Sep) & fishing
available

Min£50 Max£110pw (Low)
£150pw (High)

C Kibrannan Cottage
for bookings Mrs S A Oakes, Creggan,
Skipness, Tarbert, Argyll PA29 6YG
☎Skipness(08806)225

Originally two cottages, this stone-built
house with fenced garden stands in the
centre of the village opposite the beach.
Practically furnished with lino flooring in
some rooms. Two steep spiral staircases
lead to two attic bedrooms with skylights.
Ground floor comprises of small lounge,
kitchen, dining room, one double bedroom
and bathroom.

Allyear MWB out of season 1wkmin,
6wksmax, 1unit, 1–8persons [◆] ⑨
fridge Electric & coal Elecinclusive (high
season & metered in low) 🅛can be hired
by overseas visitors ☎(150yds) Iron &
Ironing board in unit ⊕3pin square P
🏊(100yds) Dinghy (Apr–Sep) & fishing
available

Min£70 Max£240pw

SKYE, ISLE OF
Highland Inverness-shire
Map**13**

ARDVASAR
Map**13** NG60

Ch Half Eleven Caligarry
for bookings Mrs R L Wright, Manninagh,
Mold Road, Bodfari, Clwyd LL16 4DS
☎Bodfari(0745)75363

A small timber 'A' plan chalet situated on a
hillside overlooking the Sound of Sleat
and Mallaig on the mainland. A small
garden surrounds the chalet.
Accommodation comprises open plan
lounge/diner with well-equipped kitchen
and breakfast bar, one small bunk
bedroom and an open plan double-
bedded room on the upper floor; shower
room on ground floor.

Allyear 1wkmin, 1unit, 4persons ⑨
fridge Electric Elec inclusive
🅛available on request ☎ WM & TD in
unit Iron & Ironing board in unit ☺ ⑨
CTV ⊕3pin square 2P 🏊(300yds)
⊕ ♨(500yds)

Min£160 Max£200pw

CARBOST
Map**13** NG45

B Arduaine
for bookings Miss M Steele, 75 Fife Street,
Keith, Banffshire, Grampian AB5 3EG
☎Keith(05422)2072 or 2461

A small detached bungalow on the
outskirts of the village which boasts the
famous Talisker Distillery. Accommodation
is modest but homely and comprises well-
equipped kitchen, dining room, sitting
room, one double and one single
bedroom, and bathroom. Further
accommodation of one single and one
twin bedroom and WC are found in an
annexe building to the rear of bungalow.

Allyear 1wkmin, 1unit, 6persons
no pets ⑨ fridge electric & coal fire
Elec metered 🅛not provided
☎(100yds) WM & SD in unit Iron &
Ironing board in unit TV ⊕3pin round
3P 🏊(100yds)
⊕ ♨(100yds)

Min£100 Max£120pw

DUNVEGAN
Map**13** NG24

F Roskhill Barn Flats
for bookings Mrs I E Hutchinson,
Sherwood Lodge, 3 The Gowans, Sutton
on Forest, North Yorkshire

Two self-contained flats in a recently
converted barn. Each has lounge/dining
room/kitchen and bathroom. Ground-
floor flat has one double bedroom with a
single folding bed in lounge. First-floor flat
has two double bedrooms plus a double
bed-settee in lounge.

Mar–Oct 1wkmin, 5wks max, 2units,
2–6persons no pets ⑨ fridge
Electric Elec metered 🅛inclusive
☎(350yds) Iron & Ironing board in unit
TV ⊕3pin square P 🏊(2½m)
⊕ ♨(2½m) 🎵(2½m)

Min£80 Max£105pw (Low)
Min£95 Max£150 (High)

ISLE ORNSAY
Map**13** NG61

***B* Culleag**
for bookings Miss M M Fraser, Old Post Office House, Isle Ornsay, Isle of Skye
☎Isle Ornsay(04713)201

A modern slate-roofed bungalow standing on elevated site with hill backdrop and magnificent views over Sound of Sleat and Mouth of Loch Hourn. A well decorated and furnished unit with one twin bedroom and one family room (double and single bed), sitting room/dining room/kitchen and modern bathroom. From A851 turn into village, then right on Camus Cross Road. Bungalow next to post office.

Allyear 1wkmin, 1mthmax, 1unit, 2–5persons ◈ ◎ fridge Electric Electric metered 🄻not provided ☎(200yds) Iron & Ironing board in unit ⊙ ⊕3pin square P ⌂(200yds) Fishing

⊖ ♀(200yds)

Min£60 Max£100pw

KNOCK
Map**13** NG60

***B* Knockview Bungalows**
for bookings Mr G Abernethy, Toravaig House, Hotel Knock, Isle of Skye, Inverness-shire IV44 8RJ
☎Isle Ornsay(04713)231

Two modern bungalows situated in the hotel grounds close to a mature wood with views over the ruins of Knock Castle to Mallaig. The accommodation is comfortable and comprises of open plan kitchen/diner/sitting room with convertible single bed, two bedrooms and a bathroom.

Mar–Oct 3daysmin, 4wksmax, 2units, 1–5persons ◈ ◎ fridge Electric Elec metered 🄻inclusive ☎(50yds) Iron & Ironing board in unit ⊙ CTV ⊕3pin square 2P ⌂(½m) Fishing, children's play area

⊖ ♀(50yds)

Min£50 Max£90pw (Low)
Min£100 Max£140pw (High)

PORTREE
Map**13** NG44

***B* Beechwood Holiday Homes**
Woodpark, Dunvegan Road
for bookings Hugh Murray Ltd, Dunvegan Road, Portree, Isle of Skye
☎Portree(0478)2634

Five modern, timber-framed concrete-block bungalows set in tree-studded area on outskirts of town. The bungalows offer up to date fittings and modern furniture. One bedroom with three single beds, one double-bedded room, combined lounge, dining area with convertible settee sleeping two. A very well-equipped kitchen with dishwasher and modern bathroom. On reaching Portree, turn left on A856 Dunvegan road. Access to bungalows on right.

Allyear MWB out of season 1wkmin, 5wksmax, 5units, 2–7persons ◈ ◎ fridge Electric & open fires Elec metered 🄻inclusive ☎(½m) ⊙ CTV ⊕3pin square P ▥ ⌂(½m)

⊖ ♀(½m) ♫(½m) ♬(½m)

Min£86.25 Max£207pw

SLAPTON
Devon
Map**3** SX84

C, Ch & F Mr & Mrs Rothwell **Gara Mill**
Slapton, Kingsbridge, Devon TQ7 2RE
☎Stoke Fleming(0803)770295

***Eight Cedar Lodges** with kitchen/lounge/diner, two bedrooms, and shower/WC. **Miller Cottage** and **Granary Flat** are both modernised and converted with the flat comprising kitchen, lounge/diner, bathroom/WC and two bedrooms sleeping up to six people. The cottage sleeps two plus child in one large bedroom and comprises living room with stone fireplace and kitchen recess, bathroom/WC. All are carefully sited in 4 acres overlooking river and woods. Close to beaches.*

Etr–Nov Allyear (flat & cottage) MWB out of season 3daysmin, 3mthsmax, 10units, 2–6persons [◇] ◈ ◆ ◎ fridge Electric Elec metered 🄻inclusive (in 5 lodges) 🄻can be hired Iron & Ironing board on premises [Launderette on premises] ⊙ ⊕3pin square 20P ▥ ⌂(2m) Games/TV room, fishing

⊖ ♀(2m) ♫(4m) ♬(4m)

Min£64.04 Max£83.95pw (Low)
Min£126.50 Max£192.05pw (High)

SMALLRIDGE
Devon
Map**3** SY39

***C* Lilac Cottage**
for bookings Mrs W P Stuart-Bruges, Quarley Down, Cholderton, Salisbury, Wiltshire SP4 0DZ
☎Cholderton(098 064)235

Detached stone-built old-world cottage with lawned garden. It has been carefully modernised keeping its original character by restoring the inglenook fireplace and exposing old beams. Leave A358 at Weycroft Mill towards Smallridge. In 1m turn right. Lilac Cottage is 100yds on left.

Allyear MWB out of season 4daysmin, 6mthsmax, 1unit, 2–6persons ◈ ◎ fridge ▦ Elec metered 🄻not provided Iron & Ironing board on premises ⊙ CTV ⊕3pin square P ⌂ ⌂

⊖ ♀(½m) ♫(1m)

Min£45 Max£100pw (Low)
Min£120 Max£185pw (High)

See advertisement under Axminster

SMEATON, GREAT
North Yorkshire
Map**8** NZ30

***B* Dunmar**
for bookings Mrs N Hall, Smeaton East Farm, Great Smeaton, Northallerton, North Yorkshire DL6 2ET
☎Great Smeaton(060981)336

A modern type semi-detached bungalow on the A167 with front and rear gardens. It sleeps four people in two bedrooms, kitchen and bathroom/WC. In a rural situation on the edge of the village, with lovely views, ideally situated between moors and dales, and York and Durham city.

Allyear 1wkmin, 3mthsmax, 1unit, 1–4persons ◈ ◎ fridge ▦& Electric fires Elec metered 🄻can be hired ☎ WM & SD in unit Iron & Ironing board in unit CTV ⊕3pin square 4P 1⌂ ▥ ⌂(100yds)

⊖ ♀(200yds)

Min£65 Max£75pw (Low)
Min£75 Max£100pw (High)

SOLVA
Dyfed
Map**2** SM72

C & H Mr A A Rees **Cerbid Quality Cottages** Solva, Haverfordwest, Dyfed
☎Croesgoch(03483)240 or 573

*Cerbid Holiday Cottagers are a grouping of period farmhouses and cottages on the scenic, unspoilt St David/Solva peninsula; situated in a private hamlet offering privacy in extensive grounds. **Calves Cottage** is a charming restored property with good views accommodating up to 11 people; comprising living room with open fireplace, kitchen/diner. **Cerbid House** is a Georgian farmhouse with extensive grounds offering large kitchen/diner, living room with log fires, four bedrooms and bathroom/WC. **Cerbid Old Farmhouse** is a traditional 16th-century Welsh-style property comprising living room with open fireplace, dining area, kitchen and sleeping up to eight people. **Cwm Elthin** is a stone cottage converted from a 17th-century building with spacious living room with open fireplace, kitchen/diner, three bedrooms. No steps. **Granary**, now a spacious house of Welsh stone, is set in an acre of grounds comprising living room with bay window, pine panelled kitchen/diner and sleeps up to 10 people. **No Name Cottage** has pleasant country aspects and a gallery reached by a circular staircase. It has a spacious living room, kitchen/diner, bathroom/WC, shower/WC and sleeps up to 12 people. **Stable Corner** has been transformed from a range of 18th-century stables and barns with own lawn and patio. No steps. Large*

living room with bay windows, kitchen/
dining room, master bedroom with four-
poster, three other bedrooms, bathroom/
WC and shower/WC. All the properties
have a dishwashing machine.

All year MWB out of season 2days min,
7units, 1–12persons [◇] ◈ ◆ ◎
microwaves fridge Electric & log fires
Ⓛinclusive ☎ WM TD Iron & Ironing
board in unit ☺ CTV ⑫3pin square
P 🏠 ▥ ♨(3m)
Adventure playground
↔ ♀(3m)

Min£70 Max£295pw (Low)
Min£150 Max£550pw (High)

See advertisement under St Davids

H Wincroft
for bookings Coastal Cottages of
Pembrokeshire, Seaview, Abercastle,
Mathry, Dyfed SA62 5HJ
☎Croesgoch(03483)7742

A spacious, detached house set in a large
garden overlooking St Brides Bay and
Solva Harbour. It is well equipped and
comfortable and comprises lounge with
open fire, sun lounge, dining room,
kitchen, WC, two single bedrooms on the
ground floor and upstairs three double
bedrooms, one twin-bedded room and
bathroom/WC.

All year MWB out of season 4days min,
2mths max, 1unit, 4–10persons ◈ ◆
no pets ◎ fridge ▥ Elec metered
Ⓛnot provided ☎ WM & SD in unit
Iron & Ironing board in unit ☺ CTV
⑫3pin square 4P 2🏠 ▥ ♨(300yds)
↔ ♪(3m) ♀(400yds)

Min£85 Max£395pw

SOUTH CAVE
Humberside
Map**8** SE83

C Mrs P Greenwood Wolds Way
Cottages Rudstone Walk Farm,
Southcave, Brough, Humberside
HU15 2AH
☎Southcave(04302)2230

A pair of country cottages in their own
gardens, overlooking the Humber Estuary
and surrounding countryside near to
Beverly. Accommodation comprises
spacious lounge, kitchen/diner, ground-
floor WC, one single one twin and one
double bedroom and bathroom/WC.

All year MWB out of season 1wk min,
2units, 5persons [◇] ◈ ◆ ◎
fridge ▥ Elec inclusive Ⓛinclusive
☎(1m) WM in unit Iron & Ironing board

Solva
—
Southleigh

in unit ☺ ⑬ CTV ⑫3pin square P
▥ ♨(1m)
↔ ♀(1m) Sports centre(2m)
Min£80 Max£140pw

SOUTH CREAKE
Norfolk
Map**9** TF83

C The Manse
for bookings Mr C L Gill, 13 Haslemere
Road, Winchmore Hill, London N21
☎01-886 0424

The Manse is a three bedroomed
detached period cottage, situated on the
edge of the village. It can sleep up to 10
people in three bedrooms (plus a
convertible sofa in the lounge), and has
lounge with open fire, dining room and
kitchen.

All year MWB out of season 3days min,
4mths max, 1unit, 1–10persons ◆ ◎&
wood burning stove (coal & logs free)
fridge ▥ Elec metered ☎ Iron &
Ironing board in unit ☺ CTV
⑫3pin square 3P ▥ ♨(½m)
↔ ♀(½m)

Min£65 Max£240pw

SOUTHEND-ON-SEA
Essex
Map**5** TQ88

F Clifton Court Flats 5 & 8
for bookings Hudsons Regency
Apartments, 10 Royal Terrace, Southend-
on-Sea, Essex SS1 1DU
☎Southend-on-Sea(0702)331164

Two flats with sea views on cliff top in
residential area, close to seafront and its
amenities. Both contain a lounge, two
bedrooms, bathroom and kitchen. They
are comfortable, modern and well-
equipped to a high standard with daily
cleaning services provided.

All year MWB 2days min, 5mths max,
2units, 1–6persons [◇] ◈ ◆ ◢
fridge ▥ Gas/Elec inclusive
Ⓛinclusive TD on premises Iron in unit
☺ CTV ⑫3pin square 3P 3🏠 ▥
♨(200yds)
↔ ♪(3m) ♀(100yds) ▣(½m)
♫(½m) ☖(200yds)

Min£120 Max£150pw (Low)
Min£135 Max£185pw (High)

SOUTHLEIGH
Devon
Map**3** SY29

F Flats A & B
for bookings Mrs M E Chichester,
Wiscombe Park, Colyton, Devon
☎Farway(040 487)252

Two second-floor flats situated within a
country mansion in a 600-acre country
park, 2m from the A3052. They are
approached by a side door and two flights
of rather steep stairs. Flat A has kitchen/
dining area, bathroom with WC, 30ft living
room with double bed-settee, and three
bedrooms (two with two single beds, the
other with a double and a single bed). Flat B
has a living room with kitchen area,
bathroom with WC, and two bedrooms
(one with three single beds, the other with
a double and a single bed).

Etr–Dec MWB 2units, 1–9persons
& 1–6persons ◎ fridge
Electric Gas & Elec metered Ⓛnot
provided ☎ Iron & Ironing board in
unit ☺ TV can be hired
⑫3pin square ⑬3pin round 3P
▥(4m)
↔ ♀(3m)

Details not confirmed for 1987

See advertisement under Sidmouth

F Side Wing
for bookings Mrs M E Chichester,
Wiscombe Park, Colyton, Devon
☎Farway(040 487)252

Situated in a country mansion but with a
separate entrance, the wing has kitchen/
dining room and bathroom with WC on the
ground floor. The first floor has living room
(with bed-settee) and two bedrooms (one
with a double and two single beds, the
other with three singles).

Etr–Dec 1unit, 1–9persons ◆
◎ fridge Electric Elec metered
Ⓛnot provided ☎ Iron & Ironing board
in unit ☺ TV can be hired
⑫3pin square ⑬3pin round 3P
▥(4m)
↔ ♀(3m)

Details not confirmed for 1987

See advertisement under Sidmouth

F Flat D (Stable Flat)
for bookings Mrs M E Chichester,
Wiscombe Park, Colyton, Devon
☎Farway(040 487)252 →

A first-floor flat in a converted stable block 200yds from the main house. The accommodation comprises living room (with bed-settee), kitchen/diner, bathroom and WC and two bedrooms (one with two single beds, the other with a double bed and a child's bed).

Etr–Dec 1wk min, 1mth max, 1unit, 1–6persons ◆ ⌀ fridge Electric Gas/Elec metered ⌷not provided ☎ Iron & Ironing board in unit ☉ TV can be hired ⊕3pin square ⊕3pin round 3P ⩙(4m)

⊖ ♨ (3m)

Details not confirmed for 1987

See advertisement under Sidmouth

F Flat E
for bookings Mrs M E Chichester, Wiscombe Park, Colyton, Devon
☎Farway(040 487)252

First-floor flat comprising lounge with bed-settee and kitchen at one end, shower room with WC, and bedroom with large antique half-tester bed and two single beds.

Etr–Dec 1unit, 1–4persons ◆ ◎ fridge Electric Elec metered ⌷not provided ☎ Iron & Ironing board in unit TV can be hired ⊕3pin round 3P ⩙(4m)

⊖ ♨ (3m)

Details not confirmed for 1987

See advertisement under Sidmouth

C Whitmoor
for bookings Mrs M E Chichester, Wiscombe Park, Colyton, Devon
☎Farway(040 487)252

The cottage stands alone ½m up the Wiscombe valley. It is stone-built and all the rooms face south; there is a stream close by. The ground floor comprises small hall, stone-flagged lounge with large, open fireplace, kitchen/dining room (with stone fireplace) and WC. On the first floor there are three bedrooms (one with antique half-tester bed and one single; one twin-bedded room and a large bedroom with three single beds). There is

Southleigh
—
Southwold

an extra double bed-settee on the ground floor.

Etr–Dec 1unit, 1–10persons ◆ ◎ fridge Gas & Elec metered ⌷not provided ☎ ☉ ⊕3pin square ⊕3pin round 3P ⩙(4m)

⊖ ♨ (3m)

Details not confirmed for 1987

See advertisement under Sidmouth

SOUTHPORT
Merseyside
Map7 SD31

F Mrs J Gregory Cairn House 18 Knowsley Road, Southport, Merseyside PR9 0HG
☎Southport(0704)42878

Three spacious flats within a large red-brick house, near the seafront at the north end of Southport. Each unit contains one double and one twin-bedded room. (One flat will also take twin bunks suitable for children.) Conveniently situated for shopping centre and resort facilities.

All year MWB out of season 1wk min, 1mth max, 3units, 2–6persons ◆ ◆ ◎ fridge Electric Elec metered ⌷inclusive ☎(400yds) TV ⊕3pin square 4P 𝄞 ⩙(200yds)

⊖ δ(½m) ♨(½m) 🎵(½m) 🎵(½m) ▓(½m)

Details not confirmed for 1987

F Courtyard Flats 57 London Street
for bookings Mrs A E Mardon, 5 Prestwick Drive, Liverpool L23 7XB
☎051-924 6996

Two compact but well-designed flats, close to railway station and shops. Each comprises one bedroom, bathroom, open-plan lounge and kitchen dinette.

All year MWB out of season 2units, 1–2persons, nc no pets ◎ fridge

Electric & Calor gas Elec metered ⌷can be hired ☎(20yds) SD in unit Iron & Ironing board in unit ☉ TV ⊕3pin square

⊖ δ(1m) ♨(10yds) 🎵(50yds) 🎵(500yds) ▓(500yds)

Min£40 Max£65pw (Low)

F Mrs M Fenner Fenner's Holiday Flats 30 Talbot Street, Southport, Merseyside PR8 1HS
☎Southport(0704)30655

Four flats situated within a semi-detached house in a quiet side road close to town centre. Each comprises lounge with bed-settee or 'Z'-bed, one bedroom, kitchen, shower room and WC. The furnishings are of a good modern standard.

All year MWB out of season 1wk min, 1mth max, 4units, 2–5persons ◆ ◎ fridge Electric Elec metered ⌷inclusive ☎ Iron & Ironing board in unit [Launderette within 300yds] ☉ TV ⊕3pin square 4P 𝄞 ⩙(100yds)

⊖ δ(1m) ♨(100yds) 🎵(500yds) 🎵(500yds) ▓(300yds)

SOUTHWOLD
Suffolk
Map5 TM57

F Mr A C Laight The Craighurst North Parade, Southwold, Suffolk IP18 6LP
☎Southwold(0502)723115

Eight flats, one suitable for the disabled, located on the seafront above a licensed bar and restaurant. They are all of similar style, ranging from one three-bedroomed family flat to one with one bedroom. All have lounge with put-u-up, kitchen/diner, shower and WC.

All year MWB out of season 2nights min, 5mths max, 8units, 1–7persons [◆ ◆] ◎ fridge Electric Elec metered ⌷can be hired ☎(100yds) Iron & Ironing board on premises ☉ ⊛ CTV ⊕3pin square 𝄞 ⩙(½m)

⊖ δ(1m) ♨(10yds) 🎵(½m)

Min£70 Max£110pw (Low)
Min£140 Max£205pw (High)

SOUTH ZEAL
Devon
Map**3** SX69

F Mr & Mrs M W Harbridge **The Old Barn
Flats** Poltimore Guest House, South Zeal,
Okehampton, Devon
☎Okehampton(0837)840209

*Ground- and second-floor flats in
converted barn in an attractive setting
close to Dartmoor, off the A30. Both
comprise lounge, kitchen/diner, two
bedrooms and bathroom/WC. Well-
decorated and furnished.*

All year MWB out of season 1wk min,
1mth max, 2units, 1–6persons ◈ ⊚
fridge Electric Elec metered Ⓛcan be
hired ☎(10yds) Iron & Ironing board in
unit ☺ CTV ⊕3pin square 3P Ⓜ
♨(½m)
⊖ ☎(10yds) ♫(¼m)
Min£40 Max£155pw

SPARK BRIDGE
Cumbria
Map**7** SD38

H **Dicky Cragg**
for bookings Mrs B Bailey, Down Court, 12
Courtshill Road, Haslemere, Surrey
☎Haslemere(0428)3993

*An old store barn converted into two
modern open-plan houses and situated
on the outskirts of Spark Bridge, 3m S of
Coniston Water. Accommodation
comprises lounge, kitchen, with open-plan
staircase to bedrooms and separate
bathroom. One has three bedrooms and
the other house has four.*

All year MWB out of season 1wk min,
4wks max, 2units, 2–10persons [◇]
◈ ◆ ⊚ fridge ♨ Elec inclusive
Ⓛinclusive (except towels) ☎ WM, SD
& TD on premises Iron & Ironing board
on premises ☺ TV ⊕3pin square P
🏠 Ⓜ ♨(2m)
⊖ ☎(100yds)
Min£100 Max£140pw (Low)
Min£220 Max£280pw (High)

SPEAN BRIDGE
Highland *Inverness-shire*
Map**14** NN28

Ch Mrs S M Parrish **Pine Cottage** Spean
Bridge, Inverness-shire
☎Spean Bridge(039781)404

*Two compact aluminium-clad chalets in
the grounds of Pine Cottage, a secluded
location bordering the River Spean.
Accommodation comprises two
bedrooms, open-plan kitchen/diner/sitting
room with convertible couch and a
bathroom/WC. Access is from an unclass
road off the A82 at Spean Bridge hotel.*

Etr–Oct MWB out of season 1wk min,
2units, 4–6persons ◈ ⊚ fridge
Electric Elec metered Ⓛcan be hired
☎(400yds) ☺ TV ⊕3pin square P
Ⓜ ♨(400yds) Bicycle hire
⊖ 𝄞 ☎(¼m)
Min£50 Max£110pw

South Zeal
—
Staveley

STAFFORD
Staffordshire
Map**7** SJ92

H **Tixall Gatehouse**
for bookings The Landmark Trust,
Shottesbrooke, Maidenhead, Berkshire
SL6 3SW
☎Littlewick Green(062882)5925

*Built in 1580, visitors can envelop
themselves in comfort that Mary Queen of
Scots would have enjoyed during her
imprisonment here in 1586. A spiral
staircase leads to the first floor where the
hallway gives access to a huge sitting
room furnished in a style that closely
matches the Elizabethan period. Two
bedrooms with bath/WC en-suite and a
kitchen/diner completes this floor. Stone
steps lead to the second floor which
comprises one large room which has a
table tennis table and two single
bedrooms tucked into the corner turrets
and sharing a bathroom/WC.*

All year MWB out of season 1night min,
3wks max, 1unit, 1–6persons ◈
no cats ⊚ fridge Storage heaters &
electric fires Elec inclusive
Ⓛnot provided ☎(200yds) Iron &
Ironing board in unit ☺ ⊕3pin square
2P ♨(2m)
⊖ 𝄞(2m) ☎(2m)
Min£189 Max£300pw (Low)
Min£215 Max£325pw (High)

STANTON
Gloucester
Map**4** SP03

C J W & K J Ryland **Charity Cottage**
Charity Farm, Stanton, Broadway,
Worcester
☎Stanton(038673)339

*An attractive Cotswold stone cottage with
a small garden. It comprises open-plan
kitchen/dining room, sitting room,
bathroom/WC and sleeping
accommodation for six people in three
bedrooms.*

All year 1wk min, 1unit, 2–6persons ◈
◆ ♃ fridge ♨ Electric & log fires
Gas/Elec inclusive Ⓛcan be hired ☎
Iron & Ironing board in unit ☺ CTV
⊕3pin square P Ⓜ ♨ ⌂
⊖ 𝄞(3m) ☎(500yds)
Min£75 Max£170pw

STANTON
Staffordshire
Map**7** SK14

C **Town Head Cottages**
for bookings Mrs J Clayton, 'The Flatts',
Marston Montgomery, Ashbourne,
Derbyshire
☎Rocester(0889)590228

---

*A pair of well-maintained semi-detached
stone-built cottages comprising cosy
lounge, dining room (No 1 has combined
lounge/diner), modern compact kitchen, a
double and a single-bedded room (twin-
bedded room in No 2) and bathroom/WC
(shower No 2). Simple, but clean and tidy
accommodation on the edge of a peaceful
rural village.*

All year MWB out of season 1wk (in
season) min, 3mths max, 2units,
3–4persons ◈ no pets ⊚ fridge
Electric & solid fuel Elec metered
Ⓛinclusive ☎(500yds) ☺ CTV
⊕3pin square 2P Ⓜ ♨(1½m)
⊖ 𝄞(3m) ☎(1½m) ♫(3m)
£50pw (Low)
Min£75 Max£90pw (High)

STANTON IN PEAK
Derbyshire
Map**8** SK26

C **Woodview**
for bookings Mr A Twyford, The Mount,
Stanton-in-Peak, Matlock, Derbyshire
☎Youlgrave(062986)358

*Semi-detached stone-built cottage,
located on village hillside, enjoying fine
views of surrounding countryside and
Haddon Hall from the bedrooms. The
accommodation consists of lounge,
kitchen/dining area, two bedrooms, and
bathroom/WC. The bedrooms comprise of
one family room having a double and
single bed, and one double-bedded room.*

All year MWB out of season 1wk min,
3mths max, 1unit, 1–5persons ◈ ◆
⊚ fridge Electric Elec metered
Ⓛnot provided ☎(200yds) Iron &
Ironing board in unit ☺ TV
⊕3pin square 2P Ⓜ ♨(200yds)
⊖ ☎(220yds)
Min£65 Max£85pw

STAVELEY
Cumbria
Map**7** SD49

H **Browfoot Dale & Browfoot Fell**
Browfoot Farm
for bookings Mrs Grange, Thornhill Farm,
Malmesbury, Wiltshire
☎Malmesbury(06662)2219

*This 17th-century farmhouse has been
divided into two and comprises two twin-
bedded rooms and one room with bunk
beds. The houses retain their original
character and are situated in the beautiful
Kentmere Valley on an unclassified road,
2m NW of Staveley Village.*

All year MWB out of season 1wk min,
1mth max, 2units, 2–6persons ◈ ◆
no cats ⊚ fridge Electric & open fires
Elec metered Ⓛnot provided ☎ Iron &
Ironing board in unit ☺ TV
⊕3pin square P ♨(1½m)
⊖ ☎(1½m)
Min£102 Max£160pw(Low)
Min£114 Max£207pw(High)

H   Low Brow House Browfoot Farm
for bookings Mrs Grange, Thornhill Farm,
Malmesbury, Wiltshire
☎Malmesbury(06662)2219

*A renovated, traditional stone-built
Lakeland farmhouse with four bedrooms –
three have twin beds and the fourth has
bunk beds. Situated in the beautiful
Kentmere Valley on an unclassified road,
2m NW of Staveley village.*

Allyear   MWB out of season   1wk min,
4wks max, 1unit, 2–8persons ◆ ◆
no cats ◎ fridge Electric & open fires
Elec metered ⌷ not provided ☎ Iron in
unit Ironing board in unit ☉ TV
⊕3pin square P ⅏(1½m)

⊖) ♀(1½m)

Min£145 Max£250pw (Low)
Min£153 Max£348pw (High)

STELLING MINNIS
Kent
Map**5** TR14

B   The Old Stables
for bookings Mrs P Topping, Misling Farm,
Stelling Minnis, Stone Street, Canterbury,
Kent CT4 6DE
☎Stelling Minnis(022787)256

*Converted stabling comprising kitchen,
bathroom, one double, one family
bedroom, spacious living room, bordering
paddocks and woodland. Convenient for
Channel ports.*

Allyear   1wk min, 4mths max, 1unit,
2–7persons [◇] ◆ ◆ ◎ fridge
Electric & gas Gas/Elec metered
⌷ inclusive ☎(1½m) [Launderette on
premises] Iron & Ironing board in unit
☉ CTV ⊕3pin square 7P 🆔
⅏(1½m)

⊖) ♀(¼m)

Min£80 Max£100pw (Low)
Min£110 Max£150pw (High)

STENNESS
See **Orkney**

STEPASIDE
Dyfed
Map**2** SN01

B   Merrixton
for booking Powell's Cottage Holidays,
55 High Street, Saundersfoot, Dyfed
☎Saundersfoot(0834)812791

*A modern bungalow in an isolated
position adjacent to a farm.
Accommodation comprises lounge, dining
room, kitchen, bathroom, WC, three
bedrooms one double, one twin and one
with bunk beds.*

1wk min, 1unit, 6persons [◇] ◆
no pets ◎ fridge/freezer 🍴
Elec inclusive ☎(1m) WM in unit Iron &
Ironing board in unit ☉ CTV
⊕3pin square 2P 🆔 ⅏(¾m)

⊖) ♀(¾m)

Min£93 Max£210pw

Staveley
—
Stithians

C   Ranch Cottage
for bookings Powell's Cottage Holidays,
55 High Street, Saundersfoot, Dyfed
☎Saundersfoot(0834)812791

*A cottage in a remote location where the
owners operate a Welsh weaving cottage
industry. Accommodation comprises
lounge, kitchen/diner, bathroom with WC,
two bedrooms one with double bed and
one with double and single.*

1wk min, 1unit, 5persons [◇] ◆
no pets ◎ fridge 🍴 Elec inclusive
☎(on premises) Iron & Ironing board in
unit ☉ CTV ⊕3pin square 6P 🆔
⅏(1½m)

⊖) ♀(¾m)

Min£93 Max£210pw

B   Sea Break Pleasant Valley
for bookings Powell's Cottage Holidays,
55 High Street, Saundersfoot, Dyfed
☎Saundersfoot(0834)812791

*A large modern bungalow in a quiet
residential area a short distance from
Wiseman's Bridge. It sleeps up to six and
has a kitchen, dining room, lounge, and
three bedrooms.*

May–Sep   MWB out of season   1wk min,
4wks max, 1unit, 2–6persons ◆
no pets ◎ fridge 🍴 Elec metered
⌷ not provided ☎(½m) Iron & Ironing
board in unit Launderette within 300yds
CTV ⊕3pin square P 🆔 ⅏(300yds)

⊖) ♀(½m) 🎬(2m) 🎵(2m)

Min£99 Max£222pw

STEYNING
West Sussex
Map**4** TQ11

**F   Mr & Mrs A Barnicott Down House
Flats** King's Barn Villas, Steyning, W
Sussex BN4 3FA
☎Steyning(0903)812319

*One ground- and one first-floor flat in
Edwardian house with well-kept gardens
and in rural setting. Ground-floor flat
consists of one double- and one twin-
bedded room, lounge/diner, kitchen and
bathroom/WC. First-floor flat has one twin
bedroom, lounge/diner with sofa/bed,
kitchen and bathroom/WC.*

Allyear   MWB out of season   1wk min,
3mths max, 2units, 1–4persons, nc5 ◎
fridge 🍴 Gas/Elec inclusive (high
season only) ⌷ inclusive ☎ Iron &
Ironing board in unit ☉ CTV
⊕3pin square 2P 🆔 ⅏(½m)

⊖) ♀(½m)

Min£52 Max£57pw (Low)
Min£84.50 Max£125pw (High)

C & F   Miss J Elsden **Nash** Horsham
Road, Steyning, W Sussex
☎Steyning(0903)814988

---

*Two self-contained flats and a modern
cottage attached to an old country house
in 8 acres of ground with a swimming pool,
tennis court and vineyard. The flats
consist of 1–2 bedrooms, lounge/diner,
kitchen, separate bath and WC. The
cottage can accommodate three to five
people in two bedrooms and has a
lounge/dining room, kitchen and
bathroom. 1½m N of Steyning (A283) on
the E side off B2135.*

Allyear   MWB   1wk min, 6mths max,
3units, 2–5persons ◆ ◆ ◎
fridge 🍴 Elec inclusive ⌷ can be
hired ☎ WM & SD on premises Iron &
Ironing board on premises ☉ TV can be
hired ⊕3pin square 22P 🆔 ⅏(1½m)
⊅ ⚓Hard

⊖) ♀(1m)

Min£75 Max£170pw (Low)
Min£85 Max£170pw (High)

STIRLING
Central *Stirlingshire*
Map**11** NS79

Ch & F   Vacation Letting Department
University of Stirling Stirling FK9 4LA
☎Stirling(0786)73171 ext2033

*One hundred well-maintained flats and 10
chalets situated within this attractive
University campus. The flats have up to 10
bedrooms and are functional. The chalets
are situated in a quiet corner of the
campus and comprise open-plan lounge/
kitchen/dining area, one double bedroom
and four singles.*

14Jun–12Sep   4days min, 4wks max,
110units, 1–10persons [◇ ◆ ◆]
no pets ◎ fridge Electric
Elec inclusive ⌷ inclusive ☎(200yds)
Iron & Ironing board on premises
[Launderette on premises] ☉ CTV can
be hired ⊕3pin square P 🆔
⅏(400yds) ▭ ⚓Hard putting green

⊖) ♙(½m) ♀ 🎬 🎵 🎯

£150pw (Low)
£220pw (High)

STITHIANS
Cornwall
Map**2** SW73

**F, C, B   Higher Trewithen Flats &
Cottages**
for bookings Mr & Mrs B J de Lange,
Higher Trewithen, Stithians, Truro,
Cornwall TR3 7DR
☎Stithians(0209)860863

*An attractive conversion of farm buildings
offering; four terraced cottages with open
plan kitchen/lounge/diner, bathroom, WC,
and two bedrooms (one double, one
single/twin or triple, according to size);
one bungalow with kitchen/breakfast
room, lounge/diner, bathroom, separate
WC and three bedrooms; and five flats
with kitchen/diners, lounge, bathroom/WC
or separate WC and two or three
bedrooms. Licensed bar and shop on
premises during main season.*

All year (3 units) 7Mar–7Jan (7units)
MWB out of season   4days min, 6wks max,

10units, 1–6persons [◇ ◆] ◎
fridge night storage & electric heaters
Elec metered Ⓛcan be hired ☎ [WM &
TD on premises] Iron & Ironing board in
unit ☻ CTV ⊕3pin square P ▥
♨(1¼m)
↔ 𝄞(3m) ♀ ♫(3m) ♪(3m)
🐾(3m)

Min£54 Max£146pw (Low)
Min£156 Max£224pw (High)

STOKE FLEMING
Devon
Map3 SX84

B Mr Ian Longrigg **Cliff Top & Bay View
Bungalows** Leonards Cove, Stoke
Fleming, Dartmouth, Devon TQ6 0NR
☎Stoke Fleming(0803)770206

*Eighteen self contained linked bungalows,
built on the cliff edge, make up this small
holiday complex. The nine **Cliff Top**
bungalows have a door leading onto the
balcony and give magnificent coastal
views. It has a small lobby, bathroom,
lounge/dining room with convertible sofa
bed, well-equipped kitchen and two
bedrooms, one double and one with either
twin or bunk beds. The nine **Bay View**
bungalows are situated on a higher
terrace and offer lovely views.
Accommodation comprises lounge/dining
room with sofa bed, compact kitchen,
bathroom, one double bedroom and one
twin bedroom.*

Stithians
—
Stokenham

Mar–Oct MWB out of season 3days min,
6wks max, 18units, 4–6persons [◇]
◇ ◆ no pets ◎ fridge
Electric convectors Elec metered Ⓛcan
be hired ☎ [WM & TD on premises]
[Iron on premises] [Ironing board on
premises] [Launderette on premises]
☻ TV ⊕3pin square P ♨(200yds)
↔ ♀ (200yds) ♫(1m) ♪(1m)
🐾(2m)

Min£70 Max£195pw
See advertisement under Dartmouth

STOKE LACEY
Hereford & Worcester
Map3 SO64

C **Merryfield Cottage**
for bookings Mrs Sadler, Wyvern Cottages,
60 East Road, Stoney Hill, Bromsgrove,
Worcester
☎Bromsgrove(0527)73734
*A detached cottage standing in its own
grounds with extensive views across to the
Brecon Beacons. Accommodation
comprises lounge, dining room, kitchen*

Etr–Oct 1wk min, 4wks max, 1unit,
5persons ◆ ◎ fridge 🍳
Elec metered Ⓛnot provided ☎(½m)
Iron in unit TV ⊕3pin square 3P
♨(½m)
↔ ♀ (½m)
Details not confirmed for 1987

STOKENHAM
Devon
Map3 SX84

F C & R Robinson **Stokeley Coach
House** Stokenham, Kingsbridge, Devon
TQ7 2SE
☎Kingsbridge(0548)580340

*Four flats tastefully converted from an old
coach house with **Buggy**, **Gig** and
Hansom, which is two ground and one
first-floor sleeping up to four people.
Landau is a first-floor flat, sleeping up to
seven people in three bedrooms. All of the
properties comprise lounge/diner, kitchen
and bathroom/WC; located within the
extensive grounds of the manor house
with distant sea views. Supper and
children's evening menus.*

All year MWB out of season 2 days min,
4units, 1–7persons plus baby ◇ ◆
◆ ◎ fridge Electric Elec metered
Ⓛinclusive ☎ Iron & Ironing board in →

unit [Launderette on premises] ☺ Ⓥ
CTV ⊕3pin square P 🅸 ♨(½m) ⏚
Games room

⊖ 🎵(1m)

Min£84 Max£140pw(Low)
Min£259 Max£294pw(High)

STONE
Gloucestershire
Map**3** ST69

H Elms Coach House
for bookings Mr L R Duncum, The Elms
Guest House, Stone, Berkeley,
Gloucestershire
☎Falfield(0454)260995

*Modernised coach house situated 1m
from M5 (junction 14) motorway.
Accommodation comprises one twin-
bedded room, one family bedroom, with
wash hand basin, ground-floor bedroom,
with own WC, wash hand basin and
shower, suitable for disabled or older
person. Lounge, large kitchen/diner and
bathroom. Décor is bright and clean. All of
the the ground floor is suitable for
wheelchairs.*

All year 1unit, 5persons ◈ ◉ fridge
Electric Elec metered 🔲 inclusive ☎
Iron Ironing board ☺ Ⓥ TV
⊕3pin square P ♨(1½m)

⊖ 🍽

£110pw(Low)
£130pw(High)

STRAITON
Strathclyde *Ayrshire*
Map**10** NS30

C Bishopland Lodge
for bookings Mr J Hunter Blair, Blairquhan
Estate Office, Straiton, Maybole, Ayrshire
KA19 7LZ
☎Straiton(06557)239

*Modernised stone-built cottage dating
back to c 1800. Accommodation consists
of kitchen/dining room, one bedroom with
twin beds, living room with three
convertible sofas. In a quiet location with
fine views of the surrounding countryside.*

All year MWB out of season 1wk min,
6mths max, 1unit, 1–5persons ◈ ◆
◉ fridge Electric & coal Elec inclusive
🔲not provided ☎(½m) Iron & Ironing
board in unit ☺ ⊕3pin square P 🏠
♨(2m) Fishing

⊖ 🍽(2m)

Min£64.60 Max£85.75(Low)
Min£96.85 Max£141.30pw(High)

Stokenham
—
Stratford-upon-Avon

**C Farrer, McIntyre & Wauchope
Cottages**
for bookings Mr J Hunter Blair, Blairquhan
Estate Office, Straiton, Maybole, Ayrshire
KA19 7LZ
☎Straiton(06557)239

*A converted stable with cottages leading
off the courtyard, built in 1820–24.* **Farrer
Cottage** *has a dining room and two
bedrooms and sleeps up to eight people.*
McIntyre *has a kitchen/dining room with
two bedrooms and sleeps up to six people.*
Wauchope *has a kitchen/dining room and
two bedrooms, one leading off the other,
sleeping up to five people.*

All year MWB out of season 1wk min,
1mth max, 3units, 1–8persons ◈ ◆
◉ fridge Electric & open fires
Elec inclusive 🔲not provided ☎ Iron &
Ironing board in unit ⊕3pin square P
🅸 ♨(1m) Fishing

⊖ 🍽(1m)

Min£64.60 Max£91.60pw(Low)
Min£108.95 Max£177.60pw(High)

C Kennedy Cottage
for bookings Mr J Hunter Blair, Blairquhan
Estate Office, Straiton, Maybole, Ayrshire
KA19 7LZ
☎Straiton(06557)239

*The cottage is on one side of a courtyard
forming part of Blairquhan Castle and
dates back to 1575. The cottage itself is
fully modernised and decorated to a very
high standard. It sleeps seven in two twin-
bedded rooms and one double-bedded
room and has a lounge with bed-settee,
kitchen and bathroom.*

All year MWB out of season 1wk min,
1mth max, 1unit, 1–7persons ◈ ◆
◉ fridge Electric & open fires
Elec inclusive 🔲not provided ☎ Iron &
Ironing board in unit ☺ ⊕3pin square
4P 🅸 ♨(1m) Fishing

⊖ 🍽(1m)

Min£87.40 Max£118.65pw(Low)
Min£134 Max£199pw(High)

C McDowall Cottage
for bookings Mr J Hunter Blair, Blairquhan
Estate Office, Straiton, Maybole, Ayrshire
KA19 7LZ
☎Straiton(06557)239

*A late conversion of a garden bothy
situated in the wall of Blairquhan gardens.*

---

*The accommodation comprises a double-
bedded room, a twin-bedded room, living
room with sofa/bed, kitchen and
bathroom. The estate is on the B741 near
the village.*

All year MWB out of season 1wk min,
1mth max, 1unit, 1–5persons ◈ ◆
◉ fridge Electric & open fires
Elec inclusive 🔲not provided ☎ Iron &
Ironing board in unit ☺ ⊕3pin square
6P 🅸 ♨(1m) Fishing

⊖ 🍽(1m)

Min£73.85 Max£98.60pw(Low)
Min£111.60 Max£163.85pw(High)

STRATFORD-UPON-AVON
Warwickshire
Map**4** SP25

C Lord Nelson Cottage 35 Great William
Street
for bookings Mr & Mrs M W Spencer,
Moonraker House, 40 Alcester Road,
Stratford-upon-Avon, Warwickshire
☎Stratford-upon-Avon(0789)67115

*A converted public house forming part of
a line of terraced cottages, in one of
Stratford's quaint back streets. The
modern interior comprises kitchen/diner,
large lounge, bathroom/WC and sleeps up
to five persons.*

All year 1wk min, 6mths max, 1unit,
1–5persons 🏃 fridge 🍳
Gas inclusive 🔲inclusive ☎(250yds)
WM in unit Iron & Ironing board in unit
☺ CTV ⊕3pin square 🅸 ♨(40yds)

⊖ 🚗(1m) 🍽(250yds) 🎵(1m)
🎵(300yds) 🍺(1m)

Min£60 Max£150pw

H Sandfields Cottage Luddington
for bookings Mrs P Boswell, Sandfields
Farm, Luddington, Stratford-upon-Avon,
Warwickshire CV37 9SW
☎Stratford-upon-Avon(0789)750202

*Semi-detached house surrounded by
farmland and orchards. The downstairs
accommodation comprises lounge,
kitchen/diner, bathroom and WC. Upstairs
there are three bedrooms, one double, one
twin-bedded and one with bunks. 2½m W
off A439.*

All year MWB out of season 2nights min,
1mth max, 1unit, 1–6persons ◈
no pets ◉ fridge Electric
Elec inclusive 🔲inclusive (except sheets
& pillowcases) ☎(½m) Iron & Ironing
board in unit ☺ TV ⊕3pin square 2P

⊖ 🍽(2m) 🎵(2½m) 🎵(2½m) 🍺(2½m)

Min£80 Max£97.75pw

H Shottery 85 Shottery Road
for bookings Mrs M Corfield, Brookside,
Tamworth Lane, Henley-in-Arden, Solihull, `
West Midlands B95 5QZ
☎Henley in Arden(05642)2050

A modern cottage style detached house in
a suburban road within ½m of centre of
Stratford. It comprises large kitchen,
lounge/dining room with french windows
leading to patio and large garden. The
first floor comprises two bedrooms,
bathroom and WC.

All year 1wk min, 1mth max, 1unit,
1–4persons, nc10 ◎ fridge Electric
Elec metered ⊡inclusive ☎(300yds)
Iron & Ironing board in unit ☺ CTV
⊕3pin square 2P Ⅲ ♨(200yds)
↤ δ(2m) ♀(300yds) ♫(1m)
♫(1m) ☝(1m)

Min£59 Max£119pw (Low)
Min£99 Max£139pw (High)

STRONTIAN
Highland Argyllshire
Map**14** NM86

Ca Seaview Grazings Holiday Homes
for bookings Mr Peter Howland, Seaview
Grazings (Strontian) Ltd, Strontian,
Acharacle, Argyll PH36 4HZ
☎Fort William(0397)2496

Traditional Scandinavian log houses, set
together on an uncultivated hillside. Each
one has magnificent loch and mountain
views, are very spacious, attractive and
equipped to a high standard, including
double glazing. They have either two or
three good sized bedrooms, living room
with double bed-settee and fully fitted
kitchen.

All year MWB out of season 3days min,
14units, 1–6persons ◆ ◆ ◎ fridge
Electric Elec inclusive ⊡can be hired
☎ WM in unit Iron & Ironing board in
unit ☺ CTV ⊕3pin square P
♨(½m) Fishing & boat hire
↤ ♀(½m)
Min£115 Max£285pw

STURMINSTER NEWTON
Dorset
Map**3** ST81

B The Cottage
for bookings Mrs Wingate-Saul, Holbrook
Farm, Lydlinch, Sturminster Newton,
Dorset
☎Hazelbury Bryan(02586)348

Modern detached bungalow located in the
beautiful Blackmore Vale, comprising two
twin-bedded rooms, one with bunk beds,
lounge, kitchen/diner (with dishwasher),
separate bath and WC. Situated 1m from
centre of Lydlinch, 3m W off A357
Stalbridge road.

Apr–Oct 1wk min, 1mth max, 1unit,
2–6persons ◆ ◆ ◎ fridge
Electric Elec metered ⊡can be hired
☎ Iron & Ironing board in unit ☺

Stratford-upon-Avon
—
Swanage

CTV ⊕3pin square 4P 1🏠 ♨(1m)
⊿ Clay pigeon shooting
↤ ♀(1m)
Min£92 Max£166.75pw

SUTTON ST NICHOLAS
Hereford & Worcester
Map**3** SO54

H Lane Farm Cottage
for bookings Mr R Andrews, Court Farm
Sutton St Nicholas, Hereford
☎Sutton St Nicholas(043272)224 or 708

An 18th-century, half-timbered stone
farmhouse, ideal for a peaceful holiday.
The ground-floor consists of a kitchen/
diner, lounge, and WC, whilst the first-floor
contains three bedrooms and a
bathroom/WC.

Mar–Oct MWB out of season 6wks max,
1unit, 1–6persons [◇] ◆ ◎ fridge
Electric Elec metered ⊡can be hired
☎(½m) Iron & Ironing board in unit
CTV ⊕3pin square 3P Ⅲ ♨(½m)
Fishing
↤ ♀(½m)
Min£50 Max£110pw

SWANAGE
Dorset
Map**4** SZ07

F Mr Fowler Alexander Court Grosvenor
Road, Swanage, Dorset
☎Swanage(0929)424606

Modern purpose-built block of flats in
elevated position overlooking town and
Swanage Bay. Compact and self-
contained with carpeting and modern
furniture. Fully-equipped to requirements.

All year 1wk min, 1mth max, 5units,
6–8persons ◆ ◆ ◎ no pets ◎
fridge 🍴 Elec metered ⊡can be
hired ☎(100yds) TV ⊕3pin square
P 🏠 Ⅲ ♨(500yds)
↤ ♀(500yds) ♫(500yds)
♫(500yds) ☝(½m)

Min£55 Max£75pw (Low)
Min£120 Max£240pw (High)

F Mrs J Blanchard Carlton Lodge 22
Ulwell Road, Swanage, Dorset
☎Swanage(0929)423295

Four flats situated within a detached,
modern brick and stucco building on the
Ulwell Road, 1m from Swanage town
centre. Flat 1 on the first-floor sleeps up to
eight people in two bedrooms plus a
double put-u-up in the lounge, kitchen/
dining room and bathroom/WC. Flat 2
also on the first-floor, sleeps six people in
three bedrooms (two of which have hand
wash basins), and has lounge, kitchen
and bathroom/WC. Flat 3 on the second
floor has two bedrooms plus double put-u-
up in lounge, kitchen/dining room and
bathroom/WC. Flat 4 also on the second

floor, has two bedrooms, lounge, kitchen
and bathroom/WC.

All year MWB out of season 3days min,
2mths max, 4units, 2–8persons [◆ ◆]
no pets ◎ fridge Electric
Elec metered ⊡provided ☎ SD in
unit Iron & Ironing board in unit ☺
CTV ⊕3pin square 4P Ⅲ ♨(500yds)
↤ δ(3m) ♀(100yds) ♫(500yds)
☝(1½m)

Min£50 Max£80pw (Low)
Min£170 Max£200pw (High)

F Gulls Way Flat 4 Osborne House,
Seymer Road
for bookings Mr P G Hill-Turner, Ivy
Cottage, 20 Mount Scar, Swanage, Dorset
BH19 2EZ
☎Swanage(0929)426360

A neat, well-maintained second-floor flat
with fine views of coastline.
Accommodation comprises modern fitted
kitchen, small comfortable lounge/diner
with double put-u-up, two bedrooms (one
double, one twin) and bathroom/WC and
shower. Close proximity of town centre
and beach.

15Mar–31Oct MWB out of season
4days min, 3mths max, 1unit, 2–6persons
[◆ ◆] fridge 🍴 Elec inclusive
⊡can be hired ☎(250yds) Iron &
Ironing board in unit [Launderette within
300yds] ☺ CTV ⊕3pin square 1P
♨(200yds)
↤ δ(3m) ♀(200yds) ♫(200yds)
♫(200yds) ☝(350yds)
Min£60 Max£205pw

F Mrs D Alexander Marston Flats 16
Burlington Road, Swanage, Dorset
BH19 1LS
☎Swanage(0929)422221

This detached Purbeck stone and tile-
hung gabled house provides three self-
contained flats. A fourth flat is occupied by
the proprietors. The house is situated in a
quiet residential area on a cliff top
location. Burlington Road can be found
off Ulwell Road. The flats are quite similar
with lounge, kitchen, two bedrooms and
either a bath or shower with WC. A total of
five people can be accommodated in each
flat. Two flats overlook the sea.

11Apr–Oct MWB out of season
2nights min, 4wks max, 3units,
2–5persons, nc7 no pets ◎ fridge
Electric Elec metered ⊡inclusive
☎(½m) Iron & Ironing board in unit ☺
CTV ⊕3pin square P Ⅲ ♨(½m)
↤ δ(3m) ♀(250yds) ☝(½m)

Min£50 Max£155pw (Low)
Min£130 Max£250pw (High)

F Waveney Park Road
for bookings Mr Fowler, Alexander Court,
Grosvenor Road, Swanage, Dorset
☎Swanage(0929)424606

Brick and stone Victorian villa in elevated
position overlooking town and Swanage
Bay, with converted modernised interior.

All year MWB out of season 1wk min,
1mth max, 2units, 4–10persons ◆ ◆→

no pets ◎ fridge Electric Gas/ Elec metered Ⓛ can be hired ☎(100yds) TV ⊕3pin square P ⌂ Ⓜ ♣(500yds)
⊖ ♀(500yds) ♫(500yds) ♬(500yds) 🎬(½m)
Min£55 Max£75pw (Low)
Min£120 Max£240pw (High)

SWANTON MORLEY
Norfolk
Map**9** TG01

C *Clematis & Rose Cottages*
for bookings John Carrick, Park Farm, Swanton Morley, Dereham, Norfolk NR20 4JU
☎Swanton Morley(036283)457 & 507
Semi-detached brick-built cottages in an isolated position, ½m from the village. Accommodation comprises two bedrooms, bathroom/WC on the first floor and lounge/dining area with kitchen on the ground floor. Coarse and lake fishing nearby.
Allyear 1wk min(Jun–Sep), 1mth min(Oct–May), 6mths max, 2units, 1–4persons ◈ ◆ ◎ fridge Electric & open fires Elec metered Ⓛ not provided ☎(½m) WM in unit Iron & Ironing board in unit TV ⊕3pin square 2P ♣(½m)
⊖ ♂(2¾m) ♀(½m) ♫(2¾m) ♬(2¾m)
Details not confirmed for 1987

C *Lavender Cottage* 3 Elsing Road
for bookings John Carrick, Park Farm, Swanton Morley, Dereham, Norfolk NR20 4JU
☎Swanton Morley(036 283)457 & 507
A 200-year-old brick-built cottage located in a side street in the village. It comprises two bedrooms, bathroom, lounge/dining area and fully-equipped kitchen. Coarse and lake fishing nearby.
Allyear 1wk min(Jun–Sep), 1mth min(Oct–May), 6mths max, 1unit, 1–4persons ◈ ◆ ◎ fridge ♨ Elec metered Ⓛ not provided ☎(20yds) Iron & Ironing board in unit TV ⊕3pin square P Ⓜ ♣(50yds)
⊖ ♂(2¾m) ♀(25yds) ♫(2¾m) ♬(2¾m) 🎬(2¾m)
Details not confirmed for 1987

C *Lilac Cottage* 4 Town Street
for bookings John Carrick, Park Farm, Swanton Morley, Dereham, Norfolk NR20 4JU
☎Swanton Morley(036 283)457 & 507
Brick-built end of terrace cottage overlooking the village green comprising three bedrooms, lounge, dining room, kitchen and bathroom. Coarse and lake fishing nearby.
Allyear 1wk min(Jun–Sep), 1mth min(Oct–May), 6mths max, 1unit, 1–8persons ◈ ◆ ◎ fridge ♨ Elec metered Ⓛ not provided ☎(25yds) Iron & Ironing board in unit ⊙ CTV ⊕3pin square 3P ♣(25yds)
⊖ ♂(2¾m) ♀(25yds) ♫(2¾m) ♬(2¾m) 🎬(2¾m)
Details not confirmed for 1987

C *River Cottage* Castle Farm
for bookings John Carrick, Park Farm, Swanton Morley, Dereham, Norfolk NR20 4JU
☎Swanton Morley(036 283)457 & 507
Detached brick-built cottage occupying a superb position near the banks of the River Wensum, ¾m from the village. Accommodation comprises kitchen, utility room, cloakroom, lounge and dining room on the ground floor plus three bedrooms and bathroom on the first floor.
Allyear 1wk min(Jun–Sep), 1mth min(Oct–May), 6mths max, 1unit, 1–7persons ◈ ◆ no pets ◎ fridge ♨ Elec metered Ⓛ not provided ☎(¾m) WM in unit Iron & Ironing board in unit ⊙ CTV ⊕3pin square 6P 2⌂ ♣(1¼m)
⊖ ♀(¾m)
Details not confirmed for 1987

C *Woodgate Cottage*
for bookings John Carrick, Park Farm, Swanton Morley, Dereham, Norfolk NR20 4JU
☎Swanton Morley(036 283)457 & 507
Newly renovated, brick-built cottage, ¾m from the village, occupying a very quiet position surrounded by meadowland. The accommodation is for six persons. Coarse and lake fishing nearby.
Allyear 1wk min(Jun–Sep), 1mth min(Oct–May), 6mths max, 1unit, 1–6persons ◈ ◆ ◎ fridge ♨ Elec metered Ⓛ not provided ☎(1m) WM in unit Iron & Ironing board in unit ⊙ CTV ⊕3pin square 2P 1⌂ ♣(1m)
⊖ ♂(3m) ♀(¾m)
Details not confirmed for 1987

SWIMBRIDGE
Devon
Map**2** SS63

C JFH B1012B
for bookings John Fowler Holidays, Dept 58, Marlborough Road, Ilfracombe, Devon EX34 8PF
☎Ilfracombe(0271)66666
Rambling 15th-century cottage forming part of a Devon longhouse with open fire places and exposed beams. It comprises a large lounge with bed-settee, dining area, kitchen, bathroom with shower unit, two large family bedrooms and one single room with bunk beds.
Mar–Oct MWB out of season 1wk min, 1mth max 1unit, 12persons ◈ ◎ fridge Calor gas, log fires Elec metered Ⓛ not provided ☎(½m) WM & SD in unit Iron & Ironing board in unit CTV ⊕3pin square 6P ♣(½m)
⊖ ♀(½m)
Min£79.35 Max£205.85pw

TALGARTH
Powys
Map**3** SO13

C Genffordd Farm Cottage
for bookings Mrs B Prosser, Upper Genffordd Farm, Talgarth, Brecon, Powys LD3 0EN
☎Talgarth(0874)711360
Delightful single storey cottage located on family farm and standing in its own grounds offering a spacious lounge with open fire and semi-beamed ceiling, dining area, farmhouse-style kitchen and large balcony. Bedrooms consist of one double, one double with single bed and one twin-

*bedded room, separate bathroom/WC.
Located 3m S of Talgarth on A479 with
views over the Brecons. Shooting available
on farm. The proprietor also runs a
guesthouse where bed and breakfast is
available.*

All year MWB out of season 3 days min,
1 unit, 1–7 persons ◆ ◎ fridge
Electric Elec metered Ⓛcan be hired
☎(200yds) Iron & Ironing board in unit
☉ CTV ⊕3pin square 4P Ⅲ ⚎(3m)
⊖ ⚏ (¼m)

Min£80pw (Low)
Min£130pw (High)

TARLAND
Grampian *Aberdeenshire*
Map15 NJ40

H Wardfold
for bookings Holiday Dept 6, Estate Office,
Dinnet, Aboyne, Aberdeenshire AB3 5LL
☎Dinnet(033985)341

*This characterful house was originally an
inn and then a farmhouse. It sits quietly at
the end of a mile long single track road,
formerly an old drove road parts of which
are badly surfaced. The house is lined with
pine and accommodation comprises living
room/diner, small kitchen with larder, large
bathroom with wash hand basin & WC,
separate WC and double bedroom on the
ground floor with two twin-bedded rooms
on the first floor.*

Mar–25 Oct 1 wk min, 1 mth max, 1 unit,
1–8 persons ◆ ◎ fridge
Elec inclusive Ⓛcan be hired ☎ WM,
Iron & Ironing board in unit CTV
⊕3pin square P ⚎(1m)

£120pw (Low)
£135pw (High)

TARLTON
Gloucestershire
Map3 ST99

H Edgeley Barn
for bookings Hon Mrs G B Bathurst,
Hullasey House, Tarlton Cirencester,
Gloucestershire GL7 6PA
☎Kemble(028577)274

*This converted Cotswold-Stone barn
provides spacious well appointed
accommodation yet retains its exposed
timbers and natural stonework.
Comprising on ground floor: lounge with
kitchen/diner and cloakroom. First floor,
four double bedrooms two of which are
en-suite. Second floor a twin bedded room
for the agile only approached via a wall
fitted ladder.*

All year MWB 4 days min, 6 wks max,
1 unit, 2–10 persons, nc5 years ◎
fridge storage & open fires
Elec inclusive Ⓛinclusive ☎metered
telephone SD & TD in unit Iron & Ironing
board in unit ☉ ◍ CTV
⊕3pin square 5P Ⅲ ⚎(4m) video &
music centre

⊖ ♪(3m) ⚏(1m)
Min£115 Max£805pw

Talgarth
—
Taynuilt

TAVERNSPITE
Dyfed
Map2 SN21

H White Lion
for bookings Powell's Cottage Holidays,
55 High Street, Saundersfoot, Dyfed
☎Saundersfoot(0834)812791

*Modern detached house with fields at rear,
situated in a quiet rural area. The property
has lounge, dining room, kitchen and four
bedrooms (one has a double, two have
double beds and bunk beds, and another
room has twin beds). The house is situated
1½m E of Tavernspite village on an unclass
road.*

May–Aug MWB out of season 1 wk min,
1 unit, 10 persons [◆] fridge Electric
Elec inclusive Ⓛnot provided ☎(1½m)
Iron in unit Ironing board in unit ☉
TV ⊕3pin square P ⌂ ⚎(1½m)
⊖ ⚏ (1½m)
Min£111 Max£237pw

TAYINLOAN
Strathclyde *Argyllshire*
Map10 NR74

F Cara & Gigha Killean House
for bookings Mr & Mrs D Attey,
Newmarche House, Thorpe-in-Balne,
Doncaster, South Yorkshire DN6 0DY
☎Doncaster(0302)883160 or Tayinloan
(05834)238

*These flats are furnished and equipped to
modern standards with Cara having two
bedrooms and a lounge/diner; Gigha,
which is on the first floor, has one double
room, a kitchenette/diner and lounge with
sofa bed. Situated on a 2000-acre estate
with private beach.*

Mar–Oct MWB out of season 3 days min
(out of season), 2 units, 1–4 persons
[◆] ◎ fridge Storage heaters
Elec metered Ⓛinclusive (except towels)
☎(150yds) [Launderette within 300yds]
CTV ⊕3pin square P ⚎(1m)
⊖ ⚏ (1m)

Min£65 Max£68pw (Low)
Min£165 Max£180pw (High)

F Jura, Islay & Arran Killean House
for bookings Mr & Mrs S D Attey,
Newmarche House, Thorpe-in-Balne,
Doncaster, South Yorkshire DN6 0DY
☎Doncaster(0302)883160 or
Tayinloan(05834)238

*Modernised and refurbished 19th-century
coach houses fully carpeted and neatly
decorated. Each comprising one double
bedroom (Jura has another room
containing a single and bunk beds. Islay's
second bedroom has three single beds,
and Arran's other bedroom has bunks)
combined Lounge/diner with kitchen area,
Arran has a shower room the other two,
baths. All situated on a 2000-acre estate
with private beach.*

Mar–Oct MWB out of season 3 days min
(out of season) 3 units, 1–5 persons
[◆] ◎ fridge Storage heaters
Elec metered Ⓛinclusve except towels
⚏ [Launderette on premises] CTV
⊕3pin square P ⚎(1m)
⊖ ⚏ (1m)
Min£65 Max£68pw (Low)
Min£165 Max£180pw (High)

H Lodge Killean House
for bookings Mr & Mrs D Attey,
Newmarche House, Thorpe-in-Balne,
Doncaster, South Yorkshire DN6 0DY
☎Doncaster(0302)883160 or
Tayinloan(05834)238

*This is the small gatehouse on the main
road at the entrance to Killean Estate.
Fully modernised with fitted carpets,
modern simple furnishings, and
comprising small kitchen/diner, lounge
and bathroom plus twin-bedded room on
ground floor. Two double bedrooms with
attic ceilings on first floor. Located on this
2000-acre estate with private beach.*

Mar–Oct MWB out of season 3 days min
(out of season), 1 unit, 1–6 persons [◆]
◎ fridge Storage heaters
Elec metered Ⓛinclusive except towels
☎(¼m) [Launderette on premises] CTV
⊕3pin square P ⚎(1m)
⊖ ⚏ (1m)
Min£107 Max£138pw (Low)
Min£164 Max£250pw (High)

**H Mayfair, Park Lane & Dolls House
Cottage** Killean House
for bookings Mr & Mrs D Attey,
Newmarche House, Thorpe-in-Balne,
Doncaster, South Yorkshire DN6 0DY
☎Doncaster(0302)883160 or
Tayinloan(05834)238

*Recently modernised 19th-century semi-
detached cottages comprising lounge,
kitchen/diner and bathroom on the
ground floor with a steep staircase
leading to two bedrooms on the first floor.
Mayfair and Park Lane have additional
double pull-down wall bed in lounge. All
situated in a 2000-acre estate with private
beach.*

Mar–Oct MWB out of season 3 days min
(out of season), 3 units, 1–6 persons [◆]
◎ fridge Storage heaters
Elec metered Ⓛinclusive ☎(1m)
[Launderette](300yds) CTV
⊕3pin square P ⚎(1m)
⊖ ⚏ (1m)
Min£84 Max£98pw (Low)
Min£195 Max£230pw (High)

TAYNUILT
Strathclyde *Argyllshire*
Map10 NN03

Ch Mrs I Olsen **Airdeny Chalets** Airdeny,
Taynuilt, Argyll PA35 1HY
☎Taynuilt(086 62)648

*Wooded chalets designed and built by the
owners who also own a nearby sawmill.
Two bedrooms, open plan living and
kitchen areas, shower with WC. High
standard of fittings, and visitors generally* →

well looked after. Situated in a quiet setting frequented by deer, facing E to Ben Cruachan (3,600ft). Take the Glen Lonan road at the Taynuilt Hotel on the A85, head S for 1m.

All year MWB out of season 1wk min, 1mth max, 4units, 1–4persons ◇ ◆
⊚ fridge 🍴 Elec metered
⊡inclusive ☎(1m) Iron in unit ⊕
CTV ⊕3pin square P 🏠(1m)
⊖ 🚿(1m)
Min£90pw(Low)
Min£220pw(High)

C&F Bonawe House
for bookings Highland Holidays, 18 Maxwell Place, Stirling, FK8 1JU
☎Stirling(0786)62519

Bonawe House is quietly set in its own mature gardens, beside the historic Bonawe Furnace and not far from Loch Etive. The House dates from 1750 and has three flats with one, two or three bedrooms. The former stables and staff quarters have been converted to provide six cottages with either one, two or three bedrooms. All units are comfortable and tastefully furnished.

All year MWB out of season 1wk min in season, 3 days out of season, 9units, 2–7persons [◇] ◆ ◆ ⊚ fridge electric Elec inclusive ⊡inclusive ☎ Iron & Ironing board in unit Launderette on premises ⊕ CTV ⊕3pin square 16P 🏠(¾m)
⊖ 🚿(¼m)
Min£81 Max£279pw

F Mr H & Miss S Grant Lonan House
Glen Lonan, Taynuilt, Argyll PA35 1HY
☎Taynuilt(08662)253

This Scottish mansion of architectural note, located 1m from Taynuilt and 12m from Oban, stands in attractive, landscaped grounds with magnificent scenic views. These nine flats vary in size with each being tastefully decorated and furnished.

All year MWB out of season 1wk min, 3wks max, 9units, 1–8persons ◆
⊚ fridge 🍴 Elec metered ⊡can be hired ☎ Iron & Ironing board on premises ⊕ CTV ⊕3pin square 16P 🏠(1m)
⊖ 🚿(1m)
Min£70 Max£135pw(Low)
Min£90 Max£250pw(High)

TEIGNMOUTH
Devon
Map**3** SX97

Taynuilt
—
Teignmouth

H CC Ref 402 ELP
for bookings Character Cottages (Holidays) Ltd, 34 Fore Street, Sidmouth, Devon EX10 8AQ
☎Sidmouth(03955)77001

A thatched house of character in a secluded position with gardens and paddock. It comprises attractive living room with period furniture, good kitchen, two tastefully decorated bedrooms, bathroom/WC, and two beds in living room.

All year MWB out of season 1wk min, 6mths max, 1unit, 2–5persons ◆ ⊚ fridge Gas Gas/Elec inclusive ⊡not provided ☎(100yds) Iron & Ironing board in unit ⊕ TV ⊕3pin square ⊕2pin round P 🏠(300yds) 🌿Grass
⊖ 🚿(1½m) 📼(1½m) 🎵(1½m)
🐾(1½m)
Min£83 Max£118pw (Low)
Min£140 Max£180pw (High)

C CC Ref 4080
for bookings Character Cottages (Holidays) Ltd, 34 Fore Street, Sidmouth, Devon EX10 8AQ
☎Sidmouth(03955)77001

A period cottage built in 1670, overlooking the village green, decorated to a high standard and well furnished with many fine items. It comprises lounge, dining room, kitchen, bathroom, WC and three bedrooms.

All year MWB out of season 1wk min, 1mth max, 1unit, 1–6persons [◇] no pets ⊚ fridge Electric Elec metered ⊡not provided
☎(50yds) Iron & Ironing board in unit ⊕ CTV ⊕3pin square 🏠 🏠(¼m)
⊖ 🚿(2m) 🚿(¼m) 📼(¼m) 🎵(¼m)
Min£91 Max£155pw (Low)
Min£188 Max£252pw (High)

C & F Clifford House Bridge Road
for bookings Mrs P O'Donnell, 2 School Lane, Shaldon, Teignmouth, Devon TQ14 0DG
☎Shaldon(0626)872314

*Two cottages and four flats on a corner site in the picturesque village of Shaldon. **Mews & Corner Cottages** comprise lounge/diner, kitchen and bathroom/WC on ground floor and two bedrooms on the*

*first floor. There is a double bed-settee in the lounge. **The flats** vary in size with three sleeping up to six people, one up to four. They have lounge, kitchen or lounge/ diner/kitchen, bathroom/WC, two bedrooms and three with bed-settee in lounge.*

May–Oct MWB out of season 1wk min, 1mth max, 6units, 2–6persons ◆ 🌙 or ⊚ fridge Electric Elec metered ⊡can be hired except tea towels ☎ TV ⊕3pin square P 🖼 🏠(50yds)
⊖ 🚿(2m) 🚿(50yds) 📼(1m) 🎵(1m)
🐾(1m)
Min£45 Max£90pw (Low)
Min£85 Max£195pw (High)

F Coachmans Flat
for bookings Mrs L B Francis, 12 Newton Road, Bishopsteignton, Teignmouth, Devon TQ14 9PN
☎Teignmouth(06267)6656

A spacious ground floor flat in semi-detached house set back from main Teignmouth–Newton Abbot road. Accommodation comprises large lounge/ diner (with divan), one twin-bedded room, shower room/WC and a modern fitted kitchen. Excellent views of estuary and hills.

All year MWB out of season 3nights min, 4wks max, 1unit, 2persons ⊚ fridge 🍴 Elec metered (except hot water) ⊡inclusive ☎(½m) SD in unit Iron & Ironing board in unit ⊕ CTV ⊕3pin square P 🖼 🏠(½m)
⊖ 🚿(3m) 🚿(½m) 📼(1m) 🎵(1m)
🐾(3m)
Min£70 Max£85pw

F Mr D Postlethwaite East Cliff Marine Parade, Shaldon, Teignmouth, Devon TQ14 0DP
☎Shaldon(062687)2334

*The three flats are located within a Georgian house, overlooking the estuary and adjacent to the beach and ferry. The **Captains Quarters** on the ground floor has a lounge, kitchen/diner, bathroom/ WC and one family bedroom. **Starboard Quarters** on the second-floor has lounge/ diner, kitchen, shower/WC and one bedroom. **Port Quarters** on the second floor, has open plan kitchen/ lounge, diner, shower/WC and one bedroom. There is a convertible lounge suite in each flat.*

30Mar–26Oct MWB out of season 1wk min, 1mth max, 3units, 2–6persons
◆ ◆ 🌙(2) 🌙(1) fridge 🍴 Gas & Elec inclusive ⊡inclusive ☎(400yds)

Ideally situated in the centre of this picturesque seaside village, this old Coaching Inn is now converted into two cottages and five self-contained flats, all with modern kitchens and equipped for between two and six persons. Write or phone for brochure.
Bernard and Pat O'Donnell, Fisherman's Cot, School Lane. Shaldon, South Devon. Telephone: (0626) 872314.

Iron & Ironing board in unit CTV
⊕3pin square 3P ▥ ▨(400yds)
↤ ♪(2m) ♨(100yds) ♫(1m)
♫(1m) ☙(1m)

Details not confirmed for 1987

F Mr & Mrs J Bowden **Grendons Flats (2,
3, 5 & 6)** 58 Coombe Vale Road,
Teignmouth, Devon TQ14 9EN
☎Teignmouth(06267)3667

*The house was built in 1870 and is located
in the built-up area of Teignmouth ½m N of
town centre. A small, attractive garden is
available. Flat 2 is located in an extension,
built in 1975 and comprises large sitting/
dining room with double-settee and
kitchenette, bedroom with double bed and
bunks, separate bathroom and WC. Flats
3 & 5 are on the first floor with lounge with
double bed-settee. Flat 5 has bedroom
with double and bunk beds, Flat 3 has
double and two single beds, kitchen and
bathroom/WC. Flat 6 has large sitting/
dining room with double bed-settee and
kitchenette. Separate bathroom/WC and
family bedroom with double and bunk
beds.*

All year MWB out of season 1wk min,
1mth max, 4units, 2–6persons ◆ ◆
♪(2units) ◎(2units) fridge Electric
Gas/Elec metered ⌶can be hired
☎(200yds) Iron & Ironing board in unit
[Launderette within 300yds] ↤ CTV
⊕3pin square 10P ▥ ▨(300yds)
↤ ♪(2½m) ♨(300yds) ♫(300yds)
♫(½m) ☙(1m)

Min£40 Max£50pw (Low)
Min£108 Max£171pw (High)

F Mr S H Marshall **Lendrick** Sea Front,
Teignmouth, Devon TQ14 8BJ
☎Teignmouth(06267)3009

*Seven flats in an end-of-terrace Victorian
house overlooking the seafront. They vary
in size with one or two bedrooms. All
rooms are large, particularly the living
rooms, and all flats have kitchens and
bathroom/WC or shower units.*

All year MWB out of season 1wk min,
7units, 2–8persons no pets ♪ ◎
fridge Electric Gas/Elec metered
⌶not provided ☎ Iron & Ironing board
on premises [Launderette within
300yds] TV can be hired ⊕3pin square
▥ ▨(50yds)

↤ ♨ ♫ ♪ ☙·

Min£35 Max£65pw (Low)
Min£60 Max£116pw (High)

F **Redsands** 24 Northumberland Place
for bookings Mr R D Smallwood, 14
Somerset Place, Teignmouth, Devon
TQ14 8EN
☎Teignmouth(06267)5221

*Terraced house that has been completely
refurbished and converted into six flats,
comfortably and tastefully appointed in
modern style. Accommodation for four to
six people in one or two bedrooms, plus
double bed-settee in lounge, lounge/
kitchen/diner and shower room/WC.*

All year MWB out of season 2days min,
4wks max, 6units, 2–6persons ◆ ◆

Teignmouth
—
Templecombe

no single sex parties ◎ fridge Electric
fan heaters Elec metered ⌶inclusive
(excluding tea towels) ☎ [WM & SD on
premises] Iron & Ironing board in unit
[Launderette within 300yds] ↤ CTV
⊕3pin square ▨(150yds)
↤ ♪(2m) ♨ ♫(150yds) ♫(20yds)
☙(300yds)

Min£50 Max£70pw (Low)
Min£155 Max£190pw (High)

TELFORD
Shropshire
Map7 SJ70

F **34 High Street**
for bookings The Landmark Trust,
Shottesbrooke, Maidenhead, Berkshire
SL6 3SW
☎Littlewick Green(062882)5925

*First-floor flat in unique position in town
centre over a former grocers shop with
stables and storehouses having access for
goods to be unloaded from river or road.
Accommodation comprises lounge, two
bedrooms, kitchen/diner and bathroom/
WC. Victorian furniture is featured and
also fireplaces and bathroom fittings of
cast-iron for which the town became world
famous. The number of stairs make it
difficult for the infirm.*

All year MWB out of season 1night min,
3wks max, 1unit, 1–5persons ◆ ◆
no cats ♪ fridge ♨ Gas & Elec
inclusive ⌶not provided ☎(50yds)
Iron & Ironing board in unit ↤
⊕3pin square ▥ ▨(50yds)
↤ ♪(2½m) ♨ (50yds)

Min£112 Max£225pw (Low)
Min£130 Max£225pw (High)

C **Honeysuckle Cottage** Ironbridge
for bookings Ironbridge Cottage Holidays,
45 Newbridge Road, Ironbridge, Telford,
Shropshire TF8 7BA
☎Telford(0952)453061

*A south facing terraced cottage with views
of Ironbridge Gorge. Comprises small
lounge with archway to kitchen/dining
room, shower/WC. Steep staircase to one
double and one twin-bedded room.*

All year 1wk min, 1mth max, 1unit,
1–4persons no pets ◎ fridge Gas &
electric fires Gas & Elec metered ⌶can
be hired ☎(½m) Iron & Ironing board in
unit CTV ⊕3pin square 1P
↤ ♪(3m) ♨ ♫ ♪

C **Music Masters House** Ironbridge
for bookings Ironbridge Cottage Holidays,
45 Newbridge Road, Ironbridge, Telford,
Shropshire TF8 7BA
☎Telford(0952)453061

*A 19th-century cottage situated on
Madeley Hill overlooking Ironbridge
Gorge. Comprises sitting room, kitchen,
dining room, one double and one twin-*

bedded room, bathroom/WC and lawned
garden.

All year 1wk min, 1mth max, 1unit,
1–4persons, nc4yrs no pets ◎ fridge
☙ Elec metered ⌶can be hired
☎(½m) Iron & Ironing board in unit ◎
CTV ⊕3pin square
↤ ♪(3m) ♨(½m) ♫(½m) ♫(½m)
☙(½m)

C **Rose & Furnace Cottages**
Coalbrookdale
for bookings Ironbridge Cottage Holidays,
45 Newbridge Road, Ironbridge, Telford,
Shropshire TF8 7BA
☎Telford(0952)453061

*These 18th-century cottages are listed
buildings and have been sympathetically
restored to retain their inglenook
fireplaces and beamed ceilings. The
accommodation comprises sitting room,
diner/kitchen, two bedrooms and
bathroom/WC.*

All year 1wk min, 1mth max, 2units,
1–5persons ◆ no pets ◎ fridge
☙ Elec metered ⌶can be hired
☎(½m) Iron & Ironing board in unit
CTV ⊕3pin square 1P
↤ ♪(3m) ♨(¾m) ♫(¾m) ♫(¾m)

TEMPLE CLOUD
Avon
Map3 ST65

B **Barton Springs**
for bookings Mrs Harris, Hillcrest Farm
Cameley, Temple Cloud, Bristol, Avon
☎Temple Cloud(0761)52423

*Modernised stone-built bungalow
comprising three bedrooms, two double
and one twin (additional bed and cot
available), lounge, kitchen and bathroom/
WC. Quiet setting in valley near historic
church.*

All year MWB out of season 1wk min,
4wks max, 1unit, 2–7persons ◆
no pets ◎ fridge Electric
Elec metered ⌶not provided ☎(¾m)
Iron & Ironing board in unit ↤ TV
⊕3pin square 4P ▥ ☙(¾m)
Trout fishing
↤ ♪(3m) ♨ (50yds)

Min£50 Max£130pw

TEMPLECOMBE
Somerset
Map3 ST72

H **Manor Farm**
for bookings Mrs M L Hunt, Blackmarsh
Farm, Sherborne, Dorset
☎Sherborne(0935)812389

*Detached modern stone-built two-storey
farmhouse situated on the outskirts of
Templecombe. Spacious, attractively
furnished accommodation with six
bedrooms, large lounge, dining room,
modern kitchen, bathroom, shower room
and two WCs.*

All year 1wk min, 6mths max, 1unit,
2–12persons ◆ ◆ ◎ fridge ☙
Elec metered ⌶can be hired →

233

☎(600yds) WM on premises Iron & Ironing board in unit ⊙ CTV ⊕3pin square P 🏠 ⛪(500yds)
⇔ ♀(500yds)
Min£80 Max£130pw (Low)
Min£175 Max£205pw (High)

TENBY
Dyfed
Map**2** SN10

F **Beaufort House** 38 Victoria Street
for bookings Mr & Mrs D R Pennington, 3 Morfa Terrace, Manorbier, Tenby, Dyfed SA70 7TH
☎Manorbier(083482)474
Four flats, some with sea views, situated close to the beach at Tenby. The accommodation varies in size, sleeping up to eight persons in two double, twin or family bedrooms, plus lounge with a convertible settee.
Apr–mid Oct MWB out of season 3days min, 1mth max, 4units, 2–8persons [◆] ◎ fridge Electric Elec metered Ⓛnot provided ☎(300yds) Iron & Ironing board in unit [Launderette within 300yds] ⊙ CTV ⊕3pin square ▥ ⛪(400yds)
⇔ ♀(1m) ♫(1m) ♪(1m) 🎥(1m)

F **Flint House** Deer Park
for bookings Mr & Mrs D R Pennington, 3 Morfa Terrace, Manorbier, Tenby, Dyfed SA70 7TN
☎Manorbier(083482)474
Three-storey house on the main road, converted into flats with good décor and furnishings.
Apr–mid Oct MWB out of season 4units, 4–7persons ◆ ◎ fridge Electric Elec metered Ⓛnot provided ☎(100yds) Iron & Ironing board in unit [Launderette within 300yds] ⊙ CTV ⊕3pin square ▥ ⛳ putting green
⇔ ♀(1m) ♪(1m)

F **Glentworth House** Southcliffe Street
for bookings Mr & Mrs D R Pennington, 3 Morfa Terrace, Manorbier, Tenby, Dyfed SA70 7TH
☎Manorbier(083482)474
Three-storey end-of-terrace house converted into four flats, located one block away from the seafront. Accommodation comprises double, twin or family bedrooms to sleep up to seven, lounge with convertible settee, kitchen and bathroom.
Apr–mid Oct 3days min, 1mth max, 4units, 2–7persons [◆] fridge Electric Elec metered Ⓛnot provided ☎(300yds) Iron & Ironing board in unit [Launderette within 300yds] ⊙ CTV ⊕3pin square P ▥ ⛪(400yds)
⇔ ♀(1m) ♫(1m) ♪(1m) 🎥(1m)

C & F Mrs J M Wright **The Old Vicarage**
Penally, Tenby, Dyfed
☎Tenby(0834)2773
The Old Vicarage consists of a small cottage, two mews flats adjoining the main house and three further flats with access to large walled gardens. Charming small garden cottage with sitting room/dining area, double bedroom with wash hand basin, kitchen and bathroom/WC. Two well-equipped flats both two bedroom, one flat comprising one double room and one with bunks and single bed. There is a sitting room, kitchen/diner, bathroom and WC. The other has one twin-bedded room and a bedroom with three singles, also kitchen, sitting room, dining room, bathroom and WC. The cottage and two of the flats have convertible single beds in the sitting room. The ***Granary*** *is a first-floor flat in converted Georgian coach house, comprising one double and one twin-bedded room, bathroom/WC and combined sitting room/diner, with kitchen area. The* ***Coach House*** *and the* ***Old Dairy*** *have similar accommodation to The Granary except the Coach House is a ground-floor flat. (2m SW A4139).*
All year MWB out of season 3days min, 6wk max, 6units, 2–7persons ◆ ◆ no pets ◎ ♨(in one mews cottage) fridge 🔥 Elec inclusive Ⓛcan be hired (overseas visitors only) ☎(250yds) [WM] Iron & Ironing board in unit ⊙ CTV ⊕3pin square P ▥ ⛪(200yds) Children's play area
⇔ ♂ ♀(200yds) ♫(¼m) ♪(400yds) 🎥(2m)
Min£85 Max£175pw (Low)
Min£180 Max£240pw (High)

Powell's Cottage Holidays 55 High Street, Saundersfoot, Dyfed
☎Saundersfoot(0834)812791
The following properties are operated by Powell's.

F **Abbey Garden Flat**
see 'Powell's Cottage Holidays' for address
☎Saundersfoot(0834)812791
First-floor flat in detached dormer bungalow situated 1½m from Tenby. Accommodation comprises kitchen, lounge/diner, bathroom, separate WC, two double bedrooms with additional single beds and one double bedroom.
May–Aug MWB out of season 1wk min, 1unit, 8persons, nc5 no pets ◎ fridge Electric Elec inclusive Ⓛnot provided Iron & Ironing board in unit ⊙ CTV ⊕3pin square 1P ▥ ⛪(50yds)
⇔ ♂(1½m) ♀(50yds) ♫(1½m) ♪(1½m) 🎥(1½m)
Min£111 Max£237pw

H **Court Vale**
see 'Powell's Cottage Holidays' for address
☎Saundersfoot(0834)812791
A converted malthouse, standing in well tended grounds. Accommodation comprises, lounge/diner, kitchen and four bedrooms, bathroom/WC and separate downstairs WC.
May–Aug 1wk min, 1unit, 4–8persons [◇] ◆ no pets ◎ fridge Electric, gas or coal fires Elec inclusive Ⓛnot provided ☎ Iron & Ironing board in unit ⊙ CTV ⊕3pin square P ▥ ⛪(10yds)
⇔ ♂(3m) ♪(3m) 🎥(3m)
Min£123 Max£276pw

F **14, 35 & 65 Croft Court**
for bookings see 'Powell's Cottage Holidays' for address
☎Saundersfoot(0834)812791
Three flats located in a multi-storey block, set on a hill with steps to the beach. All flats have lounge, dining area, kitchen and bathroom/WC. ***Flat 14*** *on the first floor has a double and a twin bedroom.* ***Flat 35*** *on the third floor has one bedroom with a double bed and bunks.* ***Flat 65*** *on the sixth floor has two bedrooms, one double, one single and an extra fold-up-bed.*
1wk min, 3units, 4persons no pets ◎ fridge Elec inclusive ☎ Iron & Ironing board in unit ⊙(35 only) TV(35) CTV(14 & 65) ⊕3pin square 1P each flat ▥ ⛪(¼m)
⇔ ♂(1½m) ♀(200yds) ♫(½m) ♪(½m) 🎥(½m)
Min£75 Max£210pw

B **Le Fylde**
for bookings see 'Powell's Cottage Holidays' for address
☎Saundersfoot(0834)812791
A bungalow in slightly elevated position with rural outlook. Accommodation comprises lounge, kitchen/diner, bath/WC, one double and one twin bedroom.
1wk min, 1unit, 4persons ◆ no pets ◎ fridge storage heaters Elec inclusive Iron & Ironing board in unit ⊙ CTV ⊕3pin square 2P ▥ ⛪(¾m)
⇔ ♂(1m) ♀(½m)
Min£84 Max£195pw

B **Sea Vista**
for bookings see 'Powell's Cottage Holidays' for address
☎Saundersfoot(0834)812791
A modern semi-detached bungalow comprising lounge, diner/kitchen, bathroom/WC, separate WC, one double, one twin and one family bedroom with a double and single bed
1wk min, 1unit, 8persons [◇] ◆ no pets ◎ fridge 🔥 Elec inclusive ☎(50yds) Iron & Ironing board in unit ⊙ CTV ⊕3pin square 2P 1🏠 ▥ ⛪(¼m)
⇔ ♀(½m)
Min£111 Max£237pw

TERRINGTON
North Yorkshire
Map**8** SE67

B **Barn Cottage** Mowthorpe Lane
for bookings Mrs S Goodrick, Brindle
Court, Terrington, York YO6 4PS
☎Coneysthorpe(065384)268 or 370

*Modern bungalow near village centre,
comprising large lounge, kitchen, sleeping
accommodation for four people and a
bathroom/WC.*

All year MWB out of season 4 days min,
1mth max, 1unit, 1–4persons ◈ ◆
no pets ◉ fridge Electric
Elec metered ⬓can be hired
☎(200yds) Iron & Ironing board in unit
⊙ CTV ⊕3pin square 2P ⛥ ▥
🎇(200yds)
⊖ ♨(250yds)

Min£55 Max£110pw (Low)
Min£120 Max£140pw (High)

C **Crossways** The Square
for bookings Mrs D Goodrick, Rose Villa,
Terrington, York, North Yorkshire YO6 4PP
☎Coneysthorpe(065384)268 or 370

*Stone-built cottage of character in the
village centre comprising comfortable
lounge, kitchen, bathroom/WC and two
bedrooms.*

All year MWB out of season 4 days min,
1mth max, 1unit, 1–4persons ◈ ◆
no pets ◉ fridge Electric fires
Elec metered ⬓can be hired
CTV ⊕3pin square 1P ▥ 🎇(100yds)
⊖ ♨(150yds)

Min£50 Max£85pw (Low)
Min£100 Max£140pw (High)

B **Green Gables**
for bookings Mrs D Goodrick, Rose Villa,
Terrington, York, North Yorkshire YO6 4PP
☎Coneysthorpe(065384)268 or 370

*Modern bungalow in mellow Yorkstone in
the village centre. Sleeping
accommodation for eight in a ground-
floor twin-bedded room and a double-
bedded room and in a first-floor double-
bedded room plus a twin-bedded room.
Fully fitted modern kitchen, a bathroom/
WC plus a separate WC. There is a sun-
porch and patio to the rear.*

All year MWB out of season 4 days min,
1mth max, 1unit, 1–8persons ◈
no pets ◉ fridge 🍴 Elec metered
⬓inclusive ☎(50yds) WM & SD in unit
Iron & Ironing board in unit CTV
⊕3pin square 2P ▥ 🎇(50yds)
⊖ ♨(100yds)

Min£90 Max£145pw (Low)
Min£155 Max£185pw (High)

C **Greystones** The Square
for bookings Mrs D Goodrick, Rose Villa,
Terrington, York YO6 4PP
☎Coneysthorpe(065384)268 or 370

*Renovated building in the village centre
with spacious beamed lounge, entrance
hall and cloakroom/WC, kitchen, three
bedrooms and bathroom/WC.*

All year MWB out of season 4 days min,
1mth max, 1unit, 1–4persons ◈ ◆
no pets ◉ fridge 🍴 & Electric
Elec metered ⬓inclusive ☎(30yds)

Terrington
—
Tewkesbury

WM & SD in unit Iron & Ironing board in
unit CTV ⊕3pin square 2P ▥
🎇(50yds)
⊖ ♨(150yds)

Min£70 Max£125pw (Low)
Min£135 Max£165pw (High)

C **Orchard Cottage** Mowthorpe Lane
for bookings Mrs D Goodrick, Rose Villa,
Terrington, York YO6 4PP
☎Coneysthorpe(065384)268 or 370

*Single storey cottage, converted from a
Victorian chapel, near the village centre. A
spacious lounge with bed-settee, one
bedroom and bathroom make up the
accommodation.*

All year MWB out of season 4 days min,
1mth max, 1unit, 1–4persons ◈
no pets ◉ fridge Electric
Elec metered ⬓can be hired
☎(200yds) Iron & Ironing board in unit
CTV ⊕3pin square 1⛥ ▥
🎇(200yds)
⊖ ♨(250yds)

Min£40 Max£75pw (Low)
Min£85 Max£105pw (High)

B **Sunningdale** Church Lane
for bookings Mrs D Goodrick, Rose Villa,
Terrington, York YO6 4PP
☎Coneysthorpe(065384)268 or 370

*Modern bungalow in yellow Yorkstone
situated close to the village centre and
with attractive gardens and small patio.
Accommodation comprises lounge with
french windows, two bedrooms, kitchen/
diner and bathroom.*

All year MWB out of season 4 days min,
1mth max, 1unit, 1–4persons ◈
no pets ◉ fridge 🍴 Elec metered
⬓inclusive ☎(500yds) WM & SD in
unit Iron & Ironing board in unit ⊙
CTV ⊕3pin square 1P 1⛥ ▥
🎇(500yds)
⊖ ♨(500yds)

Min£70 Max£105pw (Low)
Min£125 Max£165pw (High)

C Mr J M P Benton **Folly Farm** Tetbury,
Gloucestershire
☎Tetbury(0666)52358

*Kiln cottage features a kiln-like fireplace
and vaulted ceiling and consists of open
plan sitting room/dinner, kitchen unit,
private patio, one double bedroom,
bathroom/WC, plus childrens sleeping loft
reached by folding stairs. The Weigh
House and Wheelwrights are a pair of
cottages comprising hallway, spacious
living area, fitted kitchen and patio, and
on first floor bathroom/WC, one double-
and one twin-bedded room. The
Middleyard Cowbyres and Barnend, are*

*three well converted cottages constructed
from old stables. Each have
accommodation comprising of open plan
sitting/dining room, kitchen, bathroom/
WC, one double-bedded room and one
twin-bedded sleeping loft reached by an
elm staircase.*

All year MWB out of season 3 days min,
6units, 1–4persons [◇] ◈ ◆
no pets ⌀ fridge 🍴 & log fires Gas &
Elec inclusive ⬓inclusive ☎(½m) Iron
& Ironing board on premises ⊙ CTV
⊕3pin square P ▥ 🎇(½m)
⊖ ♨(2½m) ♨(½m)

Min£119 Max£140pw (Low)
Min£195 Max£247pw (High)

C **Norwood Cottages**
for bookings Mrs J R White, Hardwick
Farm, Teversal, Sutton in Ashfield,
Nottinghamshire NG17 3JR
☎Chesterfield(0246)850271

*This pair of semi-detached, mid-Victorian,
stone-built cottages were formerly estate
workers housing and are located close to
and are still part of the Hardwick Hall
Estate. They are in a pleasant rural
situation and provide modest but well
maintained accommodation.*

All year MWB out of season 1wk min,
2units, 5persons ◈ ◉ fridge electric
& solid fuel elec metered ⬓can be
hired ☎(3m) WM in unit Iron & Ironing
board in unit ⊙ ◉ CTV
⊕3pin square roadside parking 🎇(3m)
⊖ ♨(2m)

Min£55 Max£85pw

C & F **Auriol House**
for bookings H W Herford, Upper Court,
Kemerton, Tewkesbury, Gloucestershire
GL20 7HY
☎Overbury(038689)351

*Beautiful 15th-century merchant's house,
containing five fully modernised flats and
a cottage, accessible via a period iron
gate leading to the heavily studded front
door. The comfortable Flats have one or
two bedrooms, lounge and dining rooms
or areas, fitted kitchens and bathrooms,
some en-suite. The Garden Cottage
comprises kitchen, lounge/diner with
feature fireplace, bathroom and two
bedrooms.*

All year MWB 3 days min, 6units,
2–6persons [◇] ◈ ◆ Pets charged
for ◉ fridge Electric Elec metered
⬓inclusive ☎ Iron & Ironing board on
premises ⊙ CTV ⊕3pin square
🎇(15yds)
⊖ ♨(20yds) ♨(20yds) 🎵(½m)
🎵(½m) 🐾(100yds)

Details not confirmed for 1987

See advertisement on page 236

H   30 St Mary's Lane
for bookings The Landmark Trust,
Shottesbrooke, Maidenhead, Berkshire
SL6 3SW
☎Littlewick Green(062 882)5925

*Historic property extended at rear to
comprise ground-floor kitchen, dining
room, cloakroom with WC and wash
basin. Single bedroom and bright
spacious sitting room on first floor and
second floor has combined bathroom/
WC, and family bedroom. On the third
floor landing there is a single and twin
bedroom.*

Allyear MWB out of season 1day min,
1unit, 2–6persons ◊ ◆ ◎ fridge
⚱ Elec inclusive ⌷not provided
☎(100yds) Iron & Ironing board in unit
[Launderette within 300yds] ☺
⊕3pin square 🍽 ♨(50yds)

⊖ ⚱(100yds)

Min£112 Max£230pw (Low)
Min£115 Max225pw (High)

THORNAGE
Norfolk
Map**9** TG03

C   No 4 Meadow Cottages The Street
for bookings Mr C L Gill, 13 Haslemere
Road, Winchmore Hill, London N21
☎01-886 0424

*One of a row of four terraced properties,
located on the edge of the village and
overlooking the surrounding countryside
with mature garden and stream.
Accommodation comprises kitchen/diner,
lounge, bathroom, cloakroom/WC and
three bedrooms, one on the ground floor.*

Allyear MWB out of season 3days min,
3mths max, 1unit, 1–8persons ◊ ◆
no pets ◎ fridge ⚱ & open fires (coal
& logs free) Elec metered
⌷not provided Iron & Ironing board in
unit ☺ CTV ⊕3pin square 2P
♨(3m)

⊖ ⚱(2m)

Min£50 Max£180pw

THORNESS BAY
See **Wight, Isle of**

┌─────────────────────────┐
│   **Tewkesbury**   │
│   **—**   │
│   **Threlkeld**   │
└─────────────────────────┘

THORNFORD
Dorset
Map**3** ST61

C   No 1 & 2 Trill Cottages
for bookings Mrs M E J Warr, Trill House,
Thornford, Sherborne, Dorset
☎Yetminster(0935)872305

*A pair of red brick semi-detached cottages
in a rural setting in the Blackmore Vale.
They comprise lounge, dining room,
kitchen, bathroom with WC, all on ground
floor. One double and two twin bedrooms
on first floor. Leave Sherborne on A352
(Dorchester road) at town boundary turn
right, signposted Thornford.*

Allyear MWB out of season 3days min,
1mth max, 2units, 2–6persons ◊ ◆
no pets ◎ fridge Electric & open fires
Elec metered ⌷can be hired ☎(1½m)
WM in unit SD in unit Iron & Ironing
board in unit ☺ TV ⊕3pin square
6P 1🛁 🍽 ♨(1½m)

⊖ ⚱(1½m)

Min£35 Max£100pw

See advertisement under Sherborne

THORPE
Derbyshire
Map**7** SK15

C   Coldwall & Green Cottages Digmire
Lane
for bookings Mr & Mrs Bailey, 4 Woodland
Close, Thorpe, Ashbourne, Derbyshire
☎Thorpe Cloud(033 529)447

*Pair of tastefully modernised pebble-
dashed cottages, enjoying fine views of
surrounding countryside and each having
kitchen/diner, bathroom/WC and cosy
lounge.* **Coldwell Cottage** *has two
bedrooms;* **Green Cottage** *has three.*

Allyear 1wk min, 2units, 1–6persons
◊ ◆ no pets ◎ fridge Electric &
open fires Elec metered ⌷not provided

☎(125yds) ☺ TV ⊕3pin square 3P
🍽 ♨(200yds)

⊖ ♪(3m) ⚱(½m)

Min£60 Max£140pw

THRELKELD
Cumbria
Map**11** NY32

B & C   The Bungalows & The Cottage
for bookings Mr & Mrs P Sunley, The
Bungalow, Sunnyside, Threlkeld, Keswick,
Cumbria
☎Threlkeld(059 683)679

*Two attractive modern bungalows and a
modernised Lakeland stone cottage
situated at the top end of Threlkeld village.
They can accommodate up to six people
with the* **Bungalow** *having two family
rooms with one double and one single bed
in each room and the* **Cottage** *has one
family, one double and one single room.
The quality of the accommodation is very
good in these well cared for properties.
Pleasant rear garden which can be used
by guests.*

Allyear MWB out of season 3days min,
3units, 1–6persons ◊ ◆ ◎ fridge
electric radiators & open fires
Elec inclusive ⌷can be hired ☎ WM &
SD in unit Iron & Ironing board in unit
☺ CTV ⊕3pin square 9P 🍽 ♨(⅓m)

⊖ ♪(1m) ⚱(½m)

Min£80 Max£135pw

See advertisement under Keswick

C   1 & 2 Dalegarth
for bookings Mr G Walker, The Park,
Rickerby, Carlisle, Cumbria
☎Carlisle(0228)24848

*Two attractive cottages, set in their own
pretty gardens, at the west end of
Threlkeld village overlooking St Johns in
the vale. One of the cottages has a sitting
room, kitchen/dining room, one double
and two twin bedrooms. The other cottage
has a lounge, dining room, kitchen, one
double bedroom and one twin bedroom.
Both have bathrooms refurbished to a
high standard.*

Allyear MWB out of season 3days min,
3mths max, 2units, 4–6persons ◊ ◆

◎ fridge Night storage Elec inclusive
🔲 not provided ☎(200yds) Iron &
Ironing board in unit ☉ CTV
⊕3pin square 6P �📺 ♨(200yds)
↔ ♪(½m) ♨(½m)
Min£80 Max£95pw (Low)
Min£175 Max£195pw (High)

F *Netherend & T'Otherend*
for bookings Mr J N Baxter, Heathfield,
Crosthwaite Road, Keswick, Cumbria
CA12 4SZ
☎Threlkeld(059683)671 or Mrs Luccini
Keswick(0596)72407

Stone-built barn converted into two flats to
a very high standard. Both flats (one on
ground floor and one on first floor) are
modern and spacious and have three
double-bedded rooms. Located in the tiny
hamlet of Guardhouse and an ideal base
from which to explore the Lake District.

All year MWB out of season 3 nights min,
1mth max, 2units, 6persons ◇ ◆ ◙
fridge Electric Elec metered
🔲 not provided ☎(¾m) Iron & Ironing
board in unit ☉ CTV ⊕3pin square
3P ♨(2m)
↔ ♪(1m) ♨(¾m)

Details not confirmed for 1987

See advertisement under Keswick

THRESHFIELD
North Yorkshire
Map7 SD96

H *Glen Cottage*
for bookings G F & E Thompson, Wood
Nook Caravan Park, Skirethorns, Skipton,
North Yorkshire
☎Grassington(0756)752412

Solid stone converted coach house
situated within the farmyard, and
comprising two bedrooms, lounge, kitchen
and bathroom.

All year MWB out of season 1wk min,
1unit, 2–4persons ◇ no pets ◎
fridge open fire Elec metered 🔲 can be
hired ☎ [TD on premises] Iron &
Ironing board on premises CTV
⊕3pin square 1🏠 📺 ♨
↔ ♨(1m)

Details not confirmed for 1987

Threlkeld
—
Tobermory

THURSTONFIELD
Cumbria
Map11 NY35

CH Mrs S Potter **Lake Shore Lodges**
Thurstonefield, Carlisle, Cumbria CA5 6HB
☎Burgh-by-Sands(022876)552

Six pine-clad lodges on the shores of a 30-
acre lake which is run as a trout fishery, in
a peaceful wooded area, four miles west of
Carlisle. Each lodge has a double and a
twin-bedded room, open plan lounge,
dining room, kitchen and bathroom. All
are maintained to a very high standard.

All year MWB out of season 6units,
4–5persons ◇ ◆ ♿ fridge gas
fires Gas & Elec inclusive 🔲 inclusive
☎(50yds) Iron & Ironing board on
premises ☉ ◐ CTV ⊕3pin square
26P 📺 ♨(½m) trout fishing
↔ ♨(½m)
Min£96 Max£106pw (Low)
Min£210 Max£220pw (High)

TINTAGEL
Cornwall
Map2 SX08

F **CC Ref 345E**
for bookings Character Cottages
(Holidays) Ltd, 34 Fore Street, Sidmouth,
Devon EX10 8AQ
☎Sidmouth(03955)77001

A brick-built conversion, adjacent to a
hotel, containing five flats each sleeping
from two to six people. Four have two
bedrooms and a bed-settee in the lounge.
The fifth has three bedrooms. Each has a
kitchen, dining room (or dining area within
the kitchen), lounge and bathroom/WC.

All year MWB out of season 1wk min,
1mth max, 5units, 2–6persons [◇] ◆
no pets ◎ fridge Electric
Elec metered 🔲 can be hired ☎(1m)
Iron & Ironing board in unit
[Launderette] ☉ TV ⊕3pin square

⊕2pin round P 🏠 📺 ♨(200yds)
🔥Hard
↔ ♨ ♫ ♫
Min£58 Max£65pw (Low)
Min£138 Max£194pw (High)

C Mrs P K Upright **Halgabron Holiday**
Cottages Halgabron, Tintagel, Cornwall
☎Camelford(0840)770667

Five exceptionally fine cottages of which
Threshings & Chaffcutter *are conversions*
from a stone barn and to obtain the best
view the large lounge/diner and open-plan
kitchen are on the upper floor. The
sleeping accommodation comprises one
double room, one twin and one with bunk
beds and a bed-settee in lounge.
Cartwheel Cottage *is steeped in*
character, having beams and fireplace.
Accommodation comprises lounge,
kitchen/diner, small double-bedded room,
one family room with double bed and
bunks. ***Granary Cottage*** *is converted from*
a stone barn and comprises lounge,
kitchen/diner, one double-bedded room
which also contains bunk beds, separate
shower room/WC. ***The Reapers****, originally*
part of the old farmhouse, comprises
kitchen, large sitting room/dining room.
The first floor has a twin-bedded room and
connecting door leading to a double
bedroom with shower/WC off, wash hand
basin in both bedrooms. 1m E off B3263
towards Boscastle.

Mar–Dec 2 available in Jan & Feb MWB
out of season 1wk min, 9mths max, 5units,
1–8persons ◇ ◆ ◆ ◎ fridge
Electric Elec metered 🔲 inclusive
☎(½m) Iron & Ironing board in unit ☉
CTV ⊕3pin square P 📺 ♨(1m)
↔ ♨(1m) ♫(1m) ♫(3m)
Min£70 Max£125pw (Low)
Min£150 Max£285pw (High)

TOBERMORY
Strathclyde *Argyllshire*
See **Mull, Isle of**

TOMATIN
Highland *Inverness-shire*
Map14 NH82

C Dell Cottage Kyllachy
for bookings Scottish Highland Holiday
Homes, Wester Altourie, Abriachan,
Inverness
☎Dochgarroch(046386)247

*This spacious renovated cottage stands
on a quiet country road in the valley of the
River Findhorn. The ground-floor
accommodation comprises entrance hall,
large lounge/diner, kitchen with fridge/
freezer and a small sitting room. Upstairs
there are four bedrooms (two twin, one
single and one with bunks) and a
bathroom. 2m SW of Tomatin on
unclassified road.*

May–Sep MWB out of season 1wk min,
1unit, 1–6persons ⊚ fridge Electric &
open fires Elec metered ⌴not provided
☎ SD in unit Iron & Ironing board in
unit ⊕3pin square 3P 1🛏 ♨(1m)
⊖ (2m)
Min£80 Max£130pw

TORCROSS
Devon
Map3 SX84

B Mr H W Garner **Greyhomes**
Greyhomes Hotel, Torcross, Kingsbridge,
Devon TQ7 2TH
☎Kingsbridge(0548)580220

*Four holiday bungalows located within the
grounds of the Greyhomes hotel, in
secluded, elevated position with sea views.
They each comprise two bedrooms, plus
single divan in the lounge, kitchen/diner
and bathroom/WC. Facilities of hotel
available.*

Apr–Oct 1wk min, 4wks max, 4units,
2–5persons ◆ ◆ pets charged for
⊚ fridge Electric Elec metered ⌴can
be hired ☎ Iron & Ironing board on
premises ⊙ CTV ⊕3pin square P
🔟 ♨(500yds) ✿Grass
⊖ ♨
Min£60 Max£95pw (Low)
Min£130 Max£180pw (High)

Tomatin
—
Torquay

F Mrs F Signora **Torcross Apartment
Hotel** (Slapton Sands) Torcross,
Kingsbridge, Devon TQ7 2TQ
☎Kingsbridge(0548)580206

*At the waters-edge on Slapton Sands, with
direct access to the beach. All apartments
have one, two or three bedrooms, lounge,
kitchen and bathroom. Some have
additional en-suite bathrooms. All have
sea or lake views and facilities include bar
and restaurant.*

Mar–Nov MWB out of season
1night min, 4wks max, 20units,
2–8persons ◇ [◆ ◆] ⊚ fridge
🍴 Elec inclusive ⌴can be hired ☎
WM & TD Iron & Ironing board on
premises [Launderette on premises]
⊙ CTV ⊕3pin square P 🔟
♨(50yds) Boat park, games room
⊖ ♨
Min£54 Max£93pw (Low)
Min£120 Max£316pw (High)

TORE
Highland *Ross-shire*
Map14 NH65

B Mr D Bain **Moorside** Tore, Muir of Ord,
Ross-shire IV6 7RY
☎Munlochy(046381)273

*A white bungalow, modernised in 1964,
with gardens to the front and rear. It is
situated adjacent to the owner's residence
and has favourable outlooks over open
farmland. The interior is homely and
comprises a small living room with open
fires, kitchen, bathroom, one double
bedroom with additional single bed and
one twin-bedded room.*

Allyear 1wk min, 1unit, 5persons ◆
no pets ⊚ fridge Night storage & open
fire Elec metered ⌴can be hired
☎(50yds) Iron & Ironing board in unit
⊙ TV ⊕3pin square 3P 🔟 ♨(3m)
⊖ ♨ (100yds)

Min£40 Max£50pw (Low)
Min£60 Max£75pw (High)

TORPOINT
Cornwall
Map2 SX45

Ch Whitsand Bay Holiday Park Chalets
1–7, Millbrook, Torpoint, Cornwall
☎Plymouth(0752)822597

*Seven identical wooden chalets in middle
of holiday park, consisting of lounge, diner
with kitchen recess, one double bedroom,
one bunk bedroom, and bed-settee. There
is a shower room with separate WC
adjoining. Well signed from B3247.*

Apr–Oct MWB out of season 1wk min,
4wks max, 7units, 1–6persons [◆ ◆]
no pets ⊚ fridge Electric
Elec metered ⌴not provided ☎ [Iron &
Ironing board on premises] [Launderette
on premises] ⊙ CTV ⊕3pin square
7P 🔟 Games room, children's
playground
⊖ ♫(3m) ♨ 🎵 ♬
Details not confirmed for 1987

TORQUAY
Devon
Map3 SX96

F Mrs S Barber **Ashdene Holiday
Apartments** Solsbro Road, Chelston,
Torquay, Devon TQ2 6PF
☎Torquay(0803)605513

*Semi-detached Victorian villa set in a
select residential area with views towards
town and sea. The four flats within the
property are one on the ground floor and
three on the first floor sleeping from 2–8
people. All comprise lounge/diner, kitchen,
shower/WC. Three flats have double bed-
settee in lounge.*

Allyear MWB out of season 2days min,
4wks max, 4units, 2–8persons ◆ ◆
No single sex groups ⊚ fridge
Electric Elec metered ⌴inclusive
☎(200yds) Iron & Ironing board in unit
⊙ CTV ⊕3pin square 8P 🔟
♨(250yds) ♨
⊖ ♫(3m) ♨(250yds) 🎵(250yds)
☂(2m)

Min£55 Max£120pw (Low)
Min£150 Max£260pw (High)

F Mr & Mrs J Nelson **Ashfield Rise Holiday Flats** Ruckamore Road, Torquay, Devon TQ2 6HF
☎Torquay(0803)605156

A pleasantly modernised Victorian building with recently built extension, in quiet location adjacent to a public park. It stands in an elevated position with good views over the town to Torbay.

Allyear MWB out of season 1wk min, 1mth max, 8units, 2–6persons ◈ ◆ no pets ◎ fridge Electric Elec metered ⌶ can be hired ☎(450yds) Iron & Ironing board on premises ⊙ CTV ⊕3pin square P ▥ ▱(300yds)
⊖ ⓢ(350yds) ♫(600yds) ♫(½m) ▓(1m)

Min£52 Max£103pw (Low)
Min£133 Max£212pw (High)

F Mr & Mrs N T Bunting **Aster Apartments** Warren Road, Torquay, Devon TQ2 5TR
☎Torquay(0803)22747

Thirteen self-contained holiday flats with their own entrances from the main reception hall and stairways. Most have fine views, some have a balcony. The flats range in size from being one- to three-bedroomed and can sleep from one to six persons. Each flat has a hall, living room, separate kitchen, and bathroom.

Mid Mar–mid Jan MWB out of season 1wk min, 16wks max, 13units, 1–8persons [◈ ◆] no pets ◎ fridge Electric Elec metered ⌶ inclusive ⌁ [WM, SD & TD on premises] Iron & Ironing board on premises ⊙ CTV ⊕3pin square P ▥ ▱(½m)
⊖ ⓢ(2m) ⓠ(½m) ♫(½m) ♫(½m) ▓(½m)

Min£70 Max£95pw (Low)
Min£190 Max£275pw (High)

F Mrs B J Rhodes **Bay Fort Mansions** Warren Road, Torquay, Devon TQ2 5TN
☎Torquay(0803)213810

Thirteen units with superb views from elevated position across Torbay in good location for sea front and shops. Twelve of

---

Torquay

the units comprise one bedroom, lounge/ diner with double wall bed or bed-settee, kitchen and bathroom/WC. The other flat has two bedrooms and balcony, otherwise the same as the others.

Allyear MWB out of season 3days min, 3mths max, 13units, 2–6persons [◇] ◈ ◆ ◎ fridge Electric Elec metered ⌶ inclusive ⌁ Iron & Ironing board on premises [Launderette on premises] ⊙ CTV ⊕3pin square 3▣ ▥ ▱ [Private ski boat]
⊖ ⓢ(2½m) ⓠ ♫ ♫(½m) ▓(500yds)

Min£70 Max£110pw (Low)
Min£180 Max£330pw (High)

F Mr & Mrs A Ball **Bronshill Court Holiday Flats** Bronshill Road, Torquay, Devon TQ1 3HD
☎Torquay(0803)34549

Five flats situated on ground and first floors of a detached Georgian house, ½m from town centre. Flats have a twin-bedded room plus a double wall bed in lounge/diner (Flat 2 has an additional double bedroom). All have small neat kitchen and bathroom/WC.

Allyear MWB out of season 3days min, 3mths max, 5units, 2–6persons [◇] ◈ ◆ ◎ fridge ♨ Elec metered ⌶ can be hired ☎(250yds) Iron & Ironing board on premises TV ⊕3pin square 7P ▥ ▱(500yds) ⌂
⊖ ⓢ(1m) ⓠ(½m) ♫(½m) ♫(½m) ▓(½m)

Details not confirmed for 1987

F Mr & Mrs P W Archer-Moy **Chelston Hall** Old Mill Road, Torquay, Devon TQ2 6HW
☎Torquay(0803)605520

Good-quality flats in an imposing Victorian house set in an elevated position with fine views across the town to Torbay. The house stands in its own grounds in a quiet area yet within easy reach of the town centre and 800yds from the seafront.

Allyear MWB out of season 3nights min, 5mths max, 9units, 2–6persons [◈ ◆] ◎ fridge Electric Elec metered ⌶ inclusive ⌁ Iron & Ironing board in unit [Launderette within 300yds] ⊙ CTV ⊕3pin square P ▥ ▱(150yds)
⊖ ⓠ(100yds) ♫(100yds) ♫(100yds) ▓(2m)

Min£58 Max£109pw (Low)
Min£89 Max£205pw (High)

C Mr & Mrs B Payne **The Cottage & The Coach House** 'Glenfield', Old Torwood Road, Torquay, Devon TQ1 1PN
☎Torquay(0803)23039

Two cottages, one adjoining the owners' house, set in secluded garden and grounds. The Cottage comprises entrance hall/lounge/diner, kitchen, bathroom/WC and three bedrooms, one of which is on the ground floor. The Coach House comprises lounge/diner, kitchen, bathroom/WC and three first floor bedrooms.

Allyear MWB out of season 2days min, 4wks max, 2units, 2–7persons [◇] ◈ ◆ no pets ◎ fridge ♨ Elec metered ⌶ inclusive ⌁(500yds) Iron & Ironing board in unit [Launderette within 300yds] ⊙ CTV ⊕3pin square 4P ▱(500yds)
⊖ ⓢ(1½m) ⓠ(½m) ♫(½m) ♫(½m) ▓(½m)

Min£90 Max£180pw (Low)
Min£200 Max£290pw (High)

F Mr D E A Collins **Derwent Hill Superior Holiday Flats** Greenway Road, Torquay, Devon TQ2 6JE
☎Torquay(0803)606793

Five self-contained flats within an attractive Victorian house set in grounds and gardens of one acre, with sea views from most flats. Accommodation comprises lounge (with double wall bed in one flat). All flats have separate bedroom with double and twin beds, separate bathroom, WC and kitchen.

Allyear MWB out of season 1wk min in season, 3days min out of season 5mths max, 5units, 2–6persons ◈ ◆ ◎ fridge [Microwave ovens] Electric Elec metered ⌶ supplied ⌁ Iron & Ironing board on premises ⊙ CTV →

Immaculate apartments, some with Balconies. Games room, Pool table, Modern laundry room, Garaging. Neighbouring hotel facilities, including entertainments. Subtropical Gardens open onto the famous Rock Walk, to seafront, Theatre, Marina and Shops.

BAYFORT MANSIONS
The Subtropical Splendour
.of the English Riviera –
– with Breathtaking Views.

ELEGANT WINTER HOLIDAYS
Practical rates for over winter among the palm trees in our wonderful Riviera climate

Warren Road, Torquay, (0803) 213810

⊕3pinsquare 1Pperunit 3🏠 Ⓜ
🚠(500yds) [Solarium]
↩ ♪(3m) ♀(400yds) 🎵(1m)
🎶(1m) 🐾(2m)
Min£50 Max£170pw (Low)
Min£140 Max£205pw (High)

F A D Chapman **Evergreen Lodge**
Ruckamore Road, Chelston, Torquay,
Devon TQ2 6HF
☎Torquay(0803)605519

*Five flats located within a Victorian villa set
in own grounds in elevated residential
area, affording sea views. They comprise
lounge/diner with kitchen area or living
room with kitchen area. Two have
bathroom/WC, three have shower/WC.
Two sleep up to six persons, three sleep up
to four. Tastefully appointed.*

16Mar–14Jan MWB out of season
2daysmin, 4wksmax, 5units, 2–6persons
◇ ◆ ◉ fridge Electric fires
Elecmetered Ⓛcan be hired ☎(½m)
Iron & Ironing board on premises ☺
CTV ⊕3pinsquare 5P Ⓜ 🚠(½m) ⌿
↩ ♪(3m) ♀(½m) 🎵(½m) 🎶(½m)
🐾(1m)
Min£50 Max£90pw (Low)
Min£110 Max£230pw (High)

F Mr N Stavrou **Hesketh Apartments**
3 Hesketh Crescent, Meadfoot Beach,
Torquay, Devon
☎Torquay(0803)26530

*Four luxury apartments within a Regency
Crescent, which also embraces the
Osborne Hotel. They are on the ground,
first, second and third floors, all
overlooking Meadfoot Bay and each
comprise kitchen, lounge/diner,
bathroom/WC, various bedroom
combinations, and including bed-settee's.*

Allyear MWB out of season 3daysmin,
4wksmax, 4units, 2–6persons [◇] ◆
◆ ◉ fridge 🍴 Elecinclusive
Ⓛinclusive ☎ Iron & Ironing board in
unit [Launderette on premises] ☺ ◉
CTV ⊕3pinsquare Ⓜ 🚠(500yds) ⌿
↩ ♪(3m) ♀(100yds) 🎵(½m)
🎶(½m) 🐾(1m)

Details not confirmed for 1987

Torquay

F & H Mr & Mrs J Crane **'Hughenden'**,
Hughenden Lodge Woodend Road,
Wellswood, Torquay, Devon TQ1 2PZ
☎Torquay(0803)22646

*Hughenden Lodge is a lavishly equipped
house, sleeping seven persons, converted
in Georgian style from the original coach
house, it has it's own patio garden.
Hughenden is a Victorian Mansion with a
lovely garden converted into nine self
contained apartments sleeping between
two and seven persons. Each comprises
lounge or lounge/diner, kitchen, bath or
shower room/WC, one or two bedrooms
(nine units have additional concealed wall
bed in lounge). Some units have a sea
view, and are located within easy reach of
the sea.*

Allyear MWB out of season 2daysmin,
1mth max, 10units 2–7persons [◇]
◆ ◆ no single sex groups ◉ fridge
🍴 Elecmetered Ⓛinclusive ☎ Iron &
Ironing board on premises [Launderette
on premises] ☺ CTV ⊕3pinsquare
15P 🚠(300yds)
↩ ♪(2m) ♀(200yds) 🎵(½m)
🎶(½m) 🐾(½m)
Min£56 Max£98pw (Low)
Min£132 Max£228pw (High)

F **Kenilworth Court** Hillesdon Road,
Torquay, Devon
☎Torquay(0803)212790

*Six units located within large Victorian
residence, centrally positioned and giving
panoramic views across town to distant
sea views. They sleep up to five people.
Large garden/patio, terraced and
secluded.*

Allyear MWB out of season 1night min,
3mths max, 6units, 2–5persons [◆ ◆]
nopets ◉ fridge Electric
Elecmetered Ⓛinclusive ☎(300yds)
Iron & Ironing board in unit ☺ CTV
⊕3pinsquare 6P 🚠(½m)
↩ ♪(3m) ♀(300yds) 🎵(½m)
🎶(½m) 🐾(½m)

Min£55 Max£90pw(Low)
Min£115 Max£180pw(High)

F C J Robinson **Kenton Lodge** Croft Hill,
(off Abbey Road) Torquay, Devon
TQ2 5NT
☎Torquay(0803)27995

*Detached villa on corner site in elevated
position with views across Torbay,
converted into three flats. Centrally
located within easy walking distance of
seafront, shops and entertainments.*

Allyear MWB out of season 3daysmin,
4wksmax, 3units, 2–6persons ◆ ◉
fridge 🍴& Electric Elecmetered
Ⓛinclusive ☎ Iron & Ironing board in
unit [Launderette within 300yds] ☺
CTV ⊕pinsquare 4P Ⓜ 🚠(300yds)
↩ ♪(3m) ♀(300yds) 🎵(300yds)
🎶(300yds) 🐾(300yds)

Details not confirmed for 1987

F Mr & Mrs J Sode **Kingsleigh Manor**
Lower Warberry Road, Torquay, Devon
TQ1 1QY
☎Torquay(0803)25935

*A large detached manor house in its own
extensive 1½ acres of grounds, with well
laid out lawns and gardens. On an
elevated position it gives sea views
towards Brixham. Now converted into flats
with spacious rooms and modern fittings.
Each flat comprises open plan lounge/
diner/kitchen, bathroom/WC and
bedrooms vary sleeping up to eight
persons.*

Allyear MWB out of season 2daysmin,
1mth max, 6units, 2–8persons ◆ ◆
no single sex groups ◉ fridge Night
storage & electric fires
Elecinclusive (night storage only)
Elecmetered Ⓛinclusive ☎ Iron &
Ironing board on premises ☺ CTV
⊕3pinsquare 10P Ⓜ 🚠(½m)
⌿(heated)
↩ ♪(2m) ♀(½m) 🎵(½m) 🎶(½m)
🐾(½m) Sportscentre(½m)
Min£55 Max£90pw(Low)
Min£170 Max£250pw(High)

F Mrs S E Hassell **Lauderdale** Torbay
Road, Torquay, Devon TQ6 6QH
☎Torquay(0803)22592

A detached stone-built property containing three first-floor flats with good sea views and a sloping lawn to the seafront. Each flat has a lounge/diner with twin bed wall units, fully-fitted kitchens, bathroom/WC. The sleeping accommodation varies; two flats have a family bedroom, the third has two bedrooms. Dishwashing machines in all units.

All year MWB out of season 4days min, 6mths max, 3units, 2–7persons ◆ ◆
◎ fridge ☼ Elec inclusive
⌷ inclusive ☎(300yds) Iron & Ironing board in unit ⊕ CTV ⊕3pin square
P ▥ ♨(1m)
⊖ ♪(3m) ♀(100yds) ♫(½m) ☏(1m)
Min£85 Max£165pw (Low)
Min£110 Max£310pw (High)

F Mr & Mrs Truhol **Maidencombe Cross Holiday Apartments** Teignmouth Road, Torquay, Devon TQ1 4TJ
☎Torquay(0803)39014
Fifteen flats in large Victorian house, which has recently been extended and stands in 2 acres of private grounds with its own swimming pool. A licensed bar is just a few minutes' walk away.

Etr–Oct MWB out of season 1wk min, 15units, 2–6persons ◇ [◆ ◆]
fridge Electric Elec metered
⌷ inclusive ☎(100yds) WM, SD & [TD] on premises Iron & Ironing board on premises ⊕ CTV ⊕3pin square 15P
▥ ♨(50yds) ⌷
⊖ ♀ on premises ♫(1½m) ♫(1½m)
☏(3m)
Details not confirmed for 1987

F Mr & Mrs Rea **Marina Court** Warren Road, Torquay, Devon TQ2 5TP
☎Torquay(0803)27612
Originally a hotel, now converted into twelve flats with fine views, it towers above the famous Rock Walk. Seven of the flats comprise lounge/diner, kitchen, bathroom/WC, one bedroom with either two singles or a double bed and also a double bed-settee in the lounge. Four flats are very similar but have two bedrooms one with a double bedroom and one twin bedroom. The remaining flat has a full length balcony with lounge, kitchen, bathroom/WC, double bedroom en-suite, twin-bedded room and a double bed-settee in the lounge.

All year MWB out of season 1wk min, 1mth max, 12units, 4–6persons ◆ ◆
◎ fridge ☼ Elec metered
⌷ inclusive ☎ [WM & TD on premises]
Iron & Ironing board on premises
[Launderette on premises] ⊕ CTV
⊕3pin square P ▥ ♨(½m)
⊖ ♀(50yds) ♫(50yds) ♫(½m)
☏(50yds) Sports centre(½m)
Min£90 Max£400pw (Low)
Min£150 Max£600pw (High)

F Mr J K Hassell **Maxton Lodge Holiday Flats** Rousdown Road, Torquay TQ2 6PB
☎Torquay(0803)607811

Twenty-four flats in a residential area about 600yds from the seafront and 100yds from the shops. Well decorated, good fixtures and fittings.

All year MWB out of season 2days min, 24units, 2–7persons ◆ ◆ ◎
☼ Elec metered ⌷ inclusive ☎ SD & TD on premises Iron & Ironing board on premises ⊕ CTV ⊕3pin square ⊕3pin round P
▥ ♨(100yds) ⌷ ⌷ mini gym, sauna, solarium & recreation room
⊖ ♪(3m) ♀ ♫(½m) ♫(½m) ☏(1m)
Min£50 Max£140pw (Low)
Min£90 Max£290pw (High)

F Mr & Mrs G S Twigg **Moorhaven Holiday Flats** 43 Barton Road, Torquay, Devon TQ1 4DT
☎Torquay(0803)38567
Twelve purpose-built flats located in a detached building in a residential area, they are well decorated and equipped with modern furniture and fittings. The grounds contain a heated swimming pool, with patio surround, and lawns. About 1m from the sea and Oddicombe and Watcombe beaches with Babbacombe Downs nearby.

May–Oct MWB out of season 2days min, 4wks max, 12units, 2–6persons [◇] ◆ ◆ ◎ fridge
☼ & Electric Elec metered ⌷ can be hired ☎(50yds) Iron & Ironing board on premises [Launderette on premises]
⊕ CTV ⊕3pin square 50P ♨(½m)
⌷ Games room
⊖ ♪(1m) ♀(½m) ♫(½m) ♫(½m)
☏(½m)
Min£80 Max£215pw (Low)
Min£120 Max£325pw (High)

F Mrs S E Qureshi, Coach House **Overmead Cottages** Daddyhole Road, Torquay, Devon TQ1 2ED
☎Torquay(0803)212944
These beautifully furnished apartments are in a quiet setting behind the Overmead Hotel near the cliff top, walks, beaches and town-centre. **Coachman Cottage** contains a ground-floor and first-floor flat comprising lounge/diner with bed-settee, bathroom/WC and one bedroom. **Stable Cottage** also has a ground-floor and first-floor flat and comprises lounge/diner with bed-settee, kitchen, bathroom/WC and two bedrooms.

Etr–Nov MWB out of season 3days min, 1mth max, 4units, 2–6persons [◇ ◆
◆] ◎ fridge Electric Elec metered
⌷ inclusive ☎(500yds) Iron & Ironing board in unit ⊕ CTV ⊕3pin square
5P ▥ ♨(½m)
⊖ ♀(250yds) ♫(½m) ♫(½m) ☏(½m)
Min£60 Max£135pw (Low)
Min£140 Max£210pw (High)

F Mr B Jarvis **Parkland Holiday Flats** Palermo Road, Babbacombe, Torquay, Devon
☎Torquay(0803)34422
Detached villa with modernised extension converted into flats. Pleasant, comfortable and clean. Suburban location with outdoor swimming pool. Near to shops and seafront.

Mar–7Jan MWB out of season 2days min, 1mth max, 6units, 2–8persons [◆ ◆] ◎ fridge Electric
Elec metered ☎(150yds) Iron & Ironing board in unit [Launderette within 300yds] ⊕ CTV
⊕3pin square 9P ▥ ♨(200yds) ⌷
⊖ ♪(2m) ♀(20yds) ♫(2m) ♫(2m)
☏(2m)
Min£49 Max£147pw (Low)
Min£52 Max£196pw (High)

F Mr K J Hughes **Rogana Holiday Flats** Higher Warberry Road, Torquay, Devon TQ1 1SQ
☎Torquay(0803)23584
Seven flats in a detached, Edwardian-type house standing in its own grounds of lawns, shrubs and flower beds. Good décor and furnishings. Within walking distance of seafront and shops.

All year MWB out of season 1wk min, 7units, 2–7persons ◆ ◆ ◎
◎ fridge Electric Elec metered
☎(100yds) [Iron on premises] Ironing board on premises [Launderette on premises] ⊕ CTV ⊕3pin square P
▥ ♨
⊖ ♀(100yds)
Min£60 Max£200pw

F Mr & Mrs M E & J A Lewis **Rosa Pines** Higher Warberry Road, Torquay, Devon TQ1 1RY
☎Torquay(0803)25036
A mansion situated in quiet, residential area and standing in gardens of about 1 acre, carefully converted into flats. All are very comfortable, well appointed and comprise lounge, kitchen, shower room, dining area, and one or two bedrooms. Outdoor heated swimming pool.

All year MWB out of season 3days min, 4wks max, 11units, 2–8persons [◇]
[◆] [◆] no pets or single sex parties
◎ fridge Electric Elec metered
⌷ inclusive ☎ Iron & Ironing board in unit [Launderette on premises] ⊕
CTV ⊕3pin square 15P ▥ ♨(½m)
⊖ ♪(2m) ♀(½m) ♫(1m) ♫(1m)
☏(1m)
Min£50 Max£80pw (Low)
Min£150 Max£290pw (High)

F Mr & Mrs Browne **Rosa Torina Holiday Apartments** 517 Babbacombe Road, Torquay, Devon TQ1 1HJ
☎Torquay(0803)26995
Large Tudor-style property standing in its own grounds near the harbour, and yet close to town centre and amenities. The six flats are located on the ground and first →

floors and sleep up to six persons in a variety of accommodation which is tastefully appointed.

All year MWB out of season 2days min, 5mths max, 6units, 1–7persons [◇ ◈ ◆] no pets ◎ fridge Electric Elec metered ▣ inclusive ☎ Iron & Ironing board in unit [Launderette within 300yds] ☺ CTV ⊕3pin square 1🏠 🎬 ♨(300yds)
⊖ ♪(2½m) ♀(100yds) ♫(½m) ♬(½m) ☃(½m)

Min£55 Max£265pw

F Wng Cdr & Mrs C C Cooper **St Ronans Holiday Flats** Middle Warberry Road, Torquay, Devon TQ1 1RP
☎Torquay(0803)22493

Six flats located in a Victorian villa standing in its own grounds, in quiet residential area; approximately 1m from seafront and shops. Flats 2, 3 and 4 have three bedrooms, Flats 2B and 6 have two bedrooms and Flat 7 has one double bedroom and curtained area with bunk beds. All have kitchen, lounge and shower or bathroom. Some have a sofa bed in the lounge.

All year 1wk min, 6units, 2–10persons ◈ no pets ◔&◎ fridge Electric Gas & Elec metered ▣ can be hired ☎(100yds) Iron & Ironing board in unit ☺ CTV ⊕3pin square 7P 🎬 ♨(600yds)
⊖ ♪(2m) ♀(100yds) ♫(100yds) ♬(100yds) ☃(½m)

Min£60 Max£110pw (Low)
Min£80 Max£250pw (High)

F **Sandown Holiday Flats** 27 Ash Hill Road
for bookings Mr C Trethewey, Beech Hill, Middle Warberry, Torquay, Devon TQ1 3JB
☎Torquay(0803)26905

Seven purpose built holiday flats on ground and first floors of a modern detached property in a residential area. The flats have a separate and well-equipped kitchen and bathroom/WC. Six have one bedroom, plus a double wall bed in lounge, and one has three bedrooms. Situated within 500yds of the main shopping area.

All year MWB out of season 1wk min, 3mths max, 7units, 2–7persons [◇] ◈ ◆ no pets ◎ fridge Electric Elec metered ▣ can be hired ☎(500yds) Iron & Ironing board on premises ☺ CTV ⊕3pin square 7P 1🏠 🎬 ♨(500yds)
⊖ ♪(1m) ♀(250yds) ♫(250yds) ♬(250yds) ☃(½m)

Min£66 Max£122pw (Low)
Min£73 Max£274pw (High)

F Mr P W Moorhouse **South Sands Apartments** Torbay Road, Torquay, Devon TQ2 6RG
☎Torquay(0803)23521

Fifteen ground and first-floor flats located within a modern building, opposite the Promenade and beach, on main road to

Torquay

Paignton. Ten of the units sleep two people in one bedroom, and five have one bedroom plus a wall bed in the lounge. All comprise lounge/diner, modern kitchen and bathroom/WC or shower/WC.

All year MWB out of season 3days min, 3mths max, 15units, 2–5persons ◈ ◆ ◎ fridge 🍴 Elec metered ▣ inclusive ☺ CTV ⊕3pin square 18P 🎬 ♨(½m)
⊖ ♪(3m) ♀(20yds) ♫(½m) ♬(½m) ☃(1½m)

Min£69 Max£103.50pw (Low)
Min£138 Max£224.25pw (High)

F John Phelps Ltd **Sunningdale Holiday Apartments Type A & B** Babbacombe Downs Road, Torquay, Devon TQ1 3LF
☎Torquay(0803)35786

A villa-type residence set in its own grounds on top of Babbacombe Cliffs with magnificent sea views. All flats have kitchen, lounge, bathroom/WC, some flats have one double bedroom, the others are two-bedroomed.

All year MWB out of season 1wk min, 1mth max, 16units, 2–7persons ◈ ◆ no pets ◎ fridge Electric Elec metered ▣ inclusive ☎ [Launderette within 300yds] ☺ CTV ⊕3pin square P 🎬 ♨(30yds)
⊖ ♪(3m) ♀(200yds) ♫(200yds) ♬(300yds) ☃(1½m)

Min£70 Max£95pw (Low)
Min£139 Max£235pw (High)

F Mr & Mrs H J Sheldon **The Old Coach House** St Marks Road, Torquay, Devon TQ1 2EH
☎Torquay(0803)22223

The Old Coach House has been converted to provide a high standard of self catering apartments in an attractive residential area, but within easy reach of the harbour and beaches of Meadfoot and Beacon Cove. Each flat is well furnished, equipped and decorated, and accommodation comprises a lounge/diner, fitted kitchen, bathroom/WC, two of the flats have a double and a twin bedroom (one with additional bed-settee) and the third flat has a double bedroom, a double/single bedroom and a bed-settee.

All year MWB out of season 1wk min, 3mths max, 3units, 2–7persons [◇ ◈ ◆] pets by arrangement ◎ fridge 🍴& electric fires Elec metered ▣ inclusive (except towels & tea towels) ☎(150yds) WM & SD in unit Iron & Ironing board in unit ☺ CTV ⊕3pin square 6P 🎬 ♨(½m)
⊖ ♪(3m) ♀(½m) ♫(½m) ♬(½m) ☃(½m)

Min£75 Max£90pw (Low)
Min£85 Max£205pw (High)

F Mr K C Girling **Trinity Mews Holiday Flats** Trinity Hill, Torquay, Devon TQ1 2AS
☎Torquay(0803)24245

Converted Mews with inner courtyard in central but quiet location comprising kitchen, lounge, bathroom/toilet, with seven of the nine flats having two separate bedrooms. Compact and comfortably furnished ground and first-floor accommodation.

All year MWB out of season 3days min, 9units, 2–6persons [◇] ◈ ◆ ◎ fridge Electric (night storage) Elec metered ▣ inclusive ☎(50yds) [SD on premises] Iron & Ironing board on premises ☺ CTV ⊕3pin square 🏠 🎬 ♨(50yds)
⊖ ♀(20yds) ♫(100yds) ♬(100yds) ☃(800yds)

Min£92 Max£144pw (Low)
Min£115 Max£224pw (High)

F Mr & Mrs A J Dymond **Vansittart Holiday Flats** Higher Erith Road, Torquay, Devon
☎Torquay(0803)25444

Detached Victorian house with seven flats on main building and a further seven in a modern extension. Each self-contained unit has well-equipped kitchen, bathroom, lounge/diner with modern wall bed and bedrooms ranging from one twin-bedded room to three bedrooms some with sea views and balconies. Located ½m from seafront in residential area.

All year MWB 3days min, 6mths max, 14units, 2–9persons [◈ ◆] ◎ fridge Electric Elec metered ▣ inclusive ☎ Iron & Ironing board in unit [Launderette within 300yds] ☺ CTV ⊕3pin square 14P 🎬 ♨(½m)
⊖ ♪(2m) ♀(½m) ♫(½m) ♬(½m) ☃(½m)

Min£46 Max£98pw (Low)
Min£130 Max£280pw (High)

F Mr & Mrs A Turner **Villa Capri** Daddyhole Road, Meadfoot, Torquay, Devon TQ1 2ED
☎Torquay(0803)27959

This converted villa is in a quiet location giving sea views over Meadfoot Bay and Torbay and has been modernised to a high standard and has landscaped gardens. Flats 1, 4, 5 & 6 and 7, 8 and 10 are located on the ground- and first-floors and flat 12 is on the garden-floor. All have one bedroom, lounge with foldaway bed and kitchen. Flats 8, 10 & 12 have a bath, shower/WC, the others have shower/WC. Flats 2, 3, 9 & 11 on garden level, ground and upper first-floor have lounge with double wall bed, kitchen and bath/shower.

Feb–mid Dec MWB out of season 2nights min, 30days max, 12units, 2–6persons [◇] ◈ ◆ ◎ fridge 🍴 Electric fires (others) Elec metered ▣ inclusive ☎ [Launderette on premises] ☺ CTV ⊕3pin square 15P 🎬 ♨(200yds) Games room, video films to flats

◒ ♪(1½m) ♗(200yds) ♫(½m)
♫(½m) 🐾(½m)

Min£45 Max£90pw (Low)
Min£120 Max£230pw (High)

F Mr & Mrs K H Fleming **Villa Paradiso**
Higher Warberry Road, Torquay, Devon
TQ1 1RY
☎Torquay(0803)25501

*Carefully converted mansion in own
gardens with heated open-air swimming
pool. Some flats have sea views.
Accommodation includes entrance hall,
lounge, one or two bedrooms, kitchen
area, or kitchen with breakfast bar, and
fully fitted bath/shower rooms.*

All year MWB out of season 1wk min,
2mths max, 15units, 2–6persons [◇]
[◆] [◆] ⊚ fridge 🍴 Electric
Elec metered 🅛inclusive ☎ Iron &
Ironing board in unit [Launderette on
premises] ⊕ CTV ⊕3pin square P
🎦 🛁(1m) ⌸

◒ ♪(2m) ♗ ♫(2m) 🐾(2m)

Min£50 Max£120pw (Low)
Min£155 Max£255pw (High)

F Mrs Earland **Westcombe Holiday
Apartments** 31 Croft Road, Torquay,
Devon TQ2 5UD
☎Torquay(0803)23373

*Located in a central position this
converted property has good sea views
and private path leading to seafront and is
convenient for the shops. The flats have
been modernised and offer a variety of
accommodation with one or two
bedrooms, sleeping up to five persons.*

Closed Oct & Nov MWB out of season
3days min, 4wks max, 14units,
2–5persons ◇ ◆ ⊚ fridge 🍴
Elec metered 🅛inclusive ☎ ⊕ ⊛
CTV ⊕3pin square 14P 🎦
🛁(500yds) ⌸

◒ ♪(2m) ♗(100yds) ♫(100yds)
♫(100yds) 🐾(250yds)

Min£52 Max£153pw (Low)
Min£135 Max£210pw (High)

F Mr & Mrs F R Cornelius **York Villa** York
Road, Babbacombe, Torquay, Devon
☎Torquay(0803)37519

*Nine flats in modern, well-run, converted
Victorian house located on main
Babbacombe–Torquay road. Close to
shops and Babbacombe Beach.*

All year MWB out of season 9units,
2–10persons ◇ ◆ ⊚ fridge 🍴
Elec metered 🅛included ☎(30yds)
Iron & Ironing board in unit [Launderette
within 300yds] ⊕ CTV ⊕3pin square
18P 🎦 🛁(100yds)

◒ ♪ ♗(200yds) ♫(200yds)
♫(200yds) 🐾(1½m)

Min£48 Max£160pw (Low)
Min£78 Max£294pw (High)

TORRINGTON (GREAT)
Devon
Map**2** SS41

Torquay
—
Tring

Ch Mr & Mrs A Hussey **Greenways
Valley Holiday Park** Torrington, Devon
EX38 7EW
☎Torrington(0805)22153

*Chalet bungalows of modern design and
furnishings, each comprising lounge (with
studio couch) and kitchen area,
bathroom/WC, two bedrooms (one with
double bed and the other with twin or
bunk beds). Situated 1m from Torrington
in wooded valley with views of countryside.*

Apr–4Oct MWB out of season
3days min, 3mths max, 14units,
1–7persons [◆] ⊚ fridge Electric
Elec metered 🅛not provided ☎(½m)
Iron & Ironing board on premises ⊕
TV ⊕3pin square 14P 🎦 ⌸
🏊Hard Children's playground

◒ ♪(1m) ♗(1m) 🐾(1m)

Min£40 Max£78pw (Low)
Min£80 Max£150pw (High)

TOTNES
Devon
Map**3** SX86

C Messrs Hodges & Liddle **Higher
Poulston Holiday Cottages** Morleigh
Road, Halwell, Totnes, Devon TQ9 7LE
☎Harbertonford(080 423)255 or 345

*An old stone and slate farm building
converted into four cottages and set
amidst farmland and rolling hills. The
accommodation varies with numbers 1
and 2 having two bedrooms and 3 and 4
having three bedrooms. A small area of
field at the rear of the cottages is available
for the exclusive use of visitors.*

All year MWB out of season 1wk min,
8wks max, 4units, 2–8persons ◇ ◆
no pets ⊚ fridge Electric
Elec metered 🅛not provided ☎(1m)
SD in unit Iron & Ironing board in unit
⊕ CTV ⊕3pin square 12P 🎦
🛁(1m)

◒ ♗(1m)

Min£63 Max£218pw

F **Shippon**
for bookings Mr & Mrs R Miller, Buckyette
Farm, Little Hempston, Totnes, Devon
☎Staverton(080 426)638

*Converted stone-built barn on farm of 40
acres. Offers well furnished
accommodation; large lounge with
beamed end kitchen area, separate
bathroom with WC and wash basin,
one double room, one twin- and one
bunk-bedded room. 4m off A384
Buckfastleigh and Totnes.*

May–Oct MWB out of season 1wk min,
6wks max, 1unit, 1–6persons [◇] ◆
◆ no pets ⊚ fridge Electric
Elec metered 🅛not provided
☎(20yds) Iron on premises Ironing

---

board in unit TV ⊕3pin square P 🎦
🛁(1m)

◒ ♗(1m)

Min£80 Max£135pw

TREARDDUR BAY
Gwynedd
Map**6** SH27

B **Trearddur Bay Holiday Bungalows**
Fron Isalt
for bookings Hoseasons Holidays Ltd,
Sunway House, Lowestoft, Suffolk
NR32 3LT
☎Lowestoft(0502)62281

*Modern, purpose-built brick bungalows,
some semi-detached and some in groups
of four, consisting of two or three
bedrooms, large lounge/diner with bed-
settee, kitchen, bathroom and WC.
Modern furnishings and well-equipped. All
are within a short distance of the beach.*

All year MWB out of season 3days min,
6wks max, 50units, 1–6persons ◇ ◆
⊚ fridge Electric Gas & Elec inclusive
🅛inclusive ☎(100yds) Iron & Ironing
board on premises [Launderette on
premises] ⊕ CTV ⊕3pin square P
🛁(½m) Children's playground, sauna,
solarium & relayed video

◒ ♗(200yds) ♫(2m) ♫(2m)
🐾(2m)

Min£45 Max£205pw

TREGARON
Dyfed
Map**3** SN65

H Mrs M E Davies **Aberdwr** Tregaron,
Dyfed
☎Tregaron(09744)255

*Part of a farmhouse converted into a self
contained unit, comprising spacious
lounge, kitchen/diner, WC, bathroom/WC,
two double and one twin-bedded room all
with wash basins. Located ⅓ mile from
Tregaron on Aberwesin Rd.*

Mar–Oct MWB out of season 4days min,
6wks max, 1unit, 2–6persons [◇] ◆
◆ no pets ⊚ fridge electric & calor
gas Gas/Elec metered (hot water free)
🅛inclusive ☎(½m) WM & SD in unit
Iron & Ironing board in unit ⊕ CTV
⊕3pin square P 🎦 🛁(½m)

◒ ♗(½m)

Min£120 Max£150pw

TRING
Hertfordshire
Map**4** SP91

C **2 Parsonage Place**
for bookings Mr J Hendry, The White
House, Northfield Grange, Tring,
Hertfordshire
☎Aldbury Common(044 285)401

*Well kept, modernised terraced cottage,
consisting of three bedrooms, bathroom/
WC, large kitchen/diner and cosy lounge.*

All year MWB out of season 2wks min,
4mths max, 1unit, 1–5persons ◇
no pets ⊚ fridge 🍴 Elec metered →

🛏inclusive ☎ WM & SD in unit Iron & Ironing board in unit CTV
⊕3pin square 1P ▥ 🏠(20yds)
↔ 🚰(20yds) 🧺 ▨(½m)
Min£95 Max£100pw (Low)
Min£128 Max£135pw (High)

TROUTBECK
Cumbria
Map7 NY40
During the currency of this guide the dialling code for Ambleside is to change to (05394)

C Birkhead Cottages
for bookings Miss M R Dawson, Birkhead Guest House, Troutbeck, Windermere, Cumbria LA23 1PQ
☎Ambleside(0966)32288

Situated in the small peaceful village of Troutbeck. Three tastefully modernised and furnished stone-built cottages, only a few minutes drive from Windermere. Each cottage has two bedrooms and offers excellent views across the valley to the fells beyond.

All year 1wk min, 3units, 4persons ◆
◆ ◎ fridge Elec metered
🛏can be hired ☎(½m) Iron & Ironing board in unit ☉ CTV ⊕3pin square
P ▥ 🏠(½m) ♫(2½m)
Min£60 Max£80pw (Low)
Min£100 Max£110pw (High)

C Rose Cottage Robin Lane
for bookings Mrs A Kelly, 1 Robin Lane, Troutbeck, Cumbria LA23 1PF
☎Ambleside(0966)32780

Converted from an 18th-century grey slate barn and situated close to village centre with views of Troutbeck Valley. The accommodation features stripped pine doors and furnishings. It comprises flag-stone floored kitchen and dining room, comfortable lounge, three twin bedrooms one with bunk beds.

All year MWB out of season 1unit, 8persons, nc5yrs ◎ fridge Storage heating & log stove Elec metered
Heating free ☎(100yds) SD in unit Iron & Ironing board in unit ☉ TV
· ⊕3pin square 3P 🏠(100yds) Pony trekking, Fishing ⊖ 🚰(½m)
Min£95 Max£210pw

TROUTBECK BRIDGE
Cumbria
See **Windermere**

TRURO
Cornwall
Map2 SW84

F CC Ref 351 EL
for bookings Character Cottages (Holidays) Ltd, 34 Fore Street, Sidmouth, Devon EX10 8AQ
☎Sidmouth(03955)77001

Modern ground-floor flat situated in a stone-built cottage on the shoreline of an inland waterway. There are two bedrooms (one a double, the other twin bedded), separate lounge, dining room, kitchen and

---

Tring
—
Tywyn

---

bathroom/WC. Access to the cottage is reached by a very uneven farm track (½m long).

End May–Sep 1wk min, 1mth max, 1unit, 1–5persons, nc4 no pets 🍴 fridge Electric Gas/Elec inclusive 🛏inclusive
☎(1m) Iron & Ironing board in unit ☉
TV ⊕3pin square P 🏠(2m)
Boat mooring
⊖ 🚰(1m)
Min£139 Max£167pw

TWITCHEN
Shropshire
Map7 SO37

B Mrs Morgan Llan Farm Twitchen, Clunbury, Craven Arms, Shropshire SY7 0HN
☎Little Brampton(05887)277

Secluded bungalow, with modern furnishings, situated on a farm, on the slopes of a partially wooded valley. Leave the Craven Arms–Clun Road at Purslow on to the B4385 to Twitchen, where the Llan is signposted via a narrow metalled road.

All year MWB out of season 1night min, 1mth max, 1unit, 1–7persons [◇] ◆
◆ ◎ fridge 🍴 Elec inclusive
🛏inclusive ☎(150yds) SD in unit Iron in Unit ☉ TV ⊕3pin square P 🏠
🏠(2m)
⊖ 🚰(3m)
Min£90 Max£120pw

TWYNHOLM
Dumfries & Galloway *Kirkcudbrightshire*
Map11 NX65

C Glenterry Lodge
for bookings G M Thomson & Co, 27 King Street, Castle Douglas, Kirkcudbrightshire DG7 1AB
☎Castle Douglas(0556)2701 or 2973

Small stone-built single-storey lodge cottage bypassed by the A75, 2m W of Twynholm. It is located in an attractive wooded position and comprises two double rooms, living room with bed-settee, kitchen and bathroom.

All year 1wk min, 1unit, 1–6persons ◆
◎ fridge Electric & open fires
Elec inclusive 🛏can be hired ☎(2m)
WM & SD in unit Iron in unit TV
⊕3pin square ⊕3pin round P 🏠(2m)
⊖ 🚰(2m)
Min£75 Max£125pw

TYN-Y-GROES
Gwynedd
Map6 SH77

C Mrs J Langabeer Garthmor Cottage
Garthmor Farmhouse, Tyn-y-Groes, Conwy, Gwynedd
☎Tyn-y-Groes(049267)570

Modern stone-built cottage in the Conwy Valley, well-equipped and consisting of lounge/diner, kitchen, bathroom/WC and two bedrooms.

All year MWB out of season 2days min, 6wks max, 1unit, 2–4persons [◇] ◆
◆ no pets ◎ fridge Electric
Elec metered 🛏inclusive ☎(¾m) Iron & Ironing board on premises ☉ CTV
⊕3pin square 2P ▥ 🏠(¾m)
Min£45 Max£95pw

C Ty-Hwynt-ir-Firwd
for bookings N G Hudson, 125 Morley Hill, Enfield Middlesex EN2 0BQ
☎01-363 1431

Set in the beautiful, tranquil Conwy valley, this traditional Welsh farmhouse has been carefully modernised to provide comfortable accommodation. It comprises kitchen/diner, lounge, with stone fireplace, two double and one twin room and bathroom/shower room/WC.

All year MWB out of season wknd min, 6wks max, 1unit, 2–6persons ◎ fridge Electric & wood burners Elec metered
🛏not provided ☎(¼m) WM & SD in unit Iron & Ironing board in unit ☉
CTV ⊕3pin square 2P 🏠(1½m)
⊖ δ(3m) 🚰(1m) 🐾(3m)
Min£60 Max£120pw (Low)
Min£100 Max£150pw (High)

TYWARDREATH
Cornwall
Map2 SX05

C Mrs A Worne Treesmill Cottage
Treesmill Farm, Tywardreath, Par, Cornwall PL24 2TX
☎Par(072681)5781

The cottage is all on one level with approach through the gardens of Treesmill farm. The accommodation comprises lounge/dining room/kitchen, shower room with WC, two single bedrooms and one with twin beds.

Apr–Oct MWB out of season 1wk min, 3wks max, 1unit, 4persons ◆ no pets
◎ fridge Electric Elec metered
🛏not provided ☎(1m) WM & SD in unit Iron & Ironing board in unit ☉
CTV ⊕3pin square 2P 🏠(1m)
⊖ 🚰(1m)
£37pw (Low)
Min£45 Max£125pw (High)

TYWYN
Gwynedd
Map6 SH50

H 53 Sandilands Road
for bookings Mr J D Menhinnick, Beach Cottage Holidays, 10 Glandovey, Aberdovey, Gwynedd, Wales LL35 0EB
☎Aberdovey(065472)595

Semi-detached property a few minutes from the sea and with excellent views towards the mountains. Accommodation comprises lounge/diner, kitchen, two bedrooms (one double, one twin) and separate bath and WC.

Mar–Oct MWB out of season 1wk min,
4wks max, 1unit, 2–4persons ◈ ◆
◉ fridge Electric Elec metered
⌷not provided ☎(20yds) Iron & Ironing
board in unit ⊙ [TV] ⊕3pin square
1P ▥ ♨(300yds)
⊖ ♥(½m) ☙(1m)
Min£56 Max£184pw

ULLAPOOL
Highland *Ross & Cromarty*
Map**14** NH19

Ch Mr P J Fraser **Ardmair Point Chalet**
Ardmair, Ullapool, Highland IV26 2TN
☎Ullapool(0854)2054

*A single, timber clad chalet, overlooking
Ardmair Bay. It comprises a modern
sitting/dining room, well-equipped kitchen
with split level oven and hob, one double
and one twin bedroom, both pine
furnished and a modern shower room.*
All year MWB out of season 1wk min,
1unit, 4–6persons ◉ fridge
Electric convectors Elec inclusive
⌷inclusive ☎(100yds) WM in unit [SD
& TD on premises] Ironing & Ironing
board in unit CTV ⊕3pin square 2P
▥ ♨(100yds)
⊖ ♥(3m) ♫(3m) ♬(3m)
Min£100 Max£175pw

C **Ardmore**
for bookings Highland Coastal Trading
Company, Argyle Street, Ullapool, Ross-
shire
☎Ullapool(0854)2548 & 2937

*Reached from A835 from its own steep
driveway, this cottage sits on the shore of
Loch Broom 1½m NW of Ullapool. It
contains sitting/dining room, kitchen, a
double bedroom, and two three-bedded
rooms. Commands views of surrounding
countryside and has its own pebble beach
with boat.*
Mar–Oct MWB out of season 1wk min,
1unit, 1–8persons ◉ fridge Electric
Elec metered ⌷can be hired ☎(1½m)
TV ⊕3pin square P Pony trekking,
fishing & sea angling
⊖ ♥(1½m) ♫(1½m)
Min£76 Max£182pw

C & Ch **Corry Cottage & Corry Hill
Bungalow**
for bookings Highland Coastal Trading
Company, Argyle Street, Ullapool, Ross-
shire
☎Ullapool(0854)2548 or 2937

*Situated in an isolated location on a
hillside overlooking Loch Broom. The
chalet consists of kitchenette, lounge,
bathroom, one double and two twin*

Tywyn
—
Uplyme

*rooms. The cottage consists one bedroom
with double and single bed, two twin
bedrooms, lounge, kitchen/diner and
bathroom. Located just south of Ullapool
and reached by a private track.*
Mar–Oct MWB out of season 1wk min,
2units, 1–7persons ◈ ◉ fridge
Electric Elec metered ⌷can be hired
☎(2m) TV ⊕3pin square P ♨(1½m)
Pony trekking, fishing & sea angling
⊖ ♥(1m) ♫(1½m)
Min£55 Max£117pw

B **Rhue Baigh Bungalow**
for bookings Highland Coastal Trading
Company, Argyle Street, Ullapool, Ross-
shire
☎Ullapool(0854)2548 or 2937

*A modern block and tiled-built bungalow
with simple furnishing and fittings.
Accommodation consists of lounge/diner
with convertible sofa, kitchen, two twin-
bedded rooms, one double room, and
bathroom. Quietly situated with splendid
sea views in Rhue Bay. Access is by an
unclassified road 2m N of Ullapool off
A835.*
Mar–Oct MWB out of season 1wk min,
1unit, 1–8persons ◉ fridge Electric
Elec metered ⌷can be hired ☎(2m)
TV ⊕3pin square P ♨(3m) Pony
trekking, fishing & sea angling, boat
available
⊖ ♥(3m) ♫(3m)
Min£76 Max£182pw

ULVERSTON
Cumbria
Map**7** SD27

C & F Mr & Mrs Cheetham and Mrs J
Unger **The Falls** Mansrigg's, Ulverston,
Cumbria LA12 7PX
☎Ulverston(0229)53781

*Two converted stone-built barns, a
cottage and the former dairy of a 17th-
century farmstead set in peaceful
countryside with views of moorland,
mountains and sea. One barn has been
converted into a spacious cottage
sleeping 10, the other has been made into
two flats, each sleeping four. The dairy is
now a cottage sleeping four adults and
two children. Far Applethwaite is a
detached stone cottage sleeping up to
four people. The accommodation is of a
very high standard and the original*

*character of the property has been
maintained. A comprehensive food service
is available at extra charge.*
All year MWB out of season 1wk min,
5units, 2–10persons ◈ ◆ ♂ fridge
🍴 Gas & Elec inclusive ⌷inclusive
☎ WM, SD & TD on premises Iron &
Ironing board on premises ⊙ CTV
⊕3pin square P 4🏠 ▥ ♨(1½m)
⊖ ♪(3m) ♥(1½m) ♫(1½m) ☙(1½m)
Min£80 Max£140pw (Low)
Min£110 Max£275pw (High)

UPLYME
Devon
Map**3** SY39

C **Hilltop** Whalley Lane
for bookings Miss A M Crosse, 14 Miles
Road, Clifton, Bristol Avon BS8 2JW
☎Bristol(0272)736829

*Detached cottage, with pretty garden, in
quiet position with lovely views over
Uplyme and comprising three bedrooms,
sitting room, kitchen and bathroom/WC.*
All year MWB out of season 1wk min,
1mth max, 1unit, 5persons ♂ fridge
Electric Elec metered ⌷not provided
Iron & Ironing board on premises ⊙
[TV] ⊕3pin square P ▥ ♨(300yds)
⊖ ♪(2m) ♥(300yds) ☙(1m)

F Mr J M Groom **Waterside** Mill Lane,
Uplyme, Lyme Regis, Dorset
☎Lyme Regis(02974)2533

*Four flats located within a detached half-
timbered country residence set in well-kept
gardens enclosed by shrubs and trees.
They are comfortably furnished with
tasteful décor and fittings, the two ground-
floor flats both have French doors to
lawns and gardens and comprise lounge,
dining room, kitchen, bathroom/WC and
two/three bedrooms, with single or double
beds. Two flats are on the first floor, one
having large lounge, galley kitchen, two
bedrooms (one double and one twin-
bedded) shower/WC/WHB. The other flat
comprises large lounge, large kitchen/
diner, three bedrooms (one double and
two twin-bedded), the third bedroom can
only be reached via the other two,
bath/WC/WHB.*
All year MWB out of season 1wk min,
4wks max, 4units, 2–6persons [◈ ◆]
pets by arrangement ◉ fridge
Electric Elec metered ⌷can be hired
☎(½m) Iron & Ironing board in unit ⊙
CTV ⊕3pin square 🏠 ▥ ♨(½m)
⊖ ♪(½m) ♥(½m) ♫(1½m) ☙(1½m)
Min£35 Max£64pw (Low)
Min£51 Max£150pw (High)

VENTNOR
See **Wight, Isle of**

VERYAN
Cornwall
Map**2** SW94

C **Elerkey Cottage**
for bookings Mr J Price, The Anglers Rest
(Fingle Bridge Ltd), Drewsteignton, Exeter,
Devon
☎Drewsteignton(0647)21287

*A well appointed and tastefully converted
cottage with accommodation consisting
of lounge with inglenook fireplace, study/
bedroom, dining room, kitchen and utility
room. Upstairs there are three bedrooms,
bathroom and separate WC.*

All year   MWB out of season   1wk min,
6mths max, 1unit, 1–8persons   ◆   ⑨
fridge   ♨   Elec inclusive   Ⓛcan be
hired   ☎   WM & SD in unit   Iron &
Ironing board in unit   ☺   CTV
⊕3pin square   2P   Ⅲ   ♨(½m)

⊖   ♀(½m)

Min£90 Max£120pw (Low)
Min£130 Max£300pw (High)

VOWCHURCH
Hereford & Worcester
Map**3** SO33

C **Old Coach House & Mews Cottage**
for bookings Mrs A Spencer, The Croft,
Vowchurch, Hereford HR2 0QE
☎Peterchurch(09816)226

*Forming part of 'The Croft' these cottages
are entirely self-contained. The* **Coach
House** *offers lounge, kitchen/diner, two
double bedrooms and shower room/WC,
one bedroom has an en suite bathroom.*
The Mews *comprises lounge/dining room,
kitchenette, two double bedrooms both
have en suite showers. Accommodation is
of a high standard. The Coach House has
its own garden and patio.*

All year   MWB out of season   2days min,
4wks max, 2units, 1–4persons   ⑨
fridge   ♨(in Mews)   Electric & log
(Coach House)   Elec inclusive
Ⓛinclusive   ☎(½m)   WM & SD (Coach
House)   Iron & Ironing board in unit   ☺
CTV   ⊕3pin square   4P   Ⅲ   ♨(2m)

⊖   ♀(2m)

Min£80 Max£105pw (Low)
Min£125 Max£180pw (High)

WALL UNDER HEYWOOD
Shropshire
Map**7** SO59

Ventnor
—
Walwyns Castle

H **1 & 2 Cleeton Cottages**
for bookings Mrs Hotchkiss, Olde Hall
Farm, Wall under Heywood, Church
Stretton, Shropshire SY6 7DU
☎Longville(06943)253

*A pair of modern, semi-detached houses
with fine views across farmland and
Wenlock Edge. They comprise hall, large
kitchen/diner and good size lounge, one
double and two twin bedrooms, utility
room with WC plus bathroom/WC. Dairy
produce available from the farm.*

All year   MWB out of season   3days min,
1mth max, 2units, 1–6persons   [◇]   ◆
⑨   fridge   Electric fires & convectors
Elec metered   Ⓛnot provided
☎(400yds)   CTV   ⊕3pin square   3P
1🏠   ♨(4m)

⊖   ♀(½m)

Min£60 Max£125pw

B **Heywood Bungalow**
for bookings Mrs Hotchkiss, Olde Hall
Farm, Wall under Heywood, Church
Stretton, Shropshire SY6 7DU
☎Longville(06943)253

*A modern, brick bungalow with large
garden close to the village centre.
Accommodation comprises modern
kitchen/diner, lounge with dining facilities,
two bedrooms (one twin, one double plus
single bed) and a folding bed if required.
Good views to Wenlock Edge. Dairy
produce available from the farm.*

All year   MWB out of season   3days min,
1mth max, 1unit, 1–5persons   [◇]   ◆
no pets   ⑨   fridge   ♨(charge)
Elec metered   Ⓛnot provided
☎(200yds)   CTV   ⊕3pin square   3P
1🏠   ♨(4m)

⊖   ♀(½m)

Details not confirmed for 1987

WALWICK
Northumberland
Map**12** NY87

C **The Barn & Little Walwick Cottage**
for bookings Mr & Mrs A Moody, Little
Walwick, Humshaugh, Hexham,
Northumberland NE46 4BJ
☎Humshaugh (043481)247

*A comfortably converted barn adjoining
the main house and a cottage which is
built literally on the Roman Wall, both
offering comfortable accommodation. The*
Barn *comprises living room, well fitted*

---

*kitchen/dining area, one twin bedroom,
plus extra bunk beds in curtained-off
section in lounge, bathroom and WC. The*
Cottage *offers living room (with
convertible bed-settee), fitted kitchen, two
twin-bedded rooms, bathroom and WC.
Both have additional foldaway bed if
required.*

All year   1wk min, 3mths max, 2units,
2–6persons   ◆   ◆   ⑨   fridge
Electric heaters   Elec metered
Ⓛnot provided   ☎(1m)   Iron & Ironing
board in unit   ☺   TV can be hired
⊕3pin square   6P   Ⅲ   ♨(1m)

⊖   ♀(1m)

Min£45 Max£75pw (Low)
Min£85 Max£100pw (High)

WALWYNS CASTLE
Dyfed
Map**2** SM81

C & F J E Lloyd **Rosemoor Estate**
Walwyn's Castle, Haverfordwest, Dyfed
☎Broad Haven(043783)326

*Six cottages and four flats situated within
the 34-acre Rosemoor Estate, of which 20
acres is the Rosemoor Nature Reserve.
The well stocked 5½-acre lake is available
for fly-fishing.* **Apple Loft** *is a spacious flat
reached by a stone staircase; with
pinewood décor yet retaining some of the
original features of the 1700's. Open-plan
area for sitting and dining with kitchen
area at one end and sleeps up to seven.*
Coach House *is a detached red-
sandstone cottage overlooking large
walled garden with fruit trees. The
accommodation is all on the ground floor
which makes it suitable for the disabled. It
comprises open-plan living area with
kitchen and sleeps up to six people.* **First
Cottage** *is a single-storey courtyard
cottage built on modern lines all on one
level and suitable for the disabled. It
comprises lounge/diner, open-plan
kitchen and opens onto south facing
grassed garden.* **Hollytree Flat** *has its own
separate entrance from the garden. The
accommodation comprises open-plan
sitting room with a kitchen/dining area at
its far end, two bedrooms one with double
bed, one with twin beds, single bed/settee
in lounge, bath/WC.* **Gardeners Cottage** *is
built of red-sandstone offering attractively
laid out accommodation comprising
open-plan lounge/diner and kitchen area,
with sleeping arrangements for four
people.* **Orchard Cottage** *is an attractive
courtyard cottage, overlooking a large
walled garden with fruit trees. The ground
floor comprises living room with open-plan
pine fitted kitchen. The first floor has three
bedrooms sleeping up to six people.* ·

Peace Cottage is a courtyard flat which opens onto south facing grassed garden and would be suitable for disabled guests. There is a sitting room with dining area, open-plan kitchen and sleeping arrangements for up to six people. *Rose Cottage* is a single-storey courtyard cottage on one level and suitable for disabled. The well designed interior comprises sitting room with dining area, kitchen, one double bedroom with bathroom en suite plus two day beds in the sitting room if required. *Rosemoor* is a spacious ground-floor flat off the main house. Accommodation comprises large sitting room, kitchen/diner, two double bedrooms with additional single beds, also a double bed/settee in lounge and mezzanine bathroom/WC. Garden and lawn to side of house. *Spring Cottage* is two-storey and overlooks large walled garden with fruit trees, comprising open-plan sitting room, dining area and pine-fitted kitchen. It sleeps up to four people.

All year MWB out of season 1 night min, 10 units, 2−8 persons [◇] ◆ ◆ ⚙ or ◎ fridge ♨ or Calor gas/Electric/open fires Gas/Elec metered Ⓛinclusive except towels ☎ Iron & Ironing board in unit Launderette on premises ☉ ⓥ CTV ⊕3pin square P 🎲 ♨(2m) Play area
↔ 🚰

Min£34.50 Max115pw (Low)
Min£101.20 Max£299pw (High)

WASDALE
Cumbria
Map**6** NY10

F Stuart House
for bookings Mr M D Burnett, Greendale Holiday Apartments, Wasdale, Seascale, Cumbria CA20 1EU
☎Wasdale(09406)243

Six newly constructed flats on ground and first floors of this purpose-built apartment block. Three flats have one twin, one double and one small single room. The other three have one double and one twin-bedded room. The flats are situated in a picturesque rural location ½m from Lake Wast Water.

All year MWB out of season, 1wk min, 3wks max, 6units, 4−5persons ◆ ◎ fridge ♨ Elecinclusive Ⓛcan be hired ☎(2m) ☉ TV ⊕3pin square P ♨(5m)
↔ 🚰 (2m)

Min£110 Max£166pw

WATERROW
Somerset
Map**3** ST02

Ca Mr & Mrs C Rance Tone Valley Farm Lodges, Waterrow, Wiveliscombe, Somerset TA4 2AU
☎Wiveliscombe(0984)23322

Five pine cabins set back from the main A361 about 2 miles from Wiveliscombe. Accommodation comprises a balcony,

---

Walwyns Castle
—
Welton-Le-Wold

lounge with a bed-settee, large kitchen/diner, bathroom, one double and one twin bedroom.

All year MWB out of season 3days min 1mth max, 5units, 4−6persons [◇] ◆ ◆ ◎ fridge Elec metered Ⓛinclusive ☎ Iron & Ironing board on premises [Launderette on premises] ☉ CTV ⊕3pin square 10P 🎲 ♨
↔ 🚰(½m)

Min£78 Max£180pw

WEDMORE
Somerset
Map**3** ST44

C The Ciderbarn
for bookings T H & S P Squires, Hall Farm, Sand Road, Wedmore, Somerset BS28 4BZ
☎Wedmore(0934)712007

Converted cider barn with stone-built exterior, dates back some 200 years. Accommodation comprises one twin-bedded room, separate lounge with put-up and dining area, modern fitted kitchen, bathroom/WC/wash basin. All very good standard.

All year MWB out of season 1wk min, 1mth max, 1unit, 1−4persons ◆ ◆ ◎ fridge Electric Elec metered Ⓛnot provided ☎(½m) Iron & Ironing board in unit ☉ CTV ⊕3pin square P 🎲 ♨(½m)
↔ 🚰(½m)

Min£65 Max£90pw

WEEK ST MARY
Devon
Map**2** SX29

C The College
for bookings The Landmark Trust, Shottesbrooke, Maidenhead, Berks
☎Littlewick Green(062882)5925

A cottage property, the remains of one of the first schools to be founded by a woman. Accommodation comprises large lounge/dining room with polished flag stone floor, open fireplace and stone mullion windows on one-side, kitchen area, spiral staircase to two twin bedrooms and one single bedroom and separate bathroom. It is decorated and furnished all in keeping with the period.

All year MWB out of season 2days min, 1mth max, 1unit, 5persons [◇] ◆ ⚙ fridge ♨ Gasinclusive Ⓛnot provided ☎(100yds) Iron & Ironing board in unit ☉ ⊕3pin square 2P 🎲 ♨(100yds)
↔ 🚰(200yds)

Min£119 Max£245pw (Low)
Min£155 Max£245pw (High)

WELTON
Cumbria
Map**11** NY34

Ch Mrs A E Ivinson Green View Lodges
Welton, Dalston, Carlisle, Cumbria CA5 7ES
☎Raughton Head(06996)230

Two peacefully situated Scandinavian pine lodges, both with attractive lounge/diner/kitchen, three bedrooms, bathroom/WC and separate WC.

All year MWB out of season 3nights min, 3wks max, 2units, 2−6persons ◆ ◆ ◎ fridge ♨ Elec metered Ⓛinclusive ☎(30yds) WM & SD in unit Iron & Ironing board in unit ☉ CTV ⊕3pin square 2P 🎲 ♨(100yds)
↔ 🚰 (30yds)

Min£80 Max£175pw (Low)
Min£115 Max£195pw (High)

See advertisement under Carlisle

C Well Cottage
for bookings Mrs A E Ivinson, Green View, Welton, Dalston, Carlisle, Cumbria CA5 7ES
☎Raughton Head(06996)230

A charming semi-detached cottage centrally situated in a tiny village. The ground floor comprises comfortable lounge, kitchen, sun lounge and WC. The first floor has three bedrooms and bathroom and WC.

All year MWB out of season 3nights min, 1mth max, 1unit, 2−6persons ◆ ◆ ◎ fridge ♨ Elec metered Ⓛcan be hired telephone in unit ☎(20yds) WM in unit, Iron & Ironing board in unit ☉ CTV ⊕3pin square 2P 🎲 ♨(100yds)
↔ 🚰(20yds)

Min£65 Max£155pw (Low)
Min£105 Max£160pw (High)

See advertisement under Carlisle

WELTON-LE-WOLD
Lincolnshire
Map**8** TF28

C Lincolnshire Wolds Farmyard Cottage No 3
for bookings C V Stubbs & Sons, Manor Warren Farm, Welton-le-Wold, Louth, Lincolnshire LN11 0QX
☎Louth(0507)604207

A semi-detached farm worker's cottage standing on a farm just off A157, comprising one single-, one family- and one double-bedded room, a combined kitchen/diner and a separate lounge.

All year MWB out of season 1wk min, 1unit, 6persons ◆ ◎ fridge Electric Elec metered (except heating) Ⓛcan be hired ☎(1½m) TV ⊕3pin square P ♨(2m)

Min£72 Max£86pw (Low)
Min£98 Max£126pw (High)

See advertisement on page 248

H School House
for bookings C V Stubbs & Sons, Manor Warren Farm, Welton-le-Wold, Louth, Lincolnshire LN11 0QX
☎Louth(0507)604207

An unusual two-storey brick-built building, formerly the village school house. It stands →

in the centre of the small peaceful village. One double-, one single- and one family-bedded room, a lounge, dining room and kitchen provide ample accommodation for six.

All year MWB out of season 1wk min, 1unit, 6persons ◆ ◎ fridge ♨
Electric Elec metered (except heating)
ⓛcan be hired ☎(½m) TV
⊕3pin square P ♨(3½m)

Min£77 Max£92pw (Low)
Min£100 Max£130pw (High)

WEMBURY
Devon
Map**2** SX54

Ch   Churchwood Valley Holiday Estate
Churchwood, Wembury, Plymouth, Devon
PL9 0DZ
☎Plymouth(0752)862382

*An attractive complex of wood panelled cabins situated within 100 acres of wooded valley overlooking the sea and valley. Each cabin has its own patio and is fenced or hedged to ensure privacy. The **A6** cabin comprises lounge/diner with bed-settee, kitchen two twin bedrooms, bath with shower and separate WC. The **A6S** is similar to A6 but equipped to higher standard. The **A6 plus**, again similar but more spacious and with extra equipment. The **A4** a smaller cabin has only one twin-bedded room plus bed settee in lounge/diner/kitchen, shower and WC. The **A4S** similar to A4 but equipped to higher standard.*

Etr–Nov MWB in season 1wk min, 51units, 2–6persons no pets ◎ fridge
♨(A6S & A4S) Electric fires A6 & A4
Elec inclusive ⓛcan be hired ☎ WM &
SD in A6 plus only Iron & Ironing board in unit [Launderette on premises]
(SD Free) ⊕ ⑩A6S & A6plus CTV
A6S & A6plus ⊕3pin square P
♨(on site)
↔ ♪(2m) ♀(½m)
Min£86 Max£294pw

WEST AYTON
North Yorkshire
Map**8** SE98

Welton-Le-Wold
—
West Newton

C   Spikers Hill Cottage
for bookings Mrs P Marshall, Spikers Hill Farm, West Ayton, Scarborough, N Yorkshire YO13 9LB
☎Scarborough(0723)862537

Four cottages situated on a private farm site within the North York Moors National Park. One pair of these semi-detached cottages has a double room, single room and a further room with bunk beds, of the other two, cottage No 3 has double and twin bedrooms and cottage No 4 has double and twin bedrooms plus a room with bunk beds. Both have ground-floor lounge and kitchen.

Apr–Nov MWB out of season 1wk min, 1mth max, 4units, 1–6persons [◆] ◎
fridge Electric Elec metered
ⓛinclusive ☎(1½m) Iron & Ironing
board on premises ⊕(2units)
TV(2units) CTV(2units) ⊕3pin square
P ♨ ▥(1½m)
↔ ♀(1½m) ♬(1½m)

Min£86 Max£155pw (Low)
Min£182 Max£200pw (High)

WESTHOPE
Hereford & Worcester
Map**3** SO45

C   Honeycroft Westhope Hill
for bookings Mrs P Treadgold, Ashcroft, Westhope, Hereford HR4 8BU
☎Canon Pyon(043271)336

A recently fully-modernised farm cottage set on an open common with panoramic views. On the ground floor there are two bedrooms sleeping six, modern kitchen, lounge, dining room, bathroom/shower with WC and separate WC. Upstairs there are three single beds. Follow signs to Westhope, drive through village, up steep hill and follow signs to cottage.

All year MWB out of season 1wk min, 6mths max, 1unit, 1–8persons ◆ ◎
fridge ♨ & open fires Elec metered
ⓛinclusive ☎(50yds) Iron & Ironing

---

board in unit ⊕ ⑩ CTV
⊕3pin square P ♨(½m)
↔ ♀(1½m)
Min£80 Max£170pw

WEST LINTON
Borders *Peeblesshire*
Map**11** NT15

C   Loch Cottage
for bookings Mrs C M Kilpatrick, Slipperfield House, West Linton, Peeblesshire EH46 7AA
☎West Linton(0968)60401

Charming attachment to main house in secluded setting within its own wooded grounds of 100 acres with delightful outlook onto private loch. The cottage comprises lounge/dining room, small kitchen and bathroom. There are two twin-bedded rooms, one on the ground floor, the other on the first floor. Access from A702, 1m S of West Linton village.

All year MWB out of season 1wk min, 4wks max, 1unit, 2–4persons ◆ ◆
◎ fridge Electric & open fire
Elec metered ⓛcan be hired ☎(1m)
Iron & Ironing board in unit ⊕ CTV
⊕3pin square 2P ♨(1m) Trout fishing
↔ ♪(1½m) ♀(1m)
Min£85 Max£140pw

WEST NEWTON
Norfolk
Map**9** TF62

H   Appleton Water Tower
for bookings Landmark Trust, Shottesbrooke, Maidenhead, Berkshire SL6 3SW
☎Littlewick Green(062882)5925

A 'landmark' since 1877, this enchanting and unique holiday home offers accommodation of a ground floor lounge/diner, kitchen, and shower room. Twenty-three stairs lead to the first-floor bedroom and another twenty to reach the upper bedroom. A further seventy-five steps up an iron spiral staircase lead to the roof of the giant water tank, now empty.

All year MWB out of season 1night min, 3wks max, 1unit, 1–4persons ◆
no pets ◎ fridge Electric
Elec inclusive ⓛnot provided ☎(½m)

Iron & Ironing board in unit ☺
♨3pin square 2P ♨(½m)
↔ ♨ (2½m)
Min£147 Max£220pw (Low)
Min£155 Max£250pw (High)

WESTON-SUPER-MARE
Avon
Map**3** ST36

F Mrs G Williams **Moorfield Holiday Flats** 150 Milton Road, Weston-Super-Mare, Avon BS23 2UZ
☎Weston-Super-Mare(0934)23687

Semi-detached gabled and dormer constructed of stone, brick and hung tiled.
Flat 1 on second floor with lounge, kitchen/diner, bath, WC. Two bedrooms, one double and one double plus twin beds. Flat 2 & 3 on first floor has lounge/diner, kitchen, bath WC, one bedroom with double and bunk beds.

All year MWB out of season 3nights min, 3units, 2–6persons ◆ ◆ no pets
☺ fridge electric fires Elec metered (except heating & hot water) ☐inclusive (except towels) ☎(100yds) Iron & Ironing board on premises [Launderette within 300yds] ☺ CTV ♨3pin square P ▥ ♨(100yds)
↔ ♨ (50yds) ♬(½m) ♫(½m) ☷(½m) Sports centre(½m)
Min£36 Max£48pw (Low)
Min£50 Max£126pw (High)

WESTWARD HO!
Devon
Map**2** SS42

C & Ch Mr J L & Mrs U B Robb **Buckleigh Pines** Buckleigh Cross, Westward Ho! Bideford, Devon EX39 7AA
☎Bideford(02372)74783

Mid- and end-terrace cottages, with splendid sea views, each offering accommodation of lounge/diner, bathroom/WC, fitted kitchen, one or three bedrooms, the end terrace cottage having a verandah. Entrance to either cottage on a mezzamine floor. The six cedar wood and rendered chalets, arranged in a garden setting, offer comfortable accommodation of lounge/diner,

---

West Newton
—
Weymouth

bathroom/WC, kitchen and one to three bedrooms depending on size.

Apr–25Oct MWB out of season 1wk min, 4wks max, 9units, 1–8persons [◇] ◆
◆ no pets ☺ fridge Electric Elec inclusive ☐inclusive ☎ Iron & Ironing board on premises [Launderette on premises] ☺ CTV ♨3pin square 9P ▥ ♨(50yds) ⌲
↔ ♬(1m) ♨(½m) ♬(½m) ♫(½m) ☷(2½m)
Min£85 Max£150pw (Low)
Min£135 Max£295pw (High)

WEYBOURNE
Norfolk
Map**9** TG14

B **7 & 37 Priory Wood Holiday Bungalows**
for bookings J M Sharp, Woodwinds, Davey Lane, Cromer, Norfolk NR27 9JL
☎Cromer(0263)512773

Two purpose-built holiday bungalows within a select site of similar properties overlooking lawns in a quiet rural setting. Each has two double bedrooms and large open-plan living area comprising lounge/diner (with double studio couch) and kitchen.

Mar–Nov MWB out of season 1wk min,6mths max, 2units, 1–6persons [◆ ◆] ☺ fridge Electric Elec metered ☐not provided ☎(100yds) [Launderette with 300yds] ⊕ CTV ♨3pin square P ♨(100yds)
↔ ♨(½m)
Min£45 Max£64pw (Low)
Min£96 Max£138pw (High)

WEYMOUTH
Dorset
Map**3** SY67

H **4 Birch Way** Preston
for bookings Mrs J E Pankhurst, 15 Birch Way, Weymouth, Dorset DT3 6JA
☎Preston(0305)832265

Detached modern house in elevated position overlooking the bay. It comprises lounge, kitchen/diner, bathroom with WC and three bedrooms sleeping up to nine people. Situated in Preston village, a suburb of Weymouth. 2m N A353.

All year 1wk min, 4wks max, 1unit, 2–9persons [◇] ◆ ◆ ☺ fridge
🍴 Elec metered ☐can be hired ☎(50yds) Iron & Ironing board in unit CTV ♨3pin square P ♨ ▥
↔ ♬(3m) ♨(½m) ♬(½m) ♫(3m) ☷(3m)
Min£95 Max£100pw (Low)
Min£250 Max£270pw (High)

H **19 Budmouth Avenue, Preston**
for bookings J E Pankhurst, 15 Birchway, Preston, Weymouth, Dorset DT3 6JA
☎Preston(0305)832265

Situated in a residential area approximately 3 miles from Weymouth this detached house comprises kitchen, dining room, spacious lounge, WC, two double bedrooms and two large family rooms, bathroom and separate WC.

Apr–Oct 1wk min, 1mth max, 1unit, 12persons [◇] ◆ ◆ ☺ fridge
🍴 Elec metered ☐can be hired ☎(½m) SD in unit Iron & Ironing board in unit ☺ CTV ♨3pin square 2P 1♨ ▥ ♨(½m)
↔ ♬(3m) ♨(½m) ♬(3m) ♫(3m) ☷(3m) Sports centre(3m)
Min£109.25 Max£310.50pw

B **1 Cherry Way** Preston
for bookings Mrs J E Pankhurst, 15 Birch Way, Weymouth, Dorset DT3 6JA
☎Preston(0305)832265

Self-contained modern detached bungalow on a new estate on the outskirts of Weymouth with views out to sea. It comprises lounge/diner, kitchen, bath with WC and three bedrooms. 2m N A353.

All year 1wk min, 4wks max, 1unit, 2–8persons [◇ ◇] ◆ ☺ fridge
Electric Elec metered ☐can be hired ☎(500yds) Iron & Ironing board in unit CTV ♨3pin square ♨ ▥ ♨(500yds) →

⊖ δ(3m) ♀(½m) [♫](½m) ♫(3m)
🎥(3m)

Min£95 Max£100pw (Low)
Min£250 Max£270pw (High)

B **86 Oakbury Drive** Preston
for bookings Mrs J E Pankhurst, 15 Birch Way, Weymouth, Dorset DT3 6JA
☎Preston(0305)832265

A modern detached bungalow on a new estate on the outskirts of Weymouth with sea views. It comprises lounge, kitchen/diner, bathroom and WC, and three bedrooms. 2m N A353.

Allyear 1wk min, 4wks max, 1unit, 2–8persons [◇] ◈ ◆ ◎ fridge Electric Elec metered 🄻can be hired ☎(500yds) Iron & Ironing board in unit CTV ⊕3pin square P 🏠 🅼 🛒(500yds)

⊖ δ(3m) ♀(½m) [♫](½m) ♫(3m) 🎥(3m)

Min£95 Max£100pw (Low)
Min£250 Max£270pw (High)

H **16 Oak Way** Preston
for bookings Mrs J E Pankhurst, 15 Birch Way, Weymouth, Dorset DT3 6JA
☎Preston(0305)832265

Situated in Preston village, a suburb of Weymouth, overlooking the bay. This modern detached house has lounge, kitchen/diner, bathroom with WC and three double bedrooms, plus a single bed in each. 2m N A353.

Allyear 1wk min, 4wks max, 1unit, 2–9persons [◇] ◈ ◆ ◎ fridge Electric Elec metered 🄻can be hired ☎(75yds) Iron & Ironing board in unit CTV ⊕3pin square P 🏠 🅼 🛒(500yds)

⊖ δ(3m) ♀(½m) [♫](½m) ♫(3m) 🎥(3m)

Min£95 Max£100pw (Low)
Min£250 Max£270pw (High)

F Mr J Rose **Panda Holiday Flats**
12 Grosvenor Road, Weymouth, Dorset DT4 7QL
☎Weymouth(0305)773817

Six units within detached villa located in quiet area within walking distance of seafront and main shopping area.

Allyear MWB out of season 1wk min, 4wks max, 6units, 2–8persons ◈ ◆ ◎ fridge Electric Elec metered 🄻can be hired ☎(¼m) Iron & Ironing board in unit ⊙ CTV ⊕3pin square P 🏠 🅼 🛒(¼m)

⊖ δ(2m) ♀(¼m) [♫](½m) ♫(½m) 🎥(¾m)

Min£40 Max£85pw (Low)
Min£95 Max£190pw (High)

F **Sangary Court** 6A Stavordale Road
for bookings Mr A Rees, Bedford House, 9A Mitchell Street, Weymouth, Dorset DT4 8BT
☎Weymouth(0305)786060

One ground-floor and two first-floor flats all well furnished and decorated. The accommodation in each consists of a kitchen/lounge/dining area, bathroom and WC. The ground-floor flat has a double bedroom with bunks, one first-floor flat has a double room with bunks and another with twin beds; the other first-floor flat has a double- and a single-bedded room.

Allyear MWB out of season 1wk min, 1mth max, 3units, 1–6persons ◈ ◆ no pets ◎ fridge Elec fires 🔥 Elec metered 🄻inclusive ☎(100yds) Iron & Ironing board in unit [Launderette within 300yds] ⊙ CTV ⊕3pin square 6P 2🏠 🅼 🛒(100yds)

⊖ δ(3m) ♀(100yds) [♫](½m) ♫(½m) 🎥(½m)

Min£60 Max£75pw (Low)
Min£85 Max£155pw (High)

B **31 Ullswater Crescent** Radipole
for bookings Mrs J E Pankhurst, 15 Birch Way, Weymouth, Dorset DT3 6JA
☎Preston(0305)832265

A modern detached bungalow in the residential area of the suburb of Radipole. It comprises a lounge/diner, kitchen, separate bath and WC, and three bedrooms (three double and two single beds).

Allyear 1wk min, 4wks max, 1unit, 2–8persons [◇] ◈ ◆ ◎ fridge Electric Elec metered 🄻can be hired ☎(½m) Iron & Ironing board in unit CTV ⊕3pin round P 🏠 🅼 🛒(½m)

⊖ δ(1m) ♀(1½m) [♫](1½m) ♫(1½m) 🎥(1½m)

Min£95 Max£100pw (Low)
Min£250 Max£270pw (High)

F **Venesta Holiday Flats**
for booking Mrs T M Burt, 13 Icen Road, Weymouth, Dorset DT3 5JL
☎Weymouth(0305)783042

Five flats located in semi-basement and four floors of terraced brick building situated only two minutes' walk from seafront and five minutes from town centre. Recently converted, with modern furnishings and having either one or two bedrooms.

Allyear MWB out of season 3days min, 4wks max, 5units, 2–8persons [◇] ◈ ◆ no pets ◎ fridge Electric Elec metered 🄻can be hired ☎(250yds) Iron & Ironing board in unit [Launderette within 300yds] CTV ⊕3pin square 5P 🅼 🛒(300yds)

⊖ δ(2½m) ♀(200yds) [♫](500yds) ♫(¼m) 🎥(¼m)

Min£40 Max£50pw (Low)
Min£150 Max£180pw (High)

WHATSTANDWELL
Derbyshire
Map**8** SK35

C **Estate Lodge**
for bookings Mrs E George, Alderwasley Park, Whatstandwell, Matlock, Derbyshire DE4 5HP
☎Ambergate(077 385)2063

A former 18th-century gate lodge which has been much extended in recent years and situated in extensive wooded grounds. Accommodation comprises large lounge, two double-bedded rooms and a modern shower room/WC in the extension. The original part contains a double and a single room, simple kitchen/diner and a second lounge, bathroom and separate WC.

Allyear 1wk min, 1unit, 7persons ◈ ◆ ◎ fridge storage heater, gas & solid fuel fire Gas & Elec inclusive 🄻inclusive ☎(100yds) WM, SD & TD in unit Iron & Ironing board in unit ⊙ ⊛ TV & CTV ⊕3pin square 2P 🅼 🛒(¾m) fishing, shooting

⊖ ♀(½m)

Min£180 Max£250pw

WHEDDON CROSS
Somerset
Map**3** SS93

B, C & F J & D M Sims **1Triscombe Farm Estate** Triscombe Farm, Wheddon Cross, Minehead, Somerset TA24 7HA
☎Winsford(064 385)227

Triscombe Farm is set in 30 acres of beautiful countryside within the Exmoor National Park, 1m S of Wheddon Cross. The farmhouse and holiday homes are secluded from the main road and reached by ⅓m private drive. ***Garage Maisonette*** *is a converted coachman's cottage on two floors, with one bedroom and a double bed in partitioned-off sitting room.* ***Rose Cottage*** *is a semi-detached and comprises four bedrooms sleeping up to nine people.* ***Jubilee flat*** *has two bedrooms,* ***Shire*** *has one,* ***Stable*** *has three,* ***Stream*** *has two and* ***Steps*** *has four bedrooms.* ***Omega*** *bungalow has one twin-bedded room. The combination of beds varies from unit to unit and all have put-u-up settees in the lounge. Each has a kitchen and lounge or lounge/diner and a shower room or bathroom.*

Easter–End Oct MWB out of season 2days min, 3mths max, 8units, 2–9persons [◇ ◈ ◆] ◎ fridge 🔥(stream cottage) Electric Elec metered 🄻can be hired ☎(1m) Iron & Ironing board in unit ⊙ CTV ⊕3pin square & ⊕3pin round P 🅼 🛒(1m) 🎾Hard Games room

⊖ ♀(1m)

Min£100 Max£200pw

WHICHAM
Cumbria
Map**6** SD18

Ch **Brockwood Park**
for bookings Hoseasons Ltd, Sunway House, Lowestoft, Suffolk NR32 3LT
☎Lowestoft(0502)62292

Norwegian timber and cedarwood lodges set in 26 acres of woodland in the Whicham Valley. These well-furnished lodges comprise two or three bedrooms, lounge, bathroom/WC, seven of the lodges have saunas. Central feature of the site is the mansion house which comprises a bar and games room.

All year MWB out of season 4 days min, 8wks max, 30units, 2–8persons [◆ ◆] no pets ◎ fridge ♨ Elec inclusive ⌷ inclusive ☎ Iron & Ironing board on premises [Launderette on premises] ☉ CTV ⊕ 3pin square 35P ▥ ♨ ▣ childrens play area ↔ ♪(2¾m) ♀

Min£85 Max£275pw

WHITBY
North Yorkshire
Map**8** NZ81

C 2 Mill View Ruswarp
for bookings Mrs J Roberts, White Rose Cottages, 5 Brook Park, Sleights, Whitby, YO21 1RT
☎Whitby(0947)810763

One of a small row of former mill-workers cottages in an elevated position overlooking the River Esk. It sleeps up to four people in three bedrooms on the first floor and has a beamed lounge, bathroom, WC and kitchen on the ground floor.

All year MWB out of season 3 nights min, 3mths max, 1unit, 1–4persons ◆ ◆ ◎ fridge Electric Elec metered ⌷ not provided ☎(100yds) SD in unit Iron & Ironing board in unit TV ⊕ 3pin square ▥ ♨ (150yds) ↔ ♀(150yds) ♫(2m) ♪(3m) ▩(3m)

Min£75 Max£150pw

F Mrs J Griffiths **Regent House** 7 Royal Crescent, Whitby, N Yorkshire
☎Whitby(0947)602103

Five self-contained flats in a terrace of tall Regency houses. The ground-floor flat has one bedroom with double bed, and bunk beds, plus studio couch in lounge. The other flats have two bedrooms containing one double and one single bed, plus a studio couch in each lounge with separate

---

Whicham
—
Whitney

bathroom/WC and kitchen. All have excellent fittings and furnishings and good views of the sea. Lift to all floors.

All year MWB out of season 1 wk min, 1mth max, 5units, 2–8persons ◆ ◎ fridge Electric Elec metered ⌷ can be hired ☎(200yds) ☉ TV ⊕ 3pin square ▥ ♨(½m) ↔ ♀(200yds) ♫(200yds) ♪(200yds) ▩(½m)

Min£55 Max£190pw

C Rose Nook 21 Coach Road
for bookings Mrs J Roberts, White Rose Cottages, 5 Brook Park, Sleights, Whitby YO21 1RT
☎Whitby(0947)810763

A charming mid-terrace stone-built cottage in the village centre comprising a well-appointed pine kitchen/diner, comfortable lounge, one twin bedroom plus one double-bedded room and a modern bathroom.

All year MWB out of season 2 nights min, 3mths max, 1unit, 2–4persons ◆ ◆ ◎ fridge Electric fires Elec metered ⌷ not provided ☎(200yds) SD in unit Iron & Ironing board in unit TV ⊕ 3pin square ▥ ♨(20yds) ↔ ♪(3m) ♀(20yds) ♫(3m) ♪(3m)

Min£75 Max£150pw

H Southview 17 Coach Road
for bookings Mrs J Roberts, White Rose Cottages, 5 Brook Park, Sleights, Whitby YO21 1RT
☎Whitby(0947)810763

A spacious detached stone-built house set in its own gardens in the village centre. Accommodation comprises well-fitted kitchen, cloakroom with WC and wash hand basin, lounge, dining room, three bedrooms (one double, one twin plus bunk beds and one single), bathroom and WC.

All year MWB out of season 2 nights min, 3mths max, 1unit, 5–7persons ◆ ◆ ◎ fridge Electric fires Elec metered

---

⌷ not provided ☎(200yds) SD in unit Iron & Ironing board in unit ◑ TV ⊕ 3pin square 3P ▥ ♨(20yds) ↔ ♪(3m) ♀(20yds) ♫(3m) ♪(3m)

Min£85 Max£210pw

WHITEBRIDGE
Highland Inverness-shire
Map**14** NH41

Ch Highland Lodges
for bookings The House of Brandon-Bravo Ltd, Beauport Park, The Ridge, Hastings, Sussex
☎Hastings(0424)53207

Well-serviced and attractive modern 'lodges' with open plan kitchen and living room and two bedrooms. In a beautiful setting near a bend of the River Fechlin beside General Wade's Bridge. On A862 about 9m NE of Fort Augustus.

Mar–Nov 1wk min, 9units, 4–6persons ◆ ◆ ◎ fridge ♨ Elec inclusive ⌷ not provided ☎(100yds) Iron & Ironing board in unit ☉ ◑ ⊕ 3pin square P ♨(4m) Fishing, shooting & riding arranged ↔ ♀(200yds)

Min£92 Max£115pw (Low)
Min£155.25 Max£224.25pw (High)

WHITNEY
Hereford & Worcester
Map**3** SO24

C Cwm-yr-Afor
for bookings Mrs D L Williams, Cabalva Farmhouse, Whitney-on-Wye, Herefordshire HR3 6EX
☎Clifford(04973)324

Detached, secluded stone-built cottage with views across Wye Valley and Brecon Beacons. Accommodation comprises on the ground floor, kitchen, dining room, with original Victorian range and one double-bedded room. On the first floor one twin-bedded room and the sitting room to take full advantage of the scenery. The cottage is 2½m w off A438, ½m from Rhydspence and reached via a farm road.

All year MWB out of season 2 days min, 6wks max, 1unit, 1–5persons [◇] ◆ ◆ ◎ fridge Electric & open Elec inclusive ⌷ inclusive ☎(1m) Iron →

& Ironing board in unit ⊙ CTV
⊕3pin square 3P ♨(1½m) Fishing
↔ ♪(3m) ⚲(½m) 🎵(2m) 🎵(2m)
Details not confirmed for 1987

H   Wooden House
for bookings Mrs H Williams, Cabalva
Farmhouse, Whitney-on-Wye,
Herefordshire HR3 6EX
☎Clifford(04973)324

*Detached riverside cedarwood house
peacefully tucked away in a tranquil rural
setting with commanding views across
river to Black Mountains. Accommodation
comprises large lounge with open fire,
dining room with french doors to garden,
kitchen, small study/bedroom and
separate WC. The first floor has one
double and two twin-bedded rooms,
bathroom with shower and separate WC.
From Whitney-on-Wye follow A438 to
Clyro, Cabalva is 1m on left.*

All year   MWB out of season   3days min,
4wks max, 1unit, 1–7persons ◆ ◆
◎ fridge   Elec & open fires
Elec inclusive ⊔inclusive   Iron & Ironing
board in unit ⊙ CTV ⊕3pin square
2P 1🏠 🎲 ♨(2m) Fishing
↔ ⚲(½m) 🎵(2m)
Details not confirmed for 1987

WIGHT, ISLE OF

BEMBRIDGE
Map**4** SZ68

H   Home Cottage 47 Howgate Road
for bookings Mr & Mrs E I Baker,
3 Beachfield Road, Sandown, Isle of Wight
☎Sandown(0983)403958

*A detached house with rear garden,
situated in a quiet area with distant sea
views. Accommodation comprises kitchen,
breakfast room and lounge on ground
floor, with three bedrooms and bathroom/
WC on first floor.*

Apr–Sep   1wk min, 1mth max, 1unit,
2–5persons ◆ no pets ⌀ fridge
🍲 Solid fuel   Gas/Elec metered
⊔sheets & pillowcases inclusive
☎(250yds)   Iron & Ironing board in unit
⊙ TV ⊕3pin square P ♨(200yds)
↔ ♪(500yds)
Min£100 Max£175pw

COLWELL BAY
Map**4** SZ38

F   Mr & Mrs A D Cross **Solent Court
Holiday Apartments** Colwell Chine Road,
Colwell Bay, Freshwater, Isle of Wight
PO40 9NP
☎Freshwater(0983)754515

Whitney
—
Wight, Isle of

*Fourteen flats on two floors; twelve two-
bedroomed (one double and one twin),
and two with one double bedroom. All
have kitchen, bathroom/WC and lounge/
diner with studio couch. Situated 200yds
from sandy beach.*

All year   MWB   2days min, 1mth max,
14units, 1–6persons ◆ ◆ no pets
◎ fridge   Electric   Elec metered ⊔can
be hired ☎ Iron & Ironing board in unit
⊙ CTV ⊕3pin square P ♨(½m)
↔ ⚲(200yds) 🎵(2m) 🎵(2m)
Min£60 Max£180pw

FRESHWATER
Map**4** SZ38

F   Mr I T Tamplin **Cameron House**
Terrace Lane, Freshwater Bay, Isle of
Wight PO40 9QE
☎Isle of Wight(0983)752788

*Victorian house with good views of the
bay, converted to four self-contained flats
of varying sizes. Each has two double
bedrooms, simply but adequately
furnished. Some flats have kitchen/diner/
lounge whilst others have separate
kitchen, all have bathroom/WC.*

All year   MWB   2days min, 3mths max,
4units, 4persons ◆ ◆ ◎ fridge
electric fires   Elec metered ⊔can be
hired ☎(100yds)   Iron & Ironing board in
unit   TV ⊕3pin square 6P 🎲
♨(100yds)
↔ ♪(1m) ⚲(100yds) 🎵(2m)
Min£40 Max£85pw(Low)
Min£100 Max£139pw(High)

B, Ch, C, F   Mrs S Roberts **Mountfield
Holiday Park** Norton Green, Freshwater,
Isle of Wight PO40 9RU
☎Isle of Wight(0983)752993

*A complex including caravans, situated in
4½ acres of woodland, well sheltered and
1m from the beach. The **five bungalows**
have two bedrooms, lounge/diner and
bathroom/WC. The **three chalets**
comprise all with three bedrooms, lounge
and shower/WC. The **two flats** are located
in the main house and comprise of two
bedrooms, bathroom, kitchen/diner and
lounge. The **cottage** is located on the
fringe of the complex in a quiet, rural
position. Accommodation comprises of
four bedrooms, lounge, kitchen/diner and
bathroom.*

Mar–Oct   MWB   1wk min, 1mth max,
11units, 2–9persons ◆ ◆
⌀ (except flats) ◎(flats)   fridge   Gas
Gas & Elec inclusive(Bungalows &
chalets)   Gas/Elec metered (Flats &
cottage) ⊔can be hired ☎(50–80yds)
Iron & Ironing board on premises(Cottage
in unit)   [Launderette on premises]
⊙(Flats only)   TV in bungalows, flats &
cottage ⊕3pin square P 🎲
♨(50yds) ⚞(heated)   licensed club,
table tennis, pool table
↔ ♪(2m) ⚲(50yds) 🎵(2m) 🎵(2m)
Min£80 Max£155pw (Low)
Min£120 Max£225pw (High)

NITON
Map**4** SZ57

C   Bluebell Cottage Church Street
for bookings Mrs P Rogers, 30 Leyborne
Park, Kew Gardens, Richmond, Surrey
☎01-940 0293

*Attractive fully-modernised stone cottage
situated in middle of village. Upstairs there
are two bedrooms (one a double-bedded
room and the other a twin-bedded room);
one has bathroom/WC en-suite, the other
has a wash hand basin. The ground floor
comprises lounge, separate dining room
and kitchen. Good quality solid
furnishings. Second WC outside back
door.*

Mar–Dec   (ex 3wks Etr & Xmas)   1wk min,
3mths max, 1unit, 2–4persons ◆ ◎
fridge 🍲 Elec metered
⊔not provided ☎(200yds)   Iron &
Ironing board in unit   CTV
⊕3pin square 🎲 ♨(200yds)
↔ ⚲(200yds) 🎵(200yds)
Min£75 Max£80pw(Low)
Min£85 Max£95pw(High)

RYDE
Map**4** SZ59

C, F   Mrs M Hines **Solent House**
Playstreet Lane, Ryde, Isle of Wight
PO33 3LJ
☎Ryde(0983)64133

*Two self-contained flats within a Victorian
home, and one modernised cottage, set in
three acres of secluded grounds. Well
appointed units with spacious
comfortable rooms. They are either two or
three bedroomed.*

All year   1wk min (2wks min, Jul & Aug),
6mths max, 3units, 2–8persons ◆
no pets ◎ fridge   Electric
Elec metered ⊔not provided ☎(½m)
[WM & SD on premises]   Iron & Ironing

---

board in unit ☺ CTV ⊕3pin square
P ⊞ ♨(400yds)
⊖ ⬩(½m) ♫(1m) ♪(1m) ☎(1m)
Details not confirmed for 1987

ST LAWRENCE
Map**4** SZ57

F Mrs P A Knight **La Falaise** Undercliffe
Drive, St Lawrence, Ventnor, Isle of Wight
PO38 1XF
☎Ventnor(0983)853440

*Two flats in a large detached house,
comprising two double bedrooms with
double and twin beds, lounge/diner/
kitchen and bathroom with WC.
Comfortably furnished. 1½m W of Ventnor.*

All year MWB out of season 1wk min,
2units, 1–6persons ◆ ◎ fridge
Electric Elec metered ⊔inclusive
☎(25yds) Iron & Ironing board in unit
☺ TV ⊕3pin square 4P ⊞
♨(50yds)
⊖ ♪(1½m) ⬩(50yds) ♫(1½m)
☎(1½m)
Min£45 Max£80pw (Low)
Min£110 Max£180pw (High)

SEAVIEW
Map**4** SZ69

Ch, B Manager **Salterns Holiday
Bungalows** Seaview, Isle of Wight
PO34 5AQ
☎Isle of Wight(0983)712330 (due to
change to 612330)

---

*Large Holiday complex consisting of 26
chalets and 51 bungalows, all with
kitchens, lounge/diner, shower and WC.
Four chalets contain three bedrooms, two
units sleep six persons and all the
remaining units have two small bedrooms.
All units are simply furnished and set in
attractive grounds.*

2May–3Oct MWB 3nights min,
1mth max, 77units, 2–6persons [◆]
no pets ◎ fridge Electric
Elec metered ⊔can be hired ☎
[Launderette] [Iron & Ironing board on
premises] ☺ CTV ⊕3pin square P
♨
⊖ ♪(3m) ⬩(½m) ♫(3m) ♪(3m)
☎(3m) Sports centre(2m)
Min£55 Max£88pw (Low)
Min£133 Max£169pw (High)

SHANKLIN
Map**4** SZ58

Ch **Lower Hyde Leisure Park** Lower
Hyde Road, Shanklin, Isle of Wight
PO37 7LL
☎Isle of Wight(0983)866131

*Twenty-nine chalets of similar style in a
combined chalet and caravan park. They*

---

*are modern and small, with two bedrooms
(double and twin bedded) and lounge/
diner/kitchenette. The lounge has a
convertible settee, so each unit can sleep
six. Kitchenettes have immersion heaters.*

Apr–10Oct MWB 3nights min, 4wks max,
29units, 2–6persons [◆ ◆] no pets
◎ fridge Electric Elec metered ⊔can
be hired ☎ Iron & Ironing board on
premises [Launderette on premises]
☺ CTV ⊕3pin square 30P ⊞ ♨
⌣ [½Hard] Pitch & putt, take away
food, children's playground
⊖ ⬩ ♫(1m) ☎(1m)
Min£80 Max£100pw (Low)
Min£280 Max£315pw (High) Prices include
ferry fare.

F Mr A Thompson **The Priory (Flats)**
Luccombe Road, Shanklin, Isle of Wight
PO37 6RR
☎Isle of Wight(0983)862365

*Seven out of nine flats in a large Victorian
house in a quiet rural setting overlooking
the sea. Each flat has one double
bedroom, lounge/diner, well-equipped
kitchenette with microwave oven and
bathroom. There is a separate library for
guests' use.*

All year MWB out of season 1day min,
2mths max, 7units, 1–4persons
[◇ ◆ ◆] no pets ◎ fridge/freezer
▧& electric fires Elec metered ⊔can be
hired ☎ Iron & Ironing board on
premises [Launderette on premises] →

⊕ CTV ⊕3pin square 20P [symbol]
⚎(½m)
⊖ ♪(¾m) ⚲(200yds) 🎵(½m)
🎵(½m) ⚎(½m)
Min£65 Max£85pw (Low)
Min£165 Max£195pw (High)

F   South Wing Maisonettes
for bookings Mr A Thompson, The Priory, Luccombe Road, Shanklin, Isle of Wight PO37 6RR
☎Isle of Wight(0983)862365
A modern extension to this Victorian house consisting of four maisonettes, comfortably furnished, each with two double bedrooms, lounge/diner, well-equipped kitchen (with microwave oven) in recess off lounge, and bathroom. There is a library room for guests' use.
Allyear MWB out of season 1day min, 2mths max, 4units, 1–4persons [◇ ◆ ♦] no pets
Gas & Electric fires Gas & Elec metered [L]can be hired ☎ Iron & Ironing board on premises [Launderette on premises]
⊕ CTV ⊕3pin square 20P [symbol]
⚎(½m)
⊖ ♪(¾m) ⚲(200yds) 🎵(½m)
🎵(½m) ⚎(½m)
Details not confirmed for 1987

THORNESS BAY
Map4 SZ49

Ch & B   Thorness Bay Holiday Park
for bookings Haven Leisure Ltd, Haven House, Quay Street, Truro, Cornwall TR1 2UT
☎Truro(0872)40400
A large holiday complex of 220 units, with five different types of chalets and two bungalows. Excellent views of the Solent and good leisure facilities. The accommodation comprises good size lounge/diners, kitchen, bath/WC and two double bedrooms, some units also have small bunk bedroom.
May–Oct MWB out of season 3days min, 6mths max, 220units, 2–6persons [◆] [◆] ♫ fridge
Electric Gas/Elec metered [L]inclusive
☎(100yds) Iron & Ironing board in unit [Launderette on premises] ⊕ CTV
⊕3pin square P [symbol] ⚎ ⌂ ⌐
Children's playground, sauna & mini gym
mini golf 🎵
⊖ ♪(2m) ⚲ ⚎(3m)
Sports centre(3m)
Min£78 Max£266pw

VENTNOR
Map4 SZ57

F   Ashcliffe Holiday Flats The Pitts, Bonchurch
for bookings Mr W Wright, Sandford Park, Holton Heath, Poole, Dorset BH16 6JZ
☎Lytchett Minster(0202)622513
Modernised Victorian house converted into four flats, all of them having combined lounge/diner and separate kitchen. Two flats have three bedrooms, two have two bedrooms. All are quite large and well-appointed with modern kitchen equipment, bath and WC.
10May–25Oct 3days min, 1mth max, 4units, 1–8persons ◆ ◆ fridge
Electric Elec metered [L]inclusive ☎
Iron & Ironing board in unit ⊕ CTV
⊕3pin square P [symbol] ⚎(½m)
⊖ ⚲(200yds) 🎵(2m) 🎵(2m)
Min£50 Max£130pw

F   Cleeve Court Bath Road
for bookings Mrs M R Jones, Hills Lea, Bath Road, Ventnor, Isle of Wight PO38 1JY
☎Ventnor(0983)852259
Spacious two bedroomed apartments overlooking the sea, each comprises lounge, kitchen/diner, bathroom and WC, and an additional separate WC. Patio doors open onto balcony in garden.
Allyear MWB 2days min, 3wks max, 2units, 6persons [◇ ◆ ♦] no pets
fridge Elec metered [L]can be hired ☎ Iron & Ironing board in unit [Launderette on premises] ⊕ [⚡]
[CTV] ⊕3pin square P [symbol]
⚎(200yds) Children's play centre, garden to beach approach, barbeque
⊖ ♪(½m) ⚲(100yds) 🎵(½m)
Min£270 Max£350pw

F   Mrs M R Jones Hills Lea Flats Bath Road, Ventnor, Isle of Wight PO38 1JY
☎Ventnor(0983)852259
Victorian house, part of which has been converted into two large self-contained flats, plus four in an adjoining building, all of which have splendid sea views. They are all spacious and have modern comfortable furnishings.
Allyear MWB in season 2days min, 2mths max, 6units, 1–7persons [◇] ◆
♦ no pets fridge Electric Elec metered [L]can be hired ☎ WM, SD & TD on premises Iron & Ironing board on premises ⊕ [⚡] [CTV]
⊕3pin square P [symbol] ⚎
⊖ ♪ ⚲ 🎵 ✂(300yds)
Details not confirmed for 1987

C   Kings Bay Chalets
for bookings Mrs A H Giles, Kings Bay House, Kings Bay Road, Ventnor, Isle of Wight PO38 1QR
☎Isle of Wight(0983)853718

Four well-maintained chalets in the grounds of the house with large garden and good sea views. Accommodation comprises spacious lounge/diner, well-equipped kitchen, two bedrooms (one double, one twin), separate bathroom and WC.

Etr–mid Oct MWB out of season 2days min, 1mth max, 4units, 2–5persons ◇ ◈ ◆ ◎ fridge Wall fan heaters Elec metered 🄻can be hired ☎(200yds) Iron & Ironing board in unit [Launderette within 300yds] ⊙ CTV ⊕3pin square 12P ⅿ ⛟(100yds)

⊖ ♁(1m) ♀(200yds) ♫(½m) ♫(½m)

Min£60 Max£110pw (Low)
Min£140 Max£155pw (High)

C **Smugglers Cottage** 10 South Street
for bookings Mrs J Wearing, Castle Holme, Castle Road, Ventnor, Isle of Wight PO38 1LG
☎Isle of Wight(0983)852138

Small semi-detached cottage in elevated position on cliff top with sea views to rear. Modernised accommodation with bright and colourful décor.

Apr–Oct MWB out of season 5mths max, 1unit, 1–7persons ◈ no pets ◔ fridge Electric & Gas Gas/Elec metered 🄻inclusive ☎(400yds) Iron & Ironing board in unit ⊙ TV ⊕3pin square ⅿ ⛟(500yds)

⊖ ♀(20yds) ♫(½m) ♫(½m) 🎥(½m)

Min£95 Max£185pw

WINCHCOMBE
Gloucestershire
Map**4** SP02

C Mr M G Blanchard **Cockbury Court Cottages** Winchcombe, Cheltenham, Gloucestershire GL52 4AD
☎Bishops Cleeve(024267)4153

Cockbury Court *is a charming private hamlet set high in the Cotswold Hills in a peaceful setting with breathtaking views. Seven cottages, with excellent furnishings and décor, all of individual character, comprise this delightful holiday village which includes heated swimming pool, hard tennis court and croquet lawn within 10 acres of superb gardens. Located on A46, 2m SW of Winchcombe.* ***Badgers Mount*** *has ground-floor accommodation for five people in two bedrooms, lounge with dining area, kitchen, two bathrooms/WC and a patio and lawn.* ***Barn Cottage*** *is converted from a 16th-century tithe barn, sleeping four people and has a sitting room, kitchen with dining area, cloakroom with WC downstairs and bathroom/WC upstairs.* ***Cockbury Cottage*** *has two bedrooms, one double, one triple, bathroom/WC, kitchen, dining room, sitting room and cloakroom/WC. Also included is a lock-up garage and small garden.* ***The Gazebo****, an unusual building, circular in the main, built of Cotswold stone with thatched roof. The spacious open plan arrangement includes dining area, thatched bar, lounge with screened sleeping area, separate kitchen, two showers, two WC's and bedroom with bunk beds.* ***Honeysuckle*** *is a 16th-century stone cottage with a thatched roof on one level. It has a large sitting room with central gas fire, small kitchen/dining area, twin bedded room and bathroom.* ***Mole End*** *is a garden bungalow looking towards the water gardens and has a large lounge with small dining area, kitchen, bathroom/WC and one twin bedroom, ideal for two people.* ***Tithe Barn*** *is a magnificent 16th-century building with exposed beams and oak floor. A large open plan area incorporates a four poster bed, sitting area and galley kitchen, plus a large bathroom with shower and WC. Extra person by arrangement. Four of the cottages have open fires and logs are supplied in winter.*

Allyear MWB 2days min, 7units, 2–5persons [◇](Honeysuckle & Tithe Barn) ◈ ◆ no pets except Cockbury Cottage ◎ fridge ⅲ Elec inclusive 🄻inclusive ☎ Iron & Ironing board on premises ⊙ CTV ⊕3pin square P ⌂ ⛟(2m) ⛬ 🎾Hard

⊖ ♁(¼m) ♀(2m)

Min£155 Max£260pw (Low)
Min£200 Max£365pw (High)

F Mr & Mrs M Elliott **The Malt House** Corner Cupboard Inn, Winchcombe, Gloucestershire GL54 5LX
☎Winchcombe(0242)602303

The Malta House is the self-contained wing of a 14th-century inn, retaining many original features including Cotswold stone walled sitting/dining room. Kitchen, two bedrooms each with twin beds, shower/WC and a bed-settee in the sitting room if required.

Allyear MWB out of season 2nights min, 1unit, 2–6persons, nc3 no pets ◔ fridge ⅲ Gas/Elec inclusive 🄻inclusive ☎(10yds) Iron & Ironing board on premises ⊙ CTV ⊕3pin square 2P ⛟(¼m)

⊖ ♁(1½m) ♀

Min£95 Max£165pw

C & F **Postlip House Cottages**
for bookings Mr & Mrs Sparks, Postlip House, Winchcombe, Gloucestershire GL54 5AH
☎Winchcombe(0242)602390

Four cottages and two flats situated in the seven acres of grounds around a Cotswold stone Manor. The ***Courtyard*** *flat in the main house comprises kitchen/diner, shower/WC, lounge with double bed in recess off.* ***Stable Cottage*** *comprises lounge/diner, kitchen, shower/WC, one double, one twin and one single bedroom, bath/WC.* ***Tack Room Cottage, Chestnut Cottage*** *and* ***Hayloft Flat*** *all comprise lounge, kitchen/diner one double and one twin bedroom and bath/WC.* ***Paddock Cottage*** *comprises lounge/diner with open plan kitchen, one double bedroom and bath/WC.*

Allyear MWB 1mth max, 6units, 2–5persons [◇ ◈ ◆] ◔(hob) ◎(oven) fridge ⅲ Gas & Elec inclusive 🄻inclusive ☎ Iron & Ironing board on premises Launderette on premises ⊙ ⊛ CTV ⊕3pin square P ⅿ ⛟(½m) Evening meals available

⊖ ♁(2m) ♀(½m)

Min£126.50 Max£218.50pw

See advertisement on page 256

WINDERMERE
Cumbria
Map**7** SD49

F Mr & Mrs J N Pickup **Applethwaite Holiday Flats** The Heaning Lane, Windermere, Cumbria LA23 1JW
☎Windermere(09662)3453

A large Victorian stone-built house, standing in six acres of grounds, which is divided into six flats (only four are listed). These flats all have lounge, kitchen and shower room/WC. The bedroom accommodation varies from one to two bedrooms plus three with an extra fold away bed in the lounge.

Allyear MWB out of season 2nights min, 1mth max, 4units, 2–6persons, nc5 Pets by arrangement ◎ fridge Electric Elec metered 🄻can be hired ☎ Iron & Ironing board on premises [Launderette] ⊙ CTV ⊕3pin square P ⅿ ⛟(1m)

⊖ ♁(3m) ♀(1m) ♫(1½m) ♫(1½m) 🎥(2m)

Min£40 Max£170pw

C **Aarons Crag Cottages** The Heaning
for bookings Mr & Mrs J N Pickup, Heaning Lane, Windermere, Cumbria LA23 1JW
☎Windermere(09662)3453

Converted 17th-century coach house and stables situated in the grounds of a Victorian house. Each cottage has one bedroom – with some original beams, lounge, small fitted kitchen, shower room and separate WC.

Allyear MWB out of season 2nights min, 1mth max, 4units, 2–4persons, ◎ fridge Electric & storage heaters Elec metered 🄻can be hired ☎ Iron & Ironing board in unit [Launderette on premises] ⊙ CTV ⊕3pin square 4P ⅿ ⛟(1m) Croquet lawn

⊖ ♁(3m) ♀(1m) ♫(2m) ♫(1½m) 🎥(2m)

Min£60 Max£90pw (Low)
Min£95 Max£160pw (High)

See advertisement on page 257

F & B **Beaumont Holiday Homes**
Beaumont, Thronbarrow Road
for bookings Mrs C Latham-Warde, Lakelovers, The Toffee Loft, Ash Street, Windermere, Cumbria LA23 3RA
☎Windermere(09662)4464 or 5144 →

This charming Victorian house set in its own attractive gardens has been tastefully converted to provide four flats and two studios. **Windermere** on the ground floor and **Thirlmere** on the first floor, both have one double and one twin-bedded room. **Buttermere** on the first floor features a four poster and also has a double fold-away bed in the lounge. **Grasmere** on ground floor has one double room. **Wastwater & Elterwater** have a large bedroom with a double and single bed on the ground floor and living area on first floor. Also within the grounds are three single-storey cottages (suitable for elderly or disabled), they have a double room and a convertible sofa in the lounge.

Allyear MWB out of season 3days min, 9units, 2–4persons, nc8yrs no pets ⓜ fridge ♨ Elec metered Ⓛinclusive ☎ WM & TD on premises Iron & Ironing board in unit ⊕ ⊗ CTV ⊕3pin square 12P Ⓣ ♨(100yds)
⊖ δ(2m) ♨(¼m) 🎵(1m) ♩(1m) 🐾(1m)
Min£115 Max£200pw

F   Bowering Holiday Flats 6 Park Road
for bookings Mrs M Taylor, 'Belle Mere', Newby Bridge, Ulverston, Cumbria LA12 8NL
☎Newby Bridge(0448)31202

Three ground-floor flats in a house built of Lakeland stone, situated in a residential area close to all amenities. One flat sleeps

---

Windermere

two on a double fold away bed in spacious lounge. All have modern kitchens, and offer comfortable accommodation.

Allyear MWB out of season 2nights min, 6wks max, 3units, 2–6persons [◇] ◆ ⓜ fridge ♨ & electric fires Gas & Elec metered Ⓛcan be hired ☎(200yds) Iron & Ironing board in unit ⊕ CTV ⊕2pin square 3P Ⓣ ♨(¼m)
⊖ δ(2m) ♨(¼m) 🎵(1m) ♩(1m) 🐾(¼m)
Min£65 Max£120pw (Low)
Min£118 Max£134pw (High)

F   Canterbury Flats Quarry Rigg, Lake Road
for bookings Bowness Holidays (TG), 38 South Canterbury Road, Canterbury, Kent CT1 3LJ
☎Canterbury(0227)69803 or Windermere(09662)5216

Twenty-two modern comfortably furnished flats located in the centre of the village of Bowness and close to the lake and steamer pier. Some flats are above new shops, others on each side of a quiet cul-de-sac. **One bedroom flats** (16A to 19A and 21A) and the larger **one bedroom family flats** (32A and 33A) sleep two

---

persons in either twin- or double-bedded rooms; lounge/dining area, kitchen and bathroom/WC. **Two bedroom balcony flats** (19 and 22 to 27) sleep four persons in either twin- or double-bedded rooms and have lounge/dining area with french windows to balcony, open-plan kitchen and bathroom/WC. **Two bedroom centre flats** (40A, 41A, 446A) and the larger **two bedroom family flats** (40, 47) sleep four persons in twin- and/or double-bedded rooms; lounge/dining area, open plan or separate kitchen, bathroom/WC. **Three bedroom balcony flats** (10, 11, 12) sleep seven persons in twin- and double-bedded rooms and have lounge/dining area with french windows to balcony, two bathroom/WCs. All the flats have extra folding beds and extending settee. Off-peak heating and hot water included. Unsuitable for invalids. Garage or private parking. Video recorders.

Allyear MWB out of season 2nights min, 22units, 2–8persons ◆ ◆ no dogs in 9 units ⓜ fridge Electric Elec metered Ⓛinclusive ☎ or ☎ Iron & Ironing board in unit [Launderette within 300yds] ⊕ CTV ⊕3pin square P 🏠 Ⓣ ♨(100yds)
⊖ δ(2m) ♨(200yds) ♩(½m) 🐾(100yds)
Min£90 Max£207pw (Low)
Min£138 Max£285pw (High)

F Chapel Court Troutbeck Bridge (1m N A591)
for bookings Mrs A Marshall, Brackenhill, Singleton Parks Road, Kendal, Cumbria LA9 6PD
☎Kendal(0539)20469

Formerly the local chapel now tastefully converted to offer two modern apartments with good furnishings and fittings. Both comprise two bedrooms (one with three beds) with the first-floor flat having additional bed-settee.

All year MWB out of season 2 nights min, 3mths max, 2–6persons ◆ ◆ ◎ fridge ♨ Elec inclusive ⊡ not provided (except for overseas visitors) ☎ Iron & Ironing board in unit ⊖ CTV ⊕3pin square 2P ▥ ♨(100yds) ⊖ δ(2m) ♀(100yds) ♫(1m) ♫(1m) ⅛-(½m)

Min£85 Max£145pw

F & C Mrs P M Fanstone **Deloraine** Helm Road, Windermere, Cumbria LA23 2HS
☎Windermere(09662)5557

An Edwardian house converted into four flats, situated in a secluded, elevated position overlooking Windermere and the lake, in 1½ acres of garden. 'Brant' being on the ground floor with an entrance hall, bedroom with double and single beds, bathroom and shower. Lounge/dining room with two beds and bed-settee adjoins the kitchen. This flat is ideal for the disabled. 'Claife' has a hall, a large bed-

---

Windermere

sitting room with a double and two single beds, dining room/kitchenette, bathroom and separate WC. 'Scafell' has an entrance hall, kitchen, living/dining room with settee that can be converted into a double bed, one bedroom with double bed and bunk beds and a bathroom/WC. 'Bowfell' has an open-plan lounge/dining/kitchen with two sleeping places, one bedroom which has a double bed and bunk beds, shower room/WC. Birch Cottage is a traditional stone and slate cottage, it sleeps up to six people in a double-bedded and twin-bedded room, also a bed-settee in the lounge. The cottage is also ideal for the disabled.

All year MWB out of season 3days min, 5units, 2–6persons ◆ ◆ no pets ◎ fridge ♨ Elec metered ⊡ can be hired ☎ WM & SD on premises Iron available Ironing board available ⊖ CTV ⊕3pin square P ▥ ♨(¼m) ⊖ δ(2m) ♀(½m) ♫(½m) ⅛-(½m)

Min£50 Max£90pw (Low)
Min£70 Max£195pw (High)

See advertisement under Bowness-on-Windermere

F Mr & Mrs D Houghton **Fair Rigg Luxury Flats** Ferry View, Bowness-on-Windermere, Cumbria LA23 3JB
☎Windermere(09662)6242

A typical Lake District house, stone-built, pleasantly situated in rural surroundings and with good views of mountains and Lake Windermere from the three flats. The flatlet is at the back of the house. ¾m from the lakeside village of Bowness. An ideal base from which to enjoy the many attractions of the Lake District.

All year MWB out of season 3days min, 3mths max, 4units, 2–6persons, nc8 no pets ◎ fridge Night storage & electric fires Elec metered ⊡ inclusive ☎ Iron & Ironing board in unit ⊖ CTV ⊕3pin square P ▥ ♨(¾m) ⊖ δ(¼m) ♀(¼m) ⅛-(¾m)

Min£50 Max£90pw (Low)
Min£100 Max£170pw (High)

See advertisement on page 258

F Howe Foot Holiday & Tourist Flats Bowness-on-Widermere
for bookings Mrs M Thexton, Quarry Lodge, Oakthwaite Road, Windermere, Cumbria LA23 2BD
☎Windermere(09662)2792

Modern flats in an extension built on to the Howfoot Hotel, in a quiet cul-de-sac near to town centre.

All year MWB out of season 1wk min, 7units, 2–7persons ◆ no pets ◎ →

fridge Electric Elec metered
Ⓛinclusive ☎ Iron & Ironing board in unit [Launderette on premises] TV
⊕3pin square P ▥ ▦(300yds)
⊖ ☕(¼m) ☏(¼m)

Min£41.40 Max£72.45pw (Low)
Min£82.80 Max£161.50pw (High)

B Linthwaite Hotel (Bungalow)
Bowness-on-Windermere, Windermere,
Cumbria LA23 3JA
☎Windermere(09662)3688

Modern, self-contained bungalow situated in the grounds of Linthwaite Country House Hotel. Accommodation comprises one twin-bedded room with wash hand basin and WC, one twin-bedded room with wash hand basin, a bathroom and WC combined, comfortable lounge and well-equipped kitchen. High standard throughout.

Etr–Nov 1wk min, 1unit, 1–4persons,
nc8 no pets ◎ fridge ♨
Elec inclusive Ⓛinclusive ☎ Iron & Ironing board on premises ⊙ CTV
⊕3pin square P ▥ ▦(1m)
Putting green Fishing

⊖ ♪(¼m) ☕ ☏(1m) ♬(1m)
☏(1m)

Max£150pw

H 23 Meadow Road
for bookings Mr & Mrs Wiseman,
Wisemans Holiday Cottages, 37 Charles Street, Blackpool, Lancs FY1 3EY
☎Blackpool(0253)28936(day)
43471(evening)

A modern house, double glazed throughout with a delightful private wooded area to the rear and views of the mountains. There are two twin-bedded rooms.

Windermere
—
Winterbourne Whitechurch

All year MWB out of season 1 day min,
1mth max, 1unit, 4persons ◎ fridge
Elec metered Ⓛnot provided ☎(¼m)
Iron & Ironing board in unit TV
⊕3pin square 1P 1▥ ▦ ▦(¼m)
⊖ ♪(1m) ☕(¼m) ☏(¼m) ♬(¼m)
☏(¼m) Sports centre(3m)

Min£60 Max£90pw (Low)
Min£95 Max£150pw (High)

C School Cottages Troutbeck Bridge
(1m N A591)
for bookings Mrs A Marshall, Brackenhill,
Singleton Parks Road, Kendal, Cumbria
LA9 6PD
☎Kendal(0539)20469

An old stone-built school tastefully converted into four cottages with décor and furnishing of a high quality. Two units sleep six people, the other two sleep five people. In an elevated position with superb panoramic views of the Lakeland and fells. Indoor heated swimming pool within 100yds.

All year MWB out of season 2 nights min,
3mths max, 4units, 2–6persons ◇ ◆
◎ fridge ♨ Elec inclusive
Ⓛnot provided (except for overseas visitors) ☎ Iron & Ironing board in unit
⊙ CTV ⊕3pin square 4P ▥
▦(100yds)
⊖ ♪(2m) ☕(100yds) ☏(1m)
♬(1m) ☏(¾m)

Min£85 Max£145pw

F Mr R Allman-Smith **Spinnery Cottage Holiday Flats** Fairfield, Brantfell Road, Bowness-on-Windermere, Cumbria LA23 3AE
☎Windermere(09662)4884

Tastefully converted 200-year-old spinnery in quiet and secluded position a few minutes walk from the lake. Two of the flats are on the ground floor and two on the first floor, all have one bedroom, lounge/diner and kitchen. Three have bathroom/WC and one has shower room/WC.

All year MWB out of season 2 days min,
4wks max, 4units, 2–4persons ◇ ◆
no pets ♩(3) ◎(1) fridge ♨ Gas &
Elec metered Ⓛnot provided ☎(¼m)
Iron & Ironing board on premises ⊙
TV ⊕3pin square 4P ▥ ▦(¼m)
⊖ ♪(2m) ☕(¼m) ☏(¼m) ♬(¼m)
☏(¼m)

Min£58 Max£115pw (Low)
Min£125 Max£142pw (High)

WINTERBOURNE WHITECHURCH
Dorset
Map3 ST80

F Mrs A M Franklin **West Farmhouse (Flat)** Winterborne Whitechurch, Blandford Forum, Dorset DT11 9AW
☎Milton Abbas(0258)880265

A flat on two floors adjoining a farmhouse. The ground floor has a lounge/dining room with inglenook fireplace, kitchen and shower room with WC. The first floor consists of a double-bedded room and another bedroom with twin beds, plus a double put-u-up.

All year MWB out of season 1wk min,
6mths max, 1unit, 2–6persons [◇] ◇
◆ ◎ fridge Solid fuel stove & Electric
Elec metered Ⓛcan be hired

☎(440yds) WM & SD in unit Iron & Ironing board in unit ⊙ TV ⊕3pin square 3P 🛒(440yds)

⊖ 🍷(440yds)

Min£45 Max£90pw (Low)
Min£100 Max£150pw (High)

WINTERTON-ON-SEA
Norfolk
Map**9** TG42

***Ch* Winterton Valley Estate** Edward Road
for bookings Hoseasons Holidays, Sunway House, Lowestoft, Suffolk NR32 3LT
☎Lowestoft(0502)62271

Purpose-built wood/brick chalets sited on flat grassed area close to sea/beach. Accommodation is varied in lay-out. There are five basic styles, all have open-plan, lounge/kitchen and combined bathroom/WC. Well-furnished. Proceed along B1159 turn right into Edward Road, site is 200yds on right.

Apr–Sep MWB out of season 1wk min, 4wks max, 30units, 2–6persons [◆] ◎ fridge Electric Elec metered 🄻inclusive ☎ [Iron on premises] ⊙ CTV ⊕3pin square P 🛒(200yds) ⊟ Children's play area

⊖ 🍷(½m) ♫(½m) ♫(½m)

Min£40 Max£140pw

WITHLEIGH
Devon
Map**3** SS91

C Mrs H Hann **Cider Cottage** Great Bradley Farm, Withleigh, Tiverton, Devon EX16 8JL
☎Tiverton(0884)256946

A restored 17th-century cider barn attached to a farm house. The accommodation is completely self-contained and comprises of a kitchen/dining area, spacious lounge, three bedrooms, and bathroom. A very attractive and well-furnished property.

Allyear MWB out of season 1wk min, 1mth max, 1unit, 1–5persons [◇] ◆ ◆ no pets ◎ fridge Rayburn & Electric fires Elec metered 🄻inclusive ☎(1m) Iron & Ironing board in unit ⊙ CTV ⊕3pin square 2P Ⓜ 🛒(2½m)

⊖ ♂(3m) 🍷(1½m) ♫(3m) ♫(3m) 🎥(3m)

Min£75 Max£95pw (Low)
Min£105 Max£175pw (High)

WOLFERTON
Norfolk
Map**9** TF62

C Downside Cottage
for bookings Mr Walker, Downside, Wolferton, King's Lynn, Norfolk
☎Dersingham(0485)40674

Small single-storey detached cottage converted in 1974, forming part of the buildings on the former Royal railway station of Wolferton on the Sandringham estate. The cottage has a lounge/diner with double put-u-up and one double bedroom with shower room. Wooded garden and very quiet rural atmosphere. Lovely local walks and only 1¼m from the sea.

Allyear MWB 1night min, 1unit, 1–4persons [◇] ◎ fridge Electric Elec metered 🄻not provided ☎(200yds) Iron in unit TV ⊕3pin square P 🛒(100yds)

⊖ 🍷(3m)

Details not confirmed for 1987

WOOBURN GREEN
Buckinghamshire
Map**4** SU98

***H* Overleigh**
for bookings Mr P G Griffin, Myosotis, Widmoor, Wooburn Green, Buckinghamshire HP10 0JG
☎Bourne End(06285)21594

Semi-detached house comprising lounge, dining room, kitchen, bathroom, separate WC and three bedrooms.

Allyear 1wk min, 6mths max, 1unit, 1–10persons ◆ no pets ◎ fridge Electric Elec metered 🄻can be hired ☎ WM in unit Iron & Ironing board in unit ⊙ CTV ⊕3pin square 4P Ⓜ 🛒(1m)

⊖ ♂(3m) 🍷(¼m) 🎥(3m)

Min£140 Max£150pw (Low)
Min£180 Max£196pw (High)

See advertisement under London

WOODBURY
Devon
Map**3** SY08

***C* CC Ref 7651**
for bookings Character Cottages Ltd, 34 Fore Street, Sidmouth, Devon EX10 8AQ
☎Sidmouth(03955)77001

An end of terrace cottage that retains its original thatch and beams. Accommodation comprises lounge/diner with open stone fireplace and woodburning stove, kitchen area, one roomy double bedroom and bathroom with circular bath.

Allyear MWB out of season 2days min, 2mths max, 1unit, 2persons, nc no pets ◎ fridge storage heaters Elec inclusive 🄻inclusive ☎(¼m) WM & SD in unit Iron & Ironing board in unit ⊙ CTV ⊕3pin square P Ⓜ 🛒(¼m)

⊖ 🍷(¼m) ♫(3m)

Min£88 Max£150pw

WOOD DALLING
Norfolk
Map**9** TG12

***F* The Little Farmer**
for bookings Mrs E M Smalley, The Old Jolly Farmers, Wood Dalling, Norwich NR11 6AQ
☎Saxthorpe(026387)387

The stables of this former inn have been converted into a flat, facing south and overlooking spacious gardens. The lounge/bedroom/diner has its own patio and a divider screens off the bedroom area, there is a kitchenette, separate WC and shower.

Allyear MWB out of season 3days min, 4wks max, 1unit, 1–2persons no pets ◑ fridge ⅢⅢ Gas/Elec metered 🄻inclusive ☎(300yds) TV ⊕3pin square 2P 🛒(100yds) Hard

Min£52 Max£62pw

WOODHALL SPA
Lincolnshire
Map**8** TF16

B Mr P Osborne **Bainland Park Leisure Centre** Horncastle Road, Woodhall Spa, Lincolnshire LN10 GUX
☎Woodhall Spa(0526)52903

Thirteen modern brick-built bungalows situated on the outskirts of town within 48 acres of heath and parkland, containing numerous leisure facilities. They vary in size, the smallest sleeping two in one bedroom, the largest sleeps six in three bedrooms. Each contain kitchen, lounge/diner and bathroom/WC.

Mar–Nov MWB in season 4days min, 13units, 2–6persons ◆ ◆ ◎ fridge Electric Elec inclusive 🄻inclusive ☎ WM & SD on premises [Iron on premises] Ironing board in unit [Launderette within 300yds] ⊙ CTV ⊕3pin square 13P Ⓜ 🛒 ⊟ Hard Restaurant, solarium, spa bath & croquet crazy golf ♫ 🍷

Min£94 Max£138pw (Low)
Min£193 Max£340pw (High)

See advertisement on page 260

WOODLANDS
Hampshire
Map**4** SU31

***C* Merrie Downs**
for bookings Mrs B M Davidson, 132 Woodlands Road, Ashurst, Woodlands, Southampton, Hampshire SO4 2AP
☎Ashurst(042129)2309

An early 19th-century forest cottage which has been rebuilt and modernised in quiet residential area on the fringe of the New Forest. Accommodation consists of two bedrooms, lounge, kitchen/diner and bathroom/WC. ¼m off main Southampton–Cadnam road.

Allyear 1wk min, 1mth max, 1unit, 1–4persons ◆ ◑ fridge ⅢⅢ Gas/Elec metered 🄻can be hired ☎ (shared) ☎(¼m) WM, Iron & Ironing board in unit ⊙ TV ⊕3pin square ⊕2pin round Ⓜ 🛒(150yds)

⊖ 🍷(¼m)

Min£75 Max£105pw (Low)
Min£120 Max£180pw (High)

F Mrs P E Kernick **Woodlands Ridge**
191 Woodlands Road, Woodlands,
Southampton Hampshire SO4 2GL
☎Ashurst(042129)2475

*Three spacious and well decorated flats
set in peaceful wooded grounds with
excellent outdoor facilities including
swimming pool, sports area, games room,
barbecue and children's play area. Each
flat has kitchen/dining area, lounge, two
double bedrooms and bathroom/WC with*
Courtyard *and* **Tree Tops** *sleeping up to
six people and* **Coach House** *sleeping up
to eight.*

Last Wk May–End Sep 1wk min,
6mths max, 3units, 1–8persons ◊ ◈
◆ pets charged for ◎ fridge Electric
or Gas fires Gas/Elec metered
ᴸinclusive except towels ☎(20yds)
WM & SD in unit Iron & Ironing board in
unit ☺ CTV ⊕3pin square 6P ▥
▨(200yds) ⌁
↔ ♪(1m) ♀(200yds)
Min£140 Max£315pw

WOODTHORPE
Lincolnshire
Map**9** TF47

B Ash Bungalow
for bookings C W Stubbs & Sons, Manor
Warren Farm, Welton-le-Wold, Louth,
Lincolnshire LN11 0QX
☎Louth(0507)604207
*A fairly modern brick-built bungalow in
wooded grounds on B1373. The
accommodation includes two double and
one twin-bedded room, kitchen, dining
area and separate lounge.*

All year MWB out of season 1wk min,
1unit, 6persons ◊ ◎ fridge ▩
Elec inclusive ᴸcan be hired
ᴸ(500yds) TV ⊕3pin square P ▥
▨(1¼m)
↔ ♀(3½m)
Min£82 Max£98pw (Low)
Min£110 Max£137pw (High)

**C Blue Bell, Cowslip, Foxglove and
Primrose Cottages** Woodland Lane
for bookings C V Stubbs & Sons, Manor
Warren Farm, Welton-le-Wold, Louth,
Lincolnshire LN11 0QX
☎Louth(0507)604207

Woodlands
—
Woolacombe

*Four modernised, semi-detached, former
farm workers' cottages standing in a quiet
lane on farmland, off B1373. Each has a
kitchen, dining room or dining area, and a
separate lounge. They have either two or
three bedrooms and sleep up to six
persons.*

All year MWB out of season 1wk min,
4units, 4–6persons ◊ ◎ fridge ▩
Elec inclusive ᴸcan be hired ☎(½m)
TV ⊕3pin square P ▥ ▨(1¼m)
↔ ♀(¼m)
Min£74 Max£98pw (Low)
Min£100 Max£137pw (High)

F Rose Bungalow Woodland Lane
for bookings C V Stubbs & Sons, Manor
Warren Farm, Welton-le-Wold, Louth,
Lincolnshire LN11 0QX
☎Louth(0507)604207
*A fairly modern detached bungalow in its
own garden in a quiet lane on farmland,
off B1373. Comprises lounge, dining room,
kitchen, two double and one twin-bedded
room.*

All year MWB out of season 1wk min,
1unit, 6persons ◊ ◎ fridge ▩
Elec inclusive ᴸcan be hired ☎(½m)
TV ⊕3pin square P ▥ ▨(1¼m)
↔ ♀(1¼m)
Min£82 Max£98pw (Low)
Min£110 Max£137pw (High)

WOOL
Dorset
Map**3** SY88

B Braeside Lulworth Road
for bookings Mrs J E Baker, Barn End,
Duck Street, Wool, Wareham, Dorset
BH20 6DE
☎Bindon Abbey(0929)462057
*Detached small neat bungalow with large
rear garden and with fine views.
Accommodation comprises attractive
comfortable lounge, dining room, well
fitted kitchen, two bedrooms (one double,
one twin), bathroom/WC/wash hand basin*

---

*plus further separate WC/wash hand
basin. Good standard of furnishings and
well-appointed. Additional 'z' bed
available if required.*

All year MWB out of season 1wk min,
4mths max(Apr–Oct), 1unit, 2–5persons
◊ ◆ ◎ fridge ▩ Elec inclusive
(summer only) ᴸnot provided
☎(200yds) SD in unit Iron & Ironing
board in unit ☺ CTV ⊕3pin square
1P ▨(200yds)
↔ ♀(300yds)
Min£50 Max£80pw (Low)
Min£100 Max£200pw (High)

B Whitemead Lodge
for bookings Mr McCullagh, Frome
Cottage, East Burton Road, Wool, Dorset
☎Bindon Abbey(0929)462241

*Detached Swedish-style bungalow in rural
setting. Accommodation comprises
lounge, kitchen, bathroom/WC, one twin-
bedded room and one with twin beds plus
children's bunks. A cot is available. Off
A352 Dorchester/Wareham Road.*

Apr–Oct 1wk min, 4wks max, 1unit,
2–6persons [◆] no pets ◎ fridge
Electric Elec metered ᴸcan be hired
(overseas visitors only) ☎(300yds)
[Launderette within 200yds] ☺ TV
⊕3pin square 2P ▨(100yds)
↔ ♪(3m) ♀(50yds) ☃(2m)
Min£70 Max£110pw (Low)
£135pw (High)

WOOLACOMBE
Devon
Map**2** SS44

F Quarry Dene (Flats 1–5) Bay View
Road
for bookings Mr J Lymer, Altantic Hotel,
Sunnyside Road, Woolacombe, Devon
☎Woolacombe(0271)870469

*Detached, red brick house on three floors
containing five flats of varying size each
with lounge/kitchen/diner, and bathroom/
WC. Bay View Road runs parallel with the
beach, affording good sea views.*

Mar–Nov MWB out of season
3days min, 3mths max, 5units,
2–7persons [◊] ◊ ◆ ◎ fridge
Electric Elec metered ᴸcan be hired
☎(50yds) Iron & Ironing board in unit

**HORNCASTLE ROAD
WOODHALL SPA
LINCOLNSHIRE
LN10 6UX**

How about a weekend, a week or longer in the heart of Lincolnshire
Enjoy the privacy of your own bungalow surrouded by a par 3 Golf Course,
set in Parkland and Woodlands.
Other facilities include indoor heated pool, jacuzzi, solarium, sauna - Bistro,
restaurant and fully licensed bar.
STOP PRESS - or stay in our NEW HOTEL in the Park due to open SPRING 1986.

TEL: (0526) 52903

⊕ CTV ⊕3pin square 6P ⊞
🛁(300yds)
↭ ♀(300yds) ♫(300yds)
♫(300yds)
Min£70pw (Low)
Min£130 Max£210pw (High)

WORTHING
West Sussex
Map4 TQ10

F Mrs P Mahoney **Chesswood**
56 Homefield Road, Worthing, W Sussex
BN11 2JA
☎Worthing(0903)38512

*Large Victorian house, set in own well-
kept gardens, located in a quiet residential
area within close proximity to the seafront.
The ground-floor flat comprises a bed-
sitting room with pull-out double bed, and
a bedroom with three single beds. In
addition there is a bathroom/WC and
kitchen equipped with baby Belling
cooker. The first-floor flat comprises one
double bedded-room, kitchen/lounge with
Wentel bed and bathroom/WC. Both units
are similarly equipped.*

All year except Xmas 2units, 2–6persons
◎ fridge ♨ & Electric Elec metered
Ⓛcan be hired TV P
Min£55 Max£110pw

H **Hill Top** Mill Lane, High Salvington
for bookings Miss B F Green, 35
Storrington Rise, Findon Valley, Worthing,
W Sussex BN14 0HT
☎Findon(090671)3823

*Pleasant detached house which has lovely
views over the Downs and sea. Ground
floor comprises lounge, small separate
dining room, well-equipped kitchen,
bathroom and separate WC. On the first
floor are two double bedrooms, well-
furnished & comfortable. 3m N off A24*

All year MWB out of season 1wk min,
5mths max, 1unit, 5persons ◆ ⌀
fridge Storage & Electrical heaters
Elec metered Ⓛcan be hired ☎ SD
Iron & Ironing board in unit CTV
⊕3pin square 2P ⊞ 🛁(400yds)
↭ ♀(3m) ♫(3m) ♫(3m) 🐾(3m)
Min£50 Max£70pw (Low)
Min£80 Max£180pw (High)

F **Winslea Holiday Apartments**
for bookings Mr H D Potkins, 217–219
Brighton Road, Worthing, W Sussex
☎Worthing(0903)39795

*Three houses converted into 10 self-
contained flats which sleep 2–6people.
The apartments all have a southerly
aspect, are situated on the seafront
overlooking the sea and are 1m from the
town centre. Each flat has one or two
bedrooms, bathroom, lounge/dining room
with kitchenette.*

All year MWB out of season 3days min,
1mth max, 10units, 2–6persons [◆]
◆ fridge Electric Elec metered Ⓛcan
be hired ☎(50yds) Iron & Ironing board
on premises [Launderette within

Woolacombe — Ynys

300yds] ⊕ TV ⊕3pin square P
🛁(200yds)
↭ ♪(1½m) ♀(20yds) ♫(1m)
♫(1m) 🐾(1m)
Min£85 Max£138pw (Low)
Min£116 Max£245pw (High)

WROXHAM
Norfolk
Map9 TG21

Ch **Melville Bay** Brimbelow Road
for bookings Blakes Holidays, Wroxham,
Norwich, Norfolk NR12 8DH
☎Wroxham(06053)2917

*Two cedarwood Swiss/Scandinavian-style
chalets in picturesque and peaceful
location on bank of River Bure ⅜m from the
centre of Wroxham. Two double-bedded
rooms on first floor and one twin on
ground floor. Combined bathroom/WC on
ground and one separate WC on first
floor. Spacious comfortable lounge with
picture window overlooking river. Small
annexe with twin bunks available. Good
quality furnishings and décor throughout.
An ideal base for boating or touring
holidays.*

Etr–Oct MWB out of season 1wk min,
2units, 6–8persons [◆ ◆] ◎
fridge Electric Elec metered
Ⓛinclusive ☎(¾m) ⊕ CTV
⊕3pin square P ⊞ 🛁(¾m) Boats for
hire
↭ ♀(¾m)
Details not confirmed for 1987

WYCLIFFE
Co Durham
Map12 NZ11

C Mr & Mrs D S Peat *Thorpe Hall
Cottages* Thorpe Hall, Wycliffe, Barnard
Castle, Co Durham DL12 9TW
☎Teesdale(0833)27230

*Two purpose-built cottages in the
stableyard at the Hall comprising two
bedrooms, kitchen, living room and
shower/WC. The third cottage which is
part of the hall itself contains two
bedrooms, bathroom, kitchen and living
room. The estate is situated south of the
River Tees, 5m from Barnard Castle.*

Apr–Oct MWB out of season
2nights min, 4wks max, 3units,
2–4persons [◇] ◆ ◆ no cats ◎
fridge Electric Elec metered
Ⓛinclusive ☎(50yds) Iron & Ironing
board on premises ⊕ TV
⊕3pin square 3P ⊞ 🛁(4m)
Details not confirmed for 1987

YARCOMBE
Devon
Map3 ST20

H **CC Ref 687**
for bookings Character Cottages
(Holidays) Ltd, 34 Fore Street, Sidmouth,
Devon EX10 8AQ
☎Sidmouth(03955)77001

*A 15th-century thatched house with
paddock and garden adjacent to River
Flagston. Entrance hall, large oak-
beamed lounge with inglenook fireplace,
dining room and separate kitchen. Three
double bedrooms, plus cot, h/c wash
basin and one single with h/c wash basin.
Trout fishing available (charged).*

Apr–Oct 1wk min, 6mths max, 1unit,
2–7persons ◆ ◆ ◎ fridge
Electric Elec inclusive Ⓛinclusive Iron
& Ironing board in unit ⊕ TV
⊕3pin square ⊕2pin round P 🏠
🛁(2m)
↭ ♀(2m)
Min£110 Max£258pw

YELVERTON
Devon
Map2 SX56

F Mr & Mrs Parish **Drake Leat** Yelverton,
Devon PL20 6HY
☎Yelverton(0822)853463

*A top-floor apartment in a country
Victorian residence with beautiful views
overlooking Dartmoor. Accommodation
comprises a spacious kitchen, dining
area, large lounge with traditional Devon
beams, modern bathroom, one double
bedroom and one twin-bedded room.*

All year MWB 3days min, 1mth max,
1unit, 4persons, nc6 pets by
arrangement ◎ fridge Economy7
Elec metered Ⓛinclusive ☎(½m) Iron &
Ironing board in unit ⊕ CTV
⊕3pin square 4P ⊞ 🛁(½m) ⌫
🐾Hard
↭ ♪(½m) ♀(½m)
Min£80 Max£160pw

YNYS
Gwynedd
Map6 SH44

C **Byrnceri & Brynmarch**
for bookings Mr Tilley, 12 Cyprus Close,
Selly Oak, Birmingham B29 4EG
☎Birmingham 021-475 3336 or
Chwilog(076)688829

*Two semi-detached cottages built of stone
and each comprising lounge, kitchen/
diner, bathroom/WC, a twin-bedded room
and a room with both a double and a
single bed.*

Mar–Nov MWB out of season 1wk min,
3wks max, 2units, 5persons ◆ ◎
fridge Electric Elec metered
Ⓛnot provided Iron & Ironing board in
unit ⊕ CTV ⊕3pin square P ⊞
Min£60 Max£110pw

C Mrs M Jones **Ynys Graianog** Ynys,
Criccieth, Gwynedd
☎Garn Dolbenmaen(076675)234

*Two cottages set in pastureland
surrounded by woods (with facilities for →*

shooting and fishing). **Y Bedol** comprises *kitchen/diner, lounge, shower/WC and three bedrooms (one with bunk beds);* **Y Scubor** has *kitchen/diner, lounge, bathroom/WC, plus separate WC and four bedrooms sleeping up to 12 people.*

Etr–Oct MWB out of season 2units, 6–12persons [◇] ◈ ◆ ⊚ fridge Electric Elec metered ⊡not provided Iron & Ironing board on premises ⊖ TV ⊕3pin square P ▥

⊖ ⚑(2m)
Min£60 Max£185pw

YORK
North Yorkshire
Map**8** SE65
See also **Dunnington, Copmanthorpe** and **Skelton**

F Abbey House 2 St Mary's
for bookings Mrs M I'Anson, Littlethorpe Hall, Littlethorpe, Ripon, North Yorkshire HG4 3LP
☎Ripon(0765)5133 & York(0904)707211
Three flats located in a Victorian terraced property, near to the town centre. Two of the flats accommodate two people the other flat up to four. They all comprise lounge, separate dining room and kitchen plus bathroom/WC.
All year MWB in season 1night min, 6mths max, 3units, 1–4persons ◆

Ynys
—
York

no pets ⊚ fridge Electric Elec metered ⊡inclusive ☎ Iron & Ironing board in unit [Launderette within 300yds] ⊕ CTV ⊕3pin square 1P ⚐(200yds)
⊖ δ(2m) ⚑(100yds) ♫(100yds) ♬(200yds) 🐾(2m)
Min£55 Max£200pw

F Bainton House 6 St Mary's
for bookings Intermain Leisure Ltd, 7 St Mary's, Bootham, York YO3 7DD
☎York(0904)36154(am) & 707211(pm)
Four flats, two of which sleep four people in one double-bedded room with two bedchairs in the lounge, the other two flats sleep five people in one double and one single bed plus two bed-chairs in the lounge, each have shower/WC.
All year MWB in season 1night min, 6mths max, 4units, 1–5persons ◆ ⊚ fridge Gas/Elec inclusive ⊡inclusive ☎ Iron & Ironing board in unit Launderette within 300yds ⊕ CTV ⊕3pin square 1P 1⚐ ⚐(200yds)
⊖ δ(2m) ⚑(100yds) ♫(100yds) ♬(200yds) 🐾(2m)

Min£55 Max£85pw(Low)
Min£85 Max£175pw(High)

F Birch House 5 St Mary's, Bootham
for bookings Mrs M I'Anson, Littlethorpe Hall, Littlethorpe, Ripon, N Yorks HG4 3LP
☎Ripon(0765)5133 or York(0904)707211
Four flats within a Victorian town house near the town centre. The ground-floor flat sleeps two in twin beds (double beds in the other three flats), two have double bed-settees in the lounge, and two have single folding beds available. All have combined bathroom/WCs and well fitted kitchens.
All year MWB 2nights min, 6mths max, 4units, 1–4persons ◆ ⊚ fridge Electric Elec metered ⊡inclusive ☎(10yds) Iron & Ironing board in unit [Launderette within 300yds] ⊕ CTV ⊕3pin square 4P ⚐(100yds)
⊖ δ(2m) ⚑(100yds) ♬(200yds) 🐾(2m)
Min£55 Max£175pw

F 1 Bootham Terrace (Flats 1–5)
for bookings Mrs Felicity Walker, 52 North Lane, Haxby, York YO3 8JP
☎York(0904)768460
Five flats situated in an Edwardian town house near the centre of the city. They offer different types of accommodation and are situated between the basement and the third floor.
All year MWB out of season 3days min, 3mths max, 5units, 1–5persons ◆

no pets 🐕 fridge Electric & gas fires
Gas & Elec inclusive ⬜inclusive ☎
Iron & Ironing board in unit [Launderette
within 300yds] ⊕ CTV ⊕3pin square
6P ♨(25yds)

⊕ ♪(3m) ☎(100yds) ♫(500yds)
♫(500yds) 🛁(1m)
Min£95 Max£165pw

F Carlton House
for bookings Intermain Leisure Ltd, 7 St
Mary's, Bootham, York, N Yorks
☎York(0904)36154(am) & 707211(pm)
*Three flats located within a Victorian
terraced house, near the two centre. The
ground-floor flat has a twin-bedded room,
the first-floor flat sleeps six people and the
second-floor flat has two bedrooms. All
comprise bathroom/WC, kitchen and
lounge.*

All year MWB in season 1night min,
6mths max, 3units, 1–6persons ◆ ◆
@ fridge Electric Elec inclusive
⬜inclusive ☎(20yds) Iron & Ironing
board in unit Launderette within 300yds
⊕ CTV ⊕3pin square 1P 1♨
♨(200yds)

⊕ ♪(2m) ☎(100yds) ♫(100yds)
♫(200yds) 🛁(2m)
Min£55 Max£85pw (Low)
Min£85 Max£200pw (High)

F Dale House 13 St Mary's
for bookings Mrs M l'Anson, Littlethorpe
Hall, Littlethorpe, Ripon, N Yorkshire
HG4 3LP
☎Ripon(0765)5133 or York(0904)707211
*Four flats located within a Victorian
terraced house, close to town centre. The
ground-floor flat accommodates four
people in a twin-bedded room plus two
folding beds in the sitting room, while the
third-floor flat sleeps five in one double-*

*bedded room, a bunk-bedded room plus a
folding bed in the living room. The other
two flats each comprise two bedrooms
sleeping four, plus two single folding beds
in the sitting room. All have a combined
bathroom/WC and a kitchen.*

All year MWB in season 1night min,
6mths max, 4units, 1–6persons [◆] @
fridge Electric Elec metered
⬜inclusive ☎ Iron & Ironing board in
unit Launderette within 300yds ⊕
CTV ⊕3pin square P ♨ ♨(200yds)
⊕ ♪(2m) ☎(100yds) ♫(100yds)
♫(200yds) 🛁(2m)
Min£55 Max£200pw

C 58 Dale Street
for bookings Mr & Mrs W D Kimberling, 17
Ashbourne Way, Woodthorpe, York
YO2 2SW
☎York(0904)704844
*A small terraced cottage about one mile
from the Minster Well. It has been well
restored and maintained and comprises a
comfortable cosy lounge, dining room,
modern kitchen, ground-floor bathroom/
WC and shower, two bedrooms and also a
double bed-settee in the lounge.*

All year MWB out of season 3days min,
3wks max, 1unit, 6persons no pets @
fridge Gas inclusive Elec metered
⬜inclusive ☎ TD in unit Iron & Ironing
board in unit ⊕ ⦿ TV
⊕3pin square P 🛁 ♨(100yds)
⊕ ♪(3m) ☎(100yds) ♫(1m)
♫(1m) 🛁(½m) Sports centre(2m)
Min£100 Max£170pw

F Mrs West-Taylor **The Flat** Dalham
House, Heslington, York, North Yorkshire
YO1 5DX
☎York(0904)411617
*A self-contained first-floor apartment in
Dalham House – a restored and converted
farmhouse in its own grounds and
gardens two miles from the city centre.
Accommodation is for two to four people
in a twin-bedded room and on divans in
the living/dining room. There is a
bathroom/shower/WC and a separate
kitchen and it is fitted and furnished to a
high standard.*

All year 1wk min, 1unit, 1–4persons, nc5
no pets 🐕 fridge 🍴 Elec inclusive
⬜inclusive ☎(½m) SD in unit Iron &
Ironing board in unit ⊕ CTV
⊕3pin square 2P 🔲 ♨(½m)
⊕ ♪(½m) ☎(½m) ♫(2m) ♫(2m)
🛁(2m)
Min£80 Max£90pw(Low)
Min£115 Max£130pw(High)

H St Saviours House St Saviours Place
for bookings Mr T P Marks, 34 St
Saviourgate, York
☎York(0904)27230

*Spacious three-storey Victorian house
close to the town centre. Accommodation
comprises lounge, dining room, kitchen,
utility room, two bathrooms and a
cloakroom, two double-bedded rooms,
one twin-bedded, one with bunk beds and
a single room.*

All year MWB out of season 1wk min,
1mth max, 1unit, 9persons [◇] ◆ ◆
🐕 fridge Gas inclusive ⬜inclusive
☎ WM, SD & TD in unit Iron & Ironing
board in unit ⦿ CTV ⊕3pin square
1P 🔲 ♨(100yds)
⊕ ♪(1m) ☎(50yds) ♫(300yds)
♫(½m) 🛁(500yds) Sports centre(¾m)
Min£155 Max£343pw

County List

The following list of towns and villages at which self-catering accommodation listed in this guide are situated. It is arranged in three sections: England, Wales and Scotland. Each country is divided alphabetically into counties (regions in Scotland), under which places are listed in alphabetical order.

England

Avon
Bath
Bishop Sutton
Bristol
Chew Magna
Clevedon
Freshford
Hewish
Pensford
Temple Cloud
Weston-super-Mare

Buckinghamshire
Buckingham
Wooburn Green

Cambridgeshire
Burwell
Cambridge
Newton

Cleveland
Gerrick
Guisborough

Cornwall
Altarnun
Ashton
Bodmin
Boscastle
Bude
Cadgwith
Calstock
Cardinham
Crackington Haven
Crantock
Crows Nest
Cury
Downderry
East Taphouse
Falmouth
Godolphin Cross
Gooseham
Grampound
Gwinear
Gwithian
Hayle
Hellandbridge
Helston
Helstone
Kilkhampton
Lanreath

Launceston
Lelant
Lesnewth
Liskeard
Lizard
Looe
Ludgvan
Marazion
Mawgan Porth
Mevagissey
Minions
Mousehole
Mullion
Newquay
Padstow
Pelynt
Penzance
Perranporth
Pipers Pool
Polperro
Polzeath
Porthallow
Porthleven
Port Isaac
Portwrinkle
Poundstock
Redruth
Restronguet
Ruan Minor
Rumford
Ruthernbridge
St Anthony in Roseland
St Austell
St Breward
St Erth
St Gennys St Ives
St Issey
St Just
St Keverne
St Keyne
St Newlyn East
Sennen
Stithians
Tintagel
Torpoint
Truro
Tywardreath
Veryan

Cumbria
Ambleside
Appleby

Arnside
Bassenthwaite
Bewcastle
Braithwaite
Brampton
Brough
Broughton-in-Furness
Burgh by Sands
Cartmel
Catlowdy
Coniston
Dent
Eskdale
Garsdale
Grange in Borrowdale
Grange-over-Sands
Grasmere
Hawkshead
Hesket Newmarket
High Lorton
Kendal
Keswick
Killington
Kirkby Lonsdale
Kirkoswald
Langdale (Great)
Lazonby
Little Salkeld
Longsleddale
Manesty
Newlands
Penton
Roadhead
Rosthwaite
Seatoller
Sedbergh
Silecroft
Silloth
Spark Bridge
Staveley
Threlkeld
Thurstonfield
Troutbeck
Ulverston
Wasdale
Welton
Whicham
Windermere

Derbyshire
Alsop en le Dale
Birchover

Buxton
Buxworth
Calver
Edale
Fenny Bentley
Gratton Dale
Hartington
Hope
Hucklow, Great
Kniveton
Lullington
Matlock
Millers Dale
Rowsley
Stanton in Peak
Thorpe
Whatstandwell

Devon
Ashburton
Ashreigney
Ashwater
Axminster
Bampton
Barnstaple
Beacon
Beer
Berrynarbor
Bickleigh (nr Tiverton)
Bideford
Blackawton
Bovey Tracey
Branscombe
Bridgerule
Brixham
Broadwood-Kelly
Buck's Cross
Budleigh Salterton
Cadbury
Chagford
Challaborough Bay
Cheriton Bishop
Christow
Chudleigh
Churston Ferrers
Colaton Raleigh
Colyton
Combe Martin
Compton
Crediton
Dartmouth
Dawlish
Drewsteignton
East Portlemouth
East Prawle
Ermington
Exeter
Exmouth
Feniton
Fremington
Gittisham
Hartland
Hatherleigh
Hemyock
Holbeton
Holsworthy
Honiton
Horns Cross
Ilfracombe
Ivybridge
Jacobstowe
Kentisbeare
Kingsbridge
King's Nympton

County List

Kingswear
Lifton
Loddiswell
Lundy
Luppitt
Lustleigh
Lympstone
Lynton
Malborough
Mamhead
Membury
Moretonhampstead
Mortehoe
Newton Abbott
Newton Poppleford
Ottery St Mary
Paignton
Parkham
Plymouth
Salcombe
Sampford Spiney
Seaton
Shaldon
Shebbear
Sherford
Sidmouth
Slapton
Smallridge
Southleigh
South Zeal
Stoke Fleming
Stokenham
Swimbridge
Teignmouth
Torcross
Torpoint
Torquay
Torrington (Great)
Totnes
Uplyme
Week St Mary
Wembury
Westward Ho!
Withleigh
Woodbury
Woolacombe
Yarcombe
Yelverton

Dorset
Bournemouth & Boscombe
Bridport
Broadwindsor
Cerne Abbas
Charmouth
Christchurch
Holnest
Iwerne Courtney
Marnhull
Milton Abbas
Poole
Shillingstone
Sturminster Newton
Swanage
Thornford
Weymouth
Winterborne Whitechurch
Wool

Co Durham
Burnopfield
Wycliffe

Essex
Clacton-on-Sea
Coggeshall
Colchester
Cressing
Orsett
Southend-on-Sea

Gloucestershire
Aldsworth
Avening
Bledington
Blockley
Bourton-on-the-Hill
Bourton on the Water
Broad Campden
Buckland
Cheltenham
Chipping Campden
Cirencester
Drybrook
Longborough
Minchinhampton
Owlpen
Salperton
Stanton
Stone
Tarlton
Tetbury
Tewkesbury
Winchcombe

Hampshire
Ashurst
Keyhaven
Milford-on-Sea
Netley Marsh
New Milton
Plaitford
Portsmouth & Southsea
Woodlands

Hereford & Worcester
Abbey Dore
Ballingham
Bayton
Bircher
Bredon
Broadway
Bridstow
Canon Pyon
Docklow
Eckington
Evesham
Goodrich
Hereford
How Caple
Inkberrow
King's Caple
Knighton-on-Teme
Lea
Leominster
Little Hereford
Llangarron
Llangrove
Lyonshall
Malvern (Great)
Marden
Pencoyd
Ross-on-Wye

Sedgeberrow
Shucknall
Stoke Lacey
Sutton St Nicholas
Vowchurch
Westhope
Whitney
Wormbridge

Hertfordshire
Hatfield
Tring

Humberside
Bridlington
South Cave

Isle of Wight
Bembridge
Colwell Bay
Freshwater
Niton
Ryde
St Lawrence
Seaview
Shanklin
Thorness Bay
Ventnor

Kent
Acrise
Canterbury
Chillenden
Eastry
Goodnestone
Iden Green
Margate
St Mary's Bay
Stelling Minnis

Lancashire
Blackpool
Forton
Lytham St Annes
Morecambe
Scorton

Leicestershire
Braunston
Lydon
Oakham

Lincolnshire
Calcethorpe
Gate Burton
Kirkby-on-Bain
Skegness
Welton le Wold
Woodhall Spa
Woodthorpe

London, Greater
(London postal districts: see
London gazetteer entry)
Kingston upon Thames
Purley

Merseyside
Southport

West Midlands
Birmingham
Coventry

County List

Norfolk
Bacton
Blakeney
Brancaster Staithe
Briston
Burgh Castle
Clippesby
Gresham
Haddiscoe
Hemsby
Hindringham
Holt
Horning
Hunstanton
Moulton, Great
North Creake
Scratby
South Creake
Swanton Morley
Thornage
Thurne
West Newton
Weybourne
Winterton-on-Sea
Wolferton
Wood Dalling
Wroxham

Northumberland
Alwinton
Biddlestone
Byrness
Cheswick
Elsdon
Haltwhistle
Lambley
Powburn
Shilbottle
Walwick

Nottinghamshire
Epperstone
Teversal

Oxfordshire
Burford
Duns Tew
Kingham
Minster Lovell
Oxford

Shropshire
Bicton
Bridgnorth
Clee Hill
Cleobury Mortimer
Hopton Castle
Llanfair Waterdine
Longnor
Telford
Twitchen
Wall under Heywood

Somerset
Allerford
Binegar
Blue Anchor
Cheddar

Chilton Polden
Crowscombe
Dulverton
Dunster
Exford
Hatch Beauchamp
Ilchester
Templecombe
Waterrow
Wedmore
Wheddon Cross

Staffordshire
Alstonefield
Alton
Basford
Canwell
Cauldon
Flash
Ipstones
Leek
Longnor
Rudyard
Stafford
Stanton

Suffolk
Aldeburgh
Bradfield St George
Kessingland
Kettlebaston
Little Waldingfield
Lowestoft
Peasenhall
Southwold

Surrey
Egham
Laleham

Sussex (East)
Blackboys
Brighton
Burwash
Eastbourne
Eastdean
Fairwarp
Hastings
Lewes
Newhaven
Newick
Ripe
Sheffield Green

Sussex (West)
Charlton
East Preston
Littlehampton
Plummers Plain Littlehampton
Steyning
Worthing

Tyne & Wear
Cullercoats

Warwickshire
Alcester
Bearley
Darlingscott
Leamington Spa (Royal)
Pathlow
Stratford-upon-Avon

Wiltshire
Colerne
Kingston Deverill
Sandy Lane
Sherston

Yorkshire (North)
Aldfield
Bell Busk
Buckden
Burton-in-Lonsdale
Cawood
Cayton
Clapham
Copmanthorpe
Cropton
Dunnington
Filey
Fylingdales
Galphay
Gilling East
Grewelthorpe
Harrogate
Hawes
Hebden
Hellifield
Helmsley
Ingleton
Kettlewell
Kirby Hill
Kirkby Malham
Kirkbymoorside
Littlethorpe
Malham
Malton
Masham
Pickering
Primrose Valley
Richmond
Rosedale Abbey
Scarborough
Skelton
Smeaton, Great
Terrington
Threshfield
West Ayton
Whitby
York

Yorkshire (South)
Sheffield

Yorkshire (West)
Haworth
Hebden Bridge
Oxenhope
Pudsey

Channel Islands
Alderney
St Peter Port (Guernsey)
St Saviours (Guernsey)

Isle of Man
Douglas
Hillberry
Onchan

Isle of Scilly
St Mary's

County List

Wales

Clwyd
Betws-yn-Rhos
Colwyn Bay
Corwen
Llanferres
Mold
Prestatyn

Dyfed
Abercastle
Abereiddy
Aberporth
Aberystwyth
Ammanford
Amroth
Boncath
Broad Haven
Cardigan
Cenarth
Cosheston
Croesgoch
Crymych
Dale
Fishguard
Glynarthen
Haverfordwest
Hayscastle
Henllan-Amgoed
Jordanston
Keeston
Kilgetty
Landshipping
Little Haven
Llanarthney
Llandeilo
Llandygwydd
Llandyssul
Llanon
Llanstephan
Llanteg
Llwyncelyn
Llwyndafydd
Manorbier
Narberth
Nevern
Newport
New Quay
Oakford
Paran
Pendine
Pontshaen
Porthgain
Ratford Bridge
Rhandirmwyn
Sageston
St Brides
St Clears
St Davids
St Florence
St Nicholas
Saundersfoot
Solva
Stepaside
Tavernspite
Tenby

Tregaron
Walwyns Castle

Gwent
Abergavenny

Gwynedd
Aberdovey
Abergynolwyn
Abersoch
Bangor
Barmouth
Betws-y-Coed
Bontddu
Brynsiencyn
Caernarfon
Chwilog
Clynnog-fawr
Criccieth
Deganwy
Dolgellau
Ffestiniog
Glan Conwy
Harlech
Llanbedrog
Llanberis
Llandegfan
Llandudno
Llandudno Junction
Llandwrog
Llandyfrydog
Llanfairfechan
Llanfihangel-y-Pennant
Llangwnnadi
Llanrug
Llanystumdwy
Llwyngwril
Menai Bridge
Moelfre
Morfa Bychan
Nanttile
Pennal
Penrhyndeudraeth
Port Dinorwic
Pwllheli
Rhosgadfan
Rhyd-Ddu
Trearddur Bay
Tyn-y-Groes
Tywyn
Ynys

Powys
Abercraf
Berriew
Brecon
Builth Wells
Crossgates
Garthmyl
Gladestry
Hay-on-Wye
Kinnerton
Llangorse
Llangunllo
Llangynidr
Llansantffraid-ym-Mechain
Llanwrtyd Wells
Montgomery
Old Radnor
Rhayader
Talgarth

W Glamorgan
Caswell Bay

Horton
Mumbles
Oxwich
Scurlage

Scotland

Borders
Denholm
Duns
Jedburgh
Kelso
Kirkton Manor
Leadburn
West Linton

Central
Airth
Callander
Crianlarich
Kinlochard
Lochearnhead
Port of Menteith
Stirling
Strathyre

Dumfries & Galloway
Ardwell
Auchenmalg
Borgue
Castle Douglas
Caulkerbush
Crocketford
Crossmichael
Dalry
Elrig
Gatehouse of Fleet
Glen Trool
Haugh of Urr
Kippford
Kircudbright
Kirkpatrick Durham
Moffatt
Mossdale
New Galloway
Newton Stewart
Parton
Portpatrick
Port William
Rockliffe
Sandyhills
Twynholm

Fife
Auchtermuchty
Pittenweem
Rathillet
St Andrews

Grampian
Aboyne
Alford
Ballater
Banchory
Braemar
Buckie
Cornhill
Dinnet
Dufftown
Findochty
Gartly
Glenlivet
Kennethmont

Logie-Coldstone
Lumphanan
Portknockie
Portsoy
Rafford
Tarland

Highland
Alcaig
Arisaig
Ardvasar (see Skye, Isle of)
Aultbea
Aviemore
Ballachulish
Balnain
Beauly
Cannich
Carrbridge
Carbost (see Skye, Isle of)
Contin
Craobh Haven
Culbrokie
Culkein
Culloden Moor
Dornoch
Drimnin
Drumbeg
Drumnadrochit
Duirinish
Dulnain Bridge
Dunvegan (see Skye, Isle of)
Fort William
Foyers
Gairloch
Golspie
Grantown-on-Spey
Invergarry
Inverkirkaig
Invermoriston
Inverness
Isle Ornsay (see Skye, Isle of)
Kinlochewe
Kinloch Laggan
Kinlochleven
Kirkhill
Knock (see Skye, Isle of)
Lairg
Leckmelm
Lentran
Lochinver
Mellon Udrigle
Muir of Ord
Nethy Bridge
Newtonmore
Onich
Portree (see Skye, Isle of)
Roy Bridge
Salen
Scourie
Shieldaig
Shona, Isle of
Spean Bridge
Strontian
Tomatin
Tore
Ullapool
Watten
Whitebridge

Lothian
Dunbar
Edinburgh

Orkney
Finstown
Orphir
Stenness

Shetland
Whiteness

Strathclyde
Appin
Ardbrecknish
Baleromindubh (see Colonsay, Isle of)
Ballantrae
Barr
Bowmore (see Islay, Isle of)
Brodick (see Arran, Isle of)
Campbeltown
Carsaig (see Mull, Isle of)
Clachan-Seil
Coll (Isle of)
Colonsay (Isle of)
Connel
Crinan
Cullipool (See Luing, Isle of)
Dalavich
Dervalg (see Mull, Isle of)
Dougarie (see Arran, Isle of)
Dunmore
Dunsyre
Ellary
Galston
Gigha (Isle of)
Girvan
Glasgow
Gruinart (see Islay, Isle of)
Helensburgh
Hollybush
Kilchattan (see Colonsay, Isle of)
Kilmelford
Kilmory
Kilninver
Kiloran (see Colonsay, Isle of)
Kiloran Bay (see Colonsay, Isle of)
Lamlash (see Arran, Isle of)
Lendalfoot
Lochead
Newmilns
Oban
Ormsary
Pinwherry
Port Appin
Port Charlotte (see Islay, Isle of)
Rashfield
Rothesay (see Bute, Isle of)
Saddell
Salen (see Mull, Isle of)
Scalasaig (see Colonsay, Isle of)
Skipness
Straiton
Tayinloan
Taynuilt
Tobermory (see Mull, Isle of)

Tayside
Aberfeldy
Alyth
Balgedie
Bankfoot
Blair Atholl

Blairgowrie	**County List**	Kinloch Rannoch
Butterstone		Lintrathen
Calvine		Meigie
Crieff		Memus
Dollerie		Pitlochry
Dunning		
Fearnan	Glenshee (Spittal of)	**Western Isles**
Glenprosen	Killiecrankie	Castlebay (see Barra, Isle of)

Inventory of equipment for self catering accommodation

Ashtrays	2 per unit	Jugs, large and small	1 per unit
Blankets*	3 per bed	Kettle	1 per unit
Bowls/basins, mixing	2 per unit	Knife, table and dessert	1 per person
Bread/chopping board	1 per unit	Knife, vegetable	1 per unit
Bread knife	1 per unit	Oven roasting tray	1 per unit
Bread/cake plate	1 per person	Pillow*	1 per person
Broom	1 per unit	Plate, large and small	1 per person
Bucket	1 per unit	Potato peeler	1 per unit
Butter dish	1 per unit	Pot scourer/dish mop	1 per unit
Carving knife and fork	1 per unit	Refuse bin	1 per unit
Casserole dish	1 per unit	Saucepans and lids, large,	
Cereal/soup plate	1 per person	med & small	1 per unit
Coat hangers	2 per person	Spoon, dessert and tea	1 per person
Colander	1 per unit	Spoons, table	2 per unit
Condiment Set	1 per unit	Sugar basin	1 per unit
Cooking spoon	2 per unit	Tea caddy	1 per unit
Corkscrew and bottle opener	1 per unit	Teapot	1 per unit
Cup, tea, and saucer	1 per person	Tin opener	1 per unit
Doormat	1 per unit	Tray	1 per unit
Dusters	2 per unit	Tumbler	1 per person
Dustpan and Brush	1 per unit	Washing-up-bowl	1 per unit
Egg-cup	1 per person		
Fish slice	1 per unit	* Bedding must be adequate for the season when	
Floor cloth	1 per unit	the unit is let. Continental quilts are acceptable	
Food container	2 per unit	(one for 2 blankets). Extra pillows to be	
Fork, table and dessert	1 per person	available, within reason, on request.	
Fruit dish, large	1 per unit	**Note:** A carpet sweeper or equivalent must be	
Frying pan	1 per unit	readily available.	

ORDNANCE SURVEY
LEISURE GUIDES

LAKE DISTRICT

Voted the best new publication about the area in 1984, this superb guide describes the topography and traditions of the area and offers scenic drives, walks, and masses of information about what to see and where to stay, linked to large-scale Ordnance Survey maps, and illustrated throughout in colour.

NEW FOREST

Walks, drives, places to see, things to do, where to stay, all linked to large-scale Ordnance Survey mapping, with useful background information to the area. Illustrated throughout with superb colour photography.

YORKSHIRE DALES

Descriptions of scenery, history, customs and 'a day in the life of a dalesman' evoke the atmosphere of this remote and beautiful region and introduce the walks, drives and directory of places of interest. Large-scale Ordnance Survey maps and a wealth of colour photography make this guide a must for tourist and walker alike.

COTSWOLDS

Pretty villages of native limestone, impressive churches built on the wealth of the wool trade, ancient hillforts and Roman roads, rolling upland and gentle river valleys – these and much more are described and colourfully illustrated in this guide. Walks, drives and Ordnance Survey maps complete this ideal companion to the area.

SCOTTISH HIGHLANDS

Scottish Highlands – a treasure house of nature, packed with breathtaking scenery and fascinating traditions. The book captures the flavour, the scents and the grandeur of Europe's foremost 'wilderness' area. Walks, drives, things to do, places to stay are listed, with maps to show the way.

All available in hardback or paperback

Holiday Homes, Cottages & Apartments Guide

Member's report form

To: The Automobile Association
Hotel Services Dept
9th Floor
Fanum House
Basingstoke, Hants
RG21 2EA

Block Capitals Please

Name of property

Town

County

Date of visit

In the event of complaint I *do/do not* agree to allow the use of my name in correspondence with the establishment

Please make your comments overleaf

Name

Address

Signature   Date

Membership number

Comments

_____

_____

_____

_____

_____

_____

_____

_____

_____

_____

_____

_____

_____

_____

_____

_____

_____

_____

Key to Atlas

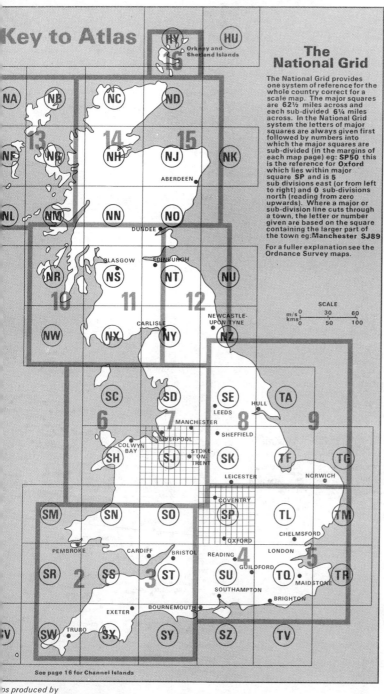

The National Grid

The National Grid provides one system of reference for the whole country correct for a scale map. The major squares are 62½ miles across and each sub-divided 6¼ miles across. In the National Grid system the letters of major squares are always given first followed by numbers into which the major squares are sub-divided (in the margins of each map page) eg: **SP50** this is the reference for **Oxford** which lies within major square **SP** and is **5** sub divisions east (or from left to right) and **0** sub-divisions north (reading from zero upwards). Where a major or sub-division line cuts through a town, the letter or number given are based on the square containing the larger part of the town eg: **Manchester SJ89**

For a fuller explanation see the Ordnance Survey maps.

SCALE

| m/s | 0 | 30 | 60 |
| kms | 0 | 50 | 100 |

See page 16 for Channel Islands

s produced by

AA Cartographic Department blications Division), Fanum House, ingstoke, Hampshire RG21 2EA

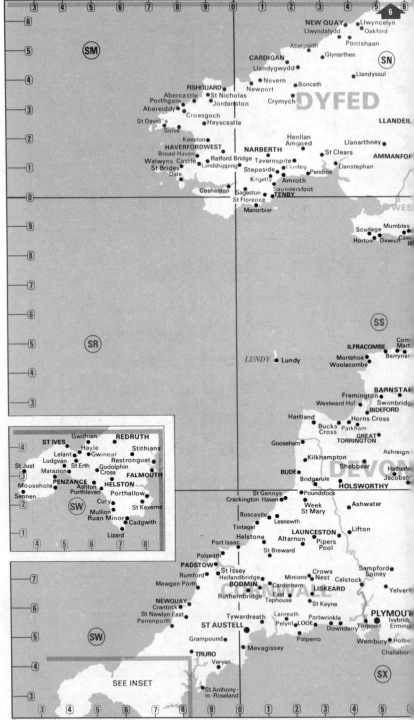

SM

SN

SR

SS

SW

SX

NEW QUAY Llwyncelyn
Llwyndafydd ● Oakford
Aberporth ● Pontshaen
CARDIGAN ● Glynarthen
Llandygwydd ● Llandyssul
● Nevern ● Boncath
FISHGUARD ● Newport ● Crymych
Abercastle ● St Nicholas
Porthgain ● Jordanston
Abereiddy ● Croesgoch
St David's ● Hayscastle
Solva ● Henllan
Keeston ● Amgoed ● Llanarthney
HAVERFORDWEST **NARBERTH** ● St Clears
Broad Haven ● Ratford Bridge ● Tavernspite
Walwyns Castle ● Landshipping ● Llanteg ● Llanstephan
St Brides ● Stepaside ● Pendine
Dale ● Kilgetty ● Amroth
● Saundersfoot
Cosheston ● Sageston **TENBY**
St Florence
Manorbier

DYFED

LLANDEIL

AMMANFO

WES

Scurlage Mumbles
Horton ● Oxwich Cas

ILFRACOMBE Com
Mart
LUNDY ● Lundy Mortehoe ● Berrynar
Woolacombe

BARNSTA
Fremington ● Swimbridg
Westward Ho! **BIDEFORD**
Hartland ● Horns Cross
Bucks ● Parkham
Cross **GREAT**
Gooseham **TORRINGTON** Ashreign

Kilkhampton
Shebbear Hatherle
BUDE Jacobsto
Bridgerule **HOLSWORTHY**

DEVON

St Gennys ● Poundstock
Crackington Haven ● Ashwater
Week
Boscastle ● St Mary
Lesnewth
Tintagel ● Helstone **LAUNCESTON** Lifton
Port Isaac ● Altarnun Pipers
Polzeath ● St Breward Pool
PADSTOW St Issey Crows Sampford
Rumford ● Hellandbridge Minions ● Nest ● Calstock Spiney
Mawgan Porth **BODMIN** Cardinham Yelver
Ruthernbridge East **LISKEARD**
NEWQUAY Taphouse ● St Keyne
Crantock Lanreath Portwrinkle **PLYMOUT**
St Newlyn East Tywardreath ● Pelynt **LOOE** Ivybridg
Perranporth **ST AUSTELL** ● Downderry Erming
Grampound Polperro Torpoint
TRURO ● Mevagissey Wembury ● Holbe
Veryan Challabor

CORNWALL

SEE INSET

St Anthony-
in-Roseland

INSET (SW):

REDRUTH
Gwithian
ST IVES Stithians
Lelant Hayle
Ludgvan ● Gwinear Restronguet
St Just Marazion St Erth Godolphin **FALMOUTH**
Cross
Mousehole **PENZANCE** Ashton **HELSTON**
Sennen Porthleven Porthallow
Cury St Keverne
Mullion
Ruan Minor ● Cadgwith
Lizard

2

For continuation pages refer to numbered arrows

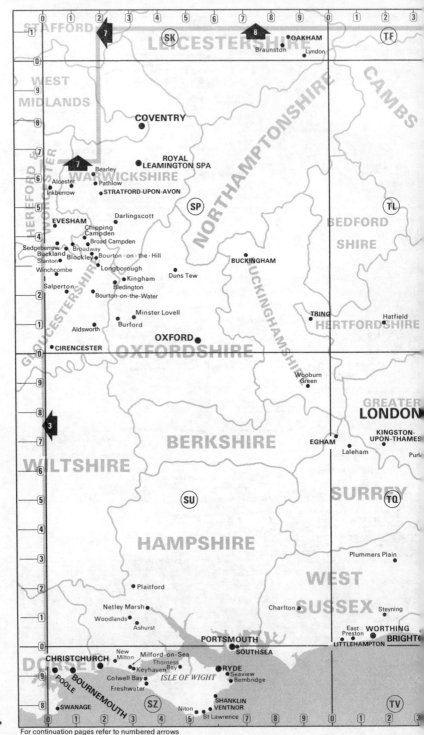

4

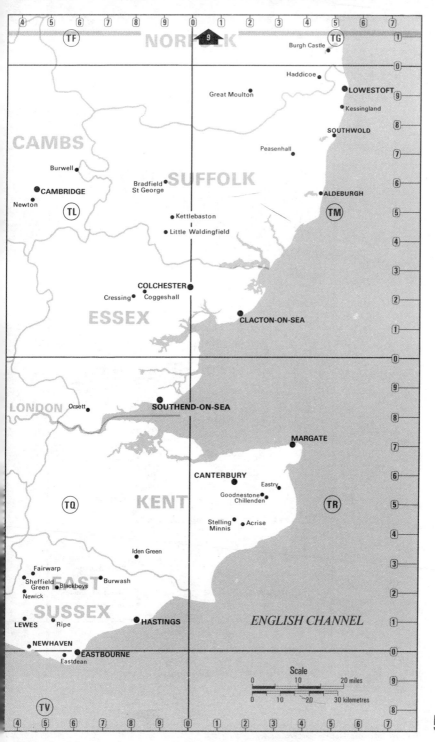

5

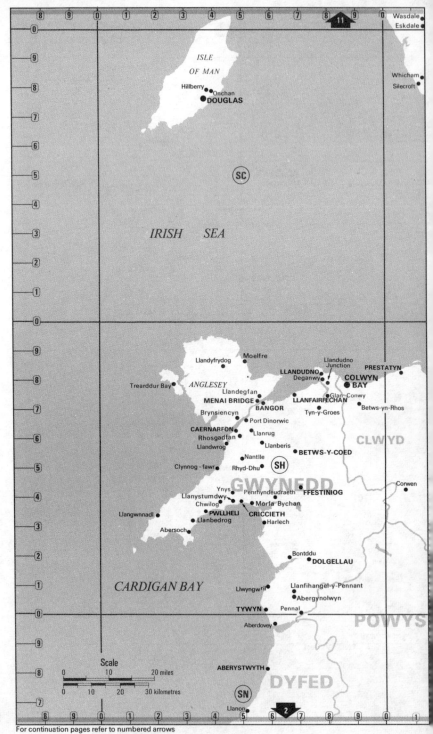

ISLE
OF MAN

Hillberry •Onchan
•DOUGLAS

Wasdale
Eskdale

Whicham
Silecroft

(SC)

IRISH   SEA

Llandyfrydog   Moelfre
Trearddur Bay   *ANGLESEY*
Llandegfan
MENAI BRIDGE
Brynsiencyn   BANGOR
Port Dinorwic
CAERNARFON
Rhosgadfan   Llanrug
Llandwrog   Llanberis
Nantlle
Clynnog - fawr   Rhyd-Dhu   (SH)
Ynys   *GWYNEDD*
Llanystumdwy   Penrhyndeudraeth
Chwilog   Morfa Bychan
PWLLHELI
Llangwnnadl   Llanbedrog   CRICCIETH
Abersoch   Harlech

Llandudno
Junction   PRESTATYN
LLANDUDNO
Deganwy   COLWYN
BAY
LLANFAIRFECHAN   Glan- Conwy
Tyn-y-Groes   Betws-yn-Rhos

CLWYD

BETWS-Y-COED

Corwen

FFESTINIOG

Bontddu
DOLGELLAU

CARDIGAN BAY

Llwyngwril   Llanfihangel-y-Pennant
Abergynolwyn
TYWYN   Pennal

Aberdovey

POWYS

Scale
0   10   20 miles
0   10   20   30 kilometres

ABERYSTWYTH   DYFED

(SN)

Llanon

6

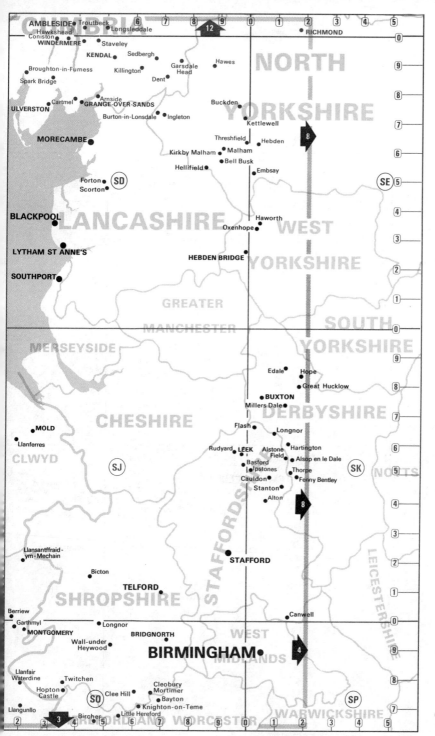

7

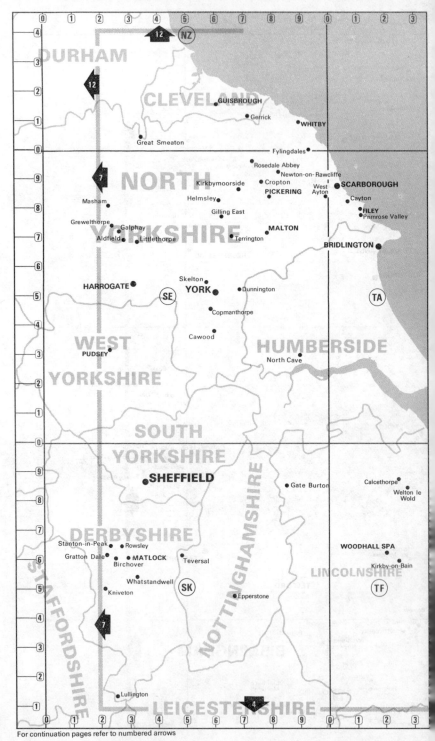

For continuation pages refer to numbered arrows

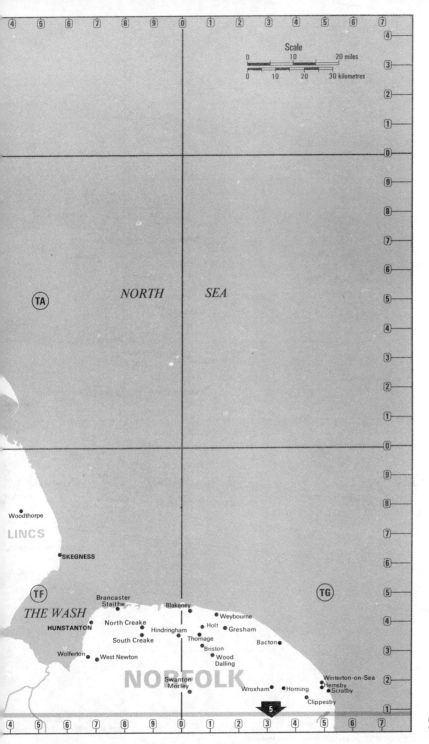

Scale

0   10   20 miles

0   10   20   30 kilometres

TA

NORTH   SEA

Woodthorpe

LINCS

SKEGNESS

TF

THE WASH

Brancaster
Staithe

Blakeney

Weybourne

HUNSTANTON

North Creake

Hindringham

Holt

Gresham

South Creake

Thornage

Briston

Bacton

Wolferton

West Newton

Wood
Dalling

TG

Winterton-on-Sea

NORFOLK

Swanton
Morley

Wroxham

Horning

Hemsby

Scratby

Clippesby

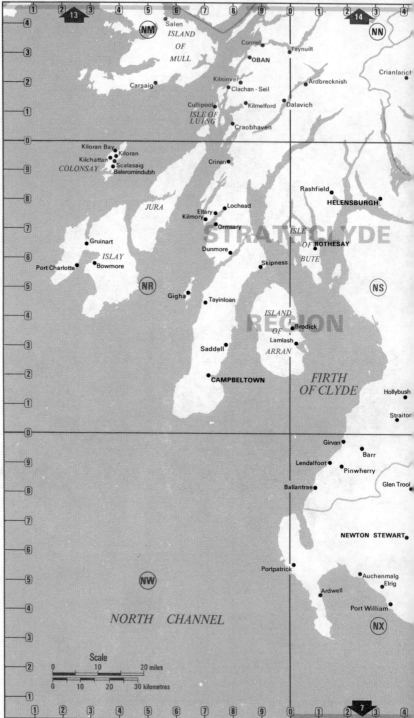

ISLAND OF MULL

NM

Salen

Carsaig

ISLE OF LUING

Cullipool

Kilninver
Clachan - Seil

Kilmelford

Craobhaven

Connel

OBAN

Taynuilt

Ardbrecknish

Dalavich

Crianlarich

NN

Kiloran Bay
Kiloran
Kilchattan
Scalasaig
COLONSAY
Baleromindubh

Crinan

Rashfield

HELENSBURGH

JURA

Gruinart

ISLAY

Bowmore

Port Charlotte

NR

Ellary
Kilmory

Lochead

Ormsary

Dunmore

STRATHCLYDE

ISLE OF ROTHESAY
BUTE

Skipness

Gigha

Tayinloan

ISLAND OF ARRAN

Brodick

REGION

Lamlash

Saddell

CAMPBELTOWN

FIRTH OF CLYDE

Hollybush

Straiton

NS

NW

NORTH CHANNEL

Scale
0   10   20 miles
0   10   20   30 kilometres

Girvan

Barr

Lendalfoot
Pinwherry

Ballantrae

Glen Trool

NEWTON STEWART

Portpatrick

Auchenmalg
Elrig

Ardwell

Port William

NX

For continuation pages refer to numbered arrows

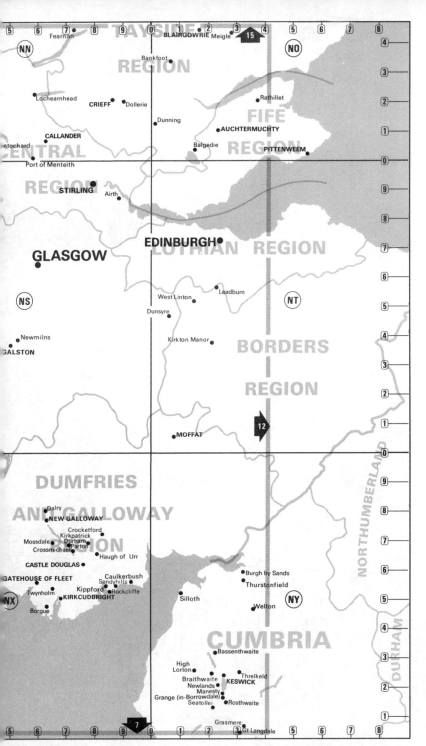

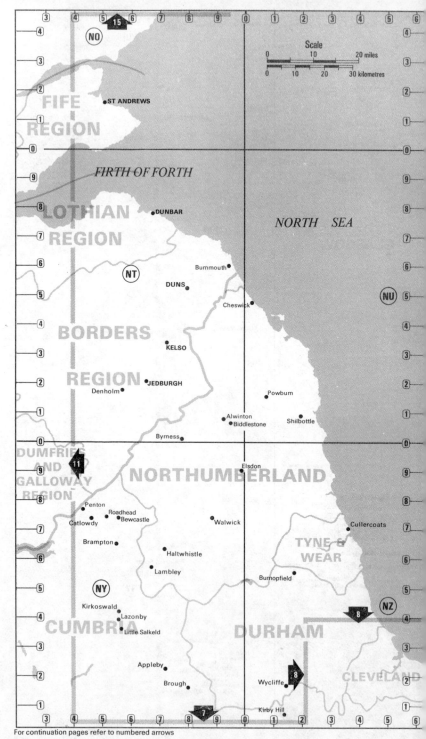

For continuation pages refer to numbered arrows

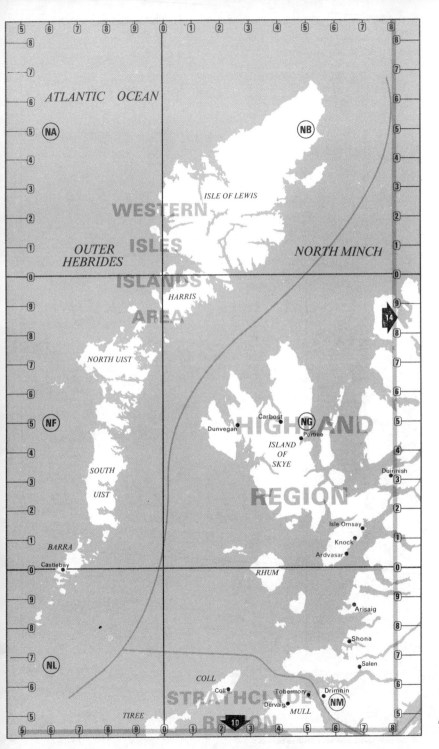

ATLANTIC OCEAN

NA

NB

ISLE OF LEWIS

WESTERN

OUTER **ISLES** NORTH MINCH
HEBRIDES

ISLANDS

HARRIS

AREA

NORTH UIST

NF

HIGHLAND
Carbost
Dunvegan **NG**
Portree
ISLAND
OF
SKYE
Duirinish

SOUTH

UIST **REGION**

Isle Ornsay

Knock
Ardvasar

BARRA
RHUM
Castlebay

Arisaig

NL
Shona

Salen

COLL
Coll
Tobermory Drimnin
STRATHCLYDE Dervaig **NM**
TIREE **REGION** MULL

14

10

13

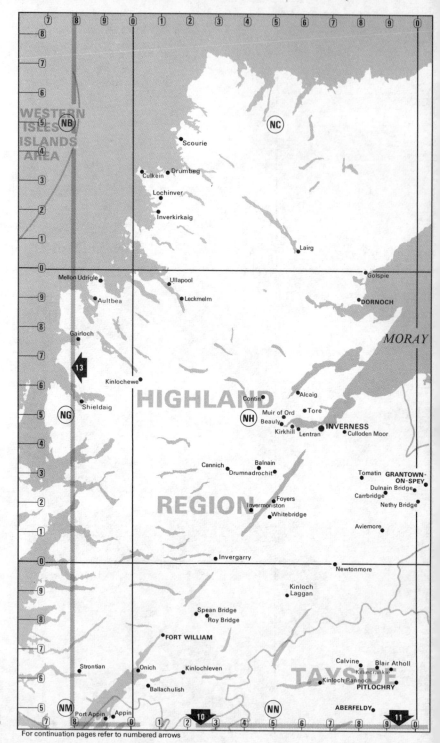

14

WESTERN ISLES ISLANDS AREA

NB

NC

Scourie

Culkein Drumbeg

Lochinver

Inverkirkaig

Lairg

Mellon Udrigle

Ullapool

Golspie

DORNOCH

Aultbea

Leckmelm

MORAY

Gairloch

13

Kinlochewe

HIGHLAND

Alcaig

Contin

NG

Shieldaig

Muir of Ord   Tore

NH   Beauly

INVERNESS

Kirkhill   Lentran   Culloden Moor

Cannich

Balnain

Drumnadrochit

Tomatin   GRANTOWN-
ON-SPEY

Dulnain Bridge

REGION

Foyers

Invermoriston

Whitebridge

Carrbridge

Nethy Bridge

Aviemore

Invergarry

Newtonmore

Kinloch
Laggan

Spean Bridge

Roy Bridge

FORT WILLIAM

Calvine   Blair Atholl

Killiecrankie

Kinloch Rannoch

TAYSIDE

Strontian

Onich

Kinlochleven

PITLOCHRY

Ballachulish

NM   Port Appin   Appin

10

NN

ABERFELDY

11

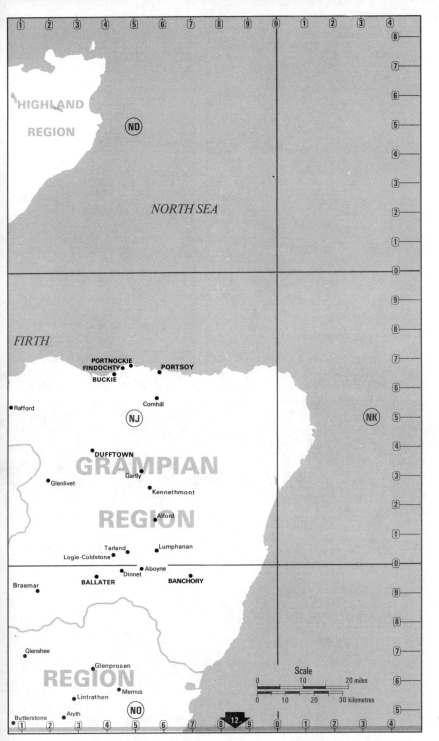

HIGHLAND
REGION

(ND)

NORTH SEA

NK

FIRTH

PORTNOCKIE
FINDOCHTY ●   ● PORTSOY
BUCKIE

● Rafford   ● Cornhill

(NJ)

● DUFFTOWN

GRAMPIAN

● Glenlivet   ● Gartly
        ● Kennethmont

REGION
        ● Alford

Tarland ●   ● Lumphanan
Logie-Coldstone ●
        ● Aboyne
    ● Dinnet
Braemar ●   BALLATER   BANCHORY

● Glenshee

REGION
    ● Glenprosen
        ● Memus
● Lintrathen
Butterstone ● ● Aiyth   (NO)

Scale

| 0 | 10 | 20 miles |
| 0 | 10 | 20 | 30 kilometres |

12

15

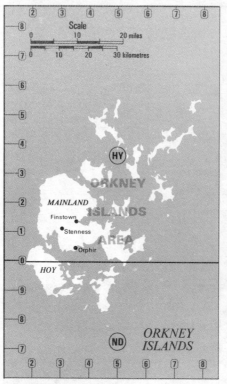

ORKNEY
ISLANDS

HY

ORKNEY
ISLANDS
AREA

MAINLAND
Finstown
Stenness
Orphir

HOY

ND

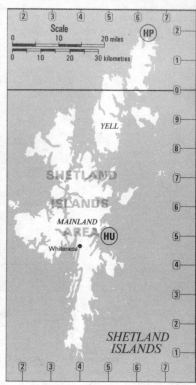

HP

YELL

SHETLAND
ISLANDS
AREA

MAINLAND
Whiteness

HU

SHETLAND
ISLANDS

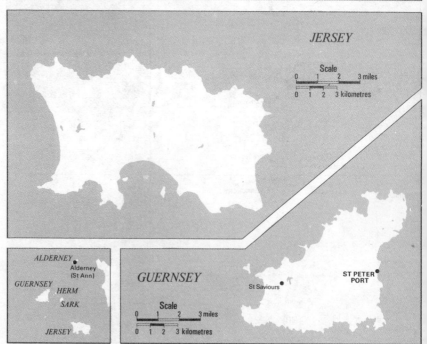

JERSEY

ALDERNEY
Alderney
(St Ann)

GUERNSEY

HERM

SARK

JERSEY

GUERNSEY

ST PETER
PORT

St Saviours

16